EDEXCEL
AS/A LEVEL
HISTORY

*Active*Book included

endorsed for
edexcel

CW00555124

Paper 1&2:
Challenges to the authority of the state in the late 18th and 19th centuries

Adam Kidson | Martin Collier | Rick Rogers |
Series editor: Rosemary Rees

ALWAYS LEARNING

PEARSON

Published by Pearson Education Limited, 80 Strand, London, WC2R 0RL.

www.pearsonschoolsandfecolleges.co.uk

Copies of official specifications for all Edexcel qualifications may be found on the website: www.edexcel.com

Text © Pearson Education Limited 2015

Designed by Elizabeth Arnoux for Pearson

Typeset and illustrated by Phoenix Photosetting, Chatham, Kent

Produced by Out of House Publishing

Original illustrations © Pearson Education Limited 2015

Cover design by Malena Wilson-Max for Pearson

Cover photo/illustration © Getty Images: Universal History Archive/UIG

The rights of Martin Collier, Adam Kidson and Rick Rogers to be identified as authors of this work have been asserted by them in accordance with the Copyright, Designs and Patents Act 1988.

First published 2015

18 17 16 15

10 9 8 7 6 5 4 3 2 1

British Library Cataloguing in Publication Data
A catalogue record for this book is available from the British Library

ISBN 978 1 447 985266

Printed in the UK by CPI

Websites
Pearson Education Limited is not responsible for the content of any external internet sites. It is essential for tutors to preview each website before using it in class so as to ensure that the URL is still accurate, relevant and appropriate. We suggest that tutors bookmark useful websites and consider enabling students to access them through the school/college intranet.

A note from the publisher

In order to ensure that this resource offers high-quality support for the associated Pearson qualification, it has been through a review process by the awarding body. This process confirms that; this resource fully covers the teaching and learning content of the specification or part of a specification at which it is aimed. It also confirms that it demonstrates an appropriate balance between the development of subject skills, knowledge and understanding, in addition to preparation for assessment.

Endorsement does not cover any guidance on assessment activities or processes (e.g. practice questions or advice on how to answer assessment questions), included in the resource nor does it prescribe any particular approach to the teaching or delivery of a related course.

While the publishers have made every attempt to ensure that advice on the qualification and its assessment is accurate, the official specification and associated assessment guidance materials are the only authoritative source of information and should always be referred to for definitive guidance.

Pearson examiners have not contributed to any sections in this resource relevant to examination papers for which they have responsibility.

Examiners will not use endorsed resources as a source of material for any assessment set by Pearson.

Endorsement of a resource does not mean that the resource is required to achieve this Pearson qualification, nor does it mean that it is the only suitable material available to support the qualification, and any resource lists produced by the awarding body shall include this and other appropriate resources.

Contents

How to use this book

STRUCTURE

This book covers Route D of the Edexcel A Level and AS Level History qualifications. Route D consists of three papers which are linked by the theme 'Challenges to the authority of the state in the late 18th and 19th centuries'.

- Paper 1: Britain c1785–c1870, democracy, protest and reform
- Paper 2a: The unification of Italy, c1830–70
- Paper 2b: The unification of Germany, c1840–71

To take Route D, you must study Paper 1, plus **one** of the two Paper 2 options. You do not need to study the other Paper 2 topic for your exam, but you might like to read it for interest – it deals with similar themes to the topics you are studying.

If you are studying for A Level History, you will also need to study a Paper 3 option and produce coursework in order to complete your qualification. All Paper 3 options are covered by other textbooks in this series.

AS LEVEL OR A LEVEL?

This book is designed to support students studying both the Edexcel AS Level and A Level qualifications. The content required for both qualifications is identical, so all the material in the papers you are studying is relevant, whichever qualification you are aiming for.

The questions you will be asked in the exam differ for the two different qualifications, so we have included separate exam-style questions and exam preparation sections. If you are studying for an AS Level, you should use the exam-style questions and exam sections highlighted in blue. If you are studying for an A Level, you should use the exam-style questions and exam sections highlighted in green.

> **AS Level Exam-Style Question Section A**
>
> Was parliament's unwillingness to modernise the electoral system the main reason for the growth in reform agitation in the years 1785–1800? (20 marks)
>
> **Tip**
> *Make sure you read the question carefully and take note of any key phrases it uses. These are clues as to how to answer it.*

> **A Level Exam-Style Question Section B**
>
> How far do you agree that the 1867 Reform Act was more significant than reform in 1832? (20 marks)
>
> **Tip**
> *When answering this question you should consider the outcomes, for different sections of society, of each Act.*

The 'Preparing for your exams' section at the end of each paper contains sample answers of different standards, with comments on how weaker answers could be improved. Make sure you look at the right section for the exam you are planning to take.

FEATURES

Extend your knowledge

These features contain additional information that will help you gain a deeper understanding of the topic. This could be a short biography of an important person, extra background information about an event, an alternative interpretation, or even a research idea that you could follow up. Information in these boxes is not essential to your exam success, but still provides insights of value.

> **EXTEND YOUR KNOWLEDGE**
>
> 'Conservatives' and 'Liberals'
> After defeat in 1832, the Tory party sought to rehabilitate itself. Under the leadership of Robert Peel in 1834 the party issued a new manifesto at Tamworth using the title 'Conservative Party'. Just as the Tories had rebranded themselves, the mostly aristocratic Whig party also began to think in terms of a more appropriate name after they were joined in parliament by a host of new non-aristocratic members following the recent reforms. With the increased reliance on these new MPs after 1850, the term 'Liberal' became a more appropriate title for the party. Collectively these new titles also nicely reflected the polarising political landscape that reform had created.

Knowledge check activities

These activities are designed to check that you have understood the material that you have just studied. They might also ask you questions about the sources and extracts in the section to check that you have studied and analysed them thoroughly.

ACTIVITY
KNOWLEDGE CHECK

How effective was the New Poor Law?

Having considered the impact of the New Poor Law which was passed in 1834, answer the following questions:

What are the three most significant features that stand out regarding its successful implementation?

What are the three most significant features that suggest its failure to address pauperism?

Summary activities

At the end of each chapter, you will find summary activities. These are tasks designed to help you think about the key topic you have just studied as a whole. They may involve selecting and organising key information or analysing how things changed over time. You might want to keep your answers to these questions safe – they are handy for revision.

ACTIVITY
SUMMARY

1 Write down with full explanations the three most important consequences of industrialisation in Germany.

2 Write a full paragraph explaining why the people in the German Confederation who were liberals might also have been nationalists.

3 Draw three mind maps about the political situation at the end of 1847, one each for Prussia, Austria and Baden.

4 Write a short essay to answer the following question:

How far would a liberal writing in May 1848 have regarded the 1848 revolutions as being successful?

Thinking Historically activities

These activities are found throughout the book and are designed to develop your understanding of history, especially around the key concepts of evidence, interpretations, causation and change. Each activity is designed to challenge a conceptual barrier that might be holding you back. This is linked to a map of conceptual barriers developed by experts. You can look up the map and find out which barrier each activity challenges by downloading the conceptual map from this website: www.pearsonschools.co.uk/ historyprogressionapproach.

conceptual map reference

THINKING HISTORICALLY | Interpretations (3a)

Differing Accounts

Carefully read extracts 3 and 4 which discuss the abolition of the slave trade.

1 For each of the historians create a summary table of their views:

Make a note of how they address the following key issues outlined below:

How important was economic motivation?

How far did political opinion influence abolition?

Make a note of the evidence they give in support of this claim

Use your notes and knowledge to give evidence which supports or challenges their interpretation

2 In pairs discuss which historian's interpretation of abolition seems to best fit with the available evidence. Which seems the most convincing?

3 Make a note of any issues which made it difficult to compare the two interpretations directly.

Challenge: Seek out another historical interpretation on the abolition of the slave trade and compare this to the views you have explored already.

Getting the most from your online ActiveBook

This book comes with three years' access to ActiveBook* – an online, digital version of your textbook. Follow the instructions printed on the inside front cover to start using your ActiveBook.

Your ActiveBook is the perfect way to personalise your learning as you progress through your AS/A Level History course. You can:

- access your content online, anytime, anywhere

- use the inbuilt highlighting and annotation tools to personalise the content and make it really relevant to you.

Highlight tool – use this to pick out key terms or topics so you are ready and prepared for revision.

Annotations tool – use this to add your own notes, for example links to your wider reading, such as websites or other files. Or, make a note to remind yourself about work that you need to do.

*For new purchases only. If the access code has already been revealed, it may no longer be valid. If you have bought this textbook secondhand, the code may already have been used by the first owner of the book.

Introduction
AS/A Level History

WHY HISTORY MATTERS

History is about people and people are complex, fascinating, frustrating and a whole lot of other things besides. This is why history is probably the most comprehensive and certainly one of the most intriguing subjects there is. History can also be inspiring and alarming, heartening and disturbing, a story of progress and civilisation and of catastrophe and inhumanity.

History's importance goes beyond the subject's intrinsic interest and appeal. Our beliefs and actions, our cultures, institutions and ways of living, our languages and means of making sense of ourselves are all shaped by the past. If we want to fully understand ourselves now, and to understand our possible futures, we have no alternative but to think about history.

History is a discipline as well as a subject matter. Making sense of the past develops qualities of mind that are valuable to anyone who wants to seek the truth and think clearly and intelligently about the most interesting and challenging intellectual problem of all: other people. Learning history is learning a powerful way of knowing.

WHAT IS HISTORY?

History is a way of constructing knowledge about the world through research, interpretation, argument and debate.

Building historical knowledge involves identifying the traces of the past that exist in the present – in people's memories, in old documents, photographs and other remains, and in objects and artefacts ranging from bullets and lipsticks, to field systems and cities. Historians interrogate these traces and *ask questions* that transform traces into *sources of evidence* for knowledge claims about the past.

Historians aim to understand what happened in the past by *explaining why* things happened as they did. Explaining why involves trying to understand past people and their beliefs, intentions and actions. It also involves explaining the causes and evaluating the effects of large-scale changes in the past and exploring relationships between what people aimed to do, the contexts that shaped what was possible and the outcomes and consequences of actions.

Historians also aim to *understand change* in the past. People, states of affairs, ideas, movements and civilisations come into being in time, grow, develop, and ultimately decline and disappear. Historians aim to identify and compare change and continuity in the past, to measure the rate at which things change and to identify the types of change that take place. Change can be slow or sudden. It can also be understood as progressive or regressive – leading to the improvement or worsening of a situation or state of affairs. How things change and whether changes are changes for the better are two key issues that historians frequently debate.

Figure 1 Fragment of a black granite statue possibly portraying the Roman politician Mark Antony.

Debate is the essence of history. Historians write arguments to support their knowledge claims and historians argue with each other to test and evaluate interpretations of the past. Historical knowledge itself changes and develops. On the one hand, new sources of knowledge and new methods of research cause *historical interpretations* to change. On the other hand, the questions that historians ask change with time and new questions produce new answers. Although the past is dead and gone, the interpretation of the past has a past, present and future.

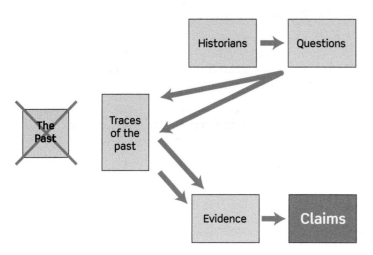

Figure 2 Constructing knowledge about the past.

THE CHALLENGES OF LEARNING HISTORY

Like all other Advanced Level subjects, A Level and AS Level history are difficult – that is why they are called 'advanced'. Your advanced level studies will build on knowledge and understanding of history that you developed at GCSE and at Key Stage 3 – ideas like 'historical sources', 'historical evidence' and 'cause', for example. You will need to do a lot of reading and writing to progress in history. Most importantly, you will need to do a lot of thinking, and thinking about your thinking. This book aims to support you in developing both your knowledge and your understanding.

History is challenging in many ways. On the one hand, it is challenging to build up the range and depth of knowledge that you need to understand the past at an advanced level. Learning about the past involves mastering new and unfamiliar concepts arising from the past itself (such as the Inquisition, Laudianism, *Volksgemeinschaft*) and building up levels of knowledge that are both detailed and well organised. This book covers the key content of the topics that you are studying for your examination and provides a number of features to help you build and organise what you know – for example, diagrams, timelines and definitions of key terms. You will need to help yourself too, of course, adding to your knowledge through further reading, building on the foundations provided by this book.

Another challenge is to develop understandings of the discipline of history. You will have to learn to think historically about evidence, cause, change and interpretations and also to write historically, in a way that develops clear and supported argument.

Historians think with evidence in ways that differ from how we often think in everyday life. In history, as Figure 2 shows, we cannot go and 'see for ourselves' because the past no longer exists. Neither can we normally rely on 'credible witnesses' to tell us 'the truth' about 'what happened'. People in the past did not write down 'the truth' for our benefit. They often had clear agendas when creating the traces that remain and, as often as not, did not themselves know 'the truth' about complex historical events.

A root of the word 'history' is the Latin word *historia*, one of whose meanings is 'enquiry' or 'finding out'. Learning history means learning to ask questions and interrogate traces, and then to reason about what the new knowledge you have gained means. This book draws on historical scholarship for its narrative and contents. It also draws on research on the nature of historical thinking and on the challenges that learning history can present for students. Throughout the book you will find 'Thinking Historically' activities designed to support the development of your thinking.

You will also find – as you would expect given the nature of history – that the book is full of questions. This book aims to help you build your understandings of the content, contexts and concepts that you will need to advance both your historical knowledge and your historical understanding, and to lay strong foundations for the future development of both.

QUOTES ABOUT HISTORY

'Historians are dangerous people. They are capable of upsetting everything. They must be directed.'

Nikita Khrushchev

'To be ignorant of what occurred before you were born is to remain forever a child. For what is the worth of human life, unless it is woven into the life of our ancestors by the records of history?'

Marcus Tullius Cicero

Britain, c1785–c1870: democracy, protest and reform

The late 18th and 19th centuries were a period of great change in Europe. It saw old empires decline and new empires grow as countries adapted to an increasingly changing world. Within this period political regimes were transformed to reflect more progressive ideas such as 'equality' and 'representation'; ideas born of the Enlightenment movement which had only recently filtered down into the public consciousness. With an increased awareness of these new ideas the authority of the old hereditary-based political order was challenged and emergent ideas like socialism, which championed the ordinary man, became more commonplace. Faced with such challenges, states undertook reform to preserve much of their authority and, in the process of making changes, transformed their states into the modern nations we recognise today.

The focus of this option is to understand these challenges to authority and to promote an appreciation as to why they occurred and what they achieved. In this chapter the focus is upon Britain and how this nation developed in the wake of considerable change undertaken during the late 18th and 19th centuries.

This was a period in which Britain came of age. It saw the nation transformed beyond recognition in social, economic and political terms and established the basis of our modern state. The single most important feature of this period was the Industrial Revolution which affected the nation profoundly. During this time Britain moved from a pre-industrial, agricultural economy, into the 'workshop of the world' and as part of this shift also witnessed the growth of a more urban-based population. These economic developments had a great impact upon the country and initiated a wider contemplation on the nature of the British state.

What emerged from this process was a more critical look at the country and a growing demand for further reforms to reflect the transformed environment. As Britain became an economically modern nation, there was an increased demand that it embrace modernity in other areas too. Between 1785 and 1870 the country was faced with new challenges from all quarters of society: the demand for voting rights, trade unionism and the abolition of the slave trade are just a few of the challenges that were presented to those in power, and these challenges were met with varied levels of success. Whether successful or not, these events and actions helped to shape modern Britain, and as such the history of that country during this period is fundamental to a broader understanding of our current experiences. In terms of what we take for granted today: the democratic process; basic necessities such as clean water; social security and fair working practices, these are things that we only enjoy because of the changes begun at the end of the 18th century. Without the demands placed upon governments of the day, these facilities may not have been implemented in Britain until much later and the development of our state might have been very different.

French Revolution	1789
Speenhamland welfare relief system adopted	1795
Combination Acts passed	1800
Abolition of the slave trade	1807
Peterloo Massacre	1819
Abolition of slavery Factory Act passed	1833
People's Charter published and Chartism begins	1838
Andover workhouse scandal	1846
Public Health Act passed	1848
Samuel Smiles publishes Self Help	1859
Second Reform Act passed	1867

1793	War with France begins
1799	Robert Owen takes over the mills at New Lanark
1804	Napoleon proclaimed emperor of France
1815	End of the Napoleonic Wars with France
1832	Great Reform Act passed
1834	Poor Law Amendment Act passed Tolpuddle 'Martyrs' tried
1844	Rochdale Pioneers founded
1847	Ten Hours Act passed
1851	Amalgamated Society of Engineers founded
1860	Chartism ends
1868	Trades Union Congress founded

SOURCE 1

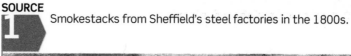

Smokestacks from Sheffield's steel factories in the 1800s.

In looking at the influences behind the evolution of modern Britain there is the opportunity to consider how ordinary people as well as great leaders effected change – the importance of determined individuals and unified collections of men and women in particular. By appreciating the roles that people can play in the story of their nation there is the acknowledgement that history is more than just dates; it is the interaction of human beings and the dynamism of actions both great and small.

1.1 The growth of parliamentary democracy, c1785–c1870

KEY QUESTIONS

- Why was the unreformed parliament criticised?
- How significant was the pressure for change between 1820 and 1852?
- What promoted further parliamentary reform after 1852?

INTRODUCTION

Political participation is a well-established feature of British democracy today. It is the foundation of our **parliamentary system** of government and ensures that the broadest elements of society are represented as effectively as possible. This principle is so universally accepted that people rarely give it a second thought as they get on with their busy lives. Such acceptance was not always present and in the late 18th century the political landscape in Britain was far removed from that which is enjoyed today.

Despite originating in ancient Greece, the concept of '**democracy**' came to Britain through a series of reforms designed to promote stability and maintain interests rather than further a political principle. Towards the end of the 1700s, industrialisation slowly began to develop in Britain and into the 19th century it spread dramatically, transforming socio-economic fortunes and unleashing new challenges that raised questions of the existing political structures. Created in the Middle Ages, these were outdated and increasingly seen as unreflective of the rapidly modernising nation. Having witnessed revolution in France, where calls for political change went unheeded, politicians in Britain became aware of the need for reform as the country began making similar demands. Over time first moderate reform was offered, and then, as society grew more 'respectable', more widespread amendments gradually transformed the political landscape.

KEY TERMS

Parliamentary system
A system of government where the people elect representatives to sit on their behalf in a parliament. The government is then drawn from whichever collection of representatives has a majority in this institution. As the embodiment of the people, parliament retains ultimate power and is the body that holds government to account.

Democracy
Originating from the Greek words *demos* and *kratos* meaning 'people' and 'power'. This concept promotes the idea that political authority is most legitimate when people are able to make their own choices.

1790 – Publication of *Reflections of the Revolution in France*

1787 – US Constitution created

1793 – Start of the Napoleonic Wars

1819 – Peterloo Massacre

| 1785 | 1790 | 1795 | 1800 | 1805 | 1810 | 1815 | 1820 | 1825 |

1783 – End of the American War

1789 – French Revolution

1792 – Publication of *Rights of Man*

1815 – End of the Napoleonic Wars; passage of new Corn Laws

1828 – Death of Lord Liverpool

The system of political power that existed in Britain towards the end of the 18th century was created over time and established by convention rather than from any specific effort to create a **codified** model like that produced by the Americans in 1787. Without the constraint of being written down, the British **constitution** promoted a more flexible approach to government, which was at the same time both an effective means for finding political solutions and also allowed for corrupt practices to go virtually without censure.

Britain's slow political evolution had created a unique system whereby the traditional role of the monarch was retained alongside more modern ideas such as government by the people. The outcome of this was that Britain had both a king who ruled with hereditary power and also a parliament that consisted of representatives of the public. The latter was separated into two 'houses': the 'House of Commons' represented the interests of the ordinary citizen, while the 'House of Lords' reflected the will of the nobility. Collectively these institutions wielded immense authority over the country and, unlike today, the monarchy and House of Lords played a more prominent role in the working of government. Although reliant upon his parliament, the king made the major policy decisions and was able to select his own ministers while the Lords had the power to block legislation proposed by the government. In this sense there was some evidence to suggest that power was reasonably divided and the system had some positive features to it.

In particular, this distribution of power appears to have the basic requirements of democracy – notably a parliament that reflects the will of the people – however, in reality parliament was anything but representative. Those who sat in each house were there primarily by virtue of wealth and influence rather than any democratic principle. To sit in the House of Lords required a peerage, while entry to the Commons was achieved through a national election, although eligibility was dependent on wealth; candidates had to own property worth at least £300 per year, depending on the constituency. If elected then the candidate would receive no salary and would serve his term without any official recompense for any expenditure incurred while carrying out his duty. Under these circumstances it was almost impossible for a man of modest means to stand for election unless he had the backing of a peer who would fund his ambitions. This practice of **patronage** eroded any pretence of democracy by giving significant influence over the Commons to the wealthier House of Lords; in 1761, for example, it was calculated that the election of 111 members to the Commons was financed by 55 peers. This activity remained the norm as elections continued and by 1801 approximately half of Britain's 658 members of parliament (MPs) owed their positions to benefactors in the Lords. The implication of this set-up was that despite the anticipated opportunity to exercise a free choice that an election presented, the idea that people were actually given a real choice when casting their votes was significantly undermined. It also gave excessive political influence to the richest strata of society, which ensured that any notion of a true and accurate representation of the breadth of British society was purely in spirit only.

KEY TERMS

Codified
A term used to describe something that has been clearly organised, usually having been written down.

Constitution
A collection of fundamental principles on which a state organises its government.

KEY TERM

Patronage
The practice of sponsoring someone's ambitions either by funding them or using influence to promote them. Given the expensive nature of election campaigning, this system was widely used in Britain before 1832.

1830	1835	1840	1845	1850	1855	1860	1865	1870

1829 – Catholic Emancipation

1833 – Slavery abolished

1838 – 'People's' Charter issued

1842 – Second Chartist Petition

1858 – Property qualifications for MPs removed

Chartism formally wound up

1866 – Hyde Park Riots

1868 – William Gladstone becomes prime minister for the first time

1832 – First Reform Act

1839 – First Chartist Petition

1848 – Third Chartist Petition

1861 – Start of the American Civil War

1867 – Second Reform Act

1865 – American Civil War ends

THE UNREFORMED PARLIAMENT AND ITS CRITICS

The pre-reform franchise

The right of men to vote in Britain was a curious affair, having also been established in the Middle Ages and based upon a range of long-standing traditions rather than any coherent structure. To make matters more complicated, the qualifications differed depending on which constituency you lived in. In Britain there were two distinct types of constituency – the counties and the boroughs. The right of women to vote was raised in parliament several times in the 19th century, but only became reality in the early 20th century.

The counties

These were the rural shires in Britain, which each elected two MPs to Westminster. The qualification in these elections was perhaps the most straightforward of all the franchise restrictions and was based upon an Act of Parliament in 1430 that set the requirement as ownership of a freehold property worth more than 40 shillings (about £2) a year. Although in Scottish counties the value was set at £100 a year, as inflation went up and the value of money went down, this became quite a wide franchise. The problem with the county vote was therefore not the numbers it excluded but rather the fact that each county returned two MPs regardless of size – in 1800, for example, Bedfordshire had a population of 2,000 while Yorkshire had grown to 20,000 and yet did not receive any more MPs.

The boroughs

If the counties seemed unrepresentative, then the borough franchise was arguably even more exclusive. Boroughs were the urban towns which had been granted administrative rights since the Middle Ages. Like the counties, they elected two MPs but, given the individuality of these towns, the franchise qualification in them was very broad. However, by the 19th century there were six generally recognised types:

Corporation:	Only members of the town council could vote.
Freemen:	Anyone with the status of 'freeman' could vote. This title could be inherited from a person's father or acquired through marriage and was bestowed if the recipient had received an honour from the local corporation or served as an apprentice in the borough.
Scot and Lot:	Anyone who paid poor rates could vote.
Burgage:	'Burgage' was an ancient form of rent applied to property in a borough and the owners of this property were able to vote.
Potwalloper:	Householders who had a hearth that was big enough to boil a pot on could vote.
Freeholder:	A similar franchise as the counties.

Parliamentary seats and elections before reform

Uncontested elections and selective representation

Understandably, the extent of the franchise varied widely in the boroughs and this lack of clarity presented great opportunities for powerful individuals to manipulate the system for personal gain, for example, in 1780 only two counties were contested as the leading families in these areas chose to divide representation among themselves rather than go to the expense of bribing voters in a contested election. Where elections did take place, the lack of a **secret ballot** meant that on election day voters were exposed to public viewing when they cast their votes. Such practice made the opportunity for intimidation particularly effective, especially if the voter depended upon the landowner or employer who was standing for election. This was evident in the counties, where the landed gentry were able to apply pressure on any of their tenants who were able to vote. However, it was most obviously the case in those boroughs where very few voters actually resided and therefore intimidation and bribery was especially effective. So common was this practice that the majority of the smallest boroughs were directly controlled by either the local landowner or by the government itself. These **pocket boroughs** were an easy way for wealthy interests to ensure their political dominance and, although the process could be expensive, it was money well spent if it meant that they could influence the political process or further their own ambitions. The pocket borough of Gatton in Surrey, for example, was 'bought' at auction in 1801 for £90,000 just so the 'owner' did not have to stand for election against a rival.

The consequence of this system was that the wealthy property owners and landowners controlled representation in the Commons. The vote, by virtue of the existing franchise qualifications, was not only distributed in different ways in boroughs and counties, but it did not adequately reflect the different interests in the country. As a result, only 11 percent of the population could take part in an election.

The inadequacies of the electoral system promoted great opportunities for corruption and the political dominance of the upper classes. In certain quarters of British society this alone would have raised questions about the need for reform; however, the system was also completely out of date. Having been created in the medieval period, the actual distribution of seats was based upon the importance of the constituency *at the time of creation* and did not necessarily reflect modern developments. By the turn of the 19th century, many of the recognised boroughs were no longer the important towns they once were. This was perhaps most famously the case with the borough of Old Sarum, just to the north of Salisbury, which by the late 1700s had all but disappeared and despite having fewer than residents still returned two MPs to Westminster. Dunwich, on the coast in Suffolk, was equally unrepresentative with 14 voters and only 32 dwellings, having lost most of its houses to the sea due to coastal erosion. These **rotten boroughs** used to be very important – Dunwich had been a thriving port before the sea swallowed up the majority of the town, and Old Sarum had been the seat of the Bishop of Salisbury in the 11th century – but clearly fortunes had changed and such over-representation was a stark indication that things needed to change. If this evidence was not enough, by contrast new towns and cities such as Manchester, which in 1831 had more than 182,000 inhabitants, and Birmingham, which boasted a population of 144,000, were not even recognised as parliamentary boroughs and had no representation at all.

> **KEY TERM**
>
> **Rotten borough**
> A small town or hamlet that used to be a prominent settlement in the Middle Ages but had over time declined in stature. Despite their reduced status rotten boroughs still retained their two MPs because of their past importance.

ACTIVITY
KNOWLEDGE CHECK

The unreformed system
Using the text and your own knowledge think about the strengths and weaknesses of the unreformed political system and write down five points that defend its continuance and five points that support its reform.

Demands for reform, c1785–1820

Given the evident problems generated by this haphazard system, there were several attempts to promote reform of parliament. Groups dedicated to this task were already common before 1785, including the London-based Society for Constitutional Information which emerged in 1780. This organisation was created by Major John Cartwright and sought to promote public awareness of the need for reform by pamphleteering. Although this group was ultimately undermined by the anti-Catholic **Gordon riots**, which scared the propertied classes and turned them away from political change, it did raise the issue of reform in a more public sphere and ensured that reform would not be forgotten. Taking up the cause in 1785 the prime minister, William Pitt, proposed disenfranchising 36 of the worst boroughs and redistributing their seats to larger counties but was defeated by 74 votes in the Commons. Despite pockets of reformers within Britain, parliamentary reform was not a popular issue during the 1780s and few MPs were motivated to change a system from which they themselves benefited. Under these circumstances, attention was turned elsewhere and the reform issue was dropped.

> **EXTEND YOUR KNOWLEDGE**
>
> **Gordon Riots (1780)**
> These were anti-Catholic riots that took place in 1780 after the passage of the 1778 Papist Act which intended to reduce Catholic discrimination in Britain. As a Protestant, Lord George Gordon had called for the repeal of the Papist Act, believing that toleration of the Catholic Church was unnecessary and his violent speech encouraged rioting against this faith.

Impact of the French Revolution

Demand for political reform presented itself again in 1789 when revolution in France broke out and in the presence of that unfolding drama – which saw aristocratic rule violently overthrown – criticisms of the British model started to re-emerge as people began to question the legitimacy of what they increasingly saw as 'rule by the rich'. Faced with this criticism, a strong defence of the unreformed electoral system ensued from conservative politicians and others who benefited from it. Primarily they argued that the system did not need to be reformed and that the criticisms levelled against it were unfounded. At the heart of this defence was a simple argument: why change something that was working well? Citing the successes of Britain in recent years – particularly the victorious wars against Napoleon and the slowly developing industrialisation of England – champions of the existing model were quick to point out that while France after its revolution had descended into violence and the 'Reign of Terror', Britain remained a stable and increasingly prosperous nation. Chief among those celebrating these virtues was the Tory politician Edmund

Burke, whose book *Reflections on the Revolution in France* had prophesied the violence abroad and blamed it on the sudden and radical political change undertaken. For him, the real virtue of the British system was its slow and adaptive nature based upon sound traditional practices and a belief that, although not all of society was able to vote, those MPs elected served as representatives of the entire nation were the best individuals in society and therefore knew how best to govern.

EXTEND YOUR KNOWLEDGE

Edmund Burke (1729-97)

Edmund Burke was the son of an Anglo-Irish solicitor who first entered politics after being appointed secretary to the **Whig** Leader Lord Rockingham. Serving as MP for Bristol between 1774 and 1780 and then for the pocket borough of Malton until his retirement in 1794, Burke became the chief exponent of conservatism. His defence of the British constitution upon the outbreak of revolution in France became the rallying cry for **Tory** politicians and his pronouncements about the importance of tradition and social order are today recognised as cornerstones of classic conservative thought.

KEY TERMS

'Whigs' and 'Tories'

These were originally terms of abuse levelled at different political factions after the 17th century. 'Whig' came from Scottish Gaelic and was a term used to describe horse thieves while 'Tory' meant a 'papist outlaw'. During the Glorious Revolution (1688–89) the terms were used to denote those who wished to deny hereditary rights to James Stuart and therefore prevent him from becoming James II ('Whigs') and those who supported his claim ('Tories'). Although both groups shared a common, gentrified, background, after 1784 the terms became more defined as political parties began to become more distinctly partisan. 'Tories' became more closely associated with religious intolerance while 'Whigs' championed the financial interests of the middle class.

SOURCE 1

From Edmund Burke's *Reflections on the Revolution in France*, published in 1790.

Our constitution... is a constitution, whose sole authority is, that it has existed time out of mind... It is a presumption in favour of any settled scheme of government against any untried project, that a nation has long flourished under it. It is a better presumption even of the choice of a nation, far better than any sudden and temporary arrangement by actual election... The multitude, for the moment, is foolish, when they act without deliberation; but when the species is wise, and when time is given to it, as a species, it almost always acts right.

SOURCE 2

From Thomas Paine's *Rights of Man*, published in 1792.

All hereditary Government is in its nature tyranny. An heritable crown, or an heritable throne, or by what other fanciful name such things may be called, have no other significant explanation than that mankind are heritable property. To inherit a Government, is to inherit the people, as if they were flocks and herds... Government ought to be a thing always in full maturity. It ought to be so constructed as to be superior to all accidents to which individual man is subject; and, therefore, hereditary succession, by being *subject to them all,* is the most irregular and imperfect of all the systems of Government.

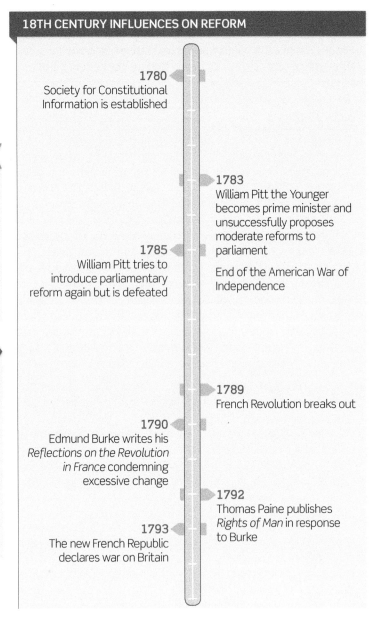

18TH CENTURY INFLUENCES ON REFORM

1780
Society for Constitutional Information is established

1783
William Pitt the Younger becomes prime minister and unsuccessfully proposes moderate reforms to parliament

End of the American War of Independence

1785
William Pitt tries to introduce parliamentary reform again but is defeated

1789
French Revolution breaks out

1790
Edmund Burke writes his *Reflections on the Revolution in France* condemning excessive change

1792
Thomas Paine publishes *Rights of Man* in response to Burke

1793
The new French Republic declares war on Britain

This defence did little to quiet the growing discontent in Britain, which by the turn of the century was given intellectual credibility by the writer Thomas Paine. Inspired by the events in France, his book *Rights of Man*, written in response to Burke, eloquently condemned the inequalities of the existing system and became a bestseller in Britain – by 1793 more than 200,000 copies had been sold. Paine's work emphasised the natural rights belonging to human beings and called for radical reform, particularly rule by the people which, in his eyes, was the only justifiable means of government. Pouring scorn on the notion of monarchy and drawing attention to the widespread corruption within British politics, *Rights of Man* inspired a raft of young reformers who sought to bring greater democracy to the country.

New organisations spread throughout Britain, including the predominantly working-class Sheffield Society for Constitutional Information formed in 1791 and the larger London Corresponding Society a year later. Like their predecessors, these groups sought to raise public awareness of reform by writing political pamphlets but they also undertook more assertive measures and in May

1792 the Sheffield Society had nearly 10,000 signatures on a national petition calling for manhood suffrage. More startling was a demonstration organised by the London Corresponding Society at Copenhagen Fields on 26 October 1795 which attracted more than 100,000 people. The more determined activities of these groups and the growing participation suggests that reform was becoming a more pressing issue for the country, particularly in the wake of revolution across the Channel. However, any threat posed by these events was quickly overshadowed by the outbreak of war with the new French Republic in 1793. Any sympathy that existed for reform was replaced by a strong sense of patriotism which reinforced the existing status quo. In addition, war brought more rigorous government control, which saw the Treason Act passed in 1795, allowing for the death penalty in the event of any treasonable activity, including political meetings and the publication of seditious material that might challenge government authority. Under such pressure, reform movements were quickly wound up and although there remained the occasional flourish in London by radicals such as Sir Francis Burdett and William Cobbett, who each raised the issue during the 1807 election, there was no sustained parliamentary reform movement until the end of the war in 1815.

SOURCE 3

Wha Wants Me? Print of Thomas Paine reading a scroll of the rights of man and appealing to Englishmen to overthrow their monarchy, dated 26 December 1792.

Demand for reform, 1815–20

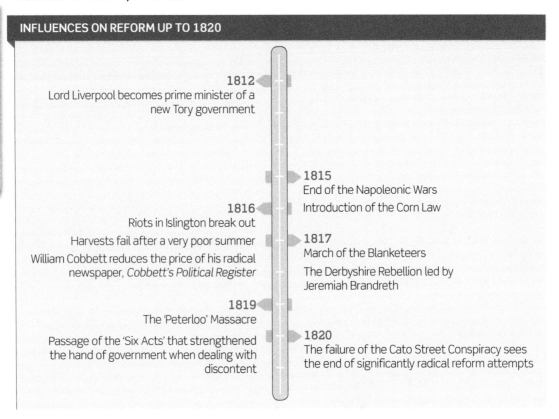

INFLUENCES ON REFORM UP TO 1820

1812
Lord Liverpool becomes prime minister of a new Tory government

1815
End of the Napoleonic Wars
Introduction of the Corn Law

1816
Riots in Islington break out
Harvests fail after a very poor summer
William Cobbett reduces the price of his radical newspaper, *Cobbett's Political Register*

1817
March of the Blanketeers
The Derbyshire Rebellion led by Jeremiah Brandreth

1819
The 'Peterloo' Massacre
Passage of the 'Six Acts' that strengthened the hand of government when dealing with discontent

1820
The failure of the Cato Street Conspiracy sees the end of significantly radical reform attempts

Demands for reform re-emerged with the end of war in 1815, when the experiences of the general population took a dramatic downturn as soldiers returned home looking for work in a depressed economic climate. This was made worse in 1816 when the harvests failed in what was one of the worst summers in British history. With basic foodstuffs in scarce supply, the cost of merely subsisting became burdensome to many of Britain's poorest people as demand forced prices higher. Coupled with a decline in wages because of the ready supply of labour provided by returning soldiers, the majority of Britain's poorer classes fell into economic distress which, only weeks after victory against Napoleon, refocused attention upon the aristocratic political regime. Economic difficulty is often the cause of protest because it affects large sections of the population and often highlights the inequalities between rich and poor. After 1815, these problems encouraged a closer look at the system of government which seemed not to be supporting those in greatest need.

Agitation from the re-awakened reform movement reflected the diversity of its members, which included both working class and also radical members of the new, commercial interests. There was an active reform press that churned out political articles and pamphlets to whoever wanted to read them; the radical newspaper *Cobbett's Political Register* was particularly popular after its owner, William Cobbett, reduced the price of his paper in November 1816 from 1s ½ d to 2d, while Thomas Wooler's *Black Dwarf* offered an ironic look at the reform issue. In support of the written word, the well-known orator Henry Hunt made rousing speeches to crowds on the topic of reform. These activities ensured that political awareness spread throughout the country at a time when people were interested in listening once again. As the message of reform was carried further north, agitation became more hardnosed; writing and making speeches was replaced by marching and attempted rebellion in those areas where distress was acutely felt. Riots at Spa Fields in Islington during 1816 (see Source 4) were trumped by weavers in Manchester organising an armed march to London in 1817 and although this 'March of the Blanketeers' was broken up by local yeomanry in Stockport, it heralded a wave of more threatening actions that sought to rock the political establishment. In Derbyshire the following year there was an attempted rebellion led by Jeremiah Brandreth, a stocking maker by trade, who later went to the gallows after the attempt failed. Across the country people were visibly criticising the ruling classes and the rising level of agitation was quite alarming for the government. When further mass demonstrations took place in 1819 their high-handed response evidenced a sense of control being lost.

SOURCE 4

Part of a pamphlet distributed at the Spa Fields meeting in December 1816.

Britons to Arms!

The whole country waits the signal from London to fly to arms! Haste, break open gunsmiths and other likely places to find arms! run all constables who touch a man of us; no rise of bread; No Regent; no Castlereagh, off with their heads; no placemen, tythes or enclosures; no taxes; no bishops.

The Peterloo Massacre

SOURCE
5

A contemporary cartoon showing the dispersing of the crowds at St Peter's Fields, Manchester, an act that became known as the 'Peterloo Massacre', August 1819.

During 1819, reform momentum increased and across the country there was a series of four political rallies held, the last of which was at St Peter's Fields in Manchester on 16 August. The speaker at the rally was Henry Hunt and it attracted upwards of 60,000 people, mostly dressed in their Sunday best clothes. In the wake of the failed rebellion in Derby the previous year and fearful of riots occurring given the large numbers concentrated in one location, local magistrates ordered the meeting to be disbanded and Hunt arrested. Using yeomanry, the crowds were forcibly dispersed by a sabre charge and in the action 18 people were killed and more than 400 wounded.

The victims of what became known as the 'Peterloo Massacre' became martyrs for reform although none was forthcoming. The immediate outcome of the event was further repression by the government through a series of Acts designed to strengthen its hand against protestors. The 'Six Acts' passed in December were introduced by the home secretary, Lord Sidmouth, and included the banning of public meetings of more than 50 people and introduced harsher punishments, including the death penalty, for **sedition**. The repressive nature of these Acts in the aftermath of the massacre suggests that the government was fearful of a violent reprisal from the more aggressive elements of the reform movement who might have seen the brutal event as an invitation to revolt. By taking such a strong position, the government hoped to crush any seed of further discontent.

For the reform movement, the Peterloo Massacre had a mixed effect. In the first instance, the shock of such brutality fractured the working- and middle-class alliance by driving much of the more conservative middle class away from the cause. After the arrest of respectable reformers such as Henry Hunt and Francis Burdett MP, many of the moderate supporters of the movement quietly dropped their reform intentions as they tried to preserve their positions in society and avoid the stiff reactionary policies of the government. For others, the massacre stirred up even greater determination to challenge the political regime and in 1820 a group of disaffected reformers, led by the London radical Arthur Thistlewood, plotted to assassinate the cabinet while they dined in Grosvenor Square. The attempt was discovered by the authorities and the group was seized at its Cato Street headquarters. The leap from public speechmaking to attempted assassination suggests that Britain was in a dangerously revolutionary position; however, this would be an overassessment of the conspiracy and state of the country.

The main source of discontent had been the declining economy. However, by 1820 this was improving once again and therefore much of the population was focusing on making the most of this good fortune rather than seeking any further reform, especially after the sharp response that met those at St Peter's Field. As a result, the conspirators at Cato Street were very much a minority acting on personal motives, rather than any altruistic community spirit. Any significance that might be applied to the event, beyond the obvious suggestion regarding its aims, perhaps lies in the brief flurry of radical activity that took place immediately after the Cato Street conspiracy. There was a woeful effort by weavers to seize Glasgow and some of their English counterparts endeavoured to take control of Huddersfield, both to no avail. In themselves, these actions were not overtly threatening to the government but they evidenced an ongoing and fairly robust feeling of animosity towards the current system, which some politicians started to take notice of (Source 6).

SOURCE

6 From a private letter written by the Tory MP Robert Peel to fellow Tory John Wilson Croker in 1820.

Do you not think that the tone of England – of that great compound of folly, weakness, prejudice, wrong feeling, right feeling, obstinacy and newspaper paragraphs, which is called public opinion – is more liberal, to use an odious but intelligible phrase, than the policy of the government?

Although violent agitation was very much in decline after 1820, kept alive only by pockets of radicals in London and the north, the message had been sent to Westminster that something needed to be done. The majority of the population might have abandoned radical reform measures after an economic revival and what many perceived to be the growing excesses of radicals, but unless steps were taken, it would not require much to push them back into the arms of reform.

The political demands of the manufacturing interests

Just as the beginning of industrialisation towards the end of the 1700s was transforming the economy, it also started to have a social impact by establishing a new class in Britain. These were the owners of the new factories, self-made men with a commercial drive that would translate into a political appetite big enough to consume the unreformed model of governance. This 'middling' class of manufacturing interests, located between the labouring classes and traditional landed aristocracy, was a collection of individuals who carried the potential to force political change as they were not only educated men, but also employers of thousands of workers who relied on their goodwill. As men of property, this interest was initially conservative and when reform had been raised in the past had generally sided with the establishment to maintain their prosperity. However, as men of business, they favoured efficiency and a *laissez-faire* approach to commerce. The latter principle was a source of contention during the wars with France when the government maintained a tight

grip on the country; at the end of the wars, when the government passed further legislation to restrict trade, vocal criticisms were raised with alarming alacrity.

KEY TERM

Laissez-faire
This is a principle that says government should have no control over economic matters. Markets should be free and people should be able to trade as they like.

The foundation of these criticisms lay with the government's decision to pass a new Corn Law to protect British farmers from foreign competition now that war was over. This law prohibited the import of foreign corn until the price of domestic corn reached ten shillings a bushel (approximately 36 litres in metric volume). Generally this was a policy designed to protect domestic markets at a time when economic fortunes were waning; the security of wartime contracts were gone and the floods of soldiers returning home was driving wages lower and lower. However, the law was seen as a stark example of how the government was 'looking after its own' and prioritising the interests of landowners. For employers in the cities the Corn Law forced up bread prices and, as this was the staple food source for many of the poor, employers were forced to raise wages so as to retain a healthy workforce.

In voicing its concerns, the commercial 'middle class' was beginning to assert its own political opinions. Entangled within the financial impact of the Corn Law was a further criticism of the inefficiency of the existing political structure. The practice of patronage itself often ensured that ineffective men found themselves in office by virtue not of their talent but rather of rich backers. To many of the self-made and determined new leaders of industry this was both aristocratic favouritism writ large and also an abject waste of talent that bred inefficiency. Worse still was the blatant unrepresentative distribution of seats in parliament which failed to reflect the huge migration of people to the cities (see pages 12–13). Increasingly it appeared to members of the growing urban middle class that, as the providers of both employment and much of Britain's resources, they perhaps merited more of a say in how the country was to be governed. In their eyes the dominance of the landed gentry was in decline; people were leaving the rural areas and moving in vast numbers to the cities for work supplied by themselves. In this sense it was logical that they, as the new elite, ought to share in the political bounty.

ACTIVITY
KNOWLEDGE CHECK

How revolutionary was Britain?
Using the material presented above about the growing agitation and demands for reform, plot a graph to provide an overall impression about the extent of threat present in Britain between 1785 and 1820.

Make the x-axis (horizontal line) the event and the y-axis (vertical line) the level of threat posed. On plotting the y-axis you should use your own judgement as to the level of threat produced, using a scale of 0 (absolutely no threat) to 10 (excessive threat).

PRESSURE FOR CHANGE AND REFORM, 1820–52

Economic and social distress; emerging popular pressure, 1820–32

In the wake of the 'Six Acts' and with the gradual improvement of the economy after 1820, popular demand for reform reduced as the country settled into a more prosperous period and trade with Europe picked up as markets became more established once again. Between 1821 and 1829, the **Gross National Product** of Britain rose by 16.8 percent while manufacturing grew by approximately 25 percent. The consequence of this prosperity was that there was now the opportunity to pursue commerce rather than public order and the Tory government was able to relax its grip upon the country.

The relaxation of government policy, which saw radicals such as Henry Hunt released from prison in 1822, has created a general impression among some historians of an administration undergoing a dramatic transformation from 'reactionism' of the 1815–21 period to 'liberalism' after 1822. This view has found much favour and encouraged the reasonable notion that with improving economic circumstances the government became more progressive in its attitudes. Within this interpretation the government was keen to stabilise the country and, having replaced controversial Tory stalwarts such as Lord Sidmouth with younger minds like that of Robert Peel, the government was endeavouring to take advantage of the prevailing positivity.

SOURCE

From an article in the *Stockport Advertiser* in June 1823.

Never in our memory was this part of the country in a state equally flourishing: our manufacturers are employed, our artisans happy and industrious, and loyalty and content have given place to **Jacobinism** and sedition, which distress had mainly contributed to foster.

KEY TERMS

Gross National Product
A term that describes the total value of services and products that a country produces in one year.

Jacobinism
A term used to describe individuals who wished to promote revolutionary ideas such as equality and were prepared to use violence to achieve their goal. The phrase comes from the Jacobin Club or, more formally, Society of the Friends of the Constitution set up at the start of the French Revolution to pursue these aims.

In terms of reform, however, this liberality of thought remained a fiction. Despite the corrupt Cornish borough of Grampound being disenfranchised in 1821 and its two seats being transferred to Yorkshire, wholesale reform of the electoral system remained a long way off. In 1822, for example, when the Whig leader Lord John Russell sought to introduce a bill designed to disenfranchise 100 of Britain's most rotten boroughs and redistribute the seats to the growing industrial cities, the motion received no support from the government and failed by a large majority. Such inaction by those in power continued to reflect the dominance of aristocratic thinking.

During this period of prosperity, political radicals were muted in their demands as the general public was contented. Towards the end of the decade, however, economic fortunes declined and, as they did, so the voice of reform was raised once more.

The basis for this decline was a series of poor harvests in 1828 and 1829. The predictable rise in food prices brought the equally predictable discontent. Between February and March of 1830 alone, there were more than 200 petitions sent to parliament from those living in rural areas demanding tax reductions. Despite receiving a positive response to this request, when conditions failed to improve, rioting broke out in the countryside and the government faced its first direct challenge. The 'Swing Riots', as they became known, lasted for more than 18 months and saw much of the south-east of England ablaze as hay ricks were burned and prominent authority figures were accused of failing the local people. These riots were not directly motivated by reform demands but did none the less inform this debate. As a massive display of public unrest in the countryside, the riots greatly alarmed the landowners in parliament who, motivated by self-preservation, began to see reform as a means to appease the discontent.

Equally disturbing was the impact of economic decline in the urban areas. Having been silent for so long, the depressed markets gave opportunity to the radical reformers once more and they were able to galvanise the distressed workers into supporting their cause. Protest marches began in earnest and the radical press found its circulations rise dramatically.

Perhaps most significant of all was the visible support for reform given by the manufacturing interests. Whereas in 1815 they had been on the fringes of the movement and quick to abandon the cause after the clampdown following the Peterloo Massacre, in 1830 the situation was different. The affluence they had attained in the economic boom of the 1820s had given them a desire for more political recognition. Furthermore, the relentless growth of industry had seen towns like Birmingham, Leeds and Sheffield expand to become major centres of commerce in Britain and yet none had direct political representation. The opinion of the middle classes in these areas, therefore, was that parliament had no real understanding about the problems they faced and that the only logical solution was an increased electorate to include those with knowledge of these issues.

The Birmingham Political Union

Established in December 1829 by the banker Thomas Attwood, the Birmingham Political Union (BPU) was created precisely to achieve greater representation for the industrial centres. Attwood believed financial reforms to be of paramount importance to British prosperity but increasingly felt that this would not be possible without first securing political reform. With this in view he set about pressurising government to make the necessary changes by uniting the working and middle classes in a respectable campaign that focused on these issues. The BPU quickly became a model for other political unions and with their combination of working-class numbers, middle-class money and, crucially, respectability, they began to yield some positive results.

Reasons for the passing of the Great Reform Act, 1832

Declining Tory hegemony

The lack of significant parliamentary change during the 1820s was certainly a feature of economic prosperity which quieted the majority of British voices, but of equal significance was the complete dominance of Tory control. Since 1812, there had been no change in leadership and Lord Liverpool was very much at the head of a party that publicly exuded confidence and assuredness of purpose. These qualities made it very difficult for the Whig opposition to mount an effective challenge and therefore the government did not feel threatened enough to consider changes.

Despite outward appearances, the Tory party was showing signs of division over the issue of Catholic Emancipation in Ireland. Since the introduction of the Penal Laws in 1691, Catholics had been barred from sitting in parliament, but among elements within the Tory membership there was increasing sympathy with the Catholic cause. The 'Catholic question' had always been a difficulty and Liverpool had made every effort to keep it off the political agenda. However, with the creation of a new protest group – the Catholic Association in Ireland in 1823 – by a determined Irish lawyer named Daniel O'Connell, the issue was thrust into the public arena where it quickly became a poisoned chalice for Liverpool's party.

Following a reshuffle of the cabinet there was a significant division among prominent members of the government, with the new home secretary, Robert Peel, an avowed anti-emancipator and the foreign secretary, George Canning, a keen supporter of the measure. Led by two of the most important ministers in government, each position became polarised to the extent that emancipation became the single most important issue in the 1826 election as Whigs saw an opportunity to break Tory dominance. Despite such a widening division, the Tories secured another term in office and what kept the party together was Liverpool himself. Though criticised as an unoriginal leader, he was generally regarded as a competent and decent person who was able to inspire trust in those around him. Using these talents in unison with his many years of political experience, he was successful in managing the more explosive characters in his government and ultimately this ensured party unity did not evaporate.

The resignation of Liverpool and Tory crisis

By 1827, the Tory party and Lord Liverpool had been in power for 15 years. However, in February, following a stroke, Liverpool resigned from office and with his departure went the ballast that had kept the party on an even keel through difficult waters. Following his resignation there was a brief power vacuum as factions in the party manoeuvred to get their candidate the leadership. The sudden vulnerability that the governing party found itself in created an opportunity for the opposition, which began to think about reform as a vehicle to achieve power and to capitalise on the growing crisis within the Tory party. The process of choosing a new leader opened up old wounds within the party which further improved the Whig cause, as in the space of 11 months the Tories had three different leaders. The third leader, the Duke of Wellington, took office in August 1828 but quickly divided the party by supporting Catholic Emancipation in 1829. This decision split party members into 'liberals' who accepted the decision and 'ultras' who rejected it. The impact of this divide reduced public confidence and the consequence was very evident in the June 1830 election when the Tory party was returned with a working majority of only 42 MPs. This was tenable if liberals could be relied upon to support government policies, but given the level of distrust and animosity that had been generated, Wellington was unable to maintain an effective government and had to step aside for the first Whig administration since 1807.

The significance of this turn of events was that reform suddenly became a political possibility, as the incoming Whig administration under the leadership of Earl Grey had been considering extending the vote as a way of enhancing their chances of attaining office. By creating the opportunity for a Whig government, the Tory leadership crisis opened the door to reform and on 1 March 1831 a bill was presented to parliament.

Middle-class pressure

The motivation for Whig reform was in one sense the desire to exploit the difficulties of the Tories, but it was also an awareness that the new middle class was increasingly wanting greater political power and the existing, outdated, system did not provide for it. This class was growing in size and economic importance as one result of industrial growth and development. It consisted, too, of the business and manufacturing interests and, increasingly, professional sections of society. As a group, its members were affluent, well educated and motivated by a strong sense of purpose, having earned their fortunes through their own hard work and determination. As a force for change, these qualities arguably made the group threatening to the authorities because it presented a thoughtful and reasoned opposition that was more difficult to deal with than mob pressure. The blunt popular agitation that was practised before 1830 could always be subdued by the use of force – evidenced by events such as Peterloo in 1819 – but the middle class presented a more challenging opponent. In part this was because of the nature of its opposition – the use of speeches and persuasion made it more difficult to apply traditional force – but of greater significance was the fact that this group was so important for the economic growth and prosperity of the country. The country was developing apace as a result of industrialisation (Chapter 1.2) and spearheading this development was the new middle class. Government was aware of the importance of this group to the expanding economy and therefore keen not to alienate its members.

Passage of the Act: the first and second bills

In March 1831, a measure of reform was presented to parliament. The bill presented was by no means an excessively radical measure and reflected the Whigs' own conservative instincts by not including either a secret ballot or uniform voting qualifications. Instead it simply proposed to disenfranchise 100 rotten and pocket boroughs and redistribute their seats to the industrial towns. Even despite this modest reform it struggled through the Commons and was then subject to rigorous amendment during the committee stage where bills were closely scrutinised before moving to the House of Lords. Although the Whigs were certainly not out-and-out reformers, it is testament to Grey's commitment to some degree of reform that, rather than accept Tory changes, he asked the king to dissolve parliament so that he might go to the people and achieve the majority he needed to get the bill passed in its current form.

The election was essentially a referendum on the issue of reform and Grey had judged the public demand accurately. The Whigs were returned with a majority of nearly 140 and the second reform bill passed the Commons only to be blocked in the Tory-dominated House of Lords in October.

Riots and a third reform bill

Following the electoral success of the reform-minded Whigs there was much excitement about the prospect of reform, such that when the bill was defeated in the Lords serious rioting broke out across the country. The most threatening of this was arguably in Bristol, which saw three days of rioting and approximately 130 people killed or wounded after a cavalry charge brought the disturbances to an end. Bristol was not an isolated case and there were additional riots in Nottingham and Derby, but given the prominence of Bristol – it was the largest port on the west coast after Liverpool and had grown substantially wealthy as a result of the slave trade – the upset that occurred in the city sent unsettling reverberations through the establishment and prompted a third bill to be presented in December.

The third bill involved substantial changes, including a reduction in the number of boroughs scheduled to lose one of their two MPs, from 41 to 30, and ten new boroughs to be given two MPs instead of the initially proposed one. These changes were aimed at securing an easier passage through parliament and by April 1832 the bill had successfully reached committee stage in the House of Lords with a slender majority of nine. If Tory peers had voted in favour of the bill after having been sufficiently shocked by the level of rioting that followed the failure of the second bill, then they rallied very quickly and blocked any further progress. To keep reform alive, Earl Grey beseeched the king to create 50 new Whig peers so that it could be forced through the upper house but his pleas fell upon deaf ears. Faced with the failure of a third attempt Grey resigned his office in May and the country erupted in protest once more.

The 'Days of May'

The resignation of Grey saw the king ask Wellington to form a new Tory government which immediately drew the condemnation of the British public. The manner in which the public responded was financial; the frustrated middle classes began to withdraw their savings and investments from banks in an attempt to destroy government finances – in ten days more than £1.8 million was removed. Although not physically threatening, the extended period over which the reform crisis had now been operating created a sense that if it continued any longer frustration would boil over into something more dangerous.

Under the prevailing circumstances Wellington found it very difficult to form a new government as many of his desired ministers were reluctant to sit with him on the government benches when the country was so against him. Unable to recruit enough supporters, Wellington had to inform the king that he could not form an administration and consequently the king asked Grey to form a government with the promise that if necessary he would have the Whig peers he needed to pass reform.

The 'Great' Reform Act, 1832 and its significance

In the event there was no need for extra peers as the opposition towards reform collapsed under public pressure. Faced with the inevitability of reform, rather than have their power in the House of Lords permanently diluted, the Tories agreed to the measure and on 4 June Britain's first Reform Act was passed by a vote of 106 to 22.

Provisions of the Act

Under the new legislation the distribution of seats was altered to reflect the modern demographical changes in Britain:

- 56 boroughs in England and Wales were disenfranchised completely with another 30 losing one of their two MPs

- 42 new borough constituencies were created

- Scotland received eight extra seats and Ireland five.

In addition the franchise was extended to include more people.

- In the counties the vote was now given to adult males who owned copyhold land worth £10 a year or rented land worth £50 a year, in addition to the existing 40 shilling freeholder.

- In the boroughs the vote was made uniform and now given to adult males who either owned or rented property worth £10 a year provided they had paid all relevant taxes, had been in possession of the property for at least one year and had not received poor relief in the previous year. Existing voters could also retain the franchise but not pass on this right to heirs.

- Voters were required to be registered.

Significance of the Act

Under this new franchise the electorate in Britain rose from 366,000 to 650,000 which equated to about 18 percent of the adult male population in England and Wales alone. On this basis the reform measure did not create democracy but simply removed the obvious injustices within the old system. Given that the men who formulated this Act were products of their unreformed environment it is reasonable to suggest that they naturally sought to retain as much continuity as possible and change only enough to appease the public clamour. Under this interpretation it is popular to view the legislation as a means of shoring up and preserving a system under threat. This idea had a lot of merit and certainly became the dominant belief in the years that immediately followed, prompting further reform demands from those who felt cheated by the limitations of the reforms.

In terms of the impact of this reform, the changes to the voting qualification it made saw the franchise being extended to include a greater proportion of people living in towns and cities. This suggested progress, but in itself was not hugely representative of the general population. Those able to vote still only amounted to 18 percent of the adult male population and, of the new electorate, the majority were middle-class business owners who did not represent the wider public. Furthermore, the number of seats in parliament that the Act redistributed still favoured the rural counties: 370 MPs came from the south of England, while only 120 came from the more densely populated and industrialised north. Given these limitations, very little had actually changed; power still remained with aristocratic landowners. Where reform had taken place, it favoured a new business group that had its own vested interests to maintain and was therefore expected to minimise political change as much as possible.

ACTIVITY
KNOWLEDGE CHECK

Why was reform passed?

Using the material presented above, create a storyboard depicting the most important events that led to the passage of the Great Reform Act in 1832.

SOURCE

From a speech made in a debate in the House of Commons on 2 March 1831 by Thomas Babington Macaulay, MP who represented the rotten borough of Calne. Macaulay is defending the Reform Bill.

[The Ministers'] principle is plain, rational and consistent. It is this – to admit the middle classes to a large and direct share in the representation, without any violent shock to the institutions of our country.

I hold it to be clearly expedient that, in a country like ours, the right of suffrage should depend on a pecuniary qualification. Every argument, sir, which would induce me to oppose universal suffrage, induces me to support the measure which is now before us. I oppose universal suffrage because I think it would produce a destructive revolution. I support this measure because I am sure that it is our best security against a revolution.

I support this measure as a measure of reform; but I support it still more as a measure of conservation. That we may exclude those whom it is necessary to exclude, we must admit those whom it is safe to admit. At present we oppose the schemes of revolutionaries with only one half, with only one quarter of our proper force. We say, and we say justly, that it is not by mere numbers, but by property and intelligence, that the nation ought to be governed. Yet, saying this, we exclude from all share in government vast masses of property and intelligence, vast numbers of those who are most interested in preserving tranquillity and who know best how to preserve it. We do more. We drive over to the side of revolution those whom we shut out of power. Is this a time when the cause of law and order can spare one of its natural allies?

Turn where we may – within, around – the voice of great events is proclaiming to us, 'Reform, that you may preserve'. Save property divided against itself. Save the multitude, endangered by their own ungovernable passions. Save the aristocracy, endangered by its own unpopular power. Save the greatest, and fairest, and most highly civilised community that ever existed, from calamities which may in a few days sweep away all the rich heritage of so many ages of wisdom and glory.

SOURCE

From a speech made in the House of Commons on 17 December 1831 by Sir Robert Peel MP in the debate on the second reading of the Second Reform Bill.

I am satisfied with the constitution under which I have lived hitherto, which I believe is adapted to the wants and habits of the people. I will continue in my opposition to the last, believing, as I do, that this is the first step, not directly to revolution, but to a series of changes which will affect the property, and totally change the character, of the mixed constitution of this country. I take my stand, not opposed to a well-considered reform of any of our institutions which need reform, but opposed to this reform in our constitution, because it tends to root up the feelings of respect, the feelings of habitual reverence and attachment, which are the only sure foundations of government. I will oppose to the last the undue encroachments of that democratic spirit to which we are advised to yield without resistance. We may make it supreme – we may establish a republic full of energy – splendid in talent – but in my conscience I believe fatal to our liberty, our security and our peace.

THINKING HISTORICALLY   Causation (3c&d)

Causation and intention

1 Work on your own or with a partner to identify as many reasons for the passage of the Great Reform Act in 1832 as you can. Write each reason on a separate card or piece of paper.

2 Divide your cards into those which represent:

   a) the actions or intentions of people

   b) the beliefs held by people at the time

   c) the contextual factors or events (i.e. political, social or economic events)

   d) states of affairs (long- or short-term situations that have developed in particular ways).

3 Focus on the intentions and actions of the key people in the run-up to the creation of the Great Reform Act. For each person draw on your knowledge to fill in the table below, identifying:

   a) their intentions

   b) the actions they took to achieve these

   c) the consequences of their actions (both intended and unintended)

   d) the extent to which their intentions were achieved.

Key figure	Intentions in 1832	Actions taken	Consequences	How far intention achieved
John Russell	To pass reform and consolidate his party. To protect the country from further reform	Introduced moderate reform	Extended the franchise Promoted expectation for more change	Short term – party was consolidated and enjoyed further success Long term – further reform took place
Duke of Wellington				
Earl Grey				

4 Discuss the following questions with a partner:

   a) Did any one party intend the Reform Act to be passed?

   b) How important are people's intentions in explaining the passage of the Great Reform Act?

The rise and fall of Chartism

Reforming reform, 1832–52

Despite things changing for many in Britain, the reality was that the passage of the Great Reform Act did not herald significant differences to the underlying political make-up of the country. Under the terms of the legislation it was primarily the propertied middle classes that benefited rather than the general public. The result of this limited change was that it caused growing discontent among the working classes and radical reformers who felt it should have been extended further.

Chartist demands

The opinion of Henry Hetherington (see Source 10) was not an isolated one and across the country many people became jaded by the sense of propertied favouritism that the 1832 Act had established. In the wake of reform, ordinary people expected their lives to improve now that parliament was more representative of them and therefore their problems. In reality, however, the immediate legislation that followed signified a large degree of vested self-interest rather than any new-found social awareness. In a country that continued to industrialise rapidly, the working and labouring classes found much cause for improvement and yet the government still failed to appreciate their

THE RISE OF CHARTISM

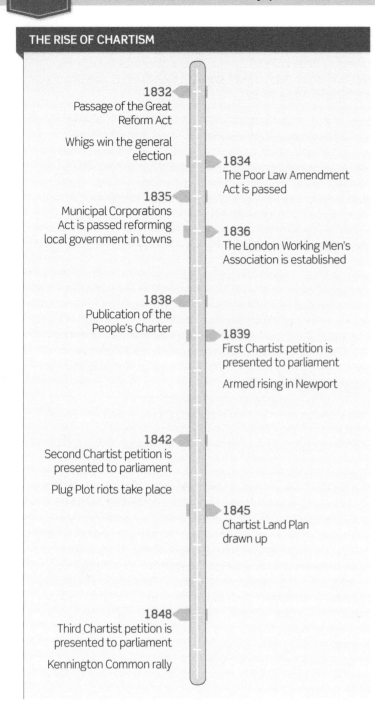

1832
Passage of the Great Reform Act

Whigs win the general election

1834
The Poor Law Amendment Act is passed

1835
Municipal Corporations Act is passed reforming local government in towns

1836
The London Working Men's Association is established

1838
Publication of the People's Charter

1839
First Chartist petition is presented to parliament

Armed rising in Newport

1842
Second Chartist petition is presented to parliament

Plug Plot riots take place

1845
Chartist Land Plan drawn up

1848
Third Chartist petition is presented to parliament

Kennington Common rally

plight. Measures such as the 1833 Factory Act were felt to benefit the newly enfranchised middle classes in that they failed to offer adequate working conditions or a maximum working day for those outside the textile industry, while the 1834 Poor Law seemed to punish rather than support those who had no work.

It was against this background of social discontent that the London Working Men's Association was founded in 1836 with the intention of demanding further political reform so that working people might be accurately represented. Founded by William Lovett and attracting familiar reform-minded names such as Henry Hetherington and Thomas Attwood, the association published its manifesto in 1838 to raise awareness of its cause.

The 'People's Charter'

The Chartists' aims were all political; by obtaining representation they hoped, among other things, to improve the economic conditions of working people.

The manifesto was known as the 'People's Charter' and it called for:

- equal representation
- universal manhood suffrage for those over 21 years old
- annual parliaments
- the removal of property qualifications for MPs
- a secret ballot
- payment of MPs.

So radical were the aims of the 'People's Charter' that the Working Men's Association quickly became better known as the 'Chartists' and once again political reform was thrust into the public eye.

The motivation behind such far-reaching demands was simple: with a more democratic system that included the rank and file and protected their vote, any successive parliament would not be able to ignore them, or at least could be held accountable if it did. Equally, by guaranteeing a wage to MPs, not only would the working classes be able to vote, they would also be able to afford to stand for election. Traditionally viewed as a privilege of the propertied classes, only once parliament had been opened up to every class would Britain finally have a governing system that operated in the interests of every person; only then in their view might government be truly representative. These were the principles of the Chartists and over the next 20 years they would endeavour to achieve them.

Chartist membership

The membership of the Chartist movement was very broad as the principles of their charter attracted a range of individuals, each with a different locus of interest. Unsurprisingly, the majority of members were working class: usually craftsmen and skilled workers from declining industries looking for protection during difficult times, although there was also a significant contingent of middle-class reformers who sought to build on the foundation laid by the 1832 Act.

The diverse nature of the movement was both its strength and its weakness. During times of economic prosperity, for example, the membership declined, as working people felt their conditions to be acceptable because they were able to earn good wages. However, during economic decline the number of members grew, as people

SOURCE

10 From an article by Henry Hetherington in his newspaper, *Poor Man's Guardian*, dated 27 October 1832.

… with a little instinctive sense of self-preservation, have the Whigs manufactured a 'great measure'. They know that the old system could not last, and desired to establish another as like it as possible, and also to keep their places, they framed the BILL, in the hope of drawing to the feudal aristocracy and yeomanry of the counties a large reinforcement of the middle class. The Bill was, in effect, an invitation to the shopocrats of the enfranchised towns to join the Whiggocrats of the country, and make common cause with them in keeping down the people, and thereby quell the rising spirit of democracy in England.

saw Chartism as a means to promote a better deal for themselves. This fluctuation has given rise to doubts as to the overall political motives of the movement, with some commentators such as J. R. Stephens suggesting that the Chartists were primarily a product of the economic climate and only sought political change to reduce economic suffering. Even if the motivation of this group is in doubt, the range of opinion it garnered generated a truly mass movement that was difficult to ignore, but such numbers needed to be carefully directed in order to maximise their effectiveness. In terms of such direction Chartism was found to be wanting.

'Physical force' and 'moral force' Chartism

At their first National Convention held in London during the winter of 1839, Chartists were immediately divided over how to achieve their aims. Men like William Lovett and Thomas Attwood were keen to use peaceful means such as pamphlets and petitions in the belief that parliament would best listen to respectful requests rather than forceful demands. These individuals became known as 'moral force' Chartists and they sought to play on the growing need for politicians to listen to the electorate. They reasoned that, given the majority of voters were now middle-class property owners, the most likely way to win favour was through behaving respectfully and not promoting the generally held image of the working class as brutish and ignorant.

By contrast, others within the organisation, such as Feargus O'Connor, James Bronterre O'Brien and George Julian Harney, were more disposed towards offering a direct challenge. These 'physical force' Chartists favoured a general strike and O'Brien and Harney in particular even considered an armed revolution to achieve their aims if the government did not listen.

The mixed attitudes of those in charge were reflected in the generally unco-ordinated and, some might say, uninspired actions of the movement which began by presenting a petition signed by 1,280,958 people to parliament in May 1839.

SOURCE 11

From the first Chartist petition presented to parliament in May 1839.

... when the State calls for defenders, when it calls for money, no consideration of poverty or ignorance can be pleaded, in refusal or delay of the call. Required, as we are universally, to support and obey the laws, nature and reason entitle us to demand that in the making of the laws, the universal voice shall be implicitly listened to. We perform the duties of freemen; we must have the privileges of freemen. Therefore, we demand universal suffrage. The suffrage, to be exempt from the corruption of the wealthy and the violence of the powerful, must be secret.

The nature of the demands echoed the same principles as *Rights of Man* had done more than 40 years before. The difference, however, was that there was no violent revolution to focus the attention of politicians and the government felt comfortable enough to reject the petition in July by a vote of 235 to 46.

With this failure, adherents of 'physical force' saw their opportunity and embarked upon what became known as the 'sacred month', which involved a general strike and protest meetings that usually turned into fights with the local authorities. More disturbing was an attempted uprising in Newport which saw approximately 5,000 miners clash with troops outside the Westgate Hotel. After a brief skirmish the Chartists fled into the night leaving more than 20 dead.

In the aftermath of the Newport rising Chartist leaders were arrested by the authorities and, between 1839 and 1841, 500 of them were held in prison. The consequence of this action was that Chartism was temporarily paralysed and after recovering in 1842 was unwilling to risk further reprisal from the government. More conservative elements sought to rehabilitate the movement by returning to its original plan of petitioning but despite a second petition attracting three million signatures, parliament was in no mood to acquiesce and rejected the new petition by an increased margin of 43.

Any remaining confidence among the Chartists was smashed by the iron resolve of parliament and after a second defeat the movement started to unravel. One leader, Feargus O'Connor, looked to a new venture that was designed to give working-class families the opportunity to own their own land and live in a rural community away from the struggles of urban life. The Land Plan was set up in 1845 and initially proved successful, attracting 70,000 subscribers by 1848. Though lacking a specific political agenda, the Land Plan is evidence that Chartism was waning and people were looking to find other solutions to their problems. Compared to the smog-ridden cities, a pleasant rural living was seen to be particularly attractive.

The Kennington Common rally and third Chartist petition

Just as Chartism was appearing to drift into terminal decline, revolution ignited the continent and cries for democracy were heard once more. In Britain this manifested itself in a massive Chartist demonstration at Kennington Common on 10 April which was to be followed by the presentation of a third petition to parliament. In the wake of revolution abroad the government declared the meeting illegal and enrolled about 150,000 special constables in anticipation of trouble. In the event, although the meeting defied the ban and went ahead, it was attended by working men and women in their Sunday best clothes and children played as speeches were made. The third petition was then driven in a carriage to parliament by O'Connor and a small group of fellow Chartists where it was politely, but firmly, declined on the basis that of the claimed five million signatures, less than half were genuine.

The failure of Chartism

Following the rejection of a third petition, Chartism was effectively over. As the revolutionary fires on the continent were extinguished so too was the Chartist movement. Although it was not formally wound up until 1860 it ceased to be a serious movement and lost support almost as quickly as it had gained it more than a decade before. There were several reasons why the movement failed.

The most popular reason offered for Chartist failures is the idea of '**hunger politics**'. This classic interpretation has its basis in the reform movement which saw levels of active support rise and fall alongside economic fortunes. In this analysis the Chartists found popular support primarily among the working class because it

SOURCE 12

A Physical Force Chartist Arming for the Fight, cartoon from *Punch*, dated 1848. *Punch* magazine was a satirical publication that commented on political events in its cartoons.

A PHYSICAL FORCE CHARTIST ARMING FOR THE FIGHT.

was they who felt the acute sense of despair during the times of economic hardship which mirrored the high points of Chartist activity; 1839, 1842 and 1848 each saw a stark decline in economic prosperity which then gave way to improved conditions when Chartism was quiet. There is merit to this argument but it does not wholly account for the failure of arguably Britain's largest working-class movement.

KEY TERM

Hunger politics
This is a phrase that is often used to describe economic hardship as the cause for unrest. It posits the idea that when people are gainfully employed and have sufficient money to feed their families then protest is unlikely to take place. During times of economic difficulty, however, when people do not earn enough to feed their families then protest is more frequent.

In addition to such conditional support, the Chartists also lacked effective leadership. Charismatic men like O'Connor were able to attract the support but were equally unable to maintain a definitive approach in the face of determined opposition and therefore the movement splintered very quickly after its first petition was defeated. Augmenting this weakness was the divisive nature of the movement from the outset. Unable to agree on the best means to proceed when the choices made were unsuccessful, dissent crept in and without decisive leadership this undermined the cohesiveness of the movement.

Perhaps most significant of all to the failure of the Chartists was their ambition. The aims they set themselves were very noble but in the mid-1800s perhaps a little ahead of their time. In a period which had only reluctantly granted the vote to a modest number of propertied and respectable members of society, the idea that only a few years after this measure the British establishment would countenance complete democratisation and hand power over to the working class is, at best, naive. A useful example of ongoing conservatism comes from the Chartists themselves. Originally when writing their charter the vote was to be extended to men and women but they baulked at such a move, believing that they would never be taken seriously if the request for genuine universal suffrage was retained. Further evidence can also be found at their first Convention where many of the middle-class attendees were put off by the talk of physical force and actually resigned before any action was taken. Given the movement itself was divided over both its aims and its methods, it was very unlikely that it was ever going to be seriously listened to, especially when what the Chartists generally agreed on was so radical and their audience so hostile to further change.

Government legislation

Despite not achieving their acclaimed goals, the idea of Chartism as a flawed movement that ultimately failed is questionable. While the authorities certainly kept close attention on the movement, through the use of government agents, they also passed legislation that arguably undermined the Chartists by improving the conditions of those who supported them. For example, in 1847, the Ten Hours Act (page 37) was passed, which limited the length of the working day of factory workers, and in 1846 the Corn Law was repealed, which had a positive effect on the price of bread. These Acts themselves were not the focus of the Chartist agenda, neither was undermining the Chartist movement the main motivating factor driving the legislation. The legislation did not address the reforms demanded in the People's Charter, but it did reduce the strength of the movement by removing many working classes sources of discontent.

The significance of this action was that much of the support for Chartism was diluted and this reduced the effectiveness of the movement. The extent to which this made Chartism a 'failure' is, however, disputable. It could be said that the motivation for their charter was to secure better political representation for the working class so that, armed with such influence, better conditions for workers could be achieved. On this basis the passage of Acts that positively affected working and social conditions could be said to have been advances that the Chartists sought in the longer term. That they themselves did not achieve the reforms they wanted is perhaps a 'failure' but the result still saw improvement overall. It would be appropriate to suggest that in helping to draw attention to the general concerns of the working class, they were perhaps successful.

Government determination

In support of this idea the ineffectiveness of Chartism could be laid at the door of the government, whose strength was considerable – particularly against perceived threats such as that posed by the Chartists. Events such as the Peterloo Massacre in 1819 (page 17) had shown the lengths to which government could go to preserve order. Throughout the 1830s and 1840s, successive governments were happy to deploy troops against any threat – a task made even easier by the growing rail network that allowed troops to be moved quickly around the country. Evidence of this attitude was the appointment of General Charles Napier to command the army in the north of England. He was charged with monitoring Chartist activity in this region and also subduing any uprising that might take place. Furthermore, in 1848, when the third petition was being presented, the government drafted in 8,000 soldiers and 150,000 special constables to prevent disorder. The presence of these men – a clear show of force by government – indicates how determined the authorities were to prevent any challenge to their administration. This determination, combined with the internal weaknesses of the movement itself, offer good reasons why Chartism was unable to enjoy direct success.

THINKING HISTORICALLY Change (4a)

Significance

Look at the two accounts of the Chartist movement in Sources 13 and 14.

1 In what ways does Elizabeth Gaskell think that the Chartist movement is significant?

2 How significant does Gaskell seem to think the movement might be in the long run?

3 Compare this to the comments made by historian Clive Behagg. What significance does Behagg ascribe to the Chartist movement?

4 Why do you think these views might differ so greatly?

SOURCE 13

Elizabeth Gaskell writing about the first Chartist petition in her novel, *Mary Barton*, published in 1848.

Besides, the starving multitudes had heard that the very existence of their distress had been denied in Parliament; and though they felt this strange and inexplicable, yet the idea that their misery had still to be revealed in all its depths, and that then some remedy would be found, soothed their aching hearts and kept down their rising fury.

So a petition was framed, and signed by thousands in the bright Spring days of 1839, imploring Parliament to hear witnesses who could testify to the unparalleled destitution of the manufacturing districts.

SOURCE 14

Clive Behagg, *Labour and Reform: Working-class Movements 1815–1914* (1991).

But Chartism was not made up of cowed and hungry simpletons. For its rank and file, as well as its leadership, radical politics represented a perfectly logical way of viewing the world and rectifying its abuses. The commitment to the vote stemmed from the brain rather than the belly. Nor does the fact that there was no formal system of education mean that these were ignorant people.

Change and continuity in post-reform Britain

With the demise of Chartism, the British radicalism settled down and there was a sense that order and stability was, once again, established. In light of this view, several historians have concluded that the reforms made at the start of the 1830s were entirely successful in securing the political establishment. By extending the franchise to the middle class, the aristocracy destroyed any alliance it may have had with the working class and instead created a strong union between the propertied interests in Britain. In forging such a bond, far from establishing a more representative system, the newly enfranchised classes simply reinforced the existing political elite.

Viewed through this lens very little had fundamentally changed in Britain. Corruption was still widely practised and without a secret ballot so too was intimidation. In the first election after the Act had passed, for example, the famed orator Henry Hunt lost his seat in Preston to a Whig–Tory coalition formed between two of the area's wealthiest families, while a young William Gladstone owed his electoral victory to the Duke of Newcastle who controlled the Newark constituency in which he stood. The failure of Chartism was evidence of a government confident in its actions and therefore without the fear that might have forced it to offer significant changes beyond that which it deemed suitable.

This is quite a bleak impression of the post-reform political landscape and only a partially accurate one. Certainly, there remained significant continuity as the reform measure was only intended to make limited changes. However, even the smallest of changes can have unintended consequences and in Britain this was without doubt the case.

The most obvious change was that more people could now vote. Not only this, but they had to be registered in order to do so. The significance of registration was that in order to ensure success, each party needed to encourage supporters to register. Political clubs such as the Tory-leaning Carlton Club and Whig-sponsored Reform Club were established to achieve this and in the bigger constituencies local party activists started to appear as part of a general effort to raise the profile of their respective parties. In effect, after 1832 the political system started to become more professional.

In direct consequence of this development, parties also became more definitive in their ideologies. Whereas in the past Tories and Whigs were from the same background and therefore generally of a similar mindset, often only differing on points of technicality, after 1832 they became more polarised, which both reduced the chances of an 'independent' candidate being successful but also established the dominance of the **two-party system**.

Most tangible of all the changes was perhaps the 1835 Municipal Corporations Act which changed the way in which local town councils were run. Prior to 1835, these bodies were self-elected and accountable to no one. Following the findings of a Royal Commission into local governance, the Whigs pushed through a bill that abolished the existing corporations and replaced them with elected councils. The franchise in these new local elections was granted to all male ratepayers, which was substantially broader than the voting qualification to parliament.

More pervasive than any other change, though, was the subtle shift in attitudes that reform engendered. After 1832, the establishment was increasingly more responsive to the electorate. Although at a national level political reform was ignored, there was substantial social and economic reform, ranging from the abolition of the slave trade to a new Poor Law, which will be considered in subsequent chapters. What is most important to remember in the post-reform landscape is that, politically, the first breach had been made and what followed was a slow awakening to the fact that Britain was becoming a modern nation that would demand an equally modern system of governance.

Although in its own lifetime Chartism had been an abject failure, having achieved none of the aims in the 'People's Charter', it was successful in keeping alive radical ideas that, as the country developed, found a more appreciative ear after 1852.

ACTIVITY
KNOWLEDGE CHECK

What impact did the 'Great' Reform Act have?
Write a list of the key features of the electoral system before 1832 and then a list of the changes that the Act made. Using these lists together with the material above, consider the impact that reform had and write a 300- to 500-word summary justifying your opinion.

'REACHING FOR DEMOCRACY'? FURTHER PARLIAMENTARY REFORM, 1852–70

Demand for political reform after 1852 was not limited to external forces and there had always been a reformist contingent in parliament, even if it was largely ineffectual during the Chartist campaigns. With the end of that pressure, however, there was an opportunity to push for moderate reforms without the excessive demands made by that working-class movement.

EVENTS IMPACTING ON PARLIAMENTARY REFORM

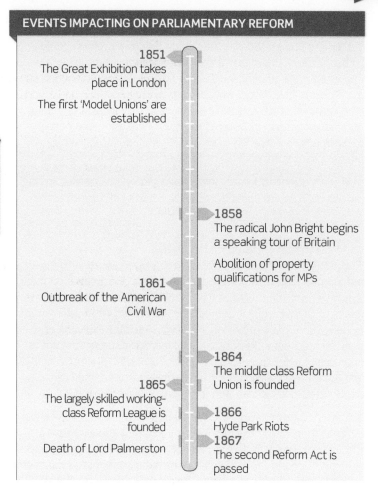

1851
The Great Exhibition takes place in London

The first 'Model Unions' are established

1858
The radical John Bright begins a speaking tour of Britain

Abolition of property qualifications for MPs

1861
Outbreak of the American Civil War

1864
The middle class Reform Union is founded

1865
The largely skilled working-class Reform League is founded

Death of Lord Palmerston

1866
Hyde Park Riots

1867
The second Reform Act is passed

EXTEND YOUR KNOWLEDGE

'Conservatives' and 'Liberals'
After defeat in 1832, the Tory party sought to rehabilitate itself. Under the leadership of Robert Peel in 1834 the party issued a new manifesto at Tamworth using the title 'Conservative Party'. Just as the Tories had rebranded themselves, the mostly aristocratic Whig party also began to think in terms of a more appropriate name after they were joined in parliament by a host of new non-aristocratic members following the recent reforms. With the increased reliance on these new MPs after 1850, the term 'Liberal' became a more appropriate title for the party. Collectively these new titles also nicely reflected the polarising political landscape that reform had created.

Many old Whigs remained positively inclined towards some further reforms, especially as politics was beginning to become more professionalised and reform would be an obvious way to enhance the fortunes of their party. For these individuals, therefore, any reform should be undertaken with careful thought as to how it would affect voting patterns and seat distributions.

In contrast to these men, there was also a more altruistic minority who sought reform as a means of purifying the system and making it more genuinely democratic. Among those who might be described as 'radical reformers' were Joseph Hume and Peter Locke King, each passionate about the need for further change; Hume, a veteran campaigner, had produced reform bills in every session of parliament between 1848 and 1852, while King was committed to extending the county franchise.

There was a third group who were also willing to accept a degree of political change. This was a growing number of new Tories who recognised, like the Whigs, that some reform could be beneficial to their party if they were seen to introduce it. This understanding had been hard earned by the Tories, now renamed the 'Conservative Party', who, between 1832 and 1852, had found themselves in office for just seven years: briefly in 1834 and then for a five-year term in 1841. The cause of this extended period in the wilderness was felt to be public gratitude for the Whig/Liberal's successful passage of reform.

In view of this development there was a growing consensus among the two main parties about the political necessity of further reform.

A modernising nation

The motive for reform has so far been suggested as primarily that of self-interested preservation brought on by acts of popular discontent that have been interpreted as threats to order. Given the limited nature of the subsequent changes, there is certainly compelling evidence for this interpretation. However, to see the evolution of parliamentary democracy simply as a reaction to pressure is not to appreciate the full story. Without doubt that motive is very persuasive and holds a lot of weight but if it was the only motive then why did the Chartists not succeed with their own political demands?

Arguably Chartism failed because it was too ambitious for the times in which it operated. The demands it made were too excessive for those in parliament and, regardless of any threat they posed, the strength of conservative thought destroyed any hope of further political improvement *at that time*. By the 1850s, however, Britain was a different country with new priorities that would open up the case for reform once more.

Population changes

Between 1821 and 1861, the population in Britain rose from just over 24 million to more than 31 million. The majority of this growing population resided in the ever-developing towns and cities and as such fell under the borough franchise qualifications which, in 1832, had been set at occupancy or ownership of property worth more than £10 a year. Under this qualification, the growing majority of working men living in the boroughs did not have the right to vote. The implication of this development was that having redrawn the electoral map in 1832, that map was now out of date. This realisation offers an additional motive for the evolution of democracy: progress. As Britain underwent fundamental structural and demographic changes, it was necessary for the political system to mirror such transformation.

Early political efforts to extend the franchise

Given the growing awareness among the Liberals and Conservatives of the potential benefits of extending the franchise, there were tentative efforts made during the 1850s by each party to do so. As early as 1852, the ageing Lord Russell proposed to reduce the existing borough qualification from £10 a year to £6. Despite popular consensus that some reform was necessary, the bill was rejected then and on two more occasions, in 1854 and 1860, when the peer had wrongly judged that enough time had passed for his bill to be acceptable. At the heart of this opposition was both an underlying fear of the working class and of partisan politics. The majority of Conservatives felt that such a low qualification would allow too many from the working class to influence politics while at the same time give the Liberals more support. Their own reform offering in 1859 retained the existing borough franchise and sought to extend it into the counties. Under this proposal, modestly respectable lodgers living in the rural areas would become enfranchised. To the Liberals this was as distasteful as Russell's bill had been to Conservatives; the counties were traditional heartlands of Conservative support and therefore it was felt they would gain the political advantage if the measure was passed.

Neither franchise proposal survived the obsessive scrutiny that party politics encouraged and, as the 1850s came to a close, with the exception of the abolition of property qualifications for MPs in 1858, further reform seemed a long way off.

Changing political attitudes

In 1859, the Liberals were returned to power under the premiership of Lord Palmerston. Under his tenure reform was largely ignored as foreign policy took priority and he was personally averse to the notion of democracy, blocking further proposed changes. Despite, or perhaps because of, Palmerston's opposition the reform question was raised once more, first by the Birmingham MP John Bright, and then by circumstances abroad.

Bright had been a moderniser throughout his political career; along with Richard Cobden he had founded the Anti-Corn Law League in 1839 and had opposed Britain's involvement in the Crimean War. Reform, however, was his main objective and in 1858 he had begun a series of public speeches aimed at promoting the issue. Although the tour faded, the message he projected concerning the rights of the working class was well heeded by those who listened and by the mid-1860s had inspired a more determined movement.

In 1860, however, the message he was conveying did not yield any significant change. Championing the virtues of the working class was not especially attractive to the aristocratic elements of both the Liberal and Conservative parties. Although open to the idea of extending the franchise, these elements were still unsure of the wisdom of allowing what they believed to be a largely self-interested body of men into the political fold. For this group, rather ironically, believed the working class was incapable of the selfless service that representative government demanded.

The American Civil War

Strangely, it was events across the Atlantic that finally debunked the commonly held myth of working-class selfishness. The economic prosperity that Britain continued to enjoy into the 1860s was in part due to the thriving textile industries in the north-west of the country. Since 1825, cotton had been Britain's biggest import and the cloth it produced accounted for a substantial part of the nation's income. More importantly, in Lancashire it provided work for 355,000 people. Much of the raw cotton was imported from the USA, but with the outbreak of the US Civil War in 1861 supplies dried up as the Republican north blockaded the Confederate Southern ports. During what became known as the 'Cotton Famine' thousands of workers were laid off and consequently found themselves upon hard times. Rather than bemoan their plight, however, these men and women stoically supported the principle of anti-slavery in the USA and made the best of what they could.

Visiting Lancashire during these difficult times was the chancellor of the exchequer, William Gladstone, who was impressed by the forbearance of the textile workers and became convinced of their readiness for the vote (Source 15).

SOURCE 15

Extracts from a speech made by William Gladstone to parliament in May 1864.

... What are the qualities which fit a man for the exercise of a privilege such as the franchise? Self-command, self-control, respect for order, patience under suffering, confidence in the law, regard for superiors... I am now speaking only of a limited portion of the working class... hearts should be bound together by a reasonable expansion... among selected portions of the people, of every benefit, and every privilege that can justly be conferred on them.

The behaviour of the Lancashire cotton workers contributed significantly to the possibility of future reform because it broadened the minds of those in power. These men had tended to retain a critical opinion of the lower classes – Palmerston had even referred to them as the 'residuum', a term referencing a substance that is left behind after processing. In tandem with the growing awareness of the value of the working class to British commerce, this new perspective gradually encouraged reluctant politicians to become more accepting of their proposed inclusion in any future extension of the franchise.

AS Level Exam-Style Question Section B

How significant was party rivalry in keeping reform alive in the years 1832–67? (20 marks)

Tip
Take careful note of the question stem at the beginning of each question as this will help you to understand what the examiner wants you to evaluate. In this case 'how significant' was the role of party rivalry?

The Reform Union and the Reform League

Reform was not only being considered in parliament. With an expanding economy and Britain's growing prominence in the world raising the general expectations of the public, attention became focused on how to capitalise on these successes and once again parliamentary reform gained fresh impetus.

Among those pushing for new reforms was a progressive middle class which felt improved political co-operation between itself and the working class would promote further stability by binding each to the other in one unified aim. By showing that there was space for commonality it was generally felt that potential divisions among employer and employed might be avoided. A group was formed in 1864 and, calling itself the 'National Reform Union', sought to extend the franchise to include all male ratepayers, promote an equal distribution of seats and establish a secret ballot.

The membership of this group was primarily liberal-minded employers such as Samuel Morley, a woollen manufacturer from Nottingham, who was later elected MP for that city in 1865. Morley was a keen advocate of liberal concerns and had been a supporter of the abolition of slavery in 1833. His participation in the Reform Union was an affirmation of his belief in the positive effects of further enfranchisement and also the greater empowerment of the working class which, he believed, would enhance British society.

The inclusion of prominent employers such as Morley gave the Reform Union a significant degree of influence which the government was reluctant to completely ignore; as a voter himself and then as an MP, Morley represented the growing influence of the upwardly mobile middle class whose position in the country was increasing each year as the economy expanded and manufacturing opportunities improved. The impact of this organisation, therefore, was as a respectable **lobby** group which was able to demand the attention of those in power.

KEY TERM

Lobby
The practice of establishing personal links with politicians in order to promote an interest.

In 1865, a similar organisation was established by members of the working class. Known as the 'Reform League', its ambitions were more radical than the Union, campaigning instead for universal manhood suffrage and a secret ballot. Although the middle-class Union had more money, the League enjoyed more widespread support and attracted many ex-Chartists and trade unionists. Generally the League was seen as a more radical group than the Reform Union but it was still very moderate in its methods. The more radical trade unionists were disallowed from joining and the president of the organisation was a barrister by the name of Edmond Beales. Under this leadership the League employed the well-worn tactic of demonstration to promote its cause. This was seen as an assertive but respectable means to gain attention in a political world where increasingly politicians were becoming more receptive to popular pressure.

The methods employed by the League were crucial to its likely success. Viewed by the government as a radical organisation, it was keen to allay this concern, in the belief that violent action would not serve its cause well and would perhaps only promote an equally hostile response. Instead, by acting in a manner perceived as acceptable and by using these methods to promote public discussion, the League might be able to take advantage of the more open political climate where politicians were more willing to listen to public issues. In this sense the League exhibited a thoughtful appreciation of the impact that reform in 1832 had produced. By extending the electorate based upon property qualifications, as the economy grew and more people were able to meet this requirement, so political parties became more aware of the need to take into account the wishes of the growing enfranchised population.

This was the basis of power for each group and both were prominent in enhancing the reform agenda by stirring up popular demand and winning the subsequent attention of politicians who were continually seeking to mine new seams of public support.

Gladstone's reform bill, 1866

With reform slowly gaining momentum during the early 1860s, it enjoyed a sudden burst of pace in 1865 when the anti-reformist prime minister, Lord Palmerston, suddenly died. His death was unexpected but, for reform, fortuitous as it brought back into office the inveterate reformer Earl (formerly Lord) John Russell.

The moderate bill presented to parliament by the chancellor of the exchequer, William Gladstone, evidenced a cautious willingness to integrate some of the working classes, and a clear party political incentive. By reducing the borough franchise to a proposed £7 a year, it was expected that more than 200,000 skilled workers would be enfranchised and that these would primarily be Liberal voters. In the counties the £50 a year rental qualification would be reduced to £14 with the hope that this would also encourage 170,000 potential Liberal voters.

Predictably, the Conservatives objected to the measure but so too did conservative elements within the Liberal party itself.

The 'Adullamites' and Liberal divisions

Within the Liberal Party there was deep-rooted division that Gladstone's reform bill exposed. Since the introduction of new MPs after 1832, the Liberals had become more inclusive, adopting a broader platform so as to establish stronger links with these new constituencies. Consequently the party became an amalgam of 'Old Whigs', radical reformers and respectable leaders of commerce. Within the more progressive environment of the 1860s, each of these groups accepted the need for further reform but differed on the extent of such change. For those most loyal to the late Lord Palmerston, Gladstone's measure was excessively liberal and threatened to enfranchise far too many of the working class. Perhaps the most able of these critics was the barrister Robert Lowe, whose argument amounted to a fear that members of the working class were unable to understand politics and enfranchising so many of them would lead to the corruption of parliament.

In an effort to dilute the bill, opponents sought an amendment that would reduce the number enfranchised. When the amendment was passed, and in the face of deep division in his party, Lord Russell resigned. Amid rising popular pressure such as the Hyde Park Riots which had been inspired by the Reform League, the Conservative Party was invited to form a minority administration.

EXTEND YOUR KNOWLEDGE

The Hyde Park Riots (1866)
Following the failure of the 1866 Reform Bill, the Reform League resolved to hold a political meeting in Hyde Park on 23 July 1866 to discuss future action in the campaign for reform. The meeting was declared illegal by the home secretary, Spencer Walpole, Hyde Park was cordoned off by police and the gates chained. Confronted by this action the large crowd that had assembled for the meeting clashed with police and was able to enter the park by swinging on the railings until they gave way.

A leap in the dark? The Second Reform Act, 1867

The role of Benjamin Disraeli

Britain was a very different place from the country that passed the first reform legislation. In every sense it was a more modern state and, to match this, the new chancellor of the exchequer, Benjamin Disraeli, was a modern politician. Fully aware of the benefits that reform could bring to the party that passed the legislation, Disraeli was happy to adopt a more pragmatic attitude and immediately sought to introduce his own bill in March 1867. Despite three of his cabinet colleagues resigning in protest, Disraeli pressed on with his modest reform package. The proposal was less progressive than the Liberal offering but over the course of its debate the chancellor accepted the radical amendments of his critics. In doing so Disraeli evidenced a keen appreciation for manipulating an opportunity. For him, political success was more important than the final shape of the bill; certainly, conservative ideology might be offended but the passage of any reform would, in his eyes, ensure the future success of that party and therefore it was imperative that the bill go through. In compromising the principles of the Conservative Party, Disraeli was, in one sense, recognising the political animal that the British public had become and, in another, was seeking to harness that emotion for the benefit of modern conservatism. Such was his belief in the necessity of this bill that he alienated several older members of his party, including Lord Cranborne, the Earl of Carnarvon and the war secretary, Jonathan Peel, who each resigned in protest in March. Despite these exits, the bill was passed in August 1867.

Political attitudes to reform in the 1860s

Provisions of the Second Reform Act

The distribution of seats involved the following changes:

- 45 seats were taken from boroughs with less than 10,000 people; seven were completely disenfranchised

- 25 of these seats went to the counties; 20 went to new boroughs; six existing boroughs got an extra seat and one seat was reserved for the University of London.

The franchise was extended to include:

- in the boroughs, all male householders provided they had lived there for at least a year and lodgers who occupied property worth at least £10 for at least one year

- in the counties, in addition to the existing franchise, all owners or leaseholders of land worth £5 a year.

SOURCE

A *Leap in the Dark*. A cartoon published by *Punch* magazine commenting on the Second Reform Act, dated August 1867.

A LEAP IN THE DARK.

The impact of the Second Reform Act

The immediate impact of the 1867 Act was electoral defeat for Disraeli in 1868. Despite enfranchising more than one million of the working class, the Conservatives lost the next general election and disproved Disraeli's own rationale for reform. In this philosophical sense, perhaps the significance of the reform was that it proved to all that members of the working class had their own minds and would vote as they saw fit. More tangibly, the British political system became more honest and professional. With more than 2.46 million voters it became almost impossible to use corrupt means to achieve votes and therefore parties began to recognise the importance of campaigning. It was perhaps the early recognition of this that gave the Liberal party greater success after 1867, as during the 1868 election members maintained a more active attempt to influence voters by speaking all over the country, while Disraeli was confident enough only to issue a printed election address to the people. In recognising and then pursuing the task of persuading voters to their causes, British parties became more representative of public interest and this was the start of a more democratic establishment.

In particular, the 1867 Act promoted a more diverse electorate. Voters after 1832 were mostly middle class and fairly conservative, but 35 years later the qualification to vote was extended to include many of the urban skilled working class, which consequently saw the voting population grow to one-third of adult males. Changes in the redistribution of several parliamentary seats to the larger cities such as Liverpool and Manchester, meant that, after 1867, and for the first time political power started to shift towards the largest section of society rather than the wealthiest. By addressing the issue of representation more accurately to reflect the social composition of the country, the Second Reform Act is often seen to make a positive contribution to establishing Britain's eventual democracy.

To suggest the Act completely eradicated 'old corruption', however, would be too optimistic. There were certainly many failings with the reform: large areas in the Midlands and the north were still under-represented while the southern counties were over-represented; property still determined the franchise in the counties; in the boroughs, a residency clause demanding occupancy for at least one year discriminated against around 30 percent of the working-class population. Additionally, a system of 'plural voting' was also permitted for those who owned property in both a borough and county and seats were reserved for prominent universities.

Clearly then, the reform was not perfect. Like the reform of 1832 before it, there was much room for improvement and over the next 15 years there would be several attempts to achieve this. But, also as in 1832, the 1867 reforms took Britain one step closer to the panacea that is democracy. Given the nation's starting point in 1785 and the enormity of this journey, small steps were perhaps the safest way of proceeding. Between 1785 and 1870 the British political system changed dramatically. During this time it witnessed a significant transformation that took power away from landed elites and placed the country onto a more democratic path which increasingly empowered ordinary people by giving them a greater political voice. The size of the electorate had grown to one-third of the adult male population and many of the new towns and cities enjoyed greater representation than they had done before. The worst excesses of the pre-reform system were largely addressed with the abolition of rotten boroughs and the provision of the vote to many among the 'respectable' working classes. These changes had been made by the passage of two reform acts that were deliberately created to address the issue of political representation. The people themselves were instrumental in promoting this action. Between 1785 and 1870, the country had witnessed the growth of public awareness and public action. Groups such as the Chartists gave a voice to working people and this helped to make parliament more aware of the need to make the House of Commons more representative. Despite these improvements, however, the country was still a long way from becoming a democracy. Representation was not completely equal: the practice of plural voting continued and, perhaps most unfair of all, women remained disenfranchised. A lot had been achieved but there was still a long way to go.

> **A Level Exam-Style Question Section B**
>
> How far do you agree that the 1867 Reform Act was more significant than reform in 1832? (20 marks)
>
> **Tip**
> *When answering this question you should consider the outcomes, for different sections of society, of each Act.*

ACTIVITY
SUMMARY

Continuity or change?

The focus of study within this paper is on developments and changes over almost 100 years of British history. In this chapter you have looked at the motivations for political change and surveyed the political system from 1785 through to 1870. Over this time there were many forces at work which prompted those in power to make significant changes to the political landscape.

Now that you have read the chapter it will be useful to take a step back and think about a broad overview of the material to get a good appreciation of the general dynamics at work.

1 Consider the following questions to help focus your reflection:

  a) What were the forces that promoted changes to be made?

  b) What were the motivations of those in power when they considered making changes to the political system?

  c) Did the reforms that were offered significantly alter the nature of the political system?

  d) Are there any strongly consistent features running through the period?

2 Having answered the questions above, now provide some examples that support each point you have made.

THINKING HISTORICALLY   Causation (3a&b)

'The might of human agency'
'Our lack of control'. Work in pairs.

1 Describe to your partner a situation where things did not work out as you had intended. Then explain how you would have done things differently to make the situation as you would have wanted. Your partner will then tell the group about that situation and whether they think that your alternative actions would have the desired effect.

'The tyranny of failed actions'. Work individually.

2 Think about Feargus O'Connor, one of the leaders of the Chartist movement after 1838, who took the third petition demanding greater political equality to parliament in 1848. Like the two previous attempts this third attempt failed and as a result Chartism fell into decline.

   a) Write down three ways in which the Chartists could have acted differently in that situation.

   b) Now imagine that you are Feargus O'Connor. Write a defence of your actions. Try to think about the things that you would have known about at the time and make sure that you do not use the benefit of hindsight.

'Arguments'. Work in groups of between four and six.

   In turn, each group member will read out their defence. Other group members suggest ways to reassure the reader that they were not a failure and that in some ways what happened was a good outcome.

3 Think about William Gladstone and his reform bill which he presented in 1866.

   a) In what ways were the consequences of the 1866 reform bill not anticipated by Gladstone?

   b) In what ways did the 1866 reform bill turn out better for Gladstone than the intended consequences?

4 Think about Benjamin Disraeli and his efforts to pass the Second Reform Act in anticipation that the Tory party would benefit from the gratitude of those newly enfranchised. Answer the following:

   a) In what ways were the consequences of the passage of the Second Reform Act not anticipated by Benjamin Disraeli?

   b) In what ways did the passage of the Second Reform Act turn out worse for Benjamin Disraeli than the intended consequences?

5 To what extent are historical individuals in control of the history they helped to create? Explain your answer with reference to specific historical examples from this topic and others you have studied.

ACTIVITY
KNOWLEDGE CHECK

How had British politics changed by 1867?
Using the material above, write down the three most important ways that Britain had changed between 1832 and 1867. Justify your answers briefly.

   WIDER READING

Belcham, J. *Popular Radicalism in Nineteenth Century Britain*, Macmillan (1995)

Evans, E. *Parliamentary Reform, c. 1770–1918*, Longman (2000)

Gash, N. *Aristocracy and People: Britain 1815–1865*, Hodder Education (1979)

Lang, S. *Parliamentary Reform 1785–1928*, Routledge (1999)

O'Gorman, F. *Voter, Patrons and Parties: The Unreformed Electorate of Hanoverian England, 1734–1832*, Oxford University Press (1989)

1.2

Industrialisation and protest, c1785-c1870

KEY QUESTIONS

- To what extent did industrialisation change Britain?
- Did working and living conditions improve for the people?
- Did protest inspire reforms to benefit the working classes?

INTRODUCTION

The Industrial Revolution has always been a popular focus for debate within British history. Credited with giving birth to the 'workshop of the world', the **industrialisation** that began towards the end of the 18th century was revolutionary in every sense of the word. Following its generally agreed conclusion by the late 1800s, the Britain it left behind was unrecognisable; as a chiefly **agrarian** nation, much of the landscape had been transformed by huge increase in the numbers of factories. In turn these 'churches of industry' generated new urban centres as a rising population sought gainful employment. With the growth of new towns and cities the centres of power in Britain were changing, which certainly had a profound effect upon the nation both politically (see Chapter 1) and economically. Perhaps the most enduring legacy of industrialisation, however, was the restructuring of society itself. Here traditional positions were challenged by the growth of a dominant working class and more particularly the emergence of a new middle class who found success as owners and managers of industry. These primarily urban groups did as much to transform the country as any technological advance at this time; as industrialisation rapidly brought the country into a modern era they prompted, and often demanded, changes to reflect their not insignificant contributions to this development. As each class pushed for recognition of its endeavours, the old foundations on which Britain was built were themselves uprooted and replaced; it seemed to many that class privilege was turned upside down and the country eventually became a more equal and open society.

KEY TERMS

Industrialisation
A term used to describe a period of social and economic change when communities, usually countries, move away from traditional, usually rural, modes of living and adopt more industrial techniques. This often sees society, and the economy in particular, dramatically transformed.

Agrarian
A term used to describe a strong focus on the land, usually in the form of farming and rural living.

					1831 –	
	1800 – Second Combination Act passed		1813 – Statute of Artificers repealed	1824 – Combination Acts withdrawn	1826 – Banking Co-partnership repealed	Outbreak of cholera in Sunderland
1795	1800	1805	1810	1815	1820	1825	1830
	1799 – Combination Act passed			1811 – Luddite protests begin	1817 – Luddism ends	1825 – New Combinations of Workmen Act passed	1830 – Swing Riots take place; start of the Ten Hours movement

THE IMPACT OF INDUSTRIALISATION IN BRITAIN

The basis for industrialisation in Britain was technological innovation combined with a burgeoning market within the expanding empire. Throughout the 18th century, these two trends dovetailed to create an environment conducive to industrial development. With the growth of the British Empire there was significant opportunity for profits to be made by creating demand for British goods. In generating this demand it became necessary to be able to produce more efficiently and during the 18th century there were several scientific developments that made this possible. Thomas Newcomen's steam engine, used in 1712 to pump water out of mines, became the prototype for steam-powered factories later in the century and the Spinning Jenny, patented in 1770, revolutionised the textile industry. Creations like these made manufacturing on a large scale achievable in Britain, enabling its transformation into the world's first industrialised nation.

Funding the revolution: the growth of banking and investment

Fundamental to industrial development was a secure financial basis that allowed for capital to be available to fund business ventures and particularly the start-up and running costs that such ventures incurred. In this field Britain had already made substantial strides that facilitated the growth of industry. In 1694, the Bank of England had been established and by 1784 there were 119 banks in the country, excluding those in London. By 1808, this number had expanded to 800, signifying both the rapid growth of this business sector and also the increasing importance of banking to the general development of the country.

Recognising the importance of banking

Banking in Britain during the 18th century was very much in its infancy and therefore largely informal, performed by private companies or individuals. The first recognised bankers in Britain were the goldsmiths, whose traditional trade of smelting and fashioning items from the precious material meant they had effective means for keeping gold safe. As faith in the Royal Mint was lost after Charles I stole from it in 1640, people chose to deposit their gold with the smiths in return for receipts or bills of exchange – the beginning of paper currency. Within London the goldsmith bankers enjoyed a flourishing trade as more and more people looked to them for both secure deposits and a means to borrow funds. During industrialisation this development helped the economy to grow considerably because it made financial transactions much easier and safer – the result of which was that new businesses could access funds more effectively so that they could become better established.

A similar system operated in the counties of England where the goldsmith bankers of London had declined to expand. Here, away from London, counties set up their own systems of banking, usually under the control of businessmen who had some degree of financial experience. Like their London counterparts these institutions accepted deposits and also offered a means of easy payment between businesses. In these dealings money would not need to be withdrawn but rather simply moved from one account to another within the bank itself. This offered a safe and efficient means of transaction which consequently encouraged further dealings that promoted mutual growth. In 1797, these county banks were granted permission to issue bank notes. This promoted the development of personal banking but, more importantly, gave employers an effective way of paying wages from a central fund. In combination with banks in the cities, these county establishments were fundamental to economic development because they offered a clear and identifiable way to manage money.

Creating a national system of banking

Despite these advances, the growth in banking was limited because of a clause within the Bank of England Charter that denied the right of note issue to banks with more than six members (Source 1). This cap prevented the creation of larger **joint-stock banks** and effectively kept banking on a localised

> **KEY TERM**
>
> Joint-stock bank
> The title given to a bank owned by several people, each with shares in the bank's capital. These individuals were only liable for debts up to the value of their shares and not the full amount in the bank.

1834 – Labourers in Tolpuddle arrested

1846 – Corn Laws repealed

1848 – Public Health Act passed

1866 – Sanitary Act passed

| 1835 | 1840 | 1845 | 1850 | 1855 | 1860 | 1865 | 1870 |

1833 – Factory Act passed

1842 – Mines Act passed

1847 – Ten Hours Act limits the length of the working day

1851 – The Great Exhibition takes place

footing. The purpose of the limit was to keep banking on a small scale. However, expanding industrialisation quickly demonstrated the need for larger financial institutions if the country was to take full advantage of the business opportunities becoming available. In 1826, the cap was removed and Britain's banks were free fully to realise their potential and contribute substantially to the country's economic development. As banks grew in size, they became more stable and investors felt more confident with the protection that joint-stock status gave them. With increased stability, the smaller private banks were absorbed into larger joint-stock enterprises. These were able to manage much greater sums of money and operate on a national scale. They therefore facilitated the growing economy that industrialisation was promoting, by establishing a financial network that spanned the country.

SOURCE

1 From the Bank of England Charter issued in 1708, which designated private joint-stock banks as being illegal.

For any political body or corporation whatsoever elected or to be elected other than the said Governor and Company of the Bank of England for or other persons whatsoever united or to be united in covenant or partnership, exceeding the number of six persons, in that part of the United Kingdom called England, to borrow, owe or take up any sum or sums of money on their bills or notes payable on demand, or any less time than six months from the borrowing therefore.

The first joint-stock bank was the Lancashire Banking Company, which was established in October 1826; other areas quickly followed and larger scale banking slowly spread across the country. The growth of these larger banks was given a further boost in 1833 when an Act of Parliament permitted joint-stock banks in London to issue cheques. By allowing people to draw on these cheques in any branch of a particular bank, the speed of commercial transactions was dramatically increased and promoted more timely business practices. As a result of this measure, banks increasingly became the easiest and most efficient way to 'do business' and they rapidly grew in number, mirroring the increased demand for the flexible services they offered. By 1866, there were 154 joint-stock banks with 850 branches nationwide.

The significance of banking for the economy'

The role of banking was important to the growing economy for several reasons. First, it provided a source of capital that allowed men with vision to establish themselves in business. This was an essential feature of the industrialisation process as it meant the emerging technological innovations could be adopted commercially and across the nation. With ready finance to buy or build new factories and furnish them with the new machines, many of the **cottage industries** on which Britain had been reliant gradually became large-scale operations. Despite some opposition from skilled craftsmen who felt threatened by this development, these industries generated significant profits as Britain became the world leader in manufacturing. One such industry was cotton. In 1761, it imported over three million pounds by weight of cotton wool yet by 1833 was importing over 300 million pounds and employing more than 833,000 people. The basis for such growth

was undoubtedly the introduction of Richard Arkwright's Water Frame in 1769 and then Samuel Crompton's Spinning Mule in 1779, which utilised the best features from Arkwright's machine and the Spinning Jenny. These machines were very effective at speeding up the process of spinning cotton but remained very expensive items that often necessitated a bank loan for their purchase, with a promise of a return with interest from the profits they would yield.

KEY TERM

Cottage industry
Small-scale industry usually performed in individual homes or small communities rather than in large factories.

An equally important function that banks served was to unite the gentleman farmer with the industrialising centres of commerce through the means of investment. The suggestion that the Industrial Revolution saw a rapid growth only of urban areas, completely separate from the counties, which continued in their traditional manner, is too simplistic. The development of the urban centres was indeed a prominent feature of the industrialisation process; however, it was supported by the counties in many respects. Foremost were the financial relationships that it fostered. Many of the landed aristocracy were not content to sit and watch their traditional incomes diminish in the face of progress. Instead, many chose to invest in the new developments. This was achieved through the banking system, which allowed them to transfer assets around relatively easily. The money they invested was often a long-term commitment and directed at developing infrastructures that aided both their own concerns directly and the urban centres secondarily. Railway investment was popular and so too was investment in building new docks to assist in the growing development of international trade. In 1839, for example, the Marquess of Bute built the docks at Cardiff Bay, while the Earl of Lonsdale has been credited with establishing Whitehaven Harbour in Cumberland. This focus on infrastructure was a specific attempt to develop their own business interests but indirectly it also contributed to the industrialisation process. More directly, many landowners bought mills to supplement their incomes and employed managers to run them on their behalf. In this manner, far from being separate from the newly developing industries, the landed gentry was very much a part of the revolution and was equally enriched by it.

The investment opportunities offered by banks were also taken up by the emerging industrial middle class. As owners of new businesses, members of this class were certainly grateful for the secure depositing facilities of banks, but they also availed themselves of the opportunity to invest their money into other ventures that might yield a good return. Members of this group initially invested in industries similar to their own or which had some direct benefit for their businesses. However, by the mid-1800s, investments were made more widely, such was the level of confidence in Britain's prosperity.

A new industrial middle class

The emergence of a new industrial middle class was one of the most significant features of industrialisation. Prior to this development a person's position in British society had been relatively straightforward. If you owned land then you were well-placed and your position was felt to be among the reasonably broad upper echelon of society, depending on how much land you controlled. If you did not own land but either rented it or worked it for somebody else then your prospects were usually less favourable and your position was significantly lower. The development of industrialisation complicated this land-centred stratification and provided alternative means for progressing in society. For those with vision and the willingness to apply themselves to the opportunities that emerging technologies offered, there was a new way to make a living which, if successful, beckoned with wealth and respectability.

The men who took advantage of these opportunities and pioneered the development of large-scale industry became known as a 'middle class' within society's lexicon. Bridging the gap between the labouring classes and the landed gentry, this new group consisted of self-made men who earned their wealth from the trades and developing service industries that grew up alongside them. The majority were small factory owners or merchants who profited from the expanding markets that industrialisation was reaching. The growth of this class was quite impressive: between 1816 and 1831 it had increased its size by 75 percent; rising from 160,000 to more than 214,000. As one of the fastest growing sectors in society, this 'middle class' demographic introduced a new dynamic to British society which would have a profound impact upon the country.

As self-made men of commerce this group sought to apply the principles of free trade which Adam Smith had advocated towards the end of the 18th century. Under this doctrine there was little room for mutual co-existence, as the means for profiteering was to dominate the market and ensure that you maintained an edge over your competitors. This fairly aggressive approach created among many employers a very hard-nosed attitude when it came to business and maintaining a profit. In terms of economic success, this attitude translated very effectively for many individuals, such as the inventor Richard Arkwright. Arkwright, who had enjoyed success with his water frame invention that harnessed the power of water for spinning yarn, is a singularly appropriate example of the self-made and commercially minded man that the middle class embodied. His early success allowed him to purchase land in the village of Cromford in Derbyshire, where he built a cotton mill. After buying out his partners, he extended across the north of England, where he built further mills powered by his water frame. Born the son of a tailor who could not afford to send him to school, Arkwright ended his life in 1792 with a personal fortune of £500,000 and a knighthood which had been bestowed in 1786. While Arkwright is an example of the success people could enjoy in the favourable circumstances of industrialising Britain, others were less fortunate. Richard Trevithick – the man who had the idea to put a steam engine on wheels, actually died penniless after making some poor business decisions. The dynamic environment that industrialisation promoted therefore presented opportunities for huge wealth to be created but it was not guaranteed. To improve their chances of success, businesses had to be managed efficiently and this sometimes brought the owners into direct confrontation with their workers.

> **EXTEND YOUR KNOWLEDGE**
>
> Adam Smith (1723–90)
> An economist and moral philosopher from Scotland, Adam Smith is most remembered for his book, *An Enquiry into the Nature and Causes of the Wealth of Nations*, which was published in 1776. In this work Smith challenged the existing ideas of economic development which advocated careful protection of domestic markets via government regulation and instead suggested that '*laissez-faire*' or 'free trade' was a more effective means to promote economic growth. Under this model, economic markets would be allowed to develop naturally without interference from government.

In terms of government relations, the immediate political impact of the new industrial middle class has already been considered in the section on the reform debate (see Chapter 1.1). More interesting in terms of the industrialisation of Britain, is the urban working class that expanded in unison with the new middle class. This group laboured in the new factories and mills that were established, attracted there by the prospect of stable and long-term employment which, in the event, was neither

> **A Level Exam-Style Question Section A**
>
> To what extent can the growth in banking be explained by the expansion of a more commercially minded nation in the years 1825–44? (20 marks)
>
> **Tip**
> *When answering this question think about how banking might be useful to a growing economy – how might commercialism benefit from it?*

stable nor long-term but which offered the only chance of reasonably regular work. As the employer of this group, the middle class enjoyed a complicated working relationship with it that was both a positive and negative influence on the development of the country. In one sense, it helped to build the new urban centres that became the bases for industrial success, but it also established a 'master and worker' identity that, as industrialisation took off, would promote a class consciousness for the labouring masses. In this sense, the growth of the industrial middle class was both a significant progression in itself and also the precursor for future social movements.

The north/south divide: economic diversity in Britain

SOURCE 2 A drawing of Stockport town and its cotton mills in the 1830s by G. Pickering.

With the development of new economies and a slow shift away from traditional modes of enterprise, the Industrial Revolution saw the landscape of Britain change quite dramatically. The traditional centres of economic power had always been the counties with their acres of fertile land, which not only fed the nation but also produced goods for trade abroad. Perhaps the best known of these goods were the woollen textiles which were shipped across the growing empire and which had been the source of British wealth since the Middle Ages. Small-scale weaving operations were located in the countryside where they had easy access to their raw materials and as a cottage industry this was a reasonably effective means of existing. However, with the introduction of more commercial interests, notably international trade, these industries began to drift closer to areas with better transportation networks. In the case of the cotton industry, Lancashire had always been well adapted to the industry due to its favourable climate which prevented the cotton thread from splitting, but Lancashire also had access to one of the biggest ports in the country: Liverpool. This access, using the Manchester to Liverpool railway built in 1830, was fundamental to the trade as it relied not only on the import of raw cotton from the USA, but also on the export of products to other parts of the Empire. Areas that were less favourably placed in terms of access to ports tended to remain small-scale enterprises, at least until the development of first the canal system and then, most importantly, the steam railway, which grew dramatically during the 1840s.

Certainly, accessibility was critical to a business if it wanted to be successful and take advantage of broader trade opportunities. Of equal importance for ambitious businesses that hoped to exploit the new technologies were the requirements of the technologies themselves. The earliest machines were powered by water and demanded constant access to this resource and therefore the first factories and mills were placed next to rivers that could generate the necessary supply. With the introduction of the steam engine after 1769, however, coal became the most important raw material. As business took advantage of the more efficient steam-powered machines, industries gravitated towards the great coalfields where access to this resource was both plentiful and less expensive. Slowly, therefore, as businesses introduced further improvements, the landscape of Britain evolved: industry became centred in the areas where supplies of vital raw materials were easily available. In the case of coal this was the Midlands and north of England, South Wales and, in Scotland, the Clyde Valley.

The increased concentration of industry in these areas throughout the 1800s established a lasting association that continues today: Sheffield Steel and the engineering plants of Birmingham that churned out motor cars during the last century are enduring examples of this ongoing association. Just as the north and the Midlands became the new centres of industry – notably engineering and manufacturing – the south became relatively unimportant, remaining very much wedded to agriculture and smaller-scale industries that maintained traditional working methods. By the mid-1800s, it is possible to discern the following broad regional differences:

- The north-west of England had become the heartland of textile manufacturing: notably cotton and wool.

- The north-east developed a strong mining industry because of the rich vein of minerals located there. It also had a healthy shipbuilding industry.

- The Midlands evolved a strong engineering tradition.

- The south-east of England, with the exception of London, remained firmly agriculturally based and continued to export grain as it always had done.

- The south-west maintained a primarily agricultural presence, although Cornwall became an important exporter of tin.

- The south also retained some of its woollen industry but after the introduction of steam power it was being out-produced by the larger enterprises in Yorkshire which had better access to coal.

To suggest the continuation of agricultural practices left the south obsolete, however, is unfair. The resources produced there were vital to maintaining the well-being of the nation and the development of farming technologies, such as Andrew Meikle's threshing machine in 1789, promoted greater productivity and ensured that the south developed, albeit at a slower pace, in line with the north. The significant difference between the south and the north, however, was that mechanisation in the south was reducing the need for human labour, while in the north it was creating a greater demand for it. The impact of this was the steady exodus of labour from the countryside into the newly developing and employment-rich towns.

ACTIVITY
KNOWLEDGE CHECK

Who were the industrial middle class?

Starting with what you have read, can you create a profile of the new industrial middle class? You should consider the following points:

- what 'middle class' means

- which people created this class

- the roles they performed

- the attitudes they held

- the impact this class had upon Britain.

The growth of industrial towns and cities

In 1750, only the cities of London and Edinburgh had populations over 50,000 and yet by 1851 there were 29 cities of this size, nine of which that had populations in excess of 100,000, including London itself with more than 2.3 million inhabitants. The vast population change undertaken during these years was undoubtedly one of the most visible effects of industrialisation and it transformed the way people lived their lives. Prior to industrial growth, Britain was a chiefly rural nation with few densely populated urban areas. With the exception of the capital, the majority of people worked on the land or in a service that directly related to it. Without a railway, travel was by horse-drawn carriage or simply by walking and could take days rather than hours and was often very expensive, as Source 3 shows.

With industrialisation came an improved and improving transport network. Canals criss-crossed the country until the middle of the 19th century, when, superseded by the expanding rail network, they began to fall into disrepair. Roads, too, were improved beyond all recognition. In these ways raw materials and finished goods were moved between factories and ports, towns and cities. The workforce, too, became more mobile.

With large numbers of people seeking employment in the new industries there was an immediate demand for housing which was usually met by the factory owners. These homes were built close to the factories and provided basic accommodation for those who worked in them. The most common style of building was known as the 'back to back' which minimised building costs by using one back wall for two properties. When used in conjunction with terracing this proved a very efficient way to house the ever-expanding urban population. The stability that came with a job and a home enabled workers to settle down and either have their families join them or begin one. In laying down roots, communities were developed and quickly small towns grew larger and large towns became cities. Perhaps the greatest of these was Manchester which had a population of 182,000 by 1831, having had one of less than 25,000 in 1772. The basis of this growth was the hugely successful cotton industry which earned Manchester the nickname 'cottonopolis'. Favourably located near to the port of Liverpool and with good transportation links to coalfields across the north, Manchester was quick to emerge as a genuinely industrialised city. It was followed very rapidly by centres such as Birmingham, Glasgow, Leeds and Bradford, which visibly evidenced the transition Britain had made into a fully fledged, urbanised industrial nation.

Government attitudes towards industrial development

The response of government to the economic and social transformation of Britain was mixed. Traditionally it has been convenient to suggest that the state did not play any significant role in industrialisation and to maintain that the changes which swept across the nation were driven by the private endeavours of the industrial middle class. This interpretation has a lot of merit, particularly before the political reforms of the 1830s; however, it is incomplete. Despite a seemingly slow rate of action, the British state did actively engage with industrialisation and ensured both its success and eventual improvement.

Given that parliament was dominated by landed interests (Chapter 1) it is fair to reason that there was some consternation about the growing power of the new urban centres, although this did not create barriers for progression. Rather, there was considered intervention where the government deemed it necessary and of mutual benefit to the state. In this sense it took a minimalist but selective, *laissez-faire* approach to industrialisation. Far from denying opportunities for greater individual enrichment, it supported this endeavour and even removed obstacles that slowed the rapid pace of profiteering. These included first, the passage of the Combination Acts in 1799 and 1800 that made it illegal to form unions and second, the Master and Servant Act in 1823, which made the failure to fulfil a contract of work a crime punishable with imprisonment. Public policy complemented private industry, especially in the development of Britain's new infrastructures such as a more robust water supply and, more noticeably, the railways. After the consolidation of private enterprise, government then undertook to regulate it to promote long-term stability.

SOURCE 3

Advertisement in *Aris's Birmingham Gazette* for coach travel between Birmingham and London, dated May 1787. For comparison of expense: the average annual family income for a labouring family in the 1780s was £24.

Safe and Elegant TRAVELLING.

Hotel and Swan Inn, Birmingham.

Paytons's Old Original well-known LONDON POST-COACH, in Sixteen Hours (with a GUARD) from the above INN, through Stratford-upon-Avon, Oxford, and High-Wycombe, to the Bull-and-Mouth Inn, London, will continue to set out every Evening, at SEVEN o'Clock; to carry four Insides, Fare 1l.11s.6d. – And Outsides at 16s. each.

Inside Passengers are allowed 14lb. Weight of Luggage, Outsides 7lb. all above to pay 1d. per 1b. – Small Parcels 1s. each; large light Boxes and Parcels charged in Proportion to their Size.

All Goods sent by this Coach, that are for the Western Part of London, will be delivered from Hand's Warehouse, the Old Green Man and Still, in Oxford-street, early the same Day.

The Proprietors beg Leave to return their Friends and the Public in general, sincere Thanks for their Support in this Business; and as the above Carriage is allowed to be equal in Expedition to any in England, they are resolved to spare no Expence or Trouble to continue it the completest of the Kind, flattering themselves that they shall still experience the generous Support of the Public.

Performed by

JOHN PAYTON, Stratford-upon-Avon.

SAMUEL WYER, Birmingham.

J. ALLEN, Wycombe, and

JOHN WILLAN and Co. London.

N.B. The Proprietors of this Coach will not be accountable for Money, Bills, Plate, Jewels, & c above Five Pounds Value, unless entered as such and paid for accordingly; nor for Passengers Luggage, unless it is properly directed and paid for when delivered.

Water supply

Before the Municipal Corporations Act of 1835, which removed local council powers from **oligarchies** and allowed the local councils to take over local utilities such as sewerage and water supply, the majority of public works were undertaken by private companies. These companies needed the permission of parliament to operate and, using this opportunity, the government established fundamental ground rules that governed their practices, notably the extent to which they could infringe upon owners' property rights when undertaking their work and also the level of competition to be allowed. Despite these provisions, the consistency of service fluctuated significantly and in the mid-1800s parliament considered **nationalising** the water utilities; however, there remained considerable opposition from water companies, who mounted a successful lobbying campaign when the idea was first suggested, and as a result the idea was shelved until later in the century.

KEY TERMS

Oligarchy
Authority concentrated into the hands of a few powerful, usually self-appointed and self-interested, people.

Nationalisation
The process whereby private businesses are taken under public ownership by the state.

The railways

Fundamental to Britain's industrial development was the creation of an effective transportation network. Certainly, towards the end of the 1700s, the use of canals had offered significant improvements for the movement of resources but this was a slow system which could not keep up with demand. More vital for the success of industrialisation was the introduction of the rail network and this was managed by private companies in partnership with the government. When the first line, the Stockton and Dartington, was conceived in the early 1820s, it needed an Act of Parliament to **incorporate** the company and also allow for the acquisition of lands for the project. By controlling these essential elements, the government was able to influence the development of this industry through judicious bargaining with the companies. In 1844, this resulted in the Railway Regulation Act, which greatly strengthened state power over the rail companies and gave it the option to nationalise the service should it want to.

KEY TERM

Incorporation
The act of giving legal recognition to a company by making it a separate legal body.

Regulation

Given the unbridled progress that was being made after the 1780s, it is easy to suggest that the government did not take a large enough interest in the economic and social developments generated by industrialisation. This is given further credence by the repeal of several laws that had promoted government intervention.

These include: 1813 Repeal of the Statute of Artificers which had, since 1563, provided some regulation of wages and working conditions; 1826 Banking Co-partnership Act which repealed the 1720 Bubble Act limiting the number of joint-stock banks; and the 1846 repeal of the Corn Laws which removed the import restrictions on that commodity. The removal of these laws promotes the idea that government very much adopted a *laissez-faire* attitude, preferring to allow market forces and private entrepreneurialism to dictate the pace of change rather than government policy. However, the implication that government was uninterested is misleading and it is equally appropriate to suggest the state was simply responding to changes in circumstance – the dynamic economic climate of the early 1800s, for example, had no need for fixed wages, while the opportunity to extend industry could only benefit from a stronger banking sector. On this basis it is just as plausible to suggest that the government was actively engaged in promoting industrialisation, saw these pieces of legislation as a hindrance and therefore sought to remove them as a barrier.

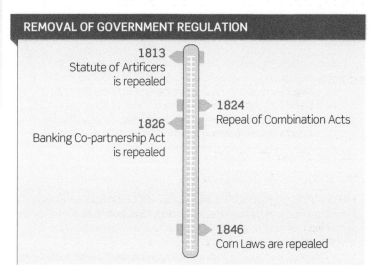

REMOVAL OF GOVERNMENT REGULATION

1813
Statute of Artificers
is repealed

1824
Repeal of Combination Acts

1826
Banking Co-partnership Act
is repealed

1846
Corn Laws are repealed

In addition, just as government removed legislation, it also introduced it. In 1799 and 1800, the Combination Acts were passed, making it illegal for men to establish **trade unions** after weavers in Lancashire had organised themselves into such an association following a decline in wage prices. The passage of this Act evidences a commitment by government to promote the unhampered development of industry and firmly placed it on the side of the entrepreneurial employers pioneering Britain's modernisation. Further efforts to regulate development included the 1844 Banking Charter Act, which placed a cap of 20 years on the lifetime of any new joint-stock bank that was created. Although both these Acts would later be repealed themselves, they demonstrate a government actively engaged with the changes being undertaken in Britain.

KEY TERM

Trade union
An association of workers from a trade who bind together to protect and improve working conditions by collective bargaining and action.

A Level Exam-Style Question Section A

How far do you agree that rapid industrial growth was primarily the result of *laissez-faire* policies? (20 marks)

Tip
When answering this question think about the term 'primarily'; what else might have encouraged rapid growth?

Clearly then, the attitude of government towards industrial development was mixed. Although in some areas it demonstrated a reasonably apathetic attitude, this belied definitive action in others where government involvement protected the sensible growth of industry. Despite showing some positive direction, however, without doubt there was need for further legislative action.

A WORKER'S PARADISE? LIVING AND WORKING IN INDUSTRIAL BRITAIN

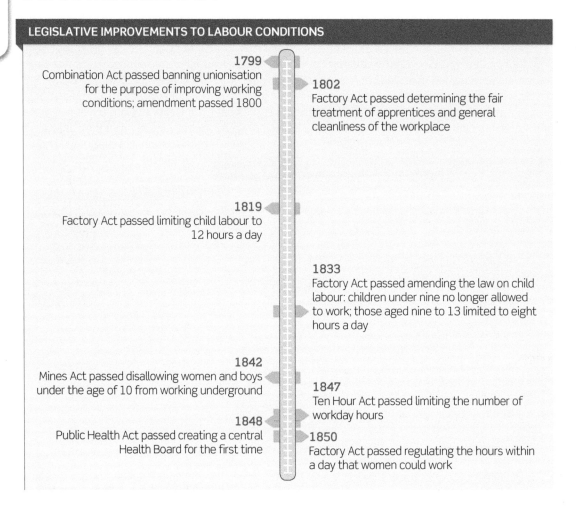

LEGISLATIVE IMPROVEMENTS TO LABOUR CONDITIONS

1799
Combination Act passed banning unionisation for the purpose of improving working conditions; amendment passed 1800

1802
Factory Act passed determining the fair treatment of apprentices and general cleanliness of the workplace

1819
Factory Act passed limiting child labour to 12 hours a day

1833
Factory Act passed amending the law on child labour: children under nine no longer allowed to work; those aged nine to 13 limited to eight hours a day

1842
Mines Act passed disallowing women and boys under the age of 10 from working underground

1847
Ten Hour Act passed limiting the number of workday hours

1848
Public Health Act passed creating a central Health Board for the first time

1850
Factory Act passed regulating the hours within a day that women could work

Industrialisation brought tremendous benefits to Britain and ensured that by the second half of the 19th century it was a significant world power. In the minds of the country's leaders there was a peculiar self-satisfied belief in the superiority of the British nation and in part this was due to the economic success that had been driven by the industrialisation process. In 1851 the Great Exhibition artfully presented the best features of Britain and its empire for the world to see, offering a platform for the nation to feel pride in its achievements. Certainly, those achievements had been great and Britain had modernised at a tremendous pace; however, there was a social cost to the rapid advances which had been made.

EXTEND YOUR KNOWLEDGE

The Great Exhibition of 1851
This was an international exhibition thought up by Queen Victoria's husband, Prince Albert, to showcase both the inventions that were promoting industrialisation and the range of quality goods then being produced. More than 100,000 objects sent by 15,000 contributors were exhibited. Although it was an international event, Britain occupied more than half the floor space.

SOURCE
4
A coloured sketch produced in Sheffield in the 1800s depicting the smokestacks from the city's steel factories.

Living conditions in the industrial towns and cities

SOURCE
5
A description of urban living in Manchester by the socialist writer Friedrich Engels after a trip to the city in 1842. Engels was a friend of Karl Marx and co-authored *The Communist Manifesto* with him in 1848.

… 350,000 working people of Manchester and its environs live, almost all of them, in wretched, damp, filthy cottages, that the streets which surround them are usually in the most miserable and filthy condition, laid out without the slightest reference to ventilation, with reference solely to the profit secured by the contractor…

Just as machines drove the economy forward, the migration of so many people to the Midlands and northern counties drove the social development of Britain. However, improvement in one was not immediately mirrored in the other. The rapid growth of towns and cities generated significant urban problems, which neither the existing systems, nor those with the authority to do so, could, or wanted to, manage. The immediate problem that was created was the pressing need to accommodate the growing workforce.

Housing – the 'back to back'

This need was met initially by employers who were eager to maintain a consistent workforce and one tied to their employ by the obligation to pay rent. Given the large numbers that began to flock to the towns and cities in the late 1700s, the main requirement for this housing was value: being able to maximise the gain with the minimal outlay. The result of this thinking was the creation of rows upon rows of cheap dwellings organised back to back so that they shared both a back wall and side walls. These 'back to backs', as they became known, were very efficient and minimised building costs but at the expense of quality (consider Source 5). Only four metres wide, these buildings were one room deep and often only had a second room above for sleeping. Aside from the cramped space, the build quality was very poor with the foundations usually only three bricks deep. The real negative feature, however, was that because they only had one wall opening onto a street there was limited natural light and they were therefore incredibly dark places, requiring the use of candles and oil lamps to provide further lighting. This created a very smoky environment which, given the obvious lack of adequate ventilation, encouraged respiratory problems that were only made worse by the smokestacks of the factories and mills.

If you lived in the 'back' house then your standard of living was even poorer. Without a street to offer a modicum of fresh air, the only means of ventilation and natural lighting came from a courtyard that allowed access to the property via narrow lanes off the street. These 'courts' were communal areas and included the wash houses and privies (toilets) that the dwellings themselves lacked. Although cheaper than those opening onto a street – rent cost 1s 10d a week compared with 2s 6d – with cesspools right outside, these properties were even more unhygienic than the 'front' houses.

Although some employers certainly did build decent houses for their workers, the efficiency offered by this style of housing made them especially attractive to the majority and as a result they became the standard housing in the cities; by 1801, two-thirds of the population of Birmingham lived in back to backs, while the smaller city of Nottingham had more than 12,600 such dwellings by 1841.

Sanitation

The speed with which towns grew and the emphasis placed upon cheap housing created excessive strain upon the local infrastructures, notably those relating to sanitation. With the vast overcrowding that urban planning generated, existing water supplies from wells and hand pumps were at a premium and what drainage systems were available were insufficient to meet rising demand. Adding to the problems of water were the communal privies that emptied into cesspits. If built without solid bottoms, these allowed liquid waste to soak into the ground and eventually contaminate the water supply and if built appropriately, they might not be emptied often enough due to the cost incurred by the landlord. The general lack of hygiene that consumed the towns often led to outbreaks of influenza and cholera which punctuated the unpleasantness of urban living and kept the population in constant fear of disease. Influenza epidemics were commonplace during the 1800s but the first major cholera outbreak in Britain was in Sunderland in 1831. Quickly spreading across the country, it killed around 32,000 people before it eventually declined the following year. Where efforts were made to improve sanitation, this enjoyed some success but there was no understanding about the spread of such diseases until the end of the century. Where improvements were made, these were almost always centred within the more affluent areas (Source 6) and therefore only served to reinforce a growing class divide.

SOURCE

 6   From the Fifth Annual Report of the Poor Law Commissioners in 1839. It was complied by Dr Thomas Southward Smith – physician in the London Fever Hospital and a friend of Edwin Chadwick whose investigations helped to raise awareness of diseases related to poverty and poor sanitation.

While systematic efforts, on a large scale, have been made to widen the streets… to extend and perfect the drainage and sewerage… in the places in which the wealthier classes reside, nothing whatever has been done to improve the condition of the districts inhabited by the poor.

Lack of communal 'free space'

The main objective that was adhered to as towns grew in the early 1800s was functionality and therefore little thought was given to the needs of people beyond their physical requirements. Indeed, before 1848 urban growth was little more than the creation of densely packed rows of houses; there was no desire to build attractive centres with promenades or public squares as these things were felt to have no utility value attached to them. The consequence of this unerring focus on function was that society as it existed in these towns became two tiered: the middle classes who could afford better houses and demanded a cleaner environment resided on the outskirts of the towns, establishing more 'respectable living' while the working classes, packed into the back to backs, were left to create their own communities and distractions in makeshift inns and chapels. The stark contrast between these two groups was softened to a small extent by several attempts to create model towns such as Saltaire, West Yorkshire, which offered better housing and even schools for workers' children and evening institutes to provide basic education for their parents, but these were often the exception rather than the norm. In separating these two classes, rather than co-existing, each developed a distinct class consciousness that increasingly promoted conflicts as one felt exploited by the other. Attempts to counter this class-separation, such as the founding of the model village of Saltaire in 1851, were few and far between.

ACTIVITY
KNOWLEDGE CHECK

Healthy development?

The urban growth that Britain underwent in the 1800s has been well documented in history books and is often cited as a fundamental aspect of industrialisation. Was this a positive development?

Consider the material you have studied so far and draw up a table on the 'Impact of urbanisation' which addresses the following points:

- Economic advantages
- Social advantages
- Economic disadvantages
- Social disadvantages
- Potential political impact.

Working conditions

Most factory owners, new to the experience, aimed to get as much work as possible from their workforce regardless of working conditions in their factories. Others, such as Robert Owen, adopted a more humanitarian approach, showing that good working conditions did not necessarily result in a fall in productivity.

Factories and foundries

The factory is perhaps the best-known feature of industrialisation in Britain and the establishment of this style of working has been credited to Richard Arkwright when he set up his cotton mill in Cromford in 1771, employing more than 300 people. Prior to this, Britain had been a nation of small cottage industries where work was carried out in the home rather than collectively in a large communal setting. The idea of the factory built upon these existing small **capitalist** industries but was revolutionary in the sense of concentrating labour in one place for the first time. The benefits of this development lay entirely with the employer who was able to closely supervise his workforce and ensure the efficient use of his expensive machines.

> **KEY TERM**
>
> Capitalism
> This is an economic concept where trade, businesses and the means of production are mostly owned privately and run for profit.

With the exception of paying better wages than agricultural work, for those working in the factory the benefits were almost non-existent. The purpose of the factory was to create profit and to achieve this employers sought to maximise output but keep costs as low as possible. This affected workers in many ways, not least the impersonality that was generated with hundreds of people crammed into the same space. Enhancing the isolation of factory work was the decline of independence as employers endeavoured to instil an efficient, automated sense of working among their workforce. Labouring under these conditions in tightly packed buildings that shuddered under the relentless noise of machines was a numbing experience for those involved. More tangible, however, were the long hours and unsafe conditions that employees faced. Before the Factory Act in 1833, there was very limited legislation regarding working hours and what existed was difficult to enforce. Employers were able to exploit their workers in the interests of increasing productivity. The working week was six days long with 14-hour days a common undertaking for men. Even after reforms were introduced, they only affected women and children; for men in factories the working day was never less than ten hours throughout the 19th century.

In addition to long working days was the discipline that workers faced. Here the main priority was efficient work practices and therefore workers faced fines for lateness or actions that reduced the speed with which they could do their work. The fine was a means by which the employer could compensate himself for loss of productivity and its value varied depending on the offence – for being ten minutes late it was not uncommon for the offender to be fined two hours' wages, while if caught talking workers were often fined one shilling, or one-fifth of their daily wage. If the employer also felt resources were being wasted, he would issue further fines: a usual sum for fixing machines under a gas lamp was two shillings as it was felt to be a waste of gas. In adopting such measures employers sought only profit and productivity; the interests of their workers were never really considered. The rationale for this position, as far as employers were concerned, was that with the payment of good enough wages the workforce had entered into an agreement with the employers allowing them the right to dictate the working day as they saw fit.

Perhaps the most unpleasant outcome of this agreement was the high injury rate that existed in factories. Certainly, tired workers having to fix moving machine parts in gloomy surroundings encouraged accidents but what made this more frequent was the general lack of safety measures that were instituted. Implementing such measures would have involved more cost, which employers were disinclined to consider; equally, establishing safe methods of working could reduce the rate of productivity. Before specific reform in 1844 therefore, there were virtually no safeguards in place to prevent injury from the machines and this cavalier attitude produced accidents on a regular basis.

Mines

Conditions in factories were certainly hazardous but mining remained a dangerous industry even though advances in safety equipment, such as the famous Davy safety lamp in 1815, had made it safer than the previous century. Working underground always carried risk – particularly of flooding, gas explosions and collapsing shafts – but as the demand for coal increased these risks were taken with greater frequency. Between 1770 and 1850, production went from six million to 55 million tons; to extract these quantities mines became deeper, extending from about 90 metres in the 18th century to about 300 metres by 1850. Working hours, like the factories, were long, with shifts of 12 hours a day, six days a week. Unlike in factories, however, until 1844 the majority of miners were not permanently employed but rather were 'bound' for agreed lengths of time. This process involved them agreeing to work for an allotted period of time, usually one year, at an agreed rate of pay. Under these terms the mine owner was not obliged to provide constant work in that period but the miner was required to present himself for work when needed. The problem with this manner of employment was that it did not guarantee miners a fixed wage and throughout the course of the 1800s, as mining became more vital to industry, this became the single most frequent source of discontent among the mining community.

The experiences of women and children

Women

The popular notion of '**separate spheres**' which gained prominence in the mid-19th century did not apply for working-class women and it can be said that industrialisation gave women more of a voice, encouraging the later suffrage and feminist movements by empowering women and highlighting the vital contribution they made to the country. In this sense economic development can be seen as an important source for political change. However, at the start of the 1800s, such ideas were far removed from the realities of women's lives.

> **KEY TERM**
>
> Separate spheres
> This is an idea that became very popular in the mid-1800s. It maintained that men and women occupied different roles and had separate functions in society. It was the function of men to work outside the home in paid employment, while women remained in the home and kept it in order for their returning men.

Although a factory wage was higher than that of an agricultural worker, wages were, on the whole, still as little as the employer could get away with – usually about 12–15 shillings a week. A steadily increasing urban population ensured that there was always sufficient demand for employment, which allowed employers to set the terms. Keeping wages as low as they could often meant workers struggled to pay for the basic necessities for living, especially when prices rose. During these periods of economic decline, employers were also able to reduce the terms of employment as they saw fit and this compounded the financial problems that working-class families already contended with. It was therefore out of necessity rather than notions of independence that women sought employment for themselves.

Women worked in all areas of the growing industrial economy, from domestic service to crawling underground as miners themselves. To the employer, women were a useful resource as they could be paid less money than male workers and would often undertake work that their male counterparts refused. One such role they performed in the mines was to operate the windlass, the winch machine that brought up coal from the seams and lowered men into them. By far the most common role for women though was that of a 'hurrier' which involved wearing a chain around their shoulders and hauling carts of coal along the shaft. This was very strenuous work and could create lasting physical injuries (Source 7).

SOURCE 7

From the testimony of Jane Watson, a miner from South Wales, given to the Royal Commission on Mining in 1842.

> A vast number of women have dead children, and false births, which is worse; they are not able to work after the latter. I have always been obliged to work below till forced to go home to bear the bairn, and so have all the other women. We return as soon as able—never longer than ten or twelve days; many less, if they are much needed. It is only horsework, and ruins the women; it crushes their haunches, bends their ankles, and makes them old women at forty.

Despite labouring under the same conditions in factories and mines, women were paid on average half the wage of men but also had to maintain a home after the working day. Only after 1833 did the working hours for women start to be reduced but even by 1878 women could still be working a 56-hour week. This inequality was a constant feature of the 19th century, standing as an example of how, in certain ways, very little changed during the economic transformation of the country.

Children

Like women, children were also valuable contributors to industrialisation and, by 1821, 49 percent of the working population were under the age of 20. Children were especially useful because of their size and in the textile factories could be employed as 'scavengers' as they could fit under the machines and collect any cotton that fell to the floor so as to reduce the wastage of raw materials. Furthermore, as 'pieceners' they could also wind together broken cotton threads without stopping the machinery. Given the dangers involved with this particular work, injuries were common but brought little sympathy. In 1859, one such scavenger in Wigan, a 13 year old by the name of Martha Appleton, caught her left hand in a working machine and severed her fingers. Rather than receive any kind of compensation, she lost her job as she could no longer perform it effectively.

Children were also employed in the mines, undertaking work as 'trappers' which involved opening trap doors in the shafts for the coal carts to pass through. They also worked as 'hurriers' like the majority of women, which took a physical toll upon particularly the youngest of children.

SOURCE 8

From a speech made in parliament by Lord Ashley, chairman of the Royal Commission into working conditions in mines, dated 7 June 1842.

> The child, it appears a girdle bound round its waist, to which is attached a chain, which passes under the legs, and is attached to the cart. The child is obliged to pass on all fours, and the chain passes under what, therefore, in that posture, might be called the hind legs; and thus they have to pass through avenues not so good as a common sewer, quite as wet, and oftentimes more contracted. This kind of labour they have to continue during several hours, in a temperature described as perfectly in-tolerable. By the testimony of the people themselves, it appears that the labour is exceedingly severe; that the girdle blisters their sides and causes great pain.

By 1842, approximately one-third of the mining workforce were children under the age of 19 and they worked the same hours as everybody else. Little thought was given to the morality of forcing children as young as six to work underground and in many cases if was felt that a good deed was being done: if children were offered employment it gave them a 'trade' and allowed them to contribute to the family income. In fact, as mining was extended during the 19th century, the practice of employing both women and children in mines was only continuing a tradition from the previous century when whole families would work together in the pit.

This practice was ended by the Mining Act of 1842, after a Royal Commission was appointed to investigate the working conditions in mines following a scandal about women and children working alongside men who, because of the extreme temperatures underground, often worked naked. Rumours spread about the loose morality being established with these practices, inspiring the investigation. Although little evidence of immorality was found, the investigation highlighted the terrible conditions women and children were forced to work under and this led to reform. Under the Mining Act women and children, including boys under the

age of ten, were no longer allowed to work underground. Further reforms followed in 1850, raising the limit for boys to 12 years and introducing official inspections, although this did little for conditions overall.

As industrialisation took a tight hold of Britain, economic demand drove the experiences of the working people and neither age nor sex affected this. Conditions remained very difficult as the owners of industry maintained their focus on profit and saw no reason to deviate from this position. Although by the mid-1800s society was starting to become more aware of the need for changes, often, though by no means totally, this was motivated by middle-class concerns about 'respectability' rather than a real sense of humanity. Changes to working conditions were slow despite the rapid evolution of working methods. If change was required it would need a more direct approach.

WORKERS UNITE? INDUSTRIAL PROTEST IN BRITAIN

AS Level Exam-Style Question Section B

How far did the Industrial Revolution adversely affect the lives of people in Britain? (20 marks)

Tip

When considering this question you should give some thought to the term 'adversely'. This is quite a judgemental phrase that you could discuss.

DIFFERING INDUSTRIAL PROTESTS

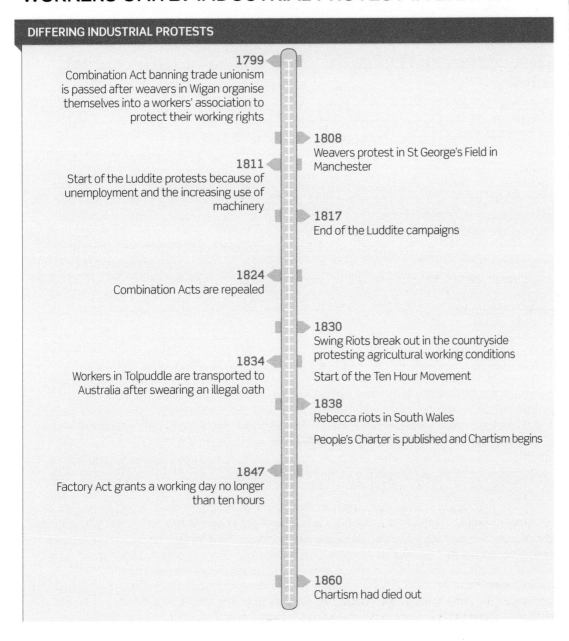

1799
Combination Act banning trade unionism is passed after weavers in Wigan organise themselves into a workers' association to protect their working rights

1808
Weavers protest in St George's Field in Manchester

1811
Start of the Luddite protests because of unemployment and the increasing use of machinery

1817
End of the Luddite campaigns

1824
Combination Acts are repealed

1830
Swing Riots break out in the countryside protesting agricultural working conditions

Start of the Ten Hour Movement

1834
Workers in Tolpuddle are transported to Australia after swearing an illegal oath

1838
Rebecca riots in South Wales

People's Charter is published and Chartism begins

1847
Factory Act grants a working day no longer than ten hours

1860
Chartism had died out

SOURCE

From Robert Owen's *Observations on the Effect of the Manufacturing System*, published in 1815. Robert Owen was a cotton-master himself in New Lanark, South Lanarkshire, Scotland.

The general diffusion of manufactures throughout a country generates a new character in its inhabitants; and as this character is formed upon a principle quite unfavourable to the individual or general happiness, it will produce the most lamentable and permanent evils, unless its tendency is counteracted by legislative interference and direction. The manufacturing system has already so far extended its influence over the British Empire as to effect an essential change in the general character of the mass of the people.

The sweeping economic and social changes that were effected during the industrialisation of Britain had a tremendous impact upon the population, and especially the working masses who toiled under extremely difficult circumstances in the interests of progress. Long working hours, harsh discipline and a generally poor wage was all this class could expect from the workplace, while at home living conditions were equally poor. As industrialisation slowly transformed the country, it placed greater importance upon the working classes because they were the driving force behind the progress being made. While scientific breakthroughs and the entrepreneurialism of the emerging middle class were making industrialisation possible, it was the labours of the working class that gave life to these ideas, fulfilling the promise with their actions. As awareness of this importance grew, the working classes adopted a more vocal presence and began to demand improvements to their lives.

The Luddites and industrial protest in early 19th-century Britain

Discontent was always a feature of the British economy as employers sought to extract the best deal for themselves and workers sought to protect what limited rights they had. Strikes and petitions were the usual methods used to extract a better deal, but during the early 19th century more extreme measures were taken as the very livelihoods of some workers were felt to be under threat with the adoption of new technology.

The most famous example of early 19th-century industrial discontent is the Luddite Movement, which began in Nottingham in 1811 and lasted for more than six years, reaching across the north of the country. Supposedly named after 'Ned Ludd', a young weaver who destroyed two knitting frames after being whipped in 1779, the 'Luddites' were mostly handloom workers who adopted aggressive action against employers who were beginning to introduce steam-powered looms, which the workers felt would damage their employment prospects. After writing threatening letters to the employers, the 'Luddites' would break into the factories and destroy the machines if their demands were refused. By February 1812, about 1,000 frames were destroyed in Nottingham at an estimated cost of between £6,000 and £10,000.

The level of destruction that Luddism promoted was so extensive that in 1812 the Frame Breaking Act was passed which made the deliberate destruction of frames a crime punishable by death. The heavy-handed response by the government demonstrated a forthright commitment to property ownership but also a fear that the working classes were considering revolution. Despite the Act, Luddite assaults and raids continued unabated in the north, raising the fears of the establishment. The direct action taken by these men drew a strong response from the mill owners and, in the case of Rawford Mill owned by William Cartwright, soldiers were brought in to protect the machines; in April 1812, the mill was attacked and in the ensuing confrontation two Luddites were killed. The significance of this act is both the length to which mill owners would go to secure their property and also the reaction of the Luddites themselves. The death of two men encouraged the Luddite movement to embrace assassination and later that month an outspoken anti-Luddite mill owner by the name of William Horsfall was shot outside Huddersfield. For many this action was a step too far and resulted in a rigorous pursuit of his killers, which was achieved in October 1812. Following their execution, along with 14 others, in January 1812, Luddite disturbances declined dramatically and although there remained isolated outbursts until 1817, Luddism was effectively over.

The murder of William Horsfall, an outspoken anti-Luddite manufacturer, in 1812. Drawing by 'Phiz' (Hablot Browne) in Captain L. Benson's *Remarkable Trials and Notorious Characters*.

On one level the actions of the Luddites can simply be explained as an economic fear – loss of employment or earnings – however, it can also be seen as an attempt by skilled craftsmen to maintain their craft rather than see it reduced to machine production which could be undertaken by an unskilled person. This alternative interpretation considers the emotional side to protest, in this case the emotive sense that livelihoods are being lost and, more importantly, identity is being lost. Under this analysis there is better understanding of the more radical aspects of Luddism, notably the assassination of William Horsfall. Prior to this action, protest had been largely peaceful and although property was damaged, lives were not deliberately targeted to achieve demands. By threatening the livelihoods, and even identities of workers, however, early industrialisation inspired emotive responses from individuals and established a precedent for aggressive protest that the government could not ignore.

'Captain Swing' and agrarian unrest

The Luddite unrest had been the reaction of skilled workers to the decline of 18th-century working practices and a general critique of the industrialisation process. In 1830, it was the turn of the agricultural workers to register discontent. The 'Swing' riots that broke out across the south of England were the product of two consecutively poor harvests which left those in the countryside with very limited money and produce. This has often prompted the impression that 'hunger politics' was the main motivating principle of these events. There is certainly merit to this argument but the riots also occurred because of the increasingly widespread introduction of new threshing machines into the countryside, which threatened to take away the winter employment of many agricultural workers.

Such is the nature of farming that work is dictated by the seasons and in autumn and winter there is less demand for workers. Consequently, during these times the majority of workers supplemented their income by threshing the corn themselves. The introduction of the **threshing** machine, however, meant that the opportunity to earn this wage was diminished as the machine could do more threshing in a day than the work of 15 men.

Threshing machines had been in existence since the late 18th century and therefore should not be seen as the only factor behind the outbreak of disturbance. In reality, the origins of the riots are best considered as a combination of factors that began with the agricultural revolution of the mid-1700s, which widened the gulf between rich and poor in the countryside. These factors then got progressively worse as wages and employment declined with the introduction of mechanisation throughout the early 19th century. The riots themselves were therefore the culmination of a difficult existence, getting progressively worse as Britain industrialised and agricultural workers were increasingly left to their own devices.

When rioting broke out in the south it was a shock to the British establishment as agricultural workers had long been considered a docile workforce in comparison with the weavers and spinners of the north. The rioters adopted the same trait of sending threatening letters to landowners as the Luddites had done, only if their demands were refused, hayricks would be burned in addition to the breaking of threshing machines. The demands varied but broadly they sought:

- wage increases or, at least, for wages to remain the same and not be reduced in times of economic difficulty
- reductions to rents
- the end of rural unemployment.

SOURCE

11 A letter from 'Captain Swing', 1830.

> Revenge for thee is on the Wing
>
> From thy determined Capt Swing.
>
> This is to inform you what you have to undergo Gentlemen if providing you Don't pull down your messhenes [machines] and rise the poor mens wages the married men give tow [two] and six pence a day a day the singel tow [two] shillings or we will burn down your barns and you in them this is the last notis.

The first burning took place in Kent during August 1830 and quickly fanned across neighbouring counties and as far north as Yorkshire. The nature of the unrest and it taking place in the countryside, on the lands and estates of the gentry, sent fear to the heart of many in parliament and almost certainly contributed to the first reform bill being presented. The riots did not end until early 1831, by which time more than 16 counties had witnessed trouble. The aftermath of the Swing Riots saw 1,976 people arrested but only 19 executed and more than 800 acquitted. The general consensus regarding this leniency is that punishment was left to local **Justices of the Peace** (JPs) and these individuals lived in the same communities as those being tried and therefore recognised the motivation behind the action. This understanding precipitated a greater degree of benevolence as many JPs actually sympathised with the aims of the rioters and felt that a subdued response would be more effective than offering up more 'martyrs'.

The Swing Riots were the first example of the strength of the rural population during industrialisation and the event highlighted the extent to which reform was necessary in the counties, particularly as a means of diffusing the evident discontent that was developing there. Although the rioters' demands were not met immediately, the riots themselves sent a strong message to those in power which precipitated reform in the future.

The Ten Hour Movement

The Luddite and Swing protests were certainly eye-catching movements but they failed to achieve any short-term, meaningful reforms in Britain. In part, this is attributable to the threatening nature of their challenge which did no more than promote a robust response from governments that were determined to maintain the pace of industrialisation amid challenging political and economic backgrounds. The lessons that the working classes drew from these events were that direct confrontation often stirred up negativity and isolated their chances of achieving the reforms they sought. This growing awareness was an important step in the development of an effective movement for worker rights as it helped to shape a more thoughtful and moderate means of protest that would present a better chance of success in the future.

The next great cause of the working people was the desire to reduce the long working days they had to endure. Regularly these days reached 16 hours during busy periods and usually averaged between 12 and 14 hours normally. The working class was not alone in seeking reforms and as early as 1802 there had been political efforts to protect younger apprentices from the uncompromising factory system. In 1825, the Whig MP John Hobhouse had sought to restrict the working day of children under 16 to 11 hours but these initiatives had been undermined by the free trade ideology that dominated British parliamentary thinking at this time. This perspective maintained the need for competitive trade and the rights of workers to sell their labour, unrestricted by government interference. Despite these forceful arguments, support for a change to working conditions did remain in a variety of quarters – not least among some mill owners themselves who saw the benefits of keeping a healthy and reasonably happy workforce.

The movement for a ten-hour day began in 1830 when workers across the Pennines organised themselves into 'short-time' committees with the intention of collaborating with trade unions to effect the changes they sought through petitioning and conventional mass meetings. The main organisers of this worker initiative were Richard Oastler and George Bull, the former a manager of a large agricultural estate in Yorkshire and the latter a vicar from Bierley, near Bradford. These were two very different men bound together by their religious convictions and sense of moral right. Each became very much disturbed by the conditions they heard about in factories and particularly concerned about the morality of working people, especially young children, labouring

so hard under them. Oastler himself was particularly forceful with his conviction about the wrongs of the factory system and his speeches left no one in doubt as to the conditions in which men, women, and especially children, worked. In September 1830, he wrote a letter to the *Leeds Mercury* in which he outlined the experiences that he had heard about and this stirred up political interest on the issue, especially as he compared the factory system to slavery.

SOURCE 12

From a letter on 'Yorkshire slavery' written by Richard Oastler to the *Leeds Mercury* in September 1830. Richard Oastler was a factory manager who sought to improve the conditions of those in his care. The paper in which he is writing circulated among the middle classes as it cost 6d to buy and therefore was beyond the means of many working people.

Let truth speak out, appalling as the statement may appear. The fact is true. Thousands of our fellow-creatures and fellow-subjects, both male and female, the miserable inhabitants of a Yorkshire town (Yorkshire now represented in Parliament by the giant of anti-slavery principles) [Henry Brougham MP for Yorkshire, 1830 and a champion of the anti-slavery movement] are this very moment existing in a state of slavery, more horrid than are the victims of that hellish system 'colonial slavery'... The very streets which receive the droppings of an 'Anti-Slavery Society' are every morning wet by the tears of innocent victims at the accursed shrine of avarice [greed], who are compelled (not by the cart-whip of the negro slave-driver) but by the dread of the equally appalling thong or strap of the over-looker, to hasten, half-dressed, but not half-fed, to those magazines of British infantile slavery – the worsted mills in the town and neighbourhood of Bradford!!!

The moral concerns these men spoke of were the driving force behind the movement's partial success because they appealed to the sensibilities of certain political figures who then took up their cause. The Tory MP Michael Sadler was very moved by the issue (Source 13) and organised a select committee to investigate the conditions in factories, before losing his seat in the 1832 election. The Tory peer Lord Ashley, who would later be instrumental in achieving reform in the mines, was the main parliamentary force for the movement and under his direction it maintained the humanitarian arguments of Oastler and Bull. Despite being strongly in favour of free trade arguments, the Whig government took up the cause of factory reform in 1833 in the belief that some kind of change was going to be necessary given the pressure being mounted. By controlling the agenda the government could offer a compromise that gave sufficient reform but neither upset the campaigners nor the owners themselves. The product of this decision was the passage of the Factory Act in 1833 which did not grant a ten-hour day but did restrict the hours of child labour and paved the way for eventually achieving the sought after ten hours in 1847.

ACTIVITY
KNOWLEDGE CHECK

The growth of industrial protest
What evidence is there to suggest that Luddism, the Swing riots, and the Ten Hours Movement were caused by industrialisation? How did these separate acts of protest differ from each other?

SOURCE

13 Extract of a campaign speech made by the Tory MP for Newark, Michael Sadler, in 1832. Sadler was in favour of factory reform but lost his seat in December 1832.

Even, at this moment, while I am thus speaking on behalf of these oppressed children, what numbers of them are still at their toil, confined to heated rooms, bathed in perspiration, stunned with the roar of revolving wheels, poisoned with the noxious effluvia of grease and gas, till at last, weary and exhausted, they turn out almost naked, plunge into the inclement air, and creep shivering to beds from which a relay of their young work-fellows have just risen; – and such is the fate of many of them at the best while in numbers of instances, they are diseased, stunted, crippled, depraved, destroyed.

The 'success' of the Ten Hour Movement fundamentally lay with the sober campaigns that it carried out and particularly the level of sympathy the cause drew from parliament itself. Rather than fighting to be heard, the desire to reduce the working day already had strong support within influential circles and this increased the effectiveness of the campaign.

REFORMING INDUSTRIAL BRITAIN, 1833–70

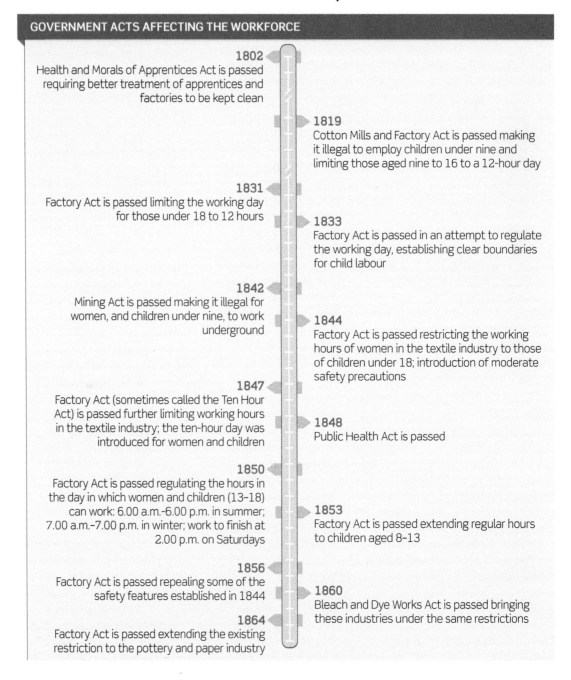

GOVERNMENT ACTS AFFECTING THE WORKFORCE

1802
Health and Morals of Apprentices Act is passed requiring better treatment of apprentices and factories to be kept clean

1819
Cotton Mills and Factory Act is passed making it illegal to employ children under nine and limiting those aged nine to 16 to a 12-hour day

1831
Factory Act is passed limiting the working day for those under 18 to 12 hours

1833
Factory Act is passed in an attempt to regulate the working day, establishing clear boundaries for child labour

1842
Mining Act is passed making it illegal for women, and children under nine, to work underground

1844
Factory Act is passed restricting the working hours of women in the textile industry to those of children under 18; introduction of moderate safety precautions

1847
Factory Act (sometimes called the Ten Hour Act) is passed further limiting working hours in the textile industry; the ten-hour day was introduced for women and children

1848
Public Health Act is passed

1850
Factory Act is passed regulating the hours in the day in which women and children (13–18) can work: 6.00 a.m.–6.00 p.m. in summer; 7.00 a.m.–7.00 p.m. in winter; work to finish at 2.00 p.m. on Saturdays

1853
Factory Act is passed extending regular hours to children aged 8–13

1856
Factory Act is passed repealing some of the safety features established in 1844

1860
Bleach and Dye Works Act is passed bringing these industries under the same restrictions

1864
Factory Act is passed extending the existing restriction to the pottery and paper industry

Factory reform: opposing views?

Growing support for reform

Pressure for reform emerged almost as soon as industrialisation and the factory system were established. The basis of this pressure was undoubtedly the working class themselves, who periodically organised in protest at the conditions they endured; organisations such the Ten Hour Movement (see above) were timely reminders of the problems facing the country's factory population. It is to be expected that this group would support reform of workplaces but support also came from other quarters of society, notably from social reformers and even some of the more humanitarian mill owners. Broadly this support was built around the morality of the factory system and cut through political party lines. Both Whigs and Tories were found to be active believers in the need for improvement and endeavoured to offer their support – the Tory Michael Sadler and Whig MP John Hobhouse in particular.

The issue of morality had different meaning for each of these groups: for many Tories it masked a fear of unbridled industrial development and the consequent decline of traditional economic practices – notably protected markets which they believed had made Britain strong. For Whigs such as Thomas Babington Macaulay, morality was inextricably linked to economic growth, particularly in regard to child labour; if working under existing conditions was unhealthy for children then they would not be able to work as effectively in later life and productivity would be compromised. For others moved by more humanitarian thinking such as Lord Ashley, it was simply the morally right thing to do considering the conditions under which people, especially children, were forced to work.

The diversity of this group was both its strength and its weakness. At once a large and forceful movement that commanded attention, when the unity of the group was scrutinised it sometimes broke down. Although bound together by a common desire to reform the factory system, each faction of the group had its own motivation for achieving this and therefore each was willing to accept different degrees of change. As reform was gradually extended after 1833, the unity of this group waxed and waned, resulting in a faltering momentum that left working conditions much improved but still with significant problems.

Opposition

Despite the growing support for factory reform, little significant headway was made before 1833 because of the dominance of the free trade argument. This had become the established theory guiding government economic policy since it was first developed at the end of the 18th century. It maintained that the most effective means of economic development was to allow markets to set their own value rather than be artificially stimulated by government regulation. This line of argument was posited mainly by the industrial middle class who reasoned that in order to be competitive it was necessary that they be left to run their factories as they did. Any changes that might be made would affect productivity and, more importantly, profits, which would have a detrimental effect on the country's economic performance. This interpretation of economics was given further credibility by the Whig economist, and prominent government advisor,

Nassau Senior who maintained that profit was only made in the last hour of a working day once expenses and capital asset deterioration were accounted for. Such was the strength of the commercial interest during the first half of the 19th century that successive governments endorsed this view and consequently only limited reforms would be achieved.

The impact of factory reform

Since 1802, there had been efforts to introduce legislation to regulate factory practices, especially regarding the use of child labour, but these had met with limited success due to the popularity of free trade principles, which demanded limited government intervention. By 1833, however, there had been sufficient protest and political pressure brought to bear that it required that some reform be made.

The Factory Act, 1833

This was perhaps the most important piece of reform legislation as it was the first *effective* law to be passed. Changes had been offered in 1802, 1819 and 1831, but these were difficult to enforce and there was insufficient will to do so. By 1833, however, the political climate was different and the Factory Act reflected a more determined, paternalistic government. Foremost it addressed the concerns that reformers had raised in relation to the use of child labour in the cotton and woollen industries in particular and set down restrictions to govern this practice:

- No child under the age of nine was allowed to be employed.

- Children between the ages of nine and 13 could only work a 48-hour week, limited to eight hours a day.

- Children between 13 and 18 could only work 12-hour days.

- All children under 13 were to receive two hours education a day.

These provisions were very important in that they set out clear guidelines for the employment of children and even presented an opportunity to improve themselves by being given access to education. This evidenced a commitment to enhance moral work practices but also a commitment to improving the prospective future of their youngest employees. In one sense the latter pledge reflected the progressive nature of industrialisation, both in terms of the need to have more skilled workers and also in the generally more modern outlook it was fostering.

As significant as these provisions were, what made the Act particularly important was that, for the first time, measures were also introduced to enforce them. An Inspectorate of Factories was established, with fining powers to ensure the compliance with the new Act. Although the department only involved four men and was not capable of inspecting the 4,000 mills it needed to reach, the attempt highlighted the more determined nature of government and laid the foundation for more effective regulation in later years.

Despite these advances, the Act retained some fundamental limitations, not least that it only applied to the textile industry, which undermined its impact on a large swathe of working children in other industries. This might be put down as a drafting error but given the strong feeling of the factory owners themselves and the Whig commitment to free trade, it would seem more likely that this was intended to limit the degree of regulation being introduced. In this interpretation it would be reasonable to suggest that the quality of life for thousands of children was compromised in the interest of profitable business.

The passage of the 1833 Factory Act therefore had established clear, but restricted, parameters for employers to operate within and also a means by which to regulate compliance. This was at once a real, significant, improvement for many workers, but also ignored others. As an individual piece of legislation it had flaws, but as a statement of intent it also symbolised a more open government that was beginning to recognise the impact of industrialisation on the people and would seek to manage that force. In this sense one could suggest somewhat optimistically that the government had listened to public concerns and effected a mutually agreeable solution.

 THINKING HISTORICALLY Change (5a)

The strands of complex change

Changes leading up to the passage of the Factory Act, 1833

Strands	Explanation of how the strand links to the passage of the Factory Act
People's increasing confidence to protest	Working people were able to show publicly how they felt towards their working conditions which placed pressure upon the government to act.
Growing maturity of the working class in presenting their concerns	Aggressive behaviour gave the government excuses either to ignore demands or to act aggressively itself. By adopting more respectable methods the working classes were able to win support from moderate sympathisers.
The growing importance of the working class within industrial Britain	Reliance on working-class labour meant that eventually some kind of reform would be likely to be necessary.
The Whigs achieving power	Having come to power on the promise of political reform, the Whig government was more open-minded about the possibility of further changes where there was a necessity for them.

Make two copies of the graph below. On the first plot the individual strands from the table above against the y-axis. Use a different colour for each. You don't need to label it with the events. On the second graph plot a single line which is a combination of all four strands (for example, at a given point two of the four strands are plotted high up on the y-axis while two are plotted lower. The combined strand would have to be plotted somewhere in the middle to represent a summary of those four individual strands).

Factory reform in Britain, 1802–33

Answer the following questions:

1 How have the strands combined to make change less or more likely?

2 Why did the Factory Act get passed in 1833, but not before?

Perhaps the most important feature of the 1833 Factory Act was that it left open the prospect of additional reform. By no means a flawless piece of legislation, it left reformers with a determination to seek further changes at a later date. This set in motion a long process of improvement that sought to address the fundamental problems with urban employment. The beginning of the century had been fertile ground for the rapid growth of industrial enterprise and the country had taken immediate advantage of this to the detriment of the people themselves. By the mid-1800s, business was well established and there was time to look at what had been created. Through the lens of the experience of the workers, the relentless pursuit of profit had established a barren environment in which humanity was barely surviving. In marked contrast to the lifestyles enjoyed by the industrial middle classes, this was a hard reality to face for those who cared to look. As the image sharpened there evolved a reformist spirit that took up the case of working conditions once again.

The effort to secure additional reforms evidenced a changing attitude about industrialisation and particularly the factory system. Having focused almost entirely upon the economic benefits of the process during the first half of the century, the reforms after 1844 show a growing awareness of the darker side of such success. In this respect the reform that takes place is important because it can be seen as an effort to counterbalance the purely economic interests of the earlier years.

The backbone of this drive for reform came initially from the Ten Hours Movement, which was a sustained campaign in the 1830s for the reduction of the hours worked in textile mills to ten per day. Led by Richard Oastler, a Tory land steward from Huddersfield, the movement was largely financed by well-established factory owners and members of the Tory urban elite. They were driven, not only by humanitarian ideals, but also by the realisation that child factory workers had to be treated well if they were to grow into effective adult factory workers. Their demands for a ten hour working day were used in the debate over child labour not only as a way of exposing the hardship experienced by children but also as a way of seeking a limitation on the working hours of adults in order that they would remain productive during all their working hours.

Further reform only came, however, with the return of a Tory government after 1841 under Sir Robert Peel. The motivating influence behind looking again at working conditions was a general wish to reduce the social distress within society. For Peel such distress affected economic growth but also undermined the moral condition of Britain. Peel was by no means a strong advocate of increased government intervention, but he did favour regulation when the moral case was compelling. In 1844, he supported the passage of another Factory Act, which restricted the hours of labour for women to the same as those of children between the ages of 13 and 18, and also introduced moderate safety precautions, which required that dangerous machinery be adequately fenced off. In stipulating specifically the safety demands and the restriction of female labour, the new Act highlighted the increasing concern with morality and social distress. Making the workplace safer had obvious moral benefits but reducing the working day for women underlines a more complex Victorian attitude about society morals.

Industrialisation and low wages had forced men, women and children into the workplace and turned them into machine operatives rather than individuals. More important than this, however, was that it kept women from the home for long hours which was felt to have a detrimental effect upon the social fabric of Britain. By restricting the working hours of females, it was felt that they would have more time to be at home and that this would promote a healthier society.

Further factory legislation after 1844 also reflected this growing commitment to promoting a greater sense of social well-being and in 1847 Oastler's desired ten-hour day was introduced for women and children. The provision was not extended to men on the basis of their right, under a free market, to sell their labour as they chose. In 1850, these hours were restricted to specific times in the day – between 6.00 a.m. and 6.00 p.m. in summer and 7.00 a.m. to 7.00 p.m. in winter, with all work on Saturdays ending at 2.00 p.m. By regularising the working day the legislation of 1850 sought to protect women and children from excessive working demands and also, for the first time, granted families an afternoon 'off'. In this manner the Act fulfilled a growing desire among social reformers for the need to consider the private lives of British men and women in addition to simply their working experiences.

The regulation that was put in place by these reforms was extended to other industries in 1860 and 1864, ensuring that by the later 19th-century working conditions were more regulated than ever before. The importance of this development was both the positive impact it had upon the physical well-being of workers, and also the attitudes that it reinforced regarding men as 'breadwinners' and women and children as being in need of protecting. After 1864, the popular Victorian idea of 'separate spheres' (see page 47) was well established and industrial working society began to conform to such a model.

Improving living conditions in Britain, 1848–70

SOURCE

14 A cartoon published in *Punch* 1848, *Lord Morpeth Throwing Pearls before — Aldermen*, about the passing of the public health bill. It was introduced into parliament by the Whig politician Lord Morpeth who then had to employ considerable talent in persuading colleagues to support it.

SANATORY MEASURES.

Lord Morpeth Throwing Pearls before ———— Aldermen.

Factory reform was not an isolated progression but rather the beginning of a raft of reforms designed to improve the social conditions of the British public. In part this motivation can be attributed to the continued pressure being applied by movements such as the Chartists, which sought political change so that working men and women might be adequately represented and their lives improved; however, it was also the product of the increased wealth that industrialisation had generated. Just as some men had become rich, this was largely at the expense of others who could not afford either the cost or time involved to improve themselves. The nature of wealth creation had locked the masses of working people into a cycle of poverty that was difficult to escape and which had promoted poor standards of living. By the mid-1800s, there had emerged a concern among the more affluent classes about the state of many of the industrial areas in Britain and particularly the health risks they promoted.

Industrialisation had created large towns and cities (see page 42 onwards) and the pace with which they grew generated significant health problems as people were forced to live in cramped houses with poor sanitation and poor water supplies. Outbreaks of cholera had been witnessed in the 1830s (page 46) but little had been done to effect change until Edwin Chadwick published his report,

The Sanitary Condition of the Labouring Population of Great Britain in 1842. The conclusions of this investigation maintained that the cause of both disease and its spread was the poor standards in which a majority of the working class lived (Source 15). Despite recognising the problem of sanitation, the government was unwilling to effect the necessary changes because of the dominant idea of limited government involvement which industrialisation had continually promoted. In the case of public health, the issue was felt to be a local one: town corporations had the responsibility to maintain sanitary conditions and arrange for the adequate supply of clean water. The reluctance of the Peel administration to take up the cause of public health is indicative of the limitations of political thought at the time. Peel was happy to consider government intervention when there was no one else to perform the necessary regulation, as with factory reform, but not when existing institutions could carry out the task. Essentially this perspective was a continuance of the long-held belief in *laissez-faire*ism which dictated that the most effective governments were those who governed least and allowed freedom of action to those in society. The findings of the report, however, would regularly influence the reform agenda until 1870.

EXTEND YOUR KNOWLEDGE

Edwin Chadwick (1800-90)

Edwin Chadwick was a lawyer and social reformer who was particularly interested in sanitary reform. Before publishing his influential report, *The Sanitary Conditions of the Labouring Population of Great Britain*, Chadwick had been a prominent member of the Poor Law Commission (1834-46) and is generally credited with creating the British workhouse system. After the passage of the Public Health Act in 1848 Chadwick served as commissioner for the Board of Health until 1854.

SOURCE

15 Extract from *The Sanitary Condition of the Labouring Population of Great Britain* by Edwin Chadwick, published in 1842.

First as to the extent and operation of the evils which are the subject of the enquiry:-

That the various forms of epidemic, endemic, and other disease caused, or aggravated, or propagated chiefly amongst the labouring classes by atmospheric impurities produced by decomposing animal and vegetable substances, by damp and filth, and close and overcrowded dwelling prevail amongst the population in every part of the kingdom, whether dwelling in separate houses, in rural villages, in small towns, in the larger towns – as they have been found to prevail in the lowest districts of the metropolis.

That such disease, wherever its attacks are frequent, is always found in connexion with the physical circumstances above specified...

The Health of Towns Association

In view of a reluctant government, the Health of Towns Association was established in 1844 to apply pressure to the administration and promote a Public Health Act. Composed of affluent and eminent individuals from across politics, the Church and academia – including the future prime minister, Benjamin Disraeli – this group was based upon the Anti-Corn Law League and like that organisation, was a single-issue movement that lobbied the government for its cause.

EXTEND YOUR KNOWLEDGE

The Anti-Corn Law League

This was a single-issue pressure group which was created in 1839 by Richard Cobden. The aim of the group was to repeal the Corn Law which, in 1815, had prevented the importation of grain until domestic produce was at a specific price. The Laws had been a source of particular controversy in Britain as they evidenced a prioritisation of landed aristocratic interest over the interests of ordinary people. After vigorous campaigning the Law was repealed in 1846.

The Public Health Act, 1848

Growing public pressure and a further outbreak of typhus in 1848 saw the introduction of Britain's first public health bill by Lord Morpeth in February of that year. The impact of this legislation was the creation of the Central Board of Health to oversee additional local Boards that would be responsible for the adequate provision of resources necessary to improve sanitation. These included: fresh water supplies; adequate drainage and sewerage; paving and the cleaning of streets. Prior to this Act these actions were nominally undertaken by the local corporations but this was very *ad hoc* and consistency was lacking. Although the new Act was not compulsory unless mortality rates were especially high, by creating a clearly distinguishable body responsible for these tasks and a centralised body to both co-ordinate and regulate them, it was hoped that public health would improve.

In the short term, the passage of the Public Health Act did little to affect the lives of the working class as, despite the powers granted to the Central Board of Health, it had no money and could not compel local corporations to adopt its recommendations. Furthermore, Local Boards of Health could only be established by consent of the inhabitants of the towns and not by default. Only in areas where there was a mortality rate of 23 in every 1,000 did a Local Board of Health have to be established and even here there was limited success without the support of the corporations themselves.

In part the limited success of the Public Health Act can be attributed to the lack of funding but also to the establishment of a centralised Board of Health which many town corporations felt promoted excessive government control. Consequently, where possible they undertook to manage their own affairs and did not seek the advice of the Board's Health Inspectors. In this sense the intentions of the new act were undermined by the government's reluctance to force local authorities' compliance. As a result the intended changes were at best patchy and, in reality, did not promote immediate improvements for the working classes.

Despite short-term failure, the Public Health Act established a precedent for the future: health and sanitation was an important feature in the improvement of people's lives. In one sense this acceptance can be ascribed to an awareness that industrialisation had promoted poor health practices and actually created much of the poor living standards that encouraged such practices. An alternative perspective is that the material improvements that industrialisation brought to many created an attitude of benevolence towards those less fortunate. In either view, the middle years of the 19th century saw a concerted effort to improve the health of the nation.

The Burial Acts, 1852–57

Increased interest in the health conditions of the British public saw attention given to the existing practices regarding burial. Although municipal cemeteries had been established in the early 1800s, the growth in population that had coincided with industrialisation had filled many of the existing plots and, given the densely populated towns and cities, the problems of where to bury people became a pressing concern. The solution for a majority of people was simply to dig shallow graves – usually about half to one metre deep – on any available piece of land, but this practice encouraged the spread of disease. In 1852, the first Burial Act was passed, which began the creation of a public network of cemeteries in London to be overseen by a Burial Board. This Board would take responsibility for the internment of bodies and maintain the cemeteries, charging the expense of such an undertaking to the **Poor Rate**. Subsequent Acts were passed in 1854 and 1857 which extended the provision across the country. The passage of the Burial Acts signified the ongoing commitment of parliament to promote health standards in Britain and reduce the frequency with which disease struck.

The Sanitary Act, 1866

The passage of the Sanitary Act marked a growing determination by government to promote better health conditions in Britain. It made sanitation inspections compulsory for local corporations and required them to maintain accurate records of these inspections. It also included a clause that made the flagrant disregard for quarantine in the case of contagious diseases punishable. The provisions within this legislation were very significant for the improvement of living conditions because they actually demanded the enforcement of sanitary practices. In the past, legislation that was issued could often be ignored as it lacked any specific enforcement mechanisms. By forcing local corporations to keep records of the inspections they were required to perform, it became difficult for them to overlook their responsibilities.

The Industrial Revolution was a very prominent event in British history and between 1785 and 1870 the country was greatly changed as a result. The course of industrialisation saw a dramatic growth in Britain's economy as the advent of technology made working practices more efficient and offered the chance of greater employment in the expanding industrial cities. This was a positive development for the country and also had a profound impact on the people. Socially it saw the demography of the nation shift as more people moved into the fast-growing cities for work, creating a sharper contrast with the rural areas, which industrialised in a gentler manner. The growth of the cities initiated further changes as working people began to assert themselves more, realising the important role they played in Britain's economic development. Facing poor living standards in overcrowded cities, people pushed for social and economic improvements, including the shortening of the working day and more regulation regarding child labour. These changes helped to transform the country into a less exploitative environment and also promoted the rights of all working men and women.

ACTIVITY
KNOWLEDGE CHECK

Effective reform?

Consider the material relating to the reforms passed in Britain between 1833 and 1870. In your opinion were these reforms effective in promoting a better standard of care for the industrial classes?

In addressing this question you should give particular attention to what these reforms actually achieved and then compare this with what they originally set out to do.

ACTIVITY
SUMMARY

Developments and changes

1 Create a spider diagram on the impact that industrialisation had upon Britain. You should include economic, geographical, and social developments.

2 Using this diagram write a brief but reasoned summary of what you feel are the most important changes that took place between 1785 and 1870.

WIDER READING

Ashton, T.S. *The Industrial Revolution 1760-1830*, Oxford University Press (1961)

Evans, E. *The Forging of the Modern State 1783-1879*, Longman (1983)

Floud, F. and Johnson, P. (eds) *The Cambridge Economic History of Modern Britain Volume 1: Industrialisation, 1700-1860*, Cambridge University Press (2004)

Griffin, E. *A Short History of the Industrial Revolution in Britain*, Macmillan (2010)

Thompson, E.P. *The Making of the English Working Class*, Penguin (1963)

1.3 | Unionism and co-operation, c1785–c1870

KEY QUESTIONS

- What, despite its opponents, was the appeal of Trade Unionism before 1834?
- How did New Model Unionism promote working-class interests?
- Why did co-operative movements become popular?

INTRODUCTION

The development of new economic processes which characterised the late 18th and 19th centuries saw a shift in the working practices of Britain's labouring classes. Previously people had worked from within their own homes in small cottage enterprises, by the late 1700s industrialisation had transformed this mode of working and replaced it with the factory system. Instead of small-scale businesses operated by groups of independent craftsmen, each with a degree of autonomy over their labour, the factory enforced collective working and set hours. It took away the independence of having a craft and made everybody work at the same pace: that of the machine. The impact of such a shift was profound and had a great affect upon the working people of Britain. It also saw the growth of two new movements designed to alleviate the resultant stresses: first, **Trade unionism**, which sought to protect workers under the new factory system industrialisation had created, and second, **co-operative movements**, which offered an alternative way of working to the competitive free trade model that depersonalised the workplace in the pursuit of profit. Each of these movements placed the well-being of its members at the centre of its activities and offered a contrast to the capitalist incentives that drove the British economy during the 19th century. By offering something different, they promoted independent thought and would influence the working relations dynamic in Britain well into the 20th century and beyond.

KEY TERMS

Trade unionism
Individual workers from the same trade or industry binding together as one force in the interest of protecting their rights and improving their work conditions.

Co-operative movement
Organisation whose primary aim is to promote the welfare of its members by working together in pursuit of mutual progress rather than for big, individual profits.

1799 – Robert Owen takes over at New Lanark

1823 – Master and Servant Act passed

1832 – National Equitable Labour Exchange formed

| 1795 | 1800 | 1805 | 1810 | 1815 | 1820 | 1825 | 1830 |

1793 – Friendly Societies Act passed

1816 – Institute for the Formation of Character set up at New Lanark

1827 – *The Co-operator* newspaper published

UNIONS AND THEIR OPPONENTS, c1785–1834

Trade societies and 'knobsticks'

Trade societies had existed as early as the 17th century but these were mostly concerned with protecting the skilled trades rather than all working people. It was not until the start of industrialisation that a more widespread network of societies grew to include those deemed 'general' or 'unskilled'. The reason for this expansion was two-fold. First, the emerging factory system created increased demand for workers. This gave them a sense of their own value to their employers because they could see the importance of their contribution to the profitability of the manufacturing interest. The preponderance of workers gathered together in one place provided a sense of unity of purpose that was often lacking in a pre-industrial age. Secondly, the expansion of the factory system was one result of the reluctance of the national government to interfere in the way **entrepreneurs** and business owners managed their businesses. Instead of regulating their various practices, the government allowed owners and employers to do as they wished and this often resulted in the exploitation of their workers. These developments were significant for the growth of trade unionism because they encouraged the expanding working classes to combine in their own interests, leading to the formation of new organisations to offer collective means of action and support.

Early organisations were known as trade societies and they undertook to provide the basic protections that their members needed. These groups were initiated by skilled tradesmen such as printers, cobblers and mechanics who sought to protect both their trade and their bargaining hand from being weakened by the growing number of unskilled interlopers that industrialisation was attracting.

These societies were primarily interested in looking after their own trades within their immediate working area rather than any universal sense of loyalty to class, and as such they remained small, locally focused organisations with little interest outside their own districts. Emphasis was placed on securing their status within their given profession and this primarily involved setting values for skilled labour above those for the unskilled and particularly ensuring that entry to the skilled professions was carefully monitored. To this end they regulated the process of apprenticeship within their trade and even embarked upon an early form of '**closed shop**' practices. In effect these societies sought to protect their own interests in the face of changing economic structures in Britain. Among the most prominent of these groups were the London printers, who in 1793 petitioned their masters for an increase in their fees given the rising cost of living. They obtained 539 signatures in support of their demands and this degree of unity was able to generate sufficient concern from their employers that it led to a successful outcome for the printers.

The early societies were generally well supported from those in the trades, and because of the skills they had, they could usually command significant improvements as their positions could not easily be replaced in the event of a stoppage of work. On this basis, therefore, from the late 18th century onwards there already existed a mechanism for workers to bind together in self-protection. Such experience was especially relevant as industrialisation expanded the economy and workers came into increasing conflict with the growing number of employers, eager to make profit.

KEY TERMS

Entrepreneur
A person who sees, and takes advantage of, a business opportunity despite the potential financial risks involved.

'Closed shop'
The practice of employing only individuals who were members of the trade union or who were in good standing with the union.

1867 – Royal Commission on Trade Units set up

1855 – Friendly Societies Act passed

1863 – Co-operative Wholesale Society set up

1871 – Trade Union Act passed

1844 – Rochdale Pioneers established

1835   1840   1845   1850   1855   1860   1865   1870

1834 – Grand National Consolidated Trades Union established; arrest of the Tolpuddle 'martyrs'

1851 – Amalgamated Society of Engineers founded

1860 – London Trades Council set up; Amalgamated Society of Carpenters and Joiners created

1868 – Foundation of the Trades Union Congress

1866 – Sheffield 'Outrages'

EARLY FACTORS EFFECTING ORGANISED LABOUR

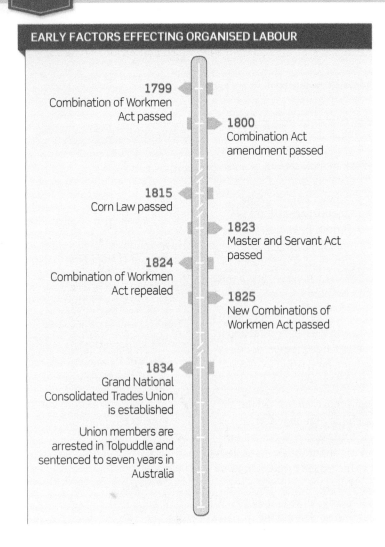

1799
Combination of Workmen Act passed

1800
Combination Act amendment passed

1815
Corn Law passed

1823
Master and Servant Act passed

1824
Combination of Workmen Act repealed

1825
New Combinations of Workmen Act passed

1834
Grand National Consolidated Trades Union is established

Union members are arrested in Tolpuddle and sentenced to seven years in Australia

'Knobsticks'

The emergence of trade societies and specific organisations to promote the interests of workers within their membership was not entirely popular and they attracted as much opposition as they did support. The strength of trade societies lay in the concept of collective bargaining and the threat of a collective withdrawal of labour in the event of a failure to agree terms. This technique offered the best way to stand up to employers because it prevented their factories or mills from operating and making money. The threat of the 'strike' or 'turnout' was very potent and such action was increasingly used by organised labour groups throughout the 18th and early 19th centuries. This approach, however, relied upon a sense of unity among the workers themselves and this was often difficult to achieve.

For every person in favour of strike action there was often another who opposed it, usually on the grounds of needing to work so as to maintain their families. Although there was an established history of paying into a strike fund, often the financial implications of refusing to work undermined the militancy of many workers. Those individuals who opposed stoppages of work and continued to carry out their duties were labelled by the unions and made pariahs in the community because their actions greatly affected the success of strike action by diluting its overall impact. In addition to those employees who chose not support union

activities, employers also had ways of neutralising strikes that took advantage of Britain's growing population.

Since the real threat of trade societies was strike action that could disrupt productivity because no one was carrying out the necessary work, employers endeavoured to minimise this threat as much as possible. A popular method was to take advantage of the growing population and draft in new immigrants to fill the void during a turnout. These individuals were usually of Irish descent and were desperate for work, having often found none in their own country. Like existing employees who did not support union action, these men were made social pariahs and were often abused by those on strike – being verbally attacked as 'knobsticks' and even physically attacked as was the case in a Saw Grinders' Union strike in Sheffield in 1866 (page 75). The readiness of alternative supplies of labour continually undermined the development of effective worker protection, and as a result the strength of employers remained almost untouched into the 19th century.

The growth of trade unions

Building upon the provisions of the early trade societies, trade unions became established to provide a more concentrated level of protection for workers. Unlike many of the societies, trade unionism was a more formal affair which organised workers into a collective and united body with the intention of achieving a common aim for the group, usually better working conditions or wages. In binding together, the intention was to create a more forceful voice with which to seek protection. In part this development was a natural progression that mirrored the growing power that employers enjoyed as industrialisation continued. The withdrawal of government intervention in the day-to-day practices of private business had given employers a free hand in the management of their affairs and the consolidation of the factory system after 1769 certainly gave workers a greater need for protection. Differing from the earlier societies, trade unions took a slightly broader interest in their given trades and this reached beyond the local districts to include others involved within that industry. In broadening their interest to the trade itself rather than just location, trade unionism started to become a more prominent movement that could better protect members.

As mentioned earlier, the birth of trade unionism was the result of a free trade mentality that emerged during the previous century and which had become government policy by the late 1700s. When employers were allowed a free hand in setting wages and working conditions, employees had to find ways to protect themselves and their own interests so that they received what they felt to be a fair remittance for their labour from those who sought only to give the bare minimum. Strike action was common practice among workers when endeavouring to extract better wages from their employers – in 1765, miners in the north-east had employed this method for that very purpose, but these actions had usually been individual ones, organised by specific groups of employees against single employers. As industrialisation continued, however, it became increasingly hard for such individual action because the position of employers became strengthened by population growth which raised the demand for

SOURCE
1
Striking workers in Liverpool maintaining a picket to prevent strike breakers or 'knobsticks' from interfering. Earlier strikes looked the same as this with men deliberately seeking to intimidate strike breakers. An unattributed engraving produced in 1846 for the *Pictorial Times* newspaper.

employment. Between 1750 and 1850, Britain's population rose from six million to over 17 million and such prolific growth reinforced the freedom of employers to set whatever conditions they wanted on the grounds that if workers were not happy with their working conditions then others could easily be found. On this basis, isolated action enjoyed limited success and therefore it was necessary to look for other ways of securing the interests of workers.

Under these difficult circumstances it was natural to look to the existing trade society model for a solution, but these were localised interests which offered limited influence outside their districts. What promoted a more universal approach to worker rights was the impact of two particular developments. The first was war with France after 1793 and the second was the relentless growth of the factory system, which forced shared grievances upon larger numbers of workers and threatened the trade of Britain's **artisan** craftsmen.

The outbreak of war with the new French Republic in 1793 was fundamental to the growth of trade unionism in Britain because it created the environment for economic discontent to grow. The rising food prices that war generated made the cost of living much greater for Britain's working population and this brought the particular issue of wages more roundly into focus for all workers, regardless of skill or industry. By 1799, weavers in Wigan, for example, had organised themselves into an association to strengthen their hand in seeking a stop to wage reductions and this practice quickly spread throughout the region. The Association of Weavers had 14 branches in Lancashire by May of 1799 and using this

KEY TERM

Artisan
A term that describes a skilled worker who uses traditional techniques in their craft. This usually involves hand-making goods rather than using machines.

united force sought to bring pressure upon parliament for redress of their concerns (Source 2). This particular group is a good example of the growing sense of mutual support as weavers were a well-regarded workforce who had commanded above-average wages and yet were motivated towards trade unionism because of the worsening economic situation brought about by war.

SOURCE

2 From an address by the Bolton committee of the Association of Weavers, dated 13 May 1799.

The present existing Laws that should protect Weavers, etc., from imposition, being trampled underfoot, for want of a union amongst them, they are come to a determination to support each other in their just and legal rights, and to apply to the Legislature of the country for such further regulations, as it may in its wisdom deem fit to make, when the real state of the cotton manufactory shall have been laid before it… [we seek] candid consideration how every necessary of life has increased in price, while the price of labour has undergone a continual decrease.

In addition to a broader awareness among traditionally secure industries, the emergence of the factory system encouraged further growth of trade unionism. The working conditions in factories have been considered in Chapter 2 and improving those conditions was undoubtedly a motivation for unionisation. What is also of particular note with regard to the factory system is the manner in which it allowed unionism to flourish. Before the emergence of factories, work was primarily conducted within the home by small units of labour – usually a master and then his **journeymen** and apprentices. In this system there was both a degree of autonomy but also a direct connection with the employer who was visibly present and often working alongside his employees. With the advent of factories, however, this direct line of communication was severed and the idea that each was working towards the same goal was lost as the employer became increasingly distanced from his workforce.

networks were developed. These advances allowed for better communications between groups and paved the way for the sharing of ideas and, eventually, collaboration which would see the establishment of a federation of unions in the Grand National Consolidated Trades Union in 1834. This particular organisation was the culmination of a broader movement during the first three decades of the 19th century to formalise and unite trade unionism in Britain. Since the establishment of the early trade societies and unions these groups had remained independent of one another but in the aftermath of the war with France, when the economy was further depressed, unions started to reach out to one another in an effort to secure a greater hand with which to negotiate on behalf of their members.

The first effort at creating a general 'union of unions' came in 1818 with the 'Philanthropic Hercules' in London and the 'Philanthropic Society' in Lancashire. These organisations sought to unite the working class from across all trades but, although very noble in principle, could not surmount the realities of trade interests among the existing unions. Unable to establish a core group these efforts were short-lived and came to an end after the arrest of five of their leaders following strike action that year. The Combination Acts of 1799 and 1800 regulated union activities before 1825, and these made it illegal for workers to join together for the purpose of cajoling employers for better conditions. In essence unions were illegal and as a consequence of this workers organisations were very restricted and therefore enjoyed little progression. A more successful endeavour came after 1825 when unions were legally recognised and John Doherty in 1829 was able to establish the Grand General Union of the Operative Spinners of Great Britain and Ireland and then the National Association for the Protection of Labour. Although these organisations each lasted less than two years they evidenced a growing determination to organise trade unionism along broader lines than ever before so as to promote a more effective platform for worker rights.

KEY TERM

Journeyman
A person who has completed an apprenticeship but not yet become a master of his trade. This individual would need to submit a master piece of work to his trade guild for examination in order to become a recognised master of his craft.

By creating a division between worker and master, the factory created an environment where mutual progress was replaced by a conflicting set of values: fair wages and respect for one, profit and productivity for the other. The only way for workers to balance these demands, given the power of the masters, was to bind together in the hope that such action would get them heard and even elicit some positive response.

The government made attempts to prevent trade unionism on behalf of the interests of employers – until 1824, membership of a union was illegal under the 1799 and 1800 Combination Acts and after 1825, when the repeal of this Act was amended, 'molestation' (pressurising fellow workers to join strikes) became a crime. Despite this, the pace of labour organisation kept up with that of industrialisation as the postal service and rail

EXTEND YOUR KNOWLEDGE

John Doherty (1798–1854)
Born in Ireland, John Doherty became a cotton spinner in 1808 and moved to Manchester in 1816. There he became a tireless campaigner for worker rights and helped to organise movements designed to improve the conditions of his fellow spinners. He was arrested in 1818 for his involvement in the Lancashire spinners strike and spent two years in prison. Elected leader of the Manchester Spinners Union in 1828, he championed a general union to win worker rights and was successful in establishing the Grand General Union of the Operative Spinners of Great Britain and Ireland in 1829.

The impact of trade unionism growth

The growth of trade unionism saw an initial rise in militancy as workers were more organised and, having established a strike fund as part of the membership fee, could afford to resort to such militancy. Major strikes by the cotton spinners of Lancashire in 1810 and again in 1818, this time also supported by the weavers, suggest a significant impact was made by trade unionism. On the face of the events themselves there is some credibility for this idea, given that the 1810 strike lasted more than four months while that of 1818 saw the action spread to other industries – including colliers and machine makers – threatening a nationwide stoppage. In the case of the 1818 strike, it was only brought to an end after the arrest of five members of the organisation. Although the aims that motivated these events were not achieved – both were defeated by the government-backed employers – the longer-term impact of this trade unionist activity was to see the existing laws restricting worker organisation abolished in 1824 when the Combinations Acts were finally repealed.

A direct consequence of this action was the emergence of a more definitive trade unionism by the later 1820s. Having steadily grown over the course of the early 19th century, in 1834 a general trades union was established which represented a high point in the history of labour organisation. The Grand National Consolidated Trades Union was the most successful of networked unions before 1834 claiming more than one million members, although this figure is difficult to confirm. The impact of the 'Grand National' was twofold. Firstly, it presented the impression of a united organisation of workers that conveyed the effect of working-class solidarity. Secondly, it generated the widespread use of 'the Document' by employers (see Source 3). In both instances the impact was mostly a negative one for trade unionism and evidenced the long way it still had to go to ensure worker rights effectively.

In the case of working-class solidarity, although the 'Grand National' had been established, it would be inaccurate to say that unionism had become a unified force with the capacity to stand up to employers with one clear voice. In reality it remained a diffuse body of independent unions that remained wedded first and foremost to their own trade interests rather than the wider concerns of all workers. In part this was due to the strength of traditional thinking but also because of the failure of the 'Grand National' to support its members effectively when they went out on strike. The reason for this failure was the meagre funds available to the organisation as it relied upon subscription fees from affiliated members, which were often not paid. Of the claimed one million members, only 16,000 had actually paid the fee and this was not enough to maintain the organisation nor fund those members who went on strike. The fragility of this predicament was first exposed in 1834 when 1,500 mill workers in Derby were locked out of their place of work for failing to abandon their union. Despite lasting out for four months even these committed union men eventually renounced the union and went back to work.

The final blow to the 'Grand National' came because of the increased use by employers of what colloquially became known as 'the Document'. The growth of unionism had not gone unnoticed by employers who moved to secure their own positions in the face of increasing organisation by their workforces. The mechanism they used was a simple piece of paper that they demanded employees sign denouncing any commitment to a union. It became a prerequisite for employment in many areas and if existing employees refused to sign it then they would usually find themselves locked out of their workplace as was the case in Derby. The 'document' essentially gave employers the power to sift out union members and secure obedience to their own demands on the threat of unemployment. So effective was this practice that by 1835 the 'Grand National' collapsed under the twin financial burden of having to support loyal members who were locked out for their union commitment and the loss of fees from those who renounced their affiliation.

SOURCE 3

An example of 'the Document' used by employers to stop employees from joining trade unions. This one was used in the building trade in 1833.

We, the undersigned… do hereby declare that we are not in any way connected with the General Union of the Building Trades and that we do not and will not contribute to the support of such members of the said union as are or may be out of work in consequence of belonging to such union.

Despite the evident growth of trade unionism between 1785 and 1834, there was no equal discussion between employers and employees. The balance of power remained firmly located with the employers who were able to exploit the financial vulnerability of the working class and maintain a tight grip on working practices. The trade unions, however, did not help themselves either. Loyalty to individual trades continued to undermine the creation of a genuinely national body that might have been able to co-ordinate an effective challenge to the dominance of the employers. At the beginning of the century, trade unionism had generated a significant amount of promise but by 1834 it had failed to deliver on those expectations.

AS Level Exam-Style Question Section A

Was the adoption of the factory system the main reason that trade unionism grew in the years 1795–1834? (20 marks)

Tip
Make sure to focus on the stated factor in this question and evaluate the other motives in light of it. In this case why is the factory system particularly relevant?

THINKING HISTORICALLY   Evidence (4a&b)

Growth of trade unionism
Sources 2 and 3 could be used by a historian to build up a picture of the growth of trade unionism. Read the sources again and then answer the following questions.

1 In what ways do Sources 2 and 3 offer two views of unionism? How might this effect their value as pieces of evidence in appraising attitudes towards unionism? Explain your answer.

Working in groups, discuss the following questions:

2 Suppose a historian had ten more accounts that agreed broadly with Source 2 and only four that agreed with Source 3. What would that tell the historian about the situation being described?

3 How far should the balance of the evidence play a role in constructing written history? What else must a historian consider about the evidence being used before drawing conclusions?

Government response to trade unions

The reaction of the British government towards the organisation of trade unions before 1834 is an exemplification of broadly conservative interest. The *laissez-faire* attitude of the establishment was grounded upon the idea that prosperity was more achievable if regulation was kept to a minimum and people were left to their own devices, but this principle very much supported the employers rather than those working for them. The growth of unionism was seen as an obstacle to wealth creation and if the economy was to be improved, employers should be able to run their businesses unfettered by organised cries for worker rights.

This general antipathy towards unionism was given further justification when first the French Revolution broke out in 1789, followed by Britain's declaration of war with that country in 1793. The revolution reinforced government's belief in the dangers of trade unionism; organised labour against employers was seen as threatening by many landowners, who were sensitive to any challenge that was presented in the immediate aftermath of the revolution. This sensitivity clouded rational thinking such that when war broke out four years later, the wage disputes that developed because of rising costs of living were mistakenly interpreted as a political attack on the British system of government.

The Combination Acts and repeal

Under wartime pressures the government of William Pitt responded to growing trade unionism by passing legislation in July 1799 making the organisation of unions illegal. There existed legislation against unionism already but this was cumbersome and time-consuming. The aim of the Combination Act 1799 was to speed up the process by allowing summary trials before a Justice of the Peace (JP), with a three-month prison term for anyone found guilty of organising. The Act was amended in 1800 (Source 4) to allow appeals in the local court sessions and also a clause forbidding employees' organisations and allowing for legally binding arbitration in wage disputes, but the legislation remained unpopular and was the source of much working-class discontent.

SOURCE 4 From the Combination Act amendment passed in 1800.

II... No journeyman, workman or other person shall at any time after the passing of this Act make or enter into, or be concerned in the making of or entering into any such contract, covenant or agreement, in writing or not in writing... and every... workman... who, after the passing of this Act, shall be guilty of any of the said offences, being thereof lawfully convicted, upon his own confession, or the oath or oaths of one or more credible witness or witnesses, before any two justices of the Peace... within three calendar months next after the offence shall have been committed, shall, by order of such justices, be committed to and confined in the common gaol, within his or their jurisdiction, for any time not exceeding 3 calendar months, or at the discretion of such justices shall be committed to some House of Correction within the same jurisdiction, there to remain and to be kept to hard labour for any time not exceeding 2 calendar months.

The purpose of the Acts had been to prevent unionisation but in fact unions continued to grow during this time because of improving modes of communication such as the postal service which allowed unions to remain in contact despite legality issues. Furthermore, the Acts themselves were poorly executed by those who sought their passage and few individuals were actually prosecuted under the legislation because older measures such as the 1797 Unlawful Oaths Act carried harsher sentences and were therefore preferable. With a view to the general lacklustre use of the Combination Acts, together with their broad unpopularity among the increasingly organised working people, it has generally been accepted by historians that their creation was primarily a reaction to the perceived dangers of the events in France. Once this threat had diminished in 1815 the Acts themselves were largely ignored. Without the motivation of this threat and in the wake of growing unionist activity, they were recognised as a failure and in 1824 were repealed.

In one sense the repeal of the Combination Acts evidences a more enlightened government attitude towards trade unionism emerging in the 1820s. Under the management of more open-minded and thoughtful MPs such as Robert Peel and Joseph Hume, the rights of workers were given more sympathetic consideration and it was felt that maintaining the Laws had been the cause of much of the discontent in the post-war years because there was no means for workers to peacefully express themselves. Their removal signalled a desire to encourage more effective outlets for workers to register their problems and the repealing of the Acts provided, among other things, for such outlets.

Government attitudes were very much influenced by circumstances and the more liberal attitude that the government adopted towards unions was motivated by a general improvement in the prosperity of the country. After 1820, food prices were more than one-third lower than the previous decade and Gross National Product rose by 16.8 percent. In this more positive economic climate, government could afford to be sympathetic. Prosperity did not reach all workers, however, and when these groups – notably the handloom weavers in Stockport whose numbers were in significant decline – sought redress the government was quick to install further legislation to limit their potential for militancy and a new Combination of Workmen Act was passed to this effect in 1825.

The Master and Servant Act, 1823

Although in repealing the Combination Acts the government evidenced a greater sense of liberal sympathy with the working class, it should not be forgotten that it maintained a stronger connection with the employers. Nowhere better is this shown than in the passage of the 1823 Master and Servant Act which made the breaking of a contract an offence punishable with imprisonment. Under the provisions of this Act a strike which resulted in the failure to complete work was considered a breach of agreement and strikers could be prosecuted. Although prosecutions under this Act before 1834 are unavailable, between 1857 and 1875 there were, on average, 10,000 prosecutions each year in England and Wales. On this basis, just as the government can be praised for beginning to consider the working-class situation, it remained resolutely in favour of employers' rights.

The Tolpuddle 'martyrs'

SOURCE

5 George Loveless, one of the Tolpuddle 'martyrs', on his way to the transportation ship that would take him to Australia following his conviction for trade union activities. An illustration by W. G. Easton, created 5 April 1834.

Government circumspection towards trade unionism remained after 1825 and although generally unionism gained from the flurry of legislation passed in the mid-1820s – organisation was now legal and unions had the right to collect fees, bargain with employers and, if necessary, go on strike – government maintained a careful eye on their activities.

The growth of trade unions and the efforts to formulate a single, general union at the end of the 1820s saw a rekindled fear within government. The attraction of a national union that reached across

A Level Exam-Style Question Section A

How far do you agree that trade unionism in the years 1785–1834 was a failure? (20 marks)

Tip
Make sure that you cover the whole of the time period specified. Here the question refers to trade unionism before 1834 so you should also consider the emergence of unionism in the years after 1785.

all trades was a potent one for many of the new workers who were not represented by the older trade societies and therefore there was a growth in membership which witnessed new rounds of strikes for the improvement of wages. What made this particularly troublesome for the government was that it was spreading unionism into the countryside at a time when the rural economy was under significant strain. Agricultural labourers were finding employment difficult following the introduction of new machinery that reduced the need for their labour and this had created a strong degree of antagonism among the rural population – antagonism which had already spilled out into violence during the Swing Riots of 1830.

In Dorset, government fears manifested themselves through the use of excessive punishment for the organisation of a trade union in the village of Tolpuddle. Intent on stamping out further discontent when it was discovered that six farm labourers had formed a union to protest at their reduced wages of six shillings a week, the 1797 Unlawful Oaths Act was invoked which carried a seven-year sentence and transportation to Australia for the men.

The punishment did not fit the crime as unionism was technically legal after the repeal of the Combination Acts in 1824, but the growth of a strong trade union network threatened the position of employers and, in the case of the emerging unions in the countryside, threatened many estates of those in government themselves. Combined with a difficult economic environment in the rural areas, it was felt that unionism would be more harmful than positive and therefore they sought to nip it in the bud before it became too strong.

NEW MODEL UNIONISM, 1850–70

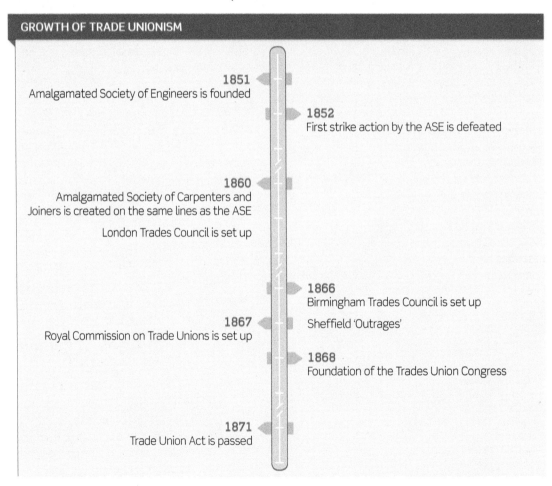

GROWTH OF TRADE UNIONISM

1851 Amalgamated Society of Engineers is founded

1852 First strike action by the ASE is defeated

1860 Amalgamated Society of Carpenters and Joiners is created on the same lines as the ASE

London Trades Council is set up

1866 Birmingham Trades Council is set up

1867 Royal Commission on Trade Unions is set up

Sheffield 'Outrages'

1868 Foundation of the Trades Union Congress

1871 Trade Union Act is passed

The first concerted efforts to establish a strong trade union movement had faltered by 1834. Despite a promising start, the early unions retained a strong local self-interest, which made the creation of a national body very difficult. What was eventually created suffered from poor support and as a result remained a fragile organisation which, under the weight of both the employers' opposition and an antipathetic government, was easily broken.

This early foray into self-protection, however, was not entirely without merit. The experiences encountered before 1834 had laid the foundations of trade unionism and invited lessons to be learned for the future. By 1850, trade unionists had been well schooled and a new model of unionism emerged.

The Amalgamated Society of Engineers

Perhaps the most important trade union to develop after 1850 was the Amalgamated Society of Engineers (ASE), which was established in 1851. This organisation was created by the binding together of three smaller independent unions – the Old Mechanics, the Steam Engine Makers' Society and the General Smiths – and as a result heralded a '**New Model Unionism**' (NMU) which would significantly influence the shape of trade unionism in the mid-19th century.

The creation of the ASE was a reaction to industrialisation and specifically the growth in unskilled labour that it generated which, in the eyes of skilled workers, was drowning industry and dragging down wages. In this sense the general significance of the union was to reassert and protect the rights of skilled labour. This endeavour both enhanced the trade union movement by offering a greater sense of direction, but also created a divide among the workers themselves. The 'new models' that were established were primarily for the benefit of the skilled trades and therefore those working in the semi-skilled or unskilled professions were still very much left to fend for themselves. In this sense, therefore, the growth of NMU through groups such as the ASE created what the social columnists and historians Sydney and Beatrice Webb described as an 'aristocracy of labour' which encouraged lingering resentments and suspicion among other workers who felt their interests were not being as well considered.

In pursuing their aim to secure skilled labour, the ASE, under the direction of its general secretary William Allan, adopted a rigid administrative system; an elected Executive Council was formally in charge, while the paid general secretary managed the day-to-day affairs of the union and also the co-ordination of the local branches. Part of the obligation of membership was a tax levied on its members for the specific purposes of securing adequate strike pay, rather than the more traditional reliance on voluntary donations. Given the better financial position that members of the ASE were in as skilled working men, this particular policy generated substantial sums of money which, in 1852, amounted to more than £12,000. With such funds the union became the most prominent in the country and was even able to support other unions in their battle for employment rights for workers.

SOURCE 6

William Allan, secretary of the Amalgamated Society of Engineers, speaking at the Royal Commission into trade unionism in 1867.

I think it [the union] has been of decided improvement in them in their position and character generally; for we have a controlling power over them; if men misconduct themselves through drinking or anything of that kind, we have the opportunity of dealing with them, and we do our best to keep them up to the mark so far as regards their position

Perhaps the most influential action the ASE took was in 1859–60 when London builders were out on strike seeking a reduction to their working day. Their demand for a nine-hour day became the arena in which the ASE was able to exhibit the fruits of its organisation. The ASE contributed three separate donations of £1,000 to the builders' strike fund, which enabled them to hold out for six months and, more importantly, forced a compromise from their employers. By using their own resources to support other union actions, the ASE showed that NMU was directly promoting working-class interests. Furthermore, this particular action more than any other informed the future of British trade unionism because it encouraged other unions to consider why the ASE was so successful and this inspired a reappraisal of the traditional model of localised, industry-specific unionisation (Source 7).

SOURCE 7

From a speech by Robert Applegarth, general secretary of the Amalgamated Society of Carpenters and Joiners after 1862, at a meeting of the Society c1870.

The London lock-out induced a number of our trade to hold an inquest on the system of 'localism', and their verdict was, 'the thing won't do'. They then decided to follow the example set by the Amalgamated Engineers, and a start was effected with eleven branches and about 350 members; but for as funds... in fact, they started without funds.

In promoting such reflection, the ASE was fundamentally important because it was able to break the belief in localised unions. At its inception, the ASE had 12,000 members and this strength was achieved by forming on a national scale within its specific industry – local borders were brushed aside in the interest of safeguarding their profession. With a headquarters based in London and branches stretching from Lancashire to Scotland, the ASE was perhaps the first genuinely national trade union and its administrative model would later be taken up by other organisations and eventually become the standard structure for British trade unionism. Following the relative success of the builders, the ASE's broader union base was adopted by the Amalgamated Society of Carpenters and Joiners (ASCJ) in 1860 – a union which would become as powerful and influential as the ASE. By offering a new way of organising and, more importantly, proving how successful this alternative could be, the ASE breathed new life into trade unionism and allowed it to compete more effectively with employers.

KEY TERM

Piecework
The practice of paying workers according to what they produce rather than a set salary.

The basis of this success not only lay in the national structure of the union but also the manner in which it conducted itself. Despite the early use of strike action in 1852, which took place in opposition to the use of **piecework** and excessive overtime, the ASE actively promoted a more moderate and prudent philosophy. In the eyes of its leaders, particularly William Allan, respectability was the way to achieve their goals – using rational negotiation based on their sought-after skills and strength in numbers to persuade employers to agree to their demands. This was a new departure for trade unionism, which had up to this point adopted a more challenging stance towards employers. It was a successful method for two specific reasons, each reflective of the changing world in which they now lived. First, the rapidly industrialising economy had made Britain the 'workshop of the world' by the 1850s and this development relied heavily on the growth of technical industries and therefore more skilled labour. As a result, the skilled unions like the ASE acquired significant leverage because their skills were in great demand. Secondly, in the increasingly moderate and respectable climate of mid-Victorian Britain, peaceful negotiations attracted more favourable responses from those with influence. They also found favour from the general public, whose lives were often inconvenienced by industrial disputes. In appealing to the public in particular, the new trade unions were able to enhance their leverage with both employers and especially politicians who were increasingly responsive to the wishes of the broader population by the later 1860s. The ASE was able to use this influence to form relationships with the Liberal party, which was both attracted and reasonably sympathetic to the moderate activities of the union. In return the Liberals could tap into the support of the large membership that the ASE commanded.

Evidently the ASE model was a very successful one but it was by no means universally adopted. The strength of the union lay primarily with the profession of its members. Skilled labour was increasingly in demand after 1850 and therefore those unions which safeguarded these skills were granted a little more latitude when it came to negotiations. In this sense the ASE had a distinct advantage over other, less skilled, organisations. For these smaller unions, the model offered by the ASE was less attractive because they could not negotiate with such a strong hand and therefore they relied more heavily upon the more traditional methods of strike action. In this case, by offering alternative modes of action, the ASE also presented a clear divide among the trade union movement: skilled professions could adopt the 'new model' offered by the ASE while the semi-skilled and unskilled professions remained reliant upon the 'old model'.

The impact of the ASE was profound. Its creation in 1851 was a watershed in union history because it transformed the nature of the entire movement. Although localised unions continued, with the success of the ASE the trend was set for the larger, national unions of NMU, which could access more funds and wield greater influence. Such was the popularity and success of this trend that by the end of 1874 the British trade union movement counted more than one million members. This figure could not be ignored by employers and had therefore finally given skilled workers, at least, an effective opportunity to promote their interests and a strong voice with which to comment on the development of the British economy and their position within it.

ACTIVITY
KNOWLEDGE CHECK

New Model Unionism
Using your own knowledge and material you have read, write a brief summary of what 'New Model Unionism' came to mean, including how it influenced the growth of the trade union movement between 1850 and 1870.

The value of evidence

Although Paper 1 does not require the use of contemporary sources, it is useful to understand the value of evidence when making judgements. Sources 6 and 7 provide evidence about the growth of New Model Unionism. Read the sources again and then complete the following tasks:

1 Write down at least three ways in which Robert Applegarth's speech is useful for establishing the growth of New Model Unionism and three ways in which William Allan's testimony is useful.

2 Compare your answers with a partner, then try to identify at least two limitations of each source for establishing the growth of NMU.

3 Discuss with a partner whether you think Applegarth or Allan is more useful for establishing the growth of NMU.

Now consider how the sources might be used to answer the question:

'What was the role of the Amalgamated Society of Engineers in the growth of NMU?'

4 Complete the diagram below to show the usefulness and limitations of Source 6 for answering this question and two questions of your own.

5 Complete a similar diagram for Source 7.

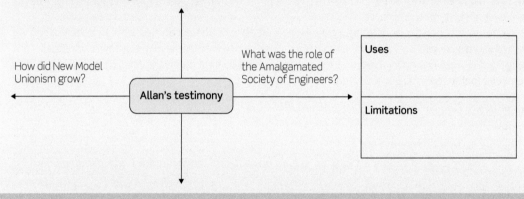

The foundation of the Trades Union Congress

With the growth of national organisations and a solid footing for the progression of worker interests, trade unionism became a more prominent feature in public affairs. Despite this, however, the movement still retained elements of individualism which prevented it from acting in a truly united fashion. Certainly, the spread of national unions was a step towards this goal but there remained a significant proportion of small, local unions that chose not to, or could not, organise in such a manner. These tended to be the semi-skilled and unskilled professions that were unable to afford the cost of creating large administrative bodies with the permanent secretaries necessary to manage affairs on a national scale. Equally the 'new models' which did adopt national structures tended to operate only within their own trades rather than in a more general manner across them. In this sense, unity was much improved but could still be enhanced if workers were to attain the best possible means of protection.

It was with this motivation in mind that efforts to create a united trades union were undertaken in the 1860s, 20 years after the failure of the first attempt at such an organisation – the Grand National Consolidated Trades Union. The idea was initially driven by George Potter, a carpenter from London who was also editor of the trade union paper *The Beehive*, and William Dronfield, a printer in Sheffield, who each saw tremendous value in bringing unions together regardless of their trade. Potter in particular believed that if the localised unions and national ones could work collectively then they would be better able to defend workers' rights. For Dronfield the motivation lay with promoting the views of the working people, which he felt were still being largely ignored – a conclusion he arrived at after a paper he gave to the middle-class National Association for the Promotion of Social Sciences defending trade unions failed to be published.

ESTABLISHMENT OF THE TRADES UNION CONGRESS

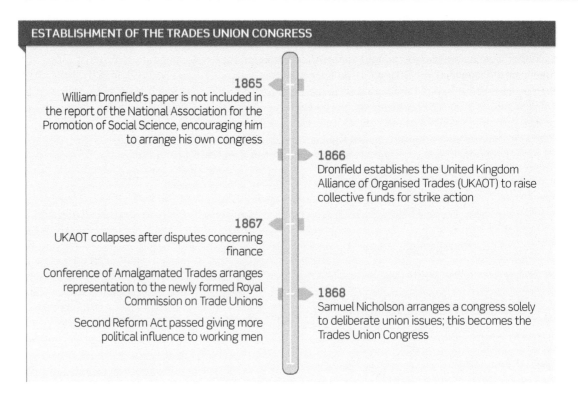

1865
William Dronfield's paper is not included in the report of the National Association for the Promotion of Social Science, encouraging him to arrange his own congress

1866
Dronfield establishes the United Kingdom Alliance of Organised Trades (UKAOT) to raise collective funds for strike action

1867
UKAOT collapses after disputes concerning finance

Conference of Amalgamated Trades arranges representation to the newly formed Royal Commission on Trade Unions

Second Reform Act passed giving more political influence to working men

1868
Samuel Nicholson arranges a congress solely to deliberate union issues; this becomes the Trades Union Congress

KEY TERM

Congress
Another term for 'conference', describing a formal meeting by representatives of different organisations.

Both of these men would be crucial to the eventual creation of the Trades Union **Congress** (TUC), but even before they began this undertaking significant inroads had already been made towards a universal body. In 1860, the London Trades Council had been formed. This sought to represent the working people of London in the absence of any other such body. This organisation was dominated by the leaders of the amalgamated unions such as the ASE and ASCJ and under their direction had amassed more than 100,000 affiliates by 1866. By this date additional trades councils were organised in other major cities in Britain although many unions still affiliated with the London branch and continued to send representatives to their headquarters in the Bell Inn at Old Bailey in London.

The growth of **Trades Councils** offered a broader forum for union activity but they still retained a degree of regional individuality which limited the scope for a truly national voice. Additionally, the dominance of the more cautious 'new model' unions frustrated many of their smaller unions who relied more heavily upon the threat of strike action to protect their interests. In consequence of this frustration there was an opportunity to organise a more universal body that actually reflected the views of all trade unions rather than simply the biggest. In this endeavour George Potter was most active and he enjoyed considerable support from the smaller, more localised organisations. Potter's idea for a Labour Parliament which would meet annually failed to impress the London Trades Council, whose leadership – described as the '**Junta**' by Sydney and Beatrice Webb in their seminal work, *The History of Trade Unionism* (1894) – felt that the idea would undermine their own control over the direction of trade unionist activities. Despite this reluctance there was considerable support from the regional unions and during 1866 a meeting in Sheffield was organised and attended by 138 delegates whose intention was to arrange an annual conference.

KEY TERMS

Trades Council
This was a grouping of local trade unions from a given geographical area that met together to promote the interests of their industry within that area. These were often city-wide organisations.

'Junta'
This was the unofficial name given to the leading members of the London Trades Council who dominated its activities. Members of the Junta included: William Allan from the ASE; Robert Applegarth from the ASCJ; Charles Coulson of the Bricklayers; Daniel Guile of the Ironfounders; George Odger of the Shoemakers.

The Sheffield meeting was arranged by William Dronfield whose own experiences had reconciled him to the need to address the lack of an adequate outlet for unionist views. After discussion the meeting produced the United Kingdom Alliance of Organised Trades, which promised to bind unions in mutual support but collapsed in 1867 due to problems of finance and the involvement of its treasurer in the 'Sheffield Outrages' the previous year. Dronfield's efforts, however, were a catalyst that prompted his friend Samuel Nicholson, president of the Manchester and Salford Trades Council, to invite the convening of a general trades congress to discuss union issues (Source 8). This meeting, which took place in June 1868, was attended by 34 delegates representing more than 118,000 members of unions from across the country and has generally been regarded as the foundation of the TUC.

SOURCE

From the proposed Congress of Trades Councils issued in Manchester on 21 February 1868.

It is proposed that the Congress shall assume the character of the annual meetings of the British Association of the Advancement of Social Sciences Association, in the transactions of which Societies the artisan class are almost entirely excluded; and that papers, previously carefully prepared, should be laid before the Congress on various subjects which at present time affect Trades Societies, each paper to be followed by discussion upon the points advanced, with a view of the merits and demerits of each question being thoroughly ventilated through the medium of the public press.

The success of this meeting lay in the skilled and unskilled unions being able to put aside their differences with regard to individual interests. Although they supported one another in principle, there had often been disagreement over the manner in which to seek worker rights. This lingering conflict had until 1868 prevented an effective organisation across the skills divide. The improved relations were influenced by a need to safeguard union funds by getting some guarantees of union status. Until 1867, it had been assumed that unions who registered under the Friendly Societies Act (1855) (page 86) were able to benefit from the security that it offered; however, following a legal judgement in 1867 this right was formally denied. The case of *Hornby v Close* had arisen after the Bradford Boilermakers' fund was stolen by its treasurer and they sought legal recompense under the Act. Following the judgement it became a matter of urgent concern for the larger amalgamated unions to protect their vast funds and therefore they were more open to the idea of a national general body.

The foundation of the TUC marked a seminal moment for trade unionism, establishing a genuinely universal mechanism for the organisation of British labour. Following 1868, unions could, with one voice, defend their members and promote the interests of the working classes. A notable addition to this classic endeavour was also the increased political motivations that the TUC exuded.

Following the passage of the second Reform Act in 1867, working men enjoyed more political influence in Britain and this acquisition was reflected in the ambitions of the TUC. When the second congress met in August 1869, a proposal set out by A. W. Walton of the Co-operative Building Society was adopted, presenting a more political role for unions. The proposal involved the creation of a working man's party that could, where two Liberal candidates stood, insist on choosing one while the middle class chose the other. In another proposal also adopted, the TUC resolved to support a new Labour Representation League which was to replace the Reform League and would seek to both send qualified working men to parliament and also support other parliamentary candidates sympathetic to the needs of the labouring classes. With the adoption of these two resolutions, the TUC took on a more politicised agenda in addition to its classic industrial one; in doing so, it placed working-class interests at the heart of British politics via a more effective trade unionist movement, which guaranteed that the voice of labour would be difficult to ignore in the future.

A Level Exam-Style Question Section B

How far do you agree that the creation of the Trades Union Congress owed more to New Model Unionism than to earlier trade union movements? (20 marks)

Tip

When answering this question it is important to consider the role that each movement played in the creation of the TUC – could one have created the Congress without the other?

Government response to New Model Unionism

The attitude of the British government towards trade unionism before 1850 had largely been negative. The domineering notion of free trade squarely placed their sympathies with the employers who, in their eyes, were making Britain a prosperous nation. Although more liberal minded politicians such as Robert Peel did begin to recognise that the experience of workers was in need of improvement and that they ought to have protection, there was limited effort by parliament to actually promote an effective means to achieve this.

The development of the 'new model' of unionism after 1851, however, encouraged a more thoughtful consideration of working men's unions and the experiences of the working classes more generally. The motivation for this was the strength that unions like the ASE and the ASCJ gave to their movements. These unions were better financed and better organised than their earlier counterparts and because they also operated on a national scale, it would be a poor government that did not take any notice of them. In addition, the methods they adopted to further their cause were more acceptable to the establishment. Whereas in the past unions had been regarded as troublesome and generally quite aggressive, New Model Unionism endorsed a considerably more respectable approach which endeared it more easily to those in power. Men like Robert Applegarth of the ASCJ and William Allan of the ASE felt progress was best made through negotiation rather than militancy and this offered the means for compromise. This had often been missing in the early trade union campaigns, which had adopted a very stark approach when fighting employers.

What made NMU especially relevant to government was the skilled trades that it embodied. By 1850, the Industrial Revolution had made Britain the strongest economy in the world with unrivalled trade opportunities. This position was achieved by the uninterrupted growth of the country's industrial capacity which was itself reliant upon the skilled trades that manufactured the new technologies providing for such success. If Britain wanted to remain the pre-eminent economy, then professions such as engineering needed to be listened to more effectively to prevent interruption from industrial disputes which, given the financial strength of the new unions, had the potential to last significant lengths of time. In the 1859–60 lockout of the London builders, the men had been able to strike for four months, which had a great impact on the fortunes of the Pimlico employer, Trollope, for whom they worked. Such sustained action, if widespread, had the potential to jeopardise Britain's economic standing and therefore the government began to take unionism more seriously in the mid-19th century.

In view of the growing importance of trade unionism, the government began to reappraise its position and granted some limited reform, which allowed unions more latitude in their undertakings. The passage of the Molestation of Workmen Act in 1859 conceded more rights to those who chose to **picket** peacefully during strikes but left the definition of 'peaceful persuasion' to the courts. In this manner the Act itself presents a good example of the mixed feelings with which government met the growing strength of trade unionism. It offered a conservative reform which recognised the increasing status of the movement, but at the same time it retained the means by which to ensure that control remained in government hands.

> **KEY TERM**
>
> Picket
> The term given to workers who stand outside the workplace during strikes to persuade others to join their cause.

This pattern of conservative reform continued throughout the mid-19th century as the government sought to maintain a positive relationship with unions at the same time as not granting them more powers, so as to ensure the continuance of middle-class prosperity. Any reform that was offered was usually a modification of an existing piece of legislation, which gave a little improvement while ultimately changing nothing of significant consequence. In the case of the Master and Servant Act of 1823, for example, unions – especially the Glasgow Trades Council – had sought the repeal of this measure since 1858 and when a new Act was finally passed in 1867 it did not rescind the earlier legislation but rather only removed the most unfair elements of it.

Despite government reluctance to accept trade unionism completely, those with political ambitions had to listen to it. The broadening of the movement onto a national level meant that the Trades Councils, particularly the dominant London Trades Council under the growing influence of Robert Applegarth and William Allan, could potentially mobilise thousands of people at General Elections. Although the majority of those in unions were unable to vote, they could still influence those who did have the franchise since elections involved public voting. Vociferous union representation for a particular candidate could assert significant pressure on voters which could in turn have decisive political implications. On the principle that the vote would enable them to secure laws to safeguard their union activities and, most importantly, their funds, many trade unionists were very interested in the political debate on franchise reform and were therefore also involved with the Reform League (see page 31) which agitated for such reform. The 1865 election saw significant grass-roots efforts by unions to facilitate an increase in parliament of radical MPs favouring franchise reform to include skilled working men. On the strength of this interest, political parties were open to such reforms which also suited their own agendas and were eventually achieved in 1867.

SOURCE

9 From *Address to the Trade Unions*, published by the Manhood Suffrage and Vote by Ballot Association in 1862. This organisation would later become part of the National Reform League.

We do not wish you to relax one iota of your efforts in reference to the amelioration of our social condition. Our advice is to be more than ever united for the purpose of reducing the hours of labour, and for advancing its price. Nor do we wish to turn our trades societies into political organisations, to divert them from their social objects; but we must not forget that we are citizens, and as such should have citizens' rights. Recollect also that by obtaining these rights we shall be able more effectually to secure our legitimate demands as Unionists.

1867 Royal Commission

Following the granting of the vote to skilled working men in 1867, the government became significantly more interested in the trade union movement. A royal commission was established later that year to investigate the 'outrages' that had occurred in Sheffield and to decide on whether to improve the legal status of unions. Under existing laws trades unions were not granted full legal rights as they were heavily associated with industrial unrest and generally stirring up trouble. Following the creation of NMU, however, this image was slowly receding as these larger unions were much more conservative in their actions and therefore there was more sympathy with extending full legality to them. The commission heard from employers as well as unions who each put forward a strong case. The unions were particularly careful to distance themselves from the 'outrages' and emphasised the benefits of unionism, using as examples the prudent and highly respectable Amalgamated Societies whose organisation and funding proved especially impressive. The conclusions of the commission were difficult to draw and produced such division among its members that two reports were drawn up: the Majority Report and the Minority Report. The former advocated a degree of legalisation with some restrictions which included the separation of strike funds from the general fund, and powers of veto on certain union rules relating to employer practices. The Minority Report suggested no such limitation and simply recommended

full legalisation together with the protections that went with it, including the security of their funds.

Within the new political climate that followed the passage of the second Reform Act in 1867, the Liberal government favoured the second report which granted trade unions complete legality and the associated protections that accompanied it. The recommendations of this report were consequently presented to parliament and eventually formulated into the Trade Union Act which was passed in 1871. After this time unions and their activities were, for the first time, entirely legal.

The response of government towards NMU was one of mixed feeling. In one sense there was the lingering desire to subdue the means of protestation by the working classes but this was diluted by a more realistic acceptance that trade unionism was now an established force. Economic and political developments between 1850 and 1870 had given opportunity to the trade union movement, opportunity which it had grasped with both hands and successfully exploited. The 'new model' that had been established created a well-resourced and well-organised union which was much better placed to promote working-class interests. If political parties were going to achieve power in the future, then their governments would need to be more sympathetic to the trade unions, which had been markedly strengthened by the advent of NMU.

THINKING HISTORICALLY   Change (4b&c)

The bird's-eye view

The growth of trade unionism

The development	Medium-term consequences	Long-term consequences
The growth of trade unionism	During industrialisation, working-class people were often exploited in order to maximise the profitability of industry.	Working people have better protection in the workplace and can go to their union in the event of a problem. Although unions are not quite as strong as they once were, they remain a significant protection for those employed.

Imagine you are looking at the whole of history using a zoomed-out interactive map like Google Maps. You have a general view of the sweep of developments and their consequences but you cannot see much detail. If you zoom in to the time of the growth of trade unionism, you can see the event in detail but will know nothing of its consequences in the medium or long term. If you zoom in to look at the medium- or long-term consequences, you will know about them in detail but will know very little about the event that caused them, for example, the creation of New Model Unionism or the establishment of the Trades Union Congress.

Look at the table above and answer the following questions:

1 What were the immediate consequences of the development?

2 In what ways are the medium-term consequences different from the long-term consequences?

Work in groups of three. Each student takes the role of the teacher for one of the above (the development, medium-term consequences or long-term consequences) and gives a short presentation to the other two. They may comment and ask questions. After each presentation, the other two members of the group write a 100-word paragraph showing how the presentation links to their own.

Then work individually and answer the following questions:

3 What happens to the detail when you zoom out to look at the whole sweep of history?

4 What are the advantages and disadvantages of zooming in to look at a specific time in detail?

5 How could you use the map in order to get a good understanding of history as a whole?

THE GROWTH OF CO-OPERATIVE ACTIVITIES

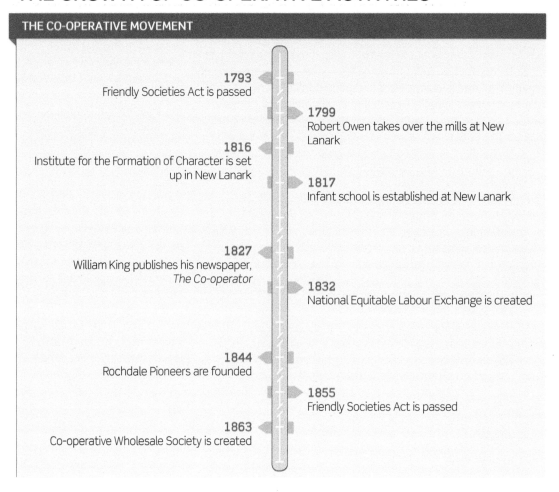

THE CO-OPERATIVE MOVEMENT

1793 Friendly Societies Act is passed

1799 Robert Owen takes over the mills at New Lanark

1816 Institute for the Formation of Character is set up in New Lanark

1817 Infant school is established at New Lanark

1827 William King publishes his newspaper, *The Co-operator*

1832 National Equitable Labour Exchange is created

1844 Rochdale Pioneers are founded

1855 Friendly Societies Act is passed

1863 Co-operative Wholesale Society is created

KEY TERM

Mutualism
The idea that well-being is dependent upon people offering mutual support rather than seeking to gain advantage by competing against each other.

Just as trade unionism developed to protect the growing working classes after the onset of industrialisation, an alternative model of protection also emerged which built on the established idea of **mutual** support for mutual benefit. In the past working people had often clubbed together to support one another in times of difficulty – the provision of benefit to a widow or a small pension to a worker no longer able to work, were common occurrences. After the general withdrawal of government intervention in the economy from the 17th century onwards, such support became even more common as people felt they could rely only upon themselves. This realisation formed the basis of mutualism and encouraged the emergence of benefit organisations, which grew in number after 1785, and also the co-operative movement, which remains in place even today. Predicated upon the idea that everyone should be able to live a good life, these developments offered significant attraction to many people in Britain where more individualistic capitalist notions of commerce and competition were increasingly taking hold.

New Lanark and co-operative activities

The most famous example of these new practices was undoubtedly that of the New Lanark mill in the Clyde Valley, operated by Robert Owen after 1799 until 1828. Owen was a committed social reformer who strongly believed in the power of education and the importance of providing welfare to employees. In contrast to the exploitative commercial attitudes of his fellow employers, though Owen was certainly interested in profit, it was not his main concern. Of more importance to him was the way people treated one another and the experiences they had. It was essential to Owen that workers were well looked after and that they were given the opportunity to improve themselves. As a result, when he took over the mills at New Lanark he sought to build upon the humane practices of its previous owner, his new father-in-law, and create a 'perfect' workplace.

SOURCE 10

The New Lanark experiment. Young girls being taught how to dance at Robert Owen's factory school, c1825.

MR OWEN'S INSTITUTION, NEW LANARK.
(Quadrille Dancing.)

EXTEND YOUR KNOWLEDGE

Robert Owen (1771–1858)

Robert Owen was born in Newton, mid-Wales and was the son of an ironmonger. Starting his career in a drapery shop, by the age of 19 he was managing a cotton mill in Manchester. Interested in social reform, Owen was an early proponent of what became known as 'utopian socialism' and sought to introduce some of its ideas into the workplace. Having bought a mill at New Lanark he put into practice some of these ideas, which saw employees treated more equally and with good working conditions. Owen also provided education and moral direction for those he employed and set up the country's first infant school in New Lanark in 1816. A tireless campaigner for the improvement of working conditions for people, Owen became president of the Grand National Consolidated Trades Union in 1834 and also sought to set up other 'New Lanarks' in Ireland and the USA.

The principle on which Owen worked was that people's characters were created by the environment around them and therefore to promote better human beings it was first necessary to improve that environment (Source 11). Features of this concept were already in existence in Britain but Owen formulated them into a clear vision and actually attempted to put theory into practice.

The means by which Owen proposed to do this was through building new communities that took care of one another and which promoted a co-operative rather than combative environment. In New Lanark Owen sought to create this idyll.

SOURCE 11

From Robert Owen's *Essay on the Formation of Character*, published in 1813.

Any general character, from the best to the worst, from the most ignorant to the most enlightened, may be given to any community, even to the world at large, by application of the proper means; which means are to a great extent at the command and under the control of those who have influence in the affairs of men.

In the early 19th century when the Industrial Revolution was driving British commercial interests to raise productivity to unprecedented levels and the factory system had been firmly established to achieve this, the nation's economy was certainly combative. Workers were treated poorly so that greater profits could be made and there was little protection available from either the government or the fledgling unionism movement to encourage any hope for change.

In New Lanark, however, this is precisely what Owen sought to do. Having taken ownership he abandoned the use of punishments as a means to raise productivity which was so popular across other institutions, and replaced them with incentives to work. The most common way of incentivising his workers was with the use of a 'silent monitor' – a wooden block that hung above every worker's station and publicly identified the quality of their efforts by means of a different coloured side: black equated to poor behaviour; blue for indifferent; yellow for good; white for excellent behaviour. These were turned daily by supervisors to regularly reflect the standard of behaviour. This simple system encouraged better performance from employees by appealing to their sense of social standing among their fellow workers rather than accentuating a master/worker division that the use of punishment often did.

In addition to the removal of punishment, New Lanark provided improved living and working standards for employees. After 1800, the working day was shortened to no more than 12 hours, including a one and a half hour meal break, and the minimum age at which children could work was set at ten years. Combined with these changes better facilities were introduced. A shop was established which sold quality goods at little more than cost price and the profit that was generated went back to the workers in the form of 'free' education for their children in the schools that were also created. Additionally, when the USA placed an embargo on cotton supplies to Britain in 1806 following a political dispute, Owen continued to pay his workers even though the mill was closed for four months. In this spirit of benevolence Owen was pioneering a new society model. The experiment at New Lanark was the beginning of what Owen hoped would become a new communal way of living: where people worked harmoniously side by side rather that at odds, and profit would be reinvested to promote the further improvement of people's lives. The concepts employed at New Lanark and the success Owen enjoyed (Source 12), drew widespread interest both at home and abroad and in 1816 the future Tsar of Russia, Grand Duke Nicholas, visited the mills.

SOURCE 12 From a letter written by Robert Owen to *The Times* in 1834.

No experiment was ever so successful as the one I conducted at New Lanark, although it was commenced and continued in opposition to all the oldest and strongest prejudices of mankind. For twenty-nine years we did without the necessity for magistrates or lawyers; without a single legal punishment; without any known poors' (sic) rate; without intemperance or religious animosities. We reduced the hours of labour, well educated all the children from infancy, greatly improved the condition of the adults, diminishing their daily labour, paid interest on capital, *and cleared upwards of £300,000 of profit.*

Co-operative activities

Of greater significance, however, was the impact that New Lanark had upon those in Britain itself. Inspired by Owen's ideas of communality and self-improvement, other progressive individuals who were disillusioned with the existing way of things sought to create similar schemes. In the declining economic climate that emerged in Britain after 1815 these efforts enjoyed a reasonable degree of popularity. In London a group of working men, including the later Chartist leader Henry Hetherington, formed a Co-operative and Economical Society in 1821 with the intention of establishing a communal house in Spa Fields. The physician William King published a newspaper entitled *The Co-operator* after 1827 and, although it only ran for two years, it had a wide readership and was able to circulate the ideas of co-operation and link disparate groups together. Through the efforts of King and others, co-operation enjoyed a steady growth and by 1829 the spirit of communalism which Owen had initially promoted had manifested itself in the form of co-operative stores across the country. These stores embodied the co-operative spirit by sharing their profits with their customers and so successful had this concept become that, by 1832, 500 such stores existed. The principle motive for this success lay with the empowerment of the people themselves. In a world where people were being exploited for personal gain, the idea of co-operation offered a real alternative that gave ordinary people control over their own lives. They could make their own choices and feel part of a larger community which, for many, was an appealing prospect in a country that was becoming very individualistic and profit-motivated.

The growth of co-operative stores rather than communal societies is indicative of the difficulties of such living in the competitive industrial world of 19th-century Britain. But with the stores the principle of collective operation was maintained. Established initially to fund the growth of new communities, these stores became popular in their own right, as other outlets for purchasing goods were often run in the interest of profit only and their owners cared little for the quality of their goods or charged exorbitant prices for them. By contrast, the co-operative stores were set up by people interested in the well-being of their customers. These individuals grouped together and pooled their resources to provide a means by which customers could buy quality goods at fair prices. The additional benefit of receiving a **dividend** for being involved with the enterprises ensured both the long-term support of these ventures and their viability.

Another interesting feature of the growing co-operative spirit was the introduction of Labour Exchange Bazaars. Although short-lived – they lasted only two years – these exchanges operated on a currency based on labour hours rather than monetary value. People would exchange goods they had produced for credit notes to the value of how many hours it took to make that product which they could then use to buy other goods to the equal time value of that labour. Two exchanges were established, one in London in September 1832 called the National Equitable Labour Exchange and the other in Birmingham in 1833. Each was well supported by the trade unions who appreciated the emphasis upon labour value but neither was able to survive in the long term due to the accumulation of unwanted goods.

Though many co-operative enterprises struggled due to lack of business sense or inability to attract new members, others were reasonably successful within their immediate localities. More important than this success, however, was the hope that they embodied for the working men and women of Britain. In the fiercely competitive world which had been created, where the poorer elements of society were continually disadvantaged, the co-operative model offered a way to dilute the iniquity of industrial capitalism. Through co-operative activities the working people had a means to improve their own condition and this paved the way for a greater equalisation of society by the end of the 1860s.

ACTIVITY
KNOWLEDGE CHECK

Unionism and co-operation

Using the material you have just read and any other knowledge you have gained, produce a Venn diagram that compares unionism and co-operation. In the overlap you should place any ideas that both concepts share.

When producing your diagram you should consider the following:

- what each concept sought to do
- how each concept was manifested in Britain
- how people responded to each idea
- the success of each idea.

The Rochdale Pioneers and co-operative economics

The seeds of co-operation that Owen sowed early in the 1800s gained momentum during the following three decades as industrialisation made the lives of workers even harder. For Owen and other socially minded individuals, co-operation had both a physical benefit for improving these lives, and also a strong moral one which reflected their own belief in self-help (Source 13). With this belief, the economically depressed years of the 1840s encouraged new co-operative activities to develop and, in 1844, a new co-operative shop was opened in the northern town of Rochdale. Although such shops were not original, the venture undertaken by the 28 men who formed The Rochdale Society of Equitable Pioneers, or simply 'Rochdale Pioneers', formalised the model of co-operative business and created the template for future such operations.

SOURCE

From the concluding address at the first Co-operative Congress held in Manchester, May 1831.

Of all the projects for raising the Workmen from the fear of pauperism, from the danger of crime, from the misery of incessant ill paid labour, or uncertain employments, none appears to us to be fraught with so many advantages and so few dangers as this. The system is rational, pious and beautiful... they will show to the world that the working classes are not only able, but are determined to follow the advice of Mr (now Sir Robert) Peel and 'TAKE THE MANAGEMENT OF THEIR AFFAIRS INTO THEIR OWN HANDS'.

KEY TERM

Dividend
A portion of the profit generated by a company and paid to those who have a financial interest in that company.

By the mid-1840s, working men's co-operatives were well established within British society but they varied in success and overall consistency. Despite good intentions, they faced considerable opposition from more traditional shops that felt they were threatening their own businesses. Often the 'co-ops' were charged excessive rents for their premises or had difficulty with their supply of goods as wholesalers refused to work with them. Such defensiveness from established traders was a natural consequence of new businesses trying to operate in the competitive economy of industrialised Britain. Many co-operatives did not have the business sense to compete effectively and therefore were unable to expand as rapidly as members wished.

SOURCE 14

Photograph taken in Rochdale in 1865 to commemorate the 13 remaining Rochdale Pioneers – the men who established the principles of modern co-operative business in Britain in 1844.

The Rochdale principles

What set the Pioneers apart from other co-operative ventures was the manner in which they sought to learn from the early efforts and to maximise their potential for longevity by applying clear rules by which to safeguard their business. These embodied the spirit of co-operation and reflected a more professional approach:

- Money should be provided by themselves and bear a fixed rate of interest.

- Only the best quality provisions procurable should be supplied to members.

- Full weight and measures should be given.

- Market value prices should be charged and no credit should be given.

- Profits should be divided pro rata upon the amount of purchases made by each member.

- The principle of 'one member one vote' should apply. Also women should be able to become members.

- The management of the organisation should be in the hands of elected leaders.

- A defined percentage of profits should be allotted to education.

- Statements and balance sheets should be available to members upon request.

Each of these principles reflected a progressive intent that had the notion of fairness at its core. In contrast to other commercial modes of business prevalent in Britain at the time, this was a positive motivation offering both a refreshing alternative and a real determination to promote a better experience for working men and women.

The principles were a new departure for co-operation because they made the concept more professional. The early efforts were largely based on goodwill and they did not have a long-term plan for their own sustainability. Where the Pioneers were different was in building a firm business structure that offered a clear pathway for ongoing development. The focus on management and profit sharing in particular evidenced a more thorough commitment to creating an effective business, which had been absent in earlier efforts.

One of the most prominent features within these 'laws' is the emphasis upon democratic principles, notably in determining the manner in which the business should be run. Democracy was not overtly practised in Britain and the national government was still very much representative of vested interests despite reform in 1832. On this basis, it is interesting that the Pioneers adopted such a progressive style. In one sense it fitted very neatly with the overall concept of co-operation: everybody being equal and working together to promote mutual benefit. In another way it also had a commercial advantage and enhanced their reputation as honest businessmen. Either way, the adoption of democratic methods was fundamental to the work of the Rochdale Pioneers as it promoted effective working relationships and underlined the very different style of commerce that they were seeking to develop.

One additional note is the specific emphasis upon quality goods with fair weights as this established a good reputation for honesty that encouraged people to use them. Other shops had often tampered with their produce to make it go further – mixing chalk into flour was a common practice – but by guaranteeing their goods the Pioneers quickly gathered a loyal following which allowed them to become established. The refusal to allow credit was also significant, for their initial success as earlier shops had fallen into financial difficulties after extending such a courtesy to their customers. Having achieved a degree of security from consistent business, the other benefits of co-operation were able to be felt.

The fundamental difference between co-operative shops and more traditional ones was the sharing of everything. People entered into partnerships and pooled their resources to buy goods at wholesale prices which could then be sold on to customers at market prices. Under the traditional model of commerce the resulting profits would then go to the owner of the business but in the co-operative model profits were divided among those who had joined the society and invested in it. The Pioneers adopted the same method of proportionality when it came to dividing up profit but they placed more importance upon the amount members spent rather than what they invested – the more you spent in the shop the more profit you received. Tying profit return to spending encouraged more customers to become members of the co-operative society and this ensured the long-term viability of the venture; it also gave customers extra money each year which made a big difference to their lives.

The model adopted by the Pioneers made them a successful business which drew a lot of attention from other societies who sought to emulate their success. By 1863, it was estimated that 332 co-operative shops were trading throughout the country, and that 251 of these were created after reading of the Pioneers shop in Rochdale. In the spirit of co-operation the Pioneers supported the growth of other outlets and were constantly sought for advice on how to set up a successful shop. In 1856, they were asked by fellow co-operative societies to provide a wholesale service to supply societies across the region. Over the next three years, the Rochdale shop expanded its business to accommodate this request and then in 1860 it undertook to set up a 'co-operative of co-operative societies' to provide this service. In 1863, the Co-operative Wholesale Society was set up and the collective trading power of this organisation meant that by 1868 it could establish overseas trading depots as far away as Australia and South America, enabling them to secure a constant supply of goods which ensured continued growth.

Co-operative economics

The basis of the Pioneers success and that of other co-operative movements was the adoption of what became known as **co-operative economics**. One of the underlying principles of this was that rather than an individual accumulating vast profits from the ownership of a business, by promoting collective ownership of that business by its customers, profit would be divided among a greater number of people. The benefit of this would be a modest improvement in individual wealth across a larger proportion of society but also the creation of a long-term interest in continuing to use that business. In this manner the business would retain and even grow its customer base which would therefore enhance further profit for those customers.

KEY TERM

Co-operative economics
A field of study which relates social equality principles implicit within co-operation thinking to economic practices.

This thinking was predicated on the idea that there is no benefit for ordinary working people to shop in traditional stores, as the wealth they generate from them only enriches the owner. By co-operating to establish their own shops which offered a return to those who used them, every penny spent by the customer would help to enrich them. Additionally, by pooling their finances they could ensure good prices by buying in bulk which would keep shop prices fair and offer further benefit to the end user – themselves.

In the self-help spirit of the mid-Victorian era this concept was an attractive one for those who recognised its potential and as such co-operation flourished – especially since it now had a clearly defined pathway. Using the blueprint of the Rochdale Pioneers, the co-operative movement grew to more than 1,000 stores by the mid-1850s and 20 years later had amassed property worth in excess of £300,000, giving it a strong footing within the British economy.

The growth of friendly societies

The expansion of the co-operation movement was in one sense a reaction to the highly individualistic nature of industrialising Britain, but the suggestion that it was an entirely new endeavour is misleading. Certainly, the commercial aspect that it prompted was original, but its social features of mutual benefit and collective working had their origins long before the onset of the Industrial Revolution.

As early as the late 17th century there had existed groups of workers who joined together to provide mutual social and financial support to one another when the need arose – usually when there was an illness or death among their cohort, in which case a fund would be provided by the workers themselves to support the families involved. In these actions there is a direct relationship with the mutual societies that exist today which provide similar services for their members. What connects these ventures is the growth of '**friendly societies**', which took place at a similar time as the reduction in government protection during the 1660s.

KEY TERM

Friendly society
Also called a 'mutual society' and sometimes a 'benevolent society', this was an organisation of men that came together to provide assistance and benefits for each other. The societies came to provide services to their members, which included insurance, saving schemes, pensions and, later, even loans.

In the absence of government protection, working men – mostly artisans and skilled workers – recognised a need to look after themselves and consequently many organised into groups that paid into a mutual fund through the use of weekly subscriptions. The fund generated was then used to support those who had paid into it in the event of the need arising, but later it also became a fund with which the members could enhance their own positions and the funds expanded into saving schemes and other financial enterprises after 1817.

The majority of these societies were born from social gatherings of men – usually in ale houses where they would congregate after work to discuss ideas and issues that affected them. Among the earliest of the 19th-century groups were the 'Royal Foresters' in Yorkshire which was formed in the 18th century, but which splintered into the 'Ancient Order of Foresters' in 1834 after a disagreement over the interpretation of their rulebook. As each society emerged, they undertook to distinguish themselves from others to provide a distinct identity and sense of belonging. There emerged an array of exotic titles, such as 'The Order of Buffaloes', the 'Hearts of Oak', designed to promote individuality, while the 'Rechabites' society, in honour of their biblical namesake, even effected a temperance policy to distinguish themselves from the others. In addition to these actions, every society came to engage in the use of sashes and banners by way of exhibiting their cohesiveness. As the anonymity of industrialisation took hold, this particular function served a social as well as financial benefit for those who joined them.

As the economy was transformed, the need for self-protection for workers increased and by the end of the 1700s there were friendly societies stretching across the country. With the growth of such organisations and the money they were pooling, the government became interested in their activities because of the perceived threat they posed to the country after the revolution in France in 1789. To the government, friendly societies appeared to exhibit some of the traits of French radicalism and were even felt by more conservative elements to be fertile ground for stirring up revolutionary feeling in Britain. Given this attitude, they sought to regulate the activities of these 'friendly groups'.

The Friendly Societies Act, 1793

Under the legislation passed in 1793 (Source 15) friendly societies were required to register themselves with local JPs and send reports of their activities every three months. As part of this process each society also had to draw up a set of rules by which to govern itself. These constitutions had to be written down and in no way challenge the interests of the government. The societies also had to lodge copies of their documents with the clerk of the court for inclusion in the rolls of that court session.

In the immediate term, the Act was an attempt by conservatives in government to regulate the activities of the emerging groups so as to keep abreast of any potential threat they may pose in the wake of first the revolution in France and then the outbreak of war. By requiring the registration of such organisations and also the production of clear guidelines, it was anticipated that these bodies would become more transparent and might even reduce in number under the administrative demands. In contrast, the passage of the Act saw a rapid growth in these organisations as there was now legal recognition for them which, by extension, also granted legal protection of their funds. This was the first time under English law that workers were able to form their own organisations in order to provide mutual benefits and they sought to take full advantage of this. By 1803, it was estimated that eight percent of the population of England were members of a 'friendly' and by 1815 these groups were able to provide support by way of insurance cover to about one-third of the population.

SOURCE

15 Text defining the role of a friendly society taken from the Encouragement and Relief of the Friendly Societies Act passed in 1793.

A society of good fellowship for the purpose of raising from time to time, by voluntary contributions, a stock or fund for the mutual relief and maintenance of all and every member thereof, in old age, sickness, and infirmity, or for the relief of widows and children of deceased members.

Although friendly societies grew at a rapid pace after 1793, it is important to recognise that membership was not open to everybody. Although they were organised by working people for their own benefit, there was a financial commitment involved which required a continuous subscription on a weekly or, more common, annual basis. The regular demand for money often excluded from membership the poorest workers, who either worked in unstable employment, such as that in the agricultural sector, or did not earn enough to enable them to pay the fees. Indeed, even if workers were able to afford membership, if they fell behind with their subscription they would often find themselves expelled from the society or unable to access its benefits. In this sense, therefore, there was a degree of exclusivity to being a member of a friendly society which belies the overall impression of benevolence that they have come to embody.

Later developments

Having obtained legal recognition friendly societies developed at a quick pace which has traditionally been ascribed to the industrialisation process. In this thesis it was generally accepted that, with the expansion of the economy in the early to mid-19th century, there was both a greater social desire for working men to organise communally and a specific financial incentive for doing so – in this case the securing of benefits in the event of injury or sickness which might prevent work. Given the 'self-help' attitude and strong sense of individualism that prevailed within British society at this time, there is significant merit to this argument and certainly much of the popularity of the friendly societies can be attributed to the financial gains membership offered. Furthermore, the demographic concentration of these societies would support the idea that it was the areas where existing and new industries were developing that societies enjoyed the greatest presence.

SOURCE

Table showing membership of friendly societies by percentage of population in the regions of Britain in 1803 and 1815.

Region	Percentage of population 1803	Percentage of population 1815
North-west	13.8	14.2
North-east	10.1	10.2
Midlands	18.3	19
South-west	7.6	9.2
South-east	4.7	5.4

In this sense the growth of friendly societies was a product of the shifting economic environment and can generally be regarded as a means of protection against the difficulties that such change might produce. This motivation for growth is extended by the co-operative nature of the societies themselves. Given the increased mobility of the industrial workforce – migration to large towns was more common during the mid-century with the development of the railroad and the need for work – the benefits of membership in a friendly society often meant that hospitality would be extended to members by other societies in that area. In the case of the United Society, for example, this organisation was simply an association of friendly societies which pledged to provide a bed and meals to any of their number who might be travelling around for work.

In addition to the social and financial benefits of joining a friendly society, there was also a convenience in doing so. Following the outbreak of war with France, the British government was very wary of working men uniting together in the fear that this would lead to revolutionary intent. As a result, the friendly societies had been regulated. The benefit of this was that because they were primarily organised by the workers, they also provided a convenient and legal means by which to undertake union activities, including in some cases collecting for strike funds, which, after 1799, had been made illegal. In this manner it is reasonable to suggest that several friendly societies grew by means of promoting trade unionism at a time when it was discouraged by government.

Friendly Societies Act, 1855

Reflecting the growth of friendly societies during the first half of the 19th century, in 1846 the practice of registering societies locally with the JP was abandoned and replaced with a central department under a new 'Registrar of Friendly Societies'. From this point on, such organisations had to register directly with this government department as part of the greater interest that the authorities were now taking. This interest was primarily due to the breadth of support friendly societies were getting – after 1815, the number of members had reached over a million and they commanded a great deal of wealth. In recognition of this the government also passed new legislation in 1855 to update the existing older Act. This new legislation related mostly to the protection of society funds and evidenced a growing degree of support for their activities. In part this was the result of the legalisation of trade unions after 1824, which gave friendly societies a more honest reputation that quieted the views of the more cynical members of parliament. More important, however, was the recognition of the welfare benefits that such societies offered to their members. In this undertaking they were actively embodying the self-help ethos that mid-Victorian sensibilities celebrated and as such the friendly societies were increasingly welcomed by those with influence.

As society became more established and the shock of industrialisation waned in the later part of the 1800s the friendly societies continued to provide benefits to the working people of Britain and in this capacity they were able to make up for the slow improvements in state provision of welfare. As wages improved so too did the membership of such societies which were increasingly able to offer social insurance to their members and, it is estimated, they outnumbered that of trade unions by four to one by 1870. With increased funds these societies began to offer improved pension provision and even savings opportunities to their members. As middle-class Britain moved towards a more comfortable style of living, the friendly societies remained buoyant and enabled significant proportions of the working classes to rest a little easier, safe in the knowledge that there was a modicum of security that would ensure their own comfort in the modern world.

Given the basic premise behind the friendly society, which advocated the mutual support of members, it is unsurprising that throughout their development there existed strong links with both the trade unions and also the emergent co-operative movement. Independently each of these organisations sought the welfare of its members, either through representation in the workplace or social and economic support during troubled times. Collectively they provided scaffolding for the lower classes in society: a structure of mutual support that could be relied upon in a world that had grown individualistic and closed off to the needs of others.

The economic changes that affected Britain in the 19th century not only improved the country's prosperity but also transformed the relationships between employers and employees; before 1785 workers were very much at the mercy of their employer but by 1870 they enjoyed much greater influence having become a more outspoken and active working class, determined to look after itself in a rapidly expanding economy. The commercialism of the Industrial Revolution arguably generated a very individualistic mentality that raised profit-making above all else. However, it also encouraged a more socially responsible society, first through the trade unions, which looked after the welfare of workers, and secondly, through broad-based co-operation, which sought to empower ordinary people in a world that had often tried to exploit them. Collectively these movements – especially unionism after 1852 – offered an alternative way for different groups in society to interact with one another instead of the traditional combative approach they had previously adopted.

ACTIVITY
KNOWLEDGE CHECK

Friendly support?

Write a summative paragraph that explains the main benefits that friendly societies offered in light of the developing social attitudes in Britain between 1785 and 1870.

ACTIVITY
SUMMARY

How much influence had the working men and women of Britain achieved by 1870?

Using the material you have read and studied, consider the impact that both unionism and co-operation (including the friendly societies) had upon the government in Britain and particularly the relationship it had with working people. Did either of these movements promote a better or worse relationship?

You should begin this task by producing a table of the key elements within each movement and then use this to address the wider question.

WIDER READING

Behagg, C. *Labour and Reform, Working Class Movements 1815–1914*, Hodder (2000)

Donnachie, I. *Robert Owen: Social Visionary*, John Donald Publishing (2005)

Fraser, W.H. *A History of British Trade Unionism 1700–1998*, Macmillan (1999)

Pelling, H. *A History of British Trade Unionism*, Macmillan (1992)

1.4 Poverty and pauperism, c1785–c1870

KEY QUESTIONS

- Why did the Old Poor Law need changing?
- What impact did the Poor Law Amendment Act have on addressing poverty in Britain?
- How much did attitudes change towards the poor and pauperism after 1834?

INTRODUCTION

The late 18th and 19th centuries witnessed substantial political and economic change in Britain. Industrialisation transformed the country: new industries emerged and people drifted towards a more urban style of living as new towns and cities grew to accommodate a growing and more mobile population. Political reform also reflected these changes and by the later 1800s Britain was a significantly more representative nation than it had ever been. These changes evidenced a country that was maturing into a modern state and the period is often viewed as having a very positive impact. Certainly, looking through the prism of economic and political development, this is a compelling image; however, as with any change there is a compromise to be made. In the case of Britain's poorest inhabitants, the rapid transformation in the economy did little to improve their lives and many found themselves worse off as the gap between rich and poor was increased. Poverty has always been present in the history of nations and in Britain it was noticeably so before 1870. As a prosperous industrial middle class emerged, it offered a stark contrast to the class beneath it. The product of a strong **self-help** ethos, the middle class accepted the conventional wisdom applied to the existence of poverty: that it was necessary to encourage self-improvement – an incentive to work hard to avoid becoming impoverished. In this sense there was reasonable acceptance of such a state. For those with influence, therefore, the problem was not poverty itself but rather **pauperism** – those who survived on state-provided poor relief. As a sense of respectability grew in society, this issue became more urgent and steps were taken to effect a solution.

KEY TERMS

Self-help
A belief in the importance of people's own abilities and determination to help themselves become successful, which was particularly influential after 1859 when the reformer Samuel Smiles published his book *Self Help*.

Pauperism
This is a general term for being poor but it also has a specific usage in English where it refers to anyone who is in receipt of state-provided relief under the Poor Laws.

1782 – Gilbert's Act passed

1795 – Speenhamland system established

1817 – Poor Employment Act passed

| 1600 | 1780 | 1785 | 1790 | 1795 | 1800 | 1805 | 1810 | 1815 | 1820 |

1601 – Elizabethan Poor Law passed

1793 – War with France begins

1815 – End of the Napoleonic wars; Corn Laws passed

THE OLD POOR LAW AND PRESSURE FOR CHANGE

The state originally took an interest in the poor during the 16th century and under Elizabeth I the basis of the Old Poor Law was established when, in 1601, legislation was formalised with the intention of managing the growth of poverty. The motivation behind this legislation was to provide social stability to prevent the spread of discontent or even rioting among the more abject members of the population. By passing the legislation, the government recognised the potential dangers of excessive poverty and therefore sought to address the issue before it threatened society at large. Even if the motivation was not entirely altruistic or born of any great sense of humanity, the passage of the Poor Law Act in 1601 evidenced the hint of a commitment by government to address the issue of poverty – a duty which has since become a primary responsibility of those in office.

The implementation and effectiveness of poor relief before 1834

The Poor Law Act of 1601 placed responsibility for dealing with poverty onto the local **parishes** and anyone seeking **poor relief** were sent back to the parish of their birth to receive this support. By the end of the 18th century, this system was under increasing pressure because of the growth in population, which consequently placed greater strain on the parishes to meet the demand for support.

Implementing poor relief, 1785–1834

The system of poor relief that was present in Britain after 1785 was still largely that introduced by Elizabethan legislation. Although improvements had been made to meet the changing needs of the destitute – orphans and the homeless, for example, could enter poorhouses which were established after 1723 – the fundamental principles remained the same. The implication of this was that as the country developed, the system of providing for its poorest inhabitants remained somewhat outdated, to the extent that by 1834 there was a need to radically transform the system.

In 1785, however, these problems were not yet anticipated and the Poor Law as it stood was felt to be an appropriate method for addressing the issue of poverty. This system was orientated around the concept of local responsibility and the main facility used to administer relief was the parish. Each county was divided up into these small church-based units and each was responsible for the people born and living within its borders. Following the Act of Settlement in 1662, membership of a particular parish was formalised as either: being born there; being resident there for a year and a day; having moved there to take up an apprenticeship or, in the case of women, if their husbands were from there. The obligations of a parish were quite broad and the cost of this obligation had to be met by the people residing within each parish. Under the existing law, the manner of relief was not specifically determined by government and therefore it was up to the parish what it did with its poor. Consequently, the quality of support was very dependent upon the extent of goodwill that existed in any given parish and this resulted in a haphazard response to a national problem.

1834 – Poor Law Amendment Act passed

1839 – Anti-Poor Law movement defeated

1844 – Outdoor Relief Prohibitory Order passed

1851 – *London Labour and London Poor* published

1859 – *Self Help* published

1869 – Charity Organisation Society formed

| 1825 | 1830 | 1835 | 1840 | 1845 | 1850 | 1855 | 1860 | 1865 | 1870 |

1832 – Royal Commission on Poor Relief set up; passage of the 'Great' Reform Act

1837 – The first part of *Oliver Twist* published; anti-Poor Law movement well underway

1842 – Outdoor Labour Test Order passed

1848 – Huddersfield workhouse scandal; *Mary Barton* published

1845 – Andover workhouse scandal

1867 – Metropolitan Poor Law Act passed

The most common mode of support that parishes offered was that of outdoor relief. This was the practice of giving money, food or clothes to the poor rather than placing them into an institution such as the poorhouses mentioned above. Originally conceived as a deterrent against idleness, these poorhouses required those within them to undertake work in return for assistance. Despite their objective to deter irresponsible claims for poor relief, by 1776 there were more than 2,000 such institutions in England, each containing between 20 and 50 inmates. These houses were very expensive to run and therefore in 1782 it was agreed in parliament that only orphaned children those who physically could not work by virtue of age, sickness or infirmity should be admitted. This became known as Gilbert's Act after Thomas Gilbert who introduced the initial bill. All other 'able-bodied' paupers should remain outside and be made to look after themselves, encouraged to find work or receive a basic provision to be determined by individual parishes.

In 1795, there was some effort to create a uniform provision for those claiming outdoor relief. This effort came from among parishes themselves and the resultant policy became known as the Speenhamland system after the Berkshire village in which it was created. This system sought to determine the value of relief to be given to those in need and it was tied to the cost of a gallon loaf of bread. Under this system the wages of a single male applicant for support would be made up to the cost of three loaves of bread. If he was married and with children, the price would be adjusted to include another one and a half loaves. For example, when a single gallon loaf of bread cost one shilling then a single man's wages would be made up to three shillings; if he had a wife and child his wages would be made up to six shillings. The money for this relief would come from the Poor Rate, which had been established in the 1601 legislation. This structure of working out the cost of relief was adopted by many parishes across the south of England and went some way to establish a sense of uniformity for managing the effects of poverty.

Although this system was very popular, it was by no means the only system employed and in other parts of the country alternative methods were developed to meet the growing demand for relief. Of particular note among these alternatives was the 'Roundsman' system, which sold the labour of paupers to local farmers or other employers at a reduced cost, with the difference being made up by the local parish from the Poor Rate. Paupers would be given tickets that they would have signed by the person employing them as they travelled around the parish seeking work and once signed for they would be paid. In many areas this system saw the auctioning of labour, with prices varying according to the time of year and the nature of the work undertaken. In addition to this system, some parishes also operated a 'labour rate' which paid money into a separate fund from the Poor Rate; the money from this fund was then used to pay paupers when they were employed to carry out work on behalf of the parish.

Each of these systems was designed to alleviate the effects of poverty while at the same time minimising the burden upon the parish ratepayers. They were generally administered by unpaid 'Overseers of the Poor' who would collect and distribute the Poor Rate under the authority of the Justice of the Peace (JP) from within the parish. However, as the population grew and the burden became even greater there was a move to formalise the process. In 1818, the Act for the Regulation of Parish Vestries and in 1819 the Act to Amend the Laws for Relief of the Poor allowed the creation of parish committees who had the power to scrutinise relief-giving and recommend the level of such provision. These committees were to be elected by the ratepayers themselves and placed greater authority with private citizens, given it was they who paid for relief. The creation of these committees tightened up the qualification for relief, as instead of needing the approval of one JP they required two; the purpose of this was to reduce the likelihood of 'soft' JPs granting relief on spurious evidence. The adoption of this particular measure signified a growing awareness of the level of demand and concern over the expense that was being incurred.

The effectiveness of poor relief, 1785–1834

The efficacy of these parish-based systems was significantly limited because of the inconsistent manner in which they operated. Since each parish acted independently and ran different systems, there was no co-ordinated country-wide response, which therefore reduced its overall effectiveness at a national level. This problem became magnified because of the rapid growth in the population, which created an overwhelming demand for relief. When the first census was taken in 1801, the population of England and Wales was officially declared at nine million – more than double that when the Elizabethan Poor Law was first established. Coupled with this increase was also the impact of industrialisation, which saw a reduction in employment opportunities for many people as their labour was supplemented by the use of machines. Although these helped to promote employment in the towns, in the countryside the already season-dependent employment of agricultural labourers was made even more fragile by the introduction of labour-saving machines, which forced workers to apply for relief more frequently. In combination, these events placed a significant strain upon the capacity to provide poor relief and this was only made worse during the wars with France between 1793 and 1815 when the cost of living rose.

During this period the inadequacies of the existing systems were brought starkly to the attention of the public. Due to the lack of foreign competition, the price of bread rose substantially and this forced more people to claim poor relief in order to feed their families. The widely adopted Speenhamland system which was tied to the price of bread placed greater strain upon the funds available and required an additional rate to be introduced in several parishes, which also raised disaffection from those having to pay this charge. Given the increasing cost it promoted, the Speenhamland system came under some criticism, not least because of the lack of incentive it encouraged for either the farmer to pay good wages or the labourer to try and earn them or to restrict his family.

EXTRACT

From Luiza Chwialkowska, 'Subsidies paid in loaves of bread in England in the 1700s', in the *National Post* (Canada), 12 December 2000.

> The first enactment of a guaranteed income may have been in 1795 in England, where the Speenhamland system extended subsidies for the infirm to include able-bodied workers... The system revealed the challenge inherent in designing such a policy; the supplement served as a subsidy that allowed employers to hire workers at below-subsistence wages, and allowed landlords to raise rents. Meanwhile, some workers found themselves better off collecting benefits than working.

Even after the conclusion of war, the British economy entered depression as trade was slow to develop again and government contracts came to an end. Additionally, the thousands of soldiers returning home needed to find employment and this was not in plentiful supply. Under these conditions applications for relief continued to remain high and the money spent on this need averaged £6.4 million between the years 1814 and 1818.

Such spending drew significant protestation from ratepayers and the owners of property as well as from the poor themselves – especially in the rural areas where they found that continued high prices due to the passage of the Corn Law (see page 18) were only made worse by the lack of employment opportunities which industrialisation had caused. The failure to provide adequately for the poor saw the outbreak of discontent and rioting become increasingly common, with the most famous example being the 'Swing Riots' that took place throughout 1830 (see page 52). These riots were mostly the result of falling wages and reduced employment, but it is interesting that the counties where they were most prevalent were also counties where the Speenhamland system of poor relief was widely used. The use of this system had meant that farmers often reduced wages, believing that the shortfall would be made up by the Poor Rate, so when further cuts were made and employment reduced, the impact in these counties was felt much more acutely. It would be too simplistic to suggest one informed the other, but given the way in which the system operated – encouraging reduced wages – it would be reasonable to consider that it at least contributed to the falling wages and lack of meaningful employment.

Urban poor relief

The need for poor relief was not confined to the rural areas and even though employment was more readily available in the new towns and cities, there was still a need for provision. Between 1802 and 1803, ten percent of those in the north received relief in contrast to around 23 percent in the south. In the case of these urban areas, wages for the most part were very low – usually not more than 12 shillings a week. During periods of economic decline, when wages were either reduced or the workforce was made temporarily unemployed, the concentrated numbers of people relying on such meagre wages found themselves having to apply for relief in order to try to cover their outgoings, which often amounted to little more than the bare necessities for living. Such was the organisation of poor relief that, during these times of increased economic hardship, the system could not sustain such concentrated demand. Disaffection would therefore emerge here also, spilling out into riots and feeding the general discontent of those people struggling to get by.

Against such a riotous background and under growing pressure for some improvement to the way poor relief was administered, the government set up a Royal Commission in 1832 to investigate the existing system and to establish whether there was a need for something new.

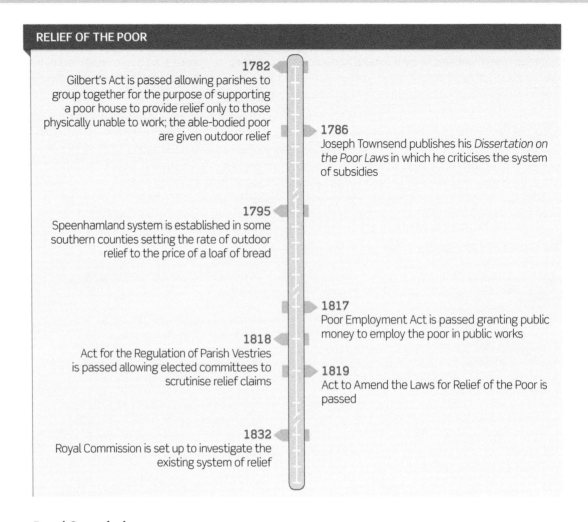

RELIEF OF THE POOR

1782
Gilbert's Act is passed allowing parishes to group together for the purpose of supporting a poor house to provide relief only to those physically unable to work; the able-bodied poor are given outdoor relief

1786
Joseph Townsend publishes his *Dissertation on the Poor Laws* in which he criticises the system of subsidies

1795
Speenhamland system is established in some southern counties setting the rate of outdoor relief to the price of a loaf of bread

1817
Poor Employment Act is passed granting public money to employ the poor in public works

1818
Act for the Regulation of Parish Vestries is passed allowing elected committees to scrutinise relief claims

1819
Act to Amend the Laws for Relief of the Poor is passed

1832
Royal Commission is set up to investigate the existing system of relief

Royal Commission

The Royal Commission was established on 1 February 1832 and the nine commissioners, including the political economist Nassau Senior and Edwin Chadwick (see pages 55 and 59), sought to make recommendations for the improvement of the Poor Law system. They gathered evidence from across the country to this effect by using 'scientific' methods, including the use of questionnaires which were sent out to 15,000 parishes, although only ten percent of these received a response.

SOURCE

A sample question from the Royal Commission into the Poor Law's questionnaire which was sent out in 1832.

> Have you any, and how many, able-bodied labourers in the employment of individuals receiving allowance or regular relief from your parish on their own account, or on that of their families: and if on account of their families, at what number of children does it begin?

There was significant criticism by advocates of the current system regarding the methods employed by the investigators – many of the questions asked were deliberately phrased awkwardly and it was claimed that Senior began writing the report before all the data were collected. The findings of the investigation were, however, very appealing for the government. The final report found that the existing system was woefully inadequate in terms of the effectiveness of its provision and also the excessive cost it demanded. The principle reasons for this, it suggested, were the lack of uniformity and the ease with which unscrupulous people could take advantage of it. In consequence the following recommendations were made:

- the removal of outdoor relief altogether

- the use of more punishing workhouses to act as a deterrent to those seeking relief

- the grouping of parishes together so that they could manage these workhouses more effectively

- the creation of a central board to implement and oversee the new system.

The recommendations proposed a radical overhaul of the present system and sought a more centralised and punishing system to replace what was believed to be a lenient and easily manipulated one.

Attitudes towards the poor

The investigation undertaken by the Royal Commission and the report of its findings is a useful barometer by which to gauge the level of feeling existing towards the poor in Britain. While there is a long history of caring for those in financial distress, towards the end of the 18th century there had emerged a more cynical attitude towards the poorer elements of Britain's increasingly affluent society. Rather than a paternalistic concern for the less fortunate, there was a harder edge to thoughts about the issue of poverty. This attitude was manifested in two distinct viewpoints: the first was a fairly fatalistic one, which simply acknowledged that in any society there is always poverty and this is a cross to bear; the second was a more moralistic approach, which maintained that poverty was the result of a weakness of character. Each of these views enjoyed significant influence throughout the late 18th and 19th centuries and certainly informed the action taken by government to address the issue at this time.

The basis of each of these positions is hard to determine specifically but certainly some of the causes lay with the rapid developments in society which took place after the start of the Industrial Revolution. Such was the magnitude of this change, which saw the rapid growth of economic prosperity, that people were fearful of it all disappearing just as quickly. For a majority of people who made their fortunes, the fear of being reduced to penury prompted them to seek out reasons why poverty befell individuals so that they might separate themselves from that situation and claim some degree of illusory protection.

Each position also carried a different level of feeling toward 'the poor'. The first involved a sense of resigned pity while the second was imbued with a greater sense of disgust, which placed blame for the condition of the poor on the poor themselves. These views reflect the range of opinion that existed between 1785 and 1870 and were perhaps influenced by earlier distinctions made about the type of people who required poor relief. By the end of the 18th century, British society had inherited the dominant belief that 'the poor' could be divided into two distinct groups: the 'deserving poor' and the 'undeserving poor'. The former were those who were unable to help themselves: the elderly or sick, orphans and the infirm. These people deserved some support and pity. The second group, however, was viewed with more scorn and deemed 'undeserving' of help. These were the able-bodied men and women who simply could not, or as was the general conception, would not find work for themselves. These people were the weak characters whose position was nobody's fault but their own. The dominance of these categories greatly informed opinions of the poor and adherence to one of them determined the manner of response offered to the claim that was made. For those deserving of help they were often found room in the poor house, while those less deserving were forced to look after themselves. They would not be left to starve and outdoor relief was provided, but they were encouraged to find employment. In this last endeavour the

government took a lead by passing the Poor Employment Act in 1817 which made public money available to employ able-bodied paupers on public works such as road building.

SOURCE
2

A Miserable Plight, a cartoon commenting on the practice of separating husbands from wives when entering the poor house. Drawn by Thomas Hood and published in *The Comic Magazine,* London 1832.

The distinction made over entitlement mirrored a broader attitude relating to poverty and its effects. Society did not have a problem with the existence of poverty itself as this was generally regarded as a necessary state to encourage hard work. In the interest of progress people needed a reason to push themselves and if there was a fear of destitution then they would continually strive to avoid falling into that situation. By contrast, the culture of dependence that pauperism encouraged was a social evil because it took away self-reliance and made people **indolent**. Here, then, it is easier to understand the mixed attitudes levelled at the poor in Britain. Those who could not provide for themselves were examples of genuine poverty which, though hard on them, provided the necessary example to others; the able-bodied 'undeserving poor' were the social menace that needed to be challenged.

KEY TERM

Indolence
A term used to describe laziness or general idleness.

Ideological pressures

Critical opinion: Thomas Malthus and Joseph Townsend

Chief among those who criticised the relief system on the grounds that it encouraged idleness were the physician and vicar of Pewsey, Joseph Townsend and, more famously, Thomas Malthus, whose work on population growth raised questions about the provision of poor relief and reflected his own judgement that there should be no such provision at all. Each of these individuals characterised the very essence of the moralistic arguments and believed that, for the general improvement of society, there was a need for a number within the population to feel the hardship that poverty brought. Townsend openly criticised the policy of poor relief in his 1786 *Dissertation on the Poor Laws* where he claimed that rather than helping society, it actively promoted its worse characteristics by denying the full extent of the lesson that real poverty could provide.

EXTEND YOUR KNOWLEDGE

Thomas Robert Malthus (1766–1834)

Thomas Malthus was an English academic who is most famous for his work on population growth and establishing the 'Malthusian catastrophe'. This theory, which he outlined in his 1798 publication *An Essay on the Principle of Population*, demonstrated that population grows exponentially while food growth does so arithmetically. Eventually, therefore, populations will outstrip the supply of food. He also maintained, however, that there were natural ways to prevent such a catastrophe and that the provision of poor relief was adding an artificial barrier to prevent these remedies. His work influenced the later field of evolutionary biology and was read by Charles Darwin among others. To this day he remains a much-discussed figure whose ideas prompt great controversy.

SOURCE

From Joseph Townsend's *Dissertation on the Poor Laws*, published in 1786.

Hunger will tame the fiercest animals, it will teach decency and civility, obedience and subjection, to the most perverse. In general it is only hunger that can spur and goad them [the poor] on to labour; yet our laws have said they shall never hunger.

The arguments of these men quickly achieved a dominant position within society during the early years of the 19th century. As industrialisation continued apace, the opportunities for employment expanded and these openings solidified the notion that pauperism was the result of laziness and a general desire among some to live off the generosity of others, rather than take advantage of the chances that the growth in new industries offered. This particular attitude would later be embodied within the 'New Poor Law' when it was introduced in 1834.

The ideas presented by Malthus and Townsend contributed to a broader ideological divide over how to deal with poverty and pauperism in Britain. The growth in population exacerbated the problem of pauperism and drew diverse opinion as to how best to manage the issue. Here there was a chasm between the Whigs and Tories who each had their own opinion. Broadly, there were three distinct views that formed the basis of the reform debate:

- those who wanted to maintain the current system

- those who wanted to change it a little

- those who wanted to transform it radically.

The first view was primarily adopted by humanitarians and paternalistic Tories who maintained that there was a humane imperative and social responsibility to provide care for the less fortunate. In part this view was also motivated by the fear that not to do so might invite greater disaffection among that class of people.

The second group adopted the same motivations as the first but was shocked at the spiralling cost and wanted to reduce this by making some changes.

The third group, broadly made up of Whigs, favoured a radical overhaul of the system, believing it to be both outdated and ineffective within industrialising Britain.

The first two groups adopted the fatalistic attitude mentioned earlier: that poverty and pauperism was inevitable and was something that those with the means had a moral obligation to help. This was very much the traditional perspective that had promoted the very concept of poor relief in previous centuries. It supported the existing system of relief on the grounds that parishes were best placed to deal with the issues in their areas.

The greatest pressure came from the third group, which was responding to the growing influence of the free market. In its view, the current system was both inefficient and not conducive to the overall improvement of society. This group adopted the arguments of the economist David Ricardo and 'wage fund theory' and attached them to the wider social attitude promoted by Townsend, which saw pauperism as being the result of idleness. This theory suggested that the money spent on relief by the employer paying the Poor Rate was reducing the amount of money that the same employer could be using to pay wages to his workers. In this analysis the poor were taking from those willing to work, which harmed both the prosperity of those workers and also the businesses in which they were employed. This argument highlighted the twin costs of relief: the real expenditure going out every week and also the potential cost to businesses in the longer term. From this perspective those claiming relief were seen as actually harming the economy and therefore they should be prevented from doing so. In the worsening economic climate of the 1830s, the merits of this argument were more readily seen by the middle and upper classes and therefore when the Royal Commission was appointed it was with the intention of establishing a motive for change.

Progressive opinion: Thomas Paine and Robert Owen

Certainly, there was a dominant trend towards thinking more critically about the way to deal with poverty, and especially pauperism, in Britain, but there were also more progressive opinions that met with some sympathy. First among these opinions was that of Thomas Paine, whose radical political beliefs outlined in his seminal work *Rights of Man* were also reflected in his attitude towards government responsibility and the general issue of poverty. As part of his vision of a democratic country, Paine believed that government should plan for the welfare of its people and within the pages of *Rights of Man* also laid out a policy for achieving this. His ideas included a pension provision for those over the age of 50 and also child benefits in the form of £4 per year for each child under 14, for 250,000 destitute families. Unlike other assessments of poverty, Paine felt that it was not the fault of the people themselves but rather the failure of government to support them adequately.

Rather than place responsibility with government, the social reformer Robert Owen promoted the idea that people would help themselves if given the chance. His belief was that character was built through a person's circumstances and this encouraged him to set up model communities where people were given the chance of self-improvement. His model factory in New Lanark in Scotland provided education as well as good working conditions with the aim of 'raising up' the working people. By offering them a means to better themselves, Owen challenged the dominant notion of indolence by suggesting that people, if given the chance, would seek to improve themselves. He maintained that through co-operative practices poverty could be challenged and people encouraged to build themselves better futures. His success at New Lanark inspired a raft of co-operative movements but his suggestions for tackling poverty specifically were ignored by the government, which found the arguments of Townsend and Malthus more persuasive and more popular.

The views of Paine and Owen found some support from individual social progressives, such as Sir Titus Salt who set up his own model community in Saltaire in 1848, but generally they were isolated affairs as the dominant ideology lay with more conservative thinkers. Placing blame on the people allowed the government to remain faithful to the idea of '*laissez-faire*ism' which influenced economic thought.

Utilitarianism: Jeremy Bentham

Another influential view that gained prominence in the early 19th century was that of Jeremy Bentham, whose theory of Utilitarianism was increasingly popular among the growing middle class. This theory was predicated on the belief that human nature was motivated by only two things: pleasure and pain. On this foundation, Bentham maintained that the only principle on which government should act was to promote the 'greatest happiness (pleasure) for the greatest number'. Bentham proclaimed that there ought to be an in-depth investigation into the needs of the poor and that any solution should be measured by reference to his happiness principle, first expounded in 1789. Using this idea, Bentham originally proposed the establishment of a National Charity Company in 1796, which would be entrusted with the responsibility of the country's poor. Workhouses would be set up along the lines of his **panopticon** prison model and the company would even be able to bring in anyone unable to prove their ability to look after themselves. Once in these workhouses the inmates would be put to work to pay for their maintenance and also provide a profit for the company shareholders. The assistance that would be provided by the company would not be more than was necessary for reasonable subsistence so that those individuals might become motivated to improve themselves upon their exit. The rationale for this quite harsh approach to poor relief was the happiness principle itself; in order to secure happiness everyone needed to be safe from the threat of starvation. By putting paupers to work, Bentham's company would also contribute to the improvement of society at large – thus supporting the happiness of the greatest number, by helping to provide new infrastructures and services that were increasingly needed. This model also took into account the expense of the current poor relief system and the prevailing attitudes relating to pauperism, offering a neat solution to both these concerns.

EXTEND YOUR KNOWLEDGE

Jeremy Bentham (1748–1832)
Jeremy Bentham was an English philosopher whose interests spanned law, economics and social reform. As an economist he supported the ideas of Adam Smith although he felt Smith failed to follow his own principles at times. He is best known for his work of 1789, *An Introduction to the Principles of Morals and Legislation*, which outlined his own theory of 'Utilitarianism' in which he maintained that people are motivated by pain and pleasure and therefore the only principles on which government should act are those which ensure the greatest happiness for the greatest number.

Utilitarianism was a significant influence upon future Poor Law relief. Its manifestation in the form of the centralised National Charity Company proposal offered a clear blueprint for the reform of the poorhouses which would take place after 1834. The real influence of Bentham's philosophy, however, lay in the simple enumeration of need that it was founded upon. The happiness principle could be reduced to a very simple equation which appealed to many reformers. If human nature was motivated by pleasure or pain then to promote less reliance on relief it would be a natural endeavour to make that relief as unpleasant as possible so as to reduce interest in it. This analysis formed the basis of the Poor Law amendment drive which took place after 1815 and it influenced the findings of the Royal Commission by adding intellectual weight to the already impressive demand for reform.

Financial pressures for change

The cost of maintaining the Old Poor Law had, by 1834, become prohibitive given the escalation in those claiming relief after 1815. The end of the French wars brought growing misery for many of Britain's poorest members: military contracts ended which affected manufacturing and returning soldiers competed for the diminishing number of jobs as industries laid off excess workers and Britain entered a depression. During these years, poor relief expenditure approached two percent of the country's Gross National Product – spending between 1815 and 1833 did not dip below £5.7 million. Very quickly questions were being asked regarding the suitability of the parish-based system of charity in meeting the high demand made upon it.

The growing financial burden was met by the ratepayers in Britain – these varied dramatically in terms of means, but were all owners of property or long-term tenants who were able to maintain consistent employment. In both cases these were reasonably influential figures who, in many cases, could also vote in general elections. With the rising cost of the Poor Rate, this group became increasingly vocal about the need to address the problem of pauperism. Much of the argument was given credibility by David Ricardo, whose exposition of 'wage fund theory' particularly appealed to the growing industrial middle class.

The return of prosperity in the 1820s saw a decline in expenditure on poor relief – after 1824 the cost per head was 9s 2d compared to 11s 7d between 1819 and 1823; however, the rising number of low-paid workers was still costing large sums in Poor Rate payments. The move towards factory working as part of the wider impact of industrialisation created a dense working population of poorly paid individuals who could not afford to insulate themselves from economic downturns.

These people were at the mercy of the economic market such that when trade was good they had employment but as soon as trade declined they were laid off in droves. Since the majority of these poorest individuals could not pay into a pension fund there was little to support them at these times other than the Poor Rate. Within agriculture the pattern was the same except here labourers had even fewer employment opportunities as they were increasingly replaced by machines.

The problems which industrialisation brought with it only served to reinforce critical opinion of the existing poor relief as dependence grew during times of economic depression and vast numbers of labourers and poorly paid workers found themselves prevailing upon the goodwill of their parishes. Under the volume of such demand the amateur nature of this goodwill found it increasingly difficult to respond effectively and the expense involved made it prohibitive to do so.

ACTIVITY
KNOWLEDGE CHECK

Criticisms of the Old Poor Law

Having read through the material above, make a list of the criticisms levelled at the Old Poor Law. Using this list, which three criticisms do you feel are the most persuasive and why?

THINKING HISTORICALLY   Cause and consequence activity (4a&b)

Fragile history

Nothing that happens is inevitable. There were causes of change which did not have to develop as they did. Something could have altered or someone could have chosen differently. What actually occurred in the past did happen but it did not have to be like that.

Work on your own and answer the questions. When you have answered the questions, discuss the answers in groups.

Perceived reasons for the passage of the Poor Law Amendment Act

Development	Event	State of affairs	Event	Trigger event
A growing population and expanding economy	The introduction of the Speenhamland system in 1795	Growing disapproval of pauperism by government	Swing Riots in 1830	1832 Royal Commission into the Old Poor Law

1 Consider the introduction of the Speenhamland system and the growing government disapproval of the time.

   a) How did the introduction of the Speenhamland system affect the views of government?

   b) Had there been no government disapproval would the Speenhamland system still have been important?

2 What other aspects of the situation existing after 1795 would have been affected had there been no government disapproval?

3 Consider the growing population and expanding economy together with the Swing Riots and Royal Commission.

   a) How important were the growing population and expanding economy as causal factors of the two events?

   b) What might have happened had the Swing Riots not taken place?

4 What other consequences came about as a result of the information in the table above? Try to identify at least one consequence for each.

5 Choose one factor from the table above. How might the Poor Law Amendment Act have developed differently if this factor had not been present?

AS Level Exam-Style Question Section A

Was the rising cost of the Poor Rate in the years 1815–33 the main reason for the reform of the Old Poor Law in 1834? Explain your answer. (20 marks)

Tip

In this question you are asked to judge what the 'main' reason for reform is so be sure to include other reasons for reform.

THE IMPACT AND EFFECTIVENESS OF THE POOR LAW AMENDMENT ACT, 1834–47

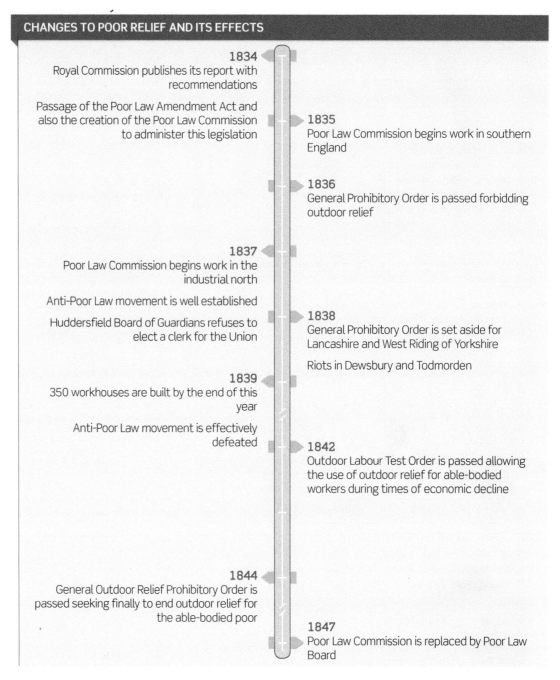

CHANGES TO POOR RELIEF AND ITS EFFECTS

1834
Royal Commission publishes its report with recommendations

Passage of the Poor Law Amendment Act and also the creation of the Poor Law Commission to administer this legislation

1835
Poor Law Commission begins work in southern England

1836
General Prohibitory Order is passed forbidding outdoor relief

1837
Poor Law Commission begins work in the industrial north

Anti-Poor Law movement is well established

Huddersfield Board of Guardians refuses to elect a clerk for the Union

1838
General Prohibitory Order is set aside for Lancashire and West Riding of Yorkshire

Riots in Dewsbury and Todmorden

1839
350 workhouses are built by the end of this year

Anti-Poor Law movement is effectively defeated

1842
Outdoor Labour Test Order is passed allowing the use of outdoor relief for able-bodied workers during times of economic decline

1844
General Outdoor Relief Prohibitory Order is passed seeking finally to end outdoor relief for the able-bodied poor

1847
Poor Law Commission is replaced by Poor Law Board

Given the limitations of the Old Poor Law, the Royal Commission's recommendations were adopted by parliament and in 1834 an Amendment Act was passed to improve the system of poor relief in Britain. Known as the Poor Law Amendment Act, this legislation outlined a much more punitive approach to relief and reflected the dominant view of those people who felt pauperism was a social evil which needed to be stemmed.

The provisions of the new Poor Law involved:

- setting up a central authority, the Poor Law Commission, to oversee the new legislation

- grouping parishes together and establishing within each cluster a workhouse that was to be the main source of relief, and in which inmates were to live in conditions that were worse than those of the poorest independent labourer; this was the principle of '**less eligibility**'

- discouraging outdoor relief for the able-bodied poor.

KEY TERM

Less eligibility
This was the term applied to the concept of deliberately making poor relief harsh so that only the most destitute and those truly unable to help themselves would apply for it.

The main feature of the legislation was the increased use of the poorhouses – now better known as workhouses – to manage the effects of poverty, although it did not specify how these were to be fully utilised. Beyond the more punitive features it encouraged, the Poor Law Amendment Act did not detail any specific guidelines for adoption and such details were left up to the **Poor Law Commission** which was established by the same Act.

The workhouse regime

Workhouses had been in existence prior to 1834 but under the Gilbert Act of 1782 they were to house only those unable to take care of themselves. Under the new legislation, however, the workhouse was to become the principal means by which to effect relief and they were intended as a deterrent to those seeking help. In this manner the traditional means of outdoor relief was to be abandoned and replaced by a strict workhouse regime designed to put off all but the most needy.

The rationale behind this policy was taken directly from the 'indolence view' of pauperism which had gained prominence during the early decades of the 19th century. Here it was believed that the allowance systems such as Speenhamland had made it too easy to claim support and even allowed people to manipulate that support for personal gain – in the case of Speenhamland by rewarding larger families. Under the new provisions any claimants would be denied outdoor relief and instead offered entry into the workhouse where they would be made less comfortable than those who chose to stay outside. On this 'test' it was believed that only the genuinely destitute would accept the workhouse and any others would seek alternative means of supporting themselves. In either case the burden upon the poor relief would be significantly reduced. This idea of self-selection by means of deterrence became known as 'less eligibility' and formed the bedrock of the New Poor Law.

To implement this policy a Poor Law Commission was established to oversee the construction and running of the new system. This commission organised the 15,000 existing parishes into 600 larger unions so as to allow for larger workhouses to be built for common usage. It also appointed boards of local men as governors of these unions to be responsible for the running of the new institutions. Known as 'guardians of the Poor Law' these men were responsible for finding the funds to build any new workhouses that were required, as the Amendment Act did not change the existing practice of each parish being responsible for its own paupers.

Funds continued to be raised through the Poor Rate and by 1839 had instituted the building of 350 workhouses. The construction of these institutions were very expensive – as an example, the workhouse in Banbury to house 300 people built in 1835 cost £6,200. There was, therefore, a general desire among guardians to keep running costs as little as possible so as to minimise the financial burden to themselves as ratepayers. Therefore the workhouses were usually very basic in their furnishing, with only bare essentials and no comforts. This was often because of the financial implications, but it also suited the harder line that these institutions were encouraged to maintain with regard to the policy of 'less eligibility'.

To promote the effectiveness of this policy, the workhouses were deliberately made unpleasant. With inmates typically working a 10-hour day excluding breaks for meals and prayers, there was no spare time. The work they were made to do varied from house to house and depended very much on what people could physically do. In the case of 'The Spike' in Guildford, vagrant inmates were made to break stones for use in road-building, while the Newbury workhouse in Berkshire ran a woollen interest which made the inmates operate each of the processes involved in the manufacture of textiles. In the interests of promoting moral behaviour many institutions, such as that in Southwell under the management of Rev. Thomas Becher, also banned the use of beer, snuff or tobacco. In return for the work undertaken by the poor they would receive a bed and a basic diet of bread, cheese and gruel (a thick porridge) while to drink all they had was water. Once a week they would get some soup, meat and potatoes and tea was a privilege reserved for the elderly. What was perhaps more debilitating than the work or diet, however, was the depersonalisation that the institutions instilled. As was common across the country, the workhouses made their inmates wear the same uniform and separated men from women; some even made distinctions between the 'deserving' and 'undeserving'. For the duration of their time on relief they would remain divided, and if families entered together once they were separated they often never saw one another until they left. Such was the nature of the workhouse regime that for many, as intended, entry became a last resort, but even so they were still filled with people, as poor wages, cold winters and fluctuating economic conditions left them with little choice.

EXTRACT

2 'A description of life in a workhouse' from *The Workhouse* by Jennie Walters.

Going into the workhouse was almost always a desperate act of last resort. It was likely to be a degrading, humiliating experience. Arriving at the workhouse gates, the prospective inmate would be interviewed by the warden or matron, then stripped, washed and given a haircut. Their clothes were taken away (sometimes burnt) and they would be issued with a uniform made from coarse, hardwearing material. Families were split up, with men, women and children housed in separate wings and not allowed to communicate with each other even in communal areas (although elderly couples could sometimes stay together).

SOURCE

4 A workhouse design to house 200 paupers, drawn by Sampson Kempthorne and issued by the Poor Law Commission in 1836. Note particularly the separate facilities presented.

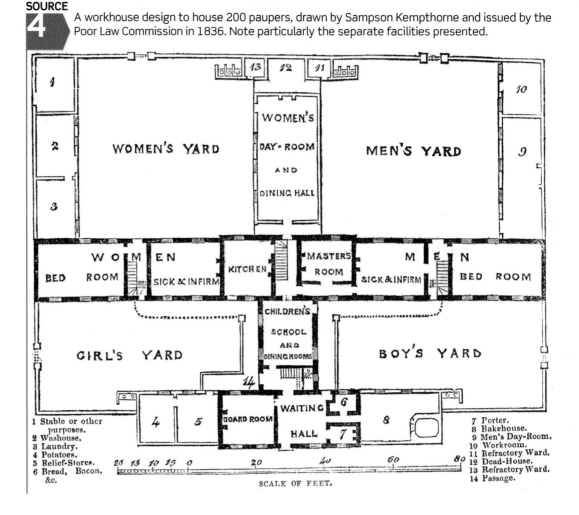

Less eligibility

Offer a brief critical assessment of this idea, using both the material provided and your own knowledge. When offering your assessment you should consider social attitudes as well as the physical impact of the idea.

The continuation of outdoor relief

Despite the intention of banning outdoor relief, the reality was that such practices continued. The New Poor Law presented the impression that relief would be more uniformly and centrally organised. However, in practice the responsibility of delivering relief remained substantially at the discretion of the locally appointed guardians. If claims were made by people who had a dwelling then often relief would still be granted even though the law stated otherwise. The motivation for this is arguably one of cost rather than any general disagreement with the law itself. The expense of running a workhouse and maintaining those in it was far more expensive than giving relief to those 'on the outside' – by 1862 it would cost 4s 8d to keep a pauper in an institution but only 2s 3d to maintain a pauper on outdoor relief. Therefore this was often preferable to the guardians whose principal aim was to reduce the cost to their parishes.

Additionally, many guardians in the north of the country where growing industry offered significant employment opportunities, resisted the demand to build expensive workhouses, on the basis that much of the poverty that affected them was cyclical and dependent upon fluctuations within the global economy. During strong economic growth, the Poor Rate here was often reduced as employers had plenty of jobs available; it was only when depression set in and markets shrank that the Poor Rates became excessive due to the vast numbers of workers then made unemployed. For the guardians in the north there was substantial reluctance to spend huge sums of money – around £6,200 if the earlier Banbury example is considered – on building workhouses, when in their eyes they would be almost empty for long periods when the economy was good.

Even in the rural areas where the Poor Rate had often been higher because of the consistent vulnerability of employment opportunities, there existed some opposition to ending outdoor relief. Here the argument was equally plain: if the cost of maintaining a pauper within the workhouse was more than offering short-term contracts and some provision of outdoor relief when labourers needed to be laid off, then this was the preferred action. The economic historian George Boyer has estimated that the cost of indoor relief was between 50 and 100 percent more expensive than outdoor provision in the countryside and therefore when faced with these charges farmers opted to retain the older practice despite the legal objection that existed. For these farmers there was also the added incentive of being able to benefit from providing some form of employment albeit short term rather than paying for the same individual to remain in the workhouse.

With such a divisive attitude prevalent across the country and coming from those who were imagined to support the measure, the New Poor Law did not achieve the immediate success its advocates had intended. Nor would it completely resolve the problem of pauperism, which saw no marked reduction in the immediate years after its introduction. Rather than create a watertight system which could offer a more effective solution, the existence of opposition meant there remained significant loopholes and, more importantly, a lack of concerted willingness to adopt the scheme. Such was the level of opposition to 'indoor relief' in Lancashire and Yorkshire that by 1838 the Poor Law Commission had sanctioned the use of traditional methods should the need arise. As suggested by H. Longley in his study of the Poor Law in 1876, without the full support of those who were entrusted to uphold the new law, that law would always struggle to achieve its intended goal. Simply put, people would not accept that it was applicable to them if the measures were not consistently applied.

A Level Exam-Style Question Section A

To what extent were the provisions of the Poor Law Amendment Act a real departure from poor relief efforts in the years 1785–1834? (20 marks)

Tip
When answering this question focus on the key words being used, in this case the phrase 'real departure' – what might this mean?

Opposition to the Poor Law

The failure of the New Poor Law to stamp out many of the old practices was indicative of the level of support it enjoyed. While it passed through parliament with limited opposition, the Act itself was a product of ideological prejudice. It ignored some realistic criticisms regarding the financial implications of building such a large-scale infrastructure. It was also determined to promote a particular message which antagonised many people in Britain who felt that the new system was excessively severe without fully recognising the problem it sought to resolve.

These criticisms were broadly felt from both those within parliament and those on the outside. Among the political opposition were Tories who objected out of a general sense of partisanship, given the measure was passed by the Whigs. They also objected to the centralised nature of this new system, particularly the co-ordination of the new legislation by Boards of Guardians under the appointment of the Poor Law Commission, which they felt undermined the existing independence of the local magistrates. In opposition to the Act, *The Times* came out publicly against it on 30 April 1834 and ran an ongoing debate on the legislation with the *Morning Chronicle*. Despite several high-profile supporters, including Robert Peel and the Duke of Wellington, Tories were generally fearful of the increasing role of government in affairs that had hitherto remained the preserve of private citizens. Part of their opposition also came from a more paternalistic sense of morality, which promoted the same sense of social responsibility that motivated William Pitt's attempt to introduce poor reform in 1796 when he tried to get the Speenhamland system adopted nationally. For these Tories the new system was a callous one which ignored the 'poor unfortunates' who had not had the same advantages as the best in society, whose duty it was, therefore, to take care of them.

Echoing a similar sentiment regarding the barbarity of the new system, radical politicians were equally disdainful of it. William Cobbett objected on the grounds that the Act removed the 'right' to relief by making those claimants for it seem like criminals. For him the New Poor Law abandoned the un-named but humane arrangement between rich and poor where one would support the other in the event of need. These views went beyond simple party politics and addressed a growing perception that those in power had little regard for the experiences of the poorest in society.

If opposition in parliament hinged on such high-minded concepts as party ideology and the nobility of social responsibility, the opposition from the people themselves was more pedestrian. Motivated by the sense that the government just wanted to save money and make their lives harder, there was substantial criticism of the Act when attempts were taken to implement it. Initial opposition came from rural areas like East Anglia and other southern counties, which saw a series of riots in 1835 against the new measures. In May, the parish union of Ampthill in Bedfordshire saw a particularly violent riot involving between 300 and 500 people. The rioters demanded 'money or blood' and attacked officials in the area. The event resulted in the **Riot Act** being read and the arrest of four men at its conclusion. Similar 'money or blood' riots occurred in East Kent, while in December the workhouse at Bulcamp in Suffolk was attacked by a mob of around 200. Specifically these events were prompted by the removal of outdoor support and the associated belief that the new laws were designed to save money rather than help the people.

KEY TERM

Riot Act
This is a piece of legislation that was passed in 1714 which allowed local authorities to declare groups of 12 or more an illegal assembly. Once the Act was read it also empowered the authorities to use punitive measures to regain order and absolved them of any criminal charges if people were injured or killed while doing so.

Despite evident disaffection with the New Poor Law, the opposition of the southern counties did not greatly affect the implementation of the legislation and by 1836 the workhouse system was generally well established in these areas. The reason for such a quick reversal can be seen in the manner of the opposition itself. The riots that took place were not well organised and nor were they united in their efforts. Despite sharing a general sympathy for the Old Poor Law, each area had operated a different system of relief and therefore what they sought to defend varied. Without effective co-ordination and a common aim the riots were effectively an emotive reaction to change, which soon 'disappeared' in the face of robust authority. The eventual submissiveness of the south, however, did not mark the end of opposition. When the commissioners undertook to introduce the scheme in the north in 1836, there was an even greater, and much more organised, defence of the old system.

The basis of the opposition in the north was irrelevance. To those in the urban centres, densely packed with workers who toiled in the mills and factories that blanketed the region, the New Poor Law had no place. It did not address the problems they encountered as their situation was entirely different from that of the agricultural south. The Poor Rate in the north was lower owing to the greater number of people employed and the permanency of the workhouse solution did not suit the pattern of cyclical unemployment that tended to occur in the region. Here, when the economy declined, everyone was temporarily out of work but this always recovered and therefore the expense of the workhouse system was felt to be unnecessary when, for the brief periods of high unemployment, the existing practice of outdoor relief would be sufficient.

Opposition was mostly organised by Tory radical reformers such as the MP Michael Sadler and Richard Oastler who had each been prominent in the campaign for factory reform in the early 1830s (see Chapter 2). The experience of these men gave the anti-Poor Law movement in the north a much more organised means of challenge, which significantly delayed the implementation of the Act in that area. In the West Riding of Yorkshire and Lancashire in particular, this movement enjoyed considerable support, and the Act was effectively attacked through public speeches and printed articles deliberately designed to raise opposition to the measures by playing on emotive fears among the population.

EXTEND YOUR KNOWLEDGE

Richard Oastler (1789–1861)

Richard Oastler was an industrial reformer and self-proclaimed Tory radical who took a prominent role in the Ten Hour Movement demanding a shortening of the working day, which eventually led to the passage of the 1847 Ten Hour Act.

Sympathetic to the plight of workers, Oastler objected to the Poor Law Amendment Act because it forced labourers to work in return for poor wages. Having spoken out publicly against the New Poor Law, he was dismissed from his employment as an Estate Manager in May 1838 and then imprisoned in 1840 for being unable to pay his debts. Friends and working people clubbed together to pay the debts on his behalf and in 1844 he was released.

SOURCE

5 From the radical newspaper *The Northern Liberator*, dated 12 January 1839, commenting on a banned propaganda pamphlet against the Poor Law entitled *The Book of Murder*. This had circulated throughout the late 1830s and intended to incite opposition by suggesting the Poor Law Commission was considering infanticide to reduce the cost of poor relief.

We see that our exposure of this shocking publication has done its work, and that the country rings with execrations of it and of its author or authors.

The Rev. Mr. Stephens amongst others, our readers will see, has made good use of it. The hack-slave *Globe* half denies its existence and then says "even if it be a bad joke, the author should be punished." We repeat WE HAVE the murder pamphlet; we quoted it *verbatim et liberatim* in our dissection of it; and it is NO JOKE!!

It is a *bona-fide*, grave, earnest, scientific proposal to murder every third infant (with a few exceptions) by "painless extinction" by means of (carbonic acid) "gas". Who may be *Marcus* its author, we know not. Certain it is that it cannot have been written by any Christian, nor by any infidel who admits the beautiful morality of the New and much of the Old Testament; nor by any person unhardened by doctrines subversive of humanity as well as charity. By a Malthusian it MUST have been written. Now Lord Brougham is a defender of Malthus to the uttermost horrors of his doctrine. Lord Howick is the same. Mr. Place, the drawer up of the horrid bill, is the same. The villainous Commissioners are their agent to carry out these execrable doctrines with effect. Amongst THE GANG then, the authorship rests. We are well read in "styles"; and we say that *Marcus,* whoever he be, has read Jeremy Bentham's works much; and that the style is tinged with that of the Malthusian sage.

ACTIVITY
WRITING

Emotive language

Emotive language is a method of eliciting an emotional response from readers by deliberately using phrases that encourage such a reaction.

Having read the extract from the newspaper article in Source 5, answer the following questions:

1 Can you identify any words and phrases that are used to generate the 'emotive impact' in the article?

2 If the intention was to be more neutral then which words could you use instead to tone down the message?

Although in the case of the 'Book of Murder' the content lacked credibility and was, in fact, entirely fictitious, the impact of methods such as these was given additional impetus when, after 1837, a trade depression set in and people in the north found themselves unemployed en masse. Under financial pressures the inflammatory speeches and articles enjoyed greater poignancy and the working people in the north reacted aggressively when they were denied the support they had traditionally been offered. Riots in Bradford during 1837 and then in Dewsbury and Todmorden in 1838 underlined conclusively the level of northern discontent and the home secretary, Lord John Russell, urged the Poor Law Commission to consider some compromise.

The northern opposition was given a more threatening demeanour than its southern counterparts because of the alliance that was formed between the middle and working class in opposition to the new legislation. The motives of the working class are well evident but the respectable middle classes were also outraged by the encroachment on their authority by the more interventionist Act. In the eyes of those who administered the Poor Rate in the North, they had always prosecuted their obligation in a humane and effective manner which had consistently maintained a stable society during depressed times. The institution of a more centralised workhouse-based system was viewed as an affront to their own authority and therefore they obstructed the new measure at any opportunity they had. Perhaps the best example of this comes from Huddersfield in 1837 when the Board of Guardians refused to elect an administrator for the newly amalgamated union of parishes and the local magistrate would not intervene to force the appointment. Despite strong pressure from the secretary of the Poor Law Commission, Edwin Chadwick, the guardians remained resolute in their defiance and no clerk was ever appointed.

In the face of such resistance, the Poor Law Commission, in 1838, allowed the Boards of Guardians to continue giving relief in the traditional manner without any judgement on the nature of relief that able-bodied paupers were to receive. By setting aside the General Outdoor Relief Prohibitory Order which had sought to ban the use of outdoor relief, the amalgamated parish unions of Lancashire and the West Riding were permitted to offer support as they saw fit and as such they never enforced the workhouse test and even granted relief in the event of inadequate wages being earned for several individuals.

By removing the obligation to deny outdoor relief to able-bodied persons, the Commission acknowledged the independence of the local guardians to make decisions based upon their own circumstances; the concept of forcing temporarily out-of-work individuals into workhouses was seen in the North as excessive and entirely unnecessary and their opposition stemmed from this belief. The compromise issued by the Commission removed the sting from the anti-Poor Law movement and after 1839 it began to fracture as new causes emerged in the form of Chartism (see Chapter 1) and many of the middle-class supporters retreated into their living rooms. Opposition to the New Poor Law had been considerable when it was first introduced after 1834 but by the end of the decade this opposition was waning. The intractability of the Poor Law Commission, driven by a strong sense of moral right, had maintained the momentum to impose the necessary changes, which were eventually accepted by the masses. The final product was certainly not that which had been envisioned by its creators; the continuation of outdoor relief was not popular with those who wanted to enforce 'less eligibility' but what had been achieved was significantly less accommodating to those deemed 'undeserving'. Despite these changes, however, outdoor relief remained the most common form of relief throughout the century.

A Level Exam-Style Question Section A

Outdoor relief continued after 1834.

To what extent did the relief of poverty change in the years 1815–47? (20 marks)

Tip
When considering this question it will be useful to think about different attitudes towards poverty which might have influenced policy decisions.

THINKING HISTORICALLY Change (5b)

Impetus and disruption
Changes in the years leading up to the passage of the Poor Law Amendment Act

Introduction of the Speenhamland system in 1795	A population that was growing significantly: in 1801 there was double the population of late 17th-century Britain.	Utilitarianism gained a significant degree of influence at the turn of the 18th century
War with France between 1793 and 1815	The Royal Commission investigation into the Poor Law in 1832	Poor harvests after 1829 which undermined economic well-being

Patterns of development consist of changes which, at given times, converge and have a bearing on one another and at other times diverge and have little in common. In the above example, the changes come together to form a pattern of development.

Work in groups.

Write each change on a small piece of paper and arrange them on a large A3 piece of paper as you think best. Then link them with lines and write along the line what it is that links the changes. Try to make sure that you think about how those links may have changed over time.

Answer the following questions individually or in pairs:

1 Why is 1795 an important year when considering the reform of the Poor Law?

2 Which changes were significant in the government's more critical attitude towards pauperism by 1834?

3 What changes were important in encouraging a reform of the Old Poor Law?

CHANGING ATTITUDES TOWARDS THE POOR AND PAUPERISM, 1834–70

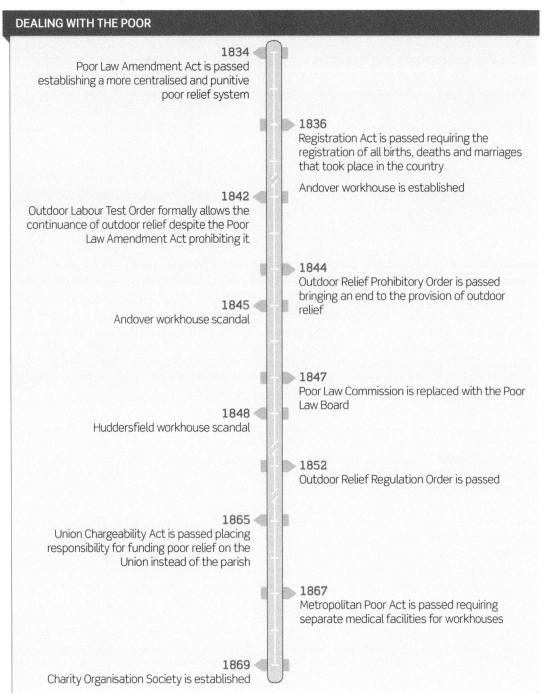

DEALING WITH THE POOR

1834
Poor Law Amendment Act is passed establishing a more centralised and punitive poor relief system

1836
Registration Act is passed requiring the registration of all births, deaths and marriages that took place in the country

Andover workhouse is established

1842
Outdoor Labour Test Order formally allows the continuance of outdoor relief despite the Poor Law Amendment Act prohibiting it

1844
Outdoor Relief Prohibitory Order is passed bringing an end to the provision of outdoor relief

1845
Andover workhouse scandal

1847
Poor Law Commission is replaced with the Poor Law Board

1848
Huddersfield workhouse scandal

1852
Outdoor Relief Regulation Order is passed

1865
Union Chargeability Act is passed placing responsibility for funding poor relief on the Union instead of the parish

1867
Metropolitan Poor Act is passed requiring separate medical facilities for workhouses

1869
Charity Organisation Society is established

The Andover workhouse scandal and national opinion

The very concept of 'less eligibility' demanded that the workhouse regime was a difficult one. The effectiveness of the new model required that workhouses act as a deterrent to those who could actually work and therefore the institutions were created as a deliberately harsh environment. Having said that, however, some institutions overstepped themselves in their zealous endeavour to achieve this effect and when they did so it gave great cause for those seeking a more humanity-centred approach.

One of the earliest examples of workhouse brutality was that of the Andover workhouse scandal which gained attention in 1845 and brought the darker side of the new regime to public attention for the first time.

SOURCE
6

Heading for the Workhouse, a drawing of the poor and destitute going to seek lodging in a union workhouse in 1846. Produced by 'T. S.' for the *Pictorial Times*, 29 August 1846.

The Andover regime

The Andover workhouse had been established in 1836 and it epitomised the belief in deterrence. Under the master of the house, Colin McDougal, who had been a sergeant-major in the military and fought at the battle of Waterloo, the workhouse gained a notorious reputation for discipline. He and his wife ran the institution like a prison camp and those who entered were treated as if they had committed a crime. In addition to the common practice of separating men and women and the compulsory wearing of uniforms, the inmates at Andover were required to eat with their fingers and if a couple tried to talk to one another then they would each be isolated in a purpose-built cell. The working day was very long and the men would be required to spend it crushing animal bones for the production of fertiliser. This was a particularly strenuous task and one which the Andover workhouse favoured over any other as it performed a useful and profitable service for the local community.

Reinforcing the penal-like system that was operated, the diet at the institution was very limited. McDougal and his wife kept expenditure to a minimum, giving only the barest minimum to those in their care. This was little more than subsistence quantities and any extra provisions that were provided by other institutions at Christmas and other special occasions, such as Queen Victoria's Coronation, were withheld at Andover. The extent of this restriction of food meant that costs were very low which kept the Board of Guardians happy as it meant that the Poor Rate could therefore be kept to a minimum.

For the inmates at Andover, however, the experience was very harsh and one which was resented by all who entered. Such was the cruelty meted out there that, between 1837 and 1846, 61 paupers were sent to prison having deliberately committed offences to escape the institution.

The scandal

Under the minimal care provided by the workhouse, inmates were constantly kept on the edge of starvation to the extent that they were driven to take extreme measures in order to survive. A common way adopted by many inmates was to supplement their meals by eating any meat left on the bones they were required to crush, or, if none was available, to break the bones in order to suck out the marrow inside. Such was the need for additional sustenance that fights would break out over particularly meaty bones that were found. During 1844–5, rumours circulated about this practice but the guardians did little to investigate them and simply voted to ban bone crushing during hot weather. This action would suggest that those charged with the supervision of the workhouse gave little regard to what went on there. In this sense, in Andover at least, the old paternalistic attitude towards poor relief was quickly replaced by a more punishing one that gave little thought to relief other than how much it cost.

The events at Andover were eventually reported when a local farmer and Poor Law guardian himself, Hugh Mundy, took his concerns to the local MP, Thomas Wakely. On 1 August 1845, he in turn asked the home secretary about the rumours which then led to a full investigation into the allegations. Undertaken by the assistant Poor Law commissioner, Henry Parker, the conclusions of the investigation found the allegations to be mostly true and that in fact things were even worse, with McDougal also abusing the female inmates. The findings of the investigation led to a public outcry and the Poor Law Commission was attacked by the public, the press and parliament for failing to supervise its institutions and allowing such an event to occur.

The impact of the Andover scandal

The events at Andover were not altogether unique but they were well publicised by critics of the New Poor Law, including the editor of *The Times*, John Walter, who ensured that the scandal was covered in great detail. The greatest impact that the event had was to expose the abuses of the workhouse system and to force a change in the way that system was administered. In 1847, the Poor Law Commission was dissolved and replaced by a Poor Law Board. The switch from Commission to Board saw the end of the broadly independent administration of relief as it was brought more clearly under government control; several cabinet ministers sat as members of the Board and the president of the new body was also an MP.

The dissolution of the Poor Law Commission marked a shift in national opinion regarding the nature of poverty and the best way to address the problem of pauperism. The 1834 Act had very much adopted the principle of deterrence, focusing only on poverty in Britain as a menace. Therefore the legislation that emerged only sought to deal with this feature rather than the greater issue itself. It applied a strict regime within the houses to punish those who ended up in them; under this system pauperism was very much seen as the product of laziness and therefore such people needed to be forced into a more proactive way of living. The abuses at Andover, however, had gone some way to soften this attitude and by the end of the 1840s there was a growing feeling of social responsibility once more.

Andover was not the seminal moment which caused this re-emergence, as in several quarters of society – especially some of the **non-conformist** churches – it was never hidden. Nor did the scandal end the general belief in the need to make people fend for themselves more effectively and the workhouse remained a central feature in the provision of poor relief. Between the years 1851 and 1866, another 100 were built to augment the 402 which had been constructed in the immediate years after 1834. Contempt of those unwilling to help themselves remained a common attitude within mid-Victorian society but this was also mixed with a strong desire for social stability. The prosperity which had been generated by this time had helped to create a dominant middle class which had mostly lost touch with its origins among the working ranks of society. This class had itself been accepted into the upper echelons of society and even been granted the vote in 1832 (see Chapter 1). In light of this rapid progression there was a strong conservative tinge to this class which sought to secure its newfound position. The events at Andover underlined to this class how the new Poor Law was not quite the ideal solution. It forced the replacement of the Poor Law Commission and showed how the stability of the workhouse system could easily be undermined without effective checks.

Non-conformist
The title given to protestant faiths such as Calvinism or Methodism which did not 'conform' to the doctrines of the Church of England nor used the Common Book of Prayer.

SOURCE

From an article 'Charity and pauperism' in the London weekly newspaper *Saturday Review*, commenting on the importance of improving relations with the poor, dated 16 January 1869.

We really can't quite button up our pockets, invest our spare cash as prudently as may be, and say to the poor man, "Starve for it serves you right",... If a pauper cannot but envy us, it is desirable that he should hate us as little as possible.

Given this realisation it can be argued that the drift towards greater social responsiveness was less a desire to improve the poor as much as a desire to secure middle-class interests. After 1834, society could generally be criticised for largely ignoring the issue of poverty as paupers were simply forced to enter the workhouse where they could not be seen. In the wake of the scandals, however, workhouse regimes came under closer scrutiny and conditions were tempered to a degree as poverty became an important topic for investigation once more. Among those who began to take an interest in pauperism was the journalist Henry Mayhew. His four-volume work, published after 1849, *London Labour and the London Poor*, concluded that it was poor wages that produced pauperism because they were insufficient to protect the recipients from unforeseen fluctuations in the economy. This work challenged the belief that idleness was the real cause of distress and briefly exposed the realities of poverty to those who could do something about it.

After 1846, there was better attention placed upon the system of poor relief and the conditions in the workhouses gradually improved, although it was a slow process and additional scandals such as that in Huddersfield in 1848 would continue to remind society of the need to maintain a more vigilant eye. The establishment of groups such as the Workhouse Visiting Society in 1858 undertook to make unofficial checks on workhouses as part of their broader interest in distributing extra food and kind words to those inside them. The information that this group collated was then used to agitate for better treatment of the sick or elderly.

Huddersfield scandal
During a typhus outbreak in 1848, the workhouse in Huddersfield was exposed as being especially poor at caring for its inmates. Such was the low level of care that ill people were made to share lice-ridden infirmary beds with dead bodies for weeks on end while others could not get their soiled bed linen changed for up to nine weeks. The revelations made at Huddersfield were deemed even more awful than those at Andover two years before. Collectively these events went a long way to promote a new approach for dealing with poverty and saw the introduction of charities. These would offer additional provisions to inmates but also carry out detailed inspections of the workhouses which would later inform the reforms in the 1880s.

Such is often the case in history that dreadful events are required before positive improvements can be made. The institution of a more rigid workhouse system after 1834 allowed society effectively to forget about the poor as they were locked away behind high walls. It took scandals such as that at Andover to remind society of its obligations and after 1846, although the workhouse system remained, it was scrutinised much more attentively and with a more socially responsible attitude.

ACTIVITY
KNOWLEDGE CHECK

How effective was the New Poor Law?

Having considered the impact of the New Poor Law which was passed in 1834, answer the following questions:

1 What are the three most significant features that stand out regarding its successful implementation?

2 What are the three most significant features that suggest its failure to address pauperism?

THINKING HISTORICALLY   Cause and consequence (5a)

Inter-relations

Causes never simply come one after another. They are often present simultaneously and have an effect on one another. Sometimes new causes develop and interact with existing ones.

Causes of the Andover workhouse scandal

New Poor Law	Conservatism	Brutal treatment	Individualism	Economic interests	Media interest

Work in groups to produce a diagram of causes and the links between them:

1 On an A3 piece of paper, write all the causes of the Andover workhouse scandal. Write these in boxes, the size of which should reflect how long they were a relevant factor. For example, if you argue that 'Conservatism' had been an important factor, then this will be quite a big box, whereas 'media interest' would be a lot smaller. Spread these boxes over the page.

2 Then make links between all the causes. Draw lines between the boxes and annotate them to explain how the causes are connected and in what ways each affected and altered the other. For example, between 'economic interests' and 'brutal treatment' you could write something like, 'Without the economic interests of the Board of Guardians dominating its decision-making, Colin McDougal's brutal treatment would not have been so apparent.'

Answer the following questions:

1 How do the causes differ in their nature? (Think in terms of events, developments, beliefs, states of affairs, etc.)

2 How do the causes differ in the roles they played in causing the scandal? (Think about whether each cause created the right conditions, was a trigger for events or acted in some other way.)

3 Write a 200-word paragraph explaining how important it is to recognise the relationships between causes. Give examples from your diagram. Try to include connective phrases such as: 'this created conditions conducive to...', 'this triggered an immediate reaction...', this made the development of that situation more/less likely...'.

The growth of charity and self-help

Part of the shifting emphasis towards a more socially responsible approach to poverty was a growth in private enterprises on behalf of the poor. These ventures were mostly organised by middle-class groups whose social conscience motivated them to help the less fortunate. In part they shared the same fears of instability if the poor continued to be ground down, but they were also imbued with a more well-meaning attitude which prosperity can sometimes promote. The growth in middle-class affluence gave rise to a stronger feeling of Christian charity which consequently informed the newfound interest in the poor. The activities of these people centred on the organisation of charity work with the intention of investigating the needs of those suffering in poverty. They then focused on alleviating the greater discomforts of poverty by supplementing the basic provision by the Poor

Law Board with additional resources and general sentiments of goodwill.

The development of charity work and other **philanthropic** enterprises was also the result of the formal end to outdoor relief for able-bodied men in 1844. Ever since the Poor Law Amendment Act had been passed it had been the intention of government to end reliance on this form of relief and yet it had remained widely in use due to fierce opposition – mostly from workers who temporarily found themselves out of work during recession and therefore relied on this provision. To force these people into workhouses seemed impractical and therefore the Outdoor Labour Test Order was passed exempting these individuals. By the mid-1840s, however, this opposition had diminished and, in an attempt to enforce the Poor Law, outdoor relief was restricted to only the sick or infirm. In 1852, a further order, the Outdoor Relief Regulation Order, was passed which limited even this provision. However, such relief remained a popular policy within the parishes and this attempt to restrict it resulted in protests by the Boards of Guardians who felt their discretionary powers were being infringed by the state. It was eventually rescinded and outdoor relief continued to be the most common form of relief throughout the century. The introduction of these measures was at once an attempt to enforce the 1834 Poor Law in its entirety and also a feature of the popular mid-Victorian belief in individual responsibility and self-help. These ideas were very prominent and had their origins in the earlier views on pauperism which laid blame for such a condition on the weak characteristics of those who found themselves in need – namely indolence and a tendency towards drink. The difference in the 1850s, however, was that these views encouraged a more proactive attitude towards pauperism. Rather than simply punish them, those in need could be helped to help themselves and therefore the new charities that emerged sought to provide the means for achieving this.

KEY TERM

Philanthropy
A term used to describe a general concern for the welfare of others, usually characterised by donations of money or other resources aimed at helping people.

An equally potent force behind the development of charity work in Britain was that it offered a way for affluent women to participate in public affairs despite the still restrictive attitudes that existed around gender roles. As with the move towards better education in the 1860s and 1870s, poor relief carried with it a perception which made it especially well suited to the assumed maternal qualities that women possessed. The roles undertaken by these women on behalf of the poor in the long term promoted their own campaign for greater recognition in the later 19th century and eventually contributed towards their political acceptance after 1918. In the 1850s, women's involvement was motivated by a wish to participate in society more fully. Among the leading figures who sought to promote the lives of the poor was Angela Burdett-Coutts, who took a particular interest in seeking to raise the opportunities of pauper children by finding them employment in the military. She also co-founded with Charles Dickens a hostel for

poor women who had turned to prostitution and funded education projects for Britain's poorest children. In this manner the purpose of charitable intervention was to furnish the poor with skills that they might then use to help themselves get out of poverty. Certainly not the only private figure motivated by a desire to alleviate the continued existence of pauperism in society, Burdett-Coutts stands as a prominent example of these attempts.

EXTEND YOUR KNOWLEDGE

Angela Burdett-Coutts (1814–1906)
The daughter of Sir Francis Burdett and his wife Sophie Coutts, Angela Burdett-Coutts became the richest woman in England when she inherited £1.8 million from her grandfather in 1837. Denied involvement in the family's banking interests due to her gender, she turned her attention to philanthropy and took great interest in helping the poor. She was a friend of Charles Dickens and together they opened a home for poor women called Urania Cottage in 1847 and she also funded education projects to promote the lives of Britain's poorest inhabitants.

Much of the charity work that was undertaken also involved the collection of statistics regarding those who found themselves in poverty. The work carried out by groups such as the Workhouse Visiting Society collected information on the experiences of the poor, allowing a much more formal approach to private relief to be organised. With solid information to back up their efforts, it allowed the rejection of the patronising 'do-gooder' mentality that motivated some of the earlier efforts.

By seeking out a more accurate knowledge of the experiences of paupers, charities pioneered a more tailored relief system, which began to focus on the specific causes of poverty rather than the blanket response that the Poor Law had instituted. In the course of their investigations, the elderly and the young were found to be the most common inhabitants of the workhouse and during the 1860s this instituted a more concerted effort of care for these groups. In 1865, the medical journal *The Lancet* undertook an investigation into the quality of medical care in London workhouses and the findings of this investigation led to the passage of the Metropolitan Poor Act in 1867. This demanded that medical facilities be separate from the workhouse itself and provided for the creation of the Metropolitan Asylum Board that took over the responsibility for caring for the sick paupers. These advances paved the way for more specialised care of the sick but also began to modernise the system of general poor relief. Much of the motivation behind greater levels of attention being paid to pauperism was to make relief more effective. By actually talking with paupers and finding out how best to help them, instead of simply locking them away in the workhouse, it marked a new departure in poor relief. It began to involve the poor themselves in finding solutions rather than treating them as the problem that needed solving. This shift in focus was both a positive step towards future welfare provision and also a clear signal that the only way dependents would get out of poverty was through helping them find their own solutions.

Self-help

The concept of self-help was not entirely new to Britain. It was an idea which was present in the 18th century and one that developed as part of the broader industrialisation of the country, which saw entrepreneurial men achieve great wealth as a result of their own efforts. The re-emphasis upon the importance of self-help in the mid-19th century was in response to a continued high level of pauperism and a desire to place responsibility for this in the hands of the paupers themselves rather than the state which, after the Andover scandal, had assumed more central responsibility. The embodiment of this principle was very much seen in the Charity Organisation Society, formed in 1869. The purpose of this organisation was to distinguish between the 'deserving' and 'undeserving' poor and then to recommend the best means by which to help those deemed 'deserving' to get back on their feet. It rejected the practice of excessive assistance which its founder believed was detrimental to society and instead sought a more targeted approach. In carrying out its role, it conducted interviews with paupers, judging each case on its own merits and the evidence obtained. On the basis of this more scientific method it sought to offer more organised and efficient assistance to those administering poor relief.

The birth of the Charity Organisation Society was the product of a growing fear among certain quarters of society that the quickly growing spirit of charity was in fact adding to the levels of dependence in Britain rather than contributing to their reduction. Put more simply they believed that charity giving was encouraging a higher degree of dependence when it was so indiscriminately. The aim of the society was to be more objective and only grant assistance to the genuine cases after a rigorous investigation of the claimant's circumstances. In this approach the organisation was echoing the earlier opinion that found voice in the 'less eligibility' doctrine. However, rather than adopt the punitive solution which had since been proven so inhumane and potentially dangerous to social stability, the society adopted a more constructive approach to address the problem. Having identified the deserving people, the organisation then directed them to the best source of help for their situation – usually to the Poor Law Board if they were in need of long-term support. On the basis of working with each deserving case and using the principle of self-help to support their improvement, the charity work which developed in the latter half of the 19th century began to adopt a more thoughtful attitude towards poverty and pauperism. This more rational approach replaced the emotive and highly critical morality-based judgements that had characterised earlier thinkers on poor relief.

A Level Exam-Style Question Section B

How far do you agree that poor relief in the years 1834–70, evidenced a more positive concern for the well-being of society? (20 marks)

Tip
When answering this question think about the different motives and methods involved with offering poor relief. How is it offered and what does this suggest about the motives?

The significance of key individuals in challenging attitudes

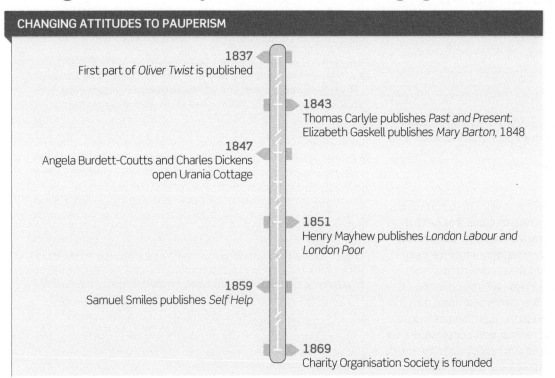

CHANGING ATTITUDES TO PAUPERISM

1837
First part of *Oliver Twist* is published

1843
Thomas Carlyle publishes *Past and Present*; Elizabeth Gaskell publishes *Mary Barton*, 1848

1847
Angela Burdett-Coutts and Charles Dickens open Urania Cottage

1851
Henry Mayhew publishes *London Labour and London Poor*

1859
Samuel Smiles publishes *Self Help*

1869
Charity Organisation Society is founded

After 1834, both public and political attitudes began to change in regard to the existence of poverty and especially pauperism. The intention behind the formulation of the New Poor Law reflected an older attitude which was largely different from that held by 1870. Changes in society mean attitudes do not remain set in stone and instead they evolve to reflect new circumstances and new information that is discovered. The cause of this evolution is often free thinking by individuals who have the confidence to voice their thoughts, demanding others then consider what they have said. Such was the enormity of the poor relief issue that many people thought and spoke about it, encouraging many ideas about the causes of poverty and the best course of action for dealing with it. With such widespread interest – especially from authors and journalists (see timeline) – existing attitudes were challenged and new perspectives were brought to bear on the system of poor relief, which met with varied success.

Opposition towards the New Poor Law had existed even during its passage through parliament. The debate on how best to deal with pauperism was one which had elicited significant interest from across society, not least from authors who each wrote, in their own way, quite extensively upon the issue.

Thomas Carlyle

Thomas Carlyle's work *Past and Present*, which was published in 1843, drew attention to the growing class divide within Britain and to the plight of workers especially, referring to workhouses as 'Poor Law prisons'. Carlyle was most interested in the spiritual growth of the country and, for this purpose, used the poor and the treatment of this group as an example of how far removed from one another members of society had become. Regarded as one of the period's great thinkers, Carlyle's ideas were well read among middle-class reformers and his words – particularly those relating to a growing divide in society – were very influential among those who were increasingly concerned about social stability.

EXTEND YOUR KNOWLEDGE

Thomas Carlyle (1795–1881)

Thomas Carlyle was a Scottish writer and historian whose works were influenced by his Calvinist upbringing. A friend of the British philosopher and economist John Stuart Mill, Carlyle took a keen interest in philosophy and much of his writing combined his strong religious influence with a more progressive social commentary on the state of society. Critical of the industrialisation of the country, Carlyle felt that it was becoming too divided and that rich and poor were losing touch with one another in the 'worship of money'. His solution was a 'spiritual rebirth' where each could learn to appreciate the other. How this was to be achieved he did not say.

Henry Mayhew

In contrast to the intellectual theorising that Carlyle offered, the work of Henry Mayhew was **empirical**. His investigation into the little-known lives of those in poverty produced a four-volume work which catalogued in more than two million words the experiences of Britain's poor. His work was perhaps the first study of this topic conducted by a private individual and its conclusions challenged the long-dominant view that idleness was the source of poverty. Instead he showed in great detail how it was insufficient wages that made people dependent upon relief. By paying such low wages the employers did not give their workers sufficient income to allow them to set aside money for those occasions when employment might be denied them for whatever reason. In reaching these conclusions, on the basis of interviews and meticulous research, Mayhew was perhaps the first person to

provide evidence of the poor wanting to earn their way but not being able to do so because of the parsimony of their employers. For a brief while the revelations offered by his publication *London Labour and London Poor* forced middle-class Victorians to consider an alternative to their long-held beliefs and in doing so encouraged new thinking about the way to treat those who found themselves upon hard times. In the immediate term this was reflected in the growth of charity work within the workhouses and the systematic inspections that began to be introduced.

KEY TERM

Empiricism
A term used to describe that which is based on evidence or observation rather than logic or theory.

Charles Dickens

Perhaps the most celebrated opponent of the New Poor Law, however, was the author Charles Dickens. Having been forced into working in a shoe blacking factory at the age of 12 after his parents entered the workhouse owing to debt, Dickens and his family had experienced first hand the realities of poverty. The episode left a strong impression upon the author and throughout his career he was committed to finding other answers to the question of pauperism. Having shared the experiences of pauperism, Dickens developed a strong social conscience and sought to give voice to the poorest in society, whose lives often went unnoticed by those in the classes above them. Throughout his work – most famously *Oliver Twist* which he wrote between 1837 and 1839 – he popularised the image of the workhouse as a place of despair and drudgery where charity was twisted into a punishment for those who had the temerity to ask for help. Although not the first writer to chronicle the experiences of the poor, he was certainly one of the most successful to do so.

SOURCE

8 From Charles Dickens's *Oliver Twist* describing the extent of hunger that the workhouse regime propagated. The story was first published in the periodical *Bentley's Miscellany* in 1837.

The room in which the boys were fed was a large stone hall, with a copper at one end; out of which the master, dressed in an apron for the purpose, and assisted by one or two women, ladled the gruel at mealtimes. Of this festive composition the boys had one porringer and no more – except on occasions of public rejoicing when he had two ounces and a quarter of bread besides. The bowls never wanted washing. The boys polished them with their spoons again till they shone again; and when they had performed this operation (which never took very long, the spoons being nearly as large as the bowls), they would sit staring at the copper, with such eager eyes, as if they could have devoured the very bricks of which it was composed; employing themselves meanwhile, in sucking their fingers most assiduously, with the view of catching up any stray splashes of gruel that might have been cast thereon. Boys have generally excellent appetites. Oliver Twist and his companions suffered the tortures of slow starvation for three months. At last they got so voracious and wild with hunger, that one boy who was tall for his age, hinted darkly to his companions that unless he had another basin of gruel, he was afraid he might some night happen to eat the boy sleeping next to him, who happened to be a weakly youth of tender age. He had a wild, hungry eye and they implicitly believed him.

The depiction of hunger and overbearing masters that appeared in *Oliver Twist* became part of a common theme within Dickens's work, throughout which he presented the public with an easily understood image of the lives of Britain's poorest subjects. In further works, such as *Hard Times* and *A Christmas Carol*, Dickens elaborated upon his theme, continually reminding his readers of the destitution that existed around them. This constant flagging up of the poor is perhaps Dickens's most significant contribution to the poor relief debate and particularly his own efforts to challenge the long-dominant moralising about 'the undeserving' paupers. By continually reminding society of this 'underclass', Dickens not only painted a vivid picture of them but also forced people to think about this group when it was all too easy to forget them. Consequently, as society developed and became more socially aware, many people looked to the ongoing suffering of the poor whom they had read about so often. This influence was also enhanced by the manner of publication through which many of Dickens's works were issued. The use of **serial novels** was a popular practice in the 19th century because it made the process of publication significantly cheaper and also allowed people to

pay as little as a shilling for each monthly instalment. In using this format, Dickens's stories became more widely read by people who might not have been able to afford to buy them in a single volume. In reaching such an audience his vision of destitution and poverty was read by many who themselves were already thinking about a more socially responsible way of proceeding.

KEY TERM

Serial novel
This was a format for publishing work – usually narrative fiction – in sections or instalments. Instead of publishing a single-volume book, a chapter would feature each month at a cost of around one shilling and then each month afterwards subsequent chapters would appear.

The works of Dickens were obviously fictional and people were not naive enough to believe that what he depicted was necessarily the truth. However, when newspapers reported on the scandals in Andover and later Huddersfield in the 1840s, fact and fiction became one, lending credibility to the stories Dickens told.

SOURCE

The title page of Charles Dickens's *Oliver Twist* which was first published between the years 1837 and 1839.

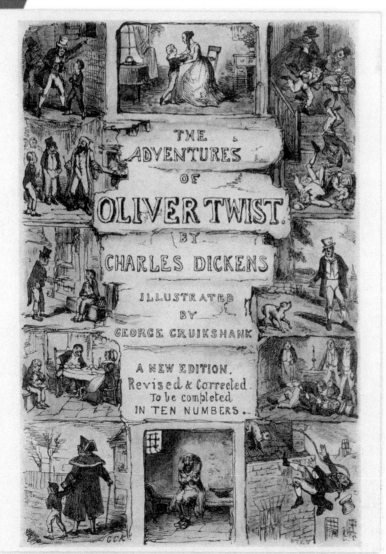

Elizabeth Gaskell

Another author who contributed to the growing awareness of poverty in Britain was Elizabeth Gaskell, whose novels, like Dickens's, offered a closer look at social problems. Her book *Mary Barton*, published in 1848, is perhaps her best-known work and in it the lives of the working class and their difficult existence amid the smoke stacks of Manchester are vividly exposed for public consumption. Her novel acquired a great deal of interest because it offered a realistic impression of the experiences of the poorer classes in Britain. Writing these realities within the framework of a fiction was not seen as a threat to established order and therefore it was able to publicise the realities of poverty to wide audiences with little controversy.

Samuel Smiles

If Elizabeth Gaskell and, more particularly, Charles Dickens, created the imagery of pauper Britain and presented the arguments against the New Poor Law, then Samuel Smiles offered the answers. Graduating with a medical degree from Edinburgh in 1832, Smiles was a social reformer who maintained a varied interest in the world around him. He supported political reform and particularly the uniting of the interests of the middle and working classes. He was briefly involved with the Chartist movement (see Chapter 2) although when it adopted 'physical force' this interest declined. His greatest influence was his publication *Self Help*. The publication of this text in 1859 was fundamental to the changing attitudes towards poor relief. The book talked about the importance of thrift and industry, placing individual determination to improve oneself as the single most important element in achieving a successful life. Published at a time when Britain enjoyed unprecedented prosperity – the fruits of industrial labour were now being born – *Self Help* epitomised the optimistic spirit of the age and it became a bestseller. By the end of the 19th century, it had sold more than 250,000 copies and effectively became a key text for anyone hoping to become successful.

SOURCE

10 From the opening chapter of Samuel Smiles's *Self Help*, published in 1859.

"Heaven helps those who help themselves" is a well-tried maxim, embodying in a small compass the results of vast human experience. The spirit of self-help is the root of all genuine growth in the individual; and, exhibited in the lives of many, it constitutes the true source of national vigour and strength. Help from without is often enfeebling in its effects, but help from within invariably invigorates. Whatever is done *for* men or classes, to a certain extent takes away the stimulus and necessity of doing for themselves; and where men are subjected to over-guidance and over-government, the inevitable tendency is to render them comparatively helpless

The emphasis on the importance of doing things for yourself and the value of doing so was particularly well regarded by mid-Victorians, who looked at the current system of relief with a more critical eye. The values expressed in Smiles's work were well understood in the economy. Indeed, many of the industrial middle-class social reformers had demonstrated the same values making their own way in life and, eventually, making their own fortunes through the very hard work and thrift that Smiles spoke of. If they could be successful by acting upon the values of self-help then the same principles could be applied to the poor, who perhaps just needed to be pointed in the right direction and shown how to support themselves. The significance of Smiles, therefore, was in publicising the principle of self-help at a time when pauperism was once again being publicly debated.

The publication of *Self Help* offered a framework for reform which groups such as the Charity Organisation Society were able to adopt as an alternative means for providing relief after 1869. In offering such a framework, Smiles was able to contribute, albeit unintentionally, an effective means to challenge the existing mode of thinking about how to deal with poverty and, more particularly, the condition of dependency it had created.

The main way in which Smiles' work influenced the discussion about poverty was in emphasising the potential of every person. He suggested that, if offered a chance to improve themselves, most people would take it and would work hard if they believed they could achieve improvement. This simple idea played to the strengths of the Victorian middle class who had reached their own positions through similar efforts – the only difference being that they had the initial belief in themselves. If the idea worked for them, then it should also work for those less fortunate. This was the logic that was applied, and added to, by business-minded individuals, who saw the possibility of further economic growth if more people could be encouraged to seek their own fortunes. An additional benefit was the anticipated reduction in cost to the rate-payers if people were encouraged to help themselves rather than seek charity or enter the workhouses. In 1862, it cost 4 shillings and 8 pence per person per week in the workhouse. By contrast, the cost of supporting that person 'on the outside' was less than half that sum. The ideas of self-help were therefore much more attractive financially, and from an ideological perspective they were in tune with the ways in which Victorian Britain perceived itself to have grown prosperous.

The evolution of poor relief between 1785 and 1870 reflects the changing attitudes within Britain towards pauperism and poverty at this time. These shifting views are the product of a country in flux; over the course of the late 18th and 19th centuries, Britain underwent dramatic change which affected the way in which society responded to problems. The issue of poverty had long been accepted as a necessary evil – a way to encourage people to work hard – but the natural consequence of pauperism was considered much less desirable. The dependence it created was seen as anathema to the Victorian ideas of self-help which preached the virtues of people making their own success. In attempting to reconcile these opposing concepts, poor relief was continually being adapted, swinging from 'less eligibility' to a more supportive approach which sought to offer a more targeted level of support. Despite alteration, basic attitudes did not change much and although a more sympathetic appreciation of poverty emerged, views on pauperism still retained a degree of cynicism.

ACTIVITY
KNOWLEDGE CHECK

Charitable goodwill?

Having read about the changing attitudes towards poverty and pauperism answer the following questions:

1 What were the underlying principles which promoted the growth in charity involvement?

2 What function did these charities perform?

3 Did the growth in charity work really reflect a new approach to poor relief?

ACTIVITY
SUMMARY

The effective evolution of poor relief

1 Write a description of poor relief before 1834 and then a second description of the same provision by 1870.

Then answer the following questions:

1 What differences do you notice between these provisions?

2 Which do you think is most effective for dealing with pauperism?

3 What were the key turning points in the development of poor relief between 1785 and 1870?

WIDER READING

Edsall, N. *The Anti-Poor Law Movement, 1834-1884*, Manchester University Press (1971)

Englander, D. *Poverty and Poor law Reform in Nineteenth Century Britain: From Chadwick to Booth*, Routledge (1998)

Murray, P. *Poverty and Welfare 1830–1914*, Hodder (1999)

Rose, M. *The Relief of Poverty 1834-1914*, Macmillan (1972)

1.5 What explains the abolition of the slave trade at the end of the period, c1785–1807?

KEY QUESTIONS

- How important was the growth in humanitarianism?
- How significant were economic and financial factors?
- What was the impact of the work of individuals?
- How important was the changing political climate?

In 1807 Britain finally abolished the **slave trade**. This had become a lucrative commercial venture in the 16th century which treated Africans as commodities that could be bought and sold much like any other goods at the time. In the case of those Africans who found themselves under the ownership of slave traders, they would then be sold for large profits into the widely practised system of **slavery** which denied these people a human identity and treated them simply as property, using them in any way deemed necessary for the benefit of their owner.

Slavery was generally seen as an acceptable practice before the mid-18th century and therefore there was felt to be no problem with establishing a business around this system: trade itself was a well-established means to promote personal and national wealth and as such the opportunities that trading in slaves offered was a natural development of existing practices.

It became a prominent feature of the British economy in the late 16th century when the Elizabethan seafarer John Hawkins hijacked Portuguese ships carrying slaves and then sold them on himself for considerable profit. After two hundred years this **Atlantic slave trade** had become an integral part

1783 – America defeats the British and becomes an independent nation; slaves are thrown overboard on the slave ship *Zong*; Quakers organise their Committee against the Slave Trade

1787 – Society for Effecting the Abolition of the Slave Trade established; Wilberforce introduced to Thomas Clarkson

1789 – Wilberforce makes his first speech to parliament on the cause of Abolition; Outbreak of the French Revolution; publication of Olaudah Equiano's *The Interesting Narrative of the Life of Olaudah Equiano*

| 1775 | 1780 | 1785 | 1790 |

1775 – American War of Independence begins

1786 – Publication of Thomas Clarkson's *Essay on the Slavery and Commerce of the Human Species*

1788 – Dolben Act passed

1791 – Haitian revolution takes plac William Wilberforce introduces the first his annual Abolition bills to parliament

of Britain's economic prosperity and therefore it enjoyed considerable support among the nation. Coastal areas like Bristol and Liverpool, with their deep water ports, grew to become important cities that channelled great wealth into the country. In the 1780s alone, more than 1,000 fully laden slave ships left these and other British ports carrying more than 300,000 Africans into bondage. Those involved with the trade who had only seen profits made, saw no reason to worry about its future and continued to run their businesses without regard to adaptation or diversification.

In spite of this certainty, within 30 years the slave trade was abolished in Britain and significant advances made towards the wider **abolition** of slavery itself. Having been established for more than 200 years, the speed with which this practice declined at the turn of the 19th century has attracted considerable interest as an indicator as to how Britain itself had developed by this time. If slavery had been a fundamental element for growth and an important part of the national economy then why did it end so quickly?

KEY TERM

Abolition
A term used to describe the end of a particular practice or event.

Different interpretations can be advanced in regard to this question and they are each influenced by different considerations: some focus upon the human dimension and point towards the more enlightened thinking that emerged into the 18th century and which subsequently promoted individual action by concerned groups. Others take a more rationalist perspective and emphasise the growing cost and risks associated with the trade. Each interpretation has validity but none is necessarily a definitive explanation. This is because each interpretation is very much a product of its time and as new evidence comes to light and new research is conducted, these interpretations are scrutinised, updated and rethought. In addition, each historian working on slavery asks subtly different questions and uses different evidence selections, methodologies and assumptions to construct their interpretations.

Evaluating interpretations of history

Since interpretations are so fluid, effectively evaluating these ideas is important so that it is possible to develop an independent view about them. This is because historians, in developing their interpretations, are often putting forward an argument that is based, partly, upon their own opinions. This is a valid starting point but opinion requires evidence to support it if it is to be convincing. Using evidence, opinion becomes judgement, as the historian weighs up the quality and consistency of the available material and uses this to reach realistic conclusions that are supportable. The most convincing interpretations are those that are rooted in the evidence provided and allow for verification by clearly setting out how judgements were developed. An interpretation without evidence is much harder to accept as there is no way of actually knowing how this position was reached, or on what basis it claims legitimacy.

1793 – Britain goes to war against the new French Republic

1799 – Slave Trade Regulation Act passed

1806 – Death of William Pitt the Younger

| 1795 | 1800 | 1805 | 1810 |

1794 – French abolish slavery and the slave trade in French colonies

1802 – Slavery and the slave trade reintroduced in French colonies by Napoleon Bonaparte

1807 – Abolition of the slave trade

THINKING HISTORICALLY | Interpretations (5a)

What I believe is how I see

Below are three descriptions of the perspectives of very famous historians. They have been written for the purposes of this exercise.

Herodotus	Leopold von Ranke	Karl Marx
• His research consisted of conversations • Identified that accounts had to be judged on their merits • Some believe that certain passages in his writing are inventions to complete the narrative.	• Believed in an evidence-based approach and relied heavily on primary sources • Desired to find out the 'facts' and discover the connections between them • Stressed the role of the individual in shaping history.	• Believed that history would go through stages leading to a state where everybody was equal • Believed that historical changes were ultimately determined by changes to the economy • Was often driven by political considerations and looked for evidence to support his point of view.

Work in groups of between three and six.

Each member or pair will take the perspective of one of the above historians and argue from that perspective. Work through the questions as a group and answer the last one individually.

1 Herodotus did not use written evidence to construct his history. Does this mean that his history is less useful than the others?

2 Ranke based his writing almost exclusively on primary sources from the time he was investigating, rather than secondary sources. How might this affect his ability to see larger patterns in history?

3 Marx put his philosophy of history, and perhaps politics, first and research second. Would this make his history weaker than the others?

4 'Colourful' individuals populate the writing of Herodotus and Ranke, while Marx concentrates on the difference between classes. Write three historical questions that each historian might ask.

5 The three historians mentioned above all had different methods and motivations and yet their writing has been valued ever since it was created. Explain how the prior knowledge that we bring to the history that we write does not invalidate it.

HOW IMPORTANT WAS THE GROWTH IN HUMANITARIANISM?

KEY TERM

Humanitarianism
A concern for the welfare of other people which is often manifested through actions to alleviate their suffering.

GROWTH OF OPPOSITION TO THE SLAVE TRADE

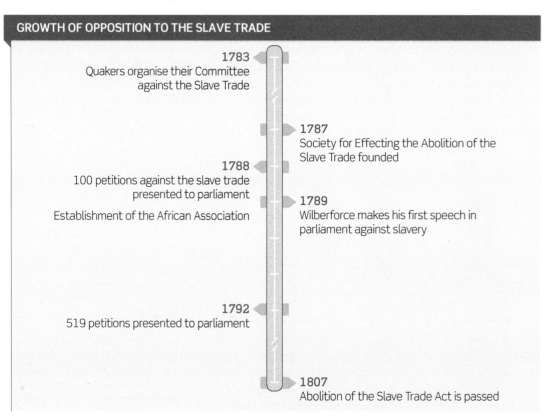

1783
Quakers organise their Committee against the Slave Trade

1787
Society for Effecting the Abolition of the Slave Trade founded

1788
100 petitions against the slave trade presented to parliament

Establishment of the African Association

1789
Wilberforce makes his first speech in parliament against slavery

1792
519 petitions presented to parliament

1807
Abolition of the Slave Trade Act is passed

Within the range of historical interpretation about the abolition of the slave trade, the importance of humanitarianism dominated traditional thought on the grounds that if it was so ingrained, then there must have been an initial impetus for change; something which prompted the first thought to reconsider the role of this trade within British society. The driving force behind this first thought has been attributed to the growth of humanitarianism in Britain and this has, in turn, become the orthodox interpretation for abolition.

Concern for people's welfare was not a new concept on an individual level but towards the end of the 18th century it enjoyed a more pronounced, widespread, appeal as **the Enlightenment**'s intellectual concerns about human rights filtered into broader society. During this period there was a substantial growth in more rational thought which began to challenge the blind obedience to existing ideas; for example, questions were raised about the legitimacy of **absolutism** on the grounds that all men by virtue of being human are fundamentally the same and therefore must enjoy the same rights as one another. This more rationalist outlook saw a growth in humanitarian campaigns in Britain which sought to address a range of issues, including the slave trade, as reformers observed the dawn of new economic and political interests through a more humane lens. In doing so they concluded that in the pursuit of modernity, the welfare of many was being ignored. The government's policy of free trade removed any significant domestic support for the poorest in society while the growth of industrialisation widened the gap between rich and poor. Throughout the later 1700s, humanitarian campaigns emerged to counter the effects of this development and in 1739 the first 'Foundling Hospital' was established to take care of abandoned children. The development of such ventures precipitated a wider sympathy among socially minded groups to care for those less fortunate than themselves in a world that was rapidly becoming very individualistic. The basis of this altruism was at once a reaction against growing self-interest but also a greater belief in the fellowship of mankind which more enlightened people increasingly adopted. This line of reasoning was extended towards the slave trade in the 1780s, first by the Religious Society of Friends – 'Quakers' – in 1783, and then by a group of similarly minded individuals who called themselves The Society for Effecting the Abolition of the Slave Trade in 1787.

The Quakers

Quakerism has a long history of humanitarian action but in the 1780s their interest focused upon the specific question of the slave trade. Having opposed the wider issue of slavery since 1657 on the grounds that everybody was equal before God, their London Yearly Meeting of 1783 presented a petition against the slave trade, signed by 273 people, to the government in June and then set up a 23-person committee to actively campaign for its abolition. By targeting this practice there was the anticipation that this would then lead into tackling the broader problem of slavery in the future. In support of this endeavour a second unofficial committee was also established in July, which undertook to publish articles highlighting the evils of slavery so as to educate the public at large on the issue. In 1784, 10,000 copies of their pamphlet *The Case of our fellow-creatures, the oppressed Africans respectfully recommended to the serious consideration of the legislature of Great Britain by the people called Quakers* was distributed among MPs, the royal family and general public to promote the cause of abolition.

The motivation for this action lay primarily with their religious belief in the existence of God inside every human being. Guided by this principle it followed that to do harm to another person would be to do harm to God himself and therefore any action that made people suffer was to be challenged whenever it occurred. In terms of the slave trade, Quakers generally felt that the notion of alleviating suffering was conveniently ignored by the public and slave interests in the pursuit of economic prosperity as there was little sympathy towards the suffering of Africans at this time. Addressing this lack of concern is where the humanitarian influence of the Quakers is especially important. By following their moral obligation they brought attention to a cause that was not broadly considered within society. In taking action they showed the way for other people who thought more carefully about the issues but who may not have known how to proceed without direction. Given the determination of the Quaker community, their organisational capabilities allowed for an effective challenge to the practice of slavery in Britain and having led the way, other people including women, who themselves were discriminated against, became motivated to take similar action, emboldened by the stand made by this religious group.

In promoting the cause of abolition, the Quakers are credited with spearheading a moral crusade against slavery which quickly found supporters as the country grew to become more aware of the injustices suffered by Africans. Although slavery in Britain had been abolished in 1772, it had become fashionable among the upper classes to have black servants in their homes and this practice upheld a lingering acceptance of discrimination. London itself was home to 10,000 Africans who had been brought back by ship's captains or returning plantation owners. In 1785, however, this tacit acceptance was increasingly challenged as the humanitarian campaign was reinforced by the involvement of other religious groups determined to end the inhuman practice of trading in lives.

Evangelical Christians

Equally unhappy with the slave trade were the Evangelical Christians – members of a multi-denominational faith who believed in the strength of repentance as a means of salvation. This belief promoted the importance of turning away from sin as the only way to reach heaven and this idea formed the bedrock of their opposition to the slave trade, which they increasingly saw as a sinful practice that should be stopped.

Among the most prominent activists were Granville Sharp and Thomas Clarkson, each avowedly against the practice of bonded service on the grounds of moral outrage and the overall inhumanity of the institution. Sharp was a veteran campaigner against slavery while Clarkson had recently been converted to the cause after researching it as an essay subject. Having written about the morality of slavery and been influenced by the more rational thinking of the Enlightenment, Clarkson was especially influential in popularising the movement after the publication of his essay in 1786.

As campaigners, Evangelical Christians were very determined; their faith required them to spread their message of repentance and as a result they were practised in public speaking and willing to do this. Clarkson is credited with encouraging the MP William Wilberforce to join the cause and become the parliamentary voice of abolition (page 125). Wilberforce, himself an Evangelical Christian, was a fine speaker and regularly spoke in parliament about the cause – introducing bills every year after 1791. Clarkson was a very diligent and effective researcher who worked tirelessly to raise support among the wider population.

The efforts of these two men would be fundamental to the eventual abolition of the slave trade and each worked intensely for this goal. The basis of their commitment was certainly their belief in the inhumanity of the trade and this was fuelled by their faith: the slave trade was a sin that needed to be ended. By providing this basis, Evangelicalism was fundamental to abolition,

contributing determined campaigners who helped to first organise, and then prosecute, the cause.

The medium through which both the Quakers and Evangelical Christians sought to achieve their goal was the founding of the Society for Effecting the Abolition of the Slave Trade in 1787. This broad-based religious organisation took up the campaign, forcing discussion of the issue in parliament in 1788.

SOURCE

From Thomas Clarkson's *An Essay on the Slavery and Commerce of the Human Species, Particularly the African* which won first prize in a Latin competition at Cambridge University in 1785 and was then published in 1786 after being translated in to English.

If any man had originally been endued with power, as with other faculties, so that the rest of mankind had discovered in themselves an *innate necessity* of obeying this particular person; it is evident that he and his descendants, from the superiority of their nature, would have had a claim upon men for obedience, and a natural right to command: but as the right to empire is *adventitious*; as all were originally free; as nature made every man's body and mind *his own*; it is evident that no just man can be consigned to *slavery*, without his own *consent*.

Neither can men, by the same principles, be considered as lands, goods, or houses, among *possessions*. It is necessary that all *property* should be inferior to its *possessor*. But how does the *slave* differ from his *master*, but by *chance*? For though the mark, with which the latter is pleased to brand him, shews, at the first sight, the difference of their *fortune*; what mark can be found in his *nature*, that can warrant a distinction?

The Society for Effecting the Abolition of the Slave Trade

The foundation of this group has given considerable weight to the traditional humanitarian and morality-based arguments offered to explain the end of the slave trade in 1807. This society was unrivalled as a lobby group and from its creation in 1787 it continually and tirelessly campaigned for abolition. Made up of social reformers with strong religious backgrounds, this group shared a collective desire to see the end of the slave trade and undertook to both raise public awareness and apply political pressure upon the British government to achieve this objective. Given the strongly religious background of the more prominent members of the Society, Clarkson, for example, became a deacon, and the abolition campaign has traditionally been cast as a moral crusade which eventually brought about the end of the slave trade thanks in main to the efforts of this small group whose consciences demanded they act.

The idea of a crusade has been maintained by several historians of the slave trade, notably by Roger Anstey who first put forward the case in an article written in 1968 which he then expanded upon in *The Atlantic Slave Trade and British Abolition 1760–1810*. This set out the case very definitively by maintaining that the abolitionists were championing a cause against a trade which, at that time, was tremendously profitable. Among much of the evidence offered by Anstey was his contention that in 1796 a bill for the immediate abolition of the broader issue of slavery was very nearly passed in the Commons; in a period when Britain was reaping the benefits of a significant sugar boom. Sugar was one of the main cash crops that slaves were used in the growing and harvesting of and, therefore, given this boom, Anstey maintained that the humanitarian argument must have been particularly strong. Although recent historians have become more sceptical of this particular thesis, preferring to focus attention upon economic and political changes, this interpretation has remained attractive because of the notion of innate goodness it still allows Britain to retain. Interpretations can also offer a perspective on the intentions of their authors and even the attitudes in the societies for which they are writing. Given the horrendous conditions under which slaves were subjected and the terrible actions of those involved with the trade – of particular note is the infamous **Zong case** in 1783 – any means to rehabilitate a sense of decency in a country who engaged in such activities enjoyed a significant following and perhaps ensured the continuation of this particular interpretation in the face of growing challenges.

EXTRACT 1

From Roger Anstey's 1968 work article, 'Capitalism and slavery: a critique' in *Economic History Review*, no. 2 vol. 21.

As of now then, the most persuasive view, in the present author's estimation, runs along these lines: the initial impulse for abolition of the slave trade came from newly acquired Christian convictions strengthened by the "reasonableness" and philanthropy of the Enlightenment. But, even despite a rich nationwide agitation, this humanitarian impulse could not immediately prevail. The shaking of the foundations of the old political order, which began with the attacks on the American war and its conduct by ministers, and from which followed the parliamentary-reform movement and a political climate somewhat favourable to other reforms, was followed by the French Revolution and the revolt in San Domingo. For more than a decade the tendency to identify reform with revolution can only have weakened the chances of carrying abolition – not so much in the Commons, perhaps, as the Lords, the persistent source of opposition. Only when political circumstances changed radically in 1806 was a successful onslaught of the slave trade possible, the new ministry containing several men committed to abolition on humanitarian grounds.

EXTEND YOUR KNOWLEDGE

The *Zong* case (1783)

This was a legal case involving the owners of the slave ship *Zong* whose Captain - Luke Collingwood - on a voyage in 1781 had ordered that 133 slaves be thrown overboard during the last stages of their journey when food supplies were running low. His intention was to sacrifice these individuals for the good of those left on board and then make an insurance claim for those who were drowned. When the insurers refused to pay the claim, a legal case was made about the insurance claim rather than the morality of killing slaves. The ruling maintained that in certain circumstances it was acceptable to kill slaves and that insurers should pay compensation but in this specific case the judge ruled against the ship owners.

The arguments in support of humanitarian campaigns are given further credibility when the experiences of the Society for Effecting the Abolition of the Slave Trade are considered more

closely. This organisation was established to end a practice that was enjoying considerable success in the 1780s: 24 percent of the country's annual income was dependent upon the trade and its associated industries and as such it was taking on a very difficult task which under the prevailing circumstances had many powerful opponents. Among this opposition was the 'West India Lobby' – a group of sugar planters in the West Indies whose business depended upon the slave trade, a trade that had made them wealthy men. This group nurtured close links with parliament and by the late 1700s it was estimated that 50 MPs were tied to the group with one even becoming Mayor of London. Despite the pro-slavery and slave trade sympathies in parliament and the odds very much stacked against them, the society remained true to its intentions and resolutely pressed their case. The strength and dedication that this group exercised in the face of such opposition has been cited as clear evidence of the humanitarian fervour that was embodied within the group. Just as religion inspired complete devotion, so too did the cause of abolition. The conviction manifested itself through an extensive education campaign which lasted for more than 20 years.

EXTRACT 2

From Adam Hochschild's *Bury the Chains: The British Struggle to Abolish Slavery* published in 2010. The quote is taken from the minutes of the first meeting of the Society for Effecting the Abolition of the Slave Trade in 1787.

"At a Meeting held for the Purpose of taking the Slave Trade into Consideration, it was resolved that the said Trade was both impolitic and unjust." Perhaps most remarkable, for it showed how much the twelve were of one mind, they promptly resolved that for conducting committee business, only three members would be needed for a quorum.

We can only imagine how the committee members felt as they dispersed to their homes that night. The task they had taken on was so monumental as to have seemed to anyone else impossible. They had to ignite their crusade in a country where the great majority of people, from farmhands to bishops, accepted slavery as completely normal. It was also a country where profits from West Indian plantations gave a large boost to the economy, where customs duties on slave-grown sugar were an important source of government revenue, and where the livelihoods of thousands of seamen, merchants, and shipbuilders depended on the slave trade. The trade itself had increased to almost unparalleled levels, bringing prosperity to key ports, including London itself. How to even begin the massive job of changing public opinion?

Among the most popular means of promoting the cause was the use of propaganda materials which emphasised the extreme nature of the trade and left no doubt as to its inhumanity. The thousands of pamphlets that were produced by the society were supported by equally emotive imagery such as the iconic plaque of a supplicant slave which was created by Josiah Wedgwood and carried the poignant title 'Am I not a man and a brother?' Equally thought-provoking was the drawing of the cross section of the slave ship *Brookes* which has since become just as iconic as Wedgwood's piece. Enduring images such as these draw attention to the moral arguments adopted by the society and also go some way to explain the success of the movement in mobilising such a forceful response by the general public. In 1792 people had signed more than 519 petitions that year alone. Indeed such was the reaction of the British public that in Manchester, a town of 50,000 people in 1787, 10,700 people had signed an abolition petition.

The importance of the humanitarian motivation lies in the common appeal it made. In the late 1700s a vast majority of people in Britain retained some form of religious belief and certainly an opinion on morality. By appealing to this universal sense the abolition campaigners were able to maintain momentum as their arguments were driven by conscience rather than tangible environmental circumstances. In this manner even when world events such as the revolution in France and then the outbreak of war with that country threatened to distract attention, the moral argument against abolition was still relevant. Although there was increased suspicion of the movement's intentions, and whispers of jacobinism were heard in discussions about the society, in the post-revolutionary years it was able to maintain a presence in parliament which ensured that the issue would not be forgotten even if it had been sidelined. The persistence of the society saw a bill in favour of abolition being presented every year between 1791 and 1799 by the MP for Hull, William Wilberforce. Although his efforts were unsuccessful, each attempt was like a candle being lit in remembrance; continual affirmation as to the nobility of the cause and the need to remember it.

SOURCE
2
'Am I Not a Man and a Brother?' Josiah Wedgwood's plaque image first produced in 1787. It became the emblem of the Society for Effecting the Abolition of the Slave Trade.

120

The role played by Wilberforce is covered in more detail in later pages but his continued efforts to present an abolition bill kept alive the interest in the cause even as it became tainted by slave revolts abroad such as the violent Haitian revolution in 1791. What his actions convey particularly well is the devotion of the movement to the cause despite difficult circumstances. In 1804 Wilberforce re-issued his bill and was able to secure the support of William Pitt whose replacement, William Grenville, in 1806 continued that support. Abolition was presented as a government measure and then subsequently passed the following year.

EXTEND YOUR KNOWLEDGE

Haitian revolution (1791)
Haiti was a French colony that grew sugar and coffee and generated significant profit for the mother country. After France's revolution many of its revolutionary ideas – notably the 'rights of man' – found their way to the island and prompted slave disturbances as they claimed the same liberties on which the revolution was fought. When the white planters refused to grant these rights open rebellion ensued under the leadership of Toussaint L'Ouverture. Around 4,000 white people were killed and 180 plantations burned to the ground. French soldiers were sent to the island but after war with Britain broke out in 1793, it was decided to free the Haitian slaves so as to maintain the possession for France.

The argument in favour of growing humanitarianism and the role of religion in the campaign for the abolition of the slave trade has come under increasing criticism in more recent years as historians widened the scope of their analysis. Despite the sense of emotion that critics suggest it plays on, it is still an important feature in abolition history. Whatever your particular perspective, the role of religion and its broader humanitarian motive did make the slave trade a political issue. By raising public awareness of the inhumanity of the trade and forcing a public debate, these groups were a trigger which set off a more critical assessment of the existing practice and therefore can be considered very relevant to the passage of the 1807 Abolition Act.

ACTIVITY
CONSOLIDATION

How effective is the humanitarian and religious argument?
After studying Extracts 1 and 2, how persuasive do you find the arguments offered by Anstey and Hochschild? Give reasons for your answer.

HOW SIGNIFICANT WERE ECONOMIC AND FINANCIAL FACTORS?

One feature of the abolition movement which has often been used to support the traditional perspective of humanitarianism is the timing employed by that group. For the writers who promote this view the attempt to end the slave trade came at a time of significant economic prosperity which was facilitated by the trade itself. This line of argument maintains that given the riches which the trade was bringing, the desire to end it must therefore have had a greater moral imperative. Despite the logical attraction of this argument, other historians have looked more closely at the economic influence as a factor for abolition. These perspectives suggest that with the growth of industrialisation and new economic theories relating to the benefits of paid labour, the slave trade was in fact a barrier to further prosperity and was therefore ended. The first person to promote this argument was the historian Eric Williams in 1944 whose book, *Capitalism and Slavery*, encouraged a reconsideration of the traditional morality thesis.

Eric Williams and the 'Decline Thesis'

The argument put forward by Williams took a very critical view of the abolitionists and particularly their 'saintly' image. For Williams these men were very selective with their efforts and if truly motivated by humanitarianism, would have broadened their gaze to include other 'crimes' such as working conditions in the mines or the poverty of the working class. Given their focus on the slave trade alone he maintained that the motivation was therefore tied to economic interests which, for him, was the motivation for any action that has been undertaken by any movement. Developing this line of argument, Williams went on to contend that the slave system was only challenged in the late 1700s because it was becoming unprofitable for those engaged with it. When profits were high as in the earlier part of the century there was no such effort to abolish either slavery or the slave trade. For him, the growth in mechanisation transformed the nature of British commerce and this ushered in a 'a greater preference' for paid labour. As profits declined it became easier to criticise the slave trade and actually promote alternative systems which were more reflective of the industrial age. These ideas challenged the existing orthodoxy and consequently fuelled further investigation by historians of British slavery.

EXTRACT 3

From Eric Williams, *Capitalism and Slavery*, published in 1944

It was the new **colonies**, crying out for labour, full of possibilities, that had to be restrained, and they were permanently crippled by abolition. That explains the support of the abolition bill by so many West Indian planters of the older islands... The war and Bonaparte's continental blockade made abolition imperative if the older colonies were to survive. "Are they not now", asked Prime Minister Grenville, "distressed by the accumulation of produce on their hands, for which they cannot find a market; and will it not therefore be adding to their distress, and leading the planters to their ruin, if you suffer the continuation of fresh importations?" Wilberforce rejoiced: West Indian distress could not be imputed to abolition. Actually, abolition was the direct result of that distress.

KEY TERM

Colony
Foreign land that was occupied by a more powerful nation with the deliberate intention of using it for economic gain.

Under scrutiny itself, the 'decline thesis' that Williams presented has been comprehensively challenged and has largely been found to be less persuasive in more recent histories. The weakness of his argument lies in the definitive assertion that economic considerations were the primary motive for abolition and that every action is motivated by it. This polemical approach reduces the importance of other factors and therefore by focusing so intently upon one feature, opens itself up to criticism. The historian Seymour Drescher in particular has challenged the central idea by showing how abolishing the trade actually did more to undermine the slave economy, rather than Williams's contention that abolition was motivated because of this decline. Such a revelation as this undermined the 'decline thesis'. However, despite this, Drescher supported the importance that Williams placed upon economic considerations and endorsed the work as a seminal text which has subsequently encouraged a more subtle consideration of why the slave trade was abolished.

EXTRACT 4

From Seymour Drescher, *Econocide: British Slavery in the Era of Abolition*, published in 2010.

The basic interpretation of the economic reality behind abolition has hitherto been that the protected empire of the early eighteenth century, with its old mercantilist-capitalist ideology, aged and was replaced, ca 1750–1830, by an informal, free-trade empire. The old system upheld slavery as well as **mercantilism**. Both were born at the same time and died at the same time. They must therefore have outlived their usefulness at the same rate. This pairing of rising laissez-faire and declining slavery is an application of the principle of concomitant variation. It is made more plausible by the fact that British slavery was an economy producing for a protected market in both 1760 and again in 1830, as it became decreasingly competitive with externally produced tropical products.

Even if we accept for the moment that British slavery, including its **metropolitan network**, was principally a component of the protected, or "forced" trade sector of the empire, the timing of abolition in 1807 becomes more rather than less mysterious. Abolition occurred at the precise peak of a movement away from free-trade principles. The shift became evident during the last year of the Pitt government and was completed by the subsequent ministry in its famous orders-in-council in 1807. The policy continued for the duration of the blockade. In 1805–1807 Britain swung towards protection of her colonial commerce, and the funnelling of the entire North Atlantic trade though either her own ships or her own ports. If ever a date represented the triumphant reassertion of mercantilism it was 1807.

KEY TERMS

Mercantilism
This is another term for commercialism, or a belief in profitable trade.

Metropolitan network
The organisation within the parent state of a colony.

THINKING HISTORICALLY | Interpretations (3a)

Differing accounts

Carefully read Extracts 3 and 4 which discuss the abolition of the slave trade.

1 For each of the historians create a summary table of their views.

   Make a note of how they address the following key issues:

   • How important was economic motivation?

   • How far did political opinion influence abolition?

   Make a note of the evidence they give in support of this claim.

   Use your notes and knowledge to give evidence which supports or challenges their interpretation.

2 In pairs discuss which historian's interpretation of abolition seems to best fit with the available evidence. Which seems the most convincing?

3 Make a note of any issues which made it difficult to compare the two interpretations directly.

Challenge: Seek out another historical interpretation on the abolition of the slave trade and compare this with the views you have explored already.

Economic considerations

The importance of the slave trade to the British economy was without question. Even before the sale of slaves or the products of their labour, the infrastructure of the trade generated prosperity. Shipbuilding and outfitting businesses grew as more than 35,000 slave voyages took place between the 16th and 19th centuries. Most of these left from Liverpool, which by the 1790s had become the biggest slave trading port in the world and claimed three-sevenths of the whole European trade. By creating such a demand for ships, the trade supported a growing economy and provided thousands of jobs for associated industries. Furthermore, the network that built up between the West Indies, Britain, the Americas and West Africa created export markets for the merchandise the country's new factories were churning out. The sugar plantation owners' homes were furnished with British imports while the slaves themselves used tools fashioned on British workbenches. With such rich opportunity, the slave ports of Britain became centres of excessive wealth, which can still be seen today in the merchant homes on Bristol's Clifton Down or Glasgow's tobacco mansions. Indeed, in the case of Bristol it was estimated that in the 1780s 40 percent of people's income in that city was slaved-based and as such the trade was very well regarded.

Throughout the mid to late 1700s, the slave trade continued to reap substantial economic rewards for the country as the trade routes expanded due to a growing demand for British goods. Between the periods 1784–1786 and 1805–1807, 87 percent of Britain's textile output went abroad with African markets taking the lion's share of this produce. The reason for this growth was that traders in slaves would first load their ships with British made goods and use these as bargaining counters when they arrived on

SOURCE

3 An extract of a petition to parliament by those who traded in African slaves presented in 1788 to assert the economic importance of their trade.

But the effects of this [African] trade to Great Britain are beneficial to an infinite extent. In its immediate effect it employs about 150 sail of shipping, which carry annually from this country upwards of a million of property, the greatest part of our own manufactures; and in its more remote effects, there is hardly any branch of commerce in which this nation is concerned that does not derive some advantage from it. But the beneficial effects of this trade have been nowhere so eminently striking as in the sugar colonies in the West Indies, where it has been proved by experience, that Europeans cannot bear the labour of the field; so that those valuable possessions would most probably have remained to this moment uncultivated and useless to a degree had they not been assisted by the African labourers...

the African coast. In return for slaves, African traders would be given these goods which included guns and ammunition as well as cloth and other textiles. This exchange of 'goods' helped to develop markets for the British wares within the African continent. During the wars with France between 1793 and 1815, British manufacturers often had to rely on these markets alone, given that their European buyers were temporarily excluded. The importance of the slave trade therefore went beyond the profiteering of slavery itself, but also promoted the growth of other industries such as textiles which, during industrialisation, became one of Britain's most successful industries.

If the slave trade offered such an opportunity to extend world markets, then why did abolition gain momentum after 1787? Certainly the moral justification has already been offered and for proponents of this argument the economic position of Britain has been used to confirm their perspective. The 'decline thesis', however, also requires some attention on the grounds of the slave trade's obvious economic significance. The argument offered here is that while the slave trade certainly contributed to the burgeoning economy, it was also undermined by it. As industrialisation took hold, there emerged a new economic principle which increasingly found favour in Britain. The economic theories of Adam Smith have been considered in earlier chapters and the *laissez-faire* approach that he endorsed is well known in terms of both economic growth and the experiences of workers. An additional feature of this perspective is his argument that slavery is neither efficient nor as cheap as free labour. The basis of this analysis is founded upon the idea that people who are happy will do their best work; if you have to force somebody to do so then they will drag their heels or try to avoid it. In terms of slavery, having to also pay for the structure of enforcement made it even more expensive and ate into the profits that were yielded. Certainly the practice had been very lucrative in previous centuries – averaging about one million pounds a year, but even though these profits had risen to nearly three million by the end of the 1700s, the attraction was beginning to wane as increased efforts were having to be made to subdue slave rebellions at great cost. In terms of the slave trade in particular, one in every ten voyages encountered some kind of slave revolt which affected profits. Although each voyage could return between 20 and 50 percent for the traders, increasingly Smith's ideas began to take hold as the British economy was transformed by the start of the new century.

This is not to say that the slave trade was in decline but rather with the advent of industrialisation and the factory system, there was an alternative mode of commerce that was showing even greater potential for the future. Industrialisation offered another means for growth which was effectively used by abolitionists to justify their cause; in this sense the economic dimension was a useful argument which could be deployed.

Financial considerations

In support of this idea was also the financial implications of the slave trade. Such was the nature of the practice that it required a vast outlay of funds to set up in the business. Ships were expensive and this was money that had to be spent out before it could generate reward. On this basis, banks extended lines of credit to traders on the understanding that the investment would yield a good return once trade had been established. Banks such as Heywood's in Liverpool, which later became part of Barclay's Bank, were prominent in funding the slave trade throughout the late 17th and 18th centuries. Given the profitable return that the trade offered, which in Liverpool was often 100 percent, financially there was felt to be minimal risk involved. Even though Liverpool was an exceptional case being the biggest slave port in the country, the average return on a single voyage was between 20 and 50 percent and it was estimated that if one ship in three came in then the owner would not lose financially. These projections only served to promote ongoing investment.

Despite the positive feeling that encouraged slave trade investment, there was also a financial cost. The practice of slaving was very expensive. Individually the costs varied depending upon the size of ship and type of cargo being used to trade slaves, but as a guide, the slave ship *Ann* undertook a voyage in 1753, having cost £3,153 to fit out. Given costs like this, traders stood to lose enormous sums of money in the event of problems at sea or a failure to get a good price for their cargo. In this sense the activity was also a very risky venture. That said however, the rewards made the risk attractive: the *Ann* earned £8,000 which, after costs were taken into account, amounted to a profit of £4,847.

Although lucrative profits could be made, the slave trade was not without its problems and on average one in every ten ships witnessed a revolt by slaves which proved costly to the traders themselves. These occurrences were also punctuated by more common problems associated with long sea voyages; damage and loss of cargo due to storms, disease or simply inadequate provisions. Each of these problems dented the profit margins of those ships and by extension those who had invested in them. Financially this was a significant cost which could often not be reclaimed despite many attempts to do so. The implications of these financial losses are that, over time, the guaranteed high profits of the slave trade became more vulnerable and as such more cautious investors, or those not able to absorb the losses, looked for other opportunities to support.

The numerous risks at sea were added to once the ships docked. Ultimately money was made by selling slaves for use on plantations, however, the cultivation of tobacco, sugar and cotton was an untested science and brought as much dismay as excitement. If successful, harvests could generate vast profits but equally if they were not then the cost of maintaining them was very high. These harvests invariably fluctuated and just as farmers today lead a somewhat fragile existence, so too did the **planters** in the Americas whose own fortunes were at the mercy of their crop. The financial burden of this variable industry was seen in the level of debt experienced by many planters. By 1776, Glasgow merchants were owed more than £1.3 million by their American partners while in Liverpool in the years between 1772 and 1778 it was estimated that the cities merchants had lost £700,000. Of the thirty leading merchant houses in this city, twelve had gone bankrupt by 1788 because of the debt owed to them.

These were the financial risks of the slave trade. It was both the maker and taker of fortunes dependent upon the extent of involvement that was adopted. Like any venture that offers rich reward, the element of risk is fundamental, but in the case of the slave trade the scale on which it operated made it more prone to uncertainty and as such the stakes were much higher. Under these circumstances it is appropriate to consider the impact of the economic arguments upon the abolition question.

KEY TERM

Planter
A term used to describe a farmer who planted crops such as sugar, tobacco and cotton on their farm or 'plantation' and used slave labour to harvest them.

Economic arguments

The slave trade was a hugely lucrative business which spread across the globe and informed the prosperity of many interested parties on both sides of the Atlantic. It also supported the growth of domestic industries such as textiles in Lancashire and Birmingham's ironmongery trade which were often the goods traded in return for slaves. Historians such as Stanley Engerman have suggested that the trade accounted for at least five percent of the nation's annual income – in addition to the vast private profits made by countless individuals. With regard to the economic argument for abolition, there is some evidence to support the claims made by Eric Williams that the trade was only ended because it became unprofitable however the sheer volume of money generated by it seems to challenge his overall conclusions. Without question the losses made by merchants across the country did make people think more carefully about investment, but the individual profits that voyages could make remained an attractive proposition for private and public investors alike. When confronted in parliament with bills to abolish the trade in the late 18th century, interested parties continued to object and every bill that was presented fell upon deaf ears. The best that was offered came in the form of the Dolben Act in 1788 which only improved the worst of the conditions on board the ships themselves. Rather than ban the trade, this Act merely restricted the number of Africans to be carried per ton and stipulated that a doctor should be present on voyages so as to maintain the health of their valuable cargo. Furthermore, the importance of the trade to other parts of the economy, particularly during the war years when European markets were closed to British commerce, made it a vital element in Britain's overall economic growth. Given the level of importance placed upon the trade in this field, to suggest the economy was the single most important reason for abolition is a difficult claim to sustain.

The 'Decline Thesis'

Outline Eric Williams's arguments relating to the abolition of the slave trade and then present three reasons which support this idea and three reasons which challenge it – do you agree with his assessment?

WHAT WAS THE IMPACT OF THE WORK OF INDIVIDUALS?

INDIVIDUAL'S CONTRIBUTION TO ABOLITION

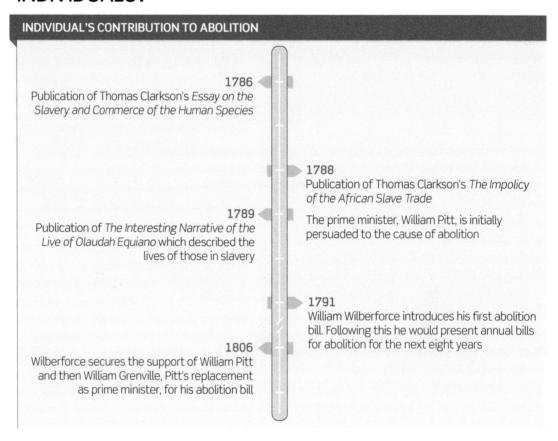

1786
Publication of Thomas Clarkson's *Essay on the Slavery and Commerce of the Human Species*

1788
Publication of Thomas Clarkson's *The Impolicy of the African Slave Trade*

The prime minister, William Pitt, is initially persuaded to the cause of abolition

1789
Publication of *The Interesting Narrative of the Live of Olaudah Equiano* which described the lives of those in slavery

1791
William Wilberforce introduces his first abolition bill. Following this he would present annual bills for abolition for the next eight years

1806
Wilberforce secures the support of William Pitt and then William Grenville, Pitt's replacement as prime minister, for his abolition bill

Perhaps most important of all to the cause of abolition were the people involved with it. While economic developments or humanitarian idealism were certainly motivating factors, it was the actions of individuals themselves that brought about the end of the slave trade. First through the experiences of the slaves themselves, who injected a human sense of moral outrage as their narratives were increasingly given a public forum, and then by the abolitionists who acted upon them with determined spirit. The movement to effect abolition was one of the earliest mass movements in Britain and by its very nature involved innumerable individuals who each contributed in their own way to bring about the end of the slave trade. These are the unknown figures of history whose contribution is only seen through statistics of petition signatures or riotous gatherings. Though they are in name forgotten, their opinions can still be found in the actions of those 'greater figures' of whom more is known. In terms of the abolition campaign, three stand out in particular for their contribution to the cause, each for different but interconnected reasons that are bound by the common goal of abolition. The first is a young graduate converted to the cause after winning an essay competition; the second is an independent member of parliament and the third an ex-slave who published a book about his personal experiences of bondage. Each from disparate backgrounds, these figures serve as examples of the significance that individuals can play in the propagation of history and the achievement of things greater than themselves.

Thomas Clarkson (1760–1846)

Thomas Clarkson perhaps epitomises the importance that men of indifferent standing can achieve if they are committed and prepared to follow through with their conviction. The son of a school headmaster bound for holy orders, he became a leading figure in the abolition movement after winning an essay competition while at Cambridge University. The topic on which he had to write was 'Is it lawful to enslave the un-consenting?' and after researching the material Clarkson became dedicated to the cause. Though not the most familiar of names in abolition history, in terms of his contribution Clarkson was second to none. His work rate for the movement was tremendous and behind the scenes he was the driving force in educating the public about the wrongs of the slave trade and ensuring that the movement gained widespread support. For the historian James Walvin, Clarkson was an 'indefatigable foot soldier' who prepared the ground for the movement's more public activities. The nature of this work meant that his was not the most acknowledged of roles, but certainly without it the movement would not have enjoyed the success it did.

EXTRACT

5 From James Walvin's *A Short History of Slavery*, published in 2007.

In 1786 the campaign was joined by the man who was to prove the catalyst for the rallying of British feeling against the slave trade. Thomas Clarkson, a young graduate and newly appointed deacon, had won a prize at Cambridge for an essay, published in 1786 as *Essay on the Slavery and Commerce of the Human Species*. This essay helped to win over William Wilberforce, a Yorkshire MP and rising political star, to the abolition cause (and at the same time to Evangelicalism). The two men, Clarkson and Wilberforce, agreed to collaborate on abolition, and the Quakers agreed to publish Clarkson's essay. Thus was a key pioneering partnership forged: Wilberforce the parliamentary leader of abolition, and Clarkson the public propagandist and indefatigable researcher, campaigning the length and breadth of Britain – and both working with the invaluable help provided by the Quakers and their well-oiled national organization. In May 1787, a small group of men, dominated by Quakers but now including Evangelical Anglicans, and reflecting a range of political interests, formed the Committee for the Abolition of the Slave Trade (afterwards the Abolition Committee).

Declaring the slave trade to be 'both impolitic and unjust', the committee planned to procure 'such information and Evidence, and for distributing Clarkson's Essay and such other publications, as may tend to the Abolition of the Slave Trade'.

ACTIVITY
WRITING

Analysing language
Analyse Extract 5.

1   Identify words and phrases used to express degrees of doubt and certainty. Write them out in order of most to least certain.

2   Identify words and phrases that show Walvin's attitude towards Thomas Clarkson. Write a short paragraph explaining this attitude using quotes form the extract to back up your points.

The significance of Clarkson was twofold; firstly his essay inspired prominent parliamentary figures like William Wilberforce to the cause of abolition, and then his talent as a public propagandist ensured that their message was well known among the British population. In terms of his essay, the passion and level of detail with which he wrote proved to be a useful and very persuasive tool which sparked greater interest in the cause of abolition. Although the Quakers had embarked upon an abolition campaign in 1783, it was not until the publication of Clarkson's work that broader interest was garnered. Ten thousand copies were printed and distributed to members of parliament and anyone who showed an interest in abolition. Among those who read this first essay, William Wilberforce was finally won over to the movement in 1787 and formally became the parliamentary leader of abolition. As an individual who sympathised with abolition, Wilberforce was slow to be won over having first taken an interest in 1784 when he helped his friend James Ramsey, a ship's surgeon, to publish a pamphlet on the experiences of slaves in the colonies. Although sympathetic, he did not feel able to lead the crusade but after reading Clarkson's essay he was persuaded to take up the banner. In helping secure a parliamentary supporter, Clarkson was fundamental in the success of the abolition movement because he established a prominent voice for its cause within the heart of British authority.

A cross-section and plan of the Liverpool slave ship *Brookes* which was created by Thomas Clarkson after finding a similar document displaying a fully loaded slave ship while on a tour in Plymouth in 1788. He reworked the plan to match the *Brookes* ship for propaganda use in 1789.

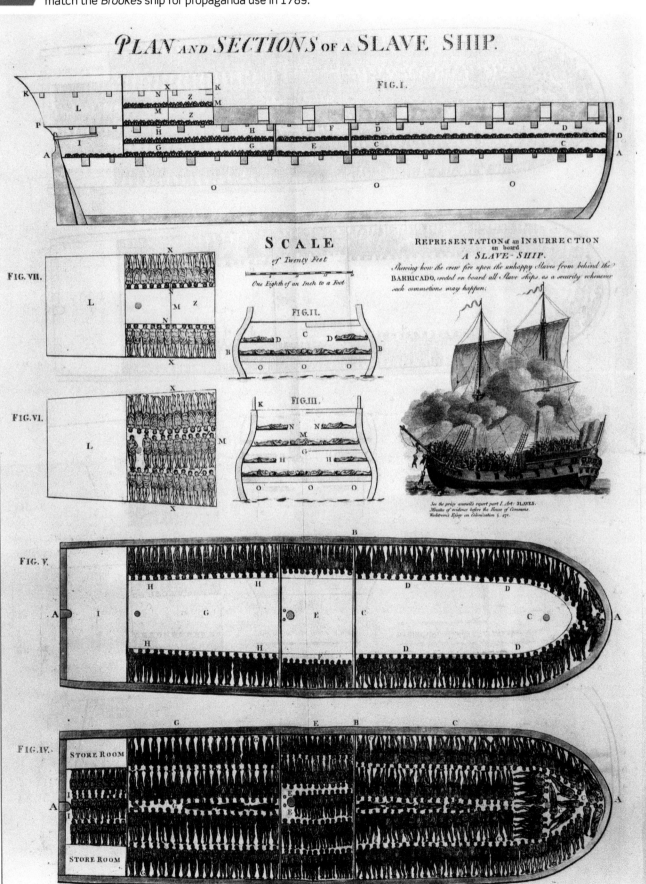

As important as this achievement was, perhaps the most important contribution that Clarkson made, however, was in both furnishing Wilberforce with details of the slave trade for use in his parliamentary speeches, and in stirring up public support. As a researcher, Clarkson was invaluable and the lengths to which he went ensured that no detail was left out. As a result the general public were well informed as to the inhumanity of the slave trade. Between 1787 and 1794 he travelled more than 35,000 miles around Britain to collect evidence about the slave trade and to deliver lectures on the subject to packed audiences. These performances were very well received as Clarkson was among the first lecturers who discovered the potency of the visual image and therefore punctuated his talks with physical objects for the audience to behold. These included items from the ships themselves such as manacles but also evidence of the culture and skills of the Africans themselves – the colourful pottery and spices in particular. His talks helped to humanise the slaves for people who had often never met any and had only ever taken for granted the perspective of the slave trader. Among the most poignant of images he acquired was the cut-through section plan of a slave ship cargo hold, which starkly displayed the overcrowded conditions faced by those enslaved. This image perhaps more than any other brought the immorality of the trade into focus. In the course of his travels across Britain Clarkson helped to found 1,200 branches of the Society for Effecting the Abolition of the Slave Trade, giving the movement a broad base of popular support by 1807.

Further to his lecturing, Clarkson also undertook significant research assignments to support new publications and parliamentary speeches. This function was especially useful after 1793, when the outbreak of war brought increased hostility towards large public meetings by members of the propertied classes who feared their revolutionary intent. In 1790 he visited 317 ships and spoke to more than 3,000 sailors, including one called Isaac Parker who served on the frigate *Melampus* and gave evidence of slave poaching off the African coast. The importance of these revelations lay with the moral weight they gave to the campaign itself, and specifically the attempts by its supporters pushing in parliament for reform.

William Wilberforce (1759–1833)

Of all the abolitionists, William Wilberforce is perhaps the most famous. It was he who persistently introduced a raft of annual abolition bills to parliament after 1791 and it was his bill that eventually became the Abolition Act in 1807. For his legislative presence he is rightly regarded as a prominent figure in the movement. However, he was not alone in achieving its goal. Without Clarkson to prepare the groundwork and people like the pottery manufacturer Josiah Wedgwood who was excellent at generating publicity, Wilberforce may not have enjoyed the success he did. In this case Wilberforce is both an excellent example of individual significance and also the effectiveness of working in combination. As an individual his contribution to the wider movement was to bring the cause to the floor of the House of Commons.

It was his status as a member of parliament that made Wilberforce such an important figure in the abolition movement. His adoption of the cause after 1787 gave the movement a figurehead around which they could rally and press a more decisive campaign. Prior to Wilberforce's involvement abolition remained very much on the periphery of British politics but with him on board it gradually became a prominent feature in parliamentary sessions. After 1789 when he made his first speech to parliament on the subject, Wilberforce was able to secure a **select committee** to investigate the slave trade and this led on to his first parliamentary bill in 1791. Although this was defeated by 163 votes to 88 his effort raised the profile of the slave issue and made fellow MPs consider the impact of the trade. In this manner his contribution was very different from that of Clarkson's but equally significant: Clarkson was the diligent researcher out on the streets while Wilberforce was the parliamentary face of abolition.

As a result of this presence Wilberforce has often been praised excessively for his part in the abolition campaign. Certainly his determination is well noted: after 1791 he presented a bill in every parliamentary session until 1799 but these bills were usually introduced late in the session when members had little time to properly consider the motion, or when other issues were of more importance. Under these conditions his bills were routinely defeated and abolition was deferred time and again. Given the poor execution of Wilberforce's actions, doubt has been cast as to his overall effectiveness when compared to men like Clarkson. For commentators such as Williams, Wilberforce

KEY TERM

Select Committee
This is a parliamentary committee usually involving MPs and Lords that is established to investigate a particular subject. It can make recommendations to the government based upon the evidence uncovered.

himself has added credibility to those arguments which marginalise the 'moral' motives of abolition in favour of more tangible economic or political ones.

EXTRACT

6 From Seymour Drescher's *Econocide: British Slavery in the Era of Abolition*, published in 2010.

1791 was certainly not a likely year for a positive vote for abolition, and Parliament replied negatively to Wilberforce. On April 19, 1791, the House of Commons, after lengthy debate, rejected the first abolition bill by the decisive margin of 163 to 88, despite the backing of its two principal leaders, Pitt and Fox.

However, even in 1791, when a lively market was reinforced by a peak anti-abolition vote in Parliament, when toasts were drunk to the trade in Liverpool, and the church bells were rung in Bristol, the British polity did not deliriously abandon itself to the perpetuity of the slave system.

EXTRACT

7 From Boyd Hilton's *A Mad, Bad and Dangerous People? England 1783–1846*, published in 2006.

Slavery was one of those issues on which politicians preferred to shelter behind the coat-tails of opinion-formers, which is why Pitt and Grenville urged Wilberforce to raise it in Parliament. In 1791 the Commons threw out a bill to outlaw the trade by a large majority, but in the following year – after more than 500 petitions had registered the nation's disapproval – MPs voted by an even larger majority (230-85) in favour of gradual abolition. Campaigners were euphoric, but momentum was checked, first by stalling tactics in the Lords, then by the war and by brutal rebellions in Saint-Domingue (1791), Grenada, and St Vincent (1794-5). These sparked off an anti-black reaction, which was cleverly exploited by the West India lobby. The latter did not *look* particularly powerful – averaging sixteen planter MPs ('country gentlemen whose estates lay overseas') and eight merchants, it had less than half the strength of the rival East India interest – but pariah status lent it useful cohesion, and anyway the political system was helpful to vested interests.

THINKING HISTORICALLY | Interpretations (4a)

The weight of evidence

Work in pairs. Read Extracts 6 and 7, do the activity and answer the questions.

1 Use highlighter pens to colour code copies of the extracts. Use one colour for 'evidence', another colour for 'conclusions' and a third for language that shows the historian is 'reasoning' (e.g. 'therefore', 'so'). Alternatively, draw up a table with three columns, headed 'Evidence', 'Conclusions' and 'Reasoning language' and copy the relevant parts of the extracts into the columns.

2 How do the extracts differ in terms of the way that the evidence is used?

3 Which of these extracts do you find more convincing? Which has the best supported arguments?

4 What other information might you want in order to make a judgement about the strength of these claims?

5 Write a paragraph of 200 words explaining the importance of using evidence to support historical claims.

Wilberforce certainly had his failings. However, under the prevailing circumstances of war with France after 1793, his underlying conservatism was perhaps a valuable resource for the abolitionists. Faced with fears of revolution, the influential propertied classes in Britain were reluctant to indulge in anything remotely suggestive of radicalism which abolition was felt to be. The movement was criticised throughout the war, yet abolition was never completely defeated; he was still able to re-submit future motions on the grounds that he, like other fellow MPs, was a man of property and therefore did not wish to seek a world turned upside down. In effect his stature and political leanings enabled him to steer a course for abolition without completely alienating those around him. Certainly his aim was to abolish the slave trade but he was not about to promote revolution in Britain. In this sense Wilberforce was able to give the movement an air of respectability at a time when political movements such as theirs were increasingly looked upon as revolutionary groups with malicious intent.

Olaudah Equiano (1745–97)

As important as both Clarkson and Wilberforce were, they did not project their cause from experience and therefore the campaign derived greater moral weight from the experiences of the slaves themselves. Among the most prominent of these figures was Olaudah Equiano whose own background gave the cause significant gravitas. As an ex-slave who was eventually able to buy his own freedom, Equiano was among the first non-white abolitionists who raised the profile of their cause through speaking tours and, in 1789, publishing his own autobiography *The Interesting Narrative of the Life of Olaudah Equiano*. This offered a first-hand account of the slave trade and particularly the experiences of those forced into bondage.

The impact of Equiano's work was just as significant as that of Clarkson's essay except his publication carried a greater sense of moral weight because, for the reader, each line depicting an inhuman experience carried with it the realisation that what was being read actually happened to its author. The particular significance of Equiano's contribution therefore was to heighten the sense of moral outrage by bringing it into the realms of reality; prior to his work it was all too easy for many individuals to think only of slavery in the abstract, thereby allowing an intellectual consideration which may not have encouraged any further action.

SOURCE

5 Text describing the conditions aboard a slave ship making the voyage across the Atlantic. Taken from Olaudah Equiano, *The Interesting Narrative of the Life of Olaudah Equiano*, published in 1789.

The stench of the hold while we were on the coast was so intolerably loathsome, that it was dangerous to remain there for any time, and some of us had been permitted to stay on the deck for the fresh air; but now that the whole ship's cargo were confined together, it became absolutely pestilential. The closeness of the place, and the heat of the climate, added to the number in the ship, which was so crowded that each had scarcely room to turn himself, almost suffocated us. This produced copious perspirations, so that the air soon became unfit for respiration, from a variety of loathsome smells, and brought on a sickness among the slaves, of which many died — thus falling victims to the improvident avarice, as I may call it, of their purchasers. This wretched situation was again aggravated by the galling of the chains, now become insupportable, and the filth of the necessary tubs, into which the children often fell, and were almost suffocated. The shrieks of the women, and the groans of the dying, rendered the whole a scene of horror almost inconceivable.

Even before the publication of his autobiography Equiano was an important figure for the abolition movement. As an ex-slave he was integral to the mobilisation of others who had been or were enslaved. In 1787 he joined the Sons of Africa group with Quobna Ottobah Cugoano and other Africans. This group worked alongside the British abolitionists and publicised the cause through extensive touring and even parliamentary lobbying. In 1788 they organised a march on parliament in support of the soon-to-be-passed Dolben Act which was a piece of legislation that sought to improve conditions aboard slave ships by regulating the number of slaves to be carried on the vessels. These actions certainly went a long way to promote the cause of abolition but their real significance was in the manner in which they dispelled misconceptions of Africans. Encouraged by stories from slave traders, for many British people the continent of Africa was an uncivilised place which was the home to inveterate believers in black magic and other 'ungodly' things. Instead, men like Equiano and Cugoano presented a very cultured and respectable reality, which challenged the common image pedalled by the traders. Equiano himself married an Englishwomen and upon his death in 1797 left an estate worth £950 – about £80,000 in early 21st-century value. In presenting a real image of Africa and exposing the cruel realities of the slave trade, Equiano and his fellow men were fundamental in promoting abolition which, without them, might have taken longer to secure.

EXTRACT

8 From James Walvin's *A Short History of Slavery*, published in 2007.

Most slave deaths on board were from gastrointestinal disorders, mainly the 'blood flux'. Inevitably, untold numbers of survivors stumbled ashore in the Americas suffering from the same condition: weakened, aged (often 'bunged up' by slave traders anxious to pass them off as fit) and destined for an early grave. Slaves were shackled below, normally in small groups. They fed from communal supplies, and shuffled in chains, to the 'necessary tubs'; but when sick, they relieved themselves where they lay...

THINKING HISTORICALLY Evidence (3b)

It depends on the question

Study Sources 4 and 5 and Extract 8.

When considering the usefulness of a piece of evidence, people often think about authenticity in the case of artefacts, reliability in the case of witness statements or methodology and structure in the case of secondary accounts. A better historical approach to the usefulness of a piece of evidence would be to think about the statements that we can make about the past based on it. Different statements can be made with different degrees of certainty, depending on the evidence.

Work in small groups and answer the following questions:

1 Look at Source 4.

   a) Write three statements that you can reasonably make about life on board a slave ship based solely on Source 4.

   b) Which of the statements can be made with the greatest degree of certainty? Why is this? Which statement can be made with the smallest degree of certainty?

   c) What else might you need to increase your confidence in your statements?

2 Source 4 is a drawing and Source 5 is a witness statement. Which is more useful to the historian studying life on board a slave ship?

3 Look at Extract 8. How would the historian have gone about constructing this piece? What kinds of evidence would they have needed?

Recent historians have generally agreed on the importance of each of these individuals – particularly the role of Equiano whose voice was perhaps the most eloquent among the ex-slave community. Clarkson also enjoys continued support given his role publicising the movement and dogged determination in finding ammunition for the political assault. The individual who has come under a more critical re-assessment is Wilberforce who, as the public figure behind the movement, enjoyed the most credit once the trade was abolished. Writers such as Adam Hochschild have found him to have been much less determined than people such as Clarkson (Extract 9), while James Walvin has also praised Clarkson highly (Extract 5) and credited him with encouraging the quiet and unassuming Wilberforce.

AS Level Exam-Style Question Section C

Analyse and evaluate Extracts 5 and 7 and use your own knowledge of the issues to explain your answer to the following question.

How far do you agree with the view that William Wilberforce was the most significant individual in the campaign to abolish the slave trade in the years 1785–1807? (20 marks)

Tip

When answering this question remember to consider what the phrase 'most significant' might mean.

ACTIVITY
CONSOLIDATION

The contribution of individuals

Having read about three significant individuals in the abolition movement, identify how these people contributed to the abolition of the slave trade.

Come to a judgement on which of them you feel was most effective.

EXTEND YOUR KNOWLEDGE

Quobna Ottobah Cugoano (1757–unknown)

Quobna Cugoano was born in Ghana and was kidnapped and forced into slavery in the West Indies in 1770. Arriving in Britain in 1772 he was set free and became a leader among the African community. Cugoano became the first African to publicly demand the abolition of the slave trade when, helped by Equiano, he published his book *Thoughts and Sentiments on the Evil and Wicked Traffic of the Human Species* in 1787.

THE CHANGING POLITICAL CLIMATE

The influence of the American War of Independence

Further support for abolition came after the loss of America following the conclusion of the **American War of Independence** in 1783. The result itself saw Britain lose a significant colony, one which had for years been a vital part of the British Empire. More important for the longevity of the slave trade was the legacy that the war bestowed upon Britain's social reformers; it raised questions about liberty and the rights of men.

In the new political climate that developed after 1783, Britain's regard for the slave trade underwent a transformation which saw a less positive approach adopted. In one sense this was in part because of the loss of their colony which had bought many of the slaves being traded – in 1776 approximately 20 percent of the population of the thirteen American colonies were of African descent, but more particularly it was a reaction to the intellectual debate which the War of Independence had generated. The basis of this debate was liberty and the rights of one nation over the lives of another. Having formed part of the British Empire since the early 17th century, by the late 1700s the Americans had formed their own distinctive identity and political practices which were influenced by a growing belief in **republicanism** and individual liberty. Having fought for eight years to achieve their freedom from Britain, American revolutionaries professed notions of equality and the wrongs of keeping people in bondage for the benefit of a mother country. The parallels with slavery that this argument drew found a receptive ear both in America itself where an abolition movement began after 1790, and also in Britain where the issue became a popular topic of discussion. Having stimulated such an interest, the War of Independence left behind a new political atmosphere in which people began to think more carefully about human experiences. The emphasis that it placed upon the importance of freedom had particular significance for the abolitionists. There now existed more justification for ending the slave trade which was essentially denying Africans any freedom of their own.

In part this discussion was born of the defeat that Britain suffered. Having lost an important colony there was considerable soul-searching in Britain about its failings and slavery and the slave trade became a prominent feature in this reflection. In this sense the American revolution had sowed the seed of doubt about this trade within the minds of many Britons and this allowed the abolitionist movement to become more readily established as people became more receptive to the idea. Combined with the publication of tracts such as Equiano's autobiography about slave experiences, the movement was able to build up sufficient momentum to become a very effective organisation in this more reflective environment. It was able to make some early gains as a result which certainly made future abolition more achievable: in 1788 the Dolben Act was passed, which further restricted the number of slaves on a ship. This was renewed with improvements every year till 1799 when it was made permanent in the Slave Regulation Act.

Napoleon and the British slave trade

Just as the American revolution forced a general reappraisal of British values, the revolutionary war with France brought the slave trade directly into focus. Although the French revolutionary government had overturned slavery on the grounds of libertarian principle, after Napoleon took control of the country his reintroduction of the slave trade into French colonial possessions in 1802 encouraged a much more critical consideration of the practice by Britain. To oppose the slave trade now became a symbol of patriotic duty and as such the movement flourished – Wilberforce found greater support for his bill in the new century and was able to gain the support of the prime minister, William Pitt, in 1806 and also that of his successor, William Grenville. With such support in 1807 the slave trade finally came to an end.

To suggest that the slave trade in Britain only ended because the French re-adopted the practice at a time when the two countries were at war would be too simplistic. The timing would suggest that at best French slave activity was a contributing factor to the British decision but this would be the extent of influence. Given that the abolition movement had been actively campaigning since May of 1787, there was already a substantial interest in abolition even before the re-adoption of the slave trade in France after 1802. In this sense the re-emergence of the trade did not transform public opinion but rather reinforced it, breathing new life into a campaign that had begun to lose momentum because of the revolutionary war with France.

KEY TERMS

American War of Independence (1776–83)
A revolutionary war between Britain and its colonies in America. The victorious Americans established their own independent nation, which in 1787 became the United States of America after agreeing their Constitution.

Republicanism
An ideology which maintains a society and government where the head of state is a chosen representative of the people rather than the people being subjects of the head of state.

To assess the impact of Napoleon's decision it is necessary to consider the broader impact of the French Revolution itself. Having overthrown the monarchy in 1789, the new French government abolished slavery in 1794 as part of its wider goal of securing the principles on which their revolution was fought; liberty, fraternity and equality. To maintain the practice of slavery, having preached these principles, would have been hypocritical in the extreme and therefore the practice was abandoned. The impact of this action upon the British abolitionist movement, however, was very damaging. Having gone to war with revolutionary France in 1793, the British propertied classes were very sensitive to the revolutionary sentiment that they feared would contaminate the country and as such they were especially critical of anything that sounded even remotely dangerous. Given the French had abandoned slavery, British abolitionists therefore became tainted with the same revolutionary brush and consequently found their activities being closely watched by government agents. People were encouraged to give the movement a wide berth or else risk arrest should sufficient evidence be found. At a parliamentary level this criticism was also felt and Wilberforce found it increasingly difficult to win support from fellow MPs during 1794–1802. The movement faltered during these years as radical politics buckled under intimidating government action such as the Seditious Meeting Act of 1795 and the 'Treason Trials' of 1793 and 1794 when radicals such as Thomas Paine and Thomas Hardy (Secretary of the London Corresponding Society, see page 14) were put on trial for their opposition to government policy.

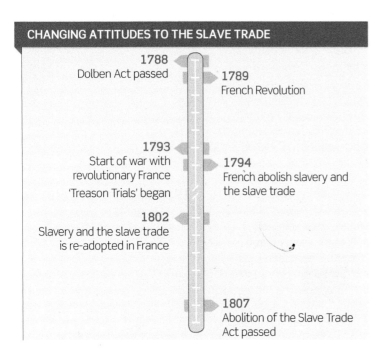

CHANGING ATTITUDES TO THE SLAVE TRADE

1788
Dolben Act passed

1789
French Revolution

1793
Start of war with revolutionary France
'Treason Trials' began

1794
French abolish slavery and the slave trade

1802
Slavery and the slave trade is re-adopted in France

1807
Abolition of the Slave Trade Act passed

During this period it became unpopular to voice abolitionist sentiment for fear of being labelled as a revolutionary. Wilberforce himself was criticised for discussing the issue and even referred to as a 'Jacobin'; the name given to the French revolutionaries whose original organisation was called the Jacobin Club. Under this degree of fear the cause of abolition lost a significant momentum, which had been building since the late 1780s and reached a considerable crescendo with the passage of the 1788 Dolben Act.

Considering this context, the importance of Napoleon Bonaparte's decision to re-introduce slavery into France's colonies becomes more noticeable. By reversing the decision of the revolutionary government, Napoleon inadvertently resurrected the fortunes of the British abolition movement by making abolition not only acceptable once more, but actually a patriotic duty to uphold. In this sense, therefore, the action transformed the political climate almost overnight and rather than hostility, actually promoted a hospitable environment in which the abolitionists could see their cause blossom by 1807.

Changing political climates and growing fears of slave resistance

As important as the abolitionists were to the end of the slave trade, the resistant actions of the slaves themselves were also a crucial influence. Under the pressurised political climate at the end of the 19th century Britain was faced with tremendous difficulties which made great demands upon the country. Not only had it lost a major colony but it was also feeling the impact of the Industrial Revolution and waging a war against a revolutionary government that threatened the very nature of the British political system. Under these conditions the additional burden of slave resistance was a problem the country could do without.

The extent to which slave resistance informed the eventual abolition of the slave trade is open to some debate. Initially it is reasonable to suggest that the threat of rebellion was a significant factor in ending the trade on the grounds of both the additional pressures it would present to the British government and the cost that such action would incur. However, when the French colony of St Domingue (present day Haiti) played host to a violent uprising by its slaves in 1791 the reaction in Britain was that of a conservative backlash against abolition and a strengthening of the pro-slavery lobby. The issue of the slave trade now fell upon deaf ears as parliament refused to countenance any change to the system in the belief that it would prompt further discontent. The motivation for this reaction largely lay with the fears associated with the rebellion; namely that economies would collapse and the threat of violence would spread to further colonies, inciting more uprisings. The staple crop on the island was sugar and this economy collapsed as slaves rose up from the plantations and attacked their owners. More than 1,000 plantations were burned and 12,000 people killed, of which 2,000 were of European descent. The level of destruction and high mortality rate gave the events in Haiti a world audience that shuddered at the extent of violence that was generated.

Although the Haitian uprising was a French issue, the British fear was that it would spark uprisings in their own colonies – slavery after all was not just a French interest. The freed men that left Haiti travelled to the Americas and also to the Caribbean where the word of revolt was passed on to other slaving areas. Mirroring the Haitian model, slave revolts erupted across British-owned possessions in the Caribbean after 1791: Grenada, St Vincent and St Lucia among others and in each case the spectre of further possessions being lost became a real concern. Hearts were hardened towards the abolitionists whose campaign against trading was, wrongly, felt to be in support of the slave revolts – William Pitt, prime minister and friend of Wilberforce, having supported his friend's cause, now shifted his support against the slaves, thereby losing the movement key support. It is because of this activity, alongside the outbreak of the French revolutionary war, that abolition momentum declined in the mid-1790s.

The slave uprisings in British possessions were by no means on the same level of destruction as the Haitian revolution, largely because of the defensive actions of the British government and its colonial governors. Having witnessed the explosion of violence in Haiti, measures were taken to minimise the likelihood of rebellion. Firstly steps were taken to improve the conditions under which slaves worked. In Jamaica, for example, after 1792 the **Colonial Assembly** resolved to abandon the use of metal collars for shackling slaves together and also the use of mutilation as a punishment. These steps were additionally reinforced by the calling out of the militia and parading in military fashion while the threat of disturbance was high. By undertaking these actions it was hoped that there would be little challenge to the existing colonial order. In the case of Jamaica again, when news of white people being murdered in their beds reached its shores, the assembly also resolved to reinforce their own militia with troops from Britain itself at a substantial cost as they were required to pay for this protection. By 1793, the island had 3,000 troops and this, together with the more lenient approach adopted by plantation owners, effectively neutralised the threat of rebellion.

KEY TERM

Colonial Assembly
This was a formal gathering of the official representatives of the British Crown in each colonial possession. These men were responsible for the running of that colony where they were resident. The assembly was headed by a Governor who acted as the highest authority on the island.

Britain did face uprisings in other colonies – for example, in the British Virgin Islands in 1790, but these were subdued relatively easily using both local militia and also regular troops. The threat of such uprisings, however, greatly affected the attitudes of those in Britain. Given the poor treatment that was meted out to slaves on board ships and also on the plantations there was a growing fear that following the Haitian revolution and smaller revolts in British possessions, the frequency of revolt was likely to increase. The cost of subduing these events was both financially substantial and also inconvenient. The interruption to trade and, more importantly, the crop economies would take time to recover and each interruption would come at considerable expense. In this sense, therefore, it could be suggested that there emerged a practical realisation that to continue this practice would be to incur further cost which both affected profits but also the lives of

SOURCE

6 'The Abolition of the Slave Trade or Inhumanity of Dealer'. A print depicting the cruelty of Captain John Kimber on board the ship *Recovery* by Isaac Cruikshank, dated 10 April 1792. Kimber was put on trial for murdering some of his cargo in 1792. The trial gave the abolition movement widespread publicity while the actions of men like Kimber encouraged slave resistance on board the slave ships.

The ABOLITION of the SLAVE TRADE.
Or the Inhumanity of Dealers in human flesh exemplified in Captn. Kimbers treatment of a Young Negro Girl of 15 for her Virjen Modesty

colonial residents. Combined with this realisation, the re-adoption of slavery by the French after 1802 gave abolitionists a new lease of life and gradually the cause gained public support once more.

Slave revolts had occurred ever since the slave trade began. In itself slave resistance was not a new experience for the British authorities and as such it was not a definitive motive for abolition. Perhaps the real significance of it was the implication of continued revolt at a time when Britain was already distracted by other problems such as war with France and domestic industrialisation. These concerns, together with growing public support and the perennial bills of Wilberforce, encouraged more sympathy for abolition which, once the initial shock of rebellion subsided, was only enhanced by the prospect of further resistance.

ACTIVITY
CONSOLIDATION

Changing political climate

1 Write down any evidence of political change you are aware of between the years 1785 and 1807.

2 How might these changes have encouraged the cause of abolition?

Assessing historical perspectives

Given the vast array of factors involved in the abolition of the slave trade and the magnitude of the event to the development of British history, it has undergone a rigorous investigation by historians to determine the real motives behind its decline. In this final section the interpretations of three historians' views relating to the abolition of the slave trade are considered and some analysis is offered regarding their conclusions.

James Walvin

Among the more recent scholars of the slave trade is James Walvin. The passage below is taken from *A Short History of Slavery* and presents an overall assessment of the abolition of the slave trade.

EXTRACT

9 From James Walvin's *A Short History of Slavery*, published in 2007.

… In March 1807 the Bill had passed all its parliamentary stages and received royal assent. The British had abolished the slave trade. To this day, however, a great deal of mystery and speculation remains about precisely why they had done so. They had, after all, abolished a form of trade that had gone virtually unchallenged for almost two centuries, which continued to profit large numbers of people and which had made possible the development of critical areas of European settlement in the tropical Americas. That it was ended, so quickly, so comprehensively and to such public acclaim remains a historical curiosity. Had it become unprofitable, even though those people most actively involved wished to continue with the trade? Had the British people changed: had they developed a previously unknown sensibility about the slave trade and its inherent cruelties? Was it largely (or simply) the work of Wilberforce and Clarkson and their unrelenting agitation? Or was it – and this is more likely – a complexity of all these and more? And what role had the slaves played in this transformation – notably those involved in the insurrection in Haiti? It is difficult to offer a satisfactory answer. And in any case, in 1807 the campaign was only half-finished. The slave trade was ended. But slavery itself survived.

The analysis offered by Walvin adopts a very broad perspective on the events leading up to abolition in 1807. The basis of his assessment lies in the premise that abolition was something not to be expected given the unprecedented level of wealth it generated and the fact that it had not been challenged for such a long period of time. Considering his qualification of the trade's unrivalled position, in this analysis he therefore seeks to offer reasons for why it came to an end when it did and rather than offer a definitive answer, instead offers a collection of factors which he maintains worked together to produce abolition. In presenting this collection of ideas he contextualises the event by identifying a range of significant elements rather than focusing on an argument that endorses any particular aspect.

The overall conclusions drawn by Walvin combine a variety of perspectives, each of which have merit. By considering them all, his analysis is acknowledging both the complexity of the issue and also the broader understanding that nothing is mono-causal; no one factor can be held as the definitive reason for an event. Certainly one factor may stand out above others, but such is the nature of things, and history particularly, that when this is the case it is very unlikely that it stands alone; factors are not often exclusive and they are themselves the product of other factors. For example, in the case of abolishing the slave trade, the classic interpretation is that it was the result of the crusading efforts of Wilberforce and his fellow abolitionists' humanitarian zeal. As an independent factor this is certainly a significant influence as it is the reason that abolition becomes a political topic having been brought to the public's attention by first the abolition society, and then Wilberforce in parliament. However, if this was the only factor then why did abolition take another 30 years to achieve after the society was first set up? Certainly it is reasonable to suggest that it takes time for people to change their opinions even if the reality is so inhumane. If this is accepted, however, why does it take so long to change? If the longer timeframe was because the public remained positively inclined towards the slave trade then what either made the population hesitant to criticise it after being faced with the realities and the government reluctant to abolish it? On this reasoning there are, logically, other factors that must have influenced the changing public and parliamentary opinion, for example, the timing of abolition. The 1790s had seen abolitionists cast into the wilderness as revolutionary France had abolished slavery and Wilberforce and his colleagues were tarred with the same revolutionary brush. Although their principle remained constant, circumstances changed which affected their campaign. After Napoleon re-introduced the slave trade in 1802, however, suddenly it became acceptable in Britain to criticise it once more and in 1807 it was finally ended. In this sense therefore, what motivated abolition was not the humanitarian cause but rather a political motivation which was exercised under a new political climate, giving greater credibility to the humanitarian campaign. Consequently, while one factor might have raised the issue, other factors must also have contributed to the final outcome, on its own the humanitarian factor was not enough.

Adam Hochschild

Another recent text on the slave trade, Adam Hochschild's *Bury the Chains: The Struggle to Abolish Slavery* focuses on the role played by abolitionists and places their actions as the main cause of success.

EXTRACT 10

From Adam Hochschild's *Bury the Chains: The Struggle to Abolish Slavery*, published in 2010.

All of the twelve [original members of the Society for Effecting the Abolition of the Slave Trade] were deeply religious, and the twenty-seven-year-old Clarkson wore black clerical garb. But they also shared a newer kind of faith. They believed that because human beings had a capacity to care about the suffering of others, exposing the truth would move people to action. "We are of the opinion," Granville Sharp wrote to a friend later that year, "that the nature of the slave-trade needs only to be known to be detested." Clarkson, writing of this "enormous evil," said that he "was sure that it was only necessary for the inhabitants of this favoured island to know it, to feel the indignation against it." It was this faith that led him to buy handcuffs, shackles and thumbscrews to display to the people he met on his travels. And that led him to mount his horse again and again to scour the countryside for witnesses who could tell Parliament what life was like on the slave ships and the plantations. The riveting parade of first-hand testimony he and his colleagues put together in the *Abstract of Evidence* and countless other documents is one of the first great flowerings of a very modern belief: that the way to stir men and women to action is not in biblical argument, but through the vivid, unforgettable description of acts of great injustice done to their fellow human beings. The abolitionists placed their hope not in sacred texts, but in human empathy.

Contrary to Walvin's assessment, in Hochschild's analysis the driving motivation is felt to be the humanitarian argument and the role of individuals such as Thomas Clarkson and, to a lesser extent, William Wilberforce. In this argument Hochschild maintains that were it not for the zeal of these figures then the slave trade would not have been abolished. The basis on which this analysis is founded is the shift in attitudes that took place between 1787 and 1807. During this time the slave trade went from being a well-established practice which few outside the non-conformist churches challenged, to an issue that attracted widespread popular discussion. In this sense, Hochschild acknowledges the 'dominant' nature of the slave trade and its supporters and seeks to explain how, given this strength, abolition was able to take place.

To a great extent the argument is an effective one because it offers a clear reason why such a shift occurred. By identifying the humanitarian dimension of abolition Hochschild lifts the general question of slavery out from the empirical data offered by historians such as Eric Williams and Seymour Drescher whose arguments focus upon the economic motivations for abolition. By doing this, he locates the argument within a more emotive field that promotes the idea that people, not statistics were most important. By focusing on this human feature the argument contends that the strength of the pro-slavery lobby was undermined because of the sheer inhumanity that it encouraged. That, when confronted with the realities of the trade by people such as Clarkson, the public quickly turned against the practice as they were exposed to the experiences of the slaves themselves. This argument has a great deal of merit because of the painstaking research that Clarkson undertook and the lengths to which he went to provide an accurate picture of the trade. When giving lectures he would provide visual aids such as shackles that he had acquired from slave ships, or examples of African culture that he would use to underline that slaves were not in fact property but actually accomplished human beings themselves. Supported by fellow-abolitionists such as Olaudah Equiano, whose published autobiography reinforced the grim realities of the slave trade, Clarkson and the emphasis upon humanitarianism was a very potent force in its eventual decline.

By placing the main cause of abolition in the hands of the abolitionists, Hochschild presents an argument which focuses on the role of individuals. On one level this offers a strong case as it is people who promote change. Events are certainly important, but what makes them so are the people who then take advantage of these events. Without Wilberforce and Clarkson to press for abolition, the more favourable climate towards abolition after 1802 would not have been so relevant. Just as Walvin suggests that it is combinations of factors that lead to abolition, Hochschild places the most emphasis upon one factor which he believes took advantage of prevailing circumstances and drove forward the cause. In this analysis he adopts a similar relational logic but places more importance upon the tangible importance of action.

A Level Exam-Style Question Section C

Study Extracts 10 and 11.

In the light of differing interpretations, how convincing do you find the view that the slave trade ended because of the efforts of humanitarian campaigners? (20 marks)

Tip
Identify the other factors that might influence abolition and evaluate them against the actions of the humanitarian campaigners – are they more or less significant?

Patrick Richardson

Writing in the late 1960s, in his *Empire and Slavery*, Patrick Richardson offers an economic analysis about the abolition of the slave trade which echoes Eric Williams.

EXTRACT 11 From Patrick Richardson's *Empire and Slavery*, published in 1968.

There were particular factors assisting the abolitionist cause. Many of the better-established West Indian planters were in favour of the abolition of the slave trade itself. They realised that the trade could supply slaves to the new British territories of Trinidad and Guiana to make them effective rivals of the older British colonies. They also felt that the British colonies were better stocked with slaves than the foreign West Indies, and that it would be in the planters' interests if there was no further supply of slaves at all. Lastly, even the port of Liverpool was becoming less concerned about the trade, which had fallen into fewer hands, and some of these big firms had felt the pinch in the last years of the trade. Other forms of trade and the very profitable practice of wartime **privateering** meant that commercial interests no longer rallied against abolition so loudly.

KEY TERM

Privateering
Privately owned ships being allowed to attack and capture vessels belonging to foreign countries when at war.

For Patrick Richardson, the motivating influence behind the abolition of the slave trade was economics. From this perspective, given the vast sums of money involved within the slave trade and slavery itself, the financial concern was most significant. In this analysis there are several interdependent motives being considered. The first lies in the suggestion that the slave trade fed an industry which, like any other, was desperate to retain a strong market presence so that greater profits could be generated. For the well-established colonies who monopolised the sugar and tobacco industries, the continuance of the slave trade could fuel competition from newly emerging British colonies. Under this interpretation what motivated the successful abolition campaign was not the humanitarian appeals of Wilberforce but rather the increasing desire of the older plantation lobbyists to prevent competition. By removing the supply of slaves, it would be harder for new colonial ventures to challenge their market dominance. This idea reduces the question of abolition to one of a simple business decision, and in the interests of existing slave owners, this decision was easy to make.

Secondly, by focusing on the economic dimension Richardson echoes Eric Williams's 'decline thesis' which places abolition as a product of slavery's receding profitability. Although several historians have shown that the slave trade and its associated economies, such as sugar, were actually growing in 1807, Richardson makes a supporting case for Williams's original argument by intimating that the great slave port of Liverpool was starting to diminish, and by identifying the increasing number of alternative ventures which were turning profit more effectively than the slave trade. In particular he suggests that wartime privateering was an attractive alternative. By offering this example,

Richardson both supports the 'decline thesis' but also forces a wider consideration of abolition because privateering was only possible during the war years. In this sense it could be suggested that timing was the overall driving force behind abolition. Having said that, however, the underlying motive remains money-based; the timing here merely presented another means to generate income, and therefore economics is still, essentially, the driving force.

Implicit to this analysis is the suggestion that the pro-slave trade lobby was substantial and that for as long as this lobby remained an obstacle then abolition would never have taken place. In this sense the fundamental importance of the economic argument is that it made those originally in favour of maintaining the practice, less motivated to do so. By reducing this interest it afforded abolitionists an easier task and as such it has perhaps also promoted that group's position in the history of British slavery. Since Wilberforce and the other abolitionists were generally seen as the instigators of abolition, the final production of the Abolition Act has usually been attributed to their action and, therefore, they have traditionally been heralded as the cause of abolition. This quickly became a popular argument because it restored some of Britain's moral authority after people were exposed to the true horrors of the trade; despite terrible actions the British people themselves saw the need to remove the slave trade and therefore found some redemption in that action. Such is the appeal of this idea that several early commentators were quick to ignore the influence of economics which actually encouraged many plantation owners to accept the end of the trade. By focusing on this feature Richardson rehabilitates Williams's thesis and promotes a more circumspect view of abolition.

In the case of abolition there are a lot of factors that informed the eventual decision to end the slave trade in 1807. Which is most prominent is both down to the significance that is applied to it and the relationship it has with the other factors. When determining which is more likely, the importance of empirical evidence is particularly relevant. Evidence is the basis on which historians base their arguments and as such it is a crucial element for making an assessment. Judgements can only be convincing if they are supported by the weight of evidence, as this is the only way that historians can be confident in suggesting what might have happened. Evidence is all that is left of the past and therefore serves as the only clue for establishing a realistic understanding of events. However, perhaps more important is the perspective of the person interpreting this evidence. In the examples cited above, each historian has a different interpretation and has applied a different emphasis upon the material available to them. Even though each would concede particular events as 'fact': William Wilberforce was the parliamentary voice for abolition; Olaudah Equiano did write his autobiography which exposed the realities of slave experiences, this does not reduce academic conflict. For the majority, these facts are accepted and yet different interpreters will ascribe different degrees of importance to them. In doing so, debate will heat up and discussion will continue about the accuracy of these interpretations. This is the beauty of history and what keeps it alive.

Between 1785 and 1807 there were substantial efforts made in Britain to end the slave trade which was the result of both a changing attitude towards the practice and also changing circumstances that made abolition more attractive. The magnitude of ending such an established practice has been the focus of considerable attention because of the varied interpretations it has generated. Humanitarian principles have generally been credited with creating abolitionism; the movement and its key individuals – Clarkson, Equiano and Wilberforce – were each motivated by a strong sense of human justice. However, they were competing against a well-established tradition, and therefore it is necessary to consider other factors that might have informed their cause. The economic performance of the trade was changing in the light of a changing economic structure – industrialisation was transforming the country – while Britain's empire was shrinking with the loss of the USA. Individually these factors are important, but collectively they are compelling and should be carefully weighed in the balance when assessing the causes of abolition.

THINKING HISTORICALLY Interpretations (4b)

Method is everything – a spectrum of historical methodology

Bad history	Good history
• Based on gut feeling • Argument does not progress logically • No supporting evidence	• Based on an interpretation of evidence • Argument progresses logically • Evidence deployed to support argument

Work in pairs.

Historical writing can reveal much about the methods by which it was constructed. Read Extracts 9 and 10 and answer the following questions.

1 Look carefully at the spectrum of methodology.

   a) Where would you place each source on the spectrum of historical practice?

   b) What evidence would you use to support your choice?

2 Look at Extract 11. How would you change it to make it the same quality of historical writing as Extract 10?

3 Use a dictionary. Explain the following words in their relation to historical writing: substantiation, deduction, inference, cross-reference.

4 How important is it that historians understand and evaluate the methods used by other historians?

ACTIVITY
CONSOLIDATION

Identifying interpretations
1 Write down the main points set out in Extracts 9, 10 and 11.

2 Provide evidence from the text and your own knowledge that supports each point you have identified.

ACTIVITY
SUMMARY

Assessing causation and motivation

Having studied the main factors that influenced the abolition of the slave trade, give each factor a colour and then plot a line graph to reflect how the impact of each factor changes between 1785 and 1807.

Your x-axis should be the time period, and the y-axis should be the extent of impact – the higher up your scale the more impact it had. Jot down any observations you make – why might these change?

📖 WIDER READING

Drescher, S. *Econocide: British Slavery in the Era of Abolition*, University of North Carolina Press (2010)

Hochschild, A. *Burying the Chains: The Struggle for the Abolition of Slavery*, Pan (2010)

Richardson, P. *Empire and Slavery*, Longman (1968)

Walvin, J. *A Short History of Slavery*, Penguin (2007)

Williams, E. *Capitalism and Slavery*, University of North Carolina Press (1944)

Preparing for your AS Level Paper 1 exam

Advance planning

1. Draw up a timetable for your revision and try to keep to it. Spread your timetable over a number of weeks, and aim to cover four or five topics each week.
2. Spend longer on topics which you have found difficult, and revise them several times.
3. Above all, do not try to limit your revision by attempting to 'question spot'. Try to be confident about all aspects of your Paper 1 work, because this will ensure that you have a choice of questions in Sections A and B.

Paper 1 overview:

AS Paper 1	Time: 2 hours 15 minutes	
Section A	Answer 1 question from a choice of 2	20 marks
Section B	Answer 1 question from a choice of 2	20 marks
Section C	Answer 1 compulsory interpretations question	20 marks
	Total marks =	60 marks

You should familiarise yourself with the layout of the paper by looking at the examples published by Edexcel. The questions for each section are followed by eight pages of lined paper where you should write your answer.

Section A questions

Section A questions ask you to analyse and evaluate either cause or consequence. You should consider either the reasons for, or the results of, an event or development. You will be asked for coverage of a period of around ten years, possibly a little longer. For example, a question for Option 1F might be 'Was the involvement of President Truman the main reason for the changing status of black Americans in the years 1945–55?' Your answer should consider the reasons given in the question, then look at other relevant points and reach a conclusion.

Section B questions

Section B questions cover a longer timespan than in Section A, at least one-third of the period you have studied. The questions take the form of 'How far…', 'How significant…', 'To what extent…' or 'How accurate is it to say…'. The questions can deal with historical concepts such as cause, consequence, change, continuity, similarity, difference and significance. Again, you should consider the issue raised in the question, consider other relevant issues, and then conclude with an overall judgement.

Section C questions

There is no choice in Section C, which is concerned with the historical interpretations you have studied linked to the question 'What explains the abolition of the slave trade at the end of the period, c1785–1807?' You will be given two sources totalling around 300 words (printed separately) and the question will take the form 'How far do you agree with the view that…?' There is no need to use source analysis skills such as making inferences or considering provenance for this Section C answers. You will need to use the extracts and your own knowledge to consider the view given in the question.

Use of time

This is an issue which you should discuss with your teachers and fellow students, but here are some suggestions for you.

1. Do not write solidly for 45 minutes on each question. For Section A and B answers you should spend a few minutes working out what the question is asking you to do, and drawing up a plan of your answer. This is especially important for Section B answers, which cover an extended period of time.
2. For Section C it is essential that you have a clear understanding of the content of each extract and the points that each extract is making. Read each extract carefully and underline important points. You could approach your answer by analysing the first extract, then the second, and then using your own knowledge before reaching an overall judgement. You might decide to spend up to ten minutes reading the sources and drawing up your plan, and 35 minutes writing your answer.

Preparing for your AS Level exams

Paper 1: AS Level sample answer with comments

Section A

These questions assess your understanding of the period in breadth. They will ask you about the content you have learned about in the four key themes, and may ask about more than one theme. For these questions remember to:

- give an analytical, not a descriptive, response
- support your points with evidence
- cover the whole time period specified in the question
- come to a substantiated judgement.

Was parliament's unwillingness to modernise the electoral system the main reason for the growth in reform agitation in the years 1785–1800? (20 marks)

Average student answer

The electoral system in Britain was very out dated and in need of improvement but the government was very reluctant to do this and therefore the people became upset to the point of establishing protest movements which aimed to force political change in the country.

The political system in Britain very much favoured the wealthy landowners who were able to use their money to bribe their way into power. Once in this position they were able to ensure that the country operated in a way that suited them rather than anybody else. They looked after themselves by passing laws like the Corn Law in 1815 which raised the price of bread by making imports expensive. This selfish attitude stopped things developing for the benefit of the whole country – for example, even though a growing manufacturing class was developing after 1785 they were not embraced by the political establishment who saw them as a threat even though they were improving the country. Since this new group was not able to get any advantages because of the closed-mindedness of those in power they began to organise themselves into a distinctive movement to make more vocal demands in the hope that they could gain the influence they felt they deserved. In this way the system did not recognise their contribution and therefore it was out-dated and this led to protest.

This introduction offers some general understanding of the question but does not acknowledge the presence of any debate. There is no clearly articulated argument and little thought is given to the need to consider other reasons.

There is some broad analysis in this paragraph and an attempt to address the question focus but this is quite limited. In places the explanation is weakened by very general evidence and some points are not sufficiently developed to promote a reasoned and closely focused response. In terms of focus, the comment about the Corn Law is outside the given timeframe and alternative evidence that fell within 1785–1800 would have been more appropriate.

Another point that supports the idea that the electoral system was outdated was the distribution of seats. This was important because the country was starting to see new cities like Manchester and Birmingham develop and yet these new cities did not have any representation. The existing system was based on medieval criteria which gave representation to towns that were important at the time. By the end of the 18th century though the majority of these towns were no longer important and some such as East Dunster had actually fallen into the sea! The existence of these 'rotten boroughs' meant that many people, particularly those who lived in the new cities, did not feel properly represented and therefore they began to get upset to the point that they would start to organise themselves into reform groups to seek the necessary changes they felt they were owed. These groups were felt to be necessary because those in parliament were not inclined to make the changes that were asked for because the current system suited them as they were the people who benefitted from it.

> This offers a reasoned point that is relevant to the question. There are descriptive passages and the evidence is a little general. The point about rotten boroughs is developed in a reasonable manner that demonstrates some appreciation of the growing motivation for reform and the reluctance of government to grant it.

Although the system was in need of changing there were other factors that also contributed to the development of protest. In France there was a revolution in 1789 which encouraged people in Britain to think about their own system and how it could be better. The revolution saw the king beheaded and a more democratic government established. This was in stark contrast to the government in Britain which was very much based on money. People in power were all landowners and believed in the righteousness of aristocratic rule as they felt these people were the best people to govern as they were the most educated. Since France was so close to Britain lower-class people heard about the French Revolution and this gave them hope for changes in their own country. People were encouraged to organise groups that used the ideas of the revolution to stir up interest for reform in Britain and in this way the system did not create protest but rather the revolution did.

> This paragraph introduces some awareness of debate and the existence of other factors which addresses the 'main reason' element of the question. The comments about the importance of the French Revolution are valid but they could be more developed in places. The comment about revolution 'stirring up interest' is nicely analytical and the paragraph ends with some clear judgement being offered. However there is no specific example of agitation identified.

In conclusion the electoral system in Britain was a very outdated one which created lots of problems for the government. People were hoping for changes to be made but this never came because those in power wanted to keep that power for themselves as it served their interests nicely. Although the French Revolution was important to developing protest groups, the people were already unhappy with the system before the revolution happened and therefore it was not as important as the system being full of weaknesses in the first place. Ultimately it was these weaknesses that encouraged the growth of the protest movements who saw that their system was poor and they wanted to change it for the better.

> The conclusion reaches a reasoned judgement which shows awareness of some of the key features of the question. It does not really address the given factor of parliament's unwillingness to grant reform and therefore it could be a little more focused.

Verdict

This is an average answer because:

- the response only partially considers the 'stated factor' of government unwillingness and therefore the focus could be more pronounced
- the reasoning offered is a little general and only supported by broad evidence
- there is some clear organisation to the answer but the precision of the argument is a little limited.

Use the feedback on this answer to rewrite it, making as many improvements as you can.

Paper 1: AS Level sample answer with comments

Section A

These questions assess your understanding of the period in breadth. They will ask you about the content you learned about in the four key themes, and may ask about more than one theme. For these questions remember to:

- give an analytical, not a descriptive, response
- support your points with evidence
- cover the whole time period specified in the question
- come to a substantiated judgement.

Was parliament's unwillingness to modernise the electoral system the main reason for the growth in reform agitation in the years 1785–1800? (20 marks)

Strong student answer

To a great extent it is reasonable to suggest that parliament's unwillingness to grant reform was the main cause for growing agitation because although the electoral system was undoubtedly out of date, this body was aware of this shortfall and had the authority to make the necessary changes if it chose to. By refusing to take action those in power were seen as being indifferent to people's needs and therefore the people were pushed to force change for themselves.

> This introduction offers a clear focus on the question demand and presents awareness of other factors while also presenting a clear argument.

Without doubt the electoral system was anachronistic and this certainly created an unfair political environment that failed to reflect the changing nature of British society. Towards the end of the 18th century industrialisation was beginning to encourage the growth of new cities such as Birmingham and Manchester which were fast growing urban centres and yet were not adequately represented. In the case of Manchester, for example, there were more than 120,000 people living there and yet they had no MPs. As these centres became more integral to the economy there was an increased awareness of their political impotence. In this sense the problem of reform was generated by economic progress however parliament was perhaps the cause of agitation because it failed to address this imbalance. Given that the majority of parliament were themselves landowners they arguably saw no incentive to introduce reform in the new towns which, in their eyes, could shift power away from their established heartlands and into the hands of the town dwellers. On these self-interested grounds there was little motivation to change the electoral system and therefore if change was to come it placed the impetus for achieving it with the people themselves.

> There is a clear point developed in this paragraph which relates well to other key features of the period. The argument is logically deployed and the reasoning well considered. In support there is some precise evidence.

In support of this argument was the failure of William Pitt to pass his reform legislation in 1785 which sought to reduce the number of 'rotten boroughs' in the country. Since the majority of these boroughs were grossly over-represented rotten boroughs and were usually under the influence of a rich landowner, there was no real incentive to pass the bill as to do so could either lose that landowner his seat, or force a contested election that could cost him thousands of pounds. The failure of this bill is particularly significant to the development of a reform movement because it evidenced very clearly the reluctance of parliament to change things and in doing so it stirred up a political consciousness amongst the population.

> This is a reasoned paragraph in support of the first point. Evidence is appropriate although the explanation could be more developed to emphasise the point about the parliamentary interest which would allow for greater focus on what the question demands.

Although this reluctance was paramount in the growth of reform agitation – after 1790 there emerged several reform groups including the Society for Constitutional Information which sought to spread the idea of political rights through pamphlets, and the London Corresponding

Society after 1792 which openly communicated with radicals abroad. The growth of these clubs dovetailed with the outbreak of the French revolution in 1789 and arguably this event was more influential. Proclaiming 'liberty' and 'equality' this revolution also killed a king and replaced monarchy with a republic. This event shook the British aristocracy and in doing so also gave reform campaigners an intellectual basis for their demands. By offering a template for reformers this revolution also created a more radical environment in Britain which arguably gave more credibility to those who sought reform and therefore raised the profile of the cause. In support of this was the publication of Thomas Paine's 'Rights of Man' which sold more than 30,000 copies and helped to spread the reform demand in Britain. By promoting this demand the revolution inspired agitation in the form of the corresponding groups in the hope that parliament would be more predisposed to consider reform given the more threatening environment that revolution had created.

> This paragraph starts to consider the debate a little more and addresses the 'main reason' element of the question by looking at other factors that might be important. These are quite well developed and also related, albeit fleetingly, to the overall argument of parliamentary inaction.

Although the revolution undoubtedly inspired agitation this was short-lived once war with France broke out in 1793 and the government adopted a more determined stance against political change. In this sense it is reasonable to suggest that the government was resolute in its determination to avoid reform and yet agitation actually died down despite this reluctance. Consequently it could be more accurate to suggest that agitation was in fact bound to other factors rather than any sense of government failing. Most prominent among these is perhaps economic difficulties as discontent only grew during times of economic depression and when employment was improved during the war years with government contracts and military demands, this discontent subsided. On this basis reform is better thought of as 'hunger politics' rather than being politically motivated and as such only challenged government when the people themselves were vulnerable. This argument has some merit but in either case the growth of agitation was encouraged by government inaction – be it politically or economically motivated.

> Here the debate is taken even further and there is some clear evaluation of why agitation developed. This paragraph offers some balance to the response and the points are reasonably substantiated.

In conclusion therefore, there was certainly a need for political change in Britain and even given the importance of revolution in France in promoting the demand for reform, the motivation primarily lay with parliament which failed to make sufficient changes to the lives of its population to the extent that people felt they had no choice but to help themselves.

> This is a confident conclusion that offers a clear judgement on reasons for the growth in agitation.

Verdict

This is a strong answer because:

- key issues relevant to the question focus are explored and developed
- sufficient knowledge is deployed and supported by mostly precise evidence from across the period up until 1800
- there is a clear argument being developed in a logical and reasonably clear manner that evidences good understanding of what the question demands
- there is a reasoned judgement that is reached.

Paper 1: AS Level sample answer with comments

Section B

These questions assess your understanding of the course in breadth and will cover a period of 30 years or more. They will ask you about the content you learned about in the four key themes, and may ask about more than one theme. The questions will also require you to explore a range of concepts, such as change over time, similarity and difference, as well as significance. For these questions remember to:

- identify the focus of the question
- consider the concepts you will need to explore
- support your points with evidence from across the time period specified in the question
- develop the evidence you deploy to build up your overall judgement
- come to a substantiated judgement that directly addresses the question set.

How significant was the rising cost of poor relief in the years 1815–33 in the decision to introduce poor law reform in 1834? (20 marks)

Average student answer

The decision to introduce poor law reform was motivated by the rising cost of providing poor relief as this figure increased dramatically in the years after 1800 and those paying for it became more critical of the existing system which, they felt, was no longer practical. Although there were also additional influences in the decision to make changes, this financial motivation was the most important factor.

In the 19th century the British population doubled in size from the time that the old poor law was introduced back in the 17th century and therefore there were more people who wanted to take advantage of the poor law provision. People were much poorer during this time as many lost their jobs because of the growing use of machines during industrialisation which was taking place. This was particularly the case in the countryside where employment was already seasonal and therefore the people were often already seeking additional support for when they did not have any work to do – usually in the winter months when harvests had been taken in. With more people needing to apply for relief the cost went up and therefore the people who paid the poor rate were forced to pay even more which encouraged them to think about changing the system so that they could reduce the amount they were being forced to spend.

Apart from the increase in population, the existing provision was not actually good enough to provide for those in need. Since 1795 the Speenhamland system had been introduced. This system involved tying the provision of relief to the cost of bread so if bread prices rose then so too would the amount of money given to the poor. Also, if you had a bigger family then you would get more money as this system was based upon being able to effectively feed your family. This system was part of the 'outdoor relief' of paupers which was effectively giving them free money which made many employers think that they could reduce wages as then their employees would get more from the poor rate which would mean that they could save money themselves. By doing this employers were able to improve their own finances but at the same time shifted more pressure onto the poor law which was not able to cope with the extra burden to the point that people began to think about changing it.

Cost was a key factor in this decision but also there were other reasons that helped to promote the idea to update the poor law too. Not least among these was the growing critical opinion among those in power who felt that pauperism was the result of lazy people who just could not be motivated to work. Chief among those who pushed this view was Joseph Townsend, a doctor

Comments (right margin):

This is a reasonably focused introduction, which identifies a clear argument in response to the question demand. It briefly acknowledges some element of debate which could be expanded a little to better show the relationship between different factors.

This paragraph identifies an important point that is relevant to the question but the explanation is a little general in places. Some thought is given to the cost implication of the growing population but the evidence supporting this is a little vague.

There is a good use of terminology here and evidence is a little more precise in places but there is some drift towards description, which limits the development of the explanation. The final sentence is clearly articulated but this could be mentioned earlier in the paragraph and made the focus as it is more clearly orientated towards what the question demands.

and vicar of Pewsey, who felt that providing relief actually stopped people making the effort to work. His belief was that by reducing, or even removing, relief provision then people would be faced with the prospect of having nothing and therefore this would be a good incentive for those people to actually make the effort to find work rather than rest safe in the knowledge that they would be taken care of in the event of having no income. This view was shared by others like Thomas Malthus, an economist, who felt that there should be no poor relief at all. Malthus was a very important person in the government as he advised them on economic policy. Such was the influence of the opinions of these men therefore that in 1832 a royal commission was set up to investigate the existing system and to make recommendations for its overhaul.

> This paragraph introduces debate although it pulls the answer into 'listing' other factors. The material is relevant but needs to be discussed in terms of its implications on 'cost'. The knowledge and explanation is quite appropriate and offers some clear understanding of the attitudes toward poor law provision.

Finally the changing attitudes of the government were important in encouraging poor law reform. With the introduction of industrialisation the economy was growing and the government felt that the best way to help the economy continue to grow was to leave it to its own devices and allow employers to maximise their profits by not really regulating them. This 'hands off' approach was called 'laissez-faireism' and the government felt they should apply this model to the provision of poor relief also.

In conclusion the decision to change the old poor law was based upon the growing cost of providing more people with relief combined with an increasingly critical opinion of the existing system. Although influential people were already critical the real motivation was the financial burden overall.

> This paragraph needs to be more developed. The point is valid but again needs linking directly to 'cost'. It also is not sufficiently explained and seems 'tacked on'. This would be a good point to relate to the previous paragraph and then use them to evaluate the impact of 'rising cost'.

> As a conclusion there is a clear judgement which is quite effective but could offer more reasoning behind why the financial burden is most important.

Verdict

This is an average answer because:

- it offers some clear focus on the question demand but the depth of analysis is a little inconsistent
- the use of evidence is a little general throughout and lacks overall precision

- there is some description within the response which detracts from the overall judgement.

Use the feedback on this answer to rewrite it, making as many improvements as you can.

Paper 1: AS Level sample answer with comments

Section B

These questions assess your understanding of the course in breadth and will cover a period of 30 years or more. They will ask you about the content you learned about in the four key themes, and may ask about more than one theme. The questions will also require you to explore a range of concepts, such as change over time, similarity and difference, as well as significance. For these questions remember to:

* identify the focus of the question
* consider the concepts you will need to explore
* support your points with evidence from across the time period specified in the question
* develop the evidence you deploy to build up your overall judgement
* come to a substantiated judgement that directly addresses the question set.

How significant was the rising cost of poor relief in the years 1815–33 in the decision to introduce poor law reform in 1834?
(20 marks)

Strong student answer

The rising cost of poor relief was certainly a significant feature in the decision to introduce reform because as the country developed in the early 19th century this burden became much greater as the population grew. By making people think about reform the rising cost is very relevant to the legislation of 1834. However this is only because it initiated a more widespread consideration. Once the idea had been established, political motive and ideological attitudes had greater influence upon the actual nature of the reforms.

The cost of providing relief is clearly a significant feature behind the reform of the poor law because ultimately governments are motivated by economic considerations such as this. With the expenditure on relief reaching more than £6.4 million between 1814 and 1818, cost was without doubt a concern of government. In this sense it is important because it raised awareness of the existing provision and forced those in power to give greater consideration of it. This was particularly significant because there were certainly problems with the existing system, including the widespread use of the Speenhamland system after 1795 which gave employers the opportunity to reduce wages in the belief that any shortfall would be made up by the poor rate. As such the rising cost was an indicator of inadequacy, which then mobilised government action to the extent that by 1834 there was wholesale reform in the shape of the Poor law Amendment Act.

Although cost was a prime consideration it only encouraged the discussion of reform but did not actually determine the shape of it. In this endeavour ideological pressures were more influential. The basis of reform was the concept of 'less eligibility' which introduced the more widespread use of workhouses, in conjunction with the ending of outdoor relief. This contrast to the old Elizabethan Poor Law was the product of a growing conservative attitude that believed pauperism was the fault of the poor themselves: that they were poor because they were indolent and did not actively seek to take care of themselves. Individuals such as Joseph Townsend and Thomas Malthus dominated this opinion and reasoned that without any relief, people would be more willing to push themselves more. Considering the more individualistic society that industrialisation and commercialism were developing, this idea enjoyed significant influence in Britain even before costs grew and as such generated much support for reforming the 'too soft' existing system.

> This is a strong opening as it contextualises the question, identifies some key features and offers a clear argument to be developed.

> There is good use of evidence here, which is spread across the timeframe and used in support of clearly developed points. The final sentence offers a clear verdict on the stated factor, which maintains a consistent focus throughout the paragraph.

> Here there is some further judgement of the stated factor and this is used to consider other influences on reform in order to demonstrate a balanced response to the question which addresses the 'how significant' requirement.

The growing dominance of this more punishing approach to poor law reform was also enhanced by the popular intellectual concept of Utilitarianism which emerged towards the end of the 18th century and which encouraged the 'greatest happiness for the greatest number'. In this sense, if applied to poor relief, it would be more beneficial to society if the few very poor people were brought into the workhouse at the expense of the many while the rest are forced to take care of themselves as this would reduce the burden on the majority. Utilitarianism offered a clear intellectual basis for reform but it also reflected the changing nature of society which increasingly supported strong individualism at the expense of those few who could not manage for themselves. In this sense the decision to reform the poor law was also perhaps motivated by a fundamental shift away from traditional government support for the vulnerable, in favour of a more individual focus which mirrored the successful economic policy – 'laissez-faireism' – that was promoting industrial growth. Given this attitude it is therefore more reasonable to suggest that the rising cost of relief was actually the pretext for adopting a new policy which was more in line with current thinking rather than the singular motive specifically.

Here the evaluation of rising cost is further challenged and the 'how significant' requirement is given more consideration. The significance of Utilitarianism is well developed and used effectively to evaluate the importance of cost in terms of other possible motivations. This shows a good appreciation of the time period and the context of the question.

On this point there is further support for this motivation as there had already been attempts to reform in line with a more conservative approach. In 1818 The Selective Vestries Act gave more scrutiny power to the parish boards with the intention of tightening up the provision. In this sense the 1834 Act was just the latest incarnation of an increasingly conservative effort to reduce dependency.

The point here is valid and made relevant although this could be more developed – perhaps a better idea here would be to incorporate this point within another paragraph above. Although there is limited development there is still some analytical comment which just needs explicitly linking to the question.

In conclusion there had been efforts to introduce reform prior to 1834. While this might be in an attempt to address the rising cost of relief, the nature of this reform suggests that cost was just one feature of generally growing disillusion with the existing system. In terms of the final reform with its heavy emphasis on punitive measures, the cost of building workhouses was excessive and therefore it is unlikely that cost was the sole motive for changing the existing system.

This conclusion reaches a reasoned judgement although new information is introduced. Overall though this demonstrates a logical argument that has focused on the stated factor and been supported.

Verdict

This is a strong answer because:

- it offers clear focus on the question demand and develops a logical argument
- the use of precise evidence and terminology is evident, demonstrating a good understanding of the material
- the points made are balanced and analytically developed
- there is a clear overall judgement that is supported by the evidence.

Paper 1: AS Level sample answer with comments

Section C

These questions require you to read and analyse two extracts carefully in order to develop a response which examines and makes an informed judgement about different interpretations. The best answers:

- need to show an understanding of the extracts and identify the key points of interpretation
- deploy own knowledge to develop points emerging from extracts and provide necessary context
- develop a judgement after developing and weighing up different interpretations.

Analyse and evaluate Extracts 5 and 7 on pages 125 and 128 and use your knowledge of the issues to explain your answer to the following question.

How far do you agree with the view that William Wilberforce was the most significant individual in the campaign to abolish the slave trade in the years 1785–1807? (20 marks)

Average student answer

The first extract by Walvin talks about the importance of Thomas Clarkson rather than Wilberforce. Clarkson developed a keen interest in the rights of people, especially those he felt were suffering exploitation and as such he won over people like Wilberforce who could make a difference. Wilberforce was important because as the source says he was the 'parliamentary leader' of abolition.

Walvin implies that Wilberforce was a very important individual because he was the MP for Yorkshire which meant that he had some political influence that could play a significant role in promoting abolition. This was because the only way to effect change was through gaining enough political influence to motivate politicians, like Wilberforce, to vote for the end of the slave trade. As someone who was present in parliament and with the opportunity to influence fellow politicians, Wilberforce was a very useful person to push the cause.

Wilberforce was won over to the cause because he was an evangelical Christian who increasingly felt that the slave trade was morally wrong. Since this issue played on his conscience it became one that he had to do something about. When Thomas Clarkson approached him Wilberforce was certainly interested in what he had to say having already read his essay on the subject as Walvin points out. Although he was a little hesitant about becoming the leader of the cause, Wilberforce's moral compass encouraged him to take the lead and consequently began to push for the necessary reform in parliament. By doing this Walvin points out that a useful partnership was formed between Clarkson and Wilberforce which ultimately helped to bring about abolition.

This opening makes the mistake of tackling the extracts separately rather than considering them together. There is some overall understanding of the question demand but the argument is a little thin.

There is some focus on Wilberforce that shows some knowledge of his importance but this is little evidence to support this. Explanation shows some appropriate direction but this could be more fully explored.

This paragraph offers some contextual basis about Wilberforce joining the fight for abolition and towards the end starts to link back to the focus of the question using references to the extract. It is quite descriptive and could be more clearly explained in regard to why Wilberforce is so important.

The second extract by Hilton suggests that Wilberforce was only of marginal importance. Instead he suggests that it was the 500 petitions that encouraged parliament to think about abolishing slavery and even then that when revolts took place these petitions were ignored. Considering the impact of petitions, this was not really the result of Wilberforce but rather Clarkson who was the man who travelled around the country stirring up support – as Walvin maintains. If the petitions were more important, then this would suggest that Clarkson, not Wilberforce was most important.

Furthermore, given that even these petitions were not effective to maintain parliament's interest once revolts took place, it is perhaps more reasonable to say that neither Wilberforce nor Clarkson were actually that effective. They each may have raised awareness of the slave trade and its horrible treatment of slaves, but actually the government was more interested in national security and therefore became more anti the abolitionists once revolts took place, threatening this security.

Overall Hilton suggests that Wilberforce was not very important because of the revolts that took place which undermined abolition, while Walvin suggest that he was quite important because he was the 'parliamentary leader'.

> There is some cross referencing here which shows awareness of the different interpretations but this is not really developed very far and the explanation offers some argument which is in need of more thorough discussion.

> The commentary on the revolts is good as it promotes argument from within the extract text but this is not sufficiently developed using own knowledge to substantiate a judgement effectively. Some examples of how these revolts upset abolition would make this stronger.

> This judgement is not very decisive but rather just says what each source suggests. It could be more thoughtful.

Verdict

This is an average answer because:

- it does not use the extracts effectively enough
- it does not relate enough to the wider movement to provide more context
- it makes a judgement but it needs more substance. There is not enough explicit focus on the question as the essay develops. It lacks the necessary sense of argument for a high level
- the candidate has not worked on the extracts sufficiently in planning the response.

Use the feedback on this answer to rewrite it, making as many improvements as you can.

Paper 1: AS Level sample answer with comments

Section C

These questions require you to read and analyse two extracts carefully in order to develop a response which examines and makes an informed judgement about different interpretations. The best answers:

- need to show an understanding of the extracts and identify the key points of interpretation
- deploy own knowledge to develop points emerging from the extract and provide necessary context
- develop judgement after developing and weighing up different interpretations.

Analyse and evaluate Extracts 5 and 7 on pages 125 and 128 and use your knowledge of the issues to explain your answer to the following question.

How far do you agree that William Wilberforce was the most significant individual in the campaign to abolish the slave trade in the years 1785–1807? (20 marks)

Strong student answer

The extracts highlight the contributions of Clarkson and Wilberforce but also indicate how they were reliant upon other factors to achieve their objectives. Extract 7, for example, emphasises the point that the legislation to abolish the slave trade was very much dependent upon circumstantial events also. In this sense, therefore, while the work of Wilberforce and his movement was crucial to promoting a parliamentary discussion, as the first extract suggests, this discussion could only lead to reform if other political factors allowed for such legislation.

Extract 5 by James Walvin certainly promotes the importance of individual action and places Wilberforce at the centre of this activity as 'the parliamentary leader'. Given the only way by which the trade could be abolished was through parliamentary legislation, having a member of parliament such as Wilberforce was undoubtedly critical for the success of such as movement. This is because it would require someone to raise the issue on their behalf and Wilberforce was very good in this regard: after 1791, for example, he introduced annual bills for abolition until the turn of the century. Although these were not necessarily successful at this time they did nonetheless promote parliamentary awareness of such a growing demand. As a 'rising political star' and the figure who drew the attention of those in power to the cause of abolition, Wilberforce, Walvin is right to suggest, was important to the abolition cause.

A focused introduction which shows a clear understanding of the key arguments put forward in the two extracts and begins to develop the argument that the success of the campaign depended on the combination of acceptable circumstances in addition to individuals.

This paragraph develops an argument that shows how important Wilberforce was. It is directly linked to the extract by developing the references to 'parliamentary leader' and, to a lesser extent, 'rising political star'. It could have developed the second point a little more but the material is supported by some good examples and there is clear thought to the extract interpretation.

In contrast to this interpretation, Extract 7 challenges the idea that Wilberforce was that important by pointing to how unsuccessful his bills were before 1807 and how in 1791 parliament had thrown out such a bill 'by a large majority'. In this sense the source suggests that the success of abolition owed less to people like Wilberforce and Clarkson, as Walvin maintained, but was only inclined to support a bill after 500 petitions had been signed. While it would be reasonable to say that this public mobilisation was the result of action by people like Clarkson who, as Extract 5 says was 'the public propagandist', it challenges the argument that Wilberforce was most important on the grounds that he did not operate so closely to the grass roots as Clarkson.

Furthermore the second extract evidences the dominance of the 'West India Lobby' which enjoyed a lot of support in parliament. This lobby is perhaps the reason that Wilberforce's bills were unsuccessful and on this note is worth considering why this might be so. The lobby was powerful because it produced substantial wealth for the country and many MPs had ties with this group of plantation owners. With such a close relationship it would be reasonable to suggest that self-interest was more persuasive than Wilberforce's moral arguments. This is further reinforced in Extract 7 when it mentions the 'brutal rebellions' which turn parliament away from abolition once they were prepared to consider it. The quick reversal of support that these rebellions promoted augments the idea that parliament was primarily motivated by self-interest. In the case of rebellion in St Domingue, any gradual change to the existing system was anticipated to stir up similar aggression in British colonies and therefore it was arguably safer to leave things as they were.

A final point that also enforces the importance of circumstance was the revolutionary war Britain was fighting with France after 1793. It is important to note that this was taking place while Wilberforce was presenting his annual abolition bills to parliament. In this sense it could be suggested that this was the reason for his failure as the slave trade kept British markets open while those in Europe were closed because of war. This would suggest that there was also an economic motivation for maintaining the trade which was perhaps more important that Wilberforce's moral arguments against abolition. Although the trade did come to an end while this war was still being fought, there was still a sufficient shift in circumstances to suggest this was more important than individual action. After 1802 Napoleon reintroduced the slave trade in France and therefore it became a point of national pride in Britain that they promote abolition. On this basis he is important in raising the issue, he was not able to achieve his aim until a sufficient shift in circumstances had taken place.

In conclusion, therefore, it is reasonable to maintain that Wilberforce was an important figure in the abolition of the slave trade because he promoted awareness in parliament of the cause and forced people to think about it. Although this was not immediately successful because of challenging circumstances, his actions did mean that when such circumstances changed, the abolitionists were well placed to take advantage.

> These paragraphs are well focused on the extract material and develop a good evaluation of the 'how convincing' element of the question. They are each supported by appropriate evidence and demonstrate some good understanding of the themes that the question draws on.

> Emphasises the contributions of Wilberforce as a dedicated leader of the campaign but also relates this to the importance of circumstance.

> A reasoned conclusion that brings together the argument that is generally sustained throughout the answer.

Verdict

This is a strong answer because:

- it uses the extracts effectively
- it mixes own knowledge with the extract use to develop ideas
- it maintains a good focus throughout the response
- there is a clear argument being developed throughout.

Preparing for your A Level Paper 1 exam

Advance planning

- Draw up a timetable for your revision and try to keep to it. Spread your timetable over a number of weeks, and aim to cover four or five topics each week.

- Spend longer on topics which you have found difficult, and revise them several times.

- Above all, do not try to limit your revision by attempting to 'question spot'. Try to be confident about all aspects of your Paper 1 work, because this will ensure that you have a choice of questions in Sections A and B.

Paper I overview:

AL Paper I	Time: 2 hours 15 minutes	
Section A	Answer I question from a choice of 2	20 marks
Section B	Answer I question from a choice of 2	20 marks
Section C	Answer I compulsory interpretations question	20 marks
	Total marks =	60 marks

You should familiarise yourself with the layout of the paper by looking at the examples published by Edexcel. The questions for each section are followed by eight pages of lined paper where you should write your answer.

Section A and Section B questions

The essay questions in Sections A and B are similar in form. They ask you to reach a judgement on an aspect of the course you have studied, and will deal with one or more historical concepts of change, continuity, similarity, difference, cause, consequence and significance. The question stems which will be used will include 'To what extent…', 'How far…', 'How significant was…' and so on. You should consider the issue raised by the question, develop your answer by looking at other relevant points, and reach a judgement in your conclusion.

The main difference between Section A and Section B questions will be the timespan of the questions. Section A questions will cover a period of ten years or more, while Section B questions will be concerned with at least one-third of the period you have studied.

A Section A question for Option 1E might read 'How far was high expenditure on the armed forces responsible for economic decline in the USSR in the years 1964–82?' Your answer should consider the issue of expenditure on the armed forces, look at

other issues such as agricultural decline, falling productivity in industry, and Brezhnev's reluctance to undertake economic reforms, before reaching an overall judgement on the question.

A Section B question on the same paper will cover a longer period of time, but have a similar shape. For example, 'How successful were the government's social policies in improving the lives of the Soviet people in the years 1917–64?' Here you should consider various successes, such as full employment, education and healthcare, but also point out policies which were less successful, such as housing and different policies towards women over time. You should conclude by reaching a judgement on the question.

Section C questions

There is no choice in Section C, which is concerned with the historical interpretations you have studied linked to the question "What explains the abolition of the slave trade at the end of the period, c1785–1807?" You will be given two extracts totalling around 400 words (printed separately) and the question will take the form "How convincing do you find the view that…?" There is no need to use source analysis skills such as making inferences or considering provenance for this Section C answers. You should approach your answer by analysing both extracts separately, and then use your own knowledge to support, and to counter, the view given in the question, before reaching an overall judgement.

Use of time

This is an issue which you should discuss with your teachers and fellow students, but here are some suggestions for you.

- Do not write solidly for 45 minutes on each question. For Section A and B answers you should spend a few minutes working out what the question is asking you to do, and drawing up a plan of your answer. This is especially important for Section B answers, which cover an extended period of time.

- For Section C it is essential that you have a clear understanding of the content of each extract and the points which each extract is making. Read each extract carefully and underline important points. You might decide to spend up to ten minutes reading the extracts and drawing up your plan, and 35 minutes writing your answer.

Preparing for your A Level exams

Paper 1: A Level sample answer with comments

Section A

These questions assess your understanding of the period in breadth. They will ask you about the content you learned about in the four key themes, and may ask about more than one theme. For these questions remember to:

- give an analytical, not a descriptive, response
- support your points with evidence
- cover the whole time period specified in the question
- come to a substantiated judgement.

How far do you agree that the work of Robert Owen at New Lanark was the most important reason for the growth of co-operation in the years 1815–65? (20 marks)

Average student answer

To a great extent Robert Owen was a significant reason for the development of co-operation ◀ after 1815 because his efforts to improve the character of his workforce at New Lanark not only resulted in economic success but also showed a different way to run industry which was felt to offer more to working people.

Robert Owen was a social reformer who believed that it was the experiences and surroundings that people had which determined their character and as such he sought to give working people ◀ better experiences so as to improve them. He sought to do this by establishing a 'model' factory in New Lanark at which he created decent accommodation and removed harsh punishment as an incentive to work. He also provided education for his workers in the form of his 'Institute for the Formation of Character', in 1816 and in 1817 even an infant school. By providing these opportunities Owen offered a better way of living to those who worked for him and therefore they worked harder and allowed Owen to be economically successful. By 1829 Owen had made more than £300,000 profit which encouraged other people to adopt similar methods.

The better working conditions that Owen created in New Lanark were more appealing to the working class and as such they were inspired to follow a similar approach. Owen's concern to ◀ support workers was manifested in the form of co-operation after 1815 which involved working people working together for their own benefit. In 1821 a Co-operative and Economical Society was set up by Henry Hetherington with the intention of forming a communal house at Spa Fields where people could live together in mutual support. Although this did not last very long it showed an increased willingness to find a way of helping themselves which was one of the basic ideas of co-operation.

By 1829 these early efforts at co-operation changed into co-operative stores which worked on the basis of sharing profits with their customers and by 1832 there were about 500 such stores in ◀ operation. These stores declined in the mid-1830s because of a general lack of business sense but they evidenced a clear effort to adopt more co-operative ideas as this kind of practice was seen as being for the benefit of the working people themselves rather than the employers who retained any profits that were generated by their shops and the labour of their employees. Although Owen did not like these stores because he felt they cheapened his overall concept, arguably they

This introduction has some direction and relates to the question reasonably well. There is a hint of awareness of other key features but this is not well drawn out.

This paragraph contains good evidence and there is some broad understanding of the impact of Robert Owen. The explanation is quite descriptive and the final sentences, though more analytical, require more substantial development.

There is a better focus on what the question demands here with some development. Material is supported by some good evidence again but the point is still quite general and could do with more explanation.

Once again there is good evidence here and some effort to offer some explanation of how Owen was important. The final sentence is quite explicit and makes the paragraph more focused.

developed because of his initial ideas and therefore he can be regarded as an important reason for their growth.

Apart from the success of Robert Owen's initiatives, there were other reasons for the growth of co-operative activities such as the success of the Rochdale Pioneers in 1844 in opening up co-op stores. This group introduced the idea of dividends which was money paid back to customers based upon what they spent in the shop. This group was very successful because they adopted clear rules by which to run their store and this allowed them to be more professionally run and therefore more profitable. The success they enjoyed was a significant reason for the growth of co-operation after 1844 and therefore they are a main reason for the development of this method of operating into the mid to late 19th century. The work of these 'pioneers' encouraged the growth of larger scale 'co-ops' that eventually allowed them to expand into world markets and become even more successful. On this basis, therefore, Owen was quite important to start with but it could be said that the Rochdale Pioneers were more important later on.

> This paragraph offers a good point that broadens the response out into a consideration of other reasons for growth. Evidence is reasonable and quite appropriate and the final judgement offers some good judgement which is broadly substantiated.

Overall therefore, Robert Owen was important to the growth of co-operation after 1815 because he introduced the initial idea which people were then able to develop in a way that best suited them. Later on the Rochdale Pioneers were maybe more important in growing co-operative activities but this was only because Owen had started the idea in the first place.

> This conclusion offers some judgement that is broadly supported in the body of the essay. The final judgement could be a little more precise.

Verdict

This is an average answer because:

- the response contains quite a lot of description which undermines the clarity of the explanation at times
- there is some attempt to consider other reasons for the growth of co-operation but this could be more developed with additional reasons to evidence greater range

- there is a reasonably substantiated judgement which is generally supported by the body of the essay.

Use the feedback on this answer to rewrite it, making as many improvements as you can.

Paper 1: A Level sample answer with comments

Section A

These questions assess your understanding of the period in breadth. They will ask you about the content you learned about in the four key themes, and may ask about more than one theme. For these questions remember to:

- give an analytical, not a descriptive, response
- support your points with evidence
- cover the whole time period specified in the question
- come to a substantiated judgement.

How far do you agree that the work of Robert Owen at New Lanark was the most important reason for the growth of co-operation in the years 1815–65? (20 marks)

Strong student answer

To a great extent Robert Owen was a significant reason for the development of co-operation after 1815 because his efforts to improve the character of his workforce at New Lanark not only resulted in economic success but his ideas offered a more positive opportunity to working people whose lives were often exploited in the increasingly individualistic and profit-motivated world that Britain in the 19th century was becoming.

Robert Owen was a significant influence upon the development of co-operation because he provided the initial inspiration for this concept. His model textile mill in New Lanark that he established after 1800 was not only profitable – earning him more than £300,000 by 1829, but it also showed how developing a more positive working relationship with employees by offering a better working environment was conducive to mutual progress. The provision of a school for children in 1817 and the adult 'Institute for the Formation of Character' the year before gave his employees more opportunities to help themselves and this arguably promoted the effectiveness of the factory itself. By clearly demonstrating the benefits of this more 'communal', people-based, approach Owen is rightly to be considered a significant cause for the growth in co-operation because not only did he introduce the general idea, but his mill offered a template for practising it.

In support of this argument after 1813 when Owen published his 'Essay of the Formation of Character' there was a rapid growth in co-operative activity which suggests that with the public dissemination of his ideas, more people were inspired by them. The primary means by which co-operation was practised was through co-operative shops which shared profits with their customers and by 1832 more than 500 were in operation. The growth of these outlets go some way to support the idea that Owen was important to the growth of co-operation as without his initial efforts at New Lanark, or the public presentation of his ideas, there may not have been such growth. In this sense his importance is that he promoted the early ideas behind co-operation and also offered a means by which it could be developed which others were then able to adopt and even adapt.

As the promoter of early co-operation, Owen is certainly significant; however, the success of this approach is perhaps also dependent on circumstances. For example, it is reasonable to suggest that his ideas were quite unusual and that they were only able to enjoy success because people saw in them a better opportunity for themselves. Given the manner in which Britain was developing, with its strong focus on commercial enterprise and individual wealth creation,

This offers a clear argument and also awareness of other motivations for why co-operation might have grown.

This is a well-developed paragraph that focuses on how Owen is important. It is supported by good evidence and offers good explanation as to why this is the case – the final sentence is a good judgement that supports the argument offered in the introduction.

There is continued focus on the role of Owen here, which is supported by good evidence. The explanation offered is analytical and is well directed, supporting a reasoned argument.

Here there is some clear evaluation of what the question demands with reference to broader issues that also influenced success.

members of the working class in particular were exploited. The benefits of co-operation that Owen promoted were arguably a means for them to improve in a world in which they were otherwise overlooked. What co-operation offered was a way for working people to look after one another and, in the context of early to mid-19th century Britain when individualism and personal success was a dominant motive, this opportunity enjoyed some popularity. In this sense Owen's ideas were dependent upon the people themselves rather than just what he did. Without the belief that they were exploited by employers perhaps co-operation would not have enjoyed as much success. Consequently it is more reasonable to suggest that Owen was important in as much as he created the idea but then the growth of this relied upon circumstances and others running with it.

This particular view is supported by the success of the Rochdale Pioneers after 1844. This group essentially made co-operation more 'professional' by introducing a clear system by which ◄ to run co-operative stores. The early stores did not last long because the personnel involved lacked real business sense and therefore by introducing such rules the pioneers were able to make this style of co-operation more effective. The outcome was that by 1863 the Co-operative Wholesale Society was created to offer a national supply for all 'co-ops' and in 1868 they were able to branch out into the world markets. By creating a definite structure, the Rochdale Pioneers devised a blueprint for the future success of co-operation and, therefore, they are also responsible for its continued growth.

In conclusion Robert Owen was certainly important to the growth of co-operation after 1815 ◄ because he introduced the initial idea and showed a way in which such an idea could be successful. This certainly encouraged the early growth of co-operation but its continued growth was more dependent upon circumstances that made people believe in the concept and the efforts of the pioneers that professionalised the concept and made it more able to develop effectively.

Here there is further discussion about how far Owen was important by considering other factors involved. By using the idea of different time frames – early on Owen was important, later on less so – there is a clear sense of evaluation being demonstrated.

This is a well-considered conclusion that draws together the different features implicit within the question demand. The argument is clearly defined and quite logical.

Verdict

This is a strong answer because:

- there is a clear argument running throughout the essay
- there is a good range of evidence and points from across the time frame
- each paragraph offers some clear explanation which is well focused on the question demand
- there is a clear judgement reached in the conclusion.

Paper 1: A Level sample answer with comments

Section B

These questions assess your understanding of the period in breadth and will cover a period of 30 years or more. They will ask you about the content you learned about in the four key themes, and may ask about more than one theme. The questions will also require you to explore a range of concepts, such as change over time, similarity and difference, as well as significance. For these questions remember to:

- identify the focus of the question
- consider the concepts you will need to explore
- support your points with evidence from across the time period specified in the question
- develop the evidence you deploy to build up your overall judgement
- come to a substantiated judgement that directly addresses the question set.

How far do you agree that political sympathies rather than popular agitation accounted for the passage of factory reform in the years 1830–1870? (20 marks)

Average student answer

To a great extent political sympathies were more important than popular agitation in encouraging factory reform between 1830 and 1870 because during this period politicians became more concerned about public welfare and agitation declined after the initial discontent from the Swing riots.

There is clear argument being offered here which shows awareness of some broad trends that are relevant to the question which could be developed within the body.

Popular agitation was very important to factory reform because the people worked in terrible conditions and many employers did not care about their workforce. This state of affairs encouraged agitation because no-one would help them and therefore they had to look after themselves. The conditions people had to work in were awful: children as young as 8 years old were forced to work really long hours; often in jobs that were very dangerous – for example, as 'scavengers' which required them to pick up the cotton threads from underneath moving machinery. This kind of job would often result in injury and the accident rate in these factories was very high. As such popular agitation from the workers themselves grew and this prompted reform after 1833.

This paragraph has a good point that relates to what the question demands but it is not sufficiently developed. There is evident awareness of the influence of difficult conditions but the explanation drifts into description, which undermines the overall point.

Popular agitation first emerged as rioting in the countryside in the form of the 'Swing' riots in 1830 and then in the form of the Ten Hours Movement the same year which sought to reduce the working day. Rioting was a very clear example of people's discontent and this did not go unnoticed by the government who became very aware of the problem – especially as much of the south-east was on fire after rioters burned hayricks in protest of their condition. The Ten Hours Movement was primarily an industrial movement that wanted to improve the conditions of working people in the factories by getting their long days reduced. It was not uncommon for people to have to work 16 hour days and men like Richard Oastler, a factory manager, felt that this was almost like slavery and therefore tried to get this reduced to 10 hours. The movement was quite broad as it included working people and also some politicians like Michael Sadler who objected to the dreadful conditions that children were forced to work in. The breadth of the movement meant that it enjoyed some real influence and this prompted factory reform.

This paragraph contains a lot of description which undermines the overall point. There is some attempt at focus here – the last sentence starts to address the question demand but this should be more specifically developed within the text. Opening with a clear point would provide the opportunity to achieve this.

Apart from popular agitation, political sympathy was also very important. In Britain the governing classes were aware of the poor conditions that people were working in because movements like that for the ten-hour day made them aware of them. Many politicians supported this desire for factory reform as they were put off by the dreadful conditions that children were forced to work in. Since these politicians were also supportive there had already been several attempts to improve working conditions before 1830 including the 1819 Factory Act which limited child labour to 12 hours a day and the 1802 Factory Act which demanded fair treatment of apprentices. Both of these Acts recognised the problems with working practices and tried to do something about them. These reforms therefore evidence the sympathies of politicians and as such offer some clear motivation for further factory reform.

> This paragraph drifts from the focus of the question and considers material that is beyond the scope of the timeframe. There is implicit relevance to the point being made but this needs to be more clearly connected to the question demand.

Of particular importance to further reform was the support of Lord Ashley who raised the issue of poor mining conditions which eventually resulted in the passage of the Mining Act in 1842. As a prominent Tory politician Ashley was able to raise awareness of the terrible conditions and give the concern significant gravitas which encouraged further consideration of additional reform between 1830 and 1870. Even when he resigned, his stance was maintained by other politicians such as John Fielden and Michael Sadler who were able to keep the push for reform alive.

> This paragraph offers some additional development of the previous point about political sympathy but it does not really focus on how this promotes further change beyond the idea of ongoing pressure. This is a valid idea but one that could be explained a little more fully.

In conclusion popular agitation was certainly an important feature in the decision to create more factory reform after 1830 but this desire was already in action because of previous efforts by politicians who were aware of the poor conditions and had already sought to address them. In this manner political sympathy is perhaps far more important as without this motivation it would be very difficult for any change to actually take place. Overall, therefore, the real motivation behind further factory reform was the parliamentary interest in doing so.

> As a conclusion this offers a reasonably substantiated judgement.

Verdict

This is an average answer because:

- there is some analysis of the question demand but this is quite general in places and includes some description
- the evidence is appropriate but lacks breadth across the period and is a little general overall
- the argument is logical and generally well communicated but it lacks precision in places
- the focus is generally evident but the full extent of the question demand is lacking.

Use the feedback on this answer to rewrite it, making as many improvements as you can.

Paper 1: A Level sample answer with comments

Section B

These questions assess your understanding of the period in breadth and will cover a period of 30 years or more. They will ask you about the content you learned about in the four key themes, and may ask about more than one theme. The questions will also require you to explore a range of concepts, such as change over time, similarity and difference, as well as significance. For these questions remember to:

- identify the focus of the question
- consider the concepts you will need to explore
- support your points with evidence from across the time period specified in the question
- develop the evidence you deploy to build up your overall judgement
- come to a substantiated judgement that directly addresses the question set.

How far do you agree that political sympathies rather than popular agitation accounted for the passage of factory reform in the years 1830–1870? (20 marks)

Strong student answer

To a great extent it is reasonable to suggest that factory reform after 1830 was primarily motivated by political sympathy rather than popular agitation because such agitation declined in intensity after the 1833 Act and that which existed was motivated toward manipulating existing political sympathies that had been evident even before agitation developed. This sympathy was more important because it created a more receptive environment for change which otherwise was not really possible. In this sense, therefore, popular agitation was important but only in stirring up sympathies which ultimately made the greatest impact.

> This offers a clear and logical argument that is well focused on the question being asked.

Popular agitation certainly played an important role in the passage of factory reform after 1830 because it kept the political authorities focused on the need for further reform. Although this agitation was very limited – after the Swing riots of 1830 the only real pressure came from the Ten Hours Movement which was led by Richard Oastler and promoted the reduction of the working day which was then achieved in 1847 – this pressure gave voice to the need for additional reform after the 1833 Factory Act. This is especially important as the 1833 Factory Act was perhaps the first major reform for working practices and as such was regarded by some as being sufficient change that would not require further revision. In this sense popular agitation was able to expose the existence of continuing problems – such as the child labour issue and overlong working day which, for Oastler writing to the 'Leeds Mercury' in September 1830, was tantamount to slavery. By ensuring those in power did not forget about this ongoing inadequacy, popular agitation was an important element in further reforms.

> This is a strong paragraph that focuses well on the issue of popular agitation and clearly explains its relevance in promoting factory reform after 1830.

Given the nature of the agitation after 1830, however, there is much to suggest that the methods employed were designed to play on existing political sympathies and therefore was only effective because they already had a reasonably receptive audience. The Ten Hours Movement, for example, did not really use aggressive tactics to achieve their goals but rather was effectively a lobby group that sought to influence parliament toward their cause. It sought and achieved the support of several prominent political figures such as Lord Ashley and the MPs Michael Sadler and John Fielden who each had existing sympathies with the cause. In part, by adopting respectable tactics like letter-writing and eliciting the support of those in parliament rather than rioting and demonstrations, the movement was aware that this might have greater success as instead of alienating individuals through radicalism, they might better attract support – particularly if they were able to exploit any pre-existing sympathetic tendencies. In this sense, therefore, the eventual success they achieved

> This continues to be well focused on the question demand and successfully develops an effective evaluation of the significance of popular pressure and political sympathy. It is illustrated by accurate, if a little general, evidence. What is also important here is that the point is related explicitly back to the question in the final sentence.

in 1847 was perhaps only possible because they were able to behave appropriately which, in turn, enabled them to mine this ready sympathy rather than alienate it.

Apart from reaching out to individuals harbouring political sympathies, popular agitation was of limited success until the political climate changed toward further factory reform. The Ten Hours Movement began in 1830 but only achieved its goal 17 years later. This would suggest they were not as successful as some may make out. Indeed, they only really made gains once Robert Peel became prime minister after 1841 and his concern about the well-being of society motivated a more receptive attitude toward reform. Peel arguably placed social welfare on the political agenda and gave it a more credible standing among policy-makers, who therefore took the issue more seriously than they had previously done. In this sense political sympathy is clearly more important as without this receptive environment, the popular demands of the movement were not able to make significant inroads for their reform. In support of the importance of this idea is the raft of additional reforms that came after 1841: the 1844 Factory Act which reduced working hours for women and children; Factory Act 1847 which achieved the ten-hour day and the Bleach and Dye Works Act of 1860 which extended the restrictions on working hours to other industries. These reforms were not necessarily possible, despite popular demand, until the government became more sympathetic towards the idea – after 1841 this was the case and therefore there is change.

> This paragraph offers greater breadth across the timeframe and evidences some good knowledge of appropriate evidence. It offers some evaluation of the different elements of the question by relating one to the other and drawing conclusions that support an overall argument.

In conclusion, therefore, popular agitation is certainly a significant force for the passage of factory reform after 1830 because it is able to exploit the individual sympathies of those in power. However, on its own this is not sufficient to motivate significant changes and reform is only really possible once the political environment became more collectively sympathetic. Only when this was the case was wholesale reform achieved and therefore this sympathy is of greatest significance.

> This is a well thought out conclusion that considers the importance of each element in the question. The argument is logical and clearly conveyed.

Verdict

This is a strong answer because:

- it is well argued throughout the entire essay
- a good range of evidence is used to support developed explanations

- there is a clear attempt to evaluate the key features of the question demand
- a logical and clearly substantiated judgement is reached.

Paper 1: A Level sample answer with comments

Section C

These questions require you to read the extracts carefully to identify the key points raised and establish the argument being put forward. For these questions remember to:

- read and analyse the extracts thoroughly remembering that you need to use them in tandem
- take careful note of the information provided about the extracts
- deploy own knowledge to develop the points and arguments that emerge from the extracts and to provide appropriate context
- develop an argument rooted in the points raised in the extracts and come to a substantial conclusion.

Study Extracts 10 and 11 on pages 135 and 136.

In the light of differing interpretations, how convincing do you find the view that the slave trade was ended because of the efforts of humanitarian campaigners? (20 marks)

Average student answer

The slave trade was an immoral activity that sought to exploit human beings in order to make vast profits for the traders and their investors. The suggestion that humanitarian campaigners were the main reason for the eventual end of this trade has some merit because of the inhuman nature of the practice.

Since the slave trade was so inhuman the argument that it came to an end because of the actions of humanitarian campaigners is quite compelling. This is because at the end of the 18th century there was a more thoughtful view towards how to treat people after the American and French revolutions had forced people to think more carefully about the rights that people had. These events impressed upon people in Britain the dangers of treating people badly and also the broader ideas of the enlightenment which encouraged more positive attitudes towards humanity. The impact of this was that by the end of the century there was a more concerted effort to promote better practices that recognised that Africans were also people instead of the previously held ideas that they were simply a commodity. By promoting this idea campaigners were able to eventually secure the end of the terrible slave trade.

The first extract supports this idea because it says that it 'relied on human empathy' and this was the main basis of the campaign. It could only rely on this empathy if people were aware of the inhumanity of the slave trade and were moved to think about the experiences of the slaves as people rather than commodities. In achieving this change of attitude the humanitarian campaigners like Thomas Clarkson were very important as they helped to persuade people to think in this way. Thomas Clarkson, for example, used to go on tours around the country where he would show people things like manacles and chains that were used to tie slaves up. He would also show them the plans of how slaves were to be put into the slave ships for transportation. They were crammed in very tightly and as such people would see how awful their conditions were. This would consequently make people feel sorry for the slaves and therefore support its abolition.

On the other hand, the second extract suggests that the end of the slave trade came about because of the other factors such as financial ones. This source maintains that these were more important than the humanitarian campaigners and this could be because the government was more likely to be motivated by things like money. In support of this point is the financial cost of the slave trade ships that would often cost around £3,000 to fit out and if they lost their cargoes then they would

> A short introduction that considers the stated factor but does not really evidence any awareness of the debate as offered in the extract material.

> These paragraphs start to develop some relevant explanation but the extract material could be used more fully in support of this. Where there is some use of the extract the material is a little more directed and some good comments are developed.

> This paragraph lacks development. The point is a good one but it is not linked to the extract material and the evidence in support of it is quite vague.

not make much money. This was perhaps more important than humanitarianism and therefore perhaps the initial interpretation is not that convincing.

In support of the financial cost of the trade is also the growth of other industries like ◄ manufacturing during the industrial revolution. This arguably made the slave trade unnecessary and, therefore, given the cost involved, it was eventually brought to an end so as to make more room for industrialisation. This idea is supported in Extract 11 when it says that even Liverpool was becoming less interested in the slave trade. Liverpool had been one of the biggest ports in the country because of the trade and yet by the end of the century it was not as interested anymore – this was possibly because of the growth of other industries instead.

Overall the humanitarian campaign was very important to the end of the slave trade but it was ◄ also because of the other things like the growth in other industries which eventually made it realistically possible.

Here there is a better reference to the extract material but the explanation does not sufficiently flesh out the point being made. The comment about the industrial revolution is quite a contextual one which is certainly appropriate but it needs to be linked more explicitly with why it promotes abolition.

A short conclusion that summarises the points made rather than offering a clear judgement.

Verdict

This is an average answer because:

- there is some awareness of different interpretations but this is not developed throughout the response
- the material does not use the extracts enough – it could have developed other lines of argument that the material comments on to promote a more balanced answer
- the argument is developed in places but the supporting evidence is a little general
- there is no reasoned judgement made in the conclusion.

Use the feedback on this answer to rewrite it, making as many improvements as you can.

Paper 1: A Level sample answer with comments

Section C

These questions require you to read two extracts carefully to identify the key points raised and establish the argument being put forward. For these questions remember to:

- read and analyse the extracts thoroughly remembering that you need to use them in tandem
- take careful note of the information provided about the extracts
- deploy own knowledge to develop the points and arguments that emerge from the extracts and to provide appropriate context
- develop an argument rooted in the points raised in the extracts and come to a substantial conclusion.

Study Extracts 10 and 11 on pages 135 and 136.

In the light of differing interpretations how convincing do you find the view that the slave trade was ended because of the efforts of humanitarian campaigners? (20 marks)

Strong student answer

The extracts offer competing views as to the cause of abolition. On the one hand Extract 10 make a strong case for the humanitarian campaigners on the grounds that they were able to exploit people's sense of morality towards the slave trade, while Extract 11 promotes a more economic motivation. Certainly the economic consideration is very important to the eventual abolition of the trade because it encouraged its supporters to abandon their position. However, that they had any position at all suggests that there were competing views on the trade and in this sense perhaps the claim that the efforts of humanitarians promoted abolition is more persuasive on the grounds that it set up the debate in the first place.

This introduction offers an argument but also identifies debate from within the extracts, setting up the direction of the essay.

The argument in favour of the humanitarian campaigners' promoting abolition is quite compelling on the basis that it forced people to consider the inhumanity of the slave trade. As Hochschild suggests when he refers to 'human empathy', the methods employed by humanitarians such as Wilberforce and Clarkson were deliberately designed to force people to see the negative nature of the practice. Clarkson, for example, would tour the country with evidence acquired from his investigations, presenting the terrible accounts he learned of to thousands of people. Using physical examples such as manacles and chains he was able to give people a vivid insight into the experiences of the slaves themselves. In addition people were also able to hear accounts by slaves themselves – Olaudah Equiano's 'Interesting narrative', for example. These actions were certainly significant in promoting the cause of abolition because they raised public awareness to such inhumanity which could then be translated into political pressure – such as the 519 petitions that were sent to parliament in 1792.

This paragraph has some precise evidence in support of a developed point. The point itself is derived from a consideration of the extract material and the significance implied by it.

Although this raised such awareness, there was no immediate abolition and in this sense perhaps Richardson's argument that financial considerations were more prevalent holds greater weight. Given that Wilberforce introduced an annual abolition bill each year after 1791 and yet was unable to secure this legislation, implies that the humanitarian campaign was perhaps not as effective at securing abolition as it was at generating support for it. The motivation for such failure could very easily be the dominant West India lobby that Richardson refers to, which, given the profits that the trade generated throughout the 1780s and 1790s, was very reluctant to see its end. In support of this idea is the close relationship that many MPs had with the lobby – and indeed, several members were actually a part of. Such was the strength of this lobby that trying to win over parliamentary support while the trade was still very profitable was a misguided action by the humanitarian campaigners who were therefore always very likely to fail. In this sense the 'human empathy' in which Hochschild places great faith, is actually dashed by economic motivations and political self-interest.

These paragraphs offer some clear explanation and development of the extract material. In support there is some good evidence in use although this could be more specific. What is particularly good, however, is that there is clear discussion of the different interpretations.

The idea of self-interest is given further credibility in Extract 11 when the author mentions that the West India lobby only supported abolition when they were challenged by new colonies. In this sense there is a self-preservation instinct among the older colonies who made up the lobby; here, given that their colonies are well-established to be able to produce their own slaves, then abandoning the trade would prevent competition from new colonies. This presents a very different view of human nature than the one Hochschild implies with the humanitarian methods playing on empathy, replacing them with coldly calculated self-interests. Having said that however, it could be supported that even the West India lobby only considered abolition because it was already being discussed – they could have simply pushed for trade exclusion for new colonies, for example, but instead supported full abolition. This, one could argue, might have been because politicians were being forced to contemplate such action as a result of the growing ground swell of public support brought about because of the humanitarian campaigners.

Equally however this might also have been because the trade itself was becoming more obsolete. By the turn of the 19th century industrialisation was well underway and new business opportunities were emerging that extolled the benefit of paid labour than that of servitude. In this sense it could be maintained that abolition was a natural consequence of Britain's progression. This is clearly borne out in Richardson's analysis, but it can also be implied in Hochschild's who maintains that the trade was inhuman and therefore not progressive but rather a hangover of a more uncivilised time. In this sense it could be argued that the humanitarian campaigners were anticipating the progression of Britain and therefore pushed for abolition on these ground also.

This paragraph broadens the debate out into a wider consideration of how the country is developing. The material is still quite mindful of the question focus and evaluates the two extract opinions although the material could do with some specific examples in support of the analysis.

In conclusion the argument in favour of humanitarianism is most compelling as it explains why the West India lobby would have chosen complete abolition and more particularly why there was a debate about the slave trade in the first place. Richardson is right to point out the economic motivation but this seems secondary to the initial demand created by the humanitarian campaign.

A clear conclusion that offers a reasoned judgement based upon the overall response.

Verdict

This is a strong answer because:

- it offers a good analysis of the source material and is consistently referring to this material
- it develops a logical argument
- it supports the explanation with specific evidence
- there is a clear judgement offered.

The unification of Italy, c1830–70

In September 1870, the troops of King Victor Emmanuel II of Italy entered Rome. Italian unification, the political unity of the different states of the Italian peninsula, was, to all intents and purposes, complete. The *Risorgimento*, the cultural and political reawakening of Italy, had reached its climax. However, the creation of the new Italian state was neither inevitable nor had it been planned. Indeed, there was, in 1861, little enthusiasm for the new state among the Italian people. In 1861, an Italian politician, Massimo d'Azeglio, remarked to Victor Emmanuel, 'Sir, we have made Italy. Now we must make Italians.' The story of what follows is of how Italy was made, but it is also a story of division and the failure to 'make Italians'.

The French Revolution of 1789 led to the absolute monarchy being swept away and the introduction of political and administrative reform. In May 1796, the French general Napoleon Bonaparte invaded Italy. From that point until 1814 (with a brief interlude in 1799) the Italian peninsula – excluding the islands of Sicily and Sardinia – lay under French rule. Under French rule, many Italians experienced a transformation in how they were governed. Instead of a patchwork of customs and feudal laws that had dominated the running of so many of the states of Italy, they enjoyed the benefits of a fairer Code of Law. Even when the French were expelled from Italy in 1814 and their laws repealed, it was difficult for many of the restored rulers – including the Austrians who controlled Lombardy and Venice – to turn back the clock. The seeds of liberalism and nationalism had been sown.

French rule in Italy was the midwife of the *Risorgimento* which, from the 1840s, promoted the cause of liberty in the Italian states. Alongside the growing demands for greater liberty was an emerging sense of national identity which was shaped and epitomised in the 1830s and 1840s by the revolutionary Giuseppe Mazzini. In these decades, the cause of national unity was to be championed by those who believed in change through revolutionary violence.

1831	1831 – Uprisings in Parma and Modena put down by the Austrians. Nationalist movement Young Italy founded by Giuseppe Mazzini.
1844	1844 – Failure of Mazzinian inspired uprising led by Bandiera brothers.
1848	1848 – Revolutions break out across Italian peninsula and in Sicily. A constitution – the *Statuto* – granted in Piedmont by Charles Albert. Piedmont declares war against Austria but is defeated at Custozza. The pope flees from Rome. Republic declared in Venice.
1850	1850 – Count Camillo Cavour becomes a minister for trade and agriculture. Anti-clerical Siccardi Laws passed by Piedmontese parliament.
1855	1855 – Piedmont joins Crimean War.
1857	1857 – The National Society formed by Giuseppe Farina, Daniele Manin and Giorgio Pallavicino.
1859	1859 – Piedmont and France wage war against Austria. Two great battles at Magenta and Solferino prove indecisive. France makes peace with Austria at Villafranca. Revolutions in Modena and Parma. Cavour resigns.
1861	1861 – The Kingdom of Italy is declared with Victor Emmauel II as king and a constitution based on the *Statuto*. Cavour dies.
1866	1866 – Italy goes to war with Austria but is heavily defeated at Custozza and Lissa. Venice is ceded to Italy by Austria after her defeat in the Austro-Prussian War.
1870	1870 – French troops abandon Rome in view of the Franco-Prussian war. Italian troops seize Rome which is subsequently annexed.

SOURCE 1

Garibaldi and his volunteers, a French drawing from 1860.

(Actualité.) **GARIBALDI ET SES VOLONTAIRES.**

1843

1843 – Publication of Vincenzo Gioberti's *On the Moral and Civil Primacy of the Italians* and Cesare Balbo's *The Hopes of Italy*.

1846

1846 – The election of Cardinal Mastai-Ferretti as Pope Pius IX.

1849

1849 – War with Austria resumed, Piedmontese forces defeated at Novara. The Piedmontese king, Charles Albert, abdicates to be succeeded by Victor Emmanuel II. Roman Republic declared and crushed by French forces. Venetian Republic capitulates to Austria.

1852

1852 – Cavour becomes prime minister of Piedmont.

1856

1856 – Cavour attends the Congress of Paris at the end of the Crimean War.

1858

1858 – Secret meeting between Cavour and French Emperor Louis Napoleon III at Plombieres.

1860

1860 – Cavour returns to office. Modena, Parma, Tuscany and Romagna vote for annexation by Piedmont. Garibaldi and the Thousand sail for Sicily. They take the island, cross to the mainland and take Naples. Garibaldi hands gains over to Victor Emmanuel at Teano. Piedmont conquers Papal States except Rome.

1862

1862 – Garibaldi wounded at the Battle of Aspromonte attempting to seize Rome.

1867

1867 – Garibaldi defeated by papal troops at Mentana attempting to seize Rome.

Ultimately, the new Italian state was not to be forged by revolutionary nationalism although the great guerrilla fighter, Giuseppe Garibaldi and his followers, were to play their part in shaping the series of events which led to unification. The new Italy was born out of war, diplomacy and alliances. It was moulded by the leaders of Italy's only liberal state, Piedmont. From the early 1850s onwards, Piedmont emerged as a modern European state; a parliamentary democracy with an increasingly industrialised economy. Piedmontese diplomatic influence, wielded primarily by prime minister Count Camillo Cavour, placed Piedmont in a position that it was able to influence events and, in 1860, impose Piedmontese rule on most of the Italian peninsula. Italian unity was not the result of a popular groundswell of support. It was political change imposed 'from above'. While by 1870 Italy had been made, it would take many decades for the rulers of Italy to make Italians.

2a.1 Challenges to the restored order and the failure of revolution, c1830–49

KEY QUESTIONS

- How significant were the challenges to the restored order, 1830–1847?
- What was the impact of Italian nationalism c1830–49?
- Why did revolution break out in 1848–49?
- Why did the revolutions of 1848–49 fail?

INTRODUCTION

The old order was restored across the Italian peninsula in 1815 by the terms of the Treaty of Vienna. **Reactionary rule** was to be guaranteed by the military might of Austria but the legacy of Napoleonic rule was not entirely lost. Those who wished for individual liberty, guaranteed rights, administrative efficiency and constitutional government were, from time to time, prepared to challenge the restored regimes through revolt and revolution. But such challenges were neither co-ordinated nor did they take place on a national scale.

The desire to create a nation state – L'Italia – was not widespread and the short-term impact of Young Italy, an organisation founded by Giuseppe Mazzini in 1831, was not significant. However, Young Italy, and to a lesser extent other secret societies, sowed the seeds of the idea of an Italian nation state based on democracy and popular consent. The progress of such an idea was limited because it represented a threat to the established order. Similarly, the popular appeal of revolutionary nationalism in the 1830s and 1840s was not great because it did not address the more fundamental issues of land ownership and day-to-day subsistence. In the 1840s, writers such as Cesare Balbo, Massimo d'Azeglio and Vicenzo Gioberti proposed more conservative suggestions for the development of the cause of national unity. However, there was no consensus as to the ideal nature or shape of an Italian state or how it might be achieved.

The ***Risorgimento*** was a cultural phenomenon centring on the concept of a national reawakening. Such an idea was expressed through literature, music, academic meetings and journals. The impact of the ideas of the *Risorgimento* was limited although there was a growing awareness of such ideas among the literate classes between the restoration in 1815 and 1848. The unifying factor for most Italian nationalists was the desire to challenge Austrian influence and expel the Austrians from the Italian peninsula.

Revolution broke out in many Italian states in 1848. Liberal constitutions were granted and, in some states, republics proclaimed. The revolutions failed because of regional differences, diversity of aims and the lack of foreign support. Ultimately they failed because of the military might of Austria with conservative rule prevailing.

1815 – June: Restoration of Italian states by Act of the Congress of Vienna

1821 – March: Rising in Piedmont against Victor Emmanuel I

1815	1820	1825	1830

1820 – July: Rising in Naples against Ferdinand I

1831 – February: Risings in Modena and Parma

1831 – March: Young Italy founded by Giuseppe Mazzini

HOW SIGNIFICANT WERE THE CHALLENGES TO THE RESTORED ORDER, 1830–47?

Political geography in 1830

The Treaty of Vienna restored the borders of a patchwork of Italian states after the disruption of the Napoleonic wars. There was no uniformity to the political geography of these states, each having its own distinct culture of government.

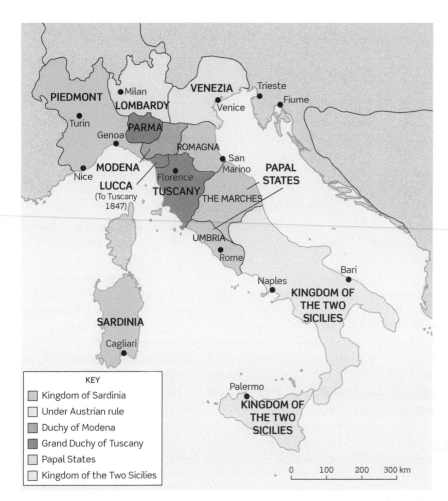

Figure 1.1 Map of the Italian peninsula c1815.

1843 – Publication of *Primato morale e civile degli Italiani* by Vincenzo Gioberti

1846 – June: Election of Pope Pius IX

1849 – August: Suppression of Venetian Republic

| 1835 | 1840 | 1845 | 1850 |

1844 – Publication of *Le speranze d'Italia* by Cesare Balbo

1848 – January: Revolution breaks out in Sicily

The Kingdom of Sardinia (Piedmont): This kingdom was made up of Piedmont on the mainland and the island of Sardinia. From its capital city of Turin, the House of Savoy ruled this relatively poor part of Italy. Sardinia was particularly backward and sparsely populated. Despite its poverty, successive rulers built up a strong army and governed with an effective civil service. The Treaty of Vienna recognised the House of Savoy as the rightful rulers of Piedmont. In 1814, Victor Emmanuel I returned to Piedmont and immediately began to restore the **absolutist state**. The Code Napoleon was repealed, as were various rights such as free and open trials. No laws passed between 1800 and 1814 were recognised and the Church was restored to its pre-Napoleonic privileged status. One important change introduced in the Treaty of Vienna was that the port and state of Genoa was granted to the House of Savoy.

Lombardy: Before the Napoleonic Wars, Lombardy had been part of the Austrian Empire. Its capital, Milan, was the second largest city of that empire. Lombardy was ruled by Austrian officials who acted in the name of the Austrian emperor. However, they were given a fair degree of freedom to act as they saw fit with the Austrian army underpinning imperial rule. It maintained a number of military strongholds known as the **Quadrilateral**, which dominated the plain of the fertile **Po Valley**. The Napoleonic conquest of Lombardy was a mere interlude, Lombardy was returned to Austrian control in 1814.

The Papal States: Stretching from the cities of Ferrara and Bologna in the north down to Benevento in the south, the Papal States (Umbria, The Marches and Romagna) dominated central Italy. They were ruled by the head of the Catholic Church, who resided in Rome. The pope was not just a spiritual leader, he also had **temporal power**. To most popes, control of the Papal States was considered essential to the protection of papal independence. However, the popes did not have a significant army and relied on Catholic countries to protect them militarily if required. Founded in the 16th century in response to the Protestant reformation, the Society of Jesus (otherwise known as the **Jesuits**) became the theological 'shock' troops of the Catholic Church. This meant that they would act to promote Catholicism wherever it was under threat. The Jesuits were the archenemies of those who opposed the power and influence of the Catholic Church. Between 1805 and 1808, Napoleon's armies took over different parts of the Papal States. Then, in 1809, Napoleon declared that Rome was to be the 'Second City of the Empire', that is, it would be incorporated into the French Empire. Pope Pius VII was to become a prisoner.

By the terms of the Treaty of Vienna, Pope Pius VII was restored to his position as spiritual and temporal ruler of the Papal States. The Code Napoleon was abolished in most parts of the Papal States and the papal legal codes re-established. However, such a move was not universal. In Romagna the Code Napoleon remained. Austrian influence over the region was considerably increased by the fact that Austrian armed forces were to be stationed in the Papal States.

Venice: Otherwise known as the Republic of St Mark, this had been a powerful independent state in the 15th and 16th centuries because its merchants dominated trade in the Mediterranean. By the 1790s, the republic had lost its importance as a trading power,

although not its architectural or artistic splendour. From 1805, Venice fell under Napoleonic rule as part of the Kingdom of Italy, but by the terms of the Treaty of Vienna, Venice was annexed by Austria.

The Central Duchies: This term refers to the independent states of Tuscany, Modena and Parma. Tuscany had been governed by part of the Habsburg family, the House of Lorraine, since the 1730s. Relatively prosperous, Tuscany had been at the heart of the Renaissance from the 14th to the 16th centuries. During the Napoleonic period the Central Duchies were amalgamated in 1801 into the Kingdom of Etruria, which was eventually annexed by France. The Treaty of Vienna left the Central Duchies firmly under Austrian influence. Grand Duke Ferdinand III, brother of the Austrian Emperor, became ruler of Tuscany. However, this did not mean that he was as conservative or as repressive as some of the other restoration rulers. Indeed, Ferdinand and his first minister, Victor Fossombroni, improved education, set up hospitals and food relief during the outbreak of typhus in 1815–16, and allowed freedom of expression, which was not permitted in the rest of Italy.

Modena and Parma were separated from Tuscany by the Apennine Mountains. These two states had a certain political independence although, like Tuscany, they were within the sphere of Austrian influence. The new ruler of Parma post-Vienna, Marie Louise of Bourbon-Parma, was equally broad-minded. She repealed the Code Napoleon in 1820, but replaced it with something similar. This was no surprise given the fact that she had been Napoleon's wife! In Modena, Duke Francis IV was far more repressive, reinstating the Jesuit order's influence over the lives of the Modenese.

The Kingdom of Naples: This kingdom was made up of Sicily and the southern part of mainland Italy. Ruled by the Bourbon family, the Kingdom of Naples was the poorest region of Italy. In 1847, the writer Luigi Settembrini wrote of it: 'No state in Europe is in a worse condition than ours … In the country that is said to be the garden of Europe, the people die of hunger and are in a state worse than beasts.' The kingdom was dominated by Naples, the largest city in Italy at the end of the 18th century with a population of 400,000. However, most of the population of Naples, and indeed the whole of the kingdom, lived in desperate poverty. In the countryside, the social structure and economic system was unchanged from medieval times. The land was owned by a few absentee landlords and the Church. The kings of Naples were absolute rulers who maintained large armies in order to control the people. From 1806, the Kingdom of Naples was ruled by Napoleon's appointees who abolished all feudal rights. Sicily was not conquered by the French and was dominated by the British, who encouraged the introduction of a constitution in 1812 to be drawn up on British lines (in other words, there was a parliament with two houses and a constitutional monarchy).

The Bourbon King, Ferdinand I, was restored to his throne in 1815 with vague promises of maintaining some of the legacy of French and British influence in Naples and Sicily respectively. However, this was not to be the case. The Church was restored to its position of power and authority. Many of the liberal projects introduced by the French, such as road building and extending education, were abandoned. In Sicily in 1816, the British-inspired constitution was destroyed; much to the frustration of many of the nobility who had enjoyed the power it had given them.

Rumblings of discontent

Although in the 1820s there were no national movements pressing for Italian unity, there were groups with serious grievances against the type of rule re-introduced after 1815. Some of the discontented joined the secret societies such as the **Carbonari**. Those who had lost out from the restoration of old monarchies, including purged army officers and civil servants, were keen on radical action. Some wished for the restoration of lost political rights and constitutions that would guarantee those rights.

Uprisings and revolutions in 1820–21 in Naples, Sicily and Piedmont reflected dissatisfaction with several rulers. But this dissatisfaction was usually related to local issues. The revolutions that took place were to challenge the legitimacy and rule of some of the restored rulers. However, they did not go so far as to challenge Austrian hegemony nor did they form the basis of a movement demanding change on a national basis.

KEY TERM

Carbonari
The origins of this secret society are unclear, but translated the name means 'charcoal burners'. Every member of the society was sworn to secrecy in a special initiation ceremony. The Carbonari was committed to the principles of the rights of the people, and was prepared to use violence and revolution as the means by which it could achieve its aims. Although the Carbonari society was an international organisation, it was strongest in Naples where it had perhaps as many as 60,000 members in the years following the restoration in 1815.

The failure of the 1830–32 revolutions

A number of Italian revolutionaries fled abroad after the failure of the 1820–21 uprisings. Many ended up in Paris and some even took part in the July Days uprising in France in 1830. The French

king, Charles X, was overthrown by a mixture of radicals, liberals and the Paris mob. He was replaced by Louis Philippe, who promised to act as a constitutional monarch. To liberals in Italy, the revolution in France raised the possibility of French support for a similar revolution in Italy. Such support, in their view, would counterbalance the power of conservative Austria.

Modena

In 1831, Enrico Misley, an academic, Italian patriot and a leading member of the Carbonari, led an uprising in Modena. Misley was also a friend of Francesco IV, the Duke of Modena. Misley tried to enlist the support of Francesco IV in return for a promise to support him in a bid to become King of Italy. Initially, Francesco seemed interested, but he was acutely aware of the danger of challenging Austrian power.

Two days before the uprising was due to begin in February 1831, Francesco IV had Ciro Menotti, one of the important members of the conspiracy, arrested. With revolution spreading, Francesco fled to Vienna to plead for support from Prince von Metternich. While he was there, he heard news that the ruler of neighbouring Parma, Marie Louise, had fled in the face of similar demands for a constitution. However, revolutionary excitement did not last long. In March 1831, Francesco returned to the Central Duchies with an Austrian army and the revolutionaries were crushed. Many of the revolutionaries, including Menotti, were executed.

EXTEND YOUR KNOWLEDGE

Klemens, Prince von Metternich
An Austrian statesman and minister of foreign affairs between 1809 and 1848, Prince von Metternich was one of the leading figures in the alliance against Napoleon at the Congress of Vienna in 1814-15. His vision for the Italian peninsula was a conservative settlement achieved through the restoration of the pre-Napoleonic War rulers. However, while Metternich was very much a conservative he was not a reactionary. Post 1815, he promoted the idea of 'amalgamation': that absolutist governments needed to innovate politically if they were to survive and prosper. Therefore, he encouraged the restoration rulers to retain features of the administrative and political reforms of the Napoleonic era which would best suit their interests. Hence in Tuscany, Naples and the Papal States post 1815, various ministers sought to create centralised and more uniform administrations as a means of creating a more efficient state. Likewise, Metternich encouraged the rulers of the restored Italian states to embark on economic reform as a means to prosperity and security.

Metternich was also the architect of the congress system of great powers which he hoped would serve to protect the status quo. His aims are summarised by his comment made before the Congress of Verona in 1821:

'The principle object of the Congress to be held [at Verona] in 1822 will be the regulation of Italian affairs so as to ward off the danger of new upheavals... an object to which I attach the greatest importance.'

Metternich had hoped that the Congress of Vienna would create a federation of Italian states but this idea failed to win the approval of the other victorious powers.

Revolution in the Papal States

Much more threatening to the established order in Italy was the outbreak of revolution in 1831 in the Papal States. The Papal States had not been touched by the 1821 revolutions but liberals were repressed and the secret societies were weaker than they were further south in Naples. In February 1831, a reactionary Church leader, Cardinal Cappellari, was elected Pope Gregory XVI.

As revolution raged in Modena and Parma, so one of its leading conspirators, Menotti, urged an uprising in the Papal States. But those in the Papal States who responded to the rallying cry for revolution were not, on the whole, nationalists but liberals who wished to challenge the clerical state and to re-establish a secular state similar to that under Napoleonic rule. In February 1831, a revolutionary army led by Colonel Giuseppe Sercognani captured the papal port of Ancona and the Umbrian capital Perugia. The following month a provisional government led by the elderly Giovanni Vicini was set up in Bologna which issued a constitution promising a reformed finance system with moderated tariffs, an elected assembly that would choose a president and cabinet and a fairer judicial system based on the Napoleonic model.

This constitution was not particularly radical, but it was too much for the Austrians. For Metternich, **revolutionary liberalism** was as much a threat to the established order as **revolutionary nationalism**. In March 1831, an Austrian army intervened and took Bologna with relative ease. The revolutionary army surrendered to papal forces believing the papal intermediary Cardinal Benvenuti when he promised an amnesty for all those who had taken up arms against papal rule. They were wrong to trust Benvenuti. Fresh revolts in the Papal States at the end of 1831 led to Austrian military intervention in January 1832 and the occupation of Ancona by the French in March 1832. To ensure that all revolutionary sentiment was crushed, papal armies swept through The Marches acting in a brutal manner that was to sow the seeds for revolution in the late 1840s.

KEY TERMS

Revolutionary liberalism
The doctrine promoting constitutional change through revolution.

Revolutionary nationalism
The doctrine espoused by Mazzini and others for the creation of the nation state through revolution.

EXTEND YOUR KNOWLEDGE

The election of Gregory XVI
The election of Pope Gregory XVI reveals the influence Austria (and Metternich specifically) had over the affairs of the Church. The death of Pius VIII in December 1830 led to the calling of the papal conclave to choose his successor. The context to the cardinals' deliberations was revolutionary ferment in the Papal States and the counter-revolutionary influence of Metternich. After 55 days of deliberation and 83 ballots, the wishes of the Austrian foreign minister prevailed. The new pope was a bitter opponent of most human rights and a staunch supporter of the political status quo.

EXTEND YOUR KNOWLEDGE

Troppau Protocol
The Congress of Troppau was a meeting of the Quintuple Alliance (Austria, Prussia, Russia and Britain) and was convened in July 1820 to consider the revolution taking place in Naples. The outcome of the meeting, the Troppau Protocol, stated that the powers of the alliance would intervene militarily to crush revolution. The British objected to the Protocol, public opinion in Britain having considerable sympathy for the cause of the Neapolitan Liberals.

Reasons for failure

The revolutionaries of 1831 failed to attract foreign support to counteract the impact of Austria. Enrico Misley had hoped for support from the government of the French king Louis Philippe, who had recently been brought to power by a similar type of liberal revolution. However, in 1831, Louis Philippe's minister, Casimir Perrier, dashed the hopes of the revolutionaries stating: 'We do not recognise the right of any people to force us to fight in its cause; the blood of Frenchmen belongs to France alone.' Without the support of a foreign power the revolutionaries had little chance of countering the might of the Austrians.

The demand of most of the revolutionaries in 1830–31 was the granting of greater constitutional liberty, not national unity. But such liberty stood in direct contrast to the wishes of Metternich and Austrian force was used as the means by which such liberty was denied. The British and French had deep reservations about the Troppau Protocol which stated that the great powers had the right to intervene to crush revolution in Europe. However, neither challenged the principle that the political stability of the Italian peninsula was the responsibility of Austria. Although the French sent a force to occupy Ancona in 1832, it was Austrian arms that eventually restored order in the Papal States and Austrian troops remained garrisoned in Bologna until 1838. Naturally, there was tension between the papacy and Austria about the extent of Austrian influence in Italy, but the events of 1831 proved that Austrian arms were still the ultimate guarantor of conservative rule in Italy.

EXTEND YOUR KNOWLEDGE

Papal temporal power
The aftermath of the 1831 revolution was of importance in the decline of papal temporal power. The fact that Austrian troops remained in Bologna until 1838 was less traumatic than the systematic pillage of The Marches and Romagna by papal troops. Indeed, such was the extent of atrocity that the historian Harry Hearder commented in Italy in the *Age of the Risorgimento 1790-1870* (1983), that the actions of the papal troops 'thereby prepared the way not only for the revolutions of 1848, but also for the ultimate extinction of the [pope's] temporal power'.

The revolutions of 1831 were a hopeless cause. They failed because they did not constitute a national uprising, but were regionally based revolts. There was little if no communication of support from revolutionaries in one region, such as Bologna, for those in another such as Modena. This was partly because the ambitions of the revolutionaries were limited by their localism. In addition, the social base of the revolutionaries was narrow; Enrico Misely was an academic, Ciro Menotti a prosperous businessman. The revolutionaries of 1831 did not have broad popular support. This was because they were normally members of exclusive secret societies such as the Carbonari and, therefore, had little interest in social change. In most cases their aims were constitutional, to extend power to their class through the granting of a constitution. This was not a cause to stir the masses.

The cultural challenge of the *Risorgimento*

The challenge of the *Risorgimento* was to forge awareness of a common cultural identity across the Italian peninsula. The roots of the concept of an Italian national identity go back to the Roman Empire when the peninsula was ruled from Rome. During the Middle Ages, when Italy was divided politically into a number of small states, there were still those who thought in terms of Italy as a cultural identity at least. Most important of these was the writer Dante, who wrote of Italia as a country. In the 16th century, one of the foremost Italian philosophers, Niccolò Machiavelli, wrote of Italia as a cultural entity. Neither Dante nor Machiavelli wrote in terms of Italy as a nation state, because such an idea did not exist during their lifetimes. It was only in the late 18th and 19th centuries that awareness of national identity began to have political significance.

EXTEND YOUR KNOWLEDGE

Dante Alighieri (1265–1321)
Dante Alighieri was born in Florence and was an Italian poet. His importance to the story of the *Risorgimento* is that he defined the Italian language as it is used today.

Niccolò Machiavelli (1469–1527)
Niccolò Machiavelli was the first great political philosopher of the Renaissance. His famous treatise, *The Prince* (written in 1513 and published in 1532), stands apart from all other political writings of the period in so far as it focuses on the practical problems a monarch faces in staying in power, rather than more speculative issues explaining the foundation of political authority. As such, it is an expression of realpolitik – that is, governmental policy based on retaining power rather than pursuing ideals.

18th- and 19th-century writers on the *Risorgimento*

The term *Risorgimento* was first used in the context of national identity by S. Bettinelli in his cultural history of Italy entitled *Del Risorgimento d'Italia dopo il mille* (1775). In the same period, the writer Vittorio Alfieri wrote in terms of national identity. The historian Carlo Denina wrote in his book *The Revolutions of Italy* (1770) about Italy as a whole rather than just Venetia or Piedmont. One should not exaggerate the impact of these writers. Their audience was small, mainly consisting of members of the upper class. However, their works contained some common themes. They wrote about the *Risorgimento* in terms of a moral revival – the struggle of good over evil. They also linked the resurrection of the culture of the Italian people with the concept of liberty.

KEY TERM

Jacobins
The most ruthless radicals of the French revolution, the Jacobins demanded universal liberty and, during the Terror of 1793–94, executed thousands of their opponents.

The first revolutions of the *Risorgimento*

The ideas of liberty were strengthened by events in France in the late 1780s and 1790s. This marks the beginning of a new phase of the *Risorgimento*, moving from a cultural and literary era to one in which political solutions were proposed. In France, **Jacobins** spoke of justice, liberty and the brotherhood of man. Italian Jacobins were involved in plots to overthrow the government in Naples and Turin in 1794. Mainly educated people, they spoke in terms of liberty for the Italian people that could only be achieved with the destruction of autocracy. These were the first revolutions of the *Risorgimento* and the leading participants paid heavily with their lives; for example, in 1794, three leaders of an uprising in Naples, including 21-year-old Emanuele de Deo were shot. Not all Italians who wanted political change were revolutionaries. Several were moderate in their tactics and their aims. Indeed, the ambitions of many, such as Francesco Melzi d'Eril who served as vice-president of the Napoleonic Italian Republic between 1802 and 1805, were limited to the demand for a greater share in ruling their regions. They were not concerned with revolutionary upheaval or with the creation of an Italian state. Instead they hoped for a more efficient administration, the removal of the last elements of feudalism and the introduction of limited social reform such as primary education. The importance of these individuals was in their desire for change, despite the fact that it was limited in its ambition.

Linguistic divisions

At the heart of cultural identity is language. An element of the *Risorgimento* was the greater awareness of a common tongue. The Italian peninsula was a patchwork of languages and regional dialects. The Italian language as we know it came from the Tuscan dialect and was only spoken in Florence. Indeed, in 1871, it is likely that it was only known and commonly used by around 630,000 out of a population of nearly 27 million. The illiteracy rate in 1871 was around two-thirds of the population, literacy being measured by the relatively straightforward task of signing one's name and reading a brief piece of text. Such linguistic diversity was at the heart of Metternich's dismissal of Italy as a 'mere geographical expression'. However, the idea that Italy was linguistically and culturally hopelessly divided is simplistic. In the years following the restoration of Austrian control of Lombardy, there were those who encouraged the use of Italian as part of their expression of the importance of national identity. The Italian language periodical *Biblioteca Italiana* was founded in Milan in 1816 and the journal *Il Politecnico* was produced in Milan between 1839 and 1845. The Austrian rulers of Lombardy were prepared to tolerate the publication of such journals because they were not openly political. But that was not the point. Such journals raised consciousness of a common culture and a common language among the educated classes.

The creation of national organisations

Equally important in the development of an Italian national consciousness was the creation of national rather than regional organisations, such as the Congresso degli Scienziata (Congress of Science). The Congresso held meetings in different parts of Italy between 1839 and 1847. Crucially, these meetings were attended by delegates from many different regions. The topics discussed were wide ranging, from the latest medical research to agricultural innovation. Importantly, the language used at the meetings was Tuscan Italian and there was a political edge to their agenda. At a Congresso meeting held in Genoa in 1846, the occasion was used to celebrate the victory of Italian arms over the Austrians in 1746. Many of the future heroes of the *Risorgimento* attended the Congresso. They provided a function as a nursery for moderate nationalist opinion. Tuscan Italian was also the common written language which, while accessible only to the literate, became more widely used as the 19th century developed. The language of Dante was the recognised language of the educated classes. It was popularised in the widely read second edition of the novel *I promessi sposi* ('The Betrothed'), published between 1840 and 1842 and written by Alessandro Massoni. Other writers including d'Azeglio also wrote in Italian rather than French, French being the conversational language of the upper class.

Patriotic themes in music and literary works

Even more important than literature to the sense of cultural unity of the class that could access the culture was opera. The outstanding composer of the period was Giuseppe Verdi. His works were performed not just in his native Parma but across Italy, again pointing to the concept of a shared culture amongst the literate classes. In Verdi's work composed in the 1840s there were clear political messages. The opera *Nabucco*, first performed in 1842 in Milan, included the famous and stirring song 'The Chorus of the Hebrew Slaves'. The parallel to be drawn between the enslavement of the Israelites and the repression of the Italians was clear for many in the audience. Equally nationalistic was the opera *I Lombardi*, first performed in 1843. The performance of Verdi's works became linked with anti-Austrian sentiment. Such was the impact of Verdi on nationalist opinion that, at times of tension, performances of his work caused outbursts of violence between Italian patriots and Austrian army officers. But Verdi's appeal was limited, because it represented the cultural expression of the Milanese nationalist middle class. His interpretation was not typical of the view of the majority of those who lived on the Italian peninsula and even those who lived in Lombardy.

Political ideas and secret societies

Secret societies

The influence of the French Revolution and the period of French dominance in Italy resulted in the emergence of secret societies. The societies were formed to plot against the French. When the French left Italy in 1815, members of the societies plotted against the restored governments. In general terms, the aims of groups such as the Carbonari and the Adelfi were the rejection of absolutist government and promotion of the rights of the people. The types of people who joined the secret societies included those who had lost out from the restoration of old monarchies, such as purged army officers and civil servants. Some wished for the restoration of lost political rights and constitutions that would guarantee those rights. They believed liberty could only be achieved with political change, either with the removal of the French or, after 1815, through revolution against the restored monarchies. Although the Carbonari was the largest secret society, there were others whose role in maintaining the revolutionary tradition should not be ignored. The Adelfi was initially a strongly anti-French society, which transformed itself into the strangely named Society of the Sublime Perfect Masters in 1818. Its main aim was the destruction of Austrian rule leading to a democratic republic. The leader of the Sublime Perfect Masters was Filippo Buonarrotti, who was an experienced revolutionary. The society's membership was based in the north, which explains why the expulsion of Austria from Italian soil was considered the primary objective. After 1815, the secret societies were able to keep the idea of political reform alive even though change did not necessarily happen as a result of their activities.

SOURCE

1

From the instructions to the Society of Guelph Knights, a secret society operating in Modena c1816.

Aims of the Order: The independence of Italy, our country. To give her a single, constitutional government, or at least to unite the various Italian governments in a confederation; all governments, however, shall be based on a constitution, freedom of the press and of worship, the same laws, currency and measures.

Methods of the Order: To spread liberal ideas and communicate them to adherents, friends and clerics, by firmly convincing them of the unfortunate state of affairs in our Mother Country. The press, gatherings and private conversations are opportune means. Cunning and perseverance are needed and, above all, the eradication of all kinds of prejudice. The unprejudiced peasant is more enthusiastic than the rich man, the property owner, and is therefore more useful.

ACTIVITY
KNOWLEDGE CHECK

Secret societies

Using Sources 1 and 2 and the information provided in the book so far, explain the nature of the secret societies. You should focus on their aims, membership and tactics.

Economic divisions and social problems

Land

The fundamental economic issue in the Italian peninsula was ownership of land. There was a significant difference in the patterns of land ownership and cultivation between the north and south. The soil in the south was inferior in quality and the region was crippled by **malaria**. Land was owned by absentee landlords and rented out by peasant farmers under a system known as the latifundia. Throughout the Italian peninsula and especially in the south, the landless majority worked as labourers and suffered from chronic underemployment. Napoleonic rule had seen the abolition of feudal laws and the sale of Church land, which further encouraged land speculation. However, this did not result in a significant broadening of land ownership. In Piedmont there was a tradition of peasant landownership that did not exist elsewhere on the peninsula. In the middle of the 19th century, there were around 800,000 estates in Piedmont, although it should be stressed that many of these were small. It is difficult to generalise about the experience of different social classes across the Italian peninsula, as there were so many regional variations. However, the period of Napoleonic rule resulted in a shift in landholding from the old aristocracy to the emerging middle class, especially in the north such as in Lombardy. One should, however, not exaggerate the extent of the decline of the nobility's economic power. Many nobles benefited from the sale of common land in the 1830s and 1840s. In the 1830s, the old nobility of Lombardy still owned around a third of the cultivated land. However, they were challenged by an emerging middle class that sought to buy land as a means of securing social status.

SOURCE

2

Profession of Faith of the Society of Sublime Perfect Masters by Filippo Buonarroti. This a series of instructions to initiates into the group, written in 1818.

The divine origin of equality is sanctioned by the social contract. By virtue of the social contract true liberty is to obey the general will of the people, that is, the true law.

Authority which derives from any other source is to be condemned as evil.

The authority of law, whether exercised by a single person or by the many, can only be conferred by election. It can never be exercised for hereditary reasons or for life.

Anyone is permitted to kill a person who challenges supreme power.

Property boundaries shall be erased, all possessions shall be reduced to communal wealth, and the one and only mistress, the patria [the nation], most gentle of mothers shall provide food, education and work to the whole body of her beloved and free children.

KEY TERM

Malaria

The impact of malaria on people living in the Italian peninsula in the 19th century was substantial. Malaria is a disease spread by mosquitos which breed in swamp conditions. The disease was lethal, accounting for around 330,000 deaths a year in the Italian peninsula. It was prevalent in in the countryside around Rome, Sicily and Sardinia. Malaria contracted in the north was often of the milder variety. Giustino Fortunato, an historian and politician who lived in the south of the peninsula, wrote of malaria that it was 'the most terrible of our afflictions'. Francesco Nitti wrote that 'Malaria lies at the root of the most important demographic and economic facts. The distribution of property, the prevailing crop system, and patterns of settlement are under the influence of this one powerful cause.'

Throughout the 19th century, changes to land ownership and how the land was exploited made matters considerably worse for the landless. Many depended on common land for fuel and food. In the 1830s, this land was sold off by local councils, enclosed and common rights lost. By the mid-1860s, about a quarter of a million acres had been sold. The critical issue was who would benefit from the sale of common land? Not surprisingly, it was sold to those close to the local prefects (administrative officers), councillors and mayors. Once they had assumed ownership of this land, they exploited it. Those who owned land generally did quite well in the years c1830–47. Improvements in agriculture led to an increase in cereal productivity of around 25 percent between the mid-1820s and late 1850s, and landowners were protected for the most part by Corn Laws which kept the price of grain artificially high. Many of the new landowners demanded higher rents and charged their tenants higher rates of interest when borrowing money to pay their rent. The peasantry, therefore, were trapped in a downward spiral of poverty and debt. The result was an alienation of the peasant from the landowner and the occasional use of direct action – land occupation or public disturbance – to resist the encroachment on common land.

Common land

The loss of common land had a devastating impact on some rural communities. In many areas the landless relied on common land for hunting, fishing, grazing and the gathering of produce. In 1839, the Austrian government declared that all uncultivated common land in Lombardy and Venice could be sold. Given recent technical improvements and the quality of the soil, the land was subsequently drained and cultivated. In Rome and the south, the enclosure of land was at the expense of cattle drovers. Across the peninsula, the poor lost ancient and historic rights to graze animals and, in some cases, access to water.

Empirical evidence for the state of the economy in the Italian peninsula

Research on Italian economic history, especially the volume of imports and exports before unification, is hampered by the lack of evidence. In *The Growth of the Italian Economy 1820-1960* (2001), Jon Cohen and Giovanni Federico point out that there are few reliable figures on the economy pre-1861 because some states did not collect the appropriate data. Others, such as Lombardy, were part of the Austrian Empire and there was a flourishing black market economy which lay outside the system.

In 1830, agriculture dominated the economies of the Italian states. Because of the lack of data there is considerable debate as to whether agricultural production grew in the period. The general consensus seems to be that production rose in line with the population increase, but that there was little or no capital investment in agricultural improvement. The dominant crops were wheat and other cereals, which were used as the basic source of food. Other important crops were silk and grapes. By 1870, almost two million hectares was under vine cultivation.

Industrial development

While there was some industrial development in certain regions in the 18th century, it was almost exclusively focused on textiles and light industry. However, the start of the 19th century saw the beginning of industrial growth. Most importantly, machines were imported from (primarily) Britain, France and Switzerland, which led to the creation of a factory-based textile industry. In 1810, for example, the entrepreneur John Muller imported the machinery necessary for cotton manufacture.

However, there were factors that limited industrial growth, not least of which was that the Italian peninsula relied on Britain for coal imports. Therefore, although cotton, wool and silk industries grew steadily, in 1844, there were only 114,000 industrial workers in Piedmont. The Apennine Mountains, which form the physical spine of the country, acted as a barrier to transport communication between the east and west of the country. The political divisions made for localised rather than nationally based economies. The restoration of 1815 reinforced this localism; trade tariffs were re-imposed, which had a negative effect on industry.

The regions of northern Italy were not integrated industrially. Indeed, because of Austrian domination of Lombardy and Venetia, the region's industries were in direct competition with neighbouring states. Some Lombard industrialists were able to lower the cost of imported cotton, making their industry more competitive but they also had to struggle with Austrian red tape which restricted growth. During the depression of 1847–48, urban centres such as Milan suffered considerably because of the lack of a broad industrial base and its dependence on the textile industry.

By 1840, the silk industry employed 70,000 workers in Lombardy alone with around 4,400 silk looms based primarily in Como and Milan. Industrial growth was very gradual, affected by the depression of 1847 and competition from China and India. The wool industry was also important in Lombardy and Venetia; as early as 1806 there were 32,000 workers in woollen mills in and around Vicenza. Gross Domestic Product (GDP) per head rose in northern and central Italy by only around 0.5 percent a year between 1830 and 1860.

If industrial growth was slow in the north, it was virtually non-existent in the south. Railways had been built in and around Naples in the 1830s. Additionally, there were some industrial enterprises in the city – mainly metalworking, shipbuilding and textiles. But the south suffered from a number of factors that hindered its development. There were few entrepreneurs with skills or capital to invest and few skilled workers. Also, industry was artisan-based in small workshops rather than factories, for the simple reason there was little natural source of power with which to run machinery. Despite these problems, silk and other textile industries were protected by a system of high tariffs and relatively low taxation.

Transport

The driving force for industrial change was the construction of the railway network. For a short period in the 1830s, the Kingdom of Naples led the way; the first railway built on the Italian peninsula was the line completed on 3 October 1839, linking Naples to the nearby suburb of Portici. The stretch of track was the first section of the Naples–Nocera–Castellammare line, and it stimulated the local engineering industry. Although the first locomotive used on the line was built in Naples from parts made in Britain, an engineering factory was set up for the construction of locomotives at Pietrarsa. But one should not exaggerate the extent of such an initiative. Whereas the city of Naples was connected to suburban districts by the railways, in 1860 over five-sixths of villages in the Kingdom of Naples were connected by tracks rather than roads. Despite the fact that the first railway was built in the south, construction was not sustained and in 1860 there was still only around 160 kilometres of operating railway track.

The state of the Italian transport system was poor. Indeed, the poverty of transport in the south acted as a break on agricultural and industrial development. In the southern region of Apulia, for example, the development of an emerging olive oil industry was stunted by the lack of any modern transport system.

Whereas in Britain, canal and rail construction and improvement had formed the basis of an integrated transport system, this was most definitely not the case in Italy. Generally there was little interest in promoting this important form of industrial transport because of Italy's topography and the lack of excess water. Ironically, it was the regions under the rule of foreign powers that led the way. In Lombardy, in 1819, the canal linking Milan to Pavia opened.

The upper and middle classes

The idea that the *Risorgimento* was a 'bourgeois' [middle class] revolution has been popular amongst historians. In addition, the relationship between the middle class and the aristocracy in Italy in the 19th century has caused some historical debate. In *The Italian Risorgimento* (1998), Martin Clark argues that the migration of many aristocrats to urban areas led to a fusion of interests between them and the middle class. To Clark this is a critical point as: 'it is the key to understanding the *Risorgimento*. It created an effective new elite, used to acting together and less beholden to the existing states.' This viewpoint is countered in *Italy: A Modern History* (1959) by Denis Mack Smith, who saw the decline in the nobility as leading to friction with the emerging middle class that sought economic and political power. He wrote that: 'the *Risorgimento* was a civil war between the old and new ruling class'. Evidence for both views can be found, depending on the regions studied. In Sicily, the nobility remained aloof and declined the opportunity to modernise, whereas in Tuscany there was a greater fusion of interest. This often helps explain the nature of the course of the *Risorgimento* in various regions. Other historians, such as Lucy Riall in *Risorgimento* (2009), have challenged the idea that the *Risorgimento* can be understood in terms of class relationships: 'it seems impossible to explain the *Risorgimento* by using a class-based analysis.'

Rich and poor

The divisions within the Italian peninsula were considerable. The lack of industry, the slow economic growth, and social and cultural division all contributed to a certain economic and social stagnation. Therefore, the dynamic for political change came from above – from a social class that benefited from the sale of cheap land, shared a common means of cultural expression and participated in the economic modernisation that did take place in this period. There was great social division between the wealthier classes and the mass of the poor. For most of those living on the Italian peninsula, the question of the day was not the political shape of Italy or of constitutions but of daily survival. The threat to that survival came from a number of sources. Add to this the diversity of language and culture, and the lack of communication and education, and one can understand why the peasantry and urban workforce were invariably the classes that resisted any political change that might make their plight worse. The main problem for many was underemployment. As a result there was emigration before 1871 on a wide scale, mainly from the northern provinces.

The greatest threats to existence were hunger and disease. The majority of the population in both the north and south lived in abject poverty. The increase in population from around 17.8 million in 1800 to over 24 million in 1850 meant that demand for food rose. As a result some marginal land was taken into cultivation but most food production was for subsistence. As a result, many regions relied on foreign imports of grain and there were periodically instances of famine.

Between 1814 and 1818, in the mid-1840s and in 1853, the peasantry were hit by widespread famine. Across much of the peninsula the peasantry lived on a diet of maize, which had potential implications for health, including vitamin deficiency and

pellagra was a permanent scourge of the peasantry. Cities such as Naples and Palermo as well as the countryside often suffered **cholera** outbreaks, the most vicious outbreak being between 1835 and 1837 (27,000 people died of cholera in Palermo alone in 1837), in 1849 and between 1854 and 1855. The countryside – most obviously in the south – was also riddled with malaria. The increasing demand for wood in the 1840s, in particular from the railway and shipbuilding industries, led to widespread deforestation. As a result, landslides and the erosion of topsoil led to the creation of swamps, which made the malaria worse. It is little wonder that peasants in the south were in a constant state of unrest.

Pellagra

Pellagra is caused by a lack of the vitamin niacin. This was common in communities whose staple diet was maize. It manifested itself in skin disorders, insanity and, occasionally, led to suicide.

Cholera

Cholera is caused by the consumption of food or water which has been contaminated with sewerage. It manifests itself in rapid and extreme dehydration which, if untreated, results in death.

Urbanisation, welfare and the Church

The enclosure of land, rural poverty and disease pushed people off the land. Limited industrialisation drew them into towns and cities, leading to urbanisation. The population of Milan grew from 139,000 in 1814 to 185,000 in 1836, and Turin from 75,000 in 1800 to 170,000 in 1860. The draw of the city was work, albeit occasional rather than permanent, and welfare. A significant proportion of urban dwellers were destitute and were increasingly catered for by local authorities or state-run welfare organisations; in 1836, Piedmont opened its first workhouses for able-bodied beggars. Before 1815, the Catholic Church was considered to be the most important charitable institution. However, the Church's position had been diminished during the Napoleonic period. A number of monasteries and religious houses which had been closed down were not reopened after 1815. Of the 1,300 monasteries and convents supressed by the French in the Kingdom of Naples, only 400 had been restored by 1821. Much of the Church's land was sold off, tithes abolished and, as a result, its income reduced. But despite these changes, the Catholic Church still played an important role in maintaining social control in rural areas. The parish priest was often still the educator and moral guardian of the local community and the Church frequently was the only provider of charitable relief, notably to the poor. The influence of the Church over the peasantry should not be underestimated.

Obstacles to the cause of Italian unity

Using the information in this section, list and explain five obstacles to the cause of Italian unity in this period.

WHAT WAS THE IMPACT OF ITALIAN NATIONALISM, c1830-49?

Mazzini and Young Italy

SOURCE
3

The execution of the Bandiera brothers, 1844. The brothers were revolutionaries and members of Young Italy. The picture was drawn in 1877.

ACTIVITY
KNOWLEDGE CHECK

Study Source 3 carefully. Where do the sympathies of the artist of this picture lie?

Young Italy

The failure of the secret societies in the 1820s and 1830s revolutions led to the founding of a new organisation, Young Italy, by Giuseppe Mazzini in 1831. Mazzini's views constituted an ideal, and a revolutionary one in an Italian peninsula dominated by conservative restoration governments. Mazzini believed in the creation of a nation state because, through the creation of such states, mankind could be best represented and mankind's interests best served. To Mazzini, nation states should be based on the principle of democracy, thereby making them fully representative

of the people who lived in, and belonged to, those states. The means of achieving this independent nation was a national revolution. Where Mazzini differed from other nationalist or secret society leaders was in the breadth of his vision. He did not just envisage a union of northern Italian states – as did so many other patriots – but a union of all Italian-speaking provinces including the south, Sicily and Sardinia. In 1829, he clearly summarised his vision: 'The fatherland of an Italian is not Rome, Florence or Milan but the whole of Italy.'

SOURCE
4

From a set of general instructions for members of Young Italy. The instructions were written by Mazzini and issued in 1831.

Young Italy is the brotherhood of Italians who believe in a law of Progress and Duty – are convinced that Italy is called to be a nation – that the failure of past attempts is due not to weakness, but to the poor leadership of the revolutionary parties – that the secret of strength lies in constancy and united effort.

Young Italy stands for republic and [national] unity. *The Republic*, because Italy has no basis for a monarchy; because the Italian tradition is wholly republican, as are its greatest memories and the progress of the nation; because monarchy was established when our decline began, and assured our downfall; because if monarchy was the aim of the Italian revolution, all the encumbrances of the monarchical system would inevitably be brought with it – concessions to foreign courts, respect for and faith in diplomacy, repression of the masses who alone have the strength to save us, and authority vested in the king's men by betraying us. This would unquestioningly destroy the revolution. *Unity*, because without unity there can be no true nation -- because by destroying the unity of the great Italian family, Federalism would destroy at its roots the mission which Italy is destined to fulfil for humanity.

The means of fulfilling the aims of Young Italy are Education and Insurrection. These two methods must be made to work in agreement and harmony. Education, by writing example and word, must always preach the necessity of insurrection, and when it succeeds must provide a principle of national education...

Convinced that Italy can free herself by her own strength – that to found a Nation it is necessary to be conscious... of nationality, and that this consciousness cannot be obtained if insurrection is achieved or triumphs through foreign hands... *Young Italy* is resolved to take advantage of foreign events, but not to allow the time and character of insurrection to depend on them.

Although Mazzini proposed democracy and wished to see the nation state built by 'the people', his views were shared by very few, most of whom belonged to the middle and upper classes. Although the membership of Young Italy set up by Mazzini in 1831 was broader than that of secret societies such as the Carbonari, it was by no means a mass movement. Many of those who took part in the Mazzinian-inspired revolutions were from privileged backgrounds, for example, the Bandiera brothers, whose gallant but flawed invasion of Calabria in 1844 led to their martyrdom (see Source 3). Young Italy was republican in its views. This did not mean that Mazzini dismissed out of hand constitutional monarchies. These were, in his view, useful as a stepping stone or 'governments of transition' on the way to the ideal: a united Italian republic. Indeed, in 1831 Mazzini wrote to the king of

Piedmont, Charles Albert, asking him to put himself at the head of the movement for a united Italy. In his letter, Mazzini asked that the king lead the nation and put on his banner 'Union, Liberty, Independence'. Charles Albert did not reply.

EXTEND YOUR KNOWLEDGE

Giuseppe Mazzini (1805–72)

Born in Genoa, Giuseppe Mazzini's training as a lawyer came a distant second in importance to his career as a revolutionary nationalist. Bored by the study of law he became interested in politics and joined the Carbonari in 1827, but became disillusioned with its secrecy and the lack of debate among members about the future of Italy. Indeed, Mazzini was eventually betrayed to the authorities in Genoa by a fellow member of the Carbonari, Raimondo Doria. While in prison in 1830, Mazzini came up with the idea of Young Italy.

Giuseppe Garibaldi (1807–82)

Giuseppe Garibaldi was the most famous soldier and patriot of the *Risorgimento*. Born in Nice, then part of Piedmont, he became a follower of Mazzini and had to flee Italy in the 1830s. He went to South America where he became involved in a number of wars. He returned to Italy in 1848 and, although a republican, joined with Charles Albert of Piedmont in his attempt to free Italy of Austrian rule. He led the army of the ill-fated Roman Republic in 1849 and after its collapse he fled to the United States of America. In 1860, he played an important part in the unification of Italy by conquering the Kingdom of Naples with his army of soldiers known as the Red Shirts. He was involved in two attempts to take Rome by force in the 1860s and in 1874 was elected to the Italian parliament. He was the hero of his day.

Young Italy did not reject all aspects of the secret societies. It looked after its members and gave them passwords, uniforms and ritual. However, there were differences in both organisation and philosophy that were to make Young Italy distinct. The organisation was accompanied by a journal, *Young Italy*, edited by Mazzini. The movement's ideas were spread from Marseilles in France (Mazzini's base) to Piedmont, the Papal States and Tuscany. In Piedmont, as circulation of *Young Italy* grew, so new adherents to the cause of revolution were recruited. However, the attempts at revolution ended in farce. In 1833, a proposed army coup was detected before it could begin. The response of Charles Albert's government was ferocious. Twelve members of Young Italy were executed out of 67 people arrested. The following year a planned attack on Piedmont fizzled out before it started. An uprising in Genoa scheduled for February 1834 and led by a new recruit to the Young Italy movement, Giuseppe Garibaldi, also failed to get off the ground. Such failures made Young Italy a laughing stock throughout Italy. Although attempts at revolution in the 1830s seemed unrealistic, Mazzini's ideas were to influence others and helped foster a developing national consciousness.

Limited influence

The uprising led by the Bandiera brothers was indicative of the limited impact of Mazzinian-inspired revolution. The problem of the Bandiera invasion of Calabria in 1844 was that there were only 19 of them and their numbers had swelled by only two by the time the authorities arrived. The Bandiera brothers were shot, but in dying they became important martyrs for the cause of national unity.

It is an irony that the appeal of Mazzinian democracy was so limited. At no time between 1830 and 1871 was the peasantry willing to support a Mazzinian-inspired uprising. This was because the Mazzinian movement had such a narrow social base of support and because it did little by way of proposing a solution to the deep social and economic poverty of many of those living in the Italian states. The most important issue for the peasantry across the Italian peninsula was not the creation of a nation state but land ownership. Indeed, the enclosure of land and the ending of feudal common land rights was a burning issue throughout the 1830s and 1840s in Italy. These had been undertaken by the middle class who were demanding political rights to complement their economic power. There was, therefore, little common ground between Mazzinian nationalists and the peasantry.

ACTIVITY
KNOWLEDGE CHECK

Mazzini

1 Using Source 4 plus information from this chapter explain in no more than 200 words the main features of Mazzinianism.

2 To further your understanding of Mazzini, find out as much as you can about Mazzini's background, political beliefs and life as a revolutionary. Once you have completed your research, explain in writing Mazzini's impact on the development of Italian nationalism.

Balbo and the rule of Charles Albert in Piedmont

The rule of Charles Albert

In 1831, Charles Albert became king of Sardinia-Piedmont. As has already been explained, he was neither a liberal nor was he sympathetic to the revolutionary nationalism of Mazzini. He was an absolute monarch who had no wish to grant any form of constitution. But Charles Albert did not object to being identified as a ruler who might, one day, expel the Austrians from the north of the Italian peninsula. Therefore, despite his dislike of popular movements, he was prepared to tolerate scientific congresses meeting in Piedmont. The significance of the congresses should not be underestimated for it was at these meetings that nationalist ideas were spread. In September 1846, the Associazione Agraria met at Mortara. Soon after, the Congresso degli Scienziati convened at Genoa. While scientific matter dominated proceedings, the meetings of both the Associazione and the Congresso were used by some as a platform to denounce Austrian influence.

Le speranze d'Italia, Balbo and d'Azeglio

Cesare Balbo was a writer whose book, *Le speranze d'Italia* ('The Hopes of Italy') was published in 1844. Balbo argued in favour of a federation of Italian states, although his view of Italy was limited to the north. Unlike others who argued for an Italian state led by the pope, Balbo suggested that the Piedmontese monarchy should take the lead in expelling the Austrians from Lombardy and Venice. His political philosophy was based on a faith in the sound judgement of princes, notably the House of Savoy. Very much a

179

writer of his time, Balbo argued that the future lay in the hands of 'educated people' rather than the masses. Therefore, he suggested that the solutions to the dilemmas raised by Italian nationalists would not be found in revolution but through diplomacy. He believed that if Austria was to be pushed out of Italy, it could look east to the Balkans for territory and influence. This was to be a prophetic suggestion.

Balbo failed to address the issue of what would happen when the Austrians decided they did not want to move out of Lombardy. This fact did not prevent his book becoming very popular in Piedmont and especially at the court of Charles Albert. Another important writer whose work strengthened the argument for more conservative political change was Massimo d'Azeglio. In September 1845, d'Azeglio was to witness first hand an attempted revolution in Romagna in the Papal States. The following year he published his account of the revolution in *Degli ultimi casi di Romagna* ('On Recent Events in Romagna'). D'Azeglio argued that those who had died in the Romagna revolution should be treated as martyrs – because they had fought against Austrian and papal tyranny – but revolution, was not the way forward. In *Degli ultimi casi di Romagna,* d'Azeglio was scathingly critical of papal rule. Nor was he in favour of revolution, believing that change would come through the weight of public opinion; in one of his most famous phrases, d'Azeglio argued for 'a conspiracy of public opinion in broad daylight'. Balbo and d'Azeglio agreed that public opinion and European opinion were crucial to the future success of Italian nationalism. If it was well informed and positive, then change would come about naturally.

The significance of Balbo's and d'Azeglio's books is in their suggestion that the liberation of the Italian peoples could and should come from above, thereby resulting in a conservative political settlement. Thus, both writers represented a significant development in the *Risorgimento*. The debate was now open to the possibility of political change engineered from above rather than through popular uprising. Such a blueprint was to attract the interest of Pius IX for at least a few years and, later, Count Cavour.

SOURCE

5 From *Primato morale e civile degli Italiani* (1843) by Vincenzo Gioberti.

I intend to prove that, mainly because of religion, Italy possesses within herself all of the necessary conditions for her national and political rebirth, and that to achieve this in practice she has no need of internal revolutions, nor of foreign invasions or imitations. And in the first place I say that before all else Italy must resurrect her life as a nation; and that national life cannot exist without political union between her various parts... That the Pope is naturally and must in practice be the civil head of Italy is a truth proven by the nature of things, confirmed by the history of many centuries, recognised on occasions by our people and princes.

SOURCE

6 Adapted from *Le speranze d'Italia* (1844) by Cesare Balbo.

No nation has been less frequently united in a single body than the Italian... The dreamers say that one can still achieve what hitherto has never been achieved... But this is childish, no more that the fantasy of rhetorical schoolboys, two-a-penny poets, drawing-room politicians... What would be the pope's position in a kingdom of Italy? That of king? But this is impossible, nobody even dreams of it. That of subject? But in that case he would be dependent.

Confederations are the type of constitution most suited to Italy's nature and history... The only obstacle to an Italian confederation – a most serious obstacle – is foreign rule, which penetrates deep into the peninsula... I maintain that an Italian confederation is neither desirable nor possible if a foreign power forms part of it.

To tell the truth, although a democratic conflagration is much threatened and feared in our days, it seems improbable, given the progress of our present democracy... In some cases democracy is tyrannical and so estranges every other class; in other cases it subjects itself to the aristocracy; in most cases it disappears within the great class of educated persons. A democratic conflagration may continue to be, for some time, the fear of the police and the hope of secret societies but it cannot enter into any assessment of the foreseeable future, it cannot be an element to be calculated as an important undertaking.

The worthy House of Savoy has upheld the sacred fire of Italian virtue for the last century and a half. All states that have come under their control have been in favour of the monarchy of Savoy and have been acquired at the expense of the House of Austria; for the most part by fighting for them.

AS Level Exam-Style Questions Section A

1 Why is Source 5 valuable to the historian for an enquiry about the development of Italian nationalism in the 1840s?

Explain your answer using the source, the information given about it and your own knowledge of the historical context. (8 marks)

2 How much weight do you give to the evidence of Source 6 for an enquiry into the attitudes towards democracy in the 1840s?

Explain your answer using the source, the information given about it and your own knowledge of the historical context. (12 marks)

Tip

Think carefully about the context of the time when answering both or either question.

Gioberti and the reforms of Pope Pius IX

Vincenzo Gioberti and *Primato*

For much of the middle part of the 19th century, the pope rather than the king of Sardinia-Piedmont was assumed to be the natural leader of any federal Italian state. Highly influential in the development of this assumption was Vincenzo Gioberti. The publication in 1843 of *Primato morale e civile degli Italiani* ('On the Moral and Civil Primacy of the Italians') was to have widespread consequences. Gioberti agreed with Mazzini that Italy should be rid of foreign influence, both French and Austrian. However, he thought Mazzini was mad and his tactics damaging. In *Primato morale e civile degli Italiani* Gioberti outlined a more moderate approach to ensuring Italian liberty. Gioberti argued in favour of Italian independence; the creation of an Italian federation under the leadership of the Pope. He believed that it was the papacy in Rome that gave Italians the moral upper hand over other European peoples. This line of thought became known as **neo-Guelph**. It appealed to many as it offered a way forward without revolution. It particularly appealed to those who disliked the idea of a French-style unitary state as suggested by Mazzini and his followers. A weakness of Gioberti's book was that it failed to mention the issue of Austrian control of Lombardy or Venetia and the fact that papal rule of the Papal States was neither popular nor effective.

Pope Pius XI

Gioberti's views appealed to Italian Catholics but were criticised by others. Writers, including Giuseppe La Farina, attacked the idea of extending papal power. The most important legacy of the *Primato morale e civile degli Italiani* was to spread the idea of a papal-led resolution to the national question. In 1846, Pope Gregory XVI died. He was succeeded by Cardinal Mastai Ferretti, who chose the title Pius IX. Immediately, Pius extended a hand of reconciliation to the liberals by declaring an amnesty for political offences, releasing some 2,000 prisoners from papal gaols. Such a move impressed the liberals, as did Pius' appointment of the liberal Cardinal Gizzi as his secretary of state. A number of reforms followed. In 1847, press censorship by the Church was ended and censorship in the Papal States was undertaken by a committee of predominantly laymen. This move allowed the creation of a relatively free press in the Papal States that was to have important consequences later on. An armed civic guard of local people was created to protect property. The guard quickly gained members who were sympathisers of Mazzinian demands for a republic. A Council of State, the Consulta, was set up in 1847 to advise the papacy on how to run the Papal States. Although its powers were limited, to many liberals it was the first step on the road to the elected parliament they so desired.

The motivation of Pius IX in allowing these reforms was to make papal rule more effective and, to a lesser extent, popular. However, in doing so he appeared to be a 'liberal pope', something that Metternich in particular found very worrying. The reaction of Metternich to the reforms of Pius IX was predictable and important. Under the Treaty of Vienna the Austrians were given the right to keep an army in the town of Ferrara, despite the fact that it was inside the Papal States. In July 1847, as a show of strength the Austrians exercised their right and militarily occupied Ferrara. Pius IX responded in a way that raised his reputation with Italian nationalists to even greater heights. He lodged a formal protest with the Austrian government claiming that the sovereignty of the Papal States had been infringed. This action momentarily made Pius IX the darling of nationalist cause. But the reality was that Pius'

politics were not the same as those seeking revolution, nor did he sympathise with the nationalist cause. At the Consulta, which met in November 1847, Pius reminded the delegates that the only power which he or they should recognise was papal sovereignty.

WHY DID REVOLUTION BREAK OUT IN 1848–49?

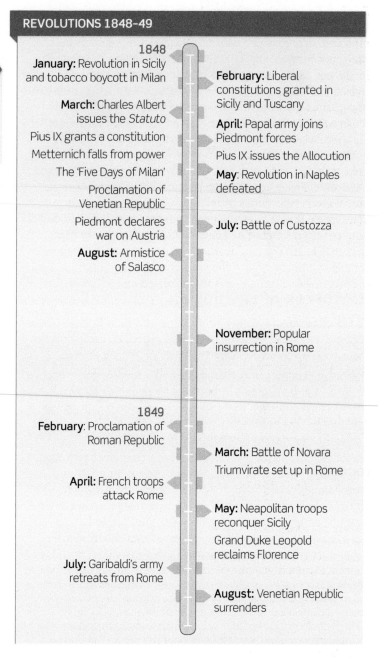

REVOLUTIONS 1848–49

1848
January: Revolution in Sicily and tobacco boycott in Milan

February: Liberal constitutions granted in Sicily and Tuscany

March: Charles Albert issues the *Statuto*
Pius IX grants a constitution
Metternich falls from power
The 'Five Days of Milan'
Proclamation of Venetian Republic
Piedmont declares war on Austria

April: Papal army joins Piedmont forces
Pius IX issues the Allocution

May: Revolution in Naples defeated

August: Armistice of Salasco

July: Battle of Custozza

November: Popular insurrection in Rome

1849
February: Proclamation of Roman Republic

April: French troops attack Rome

March: Battle of Novara
Triumvirate set up in Rome

May: Neapolitan troops reconquer Sicily
Grand Duke Leopold reclaims Florence

July: Garibaldi's army retreats from Rome

August: Venetian Republic surrenders

There were many causes of the revolutions that spread across Italy and beyond during 1848–49. The hopes and expectations of liberals for reform were heightened by the election of Pius IX in 1846. Liberals in the north of Italy were also encouraged by events in Switzerland in 1847, during which forces in favour of the introduction of a liberal constitution defeated the more conservative alliance known as the Sonderbund. Agitation for political reform was partly the result of economic problems in Italy during 1846–47. In particular, the poor harvest led to food riots from north to south and made deep-rooted economic problems worse. In southern areas such as Calabria, land enclosure had taken common land from the peasantry and their response was violence. In the north, under-employment in the textile industries resulted in workers destroying machinery. The underlying causes of unrest were economic and social, but the unrest soon turned into a political demonstration, stirred in some places by a free press. The clamour of nationalists for the destruction of Austrian power increased as the Austrian Empire seemingly faltered.

The impact of Pius IX's reforms (see page 192) on other parts of Italy was considerable. In Piedmont and Tuscany, for example, there was unrest and demand for change. The response of Charles Albert in Piedmont in October 1847 was to sack his conservative minister, Solara della Margarita, and announce a package of limited reforms. However, the emphasis should be on the word 'limited', because Charles Albert was not suddenly preparing to introduce a liberal government. None the less, he did allow press censorship to be relaxed and local government was reorganised. As is often the case, granting reform did little to satisfy liberals and radicals who simply increased their demands for reform. The same applied to Tuscany where Duke Leopold II introduced limited reforms that served to encourage radicals to demand a constitution.

Outbreak of revolution in the Italian states

Uprising in Sicily

The uprising in Sicily in 1848 was not caused by any demands for national unity. Instead, it was a reaction against the repressive regime of Ferdinand II. In 1836, an outbreak of cholera on the island killed one-tenth of the Sicilian population (some 65,000 people) and led to the belief that the disease was in some way connected to Neapolitan misrule. A lack of political debate, brutal administration and miserable living conditions provoked an uprising in Palermo on 12 January 1848. After a few days, the revolutionaries had taken control of the city and were being led by a Sicilian nobleman, Rosalino Pilo. The main demand of the revolutionaries was straightforward. They wanted the re-establishment of the 1812 constitution, which had been abolished by the King of Naples in 1816. Ferdinand II would not accept the reintroduction of such a constitution, because it would have given Sicily considerable autonomy from Naples. He offered a compromise constitution, which was refused.

The Sicilian revolutionaries consequently set up their own provisional government. The nature of this government reveals much about the nature of the revolution. A National Guard was established to ensure that the lower orders and the more militant revolutionaries did not get out of control. Hostility was maintained towards Naples and all key government posts were reserved for Sicilians. The Sicilian elections took place in March 1848. In April 1848, the newly elected parliament announced that Ferdinand was no longer king of Sicily. An Italian prince would be chosen as monarch in his place. In July 1848, the Sicilian constitution gave considerable powers to the lower house of parliament. This was not a radical revolution, but one that aimed at a constitutional settlement that would give Sicily its independence. However, this was not acceptable to Ferdinand and, in September 1848, he launched a military assault on the island, which earned him the nickname 'King Bomba'. Despite the superiority in numbers of the Neapolitan army, it took them until May 1849 to finally crush the insurrection.

Revolution in Sicily soon spread to the mainland. On 17 January 1848, an uprising of the secret societies in Salerno forced a series of concessions from Ferdinand, including the promise to free political prisoners. But this was not enough for most revolutionaries, who also wanted a constitution. A mass demonstration in Naples on 27 January in favour of their demands forced the issue. Ferdinand agreed to grant a constitution. This was due in part to the fact that he was unable to rely on Austrian support as his father had been able to do in 1820 because, as a result of Austrian behaviour in Ferarra, Pius IX refused to let Austrian troops cross the Papal States. Indeed, in making his decision to deny Austrian troops access to the Papal States, Pius IX even went so far as to ask the Lord to bless Italy. Just the utterance of the word was enough to send nationalists into a frenzy of excitement and adulation. At this point, the papacy really did seem to have put itself at the head of the nationalist cause. The constitution that was issued in February 1848 turned out to be conservative in nature. A parliament was to be created with an upper and lower chamber. The king could veto laws and could nominate members to the upper chamber of parliament. A national guard was to be created, albeit under the control of the king.

Lombardy

The Austrian rulers in Lombardy refused to respond to agitation for reform. In protest, the citizens of Milan came up with an interesting way of registering their protest. The Austrian government held the monopoly over the sale of tobacco and it has been calculated that the considerable sum of 5 million lire a year was raised in taxes from the sale of tobacco and from gambling in Lombardy. In Milan people stopped smoking and Austrian soldiers and officers seen smoking in the streets were harassed. In itself, this boycott did not constitute a full-scale uprising. It was events in Vienna in March 1848 that were to have a considerable impact on what would happen next. The February revolution in France had inspired demonstrations in favour of reform in Vienna. As popular unrest spread, the unthinkable happened. On 13 March 1848, Metternich resigned as foreign minister and this was the trigger for revolution.

The five days of Milan

On 17 March 1848, barricades were thrown up in Milan and a full-scale battle followed. On one side were the Austrian governor and troops with the initial support of the city council. On the other was a coalition of anti-Austrian forces. These included Mazzinians, liberals, around 100 priests, artisans and writers. In the light of the crisis in Vienna and ferocious opposition in Milan, the Austrian commander Field Marshal Radetzky took the decision to withdraw his troops to the safety of the fortresses of the Quadrilateral. The temporary collapse of Austrian rule left a political vacuum in Lombardy. The different opinions held in Milan about the future of Lombardy reflected some of the different strands of the *Risorgimento* already described. The more conservative moderates of the Milan City Council, led by its *podestà* (magistrate) Count Gabrio Cassati, feared an independent Lombard republic. Instead, they proposed union with Piedmont led by Charles Albert. During the uprising, the more radical Milanese formed a Council of War led by Carlo Cattaneo. Their ultimate aim was the creation of a federation of Italian republics. A provisional government was formed that was led by Cassati and dominated by the moderates. They knew that the Austrians would be back, so they asked Charles Albert for protection.

SOURCE

7   Street battle at Porta Tosa during the Milan uprising, 22 March 1848.

Demonstrations in Venice

It was not just in Lombardy that the Austrians were in trouble. In Venice, demonstrations took place demanding the release from prison of the patriot Daniele Manin. The problem for the Austrians was that many of the sailors in the Austrian navy docked in Venice were Italian, as were many of the soldiers in the Austrian garrison in the city. As such their reliability in the face of Italian nationalists was questionable. Manin was released and, on 22 March 1848, a Venetian Republic was declared by the people. Although Manin preferred Venice to stay independent until the declaration of an Italian Republic, he accepted the vote of the newly elected Venetian assembly to also ask Charles Albert for assistance.

EXTEND YOUR KNOWLEDGE

Field Marshal Count Joseph Radetzky (1766–1858)

An Austrian soldier with considerable expertise in warfare in Italy, Count Joseph Radetzky took part in the military intervention in 1831 and was put in command of the Austrian army in Italy in 1834. Radetzky introduced strict discipline into the army he commanded, but he lacked resources. In 1848, he was forced to fall back to the Quadrilateral. However, in March 1849 he led his army to victory at Novara.

Daniele Manin (1804–57)

The Venetian leader of the movement to free the north of Italy from Austrian rule. In January 1848, he was imprisoned by the Austrians but released in March after the outbreak of the revolution of 1848. He led the republic until July 1848, when the Venetian parliament voted for union with the Kingdom of Sardinia. Manin was a republican and resigned. In March 1849, he was given the powers of a dictator to organise the defence of Venice. In her pamplet *The Risorgimento* (1962), the historian Agatha Ramm summed up Manin's Venetian Republic: 'The story of the Venetian rising bears the stamp of historic moderation.' After Venice was overrun by the Austrians, he went into exile in Paris. Later he returned to Italy and became a leading member of the National Society, eventually supporting the leadership of the House of Savoy.

Causation relativity

Historical events usually have many causes. Some are crucial, while some are less important. For some historical questions, it is important to understand exactly what role certain factors played in causing historical change.

Significant factors in the timing and nature of the 1848 revolutions

Bad harvests in 1846–47 exacerbated other economic problems.	Reaction in Sicily against the repressive regime of Ferdinand II caused resentment.	The impact of Pius IX's reforms raised expectations and led to demands for change.
Successful uprising of liberals in Switzerland in 1847 encouraged liberals in the north of the Italian peninsula.	Seemingly faltering Austro-Hungarian rule led to rising expectation of Italian nationalists in Lombardy and Venice.	Risings in Sicily created a snowball effect leading to uprisings on the mainland.

Answer the following questions on your own:

The timing of the August Decrees

1 How important were bad harvests in explaining the timing of the revolutions?

2 In what ways did the Pius IX's reforms change expectations among liberals? How far did this precipitate 1848 uprisings?

3 How might have Ferdinand II prevented unrest in Sicily and Naples?

The nature of the 1848 revolutions

4 How far had the Enlightenment movement changed the attitudes of the people who were involved in writing the August Decrees?

5 What role did the above factors play in the way that the August Decrees reshaped the agricultural economy?

6 Would the nature of the August Decrees have been the same if the Bastille had not been stormed?

7 What roles did each of the above causal factors play in determining the nature and timing of the August Decrees?

The situation in Piedmont, including the First Italian War of Independence

The granting of a constitution in Naples raised expectation of liberals throughout the Italian peninsula. On 17 February 1848, Grand Duke Leopold granted an equally conservative constitution. In Piedmont, Charles Albert was far less willing to give in to liberal demands. However, he was finally persuaded that it would be better to give in to the limited demands of the more moderate liberals than to risk revolution and the potential of having to face more radical demands. The resulting *Statuto* of March 1848 had great significance in the coming years. It did not grant a full parliamentary system as the king kept hold of important powers, including the right to sanction laws that had been passed and to appoint the members of the upper house of parliament. However, it did create a constitutional monarchy with parliament given the right to introduce laws. The lower house of parliament was to be elected on a limited suffrage (only two percent of the population) and was given the power to discuss financial issues. It guaranteed civil liberties for Piedmontese citizens, for example the right to religious toleration, and it was in granting such liberties that the *Statuto* went further than other constitutions. With the issuing of the *Statuto*, Pope Pius IX found it difficult to resist calls for a constitution in the Papal States but his response was limited. In March he allowed the creation of a parliament, but one that had less power than those in the other states. He also denied the citizens of the Papal States the basic liberties promised by the Piedmontese *Statuto*. If contemporaries were looking, here was a clear sign of the limitations of Pius IX's liberal credentials.

At first, Charles Albert hesitated to assist. He disliked the revolutionary overtones of what had happened in Milan and Venice. However, one factor above all others convinced him that intervention was the correct course of action because at this moment of Austrian weakness and with Metternich gone, Lombardy was ripe for annexation. Other considerations that helped him to make his decision were the fear of military intervention by revolutionary France if he held back, and the fear that if he did not intervene, then revolution in Milan might spread to Piedmont. On 22 March 1848, Piedmont declared war on Austria. Its army, led in person by Charles Albert, invaded Lombardy. Charles Albert's hope was that he could annex Lombardy without a fight, while the Austrian government was in turmoil. At first it seemed that even if a battle had to be fought, then the Piedmontese stood a good chance of victory. Troops from across Italy converged on Lombardy to join with Charles Albert to purge Italy of the hated Austrians once and for all; columns of soldiers led by General Guglielmo Pepe came from Naples and an army led by General Giacomo Durango arrived from the Papal States. However, Durango had exceeded his orders from Pope Pius IX, who had no wish to fight with Catholic Austria. What happened next very much shaped the course of the *Risorgimento*.

Pius's Allocution, April 1848

For many conservative Italians, the pope was the natural leader of Italy. Pius IX had seemingly placed himself at the head of those who wished for an Italian federation under his leadership. However, this was a misreading of Pius IX's intentions. He was not prepared to upset Catholic Austria for the sake of Italian unity. It was not so much Piedmontese anti-clericalism (anti-Church) that led to the decline of the papacy's temporal power, but the actions of the papacy itself. A crucial turning point was the issuing of the **Papal Allocution** in April 1848. On 29 April 1848, in response to General Durango's disobedience, Pius IX issued the Allocution stating that the war against Austria did not have his blessing and highlighted the fact that Charles Albert was the aggressor in the war. The idea of a united Italy was not one supported by the papacy and the Pope did not wish to be considered as the potential leader of any **Italian Confederation**.

The Allocution shocked Italian nationalists. The critical point behind the Allocution of 1848 was that it marked the end of any dream held by moderates and those who ascribed to the ideas of Gioberti and the neo–Guelphs that the pope might lead the nationalist cause in Italy. It also severely weakened the idea of the pope as head of an Italian federation, for integral to that role was an element of antagonism towards Austria. In short, it meant that Pius had ruled himself out of the leadership of Italy. In reality, the Allocution was a statement of neutrality. Pius IX was particularly concerned that his army, led by General Durando, had marched out of the Papal States on 25 April to join the Piedmontese army in its fight against Austria. But if the aim of the Allocution was simply a reaction to this event, then its impact went far deeper. Indeed, one might argue that Pius was reacting to Durango's decision to fight the Austrians and that he was attempting to send signals to Vienna disowning the actions of his own general. However, disclaiming war against Austria severely undermined the papacy's claim to lead the Italian cause. From a military point of view, the Allocution weakened Charles Albert's cause as some soldiers in Durango's army would not go against the papal word. Worse was to come for the nationalists with the news on 15 May 1848 that Ferdinand II had re-established autocratic government in Naples. General Pepe was ordered home and although he ignored his orders, many of his troops headed south.

The loss of Lombardy

Initially, Charles Albert's army was successful in its campaign against Austria. In May 1848, it took Peschiera and won the Battle of Goito. However, the outlook for Charles Albert was distinctly worrying. A French army some 30,000 strong was amassing on the Piedmontese border. Within his own army he had a number

of troops left over from Durango's and Pepe's armies, whom he did not trust. Even more alarming was the fact that Radetzky had persuaded the Austrian government to fight for Lombardy rather than give it to Charles Albert. It was not surprising that Radetzky was keen to fight to hold on to Lombardy. He had spent most of his military career in northern Italy and understood the strategic benefits of holding the Quadrilateral. He also thought his military chances against Charles Albert's army were good. In June 1848, the Austrians ordered Radetzky to seek a negotiated peace. However, he sent Prince Felix Schwarzenberg to Vienna to persuade the government to allow him to fight, which they did. On 24 July 1848, the Austrian army overwhelmingly defeated the Piedmontese and their allies at the Battle of Custozza. Radetzky pressed home the advantage, the Piedmontese were expelled from Lombardy by 4 August and the Armistice of Salasco was brokered by 11 August. Charles Albert gave up Lombardy, although the Austrians accepted Anglo-French mediation on the understanding that it might result in territory being handed over to the Piedmontese at a later date. In reality this came to nothing.

Further defeat

In November 1848, Schwarzenberg was appointed prime minister of Austria. Schwarzenburg was in no mind to compromise. His appointment put paid to any hopes the Piedmontese might have had that the Austrians were prepared to give territorial concessions to prevent future conflict. In Piedmont, Charles Albert was persuaded by Prime Minister Gioberti and General Domenico Chiodo (who took over as prime minister in March 1849) to try one more time to defeat the Austrians. Charles Albert hoped that victory would silence the democrats and republicans in Piedmont whose popularity had increased since the Battle of Custozza. However, the outcome was further humiliation, with Radetzky crushing the Piedmontese army at Novara on 23 March 1849. The significance of this battle should not be underestimated; it marked the end of Piedmontese ambition and was a crushing blow for the nationalist cause.

In the wake of defeat, Charles Albert abdicated the throne of the Kingdom of Sardinia in favour of his son Victor Emmanuel II. When peace was signed in August 1849, Piedmont was forced to pay reparations of 65 million French francs. The defeat for Piedmont was a humiliating one and was to have important short- and long-term repercussions. Before the first campaign against the Austrians, Charles Albert had famously claimed that Italy would *fare da sè* ('go it alone'). By this he meant that Italians did not need foreign help to get rid of the Austrians. Military defeat in 1848 and 1849 proved Charles Albert wrong. To defeat the Austrians militarily, Italians would need help from abroad. As the forces of constitutional monarchy and the moderate cause were defeated on the battlefield, so those with a more radical agenda took the initiative.

Counter-revolution

As Radetsky's army entered Lombardy in the summer of 1848, it was welcomed by the cheers of many labourers in the fields who preferred Austrian rule to that of the local landlords. But it was not just in Lombardy that the Austrian forces spearheaded counter-revolution. In Tuscany, democrats had raised the prospect of radical revolt. In October 1848, the ruler of Tuscany, Grand Duke Leopold II, was forced to appoint a more 'democratic' government. The new government was led by Professor Giuseppe Montanelli, who wanted a people's war against Austria. By 1849, the atmosphere in Tuscany had become even more radical and in February Leopold fled the region. A triumvirate, of Montanelli, Francesco Domenico Guerrazzi and Giuseppe Mazzoni, took control of the government and declared a Tuscan Republic. However, the defeat of Piedmont forces at Novara led to the regaining of the upper hand by the 'moderates' in the region. They seized Florence, thereby paving the way for Leopold's return to Tuscany in April 1849, supported by Austrian troops. The constitution was suspended and press restrictions reimposed.

Although Charles Albert's army was defeated by the Austrians at Novara in March 1849, the Republic of Venice survived. Thereafter, the Republic, led by Daniele Manin, became a symbol of resistance against the Austrians for Italian nationalists, but it had little other significance. The rest of Venetia remained under Austrian control and Manin followed a policy of moderation for fear of offending Piedmont. Most Venetians looked favourably on Manin's moderation and he pursued popular policies, such as the reduction of taxes on important goods like salt and the introduction of universal suffrage. He managed to do this while not threatening with revolutionary ideas the interests of the middle class or artisans. As a result, they continued to give him their support. Despite being besieged by the Austrian army, and despite hunger and cholera in the city, Venice held out for a year, but in the end Austrian forces prevailed and on 27 August 1849 Radetsky led his army into the city.

Counter-revolution was spearheaded by the leaders of the ancien régime, but it was often supported by the masses who had little interest in constitutional reform. In Naples in May 1848, King Ferdinand launched a counter-revolution with the aim of closing down the parliament that had been granted under the terms of the constitution of January 1848. While around 300 radicals opposed Ferdinand, many of the poorest in Naples – the lazzaroni – shouted slogans in support of the king and against the constitution. By May 1849, the Bourbon army had regained control of Sicily, a move that was welcomed by many influential Sicilians, including leaders of the mafiosi. The constitution was suspended in Sicily and parliamentary leaders fled into exile. By the summer of 1849, Ferdinand was able to end the constitutional experiment. Across the Italian peninsula

peasants tired of a revolution that often meant little more than requisitioning of food and billeting of soldiers in their homes. Many members of the middle classes expressed their support for established rulers, who guaranteed order and stability if not rights. By the end of 1849, it was counter-revolution rather than revolution that had popular support in many parts of the Italian peninsula.

The Roman Republic, 1848–49

With the defeat of Piedmont at Custozza, large numbers of General Durango's troops returned to Rome. Pius IX had issued a constitution in March 1848, but was fearful of a military coup and was now openly unsympathetic to the nationalist cause. In September 1848, Pius appointed Count Pellegrino Rossi as his prime minister, hoping that Rossi would act firmly against liberal reformers and more radical democrats alike. Unfortunately for Pius, Rossi was not popular with the Roman mob and was murdered on 15 November while entering the Roman parliament. This assassination was the trigger for insurrection against the pope, who fled Rome on 24 November in fear of his life.

While Pius IX settled into temporary exile in Gaeta in the Kingdom of Naples, power in Rome was exercised by a revolutionary government led by Giuseppe Galletti. A Mazzinian and, in his youth, a revolutionary, Galletti was tried in 1844 for conspiring against Pope Gregory XVI and was sentenced to life imprisonment. Although he was a supporter of Mazzini, Galletti was moderate enough to have been appointed minister of the interior by Pius IX before his departure for Gaeta. Although his government was in a difficult position with demands for reform being made from all sides, Galletti's ministry was able to introduce some popular measures in its short period in office. The most popular reform was the abolition of the *macinato* in January 1849. Also popular was the programme of public works ordered by Galletti's government. This was partly due to the large number of people employed in the building trade in Rome and the desire of the government to keep levels of employment high. The government proposed the meeting of a Constituent Assembly, the Costituente, to decide the future of Rome and Italy, giving responsibility for the election of the Costituente to a **Giunta di Stato**. It was the task of the Giunta to invite the election of deputies from across the whole of Italy, rather than just from Rome.

The rule of the radicals

In January 1849, elections were held in Rome and the Costituente met for the first time the following month. Its membership was radical, although mainly middle class. Immediately it announced the end of the pope's power and the foundation of the Roman Republic. This was not surprising given the popularity of Mazzini's ideas among many deputies in the Costituente and it was little surprise that Mazzini was welcomed on his arrival in Rome in March. The rule of the radicals in Rome was, however, not welcomed by the pope or by his allies across Europe. At a meeting with his cardinals in April 1849 the pope called on the forces of Spain, France and the Kingdom of Naples to come to his help. He appealed to them by claiming that military intervention was necessary to liberate Rome from 'the enemies of our most holy religion and civil society'. On news of the defeat of Charles Albert at Novara in March, the Costituente chose three people to govern Rome, known as the triumvirate and Mazzini hastened to Rome. On arrival, he was given power as part of the triumvirate with Carlo Armellini and Aurelio Saffi. Mazzini was the driving force of the government. He ordered the clearing of the Roman slums and the redistribution of some Church land. He was to carry on the reforming work of Galletti's government: for example, the ending of Church control of the press and the abolition of the death penalty. The censorship of the press was abolished, as was the Church's control of education. A constitution was promised. However, it was not issued by the Costituente until June 1849, by which time it was too late because the republic was on the verge of defeat.

The March on Rome

The Roman Republic had few friends in Italy or further afield. Neither did it have a significant army with which it could defend itself. The clearest threat to the survival of the Roman Republic came from republican France. In France, the president, Louis Napoleon, wanted to win the support of Catholics and sent a force to Italy, led by General Charles Oudinot, with orders to crush the Roman Republic. On 24 April 1849, Oudinot landed at Città Vecchia and marched on Rome. The French were opposed by a makeshift force of volunteers led by perhaps the greatest hero of the *Risorgimento*, Giuseppe Garibaldi. For two months he inspired his troops to block the French army's attempt to take Rome. Meanwhile, Mazzini's attempt to appease the French was in the hope that they would not destroy the Roman Republic. By June 1849, the French had amassed an army of 20,000 at the gates of Rome. Garibaldi addressed the Costituente promising that the future for Rome's defenders was one of 'hunger, thirst, forced marches, battles and death'.

SOURCE

The siege of Rome on 1 May 1849, printed in the *London Illustrated News* on 19 May 1849.

As the French entered Rome on 3 July, Garibaldi and a force of 4,000 withdrew to San Marino to fight another day. Mazzini made one final appeal to the people of Rome before returning to exile in London. Without doubt the cause of Italian nationalism still fully relied on the attitude of foreign powers. Despite the social moderation of Mazzinian principles and the limited scope of their aims, they still posed a real threat to the dominance of the rulers of Italy. The Roman Republic was to be the high point of these principles and the moment when they were put into reality. Indeed, there was a world of difference between the clerical rule of Pope Pius IX and the enlightened but short-lived Roman Republic of 1849. What Mazzini's government of Rome proved was that his ideals could be practically realised.

SOURCE

From *Journal kept in France and Italy from 1848 to 1852* by the British economist Nassau William Senior. A government adviser and academic, Senior was well connected. In his later life he travelled extensively with the aim of observing foreign political systems and cultures.

27 November 1850 I had a long conversation with M. Buonarotti, the representative of the great artist, formerly a judge, and now Councillor of State. He spoke with great but, perhaps, not undue bitterness of the republican faction, which, by the assassination of Rossi, the Neapolitan revolt, the unjust attack on Austria, and the insurrection of Genoa, Leghorn, and Florence, has ruined the happiness of this generation, and thrown back Italy for a century. 'This little Duchy (Tuscany),' he said, 'is a specimen of Italian unity. Florence, Lucca, Sienna, and Pisa all hate one another even more than they hate Austria.' Among the mischiefs which he feared from republicanism was trial by jury.

28 November First came the Duke Serra di Falco [a Sicilian refugee in Florence]. 'I regret Sicily', he said, 'but yet I amuse myself here… Politics, on a great scale, were forced on me, and I don't think that I shall ever take them up again. Men, at least, my countrymen, are not worth the sacrifices which the attempt to serve them costs, and the attempt scarcely ever succeeds. Those who know what is right are too timid or too indolent to act on their convictions, and almost all the bold and active are ignorant and perverse. When the whole united force of all Italy was not more than was wanted to drive out the Austrian, we wasted our strength in civil war, and never were more thoroughly disunited, never feared and hated one another more deeply, that when we were proclaiming Italy united.'

5 December… I asked the Duke [Serra di Falco] if he agreed in Prince Butera's opinion that under no circumstances whatever, however liberal the Constitution, or however honest and intelligent the King, could Sicily and Naples live together comfortably under one sovereign. He answered. 'Perfectly; it is lamentable, but it is true'.

ACTIVITY
KNOWLEDGE CHECK

1849-50 revolutions

1 How useful is Source 9 to the historian researching the revolutions of 1849-50 in the Italian peninsula?

Pulling it together?

2 What were in your opinion the three most significant turning points of the 1848-49 revolutions?

WHY DID THE REVOLUTIONS OF 1848-49 FAIL?

Lack of unity

There is little evidence of a desire among the revolutionaries of 1848 to establish a united Italy. In that sense it was not a politically motivated series of revolutions. There were clearly economic grievances: the disappointing harvests of 1845 and 1846 had left grain prices high and created the context of discontent. The reformism of Pius IX in 1846–47 was a means to the end of strengthening papal rule of the Papal States. It also acted as a trigger to demands for reform in other areas of Italy, most noticeably Tuscany and Piedmont. What is most striking is the conservatism of the first wave of revolutions of 1848, not just in Italy but across Europe. The dominance of the institutions of restoration states was challenged in 1848 and 1849. However, it is clear that the nature of the challenge was varied.

- In Piedmont the challenge focused around the removal of the Austrians.

- In Sicily, the demands revolved around the resurrection of the 1812 constitution.

- In Milan, in March 1848, some of the fiercest street fighting took place, but the Milanese provisional government led by Carlo Cattaneo had little desire to call for a republic, as much for pragmatic reasons as anything else. Instead, it turned to the Piedmontese monarchy and Charles Albert for protection.

- Even though the leader of the uprising in Venice, Daniele Manin, was a 'democrat', the revolution he declared proceeded cautiously and in July 1848 he also rallied under the banner of Charles Albert.

- On the surface, the actions of the Roman Republic in 1849 were relatively moderate. The Church's power was attacked in February 1849 with the abolition of its temporal power and the announcement of Rome as a secular state.

EXTEND YOUR KNOWLEDGE

A limited revolution?
Although seemingly threatening, the revolutionaries were, in reality, limited in their political and social ambitions. In *The Risorgimento* (1962) by Agatha Ramm, the author concludes that 'the rebels of 1848–49 were not the kind of men to aim at a revolutionary shift of social power'. She is nearly, but not entirely, correct. Most of the revolutionaries who came to dominate the revolutions of 1848–49 had the limited objective of constitutional reform. Yet even Mazzini recognised there was little appetite among the masses for democratic republicanism. Even Garibaldi's army of volunteers, which performed so heroically against the French in defence of Rome in the summer of 1849, contained few labourers or peasants.

There was little significant support for the *Risorgimento* from the peasantry because often those who called for insurrection were seen as more of an opponent than the old regime. In 1848, the revolutions were mainly urban based in Milan, Rome, Venice, Florence and Turin. The support for these revolutions was drawn from the artisan class. In Sicily, the peasantry invaded the common lands and demanded their restoration. However, they were quickly thrown off the land and the new Sicilian parliament failed to pass any land reform measures. One reason why the peasantry failed to respond to the call for national unity is that it was based on a Mazzinian idealism that did not go so far as to address the issue of land. Most land was worked on the basis of subsistence farming with little capital available and primitive farming techniques.

Indeed, what is striking is the consistency of apathy among the common people of Rome for political change from 1848 to 1871. Those democrats such as Professor Montanelli, who argued in 1849 for a single constitutionally united Italy, managed to achieve the aim of the creation of a Costituente but precious little else. Although the new assembly received delegates from across the Papal States and Tuscany, it found little support elsewhere.

Austrian and French intervention

Austria
The fall of Metternich in March 1848 and the financial crisis that followed it were perceived as signs of terminal decline. The assumption of many nationalists was that Austria's influence in the affairs of the Italian states was over. But, the Austrian withdrawal was only temporary. Although Austrian forces in Italy were decimated by desertion and were forced, in March 1848, to withdraw to the Quadrilateral, they still were far too strong in battle for anything the Piedmontese and their Italian allies could throw at them. Once the control had been re-established at home, the Habsburgs were free to reassert control over Italian affairs. The crushing defeats suffered by the Piedmontese at Custozza in July 1848 and Novara in March 1849, as well as the collapse of the Venetian Republic in August 1849, reflected the continuing strength of Austria. However, it was Pius IX's issuing of the Allocution in April 1848 that revealed the reality of power in Italy. Even if Pius wished for the expulsion of Austria from Italy, Austria was too strong to be realistically challenged, even in a year of such turmoil as 1848.

France
Mazzini hoped that Louis Napoleon might have been persuaded not to attack the Roman Republic and be content with keeping an army in Italy for the purpose of deterring the Austrians from intervening. Indeed, Mazzini undertook measures including the return of French prisoners which he hoped would at least ensure French neutrality. The policy failed. While many people in France sympathised with the cause of the Roman Republic, Louis Napoleon was more interested in reassuring French Catholics than he was in supporting a revolutionary government abroad. He was able to win over doubters as to the wisdom of the French expedition in 1849 with the explanation that if the French did not intervene, the Austrians would. He was also playing on the sentiments of significant Catholic opinion in France that wanted to see the pope restored. To many in France, the deposition of Pius IX was a revolutionary action that disturbed the status quo. For this reason, the French National Assembly, which had been elected by universal suffrage, voted to send a force in 1849 to restore the pope. Despite having such an enlightened government, the Roman Republic had few friends. Although in his youth Louis Napoleon had sympathised with the cause of Italian unity, he did not allow such sentiment to cloud his judgement. The principles and priorities of domestic politics dominated and the restoration of the papacy was ultimately undertaken in order to please Catholic opinion in France. When the pope returned to Rome in April 1850, he was welcomed back by cheering crowds. Mazzini's ideas threatened to overturn the social and political order. But there were few people, either in the Italian states or abroad, who wished to see that happen.

Lack of international support
Charles Albert's announcement in March 1848 that Italy would *farà da sè* ('go it alone') was more the result of a desire to keep republican France out of northern Italy than any great conviction that Piedmont could defeat the Austrians in battle without outside support. Of foremost concern was the distinct possibility that the radically inspired unrest in Milan could spill over into Piedmont. The events in Lombardy and, to a lesser extent, Venice, had forced Charles Albert's hand, but the reality was that both France and Britain showed little interest in getting involved at this particular point. In June 1848 the British foreign secretary, Lord Palmerston,

encouraged the Austrians to abandon northern Italy. The British and the French also agreed to act as mediators between the Austrians and Piedmontese throughout the summer months, resulting in the armistice of Salasco of August 1848. But it was not mediation which the Piedmontese really needed but military support. In December 1848, Louis Napoleon was elected president of France. In the same month, Vincenzo Gioberti was appointed by Charles Albert to lead the Piedmontese government. Gioberti's miscalculation was to believe that if Piedmont went to war again with Austria it would have French support. But when, in March 1849, the Piedmontese declared war against Austria, Louis Napoleon was unmoved. The diplomatic and political reality was that neither France nor Britain wished to support Piedmont or anyone else in a war against Austria, however romantic the case. Without such support the Piedmontese were twice comprehensively defeated in battle by the Austrians, firstly at Custozza in July 1848 and then at Novara in March 1849. The lesson learned was that the Piedmontese were not strong enough militarily to expel the Austrians from the Italian peninsula; to do so they would need French support or a fundamental shift in the balance of power in Central Europe.

Reaction of the papacy

The issuing of the Papal Allocution was a fundamental turning point in the revolutions of 1848. Apart from paralysing the papal army, it made it absolutely clear that Pius IX would not support any 'national' cause nor would he countenance war against Austria. The pope would not act in such a way that would threaten the temporal power of the papacy. Indeed, he was even prepared to request support from foreign powers to restore his temporal power. Gioberti's predictions and proposals were dashed; from now on the cause of national unity would be anti rather than pro clerical. Austrian, French and Neapolitan forces all invaded the Papal States in April 1849 determined to destroy the Roman Republic and restore papal rule.

Piedmont's weaknesses

For Charles Albert of Piedmont and his successor Victor Emmanuel II, the lessons of 1848 were that foreign dominance of Italy could only be ended with outside support. Such support would only be forthcoming if Mazzinianism was kept in check. The process of the unification of Italy from 1848 to 1871 was, in part, as much to do with the defeat of Mazzinianism as it was the creation of an Italian nation state. The wars fought by Charles Albert in the 1840s were not wars of national liberation but an attempt to annex territory in northern Italy. Austrian control of parts of northern Italy and influence throughout the peninsula had been challenged but not removed. It is clear that the insurrections were mainly regional in nature. Some groups, such as the workers in Venice, hoped for revolutionary change. However, the majority were more conservative in their ambition. Those who, after 1848, were serious in support of political change in Italy began to look to Piedmont with its liberal constitution and increasingly modern economy. It was also Piedmont that would be most likely to enrol the foreign support necessary to remove Austria.

SOURCE

10 From the satirical journal *Il Don Pirlone*, issued in Rome during the Roman Republic. In this cartoon, the Mazzinian-inspired Roman Republic, Roman wolf at her side, heralds the dawn of Italian unity by ringing a bell in the shape of a cap of liberty. Pope Pius IX and Charles Albert of Piedmont are among those discomfited by the bell's sound.

SOURCE 11

From a letter by Margaret Fuller written in 1849. Fuller was an American journalist who had travelled to Europe in 1846 as a correspondent of the *New York Tribune*. Fuller met Mazzini and became romantically attached to Giovanni Ossoli, a revolutionary nationalist who fought for the Roman Republic in 1849.

On England no dependence can be placed. She is guided by no great idea; her Parliamentary leaders sneer at sentimental policy and the 'jargon' of idea... Then the Church of England, so long an enemy to the Church of Rome, feels a decided interest with it on the subject of temporal possessions. The rich English traveller, fearing to see the Prince Borghese stripped on one of his palaces for a hospital or some such low use... muses: "I hope to see them all shot yet, these rascally republicans." How I wish my own country would show some noble sympathy when an experience so like her own is going on... Order reigns – the same Order that reigned at Warsaw. Russian-Austrian clemency is yielded to those who remain to share it... The French have not redeemed one pretext by which they painted over the ugly face of their perfidy... That [foreign] intervention, the falsehood of France, the inertia of England, the entrance of Russia into Hungary – all these steps tracked in blood, which cause so much anguish at the moment, Democracy ought in fact to bless. They insure her triumphs – there is no possible compromise between her and the Old... All the more for what has happened in these sad days, will entire Europe, at the end of this century, be under Republican form of Government.

AS Level Exam-Style Question Section B

How accurate is it to assert that the cause of Italian national unity had made little progress between 1830 and 1848? (20 marks)

Tip

Before you start writing, think of the ways in which the cause of unity had made progress and the ways it had not.

A Level Exam-Style Question Section B

How far do you agree with the view that it was the lack of international support which was the main cause of the failure of the 1848–49 revolutions? (20 marks)

Tip

You will need to weigh up the significance of the lack of international support against other factors.

ACTIVITY
KNOWLEDGE CHECK

Reasons for failure

1 What do Sources 10 and 11 suggest are the reasons for the failure of the 1848–49 revolutions?

2 What reasons for the failure of the revolutions are not covered in these sources?

ACTIVITY
SUMMARY

Significant developments

Plot on a spider diagram the important turning points in the development of Italian nationalism between 1830 and 1849.

Once you have done that, explain the significance of each event.

WIDER READING

Clark, M. *The Italian Risorgimento*, Routledge (2009)

Hearder, H. *Italy in the Age of the Risorgimento 1790–1870*, Routledge (1983)

Mack Smith, D. *Mazzini*, Yale University Press (1996).

2a.2 The rise of Piedmont, 1849–56

KEY QUESTIONS

- What was the legacy of the 1848–49 revolutions?
- What were the main political developments in Piedmont?
- How did Piedmont develop economically?
- How did Piedmont's diplomatic position change between 1849 and 1856?

INTRODUCTION

One outcome of the turmoil of 1848–49 was defeat for Piedmont. The first action of the new king, Victor Emmanuel, was to negotiate and sign in August 1849 a humiliating peace with Austria. However, the Piedmontese constitution, the *Statuto*, which had been passed by Charles Albert in 1848, survived. Throughout the rest of the Italian peninsula in 1849, including in the Papal States and Kingdom of Naples, reactionary rule was restored. Many of those who had fought and were committed to the cause of Italian national unity sought exile in Piedmont. Turin and Genoa became centres of nationalist agitation.

The failure of insurrection in 1848–49 did not prevent Mazzini and some of his followers attempting further revolution. But many of those who had fought for the revolutionary cause in 1848 and 1849 subsequently questioned whether insurrection was the best means of achieving a nation state.

One consequence of the survival of the *Statuto* was the emergence of a distinct political culture in Piedmont. In November 1852, Victor Emmanuel II appointed Count Camillo Cavour as prime minister. Cavour had already held office as minister of trade and agriculture. While in post he had helped forge an alliance of centre-right and centre-left political groupings in parliament, known as the ***connubio***, which was to herald the emergence of a political culture based on pragmatism rather than ideology.

A significant issue which dominated political debate within Piedmont through the first half of the 1850s was the role of the Church. The introduction of a series of anti-clerical laws was to cause political division, but also helped to unite the parties of the *connubio*. It also informed an emerging moderate liberalism which placed the Piedmontese monarchy at the head of a future Italian state. Cavour was not an instinctive nationalist and he despised the revolutionary nature of Mazzinianism. However, over time he realised the value of placing Piedmont at the head of the movement for national unity.

1849 – August: Peace agreed between Piedmont and Austria

1851 – Issuing of papal encyclical *Ad apostolicae*

1849	1850	1851	1852

1850 – March: Siccardi Laws passed in Piedmont

1850 – October: Cavour made minister of trade and agriculture

1852 – Cavour becomes prime minister of Piedmont

Cavour was a moderniser. His support for the principles of free trade and his understanding of the significance of the railways were to lead to a transformation in the Piedmontese economy. Such a transformation was, in part, funded by French loans which helped create strong ties between Piedmont and her powerful neighbour. Cavour used diplomacy and war to promote the cause of the Italian states and of Italian unity. In 1855, Piedmont joined the Crimean War on the side of Britain and France and against Russia. Although Cavour was to return home empty handed from the peace talks in Paris in 1856, his presence at the conference had been noted and Italy's claims had been stated.

WHAT WAS THE LEGACY OF THE 1848–49 REVOLUTIONS?

Victor Emmanuel II and the *Statuto*

One reason why Piedmont, rather than any other of the states on the Italian peninsula, took the leading role in forging political unity was the distinct nature of Piedmont's political and economic development after 1848. Perhaps the most important feature of Piedmont's political system after 1848 was the constitution – the *Statuto* – first granted by Charles Albert in March 1848. The fact that a liberal constitution such as the *Statuto* survived in Piedmont, while other such constitutions across the peninsula were repressed, made Piedmont politically and constitutionally more liberal than the other Italian states.

The *Statuto*

Under the terms of the *Statuto*:

- legislation would be passed by the king in parliament – that is, with the consent of the king and two chambers (houses) of parliament (one elected, the other nominated)

- legislation on taxes would be introduced by the elected chamber of parliament

- the press would be free, albeit subject to some restraint

- individual liberty was guaranteed.

The *Statuto* gave the ruling monarch greater authority than that enjoyed by most constitutional monarchs. Under the terms of the *Statuto*, ministers were responsible to the king rather than accountable to parliament. However, in practice, the *Statuto* was more flexible and it led to the strengthening of 'parliamentary government'. The king had the power to make law by decree and choose his ministers without having to listen to them. He also chose all of the members of the Senate, which was the Upper House of the Piedmontese parliament. Article 5 of the constitution gave the king sole control over foreign policy which could be conducted without reference to either parliament, ministers or the cabinet. He was also commander-in-chief of the armed forces. All-in-all the powers vested in the executive by the *Statuto* were not inconsiderable.

1855 – Piedmont joins the Crimean War

| 1853 | 1854 | 1855 | 1856 |

1854 – Opening of a railway line linking to Milan, Turin and Genoa to the French border

1856 – Cavour attends the Congress of Paris

Victor Emmanuel and the *Statuto*

The defeat at Novara in March 1849 led to the abdication of Charles Albert. He was succeeded by his son, Victor Emmanuel II. While Victor Emmanuel was not instinctively in favour of any constitution, including the *Statuto*, he was encouraged by the Austrians to keep it. The resignation of Metternich as foreign minister in March 1848 had led to a more pragmatic Habsburg foreign policy under the direction of Prince Felix Schwarzenburg. The Piedmontese monarchy was seen by Vienna as a potential ally against more radical forces and, in the eyes of Schwarzenburg, would be strengthened by retaining the *Statuto*. In May 1849, Victor Emmanuel chose Massimo d'Azeglio to serve as his prime minster. It was d'Azeglio whom ultimately persuaded the reluctant Victor Emmanuel that keeping the *Statuto* was in his interest, persuading him that his control of the armed forces and foreign policy gave him plenty of scope for initiative in the areas which interested him most.

SOURCE

1 Victor Emmanuel, at this time king of Piedmont-Sardinia, meets the Austrian field marshal Joseph Radetzky von Radetzky after the Battle of Novara on 23 March 1849.

SOURCE

Part of a letter written by the French ambassador to Piedmont, Baron His de Buntenval, to the French foreign minister, Drouyn de Lhuys, on 16 October 1852.

King Victor Emmanuel is in no sense liberal; his tastes, his education and his whole habit of behaviour all go the other way. He tells everyone that 'my father bestowed institutions on the country which are quite unfitted to its needs and the temper of its inhabitants.' To some people he will add, 'but my father and myself have both given our word, and I will not break it.' To others, however, he will say confidently, 'I am only waiting for the *right moment to change everything*. The moment will be the outbreak of war. Whenever it comes, I shall be ready.' Any French official who finds himself alone with the King will be asked if the time has yet arrived...

Victor Emmanuel, I repeat, does not like the existing constitution, nor does he like parliamentary liberties, nor a free press. He just accepts them temporarily as a kind of weapon of war. He keeps the tricolour flag instead of restoring that of Savoy; but he looks on it not as a revolutionary standard, only as a banner of conquest. Once the conquest is over, he is over, he will bring back the old flag; but at once on the outbreak of hostilities he would suspend the constitution indefinitely. One must therefore be not deceived by any talk about the chivalrous attitude of the King and his ministers to the constitution they have sworn to observe.

ACTIVITY
KNOWLEDGE CHECK

Victor Emmanuel II

1 What image of Victor Emmanuel is given by the French ambassador in Source 2?

2 How reliable is Source 2 as evidence of Victor Emmanuel's attitude towards the *Statuto*?

EXTEND YOUR KNOWLEDGE

Victor Emmanuel II

King of Sardinia (Piedmont) from 1849 and King of Italy from 1861 until his death in 1878, Victor Emmanuel II was normally praised by contemporaries wishing to inflate his reputation in order to stave off the republican threat. Massimo d'Azeglio, as the king's prime minister, cultivated the impression of *il re galantuomo* ('the gentleman king'), but even d'Azeglio knew that historians would be less kind about Victor Emmanuel; the description below from *Modern Italy* (1997) by Denis Mack Smith is not especially kind but neither is it undeserved.

'The true picture [of Victor Emmanuel] is of a puny and usually insignificant man, good-natured and shrewd, but superstitious and ill-educated, possessing a rough-hewn and by no means despicable character but little of the lustre and aureole [shine] of majesty. He said in private that Italians were quite unsuited to parliamentary government and could only be governed by "bayonets and bribery". His own enthusiasm was chiefly reserved for women, horses and hunting.'

Freedoms

The *Statuto* allowed for a free press, religious liberty and freedom of assembly within reason. It recognised and enshrined the **rule of law**. Piedmont was unique amongst the Italian states in having such an enlightened constitution. The consequence for Piedmont of Victor Emmanuel's decision to retain the *Statuto* was profound. After the disasters of 1848–49, any of those in the Italian peninsula who craved political freedom were drawn to Piedmont. Of the 50,000 refugees who had fled to Piedmont in 1849, as many as 30,000 remained, living mainly in Turin and Genoa. Of these exiles, many were intellectuals who became highly influential in public life – for example, the economist Francesco Ferrara and the writer Giuseppe Massari. As a result, Piedmont became the centre of Italian nationalist and liberal thought. Independent newspapers and radical journalism flourished with many writers writing from an Italian, rather than Piedmontese, perspective. They were to form the basis of the National Society, the creation of which is described on pages 217–218.

KEY TERM

Rule of law
A situation where no-one is above the law, everyone is equal in the eyes of the law and an individual cannot be found guilty without going through a due legal process.

By the terms of the *Statuto*, the Catholic Church was the established church in Piedmont. However, much of the Church's power and many of its privileges, which had existed for hundreds of years, were considered by several Piedmontese politicians to be incompatible with various principles of the *Statuto*. In March 1850, a member of the government, Giuseppe Siccardi, brought in a series of bills that were passed by the Piedmontese parliament and became known as the Siccardi Laws. The laws controlled the power of the Church. In most states this was done through agreement between Church and state known as a **concordat**. What made the Siccardi Laws different was that the state passed them without consulting the Church. The range of measures aimed at the Church was broad and the impact far reaching.

KEY TERM

Concordat
An agreement signed between the papacy and a state. While the terms of the concordat vary, they inevitably included terms for the protection of Catholic Church interests in the state concerned.

The Siccardi Laws

- Separate law courts for priests and other ecclesiastical people were abolished, because their existence conflicted with Article 5 of the *Statuto*, which stated: 'All justice emanates from the king.'

- The right of criminals to seek sanctuary and protection in churches was abolished.

- Religious groups, including monasteries, were restricted in their right to buy property.

- The number of feast days on which people were forbidden to work was reduced.

The significance of these laws should not be underestimated. They reflected the determination of Piedmont's rulers to modernise and to assert the dominance of the state over the Church. This was to be a recurring theme of the next few decades.

The impact on Austrian dominance

Continuing strength

As long as Austria was militarily and diplomatically strong, the stability of the established states across the Italian peninsula was assured. But by 1848, the assumption that it was Austria's right to impose its political views on the Italian states no longer existed. Even though the fall of Metternich in March 1848 and the financial crisis that followed it were perceived as signs of terminal decline, Austrian power in Italy was to remain strong for some time after the revolutions of 1848–49. Although Austrian forces in Italy were decimated by desertion and were forced, in March 1848, to withdraw to the Quadrilateral, they were still far too strong in battle for anything the Piedmontese and their Italian allies could throw at them. The crushing defeats suffered by the Piedmontese at Custozza in July 1848 and Novara in March 1849, as well as the collapse of the Venetian Republic in August 1849, reflected the continuing military strength of Austria. However, it was Pius IX's issuing of the Allocution (see page 185) in April 1848 that revealed the reality of Austrian power in Italy. Even if Pius had wished for the expulsion of Austrian forces from the Italian peninsula, Austria was too strong to be realistically challenged, even in a year when she was relatively weak as she was in 1848.

Franz Joseph

While the Austrian Empire was the most dominant power in the Germanic world in 1848 and successfully overcame any Piedmontese opposition, at home in Austria, and particularly in Vienna, there was disorder and revolution. In December 1848, the Habsburg Emperor Ferdinand abdicated. The newly crowned emperor, Franz Joseph, attempted to reassert control. In an attempt to challenge Prussian economic dominance, in 1849 and 1852 the Habsburgs tried to create a southern Germany/middle Europe equivalent of the *Zollverein*. The attempt failed. Most of the southern German states, such as Silesia, were already closely bound into the Prussian-dominated economic system. However, the decline of Austrian political power was not apparent in the early 1850s. An attempt by Prussia to assert its leadership of at least the north of Germany with the creation of a Prussian League in 1850 led to humiliation as Austria successfully demanded the disbanding of the League by the Treaty of Olmütz in the same year.

KEY TERM

Zollverein
The *Zollverein* was a union of mainly northern German states first formed in 1834 to agree tariffs, customs and the road to economic union. The *Zollverein* was dominated by Prussia; Austria was excluded.

Relative decline

Prussia was prepared to back down in the face of Austrian political pressure up to 1850 because of the superiority of the Austrian army. Just as the Piedmontese had found, the Austrian army under Radetzky was too powerful in 1848–49 and so the Prussians were not in a position to challenge Austrian military supremacy. However, 1850 was the high point of Austrian military hegemony. For the next 14 years, Prussia consolidated its economic leadership of the Germanic world, and by doing so isolated and weakened Austrian power. In 1853, Hanover, Brunswick and Oldenburg joined the *Zollverein*, thereby completing the economic union of all of non-Austrian dominated Germany. Austrian decline was relative to the increasing power of Prussia and the roots of the change in the balance of power were economic. The development of the *Zollverein* gave the north German states an economic advantage over Austria. It was one of a number of factors that led to Prussia challenging Austria's leadership of the loose arrangement of states known as the German Confederation. Ultimately it was Austrian decline that made political change possible in Italy.

The impact on the papacy

Weakness

The impact of the 1848–49 revolutions on the papacy was considerable. The Allocution of April 1848 was a hugely significant turning point because it marked the end of any dream held by moderates and those who ascribed to the ideas of Gioberti that the pope might lead the nationalist cause in Italy. It also severely weakened the idea of the pope as head of an Italian federation. In reality, nationalist expectations of Pius IX had been inflated; while the pope had been keen to protect the integrity of the Papal States, he had no intention of leading the campaign to remove Austrian troops from Italian soil. The decision of General Durando in April 1848 to march the papal forces north to face the Austrians was taken without reference to Pius IX and was one of the main reasons for the issuing of the Allocution. Pius IX's determination to distance himself from the nationalist cause was further underlined by his offer – which followed the Allocution – to mediate between the 'German nation' (i.e. the Austrians) and the 'Italian nation' (i.e. the Piedmontese).

The flight of Pius IX to Gaeta in November 1848 and the creation of the Roman Republic in February 1849 were equally significant in that they highlighted the relative weaknesses of the papacy's temporal power. Just as Pius IX was no nationalist, neither was he by instincts a 'liberal' pope. He had been influenced by the ideas of Gioberti's *Primato morale e civile degli Italiani* (1843) and shared in the belief in the primacy of the papacy in temporal affairs. His reforms before the revolutions were examples of measures that, on the surface, seemed to point in the direction of a more liberal papacy. They included the freeing of political prisoners in 1846, the appointment of Cardinal Gizzi as secretary in the same year, the creation of the customs union and the reduction in press censorship in 1847.

Compared with his predecessor, Gregory XVI, Pius IX was relatively liberal and advanced. Gregory XVI, and his secretary, Cardinal Lambruschini, had crushed all aspirations for civil liberty. But the impulse for Pius IX's reforms was not to liberalise the papacy, because attempting to do so would only weaken its authority. Reform was undertaken to strengthen the papacy's temporal and spiritual power. However, Pius' appointments to the post of chief minister after April 1848 show his true colours more clearly. On 16 September 1848, he offered the post of prime minister to Count Pellegrino Rossi. His priority was to restore order in Rome and quell the mob. While Rossi promised limited social reform, he did not hide his contempt for Mazzinianism or the secret societies. On 15 November, Rossi was assassinated as he entered the assembly in Rome. His death sparked a series of events which led to the departure of the pope for Gaeta and the eventual proclamation of the Roman Republic. For all his reformism, Pius was not responsible to the people nor did he wish to have his hands tied by a constitution. Rossi's assassination was a symptom of the division between the papacy and those who wished for more representative government.

Cardinal Antonelli

The most significant appointment Pius IX made during his reign as pope was that of Cardinal Giacomo Antonelli as his Secretary of State in 1848. Antonelli was a conservative and his conservatism was to influence his master. With the fall of the Roman Republic

and an amnesty agreed, Pius was urged to return immediately to Rome, now occupied by French troops but he did not return until April 1850. To the French, stable government could only be assured if the papal government was to be based upon the principles of the general amnesty, the restoration of the Code Napoleon and other liberal institutions. But Pius refused, arguing that a general amnesty was impossible and administrative reform undesirable. In April 1849, Pius IX had come to the decision that the constitutional government was incompatible with the power of the papacy. In the Motu Proprio (document issued on his own initiative and signed by the pope) of September 1849, the pope promised limited administrative and judicial reforms but argued that liberalism misled the masses. After his return to Rome, Pius IX withdrew from politics and turned his mind to theological matters. The Papal States were to be governed by the reactionary Cardinal Antonelli. The most significant impact of the revolutions on the Papal States was that it ushered in a period of reaction. Antonelli stood resolutely against constitutional government, arguing that it threatened the spiritual as well as the temporal power of the papacy. Laymen were excluded from office and political prisoners were rounded up and imprisoned.

SOURCE 3
Pius IX returns to Rome 12 April 1850. Engraving by an unnamed artist, in *Spamers Illustrierte Weltgeschichte*.

Rückkehr des Papstes nach Rom am 12. April 1850.

Absolute rule

Indeed, the pope's return to Rome ushered in a period of absolute rule underpinned by harsh repression. Public execution in the Papal States by beheading was commonplace. In June 1855, there was an attempted assassination of Antonelli. The assassin, De Felici, was shown no mercy and was executed by guillotine shortly after the attempt. There was some investment in public works; some of the Pontine marshes and Ostia swamps were drained, ports improved, lighthouses were built, for example, at Ancona and Anzio, and telegraphic communication established so that by 1860 all of the main towns of the Papal States were connected. But the majority of the inhabitants of the Papal States continued to live in near abject poverty, unlike Antonelli who amassed a considerable fortune which he left to his family on his death in

1876. The government of the Papal States post 1850 was one of retrenchment, reaction and corruption.

A real significance of Antonelli was to persuade Pius to resist attacks on the Church's temporal power. In *Ad apostolicae*, which was issued in August 1851, Pius argued that temporal power was justified by the teachings of Christ and was therefore non-negotiable. In so doing, the papacy ran the risk of isolating itself diplomatically. But temporal power was reinforced by spiritual influence and vice versa. In addition, while the papacy's conservatism might not appeal to the British or French, it resonated in other European capitals. In April 1851, the restored Grand Duke Leopold II of Tuscany signed a concordat with the papacy. This was to be followed by concordats with Spain (March 1851), Bolivia (May 1851), Costa Rica (October 1852), Guatemala (October 1852) and most importantly Austria (August 1855). The 1855 Concordat with Austria was signed with the blessing of the new (and devout) Emperor Franz Joseph. By the terms of the concordat, the Church was to regain control over family law and education for Catholics as well as religious foundations. Although the concordat was to be revoked by the new Austro-Hungarian state in 1867, its stands as an example of the continuing influence of the Church.

KEY TERM

Ad apostolicae

Letter from the papacy to the faithful.

ACTIVITY
KNOWLEDGE CHECK

The pope's return 1850

Source 3 gives a clear view of the welcome received by the pope on his return to Rome in April 1850. Study the source and then consider the following questions:

1 What is the popular response according to the artist?

2 Given that the artist is unknown, how valuable is this source as evidence?

The papacy 1848 to 1856

3 What are, in your opinion, the three most significant turning points for the papacy from April 1848 up to 1856? Explain your choice of each turning point carefully and then prioritise them.

EXTEND YOUR KNOWLEDGE

Pope Pius IX

When in exile at Gaeta, Pius became increasingly preoccupied with the question of the Virgin Mary's Immaculate Conception. In February 1849, he wrote the papal letter *Ubi primum*, which asked Catholic bishops for their views on the idea that, while Mary had been conceived normally she had also, at the point of conception, been freed from original sin. In the light of much contemplation and discussion, in 1854 the dogma of the Immaculate Conception was proclaimed. The significance of Pius's work was that it identified him as a spiritual leader as well as a temporal one.

The French occupation of Rome

From the defeat of the Roman Republic in 1849 and for the next 20 years, French troops would stay in Rome to guarantee papal power. It is an irony that it was the troops of liberal France that protected the reactionary rule of Antonelli rather than the forces of the more conservative Austria. The occupation was to lead to the identification of France with conservative papal interests and was to make the French the enemy of republican and radical nationalists. On and off throughout the course of the next 20 years, Louis Napoleon would struggle with a dilemma which he failed to resolve. The French garrison in Rome shielded the papacy against change. One the one hand, he was personally sympathetic to the cause of Italian unity and wished to be seen as a champion of the nationalist cause. But to withdraw French troops from Rome would open up the possibility of challenges to the pope's temporal power, and alienating Catholic opinion at home.

The failure of Mazzini

After 1849

The German Karl Marx wrote that the Roman Republic had been 'an attempt against property, against the bourgeois order'. That 'bourgeois order', both in Italy and elsewhere, stood resolute against the development of Mazzinian principles and the emergence of a democratic Italy. The achievement of the Roman Republic was that it created a legend of heroic but worthwhile failure in direct action against perceived oppression. The 1848–49 revolutions also highlighted the weakness of Mazzinian tactics, the limited support for revolution and the unlikelihood of a 'people's war' to liberate Italy. But in the short term, the failure of the 1848–49 revolutions did little harm to Mazzini's reputation. Mazzini was feted as a hero on his return to exile in London and while in England founded the National Italian Committee which was to continue to promote the nationalist cause in Italy. He also set up the Society of the Friends of Italy in 1851, which attracted widespread support from a sizeable group of radical sympathisers.

Further revolutions

Although popular in England, the cause of nationalist revolution had lost ground in Italy. This decline was to be compounded by a series of further revolutionary conspiracies which ended in failure. A revolution in Sicily in 1851–52 failed to win support. The failure of an uprising in Milan in February 1853 seriously damaged Mazzini's reputation. Indeed, the Milan uprising was an excellent example of the weakness of Mazzini's cause and tactics. During 1851 and 1852, the Austrian authorities had infiltrated Mazzinian secret organisations and had arrested a large number of supporters. The uprising in 1853 failed because of lack of support and because the revolutionaries were poorly armed. In the immediate aftermath of the uprising, 50 of the revolutionaries were shot by the Austrians. Other insurrections also resulted in failure: Lunigiana in 1853, Massa in 1854 and Palermo in 1856. As damaging to the Mazzinian cause as the failure of the Milan uprising, was Carlo Pisacane's expedition to Sapri in 1857. Seizing a small ship, the *Cagliari*, in May 1857, Pisacane sailed for Sapri with a motley group of supporters. On arrival, his force was met by Neapolitan forces and the hostility of the locals. Pisacane was wounded and, sensing the hopelessness of his cause, killed himself. The suicide of Pisacane, apathy of the local populace, the execution of the other revolutionaries and the apparent futility of such insurrections, led many to conclude that revolution in the name of democracy was not the best means of promoting the nationalist cause. The Latin Committee in Paris was set up in 1851 to argue in favour of a federal republic and the Military Committee in Genoa in 1852 was set up by Giacomo Medici with the purpose of devising a more appropriate military strategy. The great revolutionary hero Garibaldi distanced himself from Mazzini in 1854 and in 1855 the leader of the Venetian Republic, Daniele Manin, announced his conditional support for Piedmont. That many Mazzinians were to join to National Society after its foundation in 1857 was, perhaps, the most obvious sign that the 'age of Mazzini' was at an end.

SOURCE 4

Karl Marx writing in the *New York Daily Tribune*, 8 March 1853. Marx was a revolutionary who had written *The Communist Manifesto* with Friedrich Engels in 1848.

The Milan insurrection is significant as a symptom of the approaching revolutionary crisis on the whole European continent. As the heroic act of some few proletarians the sons of Mammon were dancing, and singing, and feasting amid the blood and tears of their debased and crucified nation proletarians who, armed only with knives, marched to attack the citadel of a garrison and surrounding army of forty thousand of the finest troops in Europe, it is admirable. But as the finale of Mazzini's eternal conspiracy, of his bombastic proclamations and his arrogant *capucinades* [moralising lecture or sermon] against the French people, it is a very poor result. Let us hope that henceforth there will be an end of *révolutions improvisées*, as the French call them. Has one ever heard of great improvisators being also great poets? They are the same in politics as in poetry. Revolutions are never made to order. After the terrible experience of '48 and '49, it needs something more than paper summonses from distant leaders to evoke national revolutions.

SOURCE 5

From the British journal, *The Spectator* 21 May 1853. *The Spectator* took a liberal/radical stance but, more than anything, reflected the opinions of its founder, owner and editor, Robert Stephen Rintoul.

In the first of these proclamations, dated the 7th of February, Count Strassoldo recognizes the general peaceful and orderly conduct of the whole of the inhabitants of Milan - were acts which succeeded that recognition of the peacefulness of the citizens... After the series commences, a hint is thrown out, that the disturbers, originally a fraction of the people, but ultimately a crowd of the populace, had been seduced by persons in foreign parts; and then comes by degrees the announcement that the property of exiles will be confiscated unless they can prove their non-complicity.

The hopelessness of the Italian endeavour does not lie in the want of spirit or capacity in her people, corrupted as they have been by long oppression; but it lies in the gigantic scale of the forces arrayed against them, and in the facility which the allied powers have of suppressing every effort in detail. The mistakes which would merely enfeeble a movement in another country become fatal by the organized system which enables the enemy to take advantage of every mistake. That organized power has been gaining ground since 1848. The kingdom of Sardinia still affords a living centre and a territorial position for the Constitutional party of Italy; but it is evidently too feeble for the contest which awaits it, and before many years it must give way. With the destruction of Piedmontese independence, the flood of the waters of Absolutism will have overleaped the last dike and Italy will be thoroughly submerged.

> **A Level Exam-Style Question Section A**

How far could the historian make use of Sources 4 and 5 together to investigate the failure of the Milan uprising in 1853?

Explain your answer, using both sources, the information given about them and your own knowledge of the historical context. (20 marks)

Tip
Think very carefully about the author of each source and the line each takes about the Milan rising.

EXTEND YOUR KNOWLEDGE

Guiseppe Mazzini (1805–72)

In 1948, the historian Gaetano Salvemini wrote in his book *Mazzini*, that the unification of Italy was not the result of a harmony of ideas born of the *Risorgimento* but of a struggle: 'In reality there was in the struggle a winner and a loser; the winner was Cavour, the loser Mazzini.' However, this view is a touch simplistic. In her book *Risorgimento* (2009), Lucy Riall explains that Mazzini's contribution to political change should be understood thus: 'Above all, it is Mazzini who provides the link between nationalism as a cultural identity and nationalism as a political movement.' Riall argues that Mazzini's achievement was to give the cause of national unity credibility by developing Young Italy as a tool of propaganda, which promoted the cause and gained its support. 'His success was to have seen that the key to making the Romantic idea of Italy political was through a process of communication and that, in the post-revolutionary world, political victory lay as much in persuasion and symbolic action as it did in the control of institutional power.'

Carlo Pisacane (1818–57)

Carlo Pisacane played an important part in the revolutions of 1848–49 as a leader of the Roman Republic. He was a writer and a political thinker whose works were to have an important impact on the nature of Italian socialism as it developed later in the century. In leading the revolt of 1857, Pisacane attempted to highlight the poor conditions in which the peasantry of the south lived and he hoped to politicise them through his revolutionary example. He killed himself in 1857 when he realised that the insurrection in Naples was bound to fail (he had been injured and over 150 of his followers had been killed). The death of Pisacane robbed the *Risorgimento* of one of its more intelligent and admired leaders.

Developments in liberalism and nationalism

Moderate liberalism

The most significant development in liberalism was the compromise between liberal reform and royal power which emerged in Piedmont after 1849. Moderate liberalism involved accepting the power of the Crown and Church while promoting civil liberties. It also meant establishing a parliamentary culture which, although based on a limited suffrage and limited by various Crown powers, was autonomous. The success, therefore, of liberalism in Piedmont after 1849 was based on an identification of the monarchy with liberal reform and the acceptance of a degree of parliamentary sovereignty. This was the recipe that made economic and further political reform possible and which propelled the House of Savoy to the leadership of the nationalist movement and helped to redefine nationalism. The development of moderate liberalism stood in stark contrast to the reactionary rule in other states on the Italian peninsula and the emerging divisions and problems within the nationalist movement.

For most of the 1850s, the Piedmontese parliament was dominated by moderate liberals. They stood for parliamentary government and support for the monarch. In many senses, the most important development in liberalism in the 1850s was the emergence of a 'middle way', an alternative to the conservatism which had dominated the states restored in 1815 (including Piedmont) and revolution. Most moderate Piedmontese liberals were not nationalists; they stood for a more powerful Piedmont and, if possible, the destruction of Austrian influence. The means of change was, for the liberals of the 1850s, economic reform and free trade. But, as the 1850s progressed, there was a greater identification of nationalism with liberalism. In 1856, the leader of the Venetian Republic and erstwhile Mazzinian, Daniele Manin, met with Cavour. At this point, Cavour was still sceptical of the unification of Italy. But although the two men failed to agree on the future of Italy, their meeting was another stepping stone on the road to change. In the same year, Cavour met the adventurer Giuseppe Garibaldi and the meeting was cordial. Such contacts and the role played by the National Society became very important in later years (see pages 217–218). While nationalism influenced moderate liberals such as Cavour, moderate liberalism, in turn, changed the nature of Italian nationalism and made it more conservative and pragmatic.

EXTEND YOUR KNOWLEDGE

Changing nature of Italian nationalism

In his book *The Sterner Plan* (1963), the historian Raymond Grew identified that the changing nature of the Italian nationalism in the 1850s was of central importance. It was to shape the nature of the unification process and the nature of the new Italian state which was to follow. He writes; 'The concept of the *Risorgimento* was being changed from a revolution that would remake society to a merely political change brought about by the force of arms.' It was not a change which was envisaged or designed by any of the leading protagonists. In *Italy: A Modern History* (1959), Denis Mack Smith clearly argues how the pragmatism of Cavour was eventually able to translate 'Mazzini's dogma into practical politics'.

SOURCE

From Count Cavour, *On Railroads in Italy* written in 1846.

The division of Italy at the time of the Congress of Vienna was as arbitrary as it was imperfect. This august assemblage, acting solely on the basis of "might makes right," raised a political edifice without moral foundation. Their act was based not on any guiding principle, or on legality, which was violated in the case of Genoa and Venice, or on national interest or popular will; they recognized neither geographical situations nor the general and particular interests created by twenty years of revolution... The history of every age proves that no people can attain a high degree of intelligence and morality unless its feeling of nationality is strongly developed. This noteworthy fact is an inevitable consequence of the laws that rule human nature... Therefore, if we so ardently desire the emancipation of Italy – if we declare that in the face of this great question all the petty questions that divide us must be silenced – it is not only that we may see our country glorious and powerful but that above all we may elevate her in intelligence and moral development up to the plane of the most civilized nations... This union we preach with such ardour is not so difficult to obtain as one might suppose if one judged only by exterior appearances or if one were preoccupied with our unhappy divisions. Nationalism has become general; it grows daily; and it has already grown strong enough to keep all parts of Italy united despite the differences that distinguish them.

SOURCE

Giuseppe Mazzini, *On Nationality*, 1852.

It was not for a material interest that the people of Vienna fought in 1848; in weakening the empire they could only lose power. It was not for an increase of wealth that the people of Lombardy fought in the same year... They struggled... as do Poland, Germany, and Hungary, for country and liberty; for a word inscribed upon a banner, proclaiming to the world that they also live, think, love, and labour for the benefit of all. They speak the same language, they bear about them the impress of consanguinity, they kneel beside the same tombs, they glory in the same tradition; and they demand to associate freely, without obstacles, without foreign domination, in order to elaborate and express their idea; to contribute their stone also to the great pyramid of history. It is something moral which they are seeking; and this moral something is in fact, even politically speaking, the most important question in the present state of things. It is the organisation of the European task. The nationality of the peoples can only be founded by a common effort and a common movement; sympathy and alliance will be its result... The map of Europe has to be remade.

ACTIVITY
KNOWLEDGE CHECK

1 List ten consequences of the 1848–49 revolutions.

2 Prioritise these consequences in order of importance to the cause of Italian unity.

WHAT WERE THE MAIN POLITICAL DEVELOPMENTS IN PIEDMONT?

The rule of Victor Emmanuel II

Peace with Austria

There was little sense of a party system in the Piedmontese parliament post 1849. But what did emerge was a parliamentary system which, by and large, worked. In 1849, the lower house, the Chamber of Deputies threatened not to approve the peace treaty with Austria despite the fact that defeat on the battlefield left the king with little choice. The response of Prime Minister d'Azeglio was to dissolve parliament and call elections. The king made it perfectly clear, through what became known as the Proclamation of Moncalieri of November 1849, that if the electorate did not return deputies who would support the peace treaty then he might abolish the constitution. The electorate did as they were advised. Most deputies in the Piedmontese Chamber of Deputies were independently minded. The 1849 election resulted in the election of, on the whole, liberal minded politicians who clubbed together into loose parliamentary groupings. The 'Left' were more democratic in their instincts, the 'Right' were clerical and against liberal reforms and ideas such as free trade. Most deputies were locally minded and many had been given the opportunity to become a parliamentarian by a powerful patron. Therefore, despite belonging to groups, most deputies voted independently. As such it took a considerable amount of persuasion to get a majority to vote in favour of the peace treaty.

In October 1850, Count Camillo Cavour was made minister of trade and agriculture by Prime Minister Massimo d'Azeglio. Soon after, he was given additional responsibilities for shipping (a post that included overseeing the operation of the Piedmontese navy), in which his scientific mind resulted in technological improvement. In April 1851, he was given the important post of minister of finance. He immediately undertook reform, balancing the books and raising capital for large-scale projects. In late 1851, he borrowed heavily from the London bank of Hambro while increasing taxes. Cavour was a firm believer in free trade and, by the end of 1851, had signed trading treaties with states including Portugal, France, Britain and Belgium. The aim of these treaties was twofold – to ensure both political support and economic growth. The reduction in tariffs resulted in a growth in trade. Between 1850 and 1859, imports and exports increased by 300 percent.

As minister for trade and agriculture, Count Camillo Cavour was prepared to speak out in the Chamber of Deputies in favour of the Siccardi Laws. Cavour had been appointed in 1850 to the government led by Massimo d'Azeglio, which could be best described as centre-right in its political leanings. However, the Siccardi Laws marked a divergence of opinion with the more conservative right, led by Cesare Balbo and Thaon de Revel, voting against the first Siccardi Laws. Although the centre-right did not leave d'Azeglio's government over the issue, its disapproval was clear. In December 1851, d'Azeglio attempted to appeal to those on the right by proposing a Press Law that would reduce the freedom of the press. With the Siccardi Laws also under pressure from the pope, Cavour decided that the time was right for a realignment of Italian politics.

The *connubio*

The left minded of Piedmontese politicians had been momentarily discredited with the failure of the 1848 revolutions. But at the turn of 1851–52, Cavour made a parliamentary agreement with the leader of the centre-left, Urbano Rattazzi, and against the law restricting the freedom of the press.

The result was the creation of an alliance in the centre of Italian politics known as the *connubio*. There was some common ground between the two groups, notably their shared anti-clericalism. The first consequence of the *connubio* was the strengthening of parliament in relation to the Crown. With Cavour's support, Rattazzi was elected in May 1852 as president of the Chamber of Deputies, a job similar to the speaker of the House of Commons. Rattazzi's election took place despite the opposition of the king. Cavour was still nominally a member of d'Azeglio's government but he understood that his position as a member of the government was impossible and, in May 1852, he resigned from his role as minister of finance. Soon after, a crisis developed over the introduction of a bill introducing civil marriage. Victor Emmanuel, under pressure from the papacy, objected to the legislation which was subsequently defeated in the Senate. D'Azeglio resigned, his government being weakened by the *connubio* and the king's vigorous opposition to the proposed introduction of civil marriage.

The appointment of Cavour 1852 and its impact

In November 1852, Cavour was asked by Victor Emmanuel to become prime minister. The impact of Cavour's appointment was considerable. As prime minister he was energetic in his promotion of economic change, but he was also an important influence in the developing nature of the Piedmontese state and the decline in the impact of Mazzini and his followers. Above all else, Cavour was the master of pragmatic parliamentary politics. The *connubio* became a central feature of Piedmontese politics and it resulted in government based on the desire for political survival rather than principle. As such, Cavour was an opportunist who would happily draw into alliance any party or political grouping which would strengthen the government of the day. This was possible because the political system was relatively fluid, with groups of the so-called **Right** and **Left** dominating parliament rather than parties based on ideological or sectional interest. There were no organised political parties in Piedmont. Politicians were often elected to parliament by very small constituencies, generally of around 200 voters. Many politicians were indebted for their political success to important individuals, often landowners. In parliament, deputies switched allegiances. The range of political opinions represented in the Piedmontese parliament was, therefore, limited. The significance of Cavour's impact on shaping the political culture of Piedmont and, after 1861, of Italy should not be underestimated.

Anti-clericalism

The concept which sustained the *connubio* was anti-clericalism. Throughout his political life, Cavour exhibited a strong dislike of the Church as a dominant institution. Indeed, he commented that the Catholic Church was 'the chief cause of the misfortunes of Italy'. He saw the papacy as a natural supporter of Austria. Cavour believed in religious toleration and was quite happy to be seen as the scourge of the papacy. On becoming prime minister in 1852, Cavour pragmatically dropped proposals inherited from the d'Azeglio government in favour of civil marriage. However, his actions were less to do with personal conviction and due more to pressure from the king. Thereafter, Cavour was to pursue a resolutely anti-clerical line. The vast estates of the Church and the generous income of five million lire from the state were easy targets.

In early 1855, Cavour introduced a bill that proposed the abolition of monastic orders not involved in education or charity work. The land belonging to these orders would be taken by the state. The proposal caused a constitutional crisis; it was opposed by senate, king and papacy. Although Cavour was forced to dilute his proposals (resulting in monks and nuns from closed monasteries receiving generous pensions), he still won, despite being forced at one stage to resign as prime minister. In the 1857 election, the candidates of the right who had sympathy with the Church increased their vote. Ever the consummate parliamentary operator, Cavour ended the *connubio* and sacked Rattazzi as minister of the interior. He also had to change his attitude to the Church in order to reduce the possibility of alliances against his government. So the issue of the Church was not raised by Cavour in the late 1850s. However, his influence had been important in identifying mainstream Italian politics with anti-clericalism.

KEY TERMS

Right and Left
Those to the right in Piedmont after 1850 would have been uneasy about far-reaching reform that damaged the Church. They also disliked the policies of free trade. Right-wingers feared revolution and far-reaching reforms. Those to the left, on the other hand, were more sympathetic to reform, and supported a more democratic state and the power of parliament.

EXTEND YOUR KNOWLEDGE

Denis Mack Smith on Cavour

In the biography *Cavour* (1985), Denis Mack Smith paints a portrait of Cavour as an architect of the unification of Italy. According to Mack Smith, Cavour was the arch diplomat and a brilliant political operator. He also identifies Cavour's great strength as the ability to manage parliament. Indeed, the forging of the *connubio* was Cavour's master trick. It gave him the legitimacy of parliamentary support for his actions and from that support he derived considerable authority.

Mack Smith identifies that Cavour was a bundle of contradictions. On the one hand he was a conservative, but on the other he occasionally resorted to revolutionary action. He could also be idealistic and cynical, kind but ruthless, cautious and occasionally audacious. Mack Smith writes:

'More than anyone else he [Cavour] developed the parliamentary system in Italy, as he laid down the basic traditions that governed political behaviour thereafter. During his last years he had to fight off domestic enemies to right and left, and also survived several attempts by King Victor Emmanuel to find a more amenable and obedient Prime Minister. To the right of him were conservative opponents who wanted Italy to stay divided; to the left were Garibaldi and Mazzini whose vision of a united nation was far more radical and idealistic than his own. To succeed against such opponents, Cavour had to follow a difficult and sometimes labyrinthine path, enlisting alternately the support of both extremes against each other, and finally carrying into effect that pre-eminently difficult and almost paradoxical operation, a conservative revolution.'

Denis Mack Smith's writings have influenced a number of historians who share his view that Italian unification was the result of political rivalries rather than the emergence of any form of Italian nationalism.

Policies to create political stability

One of the first issues that Cavour had to deal with was the diplomatic impact of a Mazzinian-inspired insurrection in Austrian-controlled Milan in February 1853. So Cavour's policy was one of conciliation with the Austrian enemy, for Cavour understood that political stability would be more likely if Piedmont lived at peace with Austria – at least for the time being. Not wanting to provoke any conflict, Cavour warned Austria of the impending uprising for which he received thanks from Vienna. However, his credentials as a long-term opponent of the Austrians were saved by the next move of the Austrians, which was to seize the property of citizens of Lombardy who had fled to Piedmont. The fury this provoked distracted from the main issue, which was that Mazzini's chosen method of action had again been discredited. Cavour's policy was to stand fast against Mazzinianism. This was also the case in 1857, when insurrection in the Kingdom of Naples led by Carlo Pisacane was to end in failure. For Cavour, the added shock was that Mazzini led a simultaneous revolt in Genoa that also ended in failure. Cavour's fury at the futility of such revolutions hid the fact that they were further proof of the unlikelihood of political change in Italy being heavily influenced by Mazzini.

Liberal and nationalist influences

As the liberal influence of Cavour, as outlined above, was to strengthen Piedmont, so the nationalist cause as identified with the fortunes of Mazzini was on the wane. The leading supporters of Mazzinianism became ever more critical of Mazzini's tactics and his unwillingness to accept criticism; Antonio Mordini called him 'the tyrant of our party'. After 1849, a number of revolutionaries published accounts of the uprisings on 1848 and 1849 which painted Mazzini in a negative light. The National Society's newspaper, *Il Piccolo Corriere d'Italia* gleefully published letters written by the Carbonari leader Felici Orsini which reveal Mazzini as a dictator and cruel to those who followed his cause. Even Garibaldi turned against Mazzini; in August 1854 he was quoted in the radical newspaper *Italia e Popolo* as being against insurrection and republicanism. Garibaldi's declaration was in part fuelled by an increasing personal animosity towards Mazzini. While Garibaldi's criticism of Mazzini's methods significantly damaged the cause of national unity, even more significant were the many divisions and squabbles of which this was just one example. They came in part as a result of the failure of the 1848–49 revolutions but also in response to the emergence of a nationalism based on moderate liberalism.

SOURCE 8

Giorgio Pallavicino was a Lombard democrat who, after the revolutions of 1848–49 came to a pragmatic conclusion about the future of the Italian nation. In the following extract, from a letter dated 18 November 1851, Pallavicino is writing to General Pepe, who led the military forces of the pope in 1848.

I, like you, believe that the life of a people lies in independence more than in liberty. But as an Italian first and foremost, I seek Italian forces for an Italian war, and a popular insurrection would not be enough for the purpose. We have seen this already: a popular rising can win temporary victories within the confines of its own cities, but without a miracle it cannot fight and defeat regular troops in the open countryside.

To defeat cannons and soldiers you need cannons and soldiers of your own. You need arms, not Mazzinian chatter.

Piedmont has got soldiers and cannons; therefore I am Piedmontese. Piedmont, by ancient custom, tradition, character and duty, is today a monarchy; therefore I am not a republican. And I am content with Charles Albert's constitution. I anticipate that it will be improved in the future, not so much by men's good will as by sheer necessity.

Independence, I repeat, is the very life of the nation. First independence, then liberty. First I want to live; I will think about living well later on.

SOURCE 9

A letter by Agostino Bertani and others to Giuseppe Mazzini, January 1858. Bertani took part in the Milan uprising in March 1848 and the defence of Rome in 1849. As a physician, he also served in Genoa with Mazzini during the cholera epidemic of 1854.

We must tell you, privately but clearly, that your courses of information about public opinion are wrong. Honest they may be, but they have deceived you into thinking the whole of Italy a volcano ready to erupt, as though the courage of the revolutionaries would be enough to galvanise the country, as though a handful of unarmed men could destroy a foreign domination which has lasted for centuries. You are too credulous; you think the people are behind you, whereas unfortunately they are not nearly so restless and are certainly not permanently waiting to start a revolution. The ordinary people are neither educated enough, nor have they the strength to move or to support a revolution once it has begun; they require the immediate support of that other large social class on whom they depend for guidance, for encouragement, and even for their daily bread.

These are your mistakes, the fatal delusions which have led you from error into error, and so have caused you to forfeit the allegiance of most of our republicans who still retain the ability to think for themselves. Many of you old adherents have become so discouraged that they have turned to other parties and policies...

Your mistakes, and they are serious, are these; to impose action at a moment chosen by yourself, even without preparation and with too few people, to think that a simple insurrection can be converted quickly into an extensive revolution.

ACTIVITY
KNOWLEDGE CHECK

Define in your own words the concept of *connubio* and its impact on Piedmontese politics.

A Level Exam-Style Question Section A

How far could the historian make use of Sources 8 and 9 together to investigate the failure of Mazzinian nationalism after 1849?

Explain your answer, using both sources, the information given about them and your own knowledge of the historical context. (20 marks)

Tip
The political experience and background of both authors should be to the fore in answering this question.

AS Level Exam-Style Questions Section A

1 Why is Source 8 valuable to the historian for an enquiry into why Mazzini was deserted by some of his followers after 1849?

Explain your answer using the source, the information given about it and your own knowledge of the historical context. (8 marks)

2 How much weight do you give Source 9 for an enquiry into the problems faced by Mazzini from 1849 to the late 1850s?

Explain your answer using the source, the information given about it and your own knowledge of the historical context. (12 marks)

Tip
Try to weigh up the strengths and weaknesses of the source.

HOW DID PIEDMONT DEVELOP ECONOMICALLY?

Commercial and industrial growth

The development of the Piedmontese economy from the mid-1840s should not be underestimated in its significance in relation to Italian unification. As the introduction of the *Statuto* resulted in Piedmont enjoying a distinct political culture, so industrialisation and the building of railways in the 1850s meant that Piedmont was the first Italian region to have a partly industrialised economy. This was to further the image of Piedmont as a state in the process of modernising (which the Siccardi Laws also did). Piedmont's industrialisation did not solely rely on railways. A thriving textile industry based on the manufacture of wool, silk and cotton was firmly established by the mid-1840s. However, there were severe restrictions to the growth of industry in the north of Italy because the lack of coal hampered the development of a factory system. Both the wool and silk industries were still predominantly **domestic industries** and were labour intensive. The number employed in the silk industries was as high as 60,000 at some points in the 1840s but the cotton industry dominated – in 1844 there were approximately 114,000 domestic cotton workers in Piedmont.

> **KEY TERM**
>
> **Domestic industries**
> Industries in which the manufacturing process took place in the home. In the textile industry, for example, these processes included dyeing the cloth, spinning and weaving.

SOURCE

10 Opening of the line between Principe and Sampierdarena in 1854. Note the wide gauge railway lines.

The significance of trade agreements and the impact of the development of railways

The railways

Further development of the Piedmontese cotton and other industries relied on advances in communication, most obviously the building of railways. Cavour was very clear in his belief that railways were of critical importance to the development of Italy as a nation state. As a railway 'enthusiast' he had a personal interest in railways and in 1835 had visited Britain and seen the construction of the London to Birmingham line, designed by Robert Stephenson. He argued how the absence of railways could stunt development of a country. The best example of this was how trade was made difficult between states because of the failure of the Austrian government to build the rail line in Lombardy up to the Piedmontese border. In 1845, the Piedmontese government had begun a limited programme of railway construction spurred on by Cavour who saw the political and material benefits of doing so.

In 1846, Cavour wrote a review in the French magazine *Revue Nouvelle* of a book by Count Ilarione Pettiti with the title *The Italian Railways and an Improved Plan for Them*. In the article, Cavour argued that the railway was the 'marvellous conquest of the nineteenth century' and he tried to persuade Charles Albert and his ministers that large-scale railway construction would be of benefit to Piedmont. He argued that the railways were as important as the printing press and that their growth was inevitable. He stated that the construction of railways in Piedmont would produce economic benefits similar to those experienced in Britain and France and that they would lead to the development of a national consciousness. Cavour was keen to highlight that railway construction was under way in Naples, Tuscany and Lombardy. If Piedmont was going to lead in Italian railway construction, a commitment was needed sooner rather than later.

The impact of building the railways on the economies of Europe should not be underestimated. Similarly, the extent of railway building was a good indicator of the extent of economic modernisation in a state or country in 19th-century Europe. In 1861 (the year of Italian unification), there were only 2,404 kilometres of railway line in Italy, equivalent to 0.096 kilometres per inhabitant (in Britain the figure was 0.74). Around 40 percent of the lines were in Piedmont which gave it a claim to economic leadership. It was always Cavour's belief that economic leadership, and railway construction especially, were essential elements of political power. Although Cavour became prime minister in November 1852, he did not lose interest in developing Piedmont's economy. He was also not afraid to use public money and to borrow from France to build new railway lines. By 1858, around 280 million francs had been invested in railways in Piedmont (including Savoy). This money was used to build some highly significant lines. In 1854, the first section of the line linking Milan, Turin, Genoa and the French border was opened. This was followed by a commitment to a number of projects, including a proposed 13-kilometre railway tunnel through Mont Cenis, which gained approval from the Piedmontese parliament in 1857. The result was that by the end of the 1850s, approximately 850 kilometres of railway track were in operation in Piedmont.

Government investment in infrastructure

Free trade

Cavour aimed to stimulate economic activity through railway building, low tariffs and free trade. The move to free trade was not just an economic matter. Cavour believed that by modernising economically, he would also be promoting political liberalism, through the sweeping away of feudal economic and financial privilege. He believed that government had a part to play through direct investment, mainly in infrastructure. Cavour encouraged the investment of foreign capital into Piedmont, the majority of it being French. Indeed, the line between Turin and Genoa that was opened in 1854 was funded by French capital, in particular money invested by the French bank Rothschild. Similarly, the Mont Cenis tunnel, started in 1857, was financed by a number of Parisian-based bankers, including Laffitte and Rothschild. Indeed, Cavour had great enthusiasm for this scheme. In 1846, he wrote in his article in *Revue Nouvelle* that such a project would be 'the masterpiece of modern industry'. The political importance of the credit agreements between France and Piedmont was significant; influential French finance had an important stake in the financial and economic well-being and expansion of the Piedmontese railways and Piedmont.

But it was not just the railways that grew in the 1850s. Government subsidies to a range of enterprises resulted in significant growth. In 1853, the electric telegraph linking Turin to Paris flourished as did the textile industry, with the removal of tariffs. The building of canals, which began in 1857 with the construction of the Cavour Canal, further boosted the construction industry. Cavour also directed government investment into the navy. Up until the 1850s, the port of Genoa had served as Piedmont's naval base but Cavour was concerned that the city was a hotbed of radical sentiment. There was also limited space in the port which would potentially limit the growth of trade, so Cavour ordered the improvement to the port of La Spezia which was to serve as the main naval base. He also ordered a new naval vessel from Britain powered by screw propulsion rather than paddle steam and he introduced metric calibre naval guns. The result of such government-driven economic modernisation was debt; by 1859, the public debt stood at 725 million lire. However, such a policy changed the economic status of Piedmont for good. Piedmont was now Italy's foremost industrial region with good trading links to the rest of Europe.

The significance of Cavour

A moderniser

Cavour was an innovator in economic terms. On his estate near Trino in eastern Piedmont he introduced many practices widespread in Britain but less widely practised in Piedmont. These included crop rotation and the introduction of effective drainage.

However, his greatest foresight was in developing the economic infrastructure of Piedmont and especially the communication system. Cavour was a consummate politician, but he was also the foremost and first economic moderniser. In 1834, he had travelled to France and Britain to witness at first hand the industrialising process. He was impressed with the growth of British industry, notably the railways. He returned to Italy in 1835 an advocate of free trade and an admirer of the British political economists Adam Smith and Jeremy Bentham. As minister of finance from February 1851, Cavour was to implement changes which reflected his beliefs. The reduction of tariffs and the switch to a greater degree of free trade created better relations with countries such as Britain and France, with whom trade treaties had been signed by the end of 1851. He arranged for the indemnity owed to Austria as a result of defeat to be paid off and in the summer of 1851, Piedmont and Austria signed a commercial treaty. Cavour would not allow for enmity to get in the way of trade. The result of Cavour's policy of reducing tariffs was that Piedmontese exports and imports tripled in value between 1850 and 1859.

Equally significant as free trade was the growth in confidence in the Piedmontese economy, which was primarily the result of Cavour's intelligence and foresight. This came in part through the construction of the railways. Cavour believed that economic leadership and railway construction were a prerequisite of political power. The challenge he laid down to Charles Albert was to be the leader in that process. When he became prime minister, Cavour threw the weight of political support behind a programme of railway construction. The 1850s were an important period of political and economic development and change in Piedmont. The political system and how it operated was very much conditioned by Cavour's influence and the introduction of the *connubio*. Economic and financial reform further enhanced Piedmont's reputation as a modernised state. Both political and economic change enhanced Piedmont's role as the potential natural leader of the peninsula and the power most likely to be able to expel the Austrians from Lombardy and Venice.

Financial acumen

Cavour's financial acumen and contact bred confidence. On becoming minister of finance in 1851, he inherited a state debt of 68 million lira – which was roughly 40 percent of Piedmont's budget. Most worrying was that many of the loans had been taken out at high rates of interest, notably after the War of Independence. Cavour set about borrowing money at cheaper rates of interest which he used to repay the standing debts. Such was the confidence in Cavour across the European money markets, he was also able to secure loans which were then used to stimulate the Piedmontese economy, notably through embarking on major capital projects such as the building of the Turin to Genoa railway in 1853. He was keen to maintain a good relationship with Europe's foremost banking houses, notably Rothschild and Hambros, while ensuring that Piedmont was not financially beholden to them. A relatively small loan of 44 million lira was raised in 1854 as was a larger loan in 1858.

ACTIVITY
KNOWLEDGE CHECK

This discussion activity is to try and make you think 'outside the box'. You will probably want to discuss the following questions with someone in your class.

1 What is the relationship between economic and political change?

2 What impact did the economic changes in Piedmont have on the state's diplomatic standing?

HOW DID PIEDMONT'S DIPLOMATIC POSITION CHANGE BETWEEN 1849 AND 1856?

Relationship with Austria 1849

By the terms of the Milan Treaty agreed by Piedmont and Austria on 6 August 1849 after the Piedmont defeat in the Austro-Italian war of 1848-49, the former was obliged to pay a considerable indemnity of 65 million francs. Under the terms of the treaty, the Piedmontese agreed to re-confirm the terms of the Congress of Vienna with regards to the borders of the Italian states and the Austrians reserved their rights to interfere in Italian affairs. Importantly, however, Piedmont was not forced to cede any territory. All treaties between the two states which had been in existence before the war were fully renewed. The Austrians wished to use the Treaty of Milan to restore the status quo. However, the ending of the war marked a change in Austrian attitudes towards Lombardy. The leading supporters of the Lombard provisional government were fined and those who fled into exile, mostly to Piedmont, had their estates seized. The significance for Piedmont of a more repressive Austrian rule in Lombardy was that it accentuated the differences in the rule between the two provinces.

SOURCE

11 Part of a letter from Field Marshall Radetzky to the Austrian Prince Felix Schwartzenberg dated 13 April 1849.

I am thoroughly convinced that it is high time to stop bestowing favours on a country which all too often abuses them; that it is much more necessary and imperative to let the country feel the punitive hand of its mighty and much offended lord, since everyone knows that the Italians fear a strict but just ruler and will do his bidding, while they abuse and espies a good and indulgent one.

In my opinion this wealthy land can only be punished most severely by the removal of those means which have led it to such disobedience, for what is exile to the rich when they can take their money with them and continue to cause trouble.

To humble the disloyal rich, to protect the loyal citizen, but to praise the poorer classes of the peasantry as in Galicia, should be the principle on which from now on the government of Lombardy-Venice should be based.

I am firmly convinced that directly after the conclusion of peace... ringleaders like Casati and Borromeo and others who have suffered punitive justice will petition for clemency and the government will smother them in it. The aim of my letter is, therefore, to beseech Your Excellency beforehand, to set aside any future clemency and let justice run its course completely.

ACTIVITY
KNOWLEDGE CHECK

Radetsky's revenge

What is the message of Source 11 and why do you think that Radetsky wishes for the Austrian government to take such a hard line?

The significance of the Crimean War and Congress of Paris

Under Article 3 of the *Statuto*, foreign policy remained the prerogative of the Crown. As the king's prime minister, Cavour was given considerable power to make foreign policy as he saw fit and without parliament's approval. He was determined to exercise this power for the advancement of Piedmontese interests as he saw them. Primarily, these interests were the undermining of the 1815 Treaty of Vienna and weakening Austrian influence in the north of Italy.

The Crimean War – Austria's position

In 1854, Britain and France declared war against Russia and sent troops to fight in **the Crimea**. The cornerstone of Austrian diplomatic strength from 1815 had been the alliance with other conservative monarchies and their shared desire to keep the forces of revolutionary nationalism at bay. Of particular importance for Austria was its alliance with Russia. Importantly, this alliance collapsed during the Crimean War, a fact that was to undermine Austrian power in the long run. Austria remained neutral throughout the Crimean War and, by late 1854, it was clear that Russian antagonism towards Austria was increasing. From 1854 onwards, Austria and Russia were to vie for influence in the Balkans. In August 1854, Austria, Britain and France issued the Vienna Four Points, which effectively ended any possibility of regaining the Austro-Russian alliance in the near future. In November/December 1854, Austria signed a Four Points agreement with Britain and France aimed at forcing Russia to the negotiating table by the end of the year. For Austria to have acquired such a powerful enemy as Russia was a diplomatic benefit for Piedmont. The following month Austria made a secret treaty with Britain and France in which it was agreed that Austrian possessions in Italy be guaranteed for the duration of the war. Of course, this would have made impossible any Italian uprising in 1854 because any such uprising would have needed support from France. But an uprising was an unrealistic course of action for nationalists at this time.

Austria's close understanding with Britain and France worried Cavour. The military force that Britain and France sent to the Crimea in 1854 was ravaged by cholera. It was therefore very clear to both countries that they would need reinforcements. By mid-1854, the British and French governments placed pressure on Piedmont to join the war. Victor Emmanuel welcomed the pressure placed on Piedmont. By the beginning of 1855, the king had signified that he was prepared to appoint a more pro-war prime minister such as Count Thaon de Revel because of Cavour's reluctance for Piedmont to become involved. This reluctance for war reflected the mood of many in Piedmont who opposed the idea of conflict against Russia when the real enemy was deemed to be Austria. Other leading political figures such as the cabinet member General Vittorio Dabormida shared Cavour's reservations about going to war without first receiving firm promises of support from the allies (Britain and France). By January 1855, Cavour decided to join the war on the side of the allies. He ordered the despatch of 15,000 troops to the Crimea. Cavour took this decision for a number of reasons. His greatest fear was that if Piedmont failed to join the war on the side of the British and the French, then Austria might. Such a move on the part of Austria would have left Piedmont diplomatically isolated. Pressure from Britain and France – notably from Sir James Hudson, the British ambassador in Turin – as well as to lobbying by nationalists, convinced Cavour to agree to intervention.

War and peace

The Piedmontese troops arrived in the Crimea in the early summer of 1855. Many troops were soon struck down with the cholera that had decimated the British army in particular. However, the Piedmontese army did not disgrace itself, taking part in the victory over the Russians at Chernaya Rechka on 16 August, which led directly to the fall of Sebastopol. The battle duly won the Piedmontese army the respect and gratitude of its allies. In December 1855, Austria threatened to enter the war on the side of the allies and the Russians sued for peace. Cavour travelled to Paris where, on 7 December, he met Louis Napoleon who asked him what he could do for Italy. Cavour's response was put in a letter to the French foreign minister on 21 January 1856 (see Source 12). At the Congress of Paris of February to April 1856, neither Britain nor France was prepared to alienate Austria by addressing any Piedmontese request for a change in the status quo in the north of Italy. However, Cavour did achieve a number of diplomatic successes. His attendance at the Congress was a sign of Piedmont's growing diplomatic stature. Although Italy was not mentioned until peace had been signed, the 'Italian Question' was the main topic of discussion on 8 April. This was an important step on the road to recognition that Austrian domination of northern Italy was a diplomatic issue.

SOURCE

From a letter written by Count Cavour on 21 January 1856 to French foreign minister, Count Walewski. The letter shows Cavour's aims at the Paris Conference.

Austria, having had so great a part in the recent events, must be considered by a diplomatic fiction, to have rendered a conspicuous service to Europe, we must start by assuming that we will not ask of her, for the moment at least, any territorial sacrifice in Italy...

In the first place, while renouncing any claims on Austria for a modification of the treaty of Vienna, claims which would be in keeping with the true interests of Europe, the strong influence which the Emperor has acquired over Austria suggests to us that he could ensure that she renders justice to Piedmont, and that she adopts a less oppressive and more tolerable regime over her Italian subjects.

The ending of the military regime, which has for eight years oppressed the populations of the Lombardo-Venetian kingdom would be a real benefit to them, and would not for the moment at least, expose Austria to any true danger. Concessions made at the moment which this power (Austria) signs a favourable peace would not be interpreted as an act of weakness...

What the Emperor can obtain from Austria by friendly advice, he can impose on the King of Naples. He can, now that the preoccupations of the war no longer make vigorous diplomatic action dangerous, insist that this prince should cease from making odious the monarchical principle which is as absurd as it is violent. In forcing him to open the prisons where for so long so many illustrious and innocent victims have suffered... France will render a true service, of which Austria herself would not complain...

The state of things in the provinces which Austria possesses in Italy, like that of the Kingdom of Naples, is conditioned by the stipulations of the treaty of Vienna which for the moment the Western Powers – England at least – do not want to touch.

 Evidence (5a)

Context is everything

Work in groups using Source 12.

Take an A3 piece of paper. In the middle of it draw a circle about 18 cm in diameter. Within the circle is the evidence itself, outside the circle is the context.

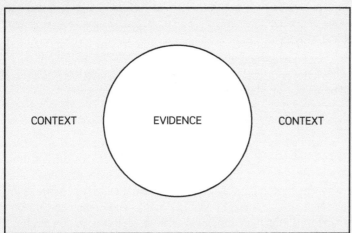

Think of a question that the source could be helpful in answering.

Inside the circle, write a set of statements giving information that can be gleaned only from the source itself without any contextual knowledge.

Outside the circle, write down statements of contextual knowledge that relate to the source.

Draw annotated lines to show links between the contextual statements and the information from the source. Does context change the nature or meaning of the information?

Now answer the following question:

Explain why knowledge of context is important when gathering and using historical evidence. Give specific examples to illustrate your point.

Relations with Britain and France

The ambassadors

In 1854, Austria signed the Vienna Four Points with Britain and France by which she gave them diplomatic support in the event of war against Russia. The possibility of a Franco-Austrian entente or even an alliance was a source of great anxiety to Cavour, but the decision to go to war against Russia was not without its drawbacks. Russia provided Piedmont with significant amounts of grain, the supply of which would be curtailed in case of war. But the French diplomatic mission in Turin, led by the Duc de Guiche, sought to persuade Victor Emmanuel that entering the war was in Piedmont's interest. He was supported in his argument by the equally influential British ambassador in Turin, Sir James Hudson. Both Britain and France were keen on Piedmont's involvement from the point of view of troop numbers, especially to reinforce the British whose troops were being decimated by disease.

British politicians had mixed views about Italian independence and their sympathies did not divide on party lines. The Tory foreign secretary in 1852 and 1858–59, Lord Malmesbury, was sympathetic whereas the Whig foreign secretary at the time of the Crimean War, Lord Clarendon, was not as enthusiastic. Lord Palmerston, who was prime minister on and off for most of the second half of the 1850s, was vigorously against Austrian influence in Italy, whereas Lord Aberdeen (prime minister from 1852 to 1855) was distinctly unsympathetic to the Italian cause. The unfounded fear of most British politicians was that support for Piedmont would lead to an unleashing of revolutionary forces. In addition, neither the British nor the French were prepared to make an explicit promise to Cavour that Piedmontese intervention in the Crimea would lead to a discussion of the Italian Question. In 1854, both Britain and France (although more so the former than the latter) still, at least on the surface, paid lip service to the idea that the 1815 settlement agreed at the Treaty of Vienna should not be disrupted.

Limited aims

At the Congress of Paris, Cavour maintained good relations with both superpowers. He maintained a diplomatically amicable correspondence with Lord Clarendon and Count Walewski, drawing their attention to the Austrian occupation of the Papal Legations and the continuing presence of foreign troops in Rome. On 8 April, Clarendon responded to Cavour's letters by raising the issue of Italy at the Congress. The two matters which he specifically addressed were the repressive rule of Ferdinand king of Naples and the issue of the Papal Legations including the Austrian presence. But the extent to which Cavour had managed to sway Britain and France behind the Italian cause in the short-term should not be exaggerated; in May 1856, France, Britain and Austria signed a secret treaty guaranteeing the independence of the Ottoman Empire. The British and French were, first and foremost, interested in maintaining good relations with the Habsburgs.

Consequences

The diplomatic consequences of the Crimean War in the longer term had an important impact on political change in Italy. In many ways, 1856 was the critical diplomatic turning point. The Crimean War and its aftermath marked the beginning of the end of the Treaty of Vienna and a watershed in Austrian power. Austria was now effectively isolated diplomatically. It had lost its great ally, Russia, and was forced to ally with an ultimately unreliable Prussia. The French and British were grateful to Piedmont for its support during the Crimean War although this gratitude did not manifest itself immediately, but it would prove to be crucial if and when Piedmont was militarily to challenge Austrian rule. Neither France nor Britain would, in the medium term, prove to be sympathetic to maintaining Austrian power in northern Italy and its dominant position over the whole peninsula. Indeed, the changing diplomatic landscape caused by the Crimean War led France in particular to adopt a far more sympathetic attitude towards the cause of Italian unity. But in the short term, neither was prepared to undermine Austria despite her isolation. Diplomacy had failed to produce the desired outcome for Piedmont. In April 1860, Cavour mused 'there is only one effective solution of the Italian question: cannon'.

The importance of diplomacy

The importance of diplomacy in forging the shape of the new Italian state should not be understated. In *The Struggle for Mastery in Europe 1848-1918* (1954), A.J.P. Taylor stresses that Cavour's greatest achievement was to recognise that: 'The Italian Question was a problem in international relations, not in domestic politics... Italy could not make herself; she could only be made by exploiting the differences between the Great Powers.' While this is an astute judgement, it does not necessarily mean that Italy was unified by diplomatic design. Instead, it is more appropriate to argue that the series of events, the change in the balance of European powers and the sympathetic attitude of many of the most significant policy-makers at the time would, together, act in favour of those who wished to see the creation of an Italian state. However, it is too simple to suggest that foreign powers intervened in Italian affairs actively to promote the cause of Italian unity, because they did not. Rather, they intervened in order to promote their own interests. Italy was, and is, strategically placed. The influence and significance of the papacy on domestic affairs in many parts of Europe was still considerable.

The significance of Cavour

The foreign policy that Cavour inherited from d'Azeglio when he became prime minister of Piedmont was well-suited to his political viewpoint. Cavour was not an instinctive Italian nationalist. However, he found the attitude of Vienna to northern Italy unsatisfactory. In its treatment of Lombardy, Cavour felt that Austria provoked revolutionaries in and outside Italy, and encouraged reactionary and conservative forces. Despite (and also because of) the reversals of 1848–49, Piedmont foreign policy priorities remained resolutely anti-Austrian. D'Azeglio had followed a 'middle-way' foreign policy, which gave encouragement to neither Mazzinians nor **Piedmontese isolationists**, but still hoped to see Austria removed from Lombardy and Venice.

Most importantly, Cavour understood that Piedmont could not dominate the north of Italy at the expense of Austria without foreign support. This was to be the cornerstone of his foreign policy.

The Crimean War confirmed Cavour's role on the diplomatic stage. It also confirmed his belief that there was considerable political advantage in speaking on behalf of Italy and against Austrian repression. Ever the political realist, Cavour understood that the extent of Piedmont's intervention meant that it was unlikely that it would get anything much from the Congress of Paris. At the Congress, the British foreign secretary, Lord Clarendon, attacked the idea of foreign troops being based in the Papal States. This attack was much to Cavour's delight given that the troops in question were Austrian, but the speech had little impact and the suggestion that, in attending the Congress, Cavour put Italy on the diplomatic map is somewhat vague and not easily substantiated. Perhaps the most significant aspect of Cavour's attendance at the Congress of Paris is that he made contact with Louis Napoleon III. While Cavour realised that there was little point in broaching the topic of the Austrian presence in Lombardy, he and Louis Napoleon III were, in time, to understand the real significance of the Crimean War and its aftermath – that through non-intervention Austria had lost diplomatic influence. It was in this context that the Treaty of Vienna could, finally, be reshaped.

Piedmontese isolationists
There were some within Piedmontese political circles in the 1850s such as Solaro della Margherita who believed that Piedmont as a nation would suffer through closer unity with other Italian states.

SOURCE

13 Count Cavour in a speech to the Piedmont Chamber of Deputies, 1858.

After the disaster of Novara and the Peace of Milan [1849], two courses were open to us. We could, bowing to adverse fate, renounce all the aspirations which had guided King Carlo Alberto during the last years of his reign, seal ourselves up within our frontiers, think only of the material and moral interests of this country [Piedmont-Sardinia]... On the other hand, we could, while accepting all the hardships imposed by accomplished facts, keep alive the faith that inspired the great actions of King Carlo Alberto, and, while declaring our firm intention to respect treaties, maintain in the political sphere the enterprise which was defeated in the military sphere [Italian unification]... In recent years, therefore, we have tried to do away with the last hindrances to our country, and we have lost no occasion to act as the spokesman and defender of the other peoples of Italy. This policy found one such occasion in the Crimean War... Our hopes were not disappointed in regard to the credit that Piedmont would acquire. As for the defence of the rights of Italy, that was our task in the course of the Congress of Paris... it was an outstanding fact that the cause of Italy was for the first time supported by an Italian power.

ACTIVITY
KNOWLEDGE CHECK

How reliable is it?

Source 13 is from a speech by Cavour in 1858. Given what it says, what you know about Cavour and what you know about the series of events, how reliable do you think this source is for a historian trying to understand Piedmontese foreign affairs?

The consequence for the cause of Italian unity was profound. As Cavour, and even Victor Emmanuel, converted to the cause of national unity, so the nature of the cause changed. Cavour was the consummate parliamentary politician and a politician of his time. In the mid-19th century, few leading political figures were prepared to accept or even foresee the advent of mass politics. Cavour's legacy was to create a political structure and culture that would suit Italy's needs for the next half century and that would only be fully undermined with the advent of mass political parties. His role as a diplomat is much highlighted and has been written about extensively. Yet it could be argued that his greatest contribution to the *Risorgimento* was not as architect of Italian unity but as moderniser of Piedmont. In helping to create a modern political state with a semi-industrial economy he helped to lay the foundations of the unification process.

AS Level Exam-Style Question Section B

How far do you agree that Piedmont's involvement in the Crimean War brought little immediate reward? (20 marks)

Tip

You will need to weigh up the evidence for and against the statement.

A Level Exam-Style Question Section B

'The rise of Piedmont in the 1850s was primarily the result of Victor Emmanuel's decision in 1849 to retain the *Statuto*'.

How far do you agree with this statement? (20 marks)

Tip

You will need to weigh the evidence for and against the statement.

ACTIVITY
SUMMARY

Summarising Cavour

Was he primarily a diplomat, economic moderniser or political fixer? After discussion with other people in your class or group, identify, in order, Cavour's strengths.

THINKING HISTORICALLY   CHANGE (6a)

Separately and together

Below are some different types of history that historians may identify.

Political History	Economic History	Social History
Religious History	Military History	Diplomatic History

These are thematic histories, where a historian focuses on a particular aspect of change. For example, an economic history of the Piedmont in the 1850s would focus on industrialisation and the building of the railways, whereas a political history would focus on, among other things, the impact of the *Statuto*.

Work in groups.

Write a definition for each type of history.

Here are some events in the period covered by this chapter.

1849	1850	1852	1854	1855	1856
Victor Emmanuel confirms the *Statuto*	Siccardi Laws passed in Piedmont	Cavour becomes prime minister of Piedmont	Opening of a railway line linking to Milan, Turin and Genoa to the French border	Piedmont joins the Crimean War	Cavour attends the Congress of Paris

Answer the following questions:

1 The first two changes can be classified as 'political' events.

   a) Why were the Siccardi Laws significant?

   b) What other area of history does this fall into?

2 What diplomatic changes came as a result of Piedmont's involvement in the Crimean War?

3 What was the social impact of the *Statuto*?

4 How did Cavour's appointment as prime minister affect Piedmont economically?

5 What was the potential significance of a railway linking Milan, Turin and the French border?

Work in pairs.

6 Write a statement attacking 'thematic history'.

7 Write three statements defending 'thematic history'.

8 Explain why 'thematic history' occurs.

WIDER READING

Clark, M. *The Italian Risorgimento*, Routledge (2009) focuses on the events of the *Risorgimento*

Hearder, H. *Cavour*, Routledge (1994) is a good biography of Cavour

Smith, M. C. *Cavour*, Alfred A Knopf (1985) is another good biography of Cavour

Riall, L. *Risorgimento*, Palgrave Macmillan (2009) identifies some of the themes of the *Risorgimento*

2a.3 The creation of the kingdom of Italy, 1856–61

KEY QUESTIONS

- Why did war against Austria break out in 1859?
- What was the impact of the war?
- What was the significance of Garibaldi?
- How did Italy unite in 1860–61?

INTRODUCTION

In 1856, Piedmont was struggling to be heard at the Paris Congress and the 'Italian Question' was not of primary importance to the leaders of Europe's great powers. But only five years later in 1861, an Italian nation state was created. How this happened is explained in this chapter.

How Italy unified is complex, with foreign powers such as France and Britain playing a part, plus the impact of Cavour and the National Society. Woven into this and of particular significance was the decline of Austria. Through the actions of these interested parties the nation state of Italy was formed from above, through political intrigue, diplomacy and war, rather than through revolution, democracy and popular consent from below.

An important turning point in the road to unification was the decision taken by Louis Napoleon and the Piedmontese government to wage war against Austria in 1859. Although the war itself did not directly lead to unification, it triggered a series of events that resulted in the most extraordinary episode in this story, the invasion of Sicily by Giuseppe Garibaldi and his guerrilla army of, initially, 1,000 volunteers. Garibaldi's ultimate aim was to seize Rome and forge a new Italian state, to be led by Victor Emmanuel of Piedmont. Whilst Cavour and Victor Emmanuel's ambitions for Italian unity were limited to the north and the expulsion of Austria, Garibaldi's invasion of Sicily and the mainland forced Cavour to respond to events. Garibaldi's significance was to turn the unification of the northern regions of Italy into unification of the whole peninsula. It was also to act as a thorn in the side of the more cautious conservatives. But it was Cavour's consummate political skill, especially in the critical years 1859 and 1860 that were of fundamental importance in shaping the Italian nation.

But the unification of Italy in 1861 had come at a price: the transfer of Nice and Savoy to France. Unification was also not complete; Venice and Rome still lay in foreign hands. The process of unification had been, to an extent, forced, and deep political divisions remained. Although the nation state had been formed, many – including the Catholic Church – had been alienated by unification.

1857 – National Society formed

1858 – July: Cavour and Napoleon III sign Pact of Plombières

1859 – April: Piedmont and France declare war on Austria

May: Battle of Magenta.

May: Revolutions in Central States and Romagna

June: Battle of Solferino

July: Treaty of Villafranca: Piedmont gains Lombardy

1860 – January: Cavour returns to office having resigned after Villafranca

| 1857 | 1858 | 1859 April | 1859 May | 1859 June | 1859 July | 1860 January |

SOURCE
1
Count Cavour meets Victor Emmanuel II, 1860. Unattributed illustration after H.C. Ademollo, in *New Age History Readers*, 1921.

WHY DID WAR AGAINST AUSTRIA BREAK OUT IN 1859?

Support from Piedmont for nationalists

The National Society

The National Society was founded in 1857 by a group of exiles living in Piedmont, which included Giuseppe La Farina, Giorgio Pallavicino and Daniele Manin. It emerged as a series of single-issue nationalist campaigns, such as the protest against the presence of Swiss mercenary

1860 March	1860 April	1860 May	1860 August	1860 September	1860 October	1861 March
	April: Savoy and Nice conceded to France		August: Garibaldi invades Naples		October: Garibaldi hands Sicily and Naples to Victor Emmanuel at Teano	
March: Plebiscites held in Central States and Romagna, which unites with Piedmont		May: Garibaldi and 'the Thousand' land at Marsala in Sicily		September: Piedmont invades Papal States and annexes Marches and Umbria		March: Proclamation of Kingdom of Italy

soldiers in Naples. The purpose of the society was to promote the cause of Italian national unity within Piedmont. It was also to encourage nationalists throughout the Italian peninsula to accept Piedmontese leadership. As a moderate liberal organisation, it used 'modern' methods of persuasion, most obviously the newspaper *Il Piccolo Corriere d'Italia* but also posters, flyers, pamphlets and meetings. The pamphlets were published in batches of up to 3,000 and distributed by post as well as being handed out or left in public places. Such tactics contrasted with the violent and revolutionary tactics associated with Mazzini and his followers. It was open in its organisation in Piedmont whereas, for obvious reasons, it was still more secretive in Lombardy and elsewhere in the Italian peninsula because of foreign rule.

For Cavour, the National Society provided a template for a style of nationalism which suited his aims and temperament – that is, conservative and pragmatic rather than radical and ideological. Its leaders, such as La Farina, were able to persuade Cavour that nationalism was both useful and politically expedient. However, Cavour's support for the National Society and the idea of the nation in the late 1850s was limited to the concept of a northern Italian state, which was economically powerful and free of Austrian dominance. As such, this form of nationalism became closely associated with political stability rather than turmoil. It appealed, therefore, to the educated middle classes among whom the concept was becoming both fashionable and respectable. It also appealed to those Mazzinians, such as Daniele Manin, who were prepared to rally to the banner of the Piedmontese monarchy as a means of promoting the cause of an Italian nation state. The creation of the National Society marked a hugely significant turning point in the cause of Italian unity.

EXTRACT

1 From *Risorgimento* by Lucy Riall, 2009.

The organisation of the National Society signals an important transformation in the aims and methods of the Italian nationalist movement. Moderate liberals and republicans may have shared the same cultural idea of Italy, and they spoke the same political language derived from this culture, but the political meanings which they attached to terms like 'nation', 'liberty' and 'resurrection' were quite distinct. The shift from revolutionary conspiracy and popular insurrection towards the respectability of parliamentary debate and diplomacy could not but alter the political nature of nationalism itself. Specifically, by allying itself to Piedmont, the National Society endorsed a conservative and monarchical political tradition, while the link between its leaders and Cavour involved their implicit acceptance of, and subordination to, essentially material ambitions. The National Society relegated revolution to a secondary phase, and deprived nationalism of its moral, regenerative force.

ACTIVITY
WRITING

Study Extract 1 carefully. Lucy Riall writes well but her language is advanced. Identify the words in this extract which you do not understand and research their meaning.

EXTEND YOUR KNOWLEDGE

The printed word
The impact of the use of printed materials by the National Society in the spread in popularity of its brand of Italian nationalism was hugely significant. In many senses, the campaign waged by the National Society was reminiscent of the tactics of the Anti-Corn Law League in Britain the previous decade. By the late 1850s, around 4,000 copies of *Il Piccolo Corriere* were circulated. In the newspaper, the leaders of the National Society gave advice as to how to set up local groups as well as taking the opportunity to attack the Austrians and the backward rule of the Bourbons in Naples. In her biography of Garibaldi (2007) Lucy Riall wrote: 'Through its publishing activities... the National Society played a crucial part in creating and marinating a common nationalist outlook amongst its members and adherents... It was to have a central organisational and propaganda role in the events on 1859-60.'

SOURCE 2

Daniele Manin's leadership of the Venetian Republic had made him a hero of the nationalist cause. Instinctively a republican, his views on how the Italian states could be best unified changed in the 1850s. From a letter written on 19 September 1855 to L. Valerio.

I am sending you herewith the original and a translation of my declaration which has already been published in the *Times* and is coming out tomorrow in the *Siècle*.

Our republican party, so bitterly criticised, thus makes one more act of abnegation and sacrifice in the national cause.

'Convinced that above all Italy must be made, that this is the first and most important question, we say to the Monarchy of Savoy: 'Make Italy and we are with you. – If not, not.'

And to the constitutionalists we say: 'Think about making Italy and not of enlarging Piedmont: be Italians and not municipalists, and we are with you. – If not, not.'

I think it is time to give up existing party divisions based on purely secondary differences; the principal, vital matter is whether we are of the unifying nationalist school of thought, or whether we belong to the separatist, municipalist school.

I, a republican, raise the banner of unity. If all those who want Italy gather round and defend it, then Italy will be.

SOURCE 3

Giorgio Pallavicino (his full name was Giorgio Pallavicino Trivulzio) was a Lombard democrat who, after the revolutions of 1848–49 came to a pragmatic conclusion about the future of the Italian nation. In the following extract, from a letter dated 1 October 1856, Pallavicino is writing to Daniele Manin.

Piedmontism is for us an extremely dangerous opponent, as implacable enemy. Everyone in Piedmont – from Count Solaro della Margarita to Angelo Brofferio – is tarred with this same brush. Instead of a single Italian nation with its centre in Rome, they would prefer a Kingdom on northern Italy with two capitals, Turin and Milan. Camillo Cavour is one of the most Piedmontese of all; and we shall harness him to our chariot only when we have a knife at his throat.

AS Level Exam-Style Questions Section A

1 Why is Source 2 valuable to the historian for an enquiry about the changing nature of nationalism in the Italian states in the 1850s?

Explain your answer using the source, the information given about it and your own knowledge of the historical context. (8 marks)

2 How much weight do you give the evidence of Source 3 for an enquiry into the obstacles facing the founders of the National Society?

Explain your answer using the source, the information given about it and your own knowledge of the historical context. (12 marks)

Tip
Before you start, you should try to define the changing nature of Italian nationalism and the obstacles facing the founders of the National Society.

Relations with Napoleon III

Cavour understood that French support for the removal of Austria would best serve Piedmont's interests. In Napoleon III, he and Piedmont had a potential useful ally. As a 22-year-old, Louis Napoleon had taken part in the uprising in Rome in 1831 and conspiracies in the Papal States and Modena. Such enthusiasm for the romantic notion of Italian liberty and nationalism was to last throughout his political life. Napoleon was grateful to Piedmont for support during the Crimean War and built a close working relationship with Cavour. After the Congress of Paris in 1856, a dialogue was maintained through intermediaries that included Napoleon's nephew Prince Jerome and Cavour's trusted assistant Costantino Niagra. However, Napoleon did not act solely with Italian interests in mind. As the inheritor of the Bonapartist title, he saw it as his duty to ensure the expansion of France. In particular, he saw the possibility of expanding into **Nice** and Savoy (which were part of the Kingdom of Sardinia) in return for help to expel the Austrians from northern Italy.

KEY TERM

Nice
The issue of the status of Nice was particularly sensitive. It was feared that if news of the potential transfer of Nice to France became public it would split opinion in national-minded circles. Most importantly, it would alienate the adventurer, soldier and patriot Giuseppe Garibaldi, who was born in Nice.

It is possible to interpret Napoleon's help for the cause of Italian unity as being less inspired by romantic ideals and more the hope that, through helping Piedmont assert itself in northern Italy, France would create a client state that would allow it greater influence in that region. Napoleon was always wary of Catholic opinion in France. In 1849, he sent French troops to Rome to help crush the Mazzinian-inspired rising and restore the papacy. This move went down well with the Catholics in France.

Napoleon never wavered from his commitment to protect the pope, a commitment that prevented the full unification of Italy until 1871. It is also likely that Napoleon envisaged a federation with the pope at its head rather than the creation of a centralised Italian state. How this would work can be seen in the planning at Plombières (see below). There is also little doubt that Napoleon hoped to further the dynastic interests of family members through engineering their appointment to kingdoms in central and southern Italy.

SOURCE

4 A memorandum about the 'Italian Question' written by Louis Napoleon for himself and his foreign minister. It is written during the time of the Congress of Paris in 1856.

The aims of all statesmen must be to avoid, as much as possible, all the ferments of dispute that still exist in Europe. Now one only has to open one's eyes to see that the country which is the greatest threat to European peace is Italy, because it political structure is such as not to satisfy any legitimate interest. To alter its structure either a revolution or a war is needed – two fatal extremities; and in any case who would be powerful enough to impose his will on so many divided countries, and which set of ideas would be accepted widely enough to unite so many states and give them a common purpose.

Nonetheless I believe that one might try something that might satisfy nearly everybody. An Italian Confederation might be set up, under the nominal leadership of the Pope, on the model of the German Confederation, i.e. a diet appointed by the various States, could meet at Rome and discuss matters of common interest, without any change to territorial boundaries or to the rights of the various rulers.

Thus Austria, by reason of its Lombard territories, would be in the same position with regard to the Italian Confederation as is Holland now, with regard to the German Confederation.

This diet would not only deal with the major issues of general interest of Italy, such as tariffs, the army, the navy, currency etc... but it would have some administrative powers, and its decisions would be sovereign on matters of general interest.

ACTIVITY
KNOWLEDGE CHECK

From all that you have read so far, what do you think were Louis Napoleon's ambitions with regards to Italy?

Significance of the Orsini Affair and Pact of Plombières

Assassination attempt

On 14 January 1858, four Italians, led by Count Felice Orsini, attempted to assassinate Napoleon as he arrived at the opera with his wife, Empress Eugénie. Orsini had hatched his plans in London, where three large bombs had been made for him. Then he travelled by train to Paris with three co-conspirators (two Mazzinians and a hired assassin). Following a tip-off, the gendarmarie (French police) had been expecting Orsini and his co-conspirators to arrive from England by road through northern France. However, the would-be assassins outwitted them by arriving via Brussels. The rationale for such action was that the assassination of Napoleon would lead to the restoration of a republic in France that would be well disposed to the creation of an Italian republic. In the event, Orsini's bomb failed to harm its target; it did, however, manage to kill seven onlookers and injure 150 others. At his trial, Orsini appealed to Napoleon to support the cause of Italian unity. By doing so, he would ensure that 'the blessings of 25 million citizens would follow him to posterity'. It has been assumed that these words in some way created a spark in Napoleon's conscience that triggered him into action and led to the arrangement of a meeting in Plombières on 20 July 1858. This assumption is dubious.

Napoleon might have wanted to use Orsini's plea as a romantic cover for what was, in reality, some hard-nosed bargaining. He wished to ensure that there were no further attempts to assassinate him. Therefore, Napoleon saw a meeting with Cavour as a way of putting pressure on Cavour to introduce repressive measures against violent nationalists living in Piedmont. Napoleon saw this as a chance to deal with a dynastic problem. He had had difficulties as leader of the Bonaparte family in finding a wife (and role in European affairs) for his cousin, Prince Jerome Bonaparte, and marriage to a Piedmont princess might be the answer. Both Cavour and Napoleon wished for war against Austria. However, a potential problem was that their motives for war differed. Cavour wanted war to remove Austrian influence from northern Italy. Napoleon wanted war to gain territory but also as part of a broader diplomatic strategy regarding Austria.

The agreement at Plombières

There is little doubt that Louis Napoleon was keen to help Piedmont in its struggle with Austria. It is correct to assume that the blueprint of a federal Italy was attractive to the French emperor, because it made likely the possibility of a French rather than Austrian-dominated peninsula. The preservation of some of the papacy's temporal power and the offer of the presidency of the Italian federation to the pope would, hopefully for Louis Napoleon, keep Catholic opinion in France relatively content. Therefore, it was agreed at the secret meeting in Plombières that France would join Piedmont in war against Austria, if war could be provoked in a way acceptable to opinion in the two countries. The aim, of course, was to use military force to drive Austria out of Italy. Other terms of the agreement were as follows.

- A kingdom of Upper Italy (ruled by the House of Savoy) would be created to cover the provinces of Piedmont, Lombardy and Venetia, and the duchies of Parma, Modena and the Papal Legations.

- A kingdom of Central Italy would be controlled by Tuscany, and would also include Umbria and the papal Marches.

- Rome and the surrounding area would remain in the control of the papacy and the pope would lead an Italian confederation.

- For the present time, the Kingdom of Naples would remain as it was. This was mainly because Napoleon feared that to unseat the Bourbons might upset the tsar, who saw himself as an ally of this similarly autocratic dynasty.

- In return for the support of 200,000 French troops, Napoleon demanded Savoy and Nice. Cavour was quite happy to accede to the request for Savoy, the majority of its population being French speaking. However, this was not the case in Nice and it took until January 1859 for Piedmont to agree.

There is also little doubt that Louis Napoleon looked for territorial gain, and Savoy was the perfect prize. All of this was anticipated by Cavour, who was not too concerned with the loss of Savoy, given that the majority of the population spoke a French dialect. It is likely that the most important aspect of the treaty for Louis Napoleon was the furthering of his dynastic ambitions with the arrangement of the marriage of his nephew Prince Jerome to Princess Clotilde, daughter of the Italian king Victor Emmanuel II.

Cavour and Plombières

The agreement at Plombières was a major diplomatic achievement for Cavour. The events of 1848–49 had proven that French military support would be essential if Austria was to be defeated. Given Cavour's satisfaction with the Plombières agreement and given his determination to see it implemented, one might assume that the political settlement it proposed was close to his own views. In that case, it is clear that Cavour was not an Italian nationalist in the sense that he agreed with the idea of the political unification of the whole peninsula. The limits of his nationalism were confined to the wish to expel the Austrians from Lombardy and Venetia, and to unite the freed provinces into a potentially wealthy political entity. At Plombières, Cavour was reluctant to discuss the French annexation of Nice because he was aware that the reaction of those nationally minded to the loss of an Italian dialect-speaking province would be considerable, especially to Garibaldi who was born in Nice. However, at the Treaty of Turin in March 1860, Cavour was content to sign over Savoy and Nice to France in return for Lombardy. This was despite the fact that he was not obliged to do so by the terms of the Plombières agreement.

EXTEND YOUR KNOWLEDGE

War against Austria

It was suggested by the historian A.J.P. Taylor in an article in the *English Historical Review* in 1936 that Napoleon might well have wanted to wage war with Austria as a means of improving diplomatic relations. He points to the fact that there had been an improvement in relations between France and Russia after the Crimean War, and that Napoleon saw no reason why this might not be the case after a war with Austria.

A more critical view of Louis Napoleon

In 1859, Louis Napoleon had redrafted a speech written by Cavour, which was to be read by Victor Emmanuel II in the wake of Plombières. The last sentence, written by Louis Napoleon, read: 'We cannot remain insensitive to the cries of pain which come to us from so many parts of Italy.' Similarly, the Plombières agreement itself, in which Louis Napoleon committed France to the cause of expelling the Austrians, can be seen as a crucial turning point.

However, the issue is one of intention. In *The Risorgimento* (1959), Agatha Ramm argues that 'Napoleon was almost equally as much a liability as an asset' to the cause of Italian unity. His desire to go to war against Austria in 1859 was not to relieve the 'cries of pain' but, as Ramm argued, 'to draw diplomatic profit from the war'. By 1859, the settlement imposed on Europe by the Treaty of Vienna was dated and crumbling. By embarking on his adventurous policy in Italy, Napoleon was recognising that Austrian power could be challenged without sparking a revolution. However, Plombières and even the events of 1831 reveal that French involvement in Italy was in part undertaken for dynastic reasons. The marriage of Prince Jerome to Clotilde was as important as any other clause to Napoleon at Plombières. He was prepared to allow for a deferment on the issue of the transferral of Nice to France, but not on the idea of securing the dynastic future of the Bonaparte family. This was a preoccupation of his uncle Napoleon I and reflected the family insecurity. As an aside, Louis Napoleon cared little for the sensitivities of the dynastic arrangements he engineered. Prince Jerome Bonaparte was a rather gentle and slow member of the Bonaparte family, with little energy or charm. His family nickname, 'Plon-plon', sums up his character rather well. When the wedding took place between 'Plon-plon' and Marie Clotilde on the eve of conflict with Austria in 1859, she was quickly labelled 'the first casualty of the war'.

More important for Napoleon than the ideal of Italian national unity was the popularity he felt he could gain at home through a successful foreign policy in Italy. Elections in France in May 1857 showed his imperial regime to be increasingly unpopular and it is this factor, more than the assassination attempt by Orsini, that can account for Napoleon's wish to be involved in a successful war against Austria. One overriding factor for Louis Napoleon was the support of French Catholics, which is why his contribution to the cause of Italian unity was limited. In 1859, as we will read later, he was a happy to sign an independent agreement with the Austrians at Villafranca because National Society uprisings in central Italy threatened the Papal States and the temporal power of the papacy.

The preparation for and outbreak of war with Austria

Preparing for war

The problem for Cavour was how to provoke war with Austria in such a way that his and France's ambitions were not made too obvious. It was agreed at Plombières that Piedmont was to be painted as the victim and Austria as the aggressor. In his opening of parliament on 12 December 1859, Victor Emmanuel II delivered a deliberately provocative speech, which included the threat: 'For while we respect treaties we are not insensitive to the cry of grief that reaches us from so many parts of Italy.' In January, the marriage of Prince Jerome to Princess Marie Clotilde as well as the military alliance between France and Piedmont was announced; but Austria was not easily provoked. Worryingly for Piedmont, at Plombières, Cavour had promised to match Napoleon's promise of an army of 200,000 with a force of 100,000. However, by the turn of 1858–59, an army of this size was proving hard to find. The National Society recruited some 20,000 volunteers, but many of these men were untrained and no match for the Austrian army. The army reserves Cavour hoped to mobilise did not exist. In the end, the Piedmontese army numbered only around 60,000.

In 1848–49, war against Austria was seen by many as a popular crusade. This time, though, things were very different; there was little popular enthusiasm for a war engineered by Cavour. When an insurrection began in the Duchy of Modena, it failed through lack of support. The failure of this insurrection was significant in that it underlined that the campaign against Austria would need to be initiated through diplomacy rather than popular insurrection. Indeed, Cavour was worried that Austrian rule in Lombardy under Archduke Maximilian was not as repressive or unpopular as it had been. In addition, war in northern Italy was unpopular with other European powers. The Prussians made it clear that their sympathies would be with Austria. In Britain, the prime minister, Lord Derby, and his foreign secretary, Lord Malmesbury, were sympathetic to the cause of Italian unity, but did not wish to see a war deliberately provoked. To many, Austrian domination in northern Italy would be replaced by French domination, which was equally undesirable. While the Russians assured France of their neutrality and goodwill, in March 1859 they called for a congress of European powers to mediate between France and Austria. To Cavour's horror, in early April, Napoleon seemed to moving towards a peaceful solution to the 'Italian Question'.

However, as the diplomatic manoeuvrings continued, so tension increased. In March 1859, the Piedmontese army was mobilised. The Austrians followed suit in April. The problem for the Austrians was that, having mobilised, they now needed to either use their army or demobilise, both of which would be costly. Therefore, on 23 April the Austrian foreign minister, Count Buol, demanded Piedmontese demobilisation within three days. When it was not forthcoming they declared war and, on 29 April, under General Franz Gyulai, the troops of the Austrian army invaded Piedmont. However, they were delayed by poor weather, which gave the French plenty of time to move their army by rail into Piedmont. Cavour's strategy had been saved by the Austrian decision to resort to war rather than diplomacy as a means of defending her empire.

The Grand Duchies

The outbreak of war stirred unrest across the peninsula. Events moved fast in the Grand Duchies (Tuscany, Modena and Parma), manipulated by the National Society which forced the pace of change.

- In April 1859, in Florence there was a popular demonstration against the Grand Duke Leopold that resulted in his flight and the creation of a provisional government led by Baron Bettino Ricasoli. Given that Ricasoli was a moderate, it is little surprise that he demanded union with Piedmont.

- In May 1859, the National Society engineered peaceful revolutions in Tuscany, Modena and Parma, and the rulers of all three fled leaving provisional governments in control.

- In June 1859, the Duke of Modena and the Duchess-Regent of Parma fled their provinces. They were replaced by a government led by Luigi Farini, which was, again, close to Piedmont. Indeed, government under Farini was akin to being ruled as a Piedmontese colony, because all major governmental decisions were approved in Turin.

There was further political unrest when, in June, insurrections took place in the Papal Legations (which were made up of the provinces of Ravenna, Ferrara and Bologna). In Bologna, Piedmontese commissioners moved in to restore government. Most of these commissioners were members of the National Society. Only in Tuscany was there any demonstration of popular support for a change in government. Despite these events, the political future of these provinces relied, in the short term, on events on the battlefield.

WHAT WAS THE IMPACT OF THE WAR?

Significance of Magenta and Solferino

Minor victories by the Piedmontese army at Palestro and by Garibaldi's **Cacciatori delle Alpi** at Como in May 1859 helped to pave the way for the two large-scale battles of the war at Magenta (4 June) and Solferino (24 June). The Piedmontese army did not take much of a part in the battle at Magenta but equipped itself well at Solferino. The Austrians were defeated at both battles, but the margin of victory for the allies in both cases was narrow. These battles mark a turning point in warfare. With the advent of new and more accurate weaponry, the deployment of large armies on the battlefield was a recipe for carnage. The casualties on both sides were considerable. At Magenta, 4,000 of the allies were killed and wounded, the Austrians just under 6,000 with a further 4,500 troops of the Imperial army taken prisoner. Such was the bloodletting at Magenta that it provided the name for a new variant of red dye. At Solferino the casualty figure of both sides combined was around 40,000. With only one doctor per 500 casualties on the allied side, the chances of survival for many of the wounded were bleak. But despite the bloodletting, the Austrians still held the Quadrilateral and showed no sign of withdrawing from northern Italy. Indeed, there was little prospect of the French and Piedmontese defeating the 150,000-strong Austrian army – which was still very well entrenched – without considerable bloodshed. The Austrian Emperor Franz Joseph could suffer a long war whereas Louis Napoleon could not.

KEY TERM

Cacciatori delle Alpi
Translated as 'Alpine Hunters', this group could be described as a private army. They were led by Garibaldi and were round 3,000 strong. They were volunteers and highly effective in their work.

SOURCE
5

Piedmontese troops advance against the Austrians. An engraving by an unnamed artist in *L'Illustration*, 1859.

Attaque générale des hauteurs de San Martino par l'armée piémontaise (24 juin 1859). (Page 47, col. 2.)

EXTEND YOUR KNOWLEDGE

Carnage at Solferino
The visitors to the Solferino battlefield included a Swiss businessman Jean-Henri Dunant. His experiences moved him to write *A Memory of Solferino*. Horrified by the agony and suffering of the soldiers left wounded on the battlefield, he called the battle 'a disaster on a European scale'. Dunant began a process which led to the establishment of the International Red Cross.

The nature of the peace settlement

Napoleon's ambition to have freed Italy 'from the Alps to the Adriatic' seemed unlikely to be fulfilled in the short term and without Cavour knowing, he sued for peace with Austria. An armistice was proposed by Napoleon on 8 July 1859. This was followed by a meeting at Villafranca on 11 July between Napoleon and Emperor Franz Joseph. Apart from his distaste for the bloodshed, Napoleon had other motives for making peace behind Piedmontese backs. He had disapproved of the turn of events in central Italy. He felt that the papacy was under threat with a National Society government friendly to Piedmont in Bologna (which was in the Papal States). He also felt that Piedmontese control of central Italy went beyond the points agreed at Plombières. Napoleon was embarrassed by the demands of French Catholics for him to act to rectify a situation that was clearly getting out of hand. Worryingly for the French, on 24 June 1859, the Prussian army mobilised an army on the banks of the Rhine in support of Austria. Indeed, Prussia had made it clear that it was willing to support Austria as long as it was allowed greater influence among the organisation of German states known as the German Confederation. Fearing that the British government would fail to support him, Napoleon sued for peace with the Austrians at Villafranca. Although Prussia was not the threat it would be ten years later, mobilisation of its army on the Rhine was enough to push Louis Napoleon into the arms of the Austrians. To the satisfaction of the Austrian emperor, Franz Joseph, the Prussians were made to 'look foolish', but he missed the point. The threat of Prussian intervention was enough to bring Napoleon to the negotiating table.

British approval

In *The Struggle for Mastery in Europe 1848-1918* (1954), A.J.P. Taylor wrote: 'Italy owed most to French armies and British moral approval.' The coming to power in Britain in June 1859 of the second ministry led by Lord Palmerston with Lord John Russell as foreign secretary had an important impact on the process of unification. Not all British politicians were keen to see the creation of a united Italy, but Palmerston and Lord John Russell, definitely were. Palmerston, who was prime minister from 1855 to 1858, then again from 1859 to 1865, made it known that he was anti-Austria south of the Alps (that is, in Italy), but pro-Austria north of the Alps. Russell was a strong supporter of Italian unification, as were most Liberals at the time. He was also a believer in free trade and argued that a free, united Italy would be a strong trading partner for Britain. His belief that the Italian Question should be solved by applying the idea of self-determination was echoed by the president of the United States of America, Woodrow Wilson, at the end of the First World War some 60 years later. Neither politician wished to see the maintenance of Austrian power in northern Italy and both were adamantly opposed to any extension of French interest in the region. However, they were restrained by domestic considerations (including the views of Queen Victoria who did not want to see Austrian interests harmed) and maintained a policy of strict neutrality. Louis Napoleon faced a potentially worrying problem as events unfolded in the summer of 1859. The government in Prussia made it known that it might lend some support to Austria by mobilising its armies along the River Rhine, thereby threatening France. The outline of a coalition as faced occasionally by his uncle Napoleon I (who faced a coalition that included Britain, Prussia, Austria and Russia) was becoming ominously clear to Napoleon III and was to be avoided at all costs.

Villafranca

The two emperors met at Villafranca in July 1859. Piedmont's ambitions were forced to play second fiddle to the diplomacy of Napoleon. Both Franz Joseph and Louis Napoleon were keen to downplay Austria's defeat in Italy and the role played by Piedmont. They also both wished to underplay nationalist sentiment. Some aspects of Plombières survived, but many did not.

- Austria agreed that Lombardy should be given to France, which might then choose to give it to Piedmont in due course. However, Venetia was to remain in Austrian hands.

- An Italian confederation was to be created with the pope as its leader.

- Piedmont was not to be given control of Modena, Tuscany or Parma and the rulers who had been forced to flee from the central Italian states were to be restored.

- Piedmont was also forbidden to annex Mantua and Peschiera (two of the military fortresses of the Quadrilateral) in Lombardy.

In groups, discuss the following question and options.

For Cavour, Villafranca was which of the following:

- a complete disaster

- as he might have expected

- a victory of sorts

- a temporary set-back

- a terrible surprise?

When your group has reached its conclusion, you should feed back to other groups.

Cavour's resignation and its significance

A possible congress

The impact on Cavour was predictable and he resigned as prime minister in disgust and disappointment. Therefore he was not present at the peace conference held in Zurich, which was to deliberate on the Italian Question. The Treaty of Zurich, signed in November 1859, formally ended the war. As part of the treaty, Napoleon suggested that the issue of central Europe was be decided by a congress of the European powers. This was a compromise that did not please the Piedmontese government, now led by Alfonso Lamarmora. However, Louis Napoleon had become a victim of his own diplomatic manoeuvrings. One consequence of Villafranca was that he had lost the initiative over Italy. His suggestion of holding a congress was in the hope that he could win it back. In December 1859, a pamphlet with the title *Le Pape et le Congrès* was published in Paris with the author being named as the Vicomte La Guéronnière. However, it was made known that the ideas in the pamphlet were those of Louis Napoleon. The main point made in the pamphlet was that the decline of the pope's temporal power was inevitable. In the pamphlet it also suggested that the pope would be the ruler of a smaller state defended by an army of an Italian confederation. The ideas outlined in *Le Pape et le Congrès* were rejected out of hand by both the papacy and the Austrians with the upshot that the idea of a congress was dead in the water. The reality of the situation was that the cause of Italian unity in the latter of part of 1859 had stalled. In addition, nationalists of all persuasions faced the distinct possibility of an understanding between the French and Austrians, which would serve to contain their ambitions.

Piedmontisation

Piedmont acquired from France responsibility for governing Lombardy in late 1859 when Cavour was out of office. The minister of the interior, Urbano Rattazzi, decided that the best course for the state was to impose a central model of government on Lombardy, despite the fact that Lombardy had been promised a Constituent Assembly to discuss the issue at the time of the **plebiscite**. The problem was that there was no common language – only two percent of all Italians spoke the Italian language, the considerable majority spoke in dialect. Lombardy had its own education system, legal system and structure of local government.

The government of Alfonso La Marmora had to decide quickly how Lombardy would be governed. It decided to impose the Piedmontese administrative model on Lombardy without any debate and by emergency degree. In Modena, in August 1860, a popular assembly controlled by Farini voted for annexation to Piedmont. However, there is little evidence to suggest that Cavour disapproved of these developments. He did nothing to reverse them when he came into power again, despite the fact that such centralisation caused considerable disquiet. In Tuscany, the imposition of Piedmontese laws was delayed for political reasons. The powerful Baron Ricasoli argued successfully for the protection of Tuscan customs and legal systems, at least in the short term. However, Tuscany was the exception rather than the rule. In most regions, the local ruling class was not able to negotiate with Piedmont from a position of strength.

Annexation of central Italian states

British influence

The British government led by Palmerston with Lord John Russell as foreign secretary had expressed its considerable displeasure at the turn of events from Villafranca onwards. It viewed the meeting between the two emperors and their subsequent agreement as being a betrayal of the cause of Italy on the part of Napoleon. However, the publication of *Le Pape et le Congrès* was a crucial turning point on the road to unification. By accepting a decline in papal power, Napoleon might have upset Catholics in France and the Austrians but he very much pleased the British. The main consequence of the pamphlet was that the idea of the Congress was dead. It was the British foreign secretary Lord John Russell who seized the moment. He proposed that the future of the Italian peninsula should be decided through the application of the principle of self-determination. This was another crucial moment. Despite the existence of a plot hatched by the king and Urbano Rattazzi aimed at preventing Cavour forming a new government, Cavour returned as prime minister on 21 January 1860 and immediately started to negotiate a deal, the Treaty of Turin, with Napoleon.

Tuscany and Emilia

The Austrians objected to the British emphasis on self-determination because it opened up the possibility of Piedmontese annexation of the Central Duchies. In a sense, Piedmontese annexation of the central Italian states had a certain inevitability about it. Despite Villafranca, Grand Duke Leopold did not return to power in Tuscany. Instead, power was held by Baron Ricasoli, who had engineered the election of a subservient local assembly, which, in August 1859, had voted to ask for annexation by Piedmont. Meanwhile, Ricasoli exercised power as a dictator. In Emilia, Luigi Carlo Farini had remained equally powerful. Through assuming dictatorial powers, Ricasoli and Farini had ensured that the political settlement in Tuscany and Emilia, both strategically important states, was to be a conservative one. In order to legitimise the annexation of central Italy, Cavour came up with the idea that it should take place through popular consent. Such an idea was, of course, in direct contradiction to his real beliefs and therefore highly cynical. The idea of self-determination, that the peoples of Italy would determine their own future, smacked of Mazzinianism. However, Cavour was wise enough to realise that he could borrow the language of popular change and some of its trappings (for example, plebiscites) for his own ends. Cavour also understood that the idea of holding plebiscites would be acceptable to the British government led by Lord Palmerston and Bonapartist France, and he was right. He also understood that the votes could be fixed through intimidation, corruption and bullying. The fact that there was an organisation, the National Society, willing to do Cavour's dirty work made it much easier for him to distance himself from some pretty strange results.

Plebiscites

On 1 March 1860, Ricasoli and Farini announced plebiscites over the question of annexation to Piedmont. Cavour recognised that there was uncertainty about the political future and that a plebiscite could pave the way to a conservative political settlement. By doing so he could prevent the possibility of a more democratic settlement on Mazzinian lines. It is no wonder that Mazzini dismissed Cavour's plans as a 'paltry, hateful programme of expediency'. But Cavour was simply doing what he did best: fulfilling the art of the possible. The plebiscites were an opportunity for them to engineer annexation with the help of the National Society, which campaigned enthusiastically. All males over 21 were given an opportunity to vote. The choice they were given was:

* annexation to the constitutional monarchy of Victor Emmanuel II, or

* a separate kingdom (the nature of the 'separate kingdom' remaining deliberately vague).

When the elections took place in March 1860, it was clear that there was widespread vote rigging. It was little surprise that the plebiscites resulted in an overwhelming victory for those in favour of annexation. The votes were as follows.

	For annexation	Against annexation
Tuscany	386,445	14,925
Emilia	427,512	756
Savoy (to France)	130,583	235
Nice	24,448	160

There was not much doubt that the plebiscites were a charade and that Cavour's government had hidden behind the cloak of popular suffrage. In reality, the annexations were the result of the diplomacy and the skills of the National Society (see pages 217–218) and the Piedmontese commissioners in the central Italian states.

Loss of Nice and Savoy

Treaty of Turin

At Plombières, Cavour had been reluctant to discuss the French annexation of Nice because he was aware that the reaction of those nationally minded to the loss of an Italian dialect-speaking province would be considerable, especially Garibaldi who was born in Nice. The British strongly objected to the French having Savoy and Nice. To Lord Palmerston and Lord John Russell it was the first step towards the creation of a new Bonapartist empire. One must remember that Napoleon I's attempts to create a European empire had been defeated only 45 years earlier. The main points of the Treaty of

Turin were that Piedmont would hand over Savoy and Nice to France and that France would accept Piedmontese annexation of the central Italian duchies, as long as the annexation was accompanied by plebiscites (popular votes). However, at Turin in March 1860, Cavour was content to sign over Savoy and Nice to France in return for Lombardy. This was despite the fact that he was not obliged to do so by the terms of the Plombières agreement, as Louis Napoleon had failed to keep his side of the bargain and push the Austrians out of Venice. However, his diplomatic instincts were sufficient to tell him that the key to Piedmontese strength was the continual support, however erratic, of Louis Napoleon. As already stated, Cavour was a pragmatist. He was also politically astute. His defining and most significant attribute was his ability to respond to events and to understand the opportunities that these events presented to Piedmont. A good example of this was the manoeuvrings which led to the annexation of the duchies and the Treaty of Turin.

ACTIVITY
KNOWLEDGE CHECK

Louis Napoleon

Using Source 4, answer the following questions:

1 To what extent did Louis Napoleon implement the ideas proposed in this memorandum?

2 How useful is such a piece of evidence to an historian trying to discover Louis Napoleon's true motivation for interfering in Italian affairs?

TIMELINE

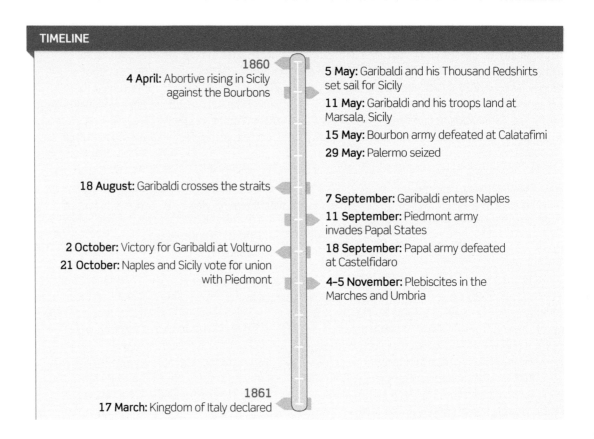

1860

4 April: Abortive rising in Sicily against the Bourbons

5 May: Garibaldi and his Thousand Redshirts set sail for Sicily

11 May: Garibaldi and his troops land at Marsala, Sicily

15 May: Bourbon army defeated at Calatafimi

29 May: Palermo seized

18 August: Garibaldi crosses the straits

7 September: Garibaldi enters Naples

11 September: Piedmont army invades Papal States

2 October: Victory for Garibaldi at Volturno

21 October: Naples and Sicily vote for union with Piedmont

18 September: Papal army defeated at Castelfidaro

4–5 November: Plebiscites in the Marches and Umbria

1861

17 March: Kingdom of Italy declared

WHAT WAS THE SIGNIFICANCE OF GARIBALDI?

Garibaldi's aims and objectives

What happened next was to turn the annexation of central Italy by Piedmont into the unification of the peninsula. The reaction of Garibaldi to the surrender of his birthplace, Nice, to the French was to organise a force to prevent its annexation. The group that became known as 'The Thousand' met near the port of Genoa. As the group increased its numbers, news broke in April 1860 of an insurrection on the island of Sicily. Although about only one-tenth of Garibaldi's force were Sicilian, he was persuaded by two of his most trusted followers, Francesco Crispi and Rosalino Pilo, to sail south. Garibaldi concurred. On 12 April, Pilo sailed on ahead to rally the Sicilian revolutionaries and inform them that help was close at hand.

Once at sea, Garibaldi declared that he was going to liberate Italy in the name of 'Italy and Victor Emmanuel'. The Mazzinians among **The Thousand** were reluctant to give their allegiance to a monarchy, but this reluctance was tempered by Mazzini's acceptance, in March 1860, of Victor Emmanuel as leader of a united Italy if that was the popular choice. As Garibaldi headed south, so Cavour was faced with a difficult dilemma. To oppose Garibaldi would make his government unpopular at home and would offend the members of the National Society, which had recently so admirably served the Piedmontese cause in central Italy. In addition, Cavour suspected that Victor Emmanuel supported Garibaldi's escapade. Elections were due to be held on 6 and 10 May, and Cavour did not wish the issue of Garibaldi to damage his political prospects in any way.

EXTEND YOUR KNOWLEDGE

Francesco Crispi (1819–1901)
Crispi had taken part in the uprising in Sicily in 1848 and thereafter went into exile. He returned in 1860 to join Garibaldi's expedition to Sicily. He became a politician in the new state and was elected to be a deputy in the Italian parliament in 1861. Crispi was twice prime minister of Italy, from 1887 to 1891 and 1893 to 1896, and became one of the most significant prime ministers of the new Italian state.

Garibaldi's relationship with Cavour and Victor Emmanuel II

Garibaldi and Cavour

Cavour was introduced to Garibaldi for the first time in 1856. Another meeting took place in December 1858 when Cavour informed Garibaldi in general terms of his hope to provoke a war with Austria. But ultimately the two leaders wanted different things. There was also no personal chemistry between the two: Cavour's ambition was to expel Austria from northern Italy and he abhorred the populism and idealism of Garibaldi. On the other hand, Garibaldi disliked Cavour's intellectual air and what he perceived as a sense of self-importance. In *The Risorgimento* (1962), the historian Agatha Ramm argued that 'it was due to Cavour that any of the aims of the *Risorgimento* were achieved, but it was due to him, some of the richness of the *Risorgimento* was inevitably lost'. This is not surprising, as Cavour stood against so much of what Garibaldi believed in and rejected the 'democratic' element of the *Risorgimento* that Garibaldi so fervently supported. It is clear that throughout the extraordinary episode which is about to be explained, Cavour struggled to regain control of the situation. In *Cavour* (1985), Denis Mack Smith suggests that Cavour's inaction in preventing Garibaldi sailing from Genoa on 6 May 1860 was part of a wider political paralysis, leaving Cavour in a dangerous predicament. If he was seen to help Garibaldi he would run the risk of alienating France and moderate opinion in Piedmont, which feared the consequences of Garibaldi's revolutionary activity. If he refused to support such a popular adventure he would be seen to be restraining action undertaken in the Italian interest. In a letter dated 16 May 1860, and addressed to fellow politician Ricasoli, Cavour clearly expressed the difficulty of his situation.

SOURCE

Letter from Cavour to Baron Ricasoli, 16 May 1860. Cavour was the prime minister of Piedmont, Ricasoli led the Tuscan moderates in favour of a union between Tuscany and Piedmont.

It is great good fortune that he [Garibaldi] gave up on the idea of attacking the Pope. He cannot be stopped from making war on the Kingdom of Naples. It may be good, it may be bad, but it was inevitable. If we had tried to restrain Garibaldi by force he would have become a real domestic problem. Now what will happen? It is impossible to predict. Will England help him? It is possible. Will France oppose him? I don't think so. And what about us? We cannot support him openly, nor can we encourage private efforts on his behalf. We have therefore decided not to allow any more sailings from Genoa or Livorno, but also not to prevent the despatch of arms and ammunition, provided they are sent off with a certain prudence. I fully recognise all of the disadvantages of the ambiguous line that we are adopting, but I cannot work out any other policy that doesn't have even greater dangers.

Garibaldi and Victor Emmanuel

Garibaldi's relationship with Victor Emmanuel was different. They met for the first time in March 1859 and they were reported to have got on well. Garibaldi was useful to a king who, on occasions, wished to circumvent his leading ministers, notably Cavour. He represented direct action as opposed to the slower and more frustrating wheels of diplomacy. Garibaldi was prepared to act in the name of the king on the understanding that he was doing so for the benefit of Italy, rather than the promotion of Piedmont's interests. Therefore, for example, Garibaldi was prepared to defer to the king for the sake of Italy. In the wake of Villafranca in the autumn of 1859, Garibaldi had the means to threaten Rome. However, he resisted moving on the city (despite encouragement from Mazzini) because he did not wish to counter the king. But, ultimately, Victor Emmanuel and Cavour both mistrusted Garibaldi's popularity. They also greatly feared the character of this popularity, especially in 1860 when Garibaldi was treated in the south as a demi-god. Both conservatives, Victor Emmanuel and Cavour perceived Garibaldi's followers to be 'red republicans' and 'socialists demagogues'. As we will see, this mistrust shaped their relationships and the nature of the unification process. The events of 1860 disillusioned Mazzini. He was to denounce the methods of Cavour as the 'Machiavellian calculations of expediency'. He also dismissed the unification process: 'I had thought to evoke the soul of Italy; all I see before me is its corpse.'

Expedition to and success in Sicily

On 11 May 1860, Garibaldi and his volunteer army landed in Marsala, Sicily. The island of Sicily was part of the Kingdom of Naples and ruled by the Bourbons. They were met with suspicion but little opposition. Luck was very much on the invaders side as the Bourbon navy had sailed southwards the previous night. The Bourbon army was routed at Calatafimi on 15 May and the locals now acclaimed the cause of 'Italia e Vittorio Emanuele'. The ranks of The Thousand were swelled with new Sicilian recruits as they marched on Palermo. Garibaldi's The Thousand may well have been poorly armed with dated muskets. However, they were well trained and superbly led. Garibaldi was a first-rate military commander who was surrounded by a small group of similarly experienced soldiers.

On 26 May, they infiltrated Palermo at night and then endured three brutal days of street fighting before seizing the capital. It was an astonishing victory against an army 20,000 strong. It was partly explained by the financial crisis which had gripped the Bourbon regime and the unsettling effect of the death of Ferdinand II in 1859 and the succession of his son Francesco. By the time of Garibaldi's invasion, the Bourbon government was unpopular and weak. Garibaldi and his guerrilla army were also ably aided by local revolutionaries and easily outfought poorly motivated Bourbon conscripts. An armistice was signed on 2 June and the island of Sicily was conquered by the end of July.

SOURCE

7 Giuseppe Garibaldi entering Palermo 27 May 1860. The artist is unknown.

ENTRATA DI GARIBALDI IN PALERMO

Reforms in Sicily

Garibaldi appointed Francesco Crispi as secretary of state in Sicily. He went about introducing a series of reforms including the abolition of the unpopular tax on milling, the *macinato*. In an assault on the feudal social structures, titles including *Eccellenza* (Your Excellency) were abolished and common land divided up. A programme of modernisation was launched which included public works, investment in education and confiscation of Church property. To the relief of the middle classes, Crispi acted to ensure that there was to be no social revolution or disorder. Local irregular troops were conscripted and looting prohibited. The problem for Garibaldi, Crispi and others was that their intervention had raised expectations. The slow redistribution of land led to land occupations and instances of banditry increased. Matters were not helped by Crispi's rather abrasive manner and clear contempt for the idea of Sicilian autonomy.

EXTEND YOUR KNOWLEDGE

Cavour's reaction

Perhaps the most contentious example of Cavour's pragmatism was his reaction to Garibaldi's invasion of Sicily and Naples in 1860.

In Denis Mack Smith's *Cavour and Garibaldi: A Study in Political Conflict* (1854) the author turned on its head the stereotype of Cavour as a far-sighted, cool statesman and Garibaldi as a hot-headed and rash freedom-fighter. Instead Mack Smith gave examples of Garibaldi's 'moderate and unrevolutionary' attitudes and his often 'cautious' 'statesmanship'. On the other hand, Cavour was represented as being often 'mistaken' and 'deceitful'. According to Mack Smith, Cavour was determined at all cost to prevent unification if it meant that popular or democratic forces were likely to gain power. He had no plan and simply reacted to events; often his reactions being characterised by outbursts of rage leading to snap decisions. The events of 1860 stand as a case in point. The government set in Sicily worried Cavour because of the predominance of Mazzinians such as Crispi.

His response was to attempt to interfere through the use of agents. Cavour sent his agent, Giuseppe La Farina, to Sicily to claim its annexation to Piedmont. However, Garibaldi was not quite ready to hand over his hard-fought gains just yet. Indeed, La Farina was not a good choice given the fact that he had supported the transfer of Nice to France. On 7 July 1860, La Farina was expelled from Sicily empty-handed. A more acceptable envoy, Agostino Depretis, was despatched instead. None the less, he failed to stop Garibaldi embarking for the mainland on 19 August. It was Cavour's ability to gamble when necessary that secured the Italy of his liking.

Invasion and takeover of Naples

Cavour reacts

For Cavour the danger was that the situation was developing out of his control. At this stage, he still did not envisage a unified Italy including the south. Even more worrying for Cavour was that Garibaldi might initially aim to invade Naples, although he knew that his ultimate target was Rome. But any threatening of Rome would result in opposition from the French, and Cavour realised that any resulting conflict would end in a French victory. The British, however, were sympathetic to Garibaldi's expedition, and the crossing of the Straits of Messina was undertaken under the watchful and sympathetic eye of the Royal Navy. Those wishing to stop Garibaldi now attempted to act, but their efforts were too little, too late. Cavour ordered Admiral Persano of the Piedmontese navy to sail to Naples and organise a pro-Piedmont insurrection before Garibaldi arrived in the city. He failed; the people of Naples were not interested. In the face of Garibaldi's success, Cavour had to reassess his attitude to the whole episode. The ruler of Naples, Francesco II, formed a liberal ministry in late June 1860 and restored the 1848 constitution in early July. He failed to convince his subjects that his political conversion was authentic. Prompted by Louis Napoleon, Cavour worked behind the scenes for an alliance with the Bourbons against Garibaldi. He also sent messages to King Francesco of Naples suggesting an alliance. At the same time, though, his agents were working hard in Naples attempting to provoke an uprising against the Bourbons that would justify Piedmontese intervention. Simultaneously, Cavour was working hard to contain the impact of Garibaldi's actions. Although he was prepared to entertain the possibility of a united peninsula, he was not prepared to accept it as a democratic Italy.

Garibaldi invades

Garibaldi launched his invasion of the Italian mainland in August 1860 in the name of 'Victor Emmanuel and Italy'. However, it was not the Italy envisaged by a far more conservative Cavour. It was Cavour's ability to gamble when necessary that secured the Italy of his liking. As Garibaldi's invasion of the mainland proved to be a success, so the urgency of the situation for Cavour became even greater. It was important for Cavour that he was seen to support Garibaldi. The king and many in the Piedmontese parliament hailed Garibaldi's actions in liberating the south from the rule of the despotic Bourbons. On 9 August 1860, Cavour wrote to the Piedmontese diplomat Costantino Nigra showing an acute understanding of Garibaldi's actions (Source 8). On 18 August, Garibaldi and a force of 3,500 crossed the sea and landed successfully on the mainland. The Bourbon forces were in disarray and fell back to a point north of Naples. The last Bourbon king of Naples, Francesco II, fled his capital on 6 September. Garibaldi was able to enter Naples without opposition which he did on 7 September 1860, taking a train from Salerno. He was met by wildly enthusiastic crowds. The Bourbon capital had fallen without a shot being fired.

SOURCE 8

Letter from Count Cavour to Costantino Nigra, 9 August 1860. Nigra was a Piedmontese diplomat and a close confidante of Cavour.

You suggest recalling parliament and having a big parliamentary battle; nothing would please me more. But even though this might succeed in saving my prestige, I think it might lose Italy. My dear Nigra, I can tell you without labouring the point that I would readily lose my popularity and reputation so long as Italy were made. But to make Italy, as things now stand, Victor Emmanuel and Garibaldi must not be set against each other.

Garibaldi has great moral power. He commands enormous prestige in Italy, and even more in the rest of Europe. In my view you are mistaken when you say that I stand as Europe's defence against him. If tomorrow I were to fight against Garibaldi, even though most of the old diplomats might approve, European public opinion would be against me, and rightly so. Garibaldi has done Italy the greatest service that a man could do; he has given the Italians self-confidence; he has proved to Europe that Italians can fight and die in battle to reconquer a fatherland.

There are only two possible occasions in which we would contemplate a fight against Garibaldi: -

1 If he wanted to drag us into a war against France.

2 If he repudiated his present programme and turned against the monarchy and Victor Emmanuel. As long as he remains loyal, we are forced to march at his side.

This notwithstanding, it would be highly desirable if a revolution in Naples came about without him, for that would reduce his influence to reasonable dimensions. If, in spite of all of our efforts, he should liberate southern Italy as he has liberated Sicily, we would have no choice but to go along with him and wholeheartedly.

HOW DID ITALY UNITE IN 1860–61?

Garibaldi's decision to take Rome and the response of Piedmont

Roma o morte

Cavour knew that Garibaldi's ultimate target was Rome, not Naples. He understood that the events of 1849 had left an indelible mark on the great adventurer's mind and that the appeal of the rallying cry 'Roma o morte' ('Rome or death') was as great in 1860 as it had been 11 years earlier. Yet an invasion of the Papal States by a democratically-inspired force would destroy Cavour's diplomatic initiative. The threat of such an invasion was real. Not only did Garibaldi possess a force some 20,000 strong (and possibly greater), but also a force some 9,000 strong led by Agostino Bertani (a supporter of Mazzini) had amassed on the border of the Papal States. Garibaldi planned to push on from Naples with the aim of entering Rome in November and before winter had set in. Cavour's clear option was to invade the Papal States in order to forestall any further action on Garibaldi's behalf. Even if this meant upsetting the pope and possibly the French, it was a risk Cavour felt he should take. On 11 September 1860, the Piedmontese army invaded the Papal States. In protest, the French government broke off diplomatic relations with Piedmont but to little avail. On 18 September, the Piedmontese forces crushed the papal army at Castelfidardo.

EXTEND YOUR KNOWLEDGE

Invasion of the Papal States

The historian Gaetano Salvemini wrote in his book *Mazzini* (1948) that the unification of Italy was not the result of a harmony of ideas born of the *Risorgimento* but of a struggle: 'In reality there was in the struggle a winner and a loser; the winner was Cavour, the loser Mazzini.' Salvemini was suggesting that the victory was that of the moderates rather than the democrats. However, he was under no illusions how this happened, claiming that Italy was unified 'by the knife of Shylock'. The invasion of the Papal States by Piedmontese forces in September 1860 was Cavour's masterstroke. On his orders, an uprising in the Papal States was engineered and the Piedmontese invited in. From that moment the creation of an Italy based on Cavour's vision rather than Garibaldi's or Mazzini's was assured.

By the middle of September, relations between Cavour and Garibaldi had all but broken down. However, Garibaldi faced an even graver threat with a counter-attack by Bourbon forces north of Naples. Despite being heavily outnumbered and despite losing more men, Garibaldi's army prevailed at the Battle of the Volturno (which lasted from 26 September to 2 October). However, it was the Piedmontese victory at Castelfidaro a month earlier that decided the fate of the south. Garibaldi's victory opened the way to a convergence of forces fighting in the name of Victor Emmanuel II.

The significance of the meeting at Teano

Meeting at Teano

From 3 October 1860, the Piedmontese army was led in person by Victor Emmanuel. On 26 October, Garibaldi and Victor Emmanuel met at the head of the two armies at Teano. The meeting was a tense affair despite the attempts of *Risorgimento* historians to claim otherwise. The crowd acclaimed Garibaldi but ignored the king, much to his disquiet. On 6 November, the king failed to turn up to a review of Garibaldi's troops at Caserta. A triumphal entry of Naples was stage-managed on 7 November, and Garibaldi formally handed his conquests over to the king. Garibaldi had demanded that he was made viceroy of the south but Victor Emmanuel refused, it was inconceivable for him to appoint someone of Garibaldi's political leanings to such a post. The king's offer to appoint Garibaldi as a general in the new Italian army was rejected. Thereafter, Garibaldi was politically isolated despite the fact he had just completed the conquest of nearly half of the Italian peninsula in the name of the Piedmontese king! In Piedmont, Garibaldi was not portrayed as a hero but as an illiberal, authoritarian figure. Indeed, he helped to encourage this image by asking for special powers to rule the south for another year. These were refused. So he left for his island home of Caprera promising, rather ominously for Victor Emmanuel, to return to free Rome and Venice, which were still in foreign hands. The meeting at Teano and the events surrounding confirmed Piedmontese annexation of the south and Garibaldi's surrendering of all of the political gains made that year. Garibaldi's revolution had been defeated and his withdrawal to Caprera meant that the democrats were without a leader at a crucial moment. It also led to divisions between moderates and democrats which were to sour the political culture and system of the new state.

SOURCE 9

Right leg in the boot at last. Giuseppe Garibaldi struggling to fit Victor Emmanuel II with the boot of Italy: 'If it won't go on, Sire, try a little more powder.' Engraving in *Punch*, 17 November 1860.

SOURCE 10

Garibaldi reflects on the events of April and May 1860 in his memoirs. His memoirs were first published in various languages between 1859 and 1861. There were revised in the 1870s at various points between1871 and 1873. They have been viewed with suspicion by most historians who believe that Garibaldi distorts the reality of what happened.

Every possible obstacle was raised in our path [by Cavour and the Piedmont government]… Some people tried to argue that the government could have stopped us and let us go, but I deny that they could have stopped us. Public opinion was irresistibly on our side from the first moment that news spread of the Sicilian rising in April 1860. It is true that the government put no absolute veto in our way; nevertheless they raised every kind of obstacle…

However, once we had taken Palermo, the liberation of all Sicily became almost certain, and the Piedmontese government therefore allowed a second expedition of volunteers to join us who proved of great help. But Cavour's new plan was still that we should go no further than Sicily, and with this purpose he sent La Farina and others to campaign in Sicily for immediate annexation to Piedmont. These men did all they possibly could to bring about their petty objective [i.e., annexation, which would have prevented Garibaldi from going on to attack Naples]…

Even greater difficulties were placed in my path at Naples. Everyone knows how Cavour sent a host of secret agents there who did what they could with the local conservative committee to bring about their own revolution before I had time to reach Naples.

SOURCE

From a letter written by Count Cavour to Costantino Nigra dated 1 August 1860. Nigra was a Piedmontese diplomat and a close confidante of Cavour. Cavour considers his options as Garibaldi threatens to invade the mainland.

If Garibaldi proceeds to the mainland of southern Italy and captures Naples just as he has already taken Sicily and Palermo, he becomes absolute master of the situation. King Victor Emmanuel would lose almost all his prestige in the eyes of nearly all Italians, who would look on him as little more than the friend of Garibaldi; and though probably he would remain king, he would merely bask in such reflected glory as this heroic adventurer might decide to allow him.

Garibaldi, if he should reach Naples, would not proclaim a republic, but he would remain dictator, and would refuse to annex southern Italy to Piedmont. His prestige would then be irresistible... We would be forced to go along with his plans and help him fight Austria...

I have no illusions about the grave and dangerous decision I am advocating, but I believe it is essential if we are to save the monarchic principle. Better than a king of Piedmont should perish in war against Austria than be swamped by the revolution. The dynasty might recover from a defeat in battle, but if dragged through the revolutionary gutter its fate would be finally sealed.

Although I have made up my mind how to act if Garibaldi reaches Naples, it is nevertheless my first duty to the king and Italy to do everything possible to prevent his success there.

SOURCE

Memo dictated by Victor Emmanuel II to an aide, Count Trecchi, on 5 August 1860 to be conveyed to Garibaldi.

Garibaldi in Naples. Will regulate himself according to opportunity, either occupying Umbria and the Marches with his troops, or allowing bands of volunteers to go. As soon as Garibaldi is in Naples he will proclaim its union to the rest of Italy as in Sicily. Prevent disorders which would harm our cause. Keep the Neapolitan army in being, for Austria will soon declare war. Let the King of Naples escape, and if he is taken by the people, save him and let him escape.

SOURCE 13

From the memoirs of Count H. d'Ideville who was secretary of the French embassy in Turin. This reflection was written in 1861 and was published in Paris in 1872.

Like all mediocre men, Victor Emmanuel is jealous and quick to take umbrage. He will find it difficult to forget the manner of his triumphal entry into Naples – he was presented to his new people by the most powerful of his subjects. People are mistaken in crediting Victor Emmanuel with a lively liking for Garibaldi.... The frankness with which the King has spoken of him on certain occasions shows the real measure of his appreciation of the man. It was in the month of June 1860; Garibaldi had just landed in Sicily, and the result of his venturesome expedition was not yet known in Turin, when the French Minister, Baron de Talleyrand, was ordered to present a note to the Turin cabinet... complaining bitterly of this fresh violation of the Law of Nations. After his audience with the sovereign, the French Minister felt convinced that His Majesty was far less pleased with the hero's attempt than people imagined. "Mon Dieu" said the monarch to M. de Talleyrand, "of course it would be a great misfortune, but if the Neapolitan cruisers were to capture and hang my poor Garibaldi he would have brought this sad fate upon himself. It would simplify things a good deal. What a fine monument we should get erected to him!"

That day, certainly, the King would have been easily consoled for the death of the Captain of the Thousand. The bold attempt succeeded, thanks to the courage and prestige of Garibaldi, greatly assisted by Neapolitan treason. Naples gave itself to Garibaldi, and Garibaldi offered his conquest to the King. But to anyone in Turin who has followed events closely, it must be evident that, far from instigating and organising the invasion of the Two Sicilies, Cavour at least at first did try to oppose it. It was not till he realised that he could not possibly put a stop to the enterprise, outflanked as had been by the Garibaldian war party, that he kept aloof, tolerating everything, and prepared to take advantage, as he did, of a conquest he rightly considered dangerous and premature.

A Level Exam-Style Question Section A

How far could the historian make use of Sources 10 and 11 together to investigate Garibaldi's invasion of the south of Italy?

Explain your answer using the sources, the information given about them and your knowledge of the historical context. (20 marks)

Tip
Make sure that you carefully consider the purpose of each author.

A Level Exam-Style Question Section A

How far could the historian make use of Sources 12 and 13 together to investigate Victor Emmanuel's role in the events of 1859–60?

Explain your answer using the sources, the information given about them and your knowledge of the historical context. (20 marks)

Tip
Assess the similarities and differences between these two sources.

THINKING HISTORICALLY Evidence (6a)

Arguments and facts

Work in groups. Read through Sources 10–13.

1 Why are facts important in history?

2 Look again at Sources 10 and 11.

　a) How do these sources agree and how do they differ?

　b) Which one do you think is more accurate? Explain your answer.

3 Look again at Sources 12 and 13.

　a) How do these sources disagree?

　b) What were Victor Emmanuel's and Cavour's attitudes towards Garibaldi's invasion of Sicily? Do you think that these authors, whose accounts differ in terms of the facts, would have viewed Victor Emmanuel's and Cavour's attitudes differently from you? Explain your answer.

4 All these sources give detailed views about the actions of other individuals but they only briefly mention the events of the invasion of Sicily. Which do you think is more important?

5 If we accept that Source 10 is highly subjective, do we discount it as being useful? Explain your answer.

Plebiscites in the south and papal territories

Garibaldi's decision

The question for Garibaldi was what he should do next. The radicals in Naples urged him to set up an assembly to negotiate terms of union with Piedmont. But Garibaldi hesitated and then decided to accept Cavour's request that a plebiscite be held to decide on whether to accept annexation by Piedmont or not. In so doing, Garibaldi accepted the likelihood of immediate annexation and the handing over of his powers to Victor Emmanuel. The plebiscites were arranged in the south with the simple question: 'One Italy, Victor Emmanuel: yes or no?' The result was not surprising, although enthusiasm for the Piedmontese king was limited. Most Sicilians and Neapolitans were voting for the end of the feudal monarchy of the Bourbon family.

The voting figures for the plebiscites held on 21 October 1860 were as follows.

	Yes	No
Sicily	432,053	667
Naples	1,302,064	10,312

The votes were held in public rather than through a secret ballot. A no vote would have suggested a desire to restore the Bourbon monarchy, which was inconceivable. Therefore, in many senses the plebiscites were little more than a charade and this was reflected in the outcome. The historian Martin Clark wrote in *The Italian Risorgimento* (1998): 'Hitler and Stalin in their heyday never received results like this.' The voting in the south was followed by plebiscites arranged in the more northerly provinces of the Marches and Umbria that were held in November 1860.

The voting figures for these ballots held in November 1860 were as follows.

	Yes	No
The Marches	133,765	1,212
Umbria	97,040	360

EXTEND YOUR KNOWLEDGE

Cavour and the plebiscites

The speed with which Cavour had plebiscites organised and the extent to which they were, again, fixed is evidence of his political effectiveness. In reality, Garibaldi was outmanoeuvred. In *Italy: A Modern History* (1959), Denis Mack Smith points out how a deputy of the Italian Parliament referred to Cavour as 'a cross between Robert Peel and Machiavelli'. He stressed, quite correctly, that Cavour's actions in 1860 were not those of a man with a desire to see Italy unified. Indeed, he acted because, as Mack Smith pointed out, 'he disliked revolutionary republicanism more than he loved national unity'. As a result, he responded to Garibaldi's invasion of the mainland with a strategy aimed at 'outdoing [the revolutionaries] at their own game'.

The kingdom of Italy established

View of the foreign powers

Few of the foreign powers showed great enthusiasm for developments in Italy. A meeting of the rulers of Austria, Prussia and Russia in Warsaw in October 1860 received the news of Piedmontese expansion coolly. It was even suggested that the Austrians might invade Lombardy while Piedmontese forces were engaged elsewhere. Although this plan came to nothing, it reveals the diplomatic tension surrounding the expansion of Piedmontese influence. Although the memories of Bonapartist expansion in Italy were, by now, more than 40 years old, they were still fresh enough to influence British foreign policy. The Villafranca agreement of 1859 between France and Austria raised the spectre of a Franco-Austrian entente over northern Italy that the British government would not accept. The Crimean War had shown that the balance of power in Europe was shifting. Palmerston and Russell were determined that part of this shifting power did not result in increased foreign domination of the Italian peninsula. The French annexation of Nice and Savoy agreed in March 1860 was bitterly opposed by Palmerston who told d'Azeglio that: '[Napoleon] has vast conceptions [ideas] which he plans to realise and which will force us to make war.'

By late 1860, the situation for Russell was critical. He was worried about the possibility of both French and Austrian expansion in Italy. As the armies of Victor Emmanuel were involved in the south in the autumn of 1860, so Russell feared some backlash against events in Italy. In October 1860, the emperors of Austria, Prussia and Russia met at Warsaw. But they failed to come up with a plan to tackle what they considered to be an Italian 'revolution'. Instead, Russia broke diplomatic relations in protest at the unseating of the ruling House of Bourbon in Naples, and Austria reinforced its army in Venetia. However, the three monarchies did not come up with a plan to prevent the unification of the peninsula. The prospect of conservative action was enough for Russell. On 27 October 1860, he issued a public note that was to have a profound impact on the course of events and, more than any other factor, was to confirm the events of the previous day, when Garibaldi met with Victor Emmanuel at Teano. While Louis Napoleon expressed concern that the papacy was under threat, Russell's pronouncements effectively destroyed the Treaty of Vienna once and for all. He asserted British support for the newly unified Italy because it was the result of the assertion of what Russell saw as the popular will. Of course, the process of unification had nothing to do with popular will, but this was not the point. Russell praised the idea of 'a people building up the edifice of their liberties'. In a second note, Russell attacked the despotic rule of the Papal States and the Kingdom of Naples, and clearly warned that if any other power intervened to undermine the new state, then Britain would intervene militarily. But the note was never sent, because Queen Victoria, who was more sympathetic to Austria, had misgivings about its content. However, the support expressed in the first note acted as a guarantee of the new state. Russell's actions should, therefore, be seen as critically important.

The Italian state

The constitution of that year imposed the legal structures, political institutions, foreign policy and cultural norms of Piedmont on the rest of Italy. In January 1861, elections were held for the parliament of the new Italian kingdom and the constitution adopted in March 1861 was based on the *Piedmontese Statuto* of 1848.

- Symbolically, the king, Victor Emmanuel, remained 'the Second' (as he was of Piedmont) rather than 'the First' (as of the new state).

- As a constitutional monarchy, the sovereign body of the state would be the king in parliament.

- The Chamber of Deputies of the parliament was elected on a minimal suffrage of approximately two percent of the population.

- The state's administrative structure was centralised. At a local level, prefects (who were often from the north) wielded considerable power and influence in the name of the Crown.

- Piedmontese taxes, weights and measures and, most important, the idea of free trade were imposed on the rest of Italy.

ACTIVITY
KNOWLEDGE CHECK

1 How did Italy unite in 1861? Choose five factors and put them on a spider chart. Compare your factors with those chosen by someone else in your class.

2 Cavour, Victor Emmanuel, Garibaldi – who should be given the most credit for Italian unification and why?

EXTEND YOUR KNOWLEDGE

Cavour and the constitution

Part of the proof of Cavour's limited nationalist ambitions was the nature of the constitution imposed on Italy in 1861. In *Cavour* (1985), Mack Smith is generous in his interpretation that the constitutional settlement was created by the speed with which unification took place between 1859 and 1861. Indeed, Mack Smith goes so far as to stress that, at heart, Cavour was a believer in 'decentralisation' of power but for pragmatic reasons acted otherwise. Mack Smith also points to Cavour's decision in 1860 to ask the ministers of the interior Luigi Farini and Marco Minghetti to conduct an investigation into the possibility of some kind of regional autonomy. Their proposals included a plan for some form of devolution with regional governors and assemblies. At a local level mayors would be elected. However, the scheme was half-hearted and eventually dismissed in 1861 by the new Italian Parliament. That said, Mack Smith does recognise that despite promising some degree of autonomy to Tuscany and Sicily for much of 1860, in the end Cavour 'never went out of his way to push it politically'.

A Level Exam-Style Question Section B

'Cavour was not so much the architect of unification but simply a politician reacting to events as they unfolded.'

How far do you agree with this statement? (20 marks)

Tip
In your plan, assess the arguments for and against and make sure that your response has balance.

AS Level Exam-Style Question Section B

How far was Garibaldi responsible for the unification of Italy in 1861? (20 marks)

Tip
Assess the extent to which Garibaldi was responsible and the extent to which he was not.

ACTIVITY
SUMMARY

Answer the following questions:

1 What are the five main events on the road to unification?

2 All of the main powers had a role to play in the unification process. Which were more significant and which were less so?

WIDER READING

Clark, M. *The Italian Risorgimento* (Seminar Studies in History), Pearson Education (2009)

di Lampedusa, G. *The Leopard*, Casa editrice Feltrinelli (1958)

Gooch, J. *The Unification of Italy* (Lancaster Pamphlets), Routledge (1986)

Hearder, H. *Italy: A Short History*, Cambridge University Press (1990)

2a.4 Consolidating the kingdom of Italy, 1861–70

KEY QUESTIONS

- How serious were the major obstacles to unity after 1861?
- How successfully was the 'Venetian Question' solved?
- How effectively was the problem of Rome resolved?
- To what extent was Italy unified in 1870?

KEY TERMS

Irredentist
An irredentist is someone who believed that lands containing Italian speakers which adjoined the new state, e.g. Trent, Trieste, Istria, should become part of Italy. The term derives from the phrase *Italia irredenta*, which means 'unredeemed Italy'.

Brigands
Bandits who lived in the forests and mountains emerging to cause havoc when they chose. Brigandage had a strong tradition in the south of Italy, most noticeably during the Napoleonic wars. To many in the south, the brigands were their protectors against the excesses of the new state. During Garibaldi's campaign in 1860, around 10,000 convicts escaped from prisons, many of them taking to the hills and becoming brigands.

INTRODUCTION

The nature of the unification of Italy – imposed from above by Piedmont – was to cause many problems for Italy. From 1861, various national institutions served and strengthened the new state. The monarchy, parliament, civil service, armed forces and local government promoted the concept of unity but the reality of Italian unity in 1861 was somewhat different. Austrian and French occupation of Venice and Rome respectively meant that, in the eyes of most nationalists, unification was not yet complete. Attempts by Garibaldi, encouraged by the king and some of his ministers, to destabilise Austrian rule in Venice came to nothing. However, in 1866, Venice was surrendered by Austria after a humiliating defeat at the hands of Prussia and a subsequent alliance between Italy and Prussia meant that Venice became part of the Italian state. In the same year a crushing defeat of Italian forces on land and sea at the hands of the Austrians was to have a negative impact on national morale and self-esteem.

Rome became part of the Italian state in similar circumstances to Venice. A war between Prussia and France led to the withdrawal of French troops from Rome and, in September 1870, troops of the Italian state marched through the gates of the Eternal City. But even with the incorporation of Venice and Rome, Italian-speaking communities continued to exist outside the borders of the new state, notably in Trieste, Trent, Istria, Nice and Fiume. Those nationalists who agitated for the inclusion of these areas in Italy, so called **irredentists**, would continue to act as critics of the new state.

On the foundation of the new Italian state, the former Piedmontese prime minister, Massimo d'Azeglio, warned: 'We have made Italy, now we must make Italians.' The task of so doing was considerable. D'Azeglio regretted the inclusion of the south in the new state and the problematic relationship between the north and southern Italy – the 'Southern Question' – would persist. The imposition of Piedmontese institutions, customs and laws on the rest of Italy, so-called Piedmontisation, was to cause considerable disquiet in a country dominated by a localist culture and mentality. In the south, thousands of so-called **brigands** took to the countryside to wage a campaign of lawlessness and terror.

1864 – September: September Convention; French agree to evacuate Rome within two years

1861 – Death of Cavour

1864 – **December:** Papacy issues the Syllabus of Errors

1861	1862	1863	1864	1865	1866

1862 – Garibaldi's unsuccessful expedition to capture Rome ends at Aspromonte

1866 – Austro-Prussian war. Venetia ceded to Italy

SOURCE
1

Plebiscite in Venice. Engraving in *L'Illustration* from a sketch by Martino Dei Don, 1866.

L'ILLUSTRATION, JOURNAL UNIVERSEL.

LE PLÉBISCITE. — Les habitants de Venise allant voter à Saint-Laurent. — D'après un croquis de M. Martino Dei Don.

But the north–south divide was not the only obstacle which hindered the development of the new state. The Catholic Church, shorn of much of its temporal power, stood as an implacable opponent to the new Italy. In response to the seizure of Rome by the forces of the new state, in October 1870, the pope declared himself a 'prisoner in the Vatican'. The opposition of the Church to the new state was of profound importance, especially given the extent of its influence. In addition, the unification of Italy, in an economic sense, was superficial at best. The removal of **tariffs** and the exposure of the southern economy to full competition was to cause considerable economic damage and was to exacerbate social unrest. It is no exaggeration to state that unification was a disaster for industry in the south and its economy as a whole.

KEY TERM

Tariff
A tariff is a tax which is raised on an item coming into a country. The result of a tariff is that the item is more expensive because of the additional tax. The purposes of tariffs are to protect the home economy and raise money.

1867 – Garibaldi's second attempt to take Rome halted by the French at Mentana

1871 – May: Law of Guarantees defines relationship between Church and state

| 1867 | 1868 | 1869 | 1870 | 1871 | 1872 |

1870 – July: Second Vatican Council proclaims doctrine of papal infallibility

August: Outbreak of war between Prussia and France leads to withdrawal of French garrison from Rome

October: Rome annexed to Italy after plebiscite

HOW SERIOUS WERE THE MAJOR OBSTACLES TO UNITY AFTER 1861?

Austrian and French influence

While the kingdom of Italy had been established, the unification of Italy was, as yet, incomplete. French troops still occupied Rome in defence of the pope and Emperor Louis Napoleon was not prepared to withdraw his support until papal power had been assured. In late 1860, Louis Napoleon proposed that if the Marches and Umbria were returned to papal control and the Abruzzi (which had been part of the Kingdom of Naples) was thrown in for good measure, then French troops would withdraw from Rome. However, such an arrangement was not satisfactory for King Victor Emmanuel or the new Italian government. Neither were prepared to cede control of territory to the papacy.

The loss of Lombardy was a real blow to the Habsburgs; it had been the jewel of their Italian possessions. But the Austrians had no intention of quitting Venice where they continued to maintain a large army. Victor Emmanuel understood that Austria's position was supported by, among others, the British (and notably Queen Victoria) who believed that a strong Austria was essential for stability in Europe. Numerous schemes, however, were hatched by others to destabilise the Austrian Empire; for example, during the Franco-Austrian war in 1859, Cavour had been in touch with Hungarian revolutionary leaders to discuss the possibility of uprisings within the empire. But such schemes came to nothing. The reality in 1861 was that France and Austria maintained their influence in Italy. They were both militarily and diplomatically more powerful than the new Italian state and both determined to preserve their position.

The papacy

In March 1861, Cavour faced fierce opposition to his government and the new state from the Catholic Church. Indeed, because of the loss of two-thirds of its land to the new state, the Catholic Church refused to recognise Italy's existence. The Church was also threatened by the belief of most Italians that Rome was the natural capital of Italy. The significance of the hostility of the Church should not be underestimated; it retrenched division and undermined the new state's legitimacy. The destruction of the papacy's temporal power had been one of the most significant aspects of the *Risorgimento*; in 1861, Cavour hoped to persuade the Church to give up its last vestige by surrendering Rome. In return he would offer the Church freedom of action. In March 1861, he made a speech promising 'a free Church in a free State'. However, the Church was unresponsive to Cavour's suggestions. It broke off any negotiations about the potential future of Rome, urging Catholics to adopt the position first coined by the editor of a leading Catholic newspaper in Turin: 'neither electors nor elected'. So began a fractious co-habitation between Church and state which was to last for many decades.

The Syllabus of Errors

The Church was not just under threat from the increasing power of the state. While the loss of temporal power as a result of the political unification of Italy was a bitter blow, its spiritual supremacy was also under attack from the advance of scientific thought and theory. The belief put forward by Charles Darwin, in *On the Origin of Species* (1859) that humankind evolved was a direct challenge to the theory of creation as explained in the Book of Genesis in the Bible. Similarly challenging was the view held by those such as the French Catholic Ernest Renan in the early 1860s that the Bible should not be treated as a completely accurate history of events. The response of the papacy was to issue the Syllabus of Errors in 1864, centred at least in part on a defence of orthodox Catholic views against Darwinism. In the Syllabus, Pius rejected most of the philosophies developed in the 19th century from communism to nationalism and liberalism to rationalism. In addition, in the Syllabus the Church:

- claimed control over the education system and all culture and science

- rejected the idea of tolerance for other religions

- asserted the idea of the continuing temporal power of the papacy.

The Syllabus was a direct criticism of the main tenets of liberalism. It attacked religious toleration, freedom of expression and thought, as well as all the 'isms' of the 19th century – including socialism, liberalism, nationalism and communism. At the heart of the Syllabus was the assertion that neither the papacy nor Catholics as a whole should accept 'progress, liberalism, and modern civilisation'. The publication of the Syllabus of Errors provoked an outburst of anti-clericalism from enemies of the Church in Italy and beyond. Mazzini suggested that the papacy had hurled down a 'gauntlet of defiance against the 19th century'. The Syllabus of Errors disappointed the more liberal Catholics who had hoped that Pius IX was still capable of modernising the Church, although it pleased the more traditionally minded. Pius IX's attempts to halt the advance of nationalism and the other 'isms' of the 19th century so roundly condemned in the Syllabus of Errors was very much 'swimming against the tide'. Yet in doing so and, meanwhile, strengthening and reinforcing its spiritual leadership, Pius laid the foundations for the future strength of the Catholic Church in Italy and beyond.

Papal infallibility

The new Italian state suppressed monastic orders and forced the Church to increase taxation payments to the state. In 1866, a law was passed demanding that most religious orders should hand over all property to the state. The tension between Church and state reflected the declining temporal power of the Church and an important shift in its priorities. From now on, the Church was to focus more heavily on its spiritual role. Without doubt, throughout the trials and tribulations of the *Risorgimento*, the overriding aim of Pius IX was to protect the power of the papacy. One of Pius's and Cardinal Antonelli's greatest concerns was that a number of Catholics across Europe were liberals who increasingly questioned the Church and its teaching. After the defeat of Austria in 1866 by Prussia, German Catholics were vulnerable to criticism by a Protestant Prussian government that might question their loyalty to the new north German state. However, Pius' concern was that, in an age of the developing nation state, Catholics would be forced to choose between the nation state and the papacy or would have to split their loyalty. In 1865, Pius IX began consulting with his cardinals about the concept of papal infallibility. A Council of the Church was summoned, the first since the 16th century, and, in 1869, the Vatican Council met. The main business of the Council was to agree the dogma of **papal infallibility** which was subsequently proclaimed in July 1870, and marked the spiritual supremacy of the pope. The increase in spiritual dominance of the papacy by 1870 was in direct contrast to the collapse of its temporal power.

KEY TERM

Papal infallibility
The idea of papal infallibility, that the pope's pronouncements on matters relating to faith and morals are indisputable, was not new in the 19th century but goes back as far as AD 519.

EXTEND YOUR KNOWLEDGE

'Legal' and 'Real' Italy
In his book *Modern Italy 1871-1995* (1996), the historian Martin Clark explains the chasm between what he terms 'legal Italy' (the state and its institutions: army, civil service, police) and 'real Italy' (those who were not part of the new 'legal Italy'). The Church, as with many other groups of political 'outsiders' – socialists, anarchists, republicans, most southerners – were alienated from the new state. The unification of Italy had been imposed from above by a political and social elite which believed that the creation of a new Italian state would be in their interests. The process of governing the new state would be tricky; 'Legal Italy' would attempt to absorb into government those who wished to be reconciled to the new state. Those groups and institutions that did not wish to be absorbed, including the Church, would be attacked and repressed.

The reaction to 'Piedmontisation', including the 'Brigands' war', 1861–65

Piedmontisation

The election of January 1861 resulted in a significant victory for Cavour's centre right group, which was now called La Destra ('The 'Right') and which dominated government until 1876. In opposition was the centre left, led by Rattazzi and Agostino Depretis; the far left, which included Garibaldians, democrats from Tuscany and those who argued for a federal state; and the far right, around 20 deputies, some of whom hoped for the restoration of the old order and others of whom were simply reactionary. From the start, the problem for the new Italian state was how to reconcile the new state, its institutions, laws and customs to large areas of Italy which found the new institutions, laws and customs to be alien. Cavour's solution was to 'Piedmontise' all institutions. The laws of the new state on all matters were to be Piedmont's laws. The taxation system, currency and civil service were to all be Piedmontese. But such Piedmontisation reinforced the belief that unification was imposed and without consent. It was acutely felt in a country rich in local tradition and marked regional variation. In addition, the constitution, based on the *Statuto*, allowed the vote to just 2.2 percent of the population. Many Italians felt isolated and betrayed by the imposition of a centralised state that was essentially Piedmont writ large.

The decision was also made that the army should be 'Piedmontised'. The issue for the army was what to do with the remnants of the defeated Bourbon forces and Garibaldi's red-shirted army. Garibaldi's army was disbanded and, in April 1861, Garibaldi appeared in the Chamber of Deputies, furious at the treatment of his soldiers. His main complaint related to the treatment of his 7,000 officers, who had not been incorporated into the Piedmontese army as Garibaldi had hoped. He attacked Cavour for wanting to start a civil war in 1860. Cavour denied the accusation. While the 2,191 officers of the Bourbon army were offered commissions in the new Italian army (they would be useful in dealing with unrest in the south) the foot soldiers were initially herded into insanitary prisoner-of-war camps and then released. Many were to take to the hills of Sicily to fight as brigands against the new regime.

EXTEND YOUR KNOWLEDGE

Cavour and Piedmontisation

As has already been suggested, Cavour was not an Italian nationalist but primarily a political pragmatist. Cavour did not always dismiss the idea of a federal Italian state. However, the ultimate motivating force in his acceptance of such a proposal was political pragmatism. At Plombières, in July 1858, Cavour struck a deal with Louis Napoleon that linked the promise of French support to expel Austria from northern Italy with the handing over to France of Savoy and, as agreed after the meeting, Nice. It was also agreed at Plombières that Italy would become a federation of states: the Kingdom of Upper Italy which was Piedmont writ large; the Kingdom of Central Italy; the Kingdom of Naples; and reduced Papal States. The leader of this federation would be the pope, mainly as compensation for the loss of land to the Kingdom of Central Italy. It is often assumed that this model of Italian political development was devised by Louis Napoleon. However, this has been disputed by some historians. In *Italy in the Age of the Risorgimento, 1790–1870* (1983), Harry Hearder asserts that 'the creative mind behind the decisions reached at Plombières was Cavour's rather than Napoleon'. His evidence is the memoranda that Cavour took with him to Plombières which accurately predicts the course and outcome of the meeting.

Part of the proof of Cavour's limited nationalist ambitions was the nature of the constitution imposed on Italy in 1861. In *Cavour* (1985), Mack Smith is generous in his interpretation that the constitutional settlement was created by the speed with which unification took place between 1859 and 1861. Indeed, Mack Smith goes so far as to stress that, at heart, Cavour was a believer in 'decentralisation' of power but for pragmatic reasons acted otherwise. Evidence to support this point lies in his decision in 1860 to ask the ministers of the interior Farini and Minghetti to conduct an investigation into the possibility of some kind of regional autonomy. Their proposals included a plan for a form of devolution with regional governors and assemblies. At a local level, mayors would be elected. However, the scheme was half-hearted and eventually dismissed in 1861 by the new Italian parliament. Despite promising some degree of autonomy to Tuscany and Sicily for much of 1860, in the end Cavour never went out of his way to push the idea through politically.

In Cavour's defence, it can be argued that the decision to impose Piedmontisation was taken when he was out of office in late 1859. The government of Alfonso La Marmora had to decide quickly how Lombardy would be governed. It decided to impose the Piedmontese administrative model on Lombardy without any debate and by emergency decree. In Modena, in August 1860, a popular assembly controlled by Farini voted for annexation to Piedmont. However, there is little evidence to suggest that Cavour disapproved of these developments. He did nothing to reverse them when he came back into power, despite the fact that such centralisation caused considerable disquiet.

In *The Italian Risorgimento* (1998), Martin Clark suggests there was so little sympathy from Cavour and politicians of his type for regional government or a federal state because of the dominant localist mentality. Clark argues that Italian politicians were concerned about their own municipalities rather than their 'regions', let alone regions elsewhere. He goes on to point out that Cavour only went to Tuscany once and never further south. Clark's line is supported by Denis Mack Smith who writes in *Modern Italy; A Political History* (1997) that Cavour: 'personally knew far more about agricultural conditions in Ireland than about those in Sicily or Sardinia, and far more about politics in Paris than in Rome'. Yet to suggest that Cavour's decisions should be attibuted to a narrow localist mentality does not sit comfortably with the fact that he was well informed and understood issues relevant to the world outside Piedmont. He also shared the view of many in the Piedmontese parliament that local autonomy equalled national collapse.

Cavour: the epitaph

After Cavour's death on 6 June 1861, his political skill was attacked. He was considered by many to be scheming and manipulative. In *Cavour* (1985), Denis Mack Smith points to the fact that the British politician and (later) prime minister Benjamin Disraeli called Cavour 'utterly unscrupulous'. While this is somewhat rich coming from Disraeli (who was often completely unscrupulous), the view from Palmerston on the other side of the British House of Commons was far warmer. He stated that Cavour was 'one of the most distinguished patriots [to] have adorned the history of any country'. However, both fell into the trap of judging Cavour by what happened during the process of unification. Cavour was not the 'patriot' Palmerston believed him to be. His ambitions were far narrower. Indeed, Mack Smith, falls into the same trap at the end of his excellent biography by stressing Cavour's 'ability to manage Parliament… [skill] in foreign policy and… sheer virtuosity in every branch of the political arts'. This list is undoubtedly accurate.

SOURCE 2

The Real Italian Brigand Chief, Punch cartoon, 24 August 1861.

PUNCH, OR THE LONDON CHARIVARI.—August 24, 1861.

THE REAL ITALIAN BRIGAND CHIEF.

The south

Many Piedmontese politicians, including Cavour, had very little understanding of the south. Its poverty, backwardness and distinct economy meant it was unsuitable for a unification with Piedmont based on Piedmontese laws. The cultural differences between north and south were huge. An illustration of incompatibility can be seen in primary school education. In 1859, the Piedmontese parliament had introduced the Casati Law which insisted on two years' free compulsory primary education. In contrast, there was no such law introduced in the south where the vast majority of the population were illiterate. Both Sicily and Naples had a long tradition of regional autonomy. Indeed, in the early summer of 1860, Cavour let it be known that he was considering some form of 'real self-government' for the southern regions after annexation to Piedmont. But 'real self-government' never materialised. In the first weeks of October 1860, Bourbon agents led thousands of peasants in pitched battles against the pro-Garibaldi national guards, their aim being to seize strategically important towns. While in Sicily, there was little enthusiasm for the Bourbon cause, there was quick disenchantment with Garibaldi (who had used force to quickly re-establish law and order) and no enthusiasm for the Piedmontese. Cavour's aim from October 1860 was to crush any opposition in the south, whether it be from those still loyal to the Bourbons, the remnants of Garibaldi's army, peasants demanding land or those hoping for some freedom. Cavour despatched Farini to the south with orders to crush opposition militarily.

THINKING HISTORICALLY   Causation (6b)

Attitudes and actions

Individuals can only make choices based on their context. Prevalent attitudes combine with individual experience and natural temperament to frame the individual's perception of what is going on around them. Nobody can know the future or see into the minds of others.

Context

The huge cultural differences between the north and the south.

Deep-seated mistrust in the north of the Bourbon dynasty.

Equally deep-seated mistrust of Garibaldi and his followers.

Continuing unrest in the south stirred up by Bourbon agents.

The failure of Cavour's agents to influence events in the south

Action

Imposition of Piedmontese rule in the south.

Answer the following questions individually and discuss your answers in a group:

1 Why might Cavour have believed that it would be difficult to bring southern Italy into a unified state? What potential problems was Cavour facing in the south in the autumn of 1860?

2 Why did he decide that self-government for the south was not an option?

3 What other information would have been useful to him to help him decide on his course of action?

4 How reasonable was Cavour's course of action given what he understood about the situation at the time?

5 How far should the historian try to understand the context of the beliefs and values of people in the past when explaining why individuals make choices in history?

The collapse of Bourbon rule in the south had left a vacuum of law and order. New taxes were introduced by the Piedmontese state to reduce the 2.5 billion lire of national debt accumulated during the recent wars. King Francis II, the deposed Bourbon king, stirred up unrest which Pope Pius IX did little to condemn. The result was the re-emergence of brigandage and a civil war, the Brigands' War, which was fought between 1861 and 1865 with great brutality and claimed more lives than the wars of unification. Made up of the unemployed, the disposed and the disillusioned, the brigands were badly managed and disorganised. They robbed, murdered and assassinated. The Piedmontese deployed an army some 120,000 strong to deal with the brigand threat, which was around half the strength of the army. In 1862, it was estimated that there were 82,000 brigands in the Neapolitan provinces. It was a war with terror deployed on both sides. By 1865, the war had subsided and brigand leaders such as Carmine Crocco had fled. But that did not prevent occasional outbursts of lawlessness and violence. In 1866, a week-long rebellion in Palermo in Sicily resulted in the murder of government officials and three days of bitter street fighting. It was another sign of the deep alienation from the new state felt in the south.

SOURCE 3

From a proclamation by Major-General Ferfinando Pinelli to his troops on 3 February 1861. Pinelli was one of the leading Piedmontese generals whose job it was to quell resistance in the south. He was, as you will read, deeply anti-clerical.

Officers and soldiers!

You have achieved a great deal already, but in war nothing has been achieved while something still remains to be done.

A troop of this brood of robbers is still hiding up in the hills. Root them out immediately, and be as merciless as fate.

Against such enemies pity is a crime. They are cowards: they will go on their knees before you when they see you in strength, but they will attack you treacherously from behind when they think you are weak, and massacre the wounded.

Indifferent to any political principles, greedy only for booty and looting, they are paid assassins; they may be currently employed by the Vicar not of Christ but of Satan, but they are ready to sell their daggers to others when the gold raised from the stupid credulity of the faithful is no longer enough to satisfy their lusts. We will annihilate them, and crush the Priestly vampire whose filthy lips have for centuries been sucking the blood of our Mother country. We shall purify with sword and fire the regions infested by its obscene slavering, and from the ashes liberty will arise in full vigour.

SOURCE 4

From the reflections of a French visitor to Naples, Maxime du Camp, who visited the city in 1862. Du Camp was a writer, traveller and early photographer who served under Garibaldi in Sicily in 1860.

Neapolitans have now accepted... that administrative reforms must be postponed .... Italy still has no real capital, no proper frontier to the northeast, and is still occupied in part by an enemy Power; hence national unity must come first. Progressive reforms will follow... but first the government must be helped to make the nation.

Only five years ago, if I asked someone if he was an Italian, he would answer: "No, I am a Neapolitan"... Today things have changed. You will be answered: "I am an Italian from Naples"... Everyone is now an Italian and feels it. In 1860, after Garibaldi's arrival at Naples, people at first saw in him just a new, easier master replacing the old; and many of the common people would cry "Long live united Italy," and then ask us "What is Italy, and what does united mean". But during May and June of this year 1862, I have spoken to many people... and all of them know about Italian unity... Anyone who knows Neapolitans, and who remembers how indifferent they used to be... will recognise that... progress has been made.

SOURCE 5

From a letter written by Massimo d'Azeglio on 2 August 1861 to a friend, Carlo Matteucci. D'Azeglio had been against the annexation of Naples; he likened it to sharing a bed with someone who has smallpox. He also disapproved of Cavour's tactics and he was a true pessimist.

In Naples we drove out a King in order to establish a government based on universal consent. But we need sixty battalions to hold southern Italy down, and even they seem inadequate. What with brigands and non-brigands, it is notorious that nobody wants us there.

What about universal suffrage you may say! I know nothing about suffrage; but I know that battalions are not necessary to the north of the Tronto river, only on the south. So there must have been some mistake somewhere. Our principles and our policy must be wrong. We must get the Neapolitans to tell us once and for all whether they want us there or not. I realise that we Italians have a right to make war against those who wish to keep the Austrians in Italy; but cannot preserve the same hostility towards Italians who, while remaining Italians, reject union with us. I think we have no right to use guns on them, unless you want to put us on the same level of expediency as Bomba [Ferdinand II] when he bombed Palermo, Messina, etc. I know that this is not the general view, but I have no intention of abandoning my right to use my reason and to say what I think.

SOURCE

6

From *Lettere Meridionali ed altri scritti sulla questione sociale in Italia*, a collection of essays by the Neapolitan historian and Italian senator Pasquale Villari. The essays were first published in Turin in 1875 and caused a stir because they exposed conditions in the south.

If we had first transformed our society, and then carried out the political revolution, we should not find ourselves in the conditions in which we now are, precisely because only a political revolution was carried out…

Brigandage is the most serious ill that can be seen in our countryside. It can correctly be described… as the consequence of an agrarian and social question which afflicts almost all of the southern provinces… In the same province one can observe that in areas where the peasant was worse off, brigandage gained much support; where his condition improve, brigandage declined or disappeared… Brigandage is not born of a brutal tendency towards crime, but of real and true desperation.

Foreigners in the southern provinces observe with amazement many populous cities in which there are a few families of rich proprietors, usually related to each other, in the midst of multitudes of proletarians, who are the peasants… Except for a few employees, there are no other categories of citizens. The countryside is deserted, its workers form the population of the city. There is no industry, there is no bourgeoisie, there is no public opinion to check the landowners who are the absolute lords of this multitude, which depends on them for its subsistence and has no other means of living if it is abandoned.

The greater part of the peasants, if they did not find themselves in the same misery and oppression as under the Bourbons, found that their fate had worsened with the new liberty.

THINKING HISTORICALLY | Interpretations (5c)

Good questions, bad questions

Above are three sources (Sources 3, 4 and 5) which are about the south of Italy. The sources are written in either 1861 or 1862. The three authors have very different views about the south. Their interpretations are all, in their own way, highly subjective. In trying to ascertain how useful these pieces of evidence are, we need to ask a number of questions.

Work in groups.

1 Devise questions which could be asked of all three sources:

e.g. What is the author's experience of the south up until the point the source was written?

2 Devise questions which are appropriate to one of the sources only:

e.g. of Source 4, to what extent did Du Camp's experiences in 1860 influence his attitude in 1862?

Now attempt one of the following questions for each source:

3 Think of a question that the source could be helpful in answering.

4 Write a set of statements giving information that can be gleaned only from the source itself without any contextual knowledge.

5 Write down statements of contextual knowledge that relate to the source.

Now try to answer the following question:

6 Explain why knowledge of context is important when gathering and using historical evidence. Give specific examples to illustrate your point.

A Level Exam-Style Question Section A

Study Sources 5 and 6.

How far could the historian make use of Sources 5 and 6 together to investigate the impact of the new Italian state on the south?

Explain your answer, using both sources, the information given about them and your own knowledge of the historical context. (20 marks)

Tip
The purposes of d'Azeglio and Villari are very different and need to be considered carefully.

The economic and social impact of the north-south divide

Finances

The wars undertaken by Piedmont from 1848 to 1860 had taken their financial toll. In 1861, the public debt stood at 2,450 million lire and was more than double that of four years later. Between 1860 and 1866, income increased steadily from 480 million to 600 million 1860. The main problem for Italy was that it needed to service the debt while also maintaining armed forces which could keep the peace in the south and could act when appropriate to seize Rome and Venice. The south was not a source of much wealth; Piedmontese officials visiting the south in the early 1860s wrote to Cavour complaining that the finances of the region were 'exhausted'. But there was the need for significant capital investment on behalf of the state, notably in the railways. By 1866, the deficit took up 60 percent of state expenditure. The government resorted to taxes to increase income. Efforts to raise money by taxing salt and tobacco had proved to be counter-productive as the sale of both goods fell. They were therefore forced to make the highly unpopular decision to reintroduce in January 1869 the *macinato* or grist tax – a tax on the milling of corn. Such was the negative reaction to the tax that two weeks after it had been reintroduced, 250 people had been killed and 1000 wounded in riots.

Land

Another way in which the state attempted to raise revenue in the second half of the 1860s was through the sale of land. The division between landowner and the middle class on the one hand, and the peasant and landless on the other, did not improve after 1861. The unification of Italy heralded the sale of large tracts of Church land. In 1867, an Act was passed that began the sale of Church land. In the next nine years, around half a million acres were sold. In the north, peasant farmers bought the land. However, in central and southern Italy it was a different story. Land was mainly bought by the middle classes and those who had capital. Those peasants who bought land often found they could not afford the interest payments on the money they borrowed. Additionally, they had little or no capital with which to improve the land and were therefore forced to sell what they had recently acquired. The process of political unification was not accompanied by significant land reform. But this was little surprise, because those who shaped the political change did so in part to avoid social change. Cavour recognised that: 'A democratic revolution has no chance of success in Italy… Active power resides almost exclusively in the middle and part of the upper class, both of which groups have ultra conservative interests to defend.'

Economic integration

In 1860, the state of the Italian transport system was still extremely poor. Whereas in Britain, canal and rail construction and road improvement had formed the basis of an integrated transport system, this was most definitely not the case in Italy. Despite the attempt of Cavour to encourage the construction of canals in Piedmont, generally there was little interest in promoting this important form of industrial transport because of Italy's topography and the lack of excess water. Ironically, it was the regions under the rule of foreign powers that led the way, notably Lombardy. Additionally, Milan was linked to a number of European cities by roads suitable for stagecoaches to travel along.

At the point of unification, Italy had 2,773 kilometres of railway. The lines had generally been built to meet the interests of the separate states, although a few railways were built across the north Italian plains and in 1857 the Venetian and Lombard railway systems had been linked together. But in Sardinia and Sicily there were no railway lines at all. It is clear that the paucity of transport in the south acted as a break on agricultural and industrial development. In the southern region of Apulia, for example, the development of an emerging olive oil industry was stunted by the lack of any modern transport system.

However, in 1860, a national transport system became not just an economic priority but a political necessity. The problem was that the government struggled to pay for the building and operation of the railways but, on the other hand, it could not afford not to. After unification, therefore, successive governments sought to build railways as a matter of priority. Such an enterprise was expensive, especially given the fact that most of the raw materials had to be imported. In 1865, the railways were transferred into private hands, but the state was still forced to provide a significant amount of capital for construction and it guaranteed profits. A national system that would allow trade to develop and would unite the disparate provinces of the country was a political priority. The effect of building the railways was considerable on the economy and Italian society. When the Mont Cenis tunnel through the Alps was completed in 1871, the Italian railway network was linked to that in France. This was of utmost importance, given the benefits of increased volume of trade between the two countries. It led to the development of engineering and iron and steel industries. But these industries were based primarily in the north, and in that sense the railways helped to encourage the development of a dual economy rather than a unified one. The building of the railways had an important effect in that it stimulated the demand for factory-made goods, because they could be transported around the country more easily. However, the impact of railway building as a whole in Italy was not as great as in the other leading industrial nations of the period.

There was little investment in road building across the Italian peninsula before 1860 and after 1860 state investment was concentrated on railway construction rather than road building. A similar situation occurred across Europe with railway construction taking precedence over roads from 1850. The Italians did have a slight advantage of still being able to use the network of roads built by the Romans.

ACTIVITY
KNOWLEDGE CHECK

Obstacles to unity

1 Give five reasons why each of the following posed an obstacle to unity:

   a) the north–south divide

   b) tensions between Church and state.

2 On a spider diagram, list the economic problems created by unification. When you have done this prioritise them in terms of importance of impact.

HOW SUCCESSFULLY WAS THE 'VENETIAN QUESTION' SOLVED?

Failure of Garibaldi, 1862–64

In December 1861, various working men's groups, patriotic and Mazzinian societies, met to form the Italian Freedom Association. This group met for the first time in March 1862 with Garibaldi as president. In his inaugural speech, Garibaldi urged those to the left in Italian politics to focus on the issues of Rome and Venice. He then embarked on a tour of Lombardy, paid for by the government. He used this tour to raise money for Venice and to whip up patriotic sentiment in favour of action. The king mooted ideas of involving Garibaldi in a scheme to stir up trouble in the Austrian Empire with the purpose of gaining access to and taking Venice. In March 1862, the new prime minister, Urbano Rattazzi, summoned Garibaldi to Turin to discuss possible action in Greece, Serbia and

Dalmatia – all areas which he presumed for be fertile territory for unrest. To help him put plans into action, he made available the sum of one million lire. However, this scheme came to nothing, partly because Garibaldi had plans of his own. But also because the government refused to sanction radical action for which it had not given prior consent. In May 1862, a group of Garibaldi supporters led by Francesco Nullo were arrested at Sarnico near the Austrian border. A demonstration in favour of the group at Brescia was fired on by government troops, killing some of the demonstrators. Garibaldi returned to Caprera (his island home) in disgust. Soon after he was to embark on another attempt to take Rome (see page 255) and the issue of Venice became secondary. In April 1864, Garibaldi embarked on an extraordinary visit to London. Welcomed by hundreds of thousands of well-wishers, he used the publicity to raise the issue of the liberation of Venice from Austrian hands.

EXTEND YOUR KNOWLEDGE

Garibaldi in England

When Garibaldi arrived in London on 11 April 1864 to thank the British for their support for Italian unification, a crowd of around half a million people turned out to greet him. It took just under six hours for his carriage to travel from Vauxhall to St James. He stayed for 12 more days in London and was mobbed wherever he went. China mementoes were made to celebrate his visit and the following year, Nottingham Forest football club adopted the red shirt in his honour. Music was composed in his honour and pubs as well as the famous Garibaldi biscuit were named after him. Garibaldi was the popular hero of the age. He was particularly popular in Britain for being anti-Catholic and liberal. He was not, however, popular with all sections of society. After his departure, Queen Victoria wrote to one of her daughters: 'Garibaldi, thank God, is gone'. In Italy, Victor Emmanuel fumed at the attention which Garibaldi received and he refused to allow the Italian ambassador to take part in proceedings.

Aims of Victor Emmanuel

Victor Emmanuel was invariably set on the idea of war as the best means of resolving diplomatic issues. The prospect of war was one that excited him. Indeed, he once informed Queen Victoria that he would 'exterminate' the Austrians if given the chance! On 6 June 1861, Cavour died aged 50 years and 10 months. He is said to have died of a fever. The death of Cavour removed an important restraint and the king, thereafter, sought to influence foreign policy, often without the approval of his government. In October 1861, Victor Emmanuel sent personal envoys across Europe with the purpose of stirring up war. One such emissary was Rattazzi, who was sent to Paris to try and persuade Louis Napoleon to help Italy wage war against Austria. He was unsuccessful in so doing, just as he was in threatening Austria with Italian-inspired insurrection in the Balkans in early 1862. Mazzini continued to agitate Victor Emmanuel to intervene in Venice and, in 1863–64, Victor Emmanuel even entered into secret discussions with the revolutionary leader. His aims – stirring up discontent with the purpose of removing the Austrians from Venice – were far-fetched. When it came to war, Victor Emmanuel was more talk than action; the reality was that Austrians would remain in Venice until events on the wider European stage dictated otherwise.

Diplomacy with Prussia and war with Austria 1866

The issue of Venice was resolved through more direct and traditional means: the use of diplomacy and war. It was also very much linked to the rise of Prussia. The accession to the Prussian throne in 1861 of Wilhelm I and his appointment of Albert von Roon as minister of war and Bismarck as minister-president in 1862 were to have an important affect on Austrian power. In March 1862, Bismarck agreed a free trade treaty between Prussia and France that excluded Austria. While allied militarily in the period 1862–64, Austria and Prussia duelled for the economic leadership of the German world. Whereas the Prussians preferred the idea of a Prussian-dominated free trading zone, the Austrians preferred a German trading zone that would include all German states and destroy the power of the *Zollverein*. The Prussians won and, in 1864, German states such as Bavaria, Nassau and Hesse, normally under the dominance of Austria, joined the *Zollverein*. The architects of change were Napoleon and the Prussian Chancellor Otto von Bismarck. In his desire for Prussian domination of Germany, Bismarck embarked on a complex diplomatic campaign to win support for an intended war against Austria.

The role of Prussia

At Biarritz, in October 1865, Bismarck met Napoleon, who promised neutrality in any forthcoming war. Napoleon also helped to broker an alliance between Bismarck and Italy, then signed a secret treaty with Austria in June 1866; Austria promised to give Venice to Napoleon in return for French neutrality in the coming war. The alliance between Prussia and Italy was completed in April 1866. By the terms of the alliance, Italy was to receive Venice for supporting Prussia in a war if it broke out in the next three months. It was to the disappointment of some Italian nationalists that Prime Minister Lamarmora failed to secure the Trentino as part of the agreement. Lamarmora knew of Louis Napoleon's treaty with Austria but still decided to go to war sensing that it would not be wise to double-cross the Prussians.

'Resolution' of the Venice issue

The area of dispute between Austria and Prussia was the Duchy of Holstein. In early June 1866 the Austrian governor of Holstein called a meeting of the Holstein Diet to discuss its future. Bismarck attacked this move as a violation of the Gastein Convention of 1865 by which joint sovereignty of Schleswig-Holstein was to be exercised by Austria and Prussia. He ordered Prussian troops into the duchy as a result. On 14 June, the Austrians engineered a vote in the Frankfurt Diet of the German Confederation against Prussia. A number of German states, including Bavaria and Saxony, sided with Austria. This had little impact on the Prussian government which declared that the federal constitution had been violated and was a reason for war.

Adhering to the terms of the alliance agreed in April, on 20 June 1866 the Italians declared war on Austria. Confidence was high. The Italians had an army of 40,000, which was far larger than the Austrian army. However, the Italians were ill-prepared and were defeated at the Battle of Custozza. Some days later, on 3 July, the Austrians were crushed by the Prussians at Sadowa. The Austrians were forced to cede Venice to France, which promptly handed it over to the Italians. The manner in which the Italians gained control over Venice was seen as humiliating. The humiliation was made worse by a crushing defeat at sea at the hands of the Austrian fleet at the Battle of Lissa on 20 July 1866. Although Venice was won, the Italian military and state were brought into some disrepute in the process. The plebiscite held in Venice to approve annexation was even more one-sided than usual, with 642,000 voting in favour and only 69 voting against. The collapse of the system of international agreement was clear after Prussia's defeat of Austria in 1866 in that there was no Congress to discuss the peace. Such was her new found strength that the terms of the peace were to be dictated by Prussia.

EXTEND YOUR KNOWLEDGE

Battle of Lissa 20 July 1866
The Battle of Lissa was one of the first battles between 'ironclad' ships. Although the Italian navy had a greater number of ships than the Austrians, the Italian commander Admiral Persano was particularly incompetent and the Austrians found little difficulty in outwitting the Italians.

Union with Venetia

The military victory of Prussian arms against Austria at Sadowa resulted in the transfer of Venice to Italy via Napoleon. Of course, this was a mere sideshow to the central issue that it confirmed Prussian dominance of Germany and the relative decline of Austria. In Venice, in October 1860, there was great rejoicing at the departure of the Austrians. To give the process of transfer from Austrian rule to Italy the same veneer of legitimacy which other regions had enjoyed, a plebiscite was held on 20 October 1866. The result was as one-sided as in previous plebiscites with 647,246 voting in favour of joining with Italy and 69 against. However, the manner in which Venice had been won, after such a humiliating defeat on land and at sea, highlighted Italy's lack of military independence and power. In short, the war of 1866 was a catastrophe which damaged the national psyche. In August 1866, Crispi wrote to his friend Agostino Bertani: 'To be an Italian was something we once longed for, now, in the present circumstances it is shameful.'

From a letter written by Garibaldi to Baron Ricasoli at Florence, 14 August 1866.

Everyone is aware that Italy is in a very dishonourable as well as a wretched condition.

The blame lies with the two ministries, those of war and the navy, or rather with those who up till now have controlled those two ministries.

As regards the navy this is obvious, because men like Ricci and La Mantica know nothing of their job. There is an absurdity about having ministers who are ignorant as well as being repugnant to honest and able men: this is why we lost the battle of Lissa with a fleet superior to the enemy's; and now myself I understand why on Lake Garda I was give six gunboats of which only one could be put into operation – and carried only one cannon at that – whereas the Austrians had eight gunboats mounting thirty-six cannon. The ministry of the navy has been wrong all through. The guilt lies with all the ministers in turn during the whole period since we first possessed a navy. And how could it be otherwise with people in office who knew nothing of naval affairs?

Italy possesses sailors in no way inferior to those of England and America.

With magnificent army material, we have nevertheless fought on land hardly any better than at sea, and this is obviously due to the same defect in leadership.

The worst of it is that nothing is being done to change the leadership. The men who led the way to the catastrophes of Lissa and Custozza are still at the head of affairs. And what guarantee is there that Italy will see herself restored to her dignity as a nation? This is the question I permit myself to put to you, dear Baron, and I would be grateful to have a reply.

A piece written by Pasquale Villari and published in the journal *Il Politecnico* in Milan in September 1866. Villairi was a respected intellectual and politician of the right.

The war is over and we possess Venice. After six years of preparation, it cost us less effort than we expected. Yet no one is content. Above all the war destroyed many illusions as well as destroying our unlimited self-confidence. The traditionally slow Germans were seen to move like lightening, while the fiery Italians crept like a tortoise. In one victory after another, Prussia annihilated the Austrian forces against whom we could do so little on land or on sea. Never again can we look at ourselves quite as we used to do.

Whose fault is it?

When trying to explain all these [military] mistakes, blame is variously placed on the political system, on general factiousness, on the reactionaries, on Piedmontism, or on the bosses. But this is not the end of the story, for you must then explain how Italy let herself be governed for so long by such men. We have a freer government than France or Prussia, to say nothing of Austria. Our ministers had the support of parliament; the deputies were elected freely without government pressure. Perhaps, then, we are just ignorant and let troublemakers lead us by the nose. Perhaps public opinion is undirected and we simply lack enough men of ability.

Italy must now begin to recognise that she has at home an enemy which is stronger than Austria. I refer to our colossal ignorance, our multitudes of illiterates, our machine bureaucrats, childish politicians, ignoramus professors, hopeless diplomats, incapable generals, unskilled workers, primitive farmers, and the rhetoric which gnaws our very bones. It was not the Austrian garrison at Mantua, Verona and the rest of the "Quadrilateral" which barred our path, as much as our seventeen million illiterates, nearly a third of whom still live in truly arcadian simplicity.

ACTIVITY
KNOWLEDGE CHECK

Read Sources 7 and 8 carefully.

1 What are Garibaldi's and Villari's criticisms of the new Italy?

2 In your opinion, how justified are these criticisms?

3 Which of the two authors is more objective in his analysis of the situation? Explain your answer.

HOW EFFECTIVELY WAS THE PROBLEM OF ROME SOLVED

The papacy and French occupation

The issue of French occupation of Rome continued to preoccupy Piedmontese leaders and French Catholic opinion. The defeat of papal forces at Castelfidaro in September 1860 caused a backlash in France, not just because of the Italian invasion and seizure of The Marches and Umbria but because Louis Napoleon's government failed to react. The response was a concerted campaign of criticism from French Catholics against their government. They forced a vote on the Roman Question in the French Chamber of Deputies and Senate in March 1861, on both occasions the government's position of maintaining troops in Rome winning by a slender majority. The contradiction of Louis Napoleon's position was best summarised by a question posed by a Catholic deputy M. Keller who asked: 'Are you revolutionaries, are you conservatives?'

Negotiations in 1864 between Victor Emmanuel and Louis Napoleon resulted in the September Convention. By the terms of the Convention the papacy would be allowed to recruit a garrison of 10,000 soldiers and French troops would leave Rome within two years. The Italian government promised in return not to attack Rome and to make Florence its capital rather than Turin. Indeed, when the Italian government (led by Marco Minghetti) agreed, Napoleon believed that the Italians had given up their claim on Rome. This was not the case. There was a storm of protest in Italy and 23 people were killed during rioting in Turin. Piedmontese deputies withdrew support from Minghetti's government. In his usual subtle style, Victor Emmanuel sacked Minghetti for not keeping him fully informed. But in 1865, the government and bureaucracy switched to Tuscany despite the fierce opposition to the move in Piedmont. In December 1866, the last French troops had departed. However, a further attempt by Garibaldi to seize Rome in 1867 led to the return of a French force to bolster papal forces. Ultimately, Louis Napoleon chose to placate French Catholics and the French garrison remained until 1870. The result was the continuation of Catholic support for the Second Empire but, also, a frosty diplomatic relationship between Italy and France which lasted until the collapse of Napoleonic rule.

SOURCE

9 From the minutes of the Council of Ministers, 10 September 1864.

Discussion was opened on which city should be the national capital. General della Rovere, Minister of War [and a Piedmontese], stressed the political reasons why it should be Turin. The Ministers Peruzzi [a Florentine], Visconti-Venosta [a Lombard], Pisanelli and Manna [both Neapolitans] advanced other political reasons why Naples should be chosen. General Cugia [from Sardinia] and General Menabrea [from Savoy], on military and political grounds, preferred Florence, and Amari [a Sicilian] agreed with them. The Prime Minister, Minghetti [a Bolognese from the Romagna], after giving his opinion in favour of Naples, then summed up the discussion. He mentioned a conversation with the King, whose preference on strategic grounds was for Florence. The cabinet then, with only one negative vote, decided for Florence; though they asked the King if he would have the matter discussed once again by an extraordinary committee of generals under His Royal Highness the Prince of Carignano.

ACTIVITY
KNOWLEDGE CHECK

Read Source 9.

The debate about the choice of Italy's capital was clearly a heated one. Source 9 gives the historian a number of clues as to why this might have been the case. What do you think was the reaction to the decision to move the capital to Florence in the following places:

a) Rome

b) Turin

c) Florence

d) Naples?

French troops leave Rome on 1 December 1866. From an engraving in *L'Illustration* from a sketch by Zwahlen.

Départ des troupes françaises de Rome. Aspect de la place Monte-Citorio, le 1ᵉʳ décembre 1866, au moment du transport des bagages du 85ᵉ régiment. — D'après un croquis de M. Zwahlen.

ACTIVITY
KNOWLEDGE CHECK

Louis Napoleon's priorities

On the one hand the impression is that Louis Napoleon was keen to support the cause of Italian unity, on the other he was resolute in his support of the papacy. What do you think Louis Napoleon's intentions and priorities were with regard to Italy? Support your answer with evidence.

The failure of Garibaldi and diplomacy, 1862–67

Aspromonte

For Italian nationalists, Italy was not complete without Rome as its capital. In June 1862, Garibaldi left Caprera for Sicily, where he raised a volunteer army with the purpose of seizing Rome. Although there was no official support from either king or government, it is highly likely that they knew of his intentions. By August, Garibaldi had raised a force of 4,000 men that crossed the Straits of Messina. The likely hope of the king and Prime Minister Rattazzi was that the French would withdraw the garrison from Rome, leaving the road open for Italian troops to march in, thereby pre-empting

Garibaldi. But Napoleon was in no mind to withdraw French troops from Rome and the government decided to halt Garibaldi in his tracks. On 26 August, an order was issued for the arrest of all those involved in the rebellion. On 29 August, Garibaldi and his men were stopped in their tracks by the regular Italian army in the mountains of Aspromonte. Garibaldi was wounded by a shot in the foot. Some of his troops who had deserted from the regular army were executed. The episode triggered a crackdown in the south which was to last well into 1863. Garibaldi was pardoned for his involvement but not before he had denounced the king for double standards. Another casualty of the Aspromonte episode was Rattazzi whose government fell in December 1862, its leader depicted as being the villain of the hour. It was a disastrous episode all round.

EXTEND YOUR KNOWLEDGE

Aspromonte 29 August 1862

Translated as 'sour mountain', Aspromonte was certainly that. The meeting between the regular army and Garibaldi's forces was not a proper battle but a brief skirmish with 12 fatalities in which Garibaldi became the hero of the hour. Later, on a ship taking him to Genoa, Garibaldi wrote a letter to the journal *Il Diritto* in which he painted himself as having defended national honour. Stories soon circulated of how, on falling wounded, he took off his hat, lit a cigar and proclaimed '*Viva l'Italia*'. The legend of Garibaldi was enhanced by the episode.

Through relentless letter writing and propaganda, Garibaldi had helped to ensure that the issue of Rome stayed high up the political agenda. In December 1866, the last French troops left Rome as had been promised in 1864. The government, led by Rattazzi, saw an opportunity and again turned to Garibaldi who toured the mainland in the early part of 1867 whipping up support, raising funds and speaking against the papacy and Church. Garibaldi again attempted to seize the moment. Government funds were paid to Romans to encourage them to rise up against the papacy. Garibaldi was sent back to Caprera but allowed to escape and, in October 1867, joined up with other volunteers in the Papal States. However, such an uprising was not forthcoming, with many Roman citizens staying stubbornly loyal to papal rule. Instead, Garibaldi's attempted invasion of Rome provoked the French into sending troops back. This was not to be taken lightly; the French army now had the new **breech**-loading chassepot rifle. At the Battle of Mentana on 3 November 1867, Garibaldi's troops were mown down. The failure of the citizens of Rome to rise in the cause of liberation led many Catholics to argue, with justification, that Rome did not wish to be part of a united Italy. Again, the government was held up to ridicule and seen to be powerless in the face of French military and diplomatic might. Garibaldi was never again to trust the king or the political establishment.

KEY TERM

Breech
The breech is the part of the gun barrel nearest the firer.

EXTEND YOUR KNOWLEDGE

Franco-Prussian War 1870

War with France came as a result of an argument over who would become king of Spain. Bismarck engineered the proposal of a Prussian candidate, Prince Leopold. France objected to this proposal, fearing an ally of Prussia the other side of the Pyrenees. Diplomatic activity ended with a demand by the French for the withdrawal of Leopold as a candidate and a determination on the part of the French to humiliate Prussia. Bismarck engineered an increase in tension, revising a report of a meeting between the French and Prussians at Ems to make it sound as if war was inevitable. On 19 July 1870, the French declared war.

The impact of the Franco-Prussian war

The Battle of Mentana and its consequences were to seriously diplomatically weaken Louis Napoleon and the French. It was increasingly clear that the greatest threat to France was the growing might of Prussia and her new allies in the North German Confederation that had been formed after the war with Austria in 1866. The logical move would have been for France to see an alliance with Austria and Italy against the Prussians. Austria would not ally herself with France unless Italy was on board because it would not wish to risk fighting a war on two fronts, as had happened in 1866. But for as long as French troops remained in Rome, an alliance involving France and Italy was highly unlikely. So Bismarck was able to use the diplomatic stalemate created by the Roman Question to Prussia's advantage. His desire to unite German states under the leadership of Prussia led him to provoke war with France in 1870. Victor Emmanuel's instincts were to support Louis Napoleon, but his government, led by Prime Minister Giovanni Lanza, wisely insisted on neutrality. As the Prussian army threatened French borders, so French troops departed from Rome leaving it defenceless except for the presence of a small papal army. The French army subsequently suffered a series of reverses at the hands of German forces, culminating in a comprehensive and final defeat at Sedan on 1 September 1870. Louis Napoleon was subject to the ultimate humiliation being taken prisoner by the Germans: the French declared a provisional republic.

The Italian takeover of Rome

The Italian government of Giovanni Lanza took the opportunity of the departure of the French to seize Rome. The papal troops briefly resisted and the Italian army, under the command of General Cardona, bombed the city walls. A breach was made at the Porta Pia on 20 September and the city was stormed. There was little enthusiasm among the Romans for the invasion. The battle was a short one with the Italian forces losing 49 men, the papal armies losing just 19. Objections to the attack were muted, indeed the only diplomatic concern registered was by the ambassador of Ecuador. Leading Catholic figures denounced the attack on Rome; in England Cardinal Manning denounced Victor Emmanuel as a second Pontius Pilate. The capitulation signed on 20 September at the Villa Albani left the Leonine City (the part of Rome surrounded by the Leonine Wall) in the hands of the pope but with the rest of the city in the control of the Italian state. A notable absentee from the events of September 1870 was Garibaldi; instead he travelled to France to fight for the new French Republic. As was the norm, the seizure of Rome was followed up with an organised display of popular approval. Support in the plebiscite held in the city on 2 October showed that 133,681 of the Eternal City's citizens approved of annexation to Italy while only 1,507 objected. Rome was pronounced the capital of the new Italy by royal decree on 9 October and its surrounding territories were seized. By the decree, the pope's personal sovereignty was assured. His response was the issuing of the encyclical *Respicientes* on 1 November by which all those involved in the invasion and seizure of Rome were excommunicated.

EXTEND YOUR KNOWLEDGE

Loss of temporal power

The loss of temporal power was virtually complete. In *The Italian Risorgimento* (1998), Martin Clark argues that the Catholic Church was 'among the big losers of the *Risorgimento*'. But we should be careful not to argue that the failure of the Church in Italy was by any means total. On the surface, Clark's view is correct with the surrender of Rome in 1870. However, temporal power had for centuries compromised and confused the Church's claim to spiritual authority. From 1870 onwards, there was to be no such ambiguity.

TO WHAT EXTENT WAS ITALY UNIFIED IN 1871?

Factors promoting unity, including the constitutional monarchy and national institutions

The monarchy

The new state was a constitutional monarchy as defined by the *Statuto*. The monarch, Victor Emmanuel, was the embodiment of the new state. As already explained on page 238, although the monarch held executive power, there were constraints on his actions; for example, he needed parliamentary approval for new taxes and no new law was valid without the signature of a minister alongside. Throughout the 1850s and 1860s, the constitutional monarchy evolved with a greater emphasis on the role of parliament. This was primarily due to Cavour's influence and very much to the monarchy's advantage. By 1870, the monarch symbolised the stability of the new state, a bulwark against republicanism and extremism. Weighed against the fact that, for many Italians, Victor Emmanuel was Piedmontese and, thereby, virtually a foreigner, was the role that he played in the process of unification and the *Risorgimento*.

The army

The army had played an important role in uniting Italy and would continue to play a significant role in national life. Expenditure on the military was relatively high at around a quarter of all national expenditure but parliament had little influence over military affairs. The rulers of Italy in 1870 kept the armed forces intentionally large so that the new state could take its place among the European great powers. The army was also seen as the means by which recruits could be made into Italians. However, perhaps most significant was the part played by the army in defeating internal enemies. While there was a degree of consent with regards to the new state, there was also considerable coercion. As already discussed, the army was used extensively in the south throughout the 1860s. By 1870, there were around 15,000 officers in the army, two-thirds of whom were Piedmontese. The army had around 215,000 soldiers with a further two million in reserve. Regiments were recruited from two different regions and were never posted for more than four years in one place. The purpose was to ensure that the loyalty of the troops was never divided. So the armed forces were the guarantor of the new state and national unity, using force if needs be to ensure its continuation and stability.

The civil service

The civil service ran the economy, education and the state's finances. Nearly all of the civil servants were Piedmontese and many of the civil service jobs in the new state were given to veterans of the Wars of Independence, the *patrioti*. The new state was run by a centralised civil service of around 30,000 bureaucrats of whom 3,100 were based in Rome. The benefit of the system was that it was relatively free of corruption. However, the system was heavily centralised and the civil servants in Rome held disproportionate influence. Any suggestion, such as that made by Prime Minister Marco Minghetti in 1864 that administration be decentralised, was rejected on the grounds that national unity could only be fostered by centralised government.

Local government

The country was divided in to 69 provinces, each with a prefect who was centrally appointed by the government in Rome. It was the job of the prefects to keep order in the provinces. They were supported in this by the main guarantor of social control in the localities, the 25,000-strong carabinieri. A military police force, the carabinieri were armed and effective. Operating mainly in the towns, the carabinieri backed up the work of around 18,000 members of the local police. The prefect also kept an eye on local government which worked, in 1871, through 8,382 *communi*. A mechanism for ensuring central control of local government was the appointment by the prefect of the mayor to run a *commune*. The *commune* was significant because it looked after education, public health as well as local taxation and public works. In reality, local government was controlled by local elites and the prefects. The latter were the key to the smooth operation of the whole political system.

The divisive effects of social and economic problems

The economic division between the north and the south was considerable and made worse by unification. Before 1860, the economy of the south was hampered by a lack of capital and skilled labour. Agriculture predominated and was based on the export of fruit and olives. But markets were distant and transport underdeveloped. Industry which did exist in the south, such as the manufacture of silk, was in the main workshop-based. One problem for southern industry was the lack of power, unlike factories and workshops in Lombardy and Piedmont which could rely on water from the Alps. Up until unification, industry in the south was protected with tariffs which were as high as 80 percent of the value of the goods. Unification led to the removal of these tariffs and the collapse of industries in the south such as the manufacture of silk which was now in direct competition with its northern counterparts. The result was widespread and prolongued de-industrialisation in the south. On the other hand, unification boosted industry in the north, notably the manufacture of cotton and wool which now had a larger market.

Unification also brought much higher levels of taxation. The wars of the *Risorgimento* had been expensive and needed to be paid for. Many of the taxes of the new state were imposed on the poorer sections of society, notably the widely hated *macinato*, the grist tax on milling. The government used the revenue from taxation to invest in public works, land reclamation and the military, the significant majority of this investment being in the north.

The level of poverty was reflected in a high child mortality rate; 22.7 percent of the children born alive in 1871 died before their first birthday and 50 percent before their fifth birthday. For many Italians, the escape from poverty, unemployment, overtaxation and lack of land was migration or emigration. Much migration was seasonal and consisted of labourers seeking work in wealthier regions of Italy or abroad in France or Switzerland. For others, the move away from home was more permanent, often to North America or South America, notably Argentina. In 1871, 120,000 Italians emigrated with many never to return to their homeland.

Papal opposition

The loss of temporal power was an important issue because, to the Church, the pope could not be governed by anyone else on earth. The humiliation of the Church was apparent after 1870 when Rome was seized. In May 1871, the state issued the Law of Guarantees, which was an attempt to define the relations between Church and state. The pope was given a degree of sovereignty in that he was granted the status of a monarch. He was allowed his own postal services, he had full liberty for his religious functions and his representatives at the Vatican were given full diplomatic status and 3,225,000 lire a year compensation for the loss of temporal lands. However, Pius IX chose to ignore the deal because the proposals were made by a state that had taken control of Rome and had seized the Papal States. He rejected the Law of Guarantees and reiterated that he believed himself to be a 'prisoner in the Vatican'. The Law served an important purpose for the Italian state in that it reassured the international community that the Church's freedom had been preserved. As a result, all major powers recognised the Italian seizure of Rome and sent representatives to the monarch's new official residence, the Quirinale Palace in Rome.

Despite international recognition, in many senses papal opposition to the new state, acted to strengthen the Church. Pius IX's stand against the Italian state was also identified as a stand against liberalism, modernity and secularism. As such it was welcomed by the devout and the faithful, many of whom felt threatened by the new state. From 1870, there were to be two courts in Rome, one at the monarch's palace, the Quirinale, and the other in the Vatican. The operation of a state within a state was to weaken the new Italy. The Church was to form its own social organisations as part of its attempt to stand apart. Perhaps the most significant impact was the refusal of Catholics to take part in the political process. In March 1871, a tribunal of the Church was asked whether it was expedient for Catholics to be involved in politics. It ruled *non expedit*, that it was not expedient. The result was that there was to be no mass conservative party on the right of Italian politics because Italy's Catholics would have sat at the heart of such a party. For at least many decades to come, the Catholics would be on the margins of the political system.

Political disunity and continued *irredenta*

Italian political culture was distinct and unique. The Italian parliament was made up of two chambers: the Senate and the Chamber of Deputies. Deputies were elected to the Chamber of Deputies to represent the interests of their constituents. However, the electorate was narrow in 1870 with only 500,000 men or 2.2 percent of the total population being eligible to vote. Only around 60 percent of those eligible to vote did so with Catholics and many Republicans abstaining on principle. Deputies sought favours and jobs from the government of the day in return for their votes. There was no party system, politicians formed into factions often centred on an influential politician. However, there were distinct differences between politicians generally considered to be on the 'Right' and those identified as being on the 'Left'. Those on the 'Right' were generally from the north and often aristocratic. They supported the monarchy and the process of improving Italy. Deputies of the 'Left' were normally from middle-class backgrounds and the south. They tended to be more anti-clerical than those on the 'Right' and they were often keener for an extension of the franchise.

The unification of Italy under the House of Savoy meant that the Republican tradition was maintained, including the occasional hopeless uprising. On 24 May 1870, a Mazzinian corporal in the Italian army, Pietro Barsanti, led an attack on an army barracks in Pavia shouting 'Long live Rome, long live the Republic, down with the monarchy'. Barsanti was arrested and shot despite a petition signed by 40,000 people pleading for him to be pardoned. In the tradition of Mazzini, Republicans were those most closely involved in promoting an irredentist agenda. For irredentists based in the north, the desire was to liberate Italians living under the yoke of the Habsburgs in territories that

SOURCE
11
Italy in Rome. *Punch* cartoon, 1 October 1870.

PUNCH, OR THE LONDON CHARIVARI.—OctOBER 1, 1870.

ITALY IN ROME.

Papa Pius (*to* King of Italy). "I MUST NEEDS SURRENDER THE *SWORD*, MY SON; BUT *I KEEP THE KEYS!!*"

were missed in 1861–66, notably Trentino, Istria and Trieste. For others, the return of Rome and the achievement of nation status meant the rebirth of Italy as a potential imperial power with an empire centred on the Mediterranean. Therefore, those on the Left were prepared to call for agitation against France. In 1870, Crispi called for the return of Nice and Savoy to Italian control. Others believed that Corsica and Malta should be part of a greater Italy. The irredentist cause was to be a thorn in the side of the new state and another indicator of continuing disunity.

SOURCE

12 From a letter written on 25 August 1871 by Giuseppe Mazzini to his friend Giuseppe Ferretti.

The Italy which we represent today, like it or not, is a living lie. Not only do foreigners own Italian territory on our frontiers with France and Germany, but even if we possessed Trieste and Nice, we should still have only the material husk, the dead corpse of Italy. The life-giving touch of God, the true soul of the nation is lacking.

Italy was put together just as though it were a piece of lifeless mosaic, and the battles which made this mosaic were fought for reasons of calculated dynastic egoism by foreign rulers who should have been loathed as our natural enemies. Lombardy, scene of the Great Five Days in 1848, allowed herself to be joined to Italy by the actions of the French despot. The Venetians, despite their heroic defence in 1849, come to us by kind permission against a German monarch. The best of us fought against France for possession of Rome; yet we remained the slaves of France so long as she was strong. Rome, therefore, had to be occupied furtively when France lay prostrate at Germany's feet, just because we feared to raise our war cry against the Vatican. Southern Italy was won by volunteers and a real movement of the people, but then it resigned its early promise and gave in to a government which still refuses to give Italy a new national constitution.

The battles fought by Italy in this process were defeats. Custoza and Lissa were thus lost because of the incompetence or worse of our leaders. Italians are now a vassal people, without a new constitution that could express their will. We can therefore have no real national existence to international policy of our own. In domestic politics we are ruled by an arbitrary violation of the law; administrative corruption has been elevated into a system; a narrow franchise means that we are governed by a few rich men who are powerless for good. Our army is not popularly based, and it is used only for internal repression. Rights of the press and of free association are fettered, and a corrupt political system inevitably is bringing a slow but growing financial collapse. Abroad we waver as before between a servile attachment now to France now to Germany. The alliance with the people has been betrayed, and our relations with Europe have thrown morality overboard just as in the worst centuries of Italian decline.

... Ordinary people are disillusioned. They had watched... as Italy, once ruler of the civilised world, began to rise again; but now they avert their gaze from what is happening and say to themselves: 'this is just the ghost of Italy'.

THINKING HISTORICALLY   Evidence (5b)

Reading between the lines

Extracts from sources can only tell the historian so much. Such extracts are fragments of evidence, it is the role of the historian to piece the fragments together so that they can be used to construct accounts of the past. But before the historian does that, he or she needs to try and understand the context of the source. The problem is that texts can have multiple contexts. Historians often debate how best to contextualise the documents that they interpret.

1 Summarise some key points from Source 12. To what extent, in Mazzini's view, has unification failed? How does he view foreign intervention? Of which aspects of the new Italian state is he most critical?

As well as noting the contents of the letter, it is important to consider who Mazzini had written the letter to. We do not know too much about Giuseppe Ferretti but for the fact that he lived in Livorno and that he was most likely an old friend and political ally. The significant fact is that Mazzini is writing to someone who has for many years shared his political ideas.

THINKING HISTORICALLY Evidence (5b) *continued*

2 The sequence of events below provides a possible context for the document in the wider story of Italian unification. Look at this timeline and then answer the question that follows.

1859 Agreement at Villafranca that Lombardy should be transferred to France and then to Piedmont

1860 Nice and Savoy ceded by Piedmont to France

1866 Italy's participation in the Austro-Prussian war; crushing defeats for Austria at Custozza and Lissa

1866 Austria cedes Venice to France which cedes to it Italy

1866 French troops withdraw from Rome

1867 French troops re-occupy Rome

1870 French troops withdraw from Rome as a result of Franco-Prussian war

How does Mazzini's critique fit into the above sequence of events? To what extent was the unification of Italy shaped by external factors as suggested by Mazzini?

The document might seem to have one kind of meaning when interpreted in the context of international intervention in the affairs of the Italian states. But contrasting interpretation appears if we locate it in another context. There is good reason to suggest that Mazzini's interpretation is shaped by his own failure, the continuing failure of his own supporters and those who supported a more radical/republican solution to the Italian question.

3 Consider the second sequence of events and answer the question that follows.

1849 The failure of the Venetian and Rome Republics

1856 Failure of Mazzinian uprisings resulting in the death of Carlo Pisacane

1860 Garibaldi turns Naples and Sicily over to Victor Emmanuel II at Teano

1861 Kingdom of Italy proclaimed as a constitutional monarchy. The new Italian constitution based on the *Piedmontese Statuto*.

1862 Attempt by Garibaldi and followers to seize Rome ended at Aspromonte

1867 Mazzini refuses a seat on the Chamber of Deputies

1867 Garibaldi's forces defeated at the Battle of Mentana

1870 Mazzini attempts to start an uprising in Sicily but is arrested and imprisoned

To what extent are Mazzini's views, as expressed in his letter to Feretti, the result of the failures of Mazzinian nationalism?

Consider both timelines together and answer the following questions:

4 Use information from both timelines to construct a possible context for why Mazzini wrote his letter of 25 August 1871 – why might he have been so critical of the new state ?

5 Why is it important for historians to spend time thinking about possible contexts for a document before they start to use it to draw conclusions about the past?

SOURCE 13

The Italian senator and writer Luigi Settembrini reflects just before he died in 1876. A liberal, Settembrini was twice imprisoned by the Bourbons, serving a total of 11 years in their gaols.

Hear what posterity will say of us. It will say that this was a generation of giants, because it carried out a task which had been impossible for many generations and many centuries. This generation made Italy, it made her by power of intellect, gathering in one and harmonizing so many discordant ideas, it re-enacted the Divine Comedy* in the real world...

Our children, born in this sacred light of liberty, will never be able to imagine the point at which this sun rose, at which day followed the terrible darkness, the point at which we became Italians, felt ourselves united and gathered together under a single standard. We suffered much in that night of servitude, but we gained equal pleasure to see that dawn, to greet that sun, to become Italians...

*'The Divine Comedy' is a famous epic poem written by Dante Alighieri.

SOURCE 14

Giosuè Carducci was considered to be the national poet of modern Italy. He was a prominent republican and critic of the new state. This speech is from 1880.

What does the Italian parliament represent?... It represents a minority with uncertain ideas; a minority which has no breadth of vision, which lacks courage... I believe that this shadow of a dream, which is Italian parliamentary life, depends precisely on the narrow, thin, fictitious, airy base on which political representation rest.

It is no longer a question of parties or of right, it is a question of the interests of Italy that the political base of the county be enlarged, so that the nation may regain its vigour, may unfold itself, so that in the end the patria may affirm itself gloriously.

We have reached such a point in Italy that all of the great ideals seem to have vanished: a sense of vulgar scepticism has seized hold of youth... Those of us who saw Mazzini and the battles of '59 and '60, those of us who saw the ardour of youth in 1866, find ourselves at a time when the 'patria' is a word with a false ring, which sounds like an archaism; when the 'nation' seems to be borrowed from the French language...

Oh, those days of sun, liberty and glory of 1860! Oh, that struggle of titans between Garibaldi and Cavour in 1861! What have we become! The epic of the infinitely great has been followed by the farce of the infinitely small, the busy little farce of ponderous clowns. For how much longer must this go on?

ACTIVITY
KNOWLEDGE CHECK

Read through Sources 13 and 14.

1 How and why do these two sources differ in their views of Italian unification?

2 Which is the more reliable for a historian investigating the aftermath of the unification?

3 With a partner, discuss and then list the main factors that caused unity in 1870 and the main factors that caused disunity.

4 To what extent would you agree with the view that, in 1870, Italian unity was superficial at best?

A Level Exam-Style Question Section B

'In 1870 Italy was unified in name only.' How far do you agree with this statement? (20 marks)

Tip
The word 'nominally' (which means 'in name only') is a good one to use when answering this question. This is very much an essay with two sides to the answer.

AS Level Exam-Style Question Section B

To what extent was Italy united by 1871? (20 marks)

Tip
Remember, you will need to answer the question so think, was Italy united to a considerable, certain or minimal extent?

ACTIVITY
SUMMARY

Answer or discuss the following questions:

1 Explain in your own words Martin Clark's analytical framework of 'legal Italy' and 'real' Italy (see page 243) and the impact that the imbalance between the two had on the governing of Italy.

2 What do Sources 2 and 9 tell us about British attitudes towards Italian politics and the Catholic Church in Italy?

3 Discuss in a group the extent to which Venice and Rome became part of Italy because of external rather than internal factors.

4. Sources 3–9 and 12–14 give a range of views about the significance of unification. Which of the sources give the most useful reflections on the impact of unification?

WIDER READING

Clark, M. *Modern Italy: 1871 to the Present*, Pearson (2008)

Duggan, C., *A Concise History of Italy*, Cambridge University Press (1994)

Smith, M. D. *Mazzini*, Yale University Press (1994)

Preparing for your AS Level Paper 2 exam

Advance planning

1. Draw up a timetable for your revision and try to keep to it. Spread your timetable over a number of weeks, and aim to cover four or five topics each week.
2. Spend longer on topics that you have found difficult, and revise them several times.
3. Above all, do not try to limit your revision by attempting to 'question spot'. Try to be confident about all aspects of your Paper 2 work, because this will ensure that you have a choice of questions in Section B.

Paper 2 overview:

AS Paper 2	Time: 1 hour 30 minutes	
Section A	Answer 1 compulsory two-part sources question	8+12 marks = 20 marks
Section B	Answer 1 question from a choice of 3	20 marks
	Total marks =	40 marks

You should familiarise yourself with the layout of the paper by looking at the examples published by Edexcel. The questions for each section are followed by eight pages of lined paper where you should write your answer.

Section A questions

Each of the two parts of the question will focus on one of the two contemporary sources provided. The sources together will total around 300 words. The (a) question, worth 8 marks, will be in the form of 'Why is Source 1 useful for an enquiry into…?' The (b) question, worth 12 marks, will be in the form of 'How much weight do you give the evidence of Source 2 for an enquiry into…?' In both your answers you should address the value of the content of the source, and then its nature, origin and purpose. Finally, you should use your own knowledge of the context of the source to assess its value.

Section B questions

These questions ask you to reach a judgement on an aspect of the topic studied. The questions will have the form, for example, of 'How far…', 'To what extent…' or 'How accurate is it to say…'. The questions can deal with historical concepts such as cause, consequence, change, continuity, similarity, difference and significance. You should consider the issue raised in the question, consider other relevant issues, and then conclude with an overall judgement.

The timescale of the questions could be as short as a single year or even a single event (an example from Option 2C.2 could be, 'To what extent was Russia's involvement in the First World War responsible for the fall of the Provisional Government in 1917?'). The timescale could be longer depending on the historical event or process being examined, but questions are likely to be shorter than those set for Sections A and B in Paper 1.

Use of time

This is an issue that you should discuss with your teachers and fellow students, but here are some suggestions for you.

1. Do not write solidly for 45 minutes on each question. For Section A it is essential that you have a clear understanding of the content of each source, the points being made, and the nature, origin and purpose of each source. You might decide to spend up to ten minutes reading the sources and drawing up your plan, and 35 minutes writing your answer.
2. For Section B answers you should spend a few minutes working out what the question is asking you to do, and drawing up a plan of your answer before you begin to write your response.

Preparing for your AS Level exams

Paper 2: AS Level sample answer with comments

Section A

Part A requires you to:

- identify key points in the source and explain them
- deploy your own knowledge of the context in which events took place
- make appropriate comments about the author/origin/purpose of the source.

Why is Source 7 (Chapter 4, page 253) valuable to historians for an enquiry about how Italy gained Venice in 1866?

Explain your answer using the source, the information given about it and your own knowledge of the historical context. (8 marks)

Average student answer

Garibaldi's letter to Baron Ricasoli is a strong attack on Italy's leaders. He uses very strong language to criticise the leaders of the navy and army as well as ministers. Garibaldi had worked tirelessly since unification in 1861 to persuade the Italian government and King Victor Emmanuel to continue to fight for those regions of Italy, most obviously Rome and Venice, which had not been included in the new state in 1861. His influence as a leading republican and nationalist can be seen by the fact that he believes himself in a position to write such a letter to Baron Ricasoli who was Italy's prime minister at the time.

The letter is directly written to Ricasoli and it demands a reply. It is personalised and subjective in that it is full of assertion. Because it is a letter, it does not include a wider context and so does not, for example, address the diplomatic issues. The important point to make about the background to the source is that it was written in August 1866 which was after the defeat of Italian forces at Lissa and Custozza but before Venice had been formally ceded by Austria. So the timing of the source is significant; it is written in the direct aftermath of military defeat and sense of national humiliation. It is not surprising, therefore, that Garibaldi comes across in the letter as so angry and that he is so critical of Italy's military and political leaders.

Overall the source, together with the background information, makes it clear that Italy gained Venice but not through the efforts of its military leaders or politicians. It is valuable because it is a letter written by a leading Italian figure at the time.

The opening paragraph focuses on the source and is aware of the main theme of Garibaldi's attack and infers that Venice had not been gained through the competence of the Italian military or ministers. The candidate deploys some effective own knowledge about Garibaldi's background but this is not used to directly answer the question.

There are some effective points about the nature of the source showing an awareness of the nature of the letter. The response also picks up on the significance of the timing of the letter. This is an important point and should be given credit. It links the tone of the letter to its timing.

The conclusion is quite general and would have been more effective if the candidate had deployed own knowledge when discussing how Italy gained Venice. There is an attempt to address the question but it is in general terms.

Verdict

This is an average answer because:

- it identifies some points from the source and makes the inference that the acquisition of Venice was not as a result of the efforts of the Italian leaders
- it discusses the nature of the source and begins to suggest the reasons behind it although this could be developed

- it deploys some own knowledge but needs to show more awareness of the reasons for the Italian acquisition of Venice
- there is an overall judgement but it needs more specific illustration and explanation to add substance.

Use the feedback on this answer to rewrite it, making as many improvements as you can.

Paper 2: AS Level sample answer with comments

Section A

Part B requires you to:

- interrogate the source
- draw reasoned inferences
- deploy your own knowledge to interpret the material in its context
- make judgement about the value (weight) of the source in terms of making judgements.

How much weight would you give to the evidence of Source 8 (Chapter 4, page 253) for an enquiry into the problems facing the united Italy the mid 1860s?

Explain your answer using the source, the information given about it and your own knowledge of the historical context. (12 marks)

Average student answer

The account by Pasquale Villari describes the many problems which faced Italy in the mid-1860s. Given his position as an intellectual and a politician, he would have had insight into the weaknesses of the state. Many of the politicians on the right wanted social progress and Villari's concern at the levels of illiteracy in Italy matched the views of his political allies. The military defeat at the hands of the Austrian navy and army in 1866 at Lissa and Custozza led to considerable soul searching in Italy.

Pasquale Villari was a respected intellectual. In the source he attempts to weigh up the different reasons given for Italy's problems. He also suggests some possible reasons for failure in 1866 which include the weaknesses of Italy's politicians; 'we simply lack enough men of ability'. Above all else, Villari identifies the most significant issue facing Italy in 1866 as being widespread illiteracy. This was a real social issue, notably in the south where the considerable majority of the peasantry could neither read nor write.

The background information informs us that Villari's article was published in September 1866. This is significant as it was just after the crushing defeats suffered at the hands of the Austrians at Lissa and Custozza. I would regard this as a valuable source about the attitudes of the politicians on the Right and the different explanations which were suggested for explaining Italy's problems.

This paragraph uses background information and states an overall conclusion but it is rather simplistic and does not deploy own knowledge to discuss what happened in Italy and why Villari became disillusioned.

This is a mixed introduction. It deploys some own knowledge re the military defeat in 1866 and how it led to political debate in Italy but does not develop it by discussing the political context beyond a general point about the wish of politicians on the right for social justice.

There is some use of background information but the opportunity to make an inference is missed and there is no discussion of the range of issues facing Italy. There is only general use of own knowledge to illustrate and explain the problems facing Italy in the mid-1860s.

Verdict

This is an average answer because:

- there is some interrogation of the source but opportunities to draw inferences are neglected
- there is some use of background information re the source but this aspect could be developed
- there is some deployment of own knowledge but a limited sense of context. In particular the political context in which Italy's problems were discussed is not explained. There could also be some reference about the external factors which helped explain the series of events which took place over the course of the summer in 1866.
- there is an overall judgement but it lacks substance.

Use the feedback on this answer to rewrite it, making as many improvements as you can.

Paper 2: AS Level sample answer with comments

Section A

Part A requires you to:

- identify key points in the source and explain them
- deploy your own knowledge of the context in which events took place
- make appropriate comments about the author/origin/purpose of the source.

Why is Source 7 (Chapter 4, page 253) valuable to historians for an enquiry about how Italy gained Venice in 1866?

Explain your answer using the source, the information given about it and your own knowledge of the historical context. (8 marks)

Strong student answer

The source is of some value to the study of how Italy gained Venice in 1866 because it reveals that the Italian military effort was poor and that the defeats at Lissa and Custozza were perceived as a national humiliation. Garibaldi has been a critic of the new state since its founding in 1861 and his comments need to be understood in this light. It is also important to point out that Garibaldi and his volunteers fought with some success in the war against Austria in 1866. Indeed, Garibaldi's success contrasted with the military humiliation suffered by the Italian army and navy. It is Garibaldi's involvement, and sympathy for his cause among influential politicians – including the king – which give his comments such weight.

The limitations of this source are, in part, a result of when it was written. The plebiscite in Venice took place over two months after Garibaldi's letter. This plebiscite attempted to gloss over the military and diplomatic humiliation which Garibaldi alludes to in his letter. In many senses the value of the letter comes from the moral authority which Garibaldi had to attack the political and military establishment in such scathing terms. That the source is an extract from a personal letter to the prime minister makes it even more pertinent. However, as an extract from a letter, it lacks the diplomatic overview, e.g. the victory of Prussia at Sadowa and the granting of Venice to Louis Napoleon which is required to provide a full account.

The source implies that Italy did not gain Venice through her own efforts and as such is highly valuable. Garibaldi's involvement in the events of 1866 and his pre-eminence as a leading nationalist, further enhance the letter's value. Taking into account the source's nature and when it was written, it is not surprising that it does not provide a full account; but that does not mean that it is not of some value to a historian.

> This is very strong opening which is sharply focused on the specific question and indicates a strong response. There is some thorough deployment of own knowledge which makes it clear why Garibaldi writes as he does and why he is so dismissive of the leading military figures and politicians.

> This section develops the analysis of the limitations of the source. It shows awareness of the purpose and nature of the evidence.

> The conclusion is to the point and answers the question.

Verdict

This is a strong answer because:

- it has sharp focus on the specific question
- it make use of evidence in the source
- it deploys appropriate own knowledge accurately and effectively.

Section A

Part B requires you to:

- interrogate the source
- draw reasoned inferences
- deploy your own knowledge to interpret the material in its context
- make judgement about the value (weight) of the source in terms of making judgements.

How much weight would you give to the evidence of the Source 8 (Chapter 4, page 253) for an enquiry into the problems facing the united Italy the mid 1860s?

Explain your answer using the source, the information given about it and your own knowledge of the historical context. (12 marks)

Strong student answer

The source would carry considerable weight and value for any enquiry into the problems facing Italy in the mid 1860s. The author was a politician who had considerable insight into the workings of the Italian political system. The fact that he is writing at the time and that he is able to explain the range of explanations for Italy's woes gives us insight into how well informed he was. Villari is also very frank as to what he believes are the problems facing Italy, ranging from military failure to widespread illiteracy and ignorance. His views may well have been representative of those on the right of Italian politics.

It is significant that Pasquale was a respected intellectual. As such he had considerable insight into the development of the new state and the events which were to shape that development. His attitude towards the 1866 war is particularly valuable in shedding light on the attitude of the intellectual class. He explains his frustrations with the new political system and all of the different elements which make up that system. It was the failings of all sections of Italian society, the political classes, the intelligentsia, the farmers as well as the military leadership of the country. This confirms the view of many that the new state was facing huge social problems and that, in some sense, unification had created huge and significant problems for the new state to overcome. Villari is biting in his criticism to the point that he borders on sarcasm at this point: 'Perhaps, then, we are just ignorant and let troublemakers lead us by the nose.'

Villari explains that, perhaps the most significant of all problems was that of illiteracy of the masses. His concerns were shared by many, in particular in the light of the Brigands War in the south of Italy. The huge expense, the considerable loss of life and the failure of the new state to end the war was a huge frustration to many in the north who had hoped that unification would have reconciled the southern peasantry to the new state.

Although the source only touches on some aspects of Italy's problems, it confirms and provides graphic illustration of some of the key features of the county at a significant moment, i.e. in the wake of the 1866 war with Austria. There are inevitable limits to the value/weight of the testimony of an individual, especially as it is brief, but in this case it can be linked to other similar accounts. We must also take into account the language Villari uses and the fact that at times, he comes across as overly dismissive. However, the source appears to be a perceptive account with some clearly weighed arguments which, on balance, make it valuable as part of an enquiry into the problems facing Italy in the mid-1860s.

> This is a focused and well balanced introduction which comments on the value of Pasquale Villari as a witness and makes effective use of specific references.

> These sections identify, illustrate and explain some of the key points emerging from the source. The candidate deploys own knowledge effectively to develop points.

> The conclusion weighs up the response and clearly answers the question.

Verdict

This is a strong answer because:

- it interrogates the source and selects and comments about key specific points
- it makes good use of the background information provided about Villari
- it brings in some own knowledge and links this source to other witness accounts and evidence from time
- it makes an overall judgement about the value of the source.

Paper 2: AS Level sample answer with comments

Section B

These questions assess your understanding of the period in some depth. They will ask you about the content you learned about in the four key themes, but may not ask about more than one theme. For these questions remember to:

- give an analytical, not a descriptive, response
- support your points with evidence
- cover the whole time period specified in the question
- come to a substantiated judgement.

How accurate is it to say that the unification process between 1859 and 1861 was shaped more by external than internal factors? (20 marks)

Average student answer

It is accurate to say that the unification process was shaped by external factors but that internal factors were also important.

Firstly, one way in which external factors shaped Italian unification was the intervention and the role played by France. The agreement of the French at Plombieres in 1858 that they would support Piedmont in a war to remove Austria from the north of the Italian peninsula was a considerable step forward. In 1859, war between Piedmont and France on one side and Austria on the other broke out. The Austrians were defeated at the battles of Magenta and Solferino in June 1859 but in July the French agreed to an armistice with the Austrians at Villafranca. At first the Piedmontese knew nothing of this armistice. Under its terms, Lombardy was given to the French who could then decide what they wanted to do with it. In January 1860 the French gave Lombardy to Piedmont in return for Nice and Savoy and they allowed Piedmont to annex the central Italian duchies. The British government objected to the French being given Savoy and Nice.

Secondly, another way in which external factors helped lead to unification was fact that the old Congress system which had, since 1815, controlled European affairs was clearly finished. At Villafranca, Louis Napoleon had agreed that the rulers of central Italy should be restored. The most significant ruler in central Italy was the pope. But in December 1859, a pamphlet written on behalf of Louis Napoleon suggested that the pope should lose some land. None of the other powers such as Prussia and Russia objected. In October 1860, the rulers of Austria, Prussia and Russia met in Warsaw. Part of their consideration was about the events which had taken place on the Italian peninsula. There was a suggestion that the Austrians might invade Lombardy but this came to nothing. The inaction of the main Congress powers was important in allowing events in Italy to take their course.

This is an example of how not to start an answer. The candidate has not made any substantial point on the question, nor is there any judgement here. A stronger opening paragraph would be longer than this single sentence, such as: 'To a certain extent, external factors did help shape unification notably the role played by Louis Napoleon and, to a lesser extent the British in supporting political change in Italy. The significance of the relative weakness of Austria should not be overlooked. However, there were many internal factors including the actions of Garibaldi and the response of Cavour which are significant. Overall, external factors were of decisive significance but the unification of north and south was mainly due to internal factors.'

This paragraph considers the importance of French support for Piedmont in 1859 and 1860 and the significance of Villafranca. While the information is given, there is very little analysis. The candidate has identified an important series of events but has failed to fully relate those events to the question.

The main point in this paragraph is clear enough, that inaction as much as action on behalf of the powers of the Congress system was to have an impact on the series of events which led to Italian unification. However, the paragraph is rather vague although the point in the last sentence is well made. Remember to always try to relate every paragraph back to the question.

Thirdly, the influence of the British government was important. Queen Victoria was pro-Austria and so the British government had to be careful what it said. But in December 1859 the British Foreign Secretary, Lord John Russell, suggested that the future of the Italian peninsula should be decided by its people. When Garibaldi crossed the Straits of Messina, the Royal Navy maintained a watchful eye. Later in the year, when the Congress powers failed to decide whether to take action or not, Lord John Russell declared on behalf of the British government that it would protect Italian unity militarily. Given that the British had the strongest navy at the time, this would have helped to prevent other powers from intervening.

> There are some relevant points made in this paragraph about the role played by the British. However, the point is too vague and there is no linkage back to the question. The candidate has organised their ideas well but has not then used this to good effect.

However, although external factors were important, so were the many internal factors. In 1859, the National Society engineered peaceful revolutions in Tuscany, Modena and Parma. In 1860, they skilfully engineered plebiscites which gave the impression of widespread popular support for union with Piedmont. They also engineered uprisings in favour of unification. The leaders of the National Society such as Farini and Ricasoli were to play a really important part. Behind the work of the National Society and the person who might be called the 'architect of unification' was the prime minister of Piedmont, Count Cavour. It was his work in persuading the French to take part in the war of 1859 which was such an important turning point. It was his actions in reaction to the actions of Garibaldi in 1860 which helped ensure that unification took place under the banner of Piedmont. Cavour made the decision to invade the Papal States in September 1860 which paved the way for the meeting at Teano in October 1860.

> This is a reasonable paragraph on the internal factors which helped lead to unification. However, it is full of information which has been rather haphazardly thrown together. Again, the information needs to be related to the question.

We should not forget that Garibaldi played a really important role. His decision to set to sea in April 1860 with his Thousand volunteers was to change the course of unification. In May 1860, Garibaldi and his troops landed in Sicily where they defeated the forces of the King of Naples. They then crossed the Straits of Messina and marched on Naples. It was Garibaldi's actions which directly led to the south becoming part of the newly unified state.

> These are accurate points, but the paragraph needs to be related to the question. It is clear that the candidate is running out of time.

Thus I have shown that there were many external factors which led to unification. These include the support of France and Britain at certain stages. The lack of involvement of the other states is important. But there were also internal factors. These included the roles played of Cavour, the National Society and Garibaldi. So although there were important external factors, there were also important internal factors as well.

> You should not use a phrase such as 'Thus I have shown' in the conclusion: a simple 'To conclude' will suffice. The candidate is attempting to reach a conclusion, but note that this is achieved by restating points made in the body of the answer. The conclusion 'sits on the fence'.

Verdict

This is an average answer because:

- there is some attempt at explanation, but there are descriptive passages, including some which do not appear directly relevant
- the material included is accurate, but is lacking in depth in several places
- there is an attempt to reach an overall judgement, but it is not entirely secure

- the answer is organised on the question, and the general trend of the argument is reasonably clear. However, a couple of paragraphs, though accurate and broadly relevant, are fairly free-standing, and could be improved with sharper links to the question overall.

Use the feedback on this answer to rewrite it, making as many improvements as you can.

Paper 2: AS Level sample answer with comments

Section B

These questions assess your understanding of the period in some depth. They will ask you about the content you learned about in the four key themes, but may not ask about more than one theme. For these questions remember to:

- give an analytical, not a descriptive, response
- support your points with evidence
- cover the whole time period specified in the question
- come to a substantiated judgement.

How accurate is it to say that the unification process between 1859 and 1861 was shaped more by external than internal factors? (20 marks)

Strong student answer

There were both external and internal factors which help explain the unification of Italy between 1859 and 1861. Undoubtedly, the role of foreign powers is highly significant in creating the circumstances within which unification could take place. France, in particular, influenced events at important points in the process. Her intervention was part of a change in the balance of power which makes unification possible. Likewise, the preeminent position of Piedmont and the role of various individuals, notably King Victor Emmanuel, Cavour and Garibaldi, are highly significant factors in the unification process. However, it is too simple to suggest that it was either internal or external factors which are more significant. The two very much work together to help explain how the new state was forged.

The role played by France and notably Louis Napoleon was key. While sympathetic to the cause of Italian unity, the French Emperor saw considerable dynastic and political advantage in supporting the cause of limited national unity. The dynastic advantage was to marry certain members of his family into royalty, the political advantage for France was to strengthen its influence in Italy. The agreements at Plombieres and Villafranca show that Louis Napoleon did not necessarily wish for the unification of the new state under Piedmont, nor did he foresee the unification of north and south. However, he clearly did envisage the removal of Austrian influence from the northern part of the Italian peninsula. And this is the important point about French involvement. Its military might, as shown at Magenta and Solferino in June 1859 helped loosen Austrian control in the north. Diplomatically, the French were prepared to act on behalf of Italian interests to a certain extent notably at Villafranca or at the Treaty of Zurich in 1859. Louis Napoleon relied on the support of Catholics in France but, in December 1859, he was prepared to argue for a decline in papal power. This was an important turning point on the road to unification and it is unlikely that the process would have taken the course it did without French influence and the support of Louis Napoleon.

This is a strong opening paragraph which places the significance of internal and external factors alongside each other. The candidate also challenges the question by suggesting that, rather than simply identifying internal or external factors as being most significant, notes that it was a combination of the two.

This is a well-developed paragraph. Louis Napoleon's aims with regard to the future of Italy and his own dynastic ambitions are made clear. The extent of French influence is well explained.

It was not just the French who were to have an influence on the series of events. The British government and notably the foreign secretary Lord John Russell were keen to support the cause of Italian unity. As such, they intervened at crucial moments to influence the course of events. An example of such intervention was the call of Russell in January 1860 for the future of Italy to be decided through self-determination, a call which helped lead to Cavour returning as prime minister and immediately opening negotiations with Louis Napoleon. Another such intervention was the role played by the Royal Navy in 1860 in helping Garibaldi seize both Sicily and Naples. However, the extent of the intervention of the British should not be exaggerated. What was perhaps more significant as a factor in shaping the unification process was the relative decline of Austria. The defeat of Austrian arms in 1859 and her failure to persuade other Congress powers to oppose Italian unity was of utmost importance. Likewise, the failure of Austria to support the Papacy in September 1866 is reflective of her weaker position relative to both France and Piedmont. It was this factor, perhaps more than any other which opened the way to the political unification of the whole peninsula.

> It would be easy simply to describe the course of events between 1859 and 1861, but the candidate here is evaluating the relative significance of the different factors. The role of the British in helping unification is noted, but the candidate suggests that the relative decline of Austrian power made matters worse.

It was the change in the status of the great powers which allowed Piedmont to take advantage of the series of events which followed the war of 1859. So external factors are of significance, but they are linked to the internal factors which also helped shape unification. The economic improvements in Piedmont and its role in the Crimean War meant that it was a more significant power militarily and diplomatically. It also meant that it was able to assume the mantle of the leading Italian state, a fact which was reinforced by the National Society which, throughout 1859 promoted the cause of national unity under Piedmont. The rigged plebiscites of March 1860 in Tuscany are very much a case in point. Although Cavour and the Piedmontese leadership were taken by surprise by Garibaldi's actions, through shrewd manoeuvring and diplomacy Cavour was able to turn the situation in late 1860 to Piedmont's advantage. The successful invasion of the Papal States and the defeat of the papal army at Castelfidaro are good examples of this point. Cavour and the Piedmontese leadership would not have been able to take advantage of events if it had not been for a change in the balance of power. But, ultimately, the process of unification was shaped by Italians.

> The candidate is making it clear that both external and internal factors are of significance. It is a good paragraph which links external and internal factors.

Therefore, the process of unification in Italy between 1859 and 1861 was partly shaped by external factors, notably the change in the balance of power and the role played by France. However, these factors inter-relate closely with the part played by various individuals and the rise of the Piedmontese state. In many senses one can argue that unification would not have happened as it did without the context of foreign intervention and non-intervention. But ultimately, unification was shaped by Garibaldi, Cavour and the Piedmontese leadership. It was Cavour who took action to contain the actions of Garibaldi and it was Cavour who manipulated the situation in 1860 to Piedmont's advantage. Therefore, while external factors are of great significance, the unification process was ultimately shaped by internal factors.

> This is a strong evaluative conclusion. The candidate notes the significance of the external factors and gives them due weight in the argument. However, internal factors, according to the candidate are ultimately the more significant in explaining how Italy was unified between 1859 and 1861.

Verdict

This is a strong answer because:

- the key issues relevant to the question are all explored
- there is a wide range of accurate material deployed to support the points made
- the argument throughout the answer is well-organised, coherent, logical and persuasive.

Preparing for your A Level Paper 2 exam

Advance planning

1. Draw up a timetable for your revision and try to keep to it. Spread your timetable over a number of weeks, and aim to cover four or five topics each week.
2. Spend longer on topics that you have found difficult, and revise them several times.
3. Above all, do not try to limit your revision by attempting to 'question spot'. Try to be confident about all aspects of your Paper 2 work, because this will ensure that you have a choice of questions in Section B.

Paper 2 overview

AL Paper 2	Time: 1 hour 30 minutes	
Section A	Answer 1 compulsory source question	20 marks
Section B	Answer 1 question from a choice of 2	20 marks
	Total marks =	40 marks

You should familiarise yourself with the layout of the paper by looking at the examples published by Edexcel. The questions for each section are followed by eight pages of lined paper where you should write your answer.

Section A questions

This question asks you to assess two different types of contemporary sources totalling around 400 words, and will be in the form of 'How far could the historian make use of Sources 1 and 2 together to investigate…?' Your answer should evaluate both sources, considering their nature, origin and purpose, and you should use your own knowledge of the context of the sources to consider their value to the specific investigation. Remember, too, that in assessing their value, you must consider the two sources, taken together, as a set.

Section B questions

These questions ask you to reach a judgement on an aspect of the topic studied. The questions will have the form, for example, of 'How far…', 'To what extent…' or 'How accurate is it to say…'. The questions can deal with historical concepts such as cause, consequence, change, continuity, similarity, difference and significance. You should consider the issue raised in the question, then other relevant issues, and conclude with an overall judgement.

The timescale of the questions could be as short as a single year or even a single event (an example from Option 2C.2 could be, 'To what extent was Russia's involvement in the First World War responsible for the fall of the Romanovs in 1917?'). The timescale could be longer depending on the historical event or process being examined, but questions are likely to be shorter than those set for Sections A and B in Paper 1.

Use of time

This is an issue that you should discuss with your teachers and fellow students, but here are some suggestions for you.

1. Do not write solidly for 45 minutes on each question. For Section A it is essential that you have a clear understanding of the content of each source, the points being made, and the nature, origin and purpose of each source. You might decide to spend up to ten minutes reading the sources and drawing up your plan, and 35 minutes writing your answer.
2. For Section B answers you should spend a few minutes working out what the question is asking you to do, and drawing up a plan of your answer before you begin to write your response.

Preparing for your A Level exams

Paper 2: A Level sample answer with comments

Section A

You will need to read and analyse two sources and use them in tandem to assess how useful they are in investigating an issue. For these questions remember to:

- spend time, up to ten minutes, reading and identifying the arguments and evidence present in the sources; then make a plan to ensure that your response will be rooted in these sources
- use specific references from the sources
- deploy own knowledge to develop points made in the sources and establish appropriate context
- come to a substantiated judgement.

How far could a historian make use of Sources 4 and 5 (Chapter 2, page 199) together to investigate the weaknesses of Mazzinian nationalism in the 1850s?

Explain your answer, using both sources, the information given about them and your own knowledge of the historical context.
(20 marks)

Average student answer

On one level the two sources present similar reactions to the Milan rising of 1853. Karl Marx attacks Mazzini and the tactics of Mazzinianism while *The Spectator* refers to the 'mistakes' of Mazzinianism. The background information about both of the sources helps to explain why there are similarities in the responses: both are written from a radical perspective although Karl Marx is a revolutionary and *The Spectator* would invariably reflect the views of its owner Robert Stephen Rintoul.

The Milan Rising of 1853 was a very good example of weaknesses of Mazzinian nationalism. Austrian agents had infiltrated the ranks of Mazzinian revolutionaries and many of Mazzini's followers had been arrested. Despite Mazzini's claims, his brand of revolution lacked popular support, either in the cities or the countryside. The revolutionaries lacked the means by which they could take on the military strength of the Austrians. Karl Marx clearly identifies the lack of adequate weaponry used by the revolutionaries; he writes of the revolutionaries being 'armed only with knives'. He also stresses that the revolutionaries did not have the means required to take on the might of the Austrian army. This point is also made by *The Spectator* which suggests that the size of the Austrian army makes the nationalism cause in 1853 'hopeless'.

Marx is a revolutionary but he clearly does not like Mazzini's tactics and he dismisses his leadership of the nationalist movement. His criticism is based on a rejection of Mazzini's 'eternal conspiracy', his revolutionary proclamations and his attacks on the French people. His view is that revolution does not come about through the type of planning which Mazzini was keen on. Marx suggests that this way of organising revolution was the problem in 1848 and 1849 and clearly continues to be the problem in 1853. Because he is a revolutionary, Marx's views are interesting and compare with the views of *The Spectator*.

This is a promising opening which works with both sources and emphasises their similar perspectives. The background information is used but the points which are made about the provenance of the sources are not especially well developed.

The points in this paragraph illustrate some of the weaknesses of the Mazzinian cause as well as the reasons why the Milan Rising failed. There is not as much contextual understanding shown and the candidate does not interrogate the evidence. The analysis of the source is simplistic and the candidate misses details and deals with the first source too simplistically. The response also misses the opportunity to deploy own knowledge to illustrate the weaknesses of Mazzinianism. However, the candidate does try to draw a comparison with the second source.

The Spectator attempts to give an objective account of the aftermath of the Milan Rising. It explains that the revolution did not have wide support 'a small party' and 'originally a fraction of the people'. It also suggests that the leadership of the Mazzinian cause was based overseas or in other parts of Italy. As a British journal and one which is sympathetic to the nationalist cause, *The Spectator*, is able to come to relatively clear judgements about Mazzini and his movement. Some of its ideas are speculative, such as that explained at the end of the source which suggested that Piedmont would eventually weaken and collapse and that Austrian and other absolutist rule would dominate.

> The basic view of *The Spectator* is set out by the candidate is this paragraph. There could be more on the nature of Mazzinianism and the judgements made about the source could be supported with greater justification.

Historians could certainly make use of the two sources to aid their investigation into the weaknesses of Mazzinian nationalism. The two writers have different perspectives but also illustrate some similarities in attitude towards Mazzinianism. Marx represents the view that the Milan Rising was another example of the failure of Mazzini's tactics of organising set piece revolutionary risings. *The Spectator* also stresses that the opponents to revolutionary nationalism were very strong and well organised. It highlights that reaction of the authorities was part of the problem for the Mazzinian cause. Both sources were written at the time and both provide a good starting point for further research.

> The concluding paragraph sums up various viewpoints about Mazzinian nationalism but continues to portray a rather simple version of the points made, especially by Marx. The evaluation of the evidence lacks development.

Verdict

This is an average answer because:

- it does identify arguments in both sources but it does not evaluate the source material with conviction – any judgement about the sources is limited and without full justification and there needs to be more cross-referencing between the sources

- it does deploy some own knowledge but it needs more range and specific illustration
- it does come to a sound overall conclusion.

Use the feedback on this answer to rewrite it, making as many improvements as you can.

277

Paper 2: A Level sample answer with comments

Section A

You will need to read and analyse two sources and use them in tandem to assess how useful they are in investigating an issue. For these questions remember to:

- spend time, up to ten minutes, reading and identifying the arguments and evidence present in the sources; then make a plan to ensure that your response will be rooted in these sources
- use specific references from the sources
- deploy own knowledge to develop points made in the sources and establish appropriate context
- come to a substantiated judgement.

How far could a historian make use of Sources 4 and 5 (Chapter 2, page 199) together to investigate the weaknesses of Mazzinian nationalism in the 1850s?

Explain your answer, using both sources, the information given about them and your own knowledge of the historical context. (20 marks)

Strong student answer

The two sources certainly provide different perspectives on the weaknesses of Mazzinian nationalism. However, there are similarities between these sources. Karl Marx is a revolutionary who is writing for an American newspaper. While supporting the idea of revolution – as was put forward in the Communist Manifesto (which was written in 1848), Marx is critical in this source of Mazzini and his methods. Indeed he does not mince his words when describing Mazzini's failures. *The Spectator* provides another view from abroad of the Milan Rising and the possible reasons why it failed. The author of the source may well be reflecting the view of Robert Stephen Rintoul who was the owner of *The Spectator*. The journal had the reputation for being sympathetic to radical causes and, as such, one would expect it to be objective in it treatment and assessment of Mazziniansim. The sources together provide an interesting contrast of analysis while giving a similar impression.

A main weakness of Mazzinian nationalism was its reliance on revolutionary insurrection against overwhelming odds. Karl Marx clearly feels that this approach and the outcome of uprisings such as that in Milan in 1853 is: 'a very poor result' while *The Spectator* is clear in view about what it calls: 'the hopelessness of the Italian endeavour'. The strength of Austrian forces based in the Quadrilateral was formidable, as Marx describes in Source 4 'a garrison and surrounding army of forty thousand of the finest troops of Europe'. The authors of both sources go out of their way to praise the heroism of the Milan revolutionaries; Marx calls the uprising a 'heroic act' and *The Spectator* refers to the 'spirit' of those who were prepared to challenge Austrian rule. It was not foreign observers such as Marx and *The Spectator* who were critical of Mazzini's tactics in the 1850s. Many of the leading republicans, such as Giorgio Pallavicino and Daniele Manin, were to become critics of his revolutionary methods.

Marx is an intellectual and a writer. His belief was that Mazzini's style of revolution was doomed to failure. Marx's analysis is supported by *The Spectator* which refers to the strength of the 'organized system' and 'organized power' lined up against the Mazzinian revolutionaries. While *The Spectator's* analysis of the future strength of the Kingdom of Sardinia proved to be wrong, the points which it and Marx make about the effectiveness of Mazzinian revolution proved to be accurate. Throughout the 1850s, Mazzinian-inspired revolutions failed. Apart from the collapse of the Milan Rising of 1853, revolutions were put down in Massa in 1854 and Palermo in 1856. The crushing of the rising led by Carlo Pisacane in 1857 and the subsequent

---

This is a strong opening paragraph which explains the background of both sources. The introduction emphasises that the first source, while being generally critical, does provide some insight and that the second source although relatively objective in its viewpoint does reflect the views of many of those who were sympathetic in general terms to Mazzinianism.

These two paragraphs identify key points made in the sources and illustrate them with specific references and some effective own knowledge. In particular, they identify the weakness of the tactic of revolutionary uprising and illustrate that the failure of the Milan uprising in 1853 was just one failure of many. It also makes clear that there were many individuals and groups who would have agreed with both sources.

suicide of Pisacane and execution of its leaders was typical of a decade of failure. The creation of the National Society and Garibaldi's criticism of Mazzini in 1854 and 1856 were further evidence of the rejection of revolutionary nationalism and the move by nationalists to different tactics.

Both sources are written in a style appropriate to their viewpoint. Marx is direct and to the point. Writing in a newspaper he is clearly expressing an opinion and his dismissal of Mazzini and his tactics is harshly put. However, it is supported by the line taken by *The Spectator* although, perhaps, this source is more balanced and even handed in its criticism. It is little surprise that the sources have such similarities, they both represent the views of informed outsiders. Neither source is positive about Mazzini or his methods but, again, that is little surprise given the recent failure of the Milan Rising. The feelings and points made in the two sources provide an effective starting point for a debate about the weaknesses of Mazzinian nationalism in the 1850s. They both react to the failure of the Milan Rising, feeling that it is a very good example of the weaknesses of a revolutionary creed which had little chance of success given the lack of popular support and poor leadership. Taken together the sources would be of considerable use to an historian.

Verdict

This is a strong answer because:

- it is rooted in the sources and identifies and illustrates their key features
- it deploys a sound range of own knowledge to support the points and provide some context

- it sustains focus and develops a clear and balanced argument
- there is a clear judgement which follows on from the arguments put forward.

Paper 2: A Level sample answer with comments

Section B

These questions assess your understanding of the period in some depth. They will ask you about the content you learned about in the four key themes, and may ask about more than one theme. For these questions remember to:

- give an analytical, not a descriptive, response
- support your points with evidence
- cover the whole time period specified in the question
- come to a substantiated judgement.

'Italy, in 1871, was still far from being united.' How far do you agree with this statement? (20 marks)

Average student answer

In many ways, by 1871 Italy was united. The country had been brought together in 1861; there was one king and one political system which governed the country. However, there were some important divisions during this period, especially between Church and State as well as between the north and the south. There was still not one economy and would not be for some time.

Italy was united in 1861. There was to be one king who was Victor Emmanuel II. The king was a constitutional monarch; the Italian parliament consisted of a Chamber of Deputies which was elected on a suffrage of 2 percent of the population and a Senate. Prefects governed locally and they were chosen by the central government. The tax system was based on the Piedmont model.

There was also economic and financial unity. Taxes were the same across all of Italy and taxes on goods sent around the country, known as tariffs, were abolished. The government was very keen to build a national railways network which could help unify the country. In 1871, the network was linked to France when the Mount Cenis tunnel was finished. With the building of a national railways system, goods which were made in the north could be transported more easily to the south. So there was greater unity in 1871 in an economic sense because the country was being brought together by better transport links.

A problem for many nationalists in 1861 was that Italy had been unified without Venice and Rome. Venice still lay under the control of Austria and Rome was guarded by French troops. Although the inhabitants of both areas spoke an Italian dialect, neither Austria nor France had any intention of handing either region over to the new state. Garibaldi tried on two occasions to use force to conquer Rome but was defeated both times; first in 1862 at the Battle of Aspromonte and secondly in 1867 at Mentana. But in 1866, Italy got Venice on the back of the Austro-Prussian War and in 1870 it got Rome after the Franco-Prussian War.

> The candidate has clearly decided to take on the issues of the extent to which Italy unified. However, there are no explicit points which address the question.

> This paragraph is stated rather than explained. The information provided by the candidate is accurate and relevant and there is some detail; however, the paragraph is not developed.

> Once again the concluding comment is not fully supported by the evidence in the paragraph. The candidate might have noted that despite the aims of successive governments to build a national economy, by 1871 there was still considerable division between north and south.

> In this paragraph the candidate runs through the issues of Venice and Rome. The point is appropriate and the detail accurate. However, yet again, the paragraph is overly descriptive and the candidate fails to really answer the question.

But there were many ways in which the country was not united by 1871. The Church did not like the new state and in 1870, the pope, Pius IX, declared himself to be 'a prisoner in the Vatican'. As the pope's temporal power declined, so he attempted to assert the spiritual power of the papacy. This was done in a number of ways. In 1864 the papacy issued the Syllabus of Errors which rejected the ideas of liberalism and nationalism. As a challenge to the new state, it claimed for the Church control over the education system. In July 1870, Pope Pius IX announced the idea of papal infallibility; that the pope was unquestionably right on all matters relating to doctrine. The Church did not recognise the new state of Italy. In response, the state passed the Law of Guarantees which gave the government control over appointing bishops.

> This is a better paragraph on the Church–State relationship, but the answer does not draw the conclusions as to how the divisions of Church and State might impact.

Perhaps the most important division was between the north and the south. As I have already said, the unification was based on the Piedmont model; the constitution which was adopted by Italy in 1861 was the Statuto which was from Piedmont. Many people in the south had hoped that the removal of the Bourbons would lead to fairer rule and the re-distribution of land. Cavour had suggested in 1860 that he would allow some kind of self-rule but it was not to be. In 1860 the south was in an uneasy state. Soldiers from Garibaldi's army and the Bourbon army roamed the countryside. The response of Cavour was to send troops from the north to keep the peace. The result was the Brigands war which was to last until 1865 but, in reality, continued for longer. An example was the uprising in Palermo in 1866 which lasted a week. The brigands were bandits who fought against the officials and army of the new state. At some point in the early 1860s it was calculated that there were as many as 80,000 brigands in the south of Italy. The war was vicious with acts of barbarity on both sides. It showed more than anything else that the new state did not have the support of everybody. The land which was given out in the south was taken from the Church. It was mainly bought by the people who could afford it like the middle classes. Often they enclosed the land which upset the peasant farmers who had hoped to have land of their own and now did not have any common land.

> The paragraph starts quite well and the explanation of the Brigands War is appropriate. However, the paragraph lacks coherence and precision. The second part of the paragraph about land is generalised and weakens the response as a result.

Overall, therefore, it is fair to say that Italy was united in many ways in 1871. The country had a united political system, a constitution and economic unity. It gained Venice in 1866 and Rome in 1870. However, these factors were weighed against the big divisions between Church and State and north and south.

> The conclusion is brief and consists largely of repetition of points made in the body of the answer.

Verdict

This is an average answer because:

- there is some attempt to explain links to the question although most of the passages are descriptive
- the knowledge deployed is mostly accurate and relevant but the material lacks range or depth
- there is an attempt to reach a judgement, but it is limited in its range and needs greater supporting material to make the judgement stand up
- the answer shows some organisation and but it lacks coherence and precision in places.

Use the feedback on this answer to rewrite it, making as many improvements as you can.

Paper 2: A Level sample answer with comments

Section B

These questions assess your understanding of the period in some depth. They will ask you about the content you learned about in the four key themes, and may ask about more than one theme. For these questions remember to:

- give an analytical, not a descriptive, response
- support your points with evidence
- cover the whole time period specified in the question
- come to a substantiated judgement.

'Italy, in 1871, was still far from being united.' How far do you agree with this statement?' (20 marks)

Strong student answer

In 1861, Massimo d'Azeglio remarked to King Victor Emmanuel II: 'We have made Italy, now we have made Italians.' However, given the nature of unification, as a political solution imposed from Piedmont, it was unlikely that true unity would have been achieved by 1871. Despite institutional uniformity and the development of a national economy, the political culture was still dominated by localism. The acquisition of Venice and Rome helped the sense of nation building but areas considered as Italian by nationalists still lay outside the borders of the new state. Above all else, the divisions between north and south and the Church and State were considerable and had not been resolved by 1871.

> This is a strong start to the answer. The candidate places the answer within the context of ten years from 1861 to 1871 as a whole, and considers factors which point to unity and those factors which do not.

The historian Martin Clark wrote about the division in 1871 between what he called 'legal' and 'real' Italy. By 1871 there was unity in a legal sense. The new country had one constitution based on the Statuto and one legal system. There was a constitutional monarchy with Victor Emmanuel II ruling as king of Italy. The army, judiciary and police were all nationally based. But despite this institutional unity, tensions emerged due to the fact that the institutions of state were based on the Piedmontese model. Regions such as Tuscany which had a long history of political autonomy found their institutions swept away. But despite the central institutions, much power still was wielded at a local level, notably by the Prefects. This localist mentality was shared by many of those who were elected as deputies to the Lower House which was the Chamber of Deputies. So while there was, by 1871, institutional unity which one might call 'legal Italy' even in this sense the suggestion that Italy was united might be qualified.

> In this paragraph the answer maintains focus, and looks at some of the aspects of institutional unity. The paragraph is well written and the reference to Martin Clark is well made. The use of own knowledge could be stronger.

Any suggestion that unification brought economic unity should be challenged. Indeed, the removal of tariffs after 1861 caused considerable economic damage to the southern economy as a whole. Unification brought financial problems. The public debt was over 5000 million lire as a result of the wars of unification and the continuing turmoil in the south. The result was that successive governments raised taxes which often disproportionately hit the poor. The most hated and divisive of taxes, the macinato, was reintroduced in 1869. The macinato was a tax on the milling of corn and it caused bitter resentment of the Piedmontese political establishment and its officials who were tasked with collecting it. The 1867 Act which led to the sale of over half a million acres of Church land benefitted, on the whole, the middle classes who had the capital to buy the land. State investment in transport infrastructure benefitted the north rather than the south. So while unification brought a uniform system of weights and measures, a national taxation system and some semblance of a national economy, it would be hard to suggest that by 1871 there was a national economic or financial system in reality.

> This paragraph contains plenty of accurate information, but it tends to jump around a bit. However, the candidate shows good overall control and, again weighs both sides within the paragraph. The concluding sentence works well and shows how effective a point of reiteration at the end of the paragraph can be.

The claim of a united Italy was advanced by the additions to the state of Venice in 1866 and of Rome in 1870. However, the nature of the acquisition of Venice was to provoke deep soul searching among Italian politicians and intellectuals: for while Venice was taken from Austria it was by force of Prussian arms. The Italian armed forces failed dismally, the navy suffering defeat at Lissa in 1866 and the army being defeated at Custozza. Likewise, Rome was acquired through the actions of the Prussian army which comprehensively defeated the French in 1870. While Rome was of huge symbolic importance, other irredentist lands such as Trent, Istria and northern Dalmatia still lay outside the borders of the new state. So while to an extent Italy had been geographically united by 1871, the manner of the acquisition of Venice and Rome and the failure to create what might be called a 'greater Italy' was to cause significant division.

> This is a secure paragraph on the acquisition of Venice and Rome and the impact of the lingering irredentism. The points in this paragraph are well made.

Indeed, one consequence of the acquisition of Rome was that it accentuated the division between Church and State. The anti-clerical Law of Guarantees in 1871 reinforced the deep distrust between the two institutions. It was impossible for the State to claim social unity with the existence of such an institution acting as a state within a state. The strengthening of the Church's spiritual control through the issuing of the Syllabus of Errors of 1864 and the pronouncement of papal infallibility in 1870 was to reinforce its control over the faithful. Likewise, the continuing division between north and south highlighted the weakness of the argument that, by 1871, Italy was united. The Brigands War between 1861 saw the south subdued by a Piedmontese army of 120,000 strong. Although, by 1871, the south had been to a considerable extent pacified the resentment in the south against the north was to linger for decades. These divisions were perhaps the strongest evidence of the failure of the new Italian state to either 'make Italians' or unify the new state.

> The impact of the divisions between Church and State and north and south are considered in this paragraph, and the candidate refers only to their impact on the Italian state. The material is accurate; the only weakness of this paragraph is that the candidate is seemingly running out of time and has not developed the point about north and south as might have been the case.

In conclusion, by 1871 there were still considerable differences between 'real' and 'legal' Italy. The unification process had led to the creation of centralised institutions of state and national systems based on the Piedmontese model. Yet this Piedmontisation meant that unification was, to a considerable extent, imposed on Italy. The continuation of a strong localist culture, irredentism, the divisions of north and south as well as Church and State mean that, to a considerable extent, Italy was unified in name only in 1871.

> A strong answer to this question must consider the factors for and against unity, and weigh these up before reaching a judgement. This is what the candidate has done in this conclusion.

Verdict

This is a strong answer because:

- it puts both sides of the case, looking at both factors which suggests unity and those which do not and it sustains a focus on the question set
- it has a wide range of evidence which is used to support the points made
- it reaches a secure concluding judgement
- it is well organised and communication of material is clear and precise; however, there is some imbalance in the emphasis on the question both within the paragraphs and from paragraph to paragraph.

The unification of Germany, c1840–71

Modern Germany has the largest population and the biggest economy in Europe but it has only been a unified country for a relatively short time. Before 1871, Germany was only a loose confederation of independent states. Each of these states had their own rulers and laws, despite some of them being very small indeed. Austria and Prussia were the largest states within the Confederation while some of the port cities like Bremen and Hamburg were states in their own right.

After the Napoleonic Wars ended in 1815, the German states were independent but 'German' affairs were influenced by an assembly made up of delegates from all the German states. This Federal Diet had very little power but much influence and it was used by the most powerful states to exercise control over the German Confederation. The most influential of these member states were Austria and Prussia and it was their view of how things should be that prevailed in the years that followed 1815. The highly conservative view of politics imposed by Austria and Prussia became known as the 'Metternich' system, after Prince Metternich, the foreign minister of Austria from 1809 and later chancellor, from 1821 until 1848.

In 1848, a series of revolutions overthrew the conservative regimes and replaced them with more liberal ones, although by 1849, the conservative regimes had regained their supremacy. What had changed, however, was not only the popular belief that a unified Germany was possible but the relationship between Austria and Prussia. Prussia was no longer willing to follow the Austrian lead within the German Confederation but wanted to challenge the Austrians and take the lead itself.

During the 1850s, the Prussians began to grow more confident, as their industry expanded and their tax income grew. At the same time, the Austrians were in political and financial crisis. In 1859, the Austrians lost a war in northern Italy against the French and the Piedmontese just as a new organisation (the *Nationalverein*) was being set up to promote German unity under Prussian leadership. The 1860s would prove to be decisive in the process of unification.

1840	1840 – The Rhine Crisis
1848	1848 – Revolution across Germany
	1848 – The Frankfurt Parliament
1859	1859 – Franco-Austrian War
	1859 – Establishment of the *Nationalverein*
1862	1862 – Appointment of Otto von Bismarck as first minister of Prussia
1866	1866 – The Seven Weeks' War between Prussia and Austria

Perhaps the most important single event was the appointment of Otto von Bismarck as first minister of Prussia in 1862. It was Bismarck's skilful management of the Prussian parliament that got through much needed army reforms and his masterful diplomacy that allowed Prussia to exploit military successes and unify Germany. Prussia fought three major wars in Europe between 1864 and 1871 and it was through these that Germany became a unified state.

The first war was against Denmark and was fought in the summer of 1864. It resolved the dispute over the duchies of Schleswig and Holstein. It also showed that the Prussian army were a powerful force and helped to give them the confidence to take on the larger Austrian army, which they would do two years later.

The Seven Weeks' War of 1866 changed the balance of power within the German Confederation. The superior Prussian army defeated the Austrian army at a series of minor engagements before winning a monumental victory at the battle of Koniggratz. As a result of this, the Austrians gave up their claim to influence within the German-speaking lands and Bismarck was able to make a new state called the North German-Confederation, which stretched from Holland in the west to Russia in the east, omitting only the states in southern Germany: Bavaria, Württemberg, Hesse Darmstadt and Baden.

In 1870, Bismarck's diplomacy was again at the centre of affairs as he provoked the French into declaring war. The Prussian army was again victorious neutralising the French army in a matter of weeks. The war only ended in January 1871, after a prolonged siege of Paris but, by this time, the German Empire had already been proclaimed with William, the King of Prussia, as the new emperor of the Germans and Bismarck as the chancellor of the new Germany, which now contained Württemberg, Baden, Bavaria and Hesse Darmstadt but still excluded the Austrian Empire.

1846–47

1846–47 - Poor harvests

1850

1850 - The Punctation of Olomouc

1860

1860 - Army reform in Prussia proposed

1864

1864 - War between the German Confederation and Denmark

1870

1870 - The Franco-Prussian War

2b.1 Popular pressure and causes of revolution, 1840–48

KEY QUESTIONS

- Why was Austria able to dominate the German Confederation in the years before 1848?
- How significant was the impact of economic and social developments in the 1840s?
- How important were the events of 1846–48?
- Why did revolution break out in 1848?

INTRODUCTION

At the beginning of the 1840s, Germany was a loose confederation of independent states. While there were organisations that covered all or a large part of the German states, every German ruler and parliament ruled their own country without outside interference. At the same time, the German states were moving closer together, both economically and culturally. In 1848, disturbances caused by economic grievances would turn into a political revolution that would question both the structure of the German **Confederation** and the nature of government in the individual states.

The map of the German states drawn up at the **Congress** of Vienna in 1815 had not changed by 1840. The German Confederation was made up of 39 independent states, the largest of which were Austria and Prussia. The Confederation had its own **constitution** (the Federal Act) and its own parliament (the **Diet**) but had little power over the governments of the independent states. The Confederation had its own ambassadors and dealt with foreign powers on behalf of its members.

THE POLITICAL SITUATION IN THE 1840s
The role of Austria

The German Confederation was not a new idea. A confederation had existed in Central Europe since the early Middle Ages and had become known as the Holy Roman Empire. At different times in its existence, it had contained parts of modern-day Germany, Switzerland, France, Italy, Austria, the Czech Republic, Slovenia, Holland, Luxembourg, Belgium and Poland. The states within the empire were ruled by individual kings, princes, dukes and archbishops and the most important of these (electors) would elect the emperor, who would oversee the empire. By the end of the Middle Ages, the election of the emperor had become a formality and was passed down through families: at first the Luxembourg family and later the Habsburgs, who were the ruling family of Austria. By the Thirty Years War (1618–48), it had become accepted that whoever was the Archduke of Austria would also be the Holy Roman Emperor.

1840 – The Rhine Crisis
Frederick William IV becomes King of Prussia

1843 – Reinstatement of press censorship by the Prussian government

| 1840 | 1841 | 1842 | 1843 | 1844 |

1841 – Friedrich List, *The National System of Political Economy*, links economic unity with political unity

1844 – Painting *Sliesian Weavers* by Wilhelm Hübner draws attention to the plight of the Prussian textile industry

SOURCE
1

The political geography of the German Confederation.

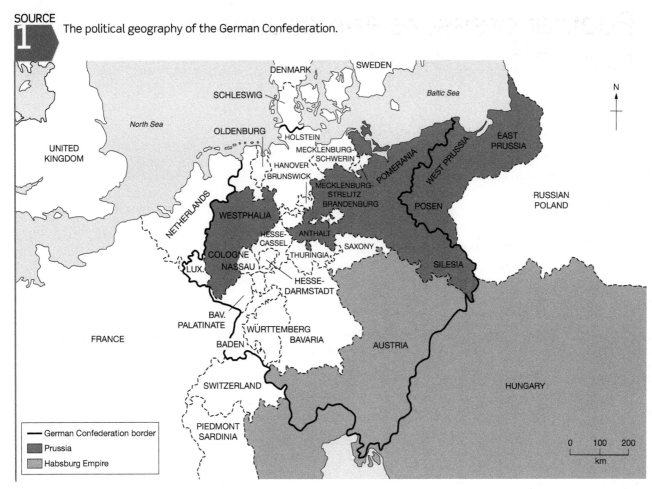

This situation persisted until the Napoleonic Wars of the early 19th century. In a two-year campaign between 1805 and 1807, the French army under Napoleon Bonaparte defeated Austria, Prussia and Russia. As part of the peace treaty, Napoleon abolished the Holy Roman Empire and redrew the map of Central Europe. The new arrangement contained the 'Confederation of the Rhine', a similar organisation of loosely connected independent states but one that excluded the two most powerful German-speaking states: Austria, the largest state in the Confederation, and Prussia.

When Napoleon was finally defeated, the Congress of Vienna (1814–15) set about the process of once again redrawing the map of Central Europe. While the Holy Roman Empire was not reinstituted, a German Confederation was created which included Prussia and the 'Germanic' parts of the Austrian Empire (Hungary and territories to the south and east were excluded, as their first language was not German). In view of its historic role (and its large population), Austria expected to be the leading state in the new German Confederation. For much of the time, this was the case and Austria was able to take a lead in German affairs. It was, however, the ambition of Prussia to be the leading state within Germany and it was this tension between the two rivals that was often at the centre of the changes that brought about the unification of Germany.

1846 – Relaxation of press censorship in Baden

Schleswig-Holstein Crisis

Poor harvests

1848 – French Revolution of February replicated in Baden

Publication of *The Communist Manifesto* by Marx and Engels

| 1845 | 1846 | 1847 | 1848 |

1847 – Meeting of the United Prussian Diet in Berlin

Large meetings of liberals at Offenburg (September) and Heppenheim (October)

Frederick William IV of Prussia recalls the Landtag (national assembly)

Prussia under Frederick William III

Prussia was a large state in the east of the German Confederation. Its main economic activity was agriculture and it was traditionally one of the largest wheat-producing areas of Europe. It also had some industry in Berlin and in the province of Silesia. In East Prussia, there were large estates owned by powerful aristocrats known as **Junkers**. It was from these families that most members of the government and most army officers were taken.

Frederick William became the King of Prussia in 1797 and it was the traumatic period at the start of his reign that did much to shape the rest of it. The French Revolutionary and Napoleonic Wars went badly for Prussia. The lowest point came in 1806 when the French army defeated the Prussians at the Battle of Jena and occupied Berlin. In the peace treaty that followed (Tilsit, 1807), Prussia lost territories along the Rhine and in the east. After the **Treaty** of Vienna, it regained those territories in western Germany and its place in European politics, but Frederick William had become nervous of change and pursued a **reactionary** policy for the rest of his reign.

Frederick William was supported in his reactionary views by the first minister of Austria, Prince Metternich. Both shared the similar view that monarchs and aristocrats should rule states and that the middle and lower classes should not concern themselves with these matters. Therefore, despite their natural rivalry, Austria and Prussia worked together within the German Confederation, bolstering autocratic rulers and thwarting reform.

One of the most significant results of Austro-Prussian co-operation were the Carlsbad Decrees from 1819. Initially a reaction to the murder of August von Kotzebue by a liberal student, eventually the decrees were a series of restrictions on university life and the freedom of the press. Drawn up by Metternich with the agreement of Frederick William at Carlsbad in Bohemia, the decrees were voted for and passed by the Federal Diet under pressure from the Austrians and became a means by which reactionary power was exerted for the next 29 years.

The Carlsbad Decrees illustrated that Austria was the dominant power within the German Confederation in the years following the end of the Napoleonic Wars. What was also clear was that it served Prussia's purpose to co-operate with Austria while they both pursued reactionary policies.

EXTEND YOUR KNOWLEDGE

Prince Klemens von Metternich (1773–1859)
Prince Metternich was the foreign minister of Austria from 1809 to 1848 and chancellor from 1821 to 1848. He was one of the most influential statesmen of the 19th century. Metternich's diplomacy was at the centre of the fall of the Napoleonic Empire and he had much to do with the redrawing of the map of Europe at the Congress of Vienna in 1814–15. Under Metternich's leadership, the congress system promoted the 'Concert of Europe' by which the leading powers co-operated in order to maintain peace on the continent.

Metternich was highly conservative and pursued a reactionary policy within both Austria and the German Confederation. He saw that Austria would have to play a leading role in holding back the forces of liberalism and nationalism.

SOURCE 2 From the Carlsbad Decrees, published in September 1819.

3. The longstanding laws against secret or unauthorised gatherings at universities should be vigorously respected and, in particular, with reference to the German Students' Association which has existed for several years, especially since this society is the root cause of the totally unauthorised links and correspondence between the different universities. Those authorised by the government should, in view of this point, pay the keenest attention, as a matter of duty to make sure that it is respected.

The government are agreed that individuals who, having been aware of the present decree, remain members of, or join secret societies, should be barred from all public office.

4. No student who is sent down because of reports by government authorities or on the recommendation of an academic senate, or who has left university in order to escape such a recommendation, should be allowed entrance to another university, nor should any student, who has left a university without a certificate of satisfactory conduct, be accepted by another university.

ACTIVITY
KNOWLEDGE CHECK

The German Confederation

1 How does the German Confederation show continuity in German politics?

2 Write a short paragraph explaining why Austria saw itself as the leading state within the German Confederation after 1815.

3 Why do you think that Prussia was willing to co-operate with Austria in the years following the Congress of Vienna?

4 Study Source 2. What does this source tell us about the attitudes of the ruling elites towards students in 1819?

Research activity

Using the map in Source 1 on page 287, find out whether the most popular religion was Protestantism or Catholicism in each of the major German states. Can you see a pattern emerging? Why might this be important for politics within the Confederation?

The growth of liberalism

The old social and political order had been challenged by two major events in the late 18th century. The creation of the USA in 1776 and the French Revolution in 1789 had raised questions about how states should be governed. At the same time, a philosophical and scientific movement – the Enlightenment – began to question the assumptions by which people had lived for centuries. Prior to this, it was widely accepted that God sent monarchs to rule states and that their will was law. Moreover, as every aspect of life was controlled by God, to go against a king was seen as going against God. Against this backdrop, monarchs and aristocrats had maintained a hold on power and many states had systems of government that had changed little since the Middle Ages.

Under the banner of 'Liberty, Fraternity, Equality', the French Revolution had unleashed violence, at first in France and then throughout continental Europe. The wars fought against France by the absolutist rulers of the central and eastern European powers were primarily focused on preventing these new ideas from gaining a foothold. Although the French were finally defeated in 1815 and the old order restored, the liberal ideas that came with the revolution would not go away. Authorities throughout Europe could not ignore the potential that **liberalism** and revolution would threaten their hold on power.

Karl Marx saw German politics as consisting of two loose parties – the party of 'movement' and the party of 'resistance'. The liberals belonged to the party of 'movement' insofar as they wanted change. This change centred around the system of government. Liberals felt that power was concentrated in the hands of a narrow elite and that it should have a broader spread. To some this meant universal manhood suffrage within either a republic or a **constitutional monarchy**; to others a greater opportunity for the middle classes to hold political office would suffice.

KEY TERM

Liberalism
A political doctrine that takes protecting and enhancing the freedom of the individual to be central to politics.

EXTEND YOUR KNOWLEDGE

Karl Marx (1818–83)
Born in Trier in Prussia, Karl Marx was a German philosopher, historian and political activist. As he was unable to pursue an academic career due to his atheism, he turned to journalism and later to philosophical writing. Marx became the editor of the liberal newspaper the *Rhenish Gazette*, but this was closed by the censors in 1843. He then moved to France and spent most of the rest of his life abroad.

When the revolutions broke out in 1848, Marx moved back to Cologne and published the *New Rhenish Gazette*, which supported the view that the workers had a right to a say in the political changes that were taking place. By 1849, it was clear to Marx that the revolutions had failed and, under threat of arrest by the Prussian authorities, he moved to London.

He continued to observe German politics from abroad, but the main focus of his work were the new ideas about history, economics and politics, which would come to be known as 'Marxism' and which gave rise to the political ideology called '**communism**'.

KEY TERMS

Constitutional monarchy
A state with a monarch who rules alongside an elected parliament. The monarch often has little or no real power.

Communism
A theoretical economic and political system characterised by the collective ownership of property and by the organisation of labour for the common advantage of all members.

SOURCE 3

From a speech by Karl von Hase, a 19-year-old student, on 18 October 1820, at a gathering to commemorate the Battle of Leipzig.

A people who fought seven years ago on this battlefield is worthy of a better fate. And if the magnificence of the great day has disappeared, if all the palms of victory have withered, if all the medals and trophies of great victories have faded, if all the hopes have been deceived – one thing remains and shall remain, that is the visions proclaimed on that day...

The first vision seems to me to be this: happiness and pleasure are not the highest aims of the people, but freedom. That is the will of God and reason.

From this it follows: the happiness and greatness of a people depend on the highest possible liberty of all citizens and the equality of all, established by laws they make themselves or that are made by their representatives.

The third, however, is a heart stirring conviction which is instinctive in every truly great person. An enthusiastic people which is willing to fight for such laws and for such a Fatherland cannot be conquered – even if there are one hundred thousand Persians standing against ten thousand heroes of Marathon...

The fourth belongs to us alone and is the most beautiful of all: Germans are well all together! There are few Saxons, few Bavarians, no more Hessians, the Franks do not wish to say much, the Prussians can be mastered; but that wonderful people from the Weichsel to the Vosges, from the North Sea over the Alps to Carpathia, made equal through speech, customs, and descent, all citizens of the Reich – a unified people of brothers is irresistible...

You, ghosts of the fallen, be our witness, ghosts of our great fathers look upon us! We swear never to flinch, never to tremble, we swear in this dark hour our loyalty to the Fatherland, loyalty to all good and beautiful, loyalty until death...

Measures like the Carlsbad Decrees were seen by reactionaries like Metternich and Frederick William III to be a key part of their struggle against liberalism. Until 1848, reactionary governments held firm, though liberals made some small gains in some parts of the Confederation.

- In the 1830s, some of the smaller German states agreed to make their constitutions more liberal. These included Brunswick, Hesse Cassel and Saxony.

- In 1833, Hanover gained its first constitution from its ruler, King William, who was also the King of Great Britain.

SOURCE 4

The Thinkers Club important question for consideration at today's meeting: how long shall we be allowed to think? A cartoon about the suppression of freedom of speech.

- In 1846, liberals in Baden made gains when press censorship was relaxed and the police and judicial service were reformed.

- In 1847, a moderate liberal newspaper, *Die Deutsche Zeitung* ('The German Newspaper') was first published in Heidelberg.

- Also in 1847, a meeting of liberals from the south-western states met at Heppenheim and demanded liberal reforms in the areas of the National Diet, the press, the armed forces and taxation.

- The King of Prussia, Frederick William IV, agreed to a meeting of the National Diet in 1847. Afraid of possible liberal ideas within it, Frederick William disbanded the Diet. This enraged Prussian liberals who subsequently became more active.

The growth of nationalism

In early societies, loyalty was a matter between people. People belonged to kinship groups or tribes. In the Middle Ages, people became tied to somebody above them in society and owed loyalty as a feudal obligation. As monarchs became more important, loyalty to the monarch became more important. People regarded their identities as being tied to their loyalty to their monarch. During wartime, soldiers fought in the king's army often in regiments led by, or named after, members of the royal family.

During the war to found the USA and the French Revolution, new concepts of belonging were needed, as monarchy and aristocracy had ceased to exist in these countries. There had been developing throughout the 18th century, a new idea that nation states were inherently a good thing and that loyalty to your group was every bit as good, if not better, than loyalty to an individual. The first line of the song 'The Marseillaise', which was to become the French nation anthem, is: 'Arise, children of the Fatherland'. At the Battle of Valmy in 1792, a French army of conscripts motivated by **nationalism** beat a professional army of Prussians fighting for their monarch. This was very practical evidence of the potency of the new idea.

In the German states, there was an important difference between the kind of nationalism that was growing in France and that which might develop in central Europe. People in the German states had to ask themselves: 'Am I Hanoverian or German?' In other words, did nationalism mean belonging to the political state that people lived in or belonging to the cultural group? The intellectuals who discussed this concept were fairly unanimous in their answer. For the writer Johann Goethe and the philosopher Johann Herder, nationalism meant belonging to the cultural group that could be identified as 'German'. As the idea of nationalism grew among the Germans, a greater degree of 'unity', political, cultural or economic, was central to the notion.

The prevalence of new ideas in the German Confederation

While there is much evidence that nationalist and liberal groups existed throughout the German Confederation, the extent to which these views were held is still at matter for historical debate. There were certainly events, such as the Hambach Festival in 1832 or the Heppenheim meeting in 1847, which drew large numbers of people. These were a clear expression of liberal and nationalist views. It is, however, problematic to ascribe the same motivation to all those who attended. Similarly, demonstrations against the state, particularly violent ones, have been cited as evidence of widely held liberal and nationalist sympathies. Often the causes of such incidents had social and economic aspects to them. It is often difficult to see the extent to which ordinary people held onto liberal and nationalist ideas when faced with more pressing needs concerning employment, poverty and housing.

KEY TERM

Nationalism
A desire by a large group of people, who may share the same culture, history, language, etc., to form a separate and independent nation of their own.

SOURCE 5

Germania, the female figure that represented the German nation, painted by Philipp Veit in 1848.

The 1840 crisis

The extent to which nationalist sentiments had permeated everyday life in Germany was not always clear, but certainly during times when other powers threatened (or occupied) parts of the German Confederation nationalist feelings came to the fore. One of these occasions was the Rhine Crisis of 1840.

Instability in the Ottoman Empire had caused the major European powers to sign a Convention in 1840 that would put an end to French interference in that area. This was a major diplomatic defeat for France and politically embarrassing for the French first minister, Adolphe Thiers. To deflect attention from this, Thiers raised the old issue about France's eastern border. During peace negotiations in 1813, it had been put forward that France's eastern boundaries should be natural features: the Alps in the south and the Rhine in the north. When Napoleon was defeated in 1814, this proposal was forgotten. Thiers revived this claim in 1840.

The German reaction to this was outrage. There were over 30,000 square kilometres of territory to the west of the Rhine that were populated by Germans and ruled by German states (mostly Prussia). The idea that the French army would occupy the Rhineland and annex it to France was unthinkable to most Germans. A wave of nationalist fervour swept not only through the Rhineland but throughout the Confederation. Nationalist groups were formed and demonstrations took place against the French. Songs were written such as 'Die Wacht am Rhein' and 'Deutschlandlied', the third stanza of which would become the German national anthem, 'Deutschland, Deutschland über Alles'.

This rise in nationalist feeling was welcome but also caused a problem for the leading powers of Austria and Prussia. On the one hand, if German nationalism could be utilised as political force against foreign powers, it could only enhance the potential standing of the German Confederation within Europe. Moreover, as nationalism had replaced liberalism in the German political psyche, particularly as German liberals had cited France as the model liberal state, then it would be easier for the reactionary governments to check the liberals. On the other hand, the danger was that German nationalism could build a momentum of its own, become uncontrollable and thereby be a threat to the status quo.

For the rulers of the German states, the response to the crisis was reassuring and alarming at the same time. The upsurge of nationalist feeling meant that the ruling elite would be confident that France would not risk an invasion against the combined might of the German Confederation led by Austria and Prussia. On the other hand, the sentiment that caused such a vigorous popular response could soon turn to the issue of a united Germany, a threat just as serious as that of a foreign invasion.

The Schleswig-Holstein crisis, 1846

Schleswig and Holstein were two duchies on the border of Denmark. For centuries, the ruler of these duchies had also been the King of Denmark. When Christian VIII became King of Denmark in 1839, there was a lot of pressure to incorporate both duchies into Denmark. The problem was that the population in these duchies was predominantly German, and Holstein, though not Schleswig, was part of the German Confederation.

Aware of the potential problems, the Federal Diet issued a proclamation in 1846 calling on the Danish king to pay due regard to the rights of the Confederation but made no reference to the 'national' characteristics of the population. At the same time, it called upon German states to control nationalist enthusiasm. Again, members of the ruling class were nervous of a diplomatic incident inciting nationalist feelings within the Confederation.

ACTIVITY
KNOWLEDGE CHECK

Liberalism and nationalism

Answer the following questions:

1 How did liberalism pose a threat to those who wished to follow a reactionary policy?

2 How did nationalism pose a threat to those who wished to follow a reactionary policy?

3 What were the differences between liberalism and nationalism?

4 How did issues abroad threaten the ruling elites within the German Confederation?

SOURCE

Part of a poem by Ernst Arndt, written in 1813, set to music in 1825 and sung often in 1840.

Wherever rings the German tongue,
And praises God the German song,

There shall it be!

There German, make your Germany
There shall the German's country lie.
Where scorn meets Gallic frippery
Where France meets hatred from the land,
And German clasps a German hand,

There shall it be!

There is the whole of Germany!
There is the whole of Germany!
Oh God, regard it from on high,
Grant German courage to us all,
That we may love it true and well,

There shall it be!

There is the whole of Germany!

AS Level Exam-Style Question Section A

Study Source 3 on page 290.

Why is this source valuable to the historian for an enquiry into the reasons why the ruling elites feared liberalism in the 1840s?

Explain your answer using the source, the information given about it and your own knowledge of the historical context. (8 marks)

Tip

Make sure you quote from the source and refer to specific context about the 1840s as you analyse the material. Don't forget to consider the purpose of the author and the ongoing reaction of his audience.

ECONOMIC AND SOCIAL DEVELOPMENTS IN THE 1840s

The economic situation within the German Confederation

The Industrial Revolution in Britain and later in Europe and North America changed the economic situation of all countries in the world. The ability to mass produce goods made items much cheaper and caused a boom in economic activity. For the German Confederation, the issue during the first half of the 19th century was the damage that could be done to German producers of manufactured goods by the potential influx of cheap goods from Britain. This meant that some favoured a **protectionist** system with high **customs duties** that would artificially inflate the price of foreign imports. On the other hand, the Agrarian Revolution meant that agricultural production was more efficient and therefore some farmers in Germany were producing record surpluses and favoured a 'free trade' policy, which meant that they could export cheap farm produce to other countries.

As the area of the German states spread from the Rhineland in the west to the Baltic states in the east, the economic activity varied by region. States in the north-west of the Confederation, such as Hanover and the western territories of Prussia around the Ruhr, were rich in natural resources and close to the large ports at Hamburg and Bremen. This provided the natural environment for heavy industry, particularly steel. When railways began to be developed from the mid-1830s onwards, this provided a further stimulus. The Krupp family started making steel in this area at the beginning of the 19th century and became one of the largest steel-producing companies in the world. Silesia in the south-western part of Prussia and Saxony also had a tradition of heavy industry. Away from these areas, the German Confederation had a very traditional economy based on agriculture. States in the south-west such as Bavaria and Württemberg depended on a wide range of agriculture, as did the eastern part of Prussia west of the Oder river. Austria had a largely agricultural economy and production of manufactured goods was extremely outdated.

The chief issue within the German Confederation's economy was for governments to choose between '**free trade**' and protectionism. Traditionally, protectionism had been in place. Not only did it protect the states' producers but it also served the needs of the ruling elites. Trades guilds favoured protectionism because it meant that their members had a relatively secure place in the market. Landowners favoured protectionism because it maintained a stable and relatively high price for agricultural produce. Monarchs liked protectionism because it was a good source of income for the royal purse. As production became more efficient, however, 'free trade' became a much more appealing policy. Landowners who could produce large surpluses needed new markets in which to sell their surplus while manufacturers who could make more, quicker and cheaper needed to export in order to maximise their profits. Broadly speaking, Prussia favoured a 'free trade' approach whereas Austrian policy was one of protectionism.

The economic dominance of Prussia

After 1815, Prussia had made territorial gains in the west, which did much to improve its political position. Having part of the western and the eastern border of the Confederation meant that it was strategically placed to intervene in matters relating to those areas. This was particularly significant when it came to dealing with France. Proximity to the French border would shape diplomacy in the 1860s and the course of the war in 1870.

The new Prussian territory also gave it an economic edge over the rest of the Confederation. It gave it a new diversity in its economic activities, which partially protected it from changes in the market and natural disasters like harvest failure. Geography had given the Prussians the ability to dominate Germany's natural resources and also control of the major rivers, the most useful means of transporting goods from cities inland to the large ports in the north like Hamburg and Kiel.

Changes in agriculture after 1815 improved Prussia's position. East Prussia had been a large wheat-growing area for centuries and improvements in production methods meant that a surplus was usually achieved in years when there was no natural threat to the crop. The newly acquired lands in the west brought diversity to the Prussian agricultural economy, with rye being a popular crop along with barley, hops and grapes. Despite the growth in population in the 19th century, Prussia tended to produce twice as much food as was needed, which gave it a regular surplus to export. This brought in foreign currency for the farmers and merchants and export duty for the government.

New territories also diversified Prussian manufacturing. Traditional Prussian manufacturing had been for the local market except for textiles and luxury goods made from amber. The acquisition of Silesia in 1740 had given Prussia more natural resources and heavier industry grew up in that area. After 1815, domination of the Ruhr and the Saar gave Prussia control of the coal resources and thereby iron production was naturally centred in these areas. Industrialisation did not take place until the 1850s but Prussia was ideally placed for this change when it occurred.

Aside from its advantages in manufacturing and agriculture, Prussia's size and position gave it an advantage. The population of Prussia provided a large market close by for businesses and merchants in other German states and many businesses became dependent on the Prussian market. Moreover, the movement of goods within the northern part of the Confederation had to go through Prussia. The three major waterways, the Elbe, the Oder and the Rhine, all went through Prussian territory and without using these rivers it was very difficult to get goods to the northern ports and an overseas market.

SOURCE

Table showing the development of agricultural production per unit of labour input (LI) in the German Confederation, 1800–50 on the basis of grain values.

Period	Production in 1,000 tonnes					
	Arable	Livestock	Total	Labour force (1,000)	Tonnes per LI	Index*
1800-10	14,500	7,555	22,055	9,525	2.32	100
1811-20	15,660	7,332	22,992	9,530	2.41	104
1821-25	19,140	8,100	27,240	10,100	2.70	116
1826-30	20,010	8,787	28,797	10,300	2.80	120
1831-35	22,910	11,205	34,115	10,600	3.22	139
1836-40	24,795	12,262	37,057	11,057	3.35	144
1841-45	26,825	13,719	40,544	11,662	3.48	150
1846-50	29,000	14,874	43,874	11,425	3.84	165

*Index shows the relative growth in output (tons per LI) from the base line of 1800 = 100.

SOURCE

Tables showing industrial growth in the German Confederation, 1815–48 (Austrian and UK figures are given for comparison).

Coal and Lignite production: annual average (in million tonnes)			
	German Confederation	Austria	UK
1815	1.2		16.2
1825-29	1.6	0.2	22.3
1835-39	3.0	0.3	28.1
1845-49	6.1	0.8	48.6

Pig Iron production: annual average (in thousand tonnes)			
	German Confederation	Austria	UK
1825-29	90	73	669
1835-40	146	103	1,142
1845-49	184	146	1,786

Length of railway line open at the end of each year (in kilometres)			
	German Confederation	Austria	UK
1835	6		544
1840	469	144	2,390
1845	2,143	728	3,931

KEY TERM

Customs union
An agreement between states to lower or abolish customs duties between them.

The *Zollverein*

The *Zollverein* was a **customs union** that would prove to play a significant part in the process by which Germany became unified. Eventually it would draw in all the German states except Austria and have its own regulatory bodies.

In the years after 1815, economies in the German Confederation began to grow, particularly the Prussian economy. The main problem was that internal customs duties were so complicated that they deterred trade within Germany. There were ancient customs duties in place within states and every time goods crossed a border into another state, customs were paid as well. This was particularly bad for those states which had territories that were split. Prussia, for example, had territory in the east and territory in the west but to get from one to the other meant travelling across at least one and often two other states. This could mean paying one or more sets of customs duties which made it very difficult for manufacturers in one part of the Confederation to sell goods in another part, even if that part were actually the same state.

In 1818, in response to pressure from manufacturers in the Rhineland, the Prussian government passed the Tariff Reform Law, which did away with all internal customs duties within Prussia. This was known as the Prussian Customs Union. The manufacturers had also pressed for a high protective duty against imports, particularly goods from Britain. The Prussian government believed that high customs duties would only serve to encourage smuggling so it kept them to a minimum. Initially, there were no duties on imported raw materials, only 10 percent on manufactured goods and 20 percent on luxury items. Prussian leaders saw that free trade would be of greater benefit to Prussia than protectionism.

Within ten years, other smaller German states had joined the Prussian Customs Union, either because they saw being a member as economically advantageous or they felt that not being a member was economically disadvantageous. Other groups, however, resisted. Bavaria and Württemberg formed a South German Customs Union and the Middle German Commercial Union consisted of Hanover, Brunswick, Saxony and several smaller states. The significance of the Middle Union was that it stood geographically between the two halves of Prussia. This meant that Prussian goods still needed to go through it in order to move from one half of Prussia to the other. Moreover, if Prussia were to control a stretch of land from the Rhine to East Prussia, it could effectively control the routes between the large cities in central and southern Germany and the sea ports in the north.

The Middle Union was determined to keep these routes free from Prussian control. It built a series of roads that would connect central and southern Germany with the ports in order to keep trade flowing outside the Prussian Customs Union. To counter this, the Prussians also financed road building and eventually joined Prussia directly with Frankfurt, Bavaria and Württemberg. In 1830, Hessen-Cassel, which was a member of the Middle Union, ran into financial difficulties and was left with no choice but to join the Prussians. Very soon the Middle German Commercial Union collapsed owing to infighting and lack of investment and most of its members joined the Prussian Customs Union.

In 1834, Bavaria and Württemberg joined and the Prussian Customs Union dropped the 'Prussian' in its title and became known simply as the Customs Union or *Zollverein*. By 1836, it covered an area with a population of 26 million people and, by 1844, only Austria, Hanover, Mecklenburg and a handful of smaller states were not members.

By the mid-1840s, when the *Zollverein* was fully in place, Austria had become economically marginalised within the Confederation. With a very backward economy, Austria favoured a highly protectionist policy which kept foreign goods out and meant that Austrian goods remained within the Austrian market. As the Austrian Empire, which included Hungary, Bohemia, Slovakia, parts of Italy and the Balkans, was so large, the protected market served the needs of Austria's basic industry. At a time, however, when the rest of Europe was making such rapid industrial progress, Austria fell behind, with what would prove to be far-reaching consequences.

SOURCE 9

Map of the *Zollverein*, c1845.

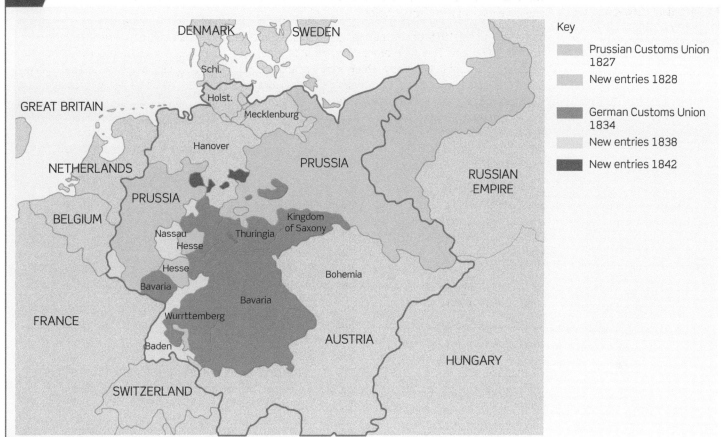

Key

- Prussian Customs Union 1827
- New entries 1828
- German Customs Union 1834
- New entries 1838
- New entries 1842

SOURCE 10

Excerpts from *On Hostility to Trade*, an essay written in 1843 by John Prince Smith, an Englishman and a Prussian citizen.

I believe that I may introduce the following propositions as irrefutable, namely:

- that government interference in the course of trade through tariffs can only *prohibit profit* or *compel loss*;

- that creating certain branches of industry through protective tariffs does not increase employment for labor and capital, but can only provide for a damaging type of employment;

- that, without this kind of artificial provision, the capital and labor to be employed in protected trades would find application in free, profit-making trades; — (because the price that the protected trades need to pay for capital and labor is the price that the unprotected trades offer for the same);

- that a protective system diminishes the funds for employing workers overall by way of destroying capital;

- that entrepreneurs in protected industries have to suffer under the general pressure that the protective system distributes across all members of the nation in the form of increased prices for articles for consumption;

- that the protective system puts exotic trades that depend upon restricted sales at home in the place of natural, home-grown branches of production that might win out in world markets;

- that an attempt at reprisal by way of protective tariffs only increases the damage to [a country's] own subjects;

- that an attempt to offset a disadvantage arising from a restriction imposed by others with a self-imposed restriction will actually increase the losses to those subjects who were disadvantaged in the first place;

- that the entire prohibitive system, which stems from ignorance, aspires to imagined advantages, without any calculation of the costs

SOURCE 11

Prince Metternich writing about the *Zollverein* in 1833. This document was written for his own purposes and only published after his death.

The German Confederation cannot be considered a really effective political institution, nor is it possible for it to maintain the high place which it has had on the European political scene, unless it remains completely faithful to the principle of equality of rights and duties among the members of the federal body. Special privileges for any powers whatsoever are banned by the Confederation, as created by the Act of the Congress of Vienna (With the exception that the presidence of the diet is officially recognised as belonging to Austria); all members should exercise with equal liberty and independence their right of voting in the diet, a right which the constitution guaranteed them...

The situation has changed as result of the formation of the Prussian Customs Union. Now a number of Independent States accept, in relation to a neighbour superior in power, the obligation of conformance with its laws, of submitting to its administrative measures and its control in a most important branch of public finance. The quality of rights of the members, as arranged in the federal acts and maintained until this time, now vanishes...

The founding of the *Zollverein* was, perhaps, the first significant point at which the balance of power between Prussia and Austria began to shift. As German economic activity began to centre on Prussia, so political activity would follow. The *Zollverein* had an advisory body which met to discuss relevant issues. Every member state had representatives. Although purely an economic and commercial body, the *Zollverein* had strong political overtones, indicating that co-operation that could take place on the economic level could also take place on the political level. In the long term, Prussian economic dominance would play an important part in the process by which German unification was achieved. In the short term, of perhaps greater immediate significance, was that the customs union led quickly to the standardising of weights and measures throughout Germany and then to the introduction of a single currency for all the member states.

SOURCE 12

Statistics indicating that Austria was a successful industrial nation in the first half of the 19th century (taken from Source 8).

Pig Iron production: annual average (in thousand tonnes)		
	German Confederation	Austria
1825-29	90	73
1835-40	146	103
1845-49	184	146

SOURCE 13

Prince Metternich, writing in 1833, explaining that everyone is equal within the German Confederation, from his *Mémoires*, 1882 (taken from Source 11).

Special privileges for any powers whatsoever are banned by the Confederation, as created by the Act of the Congress of Vienna... all members should exercise with equal liberty and independence their right of voting in the diet, a right which the constitution guaranteed them.

SOURCE 14

Friedrich List, commenting, perhaps inaccurately, about the impact of steam railways (taken from Source 17).

It promotes the hygienic condition of the community.

SOURCE 15

A happy man and his friends enjoying tossing a coin, a detail from *The Silesian Weavers* by Wilhelm Hübner, 1844 (see Source 18).

A Level Exam-Style Question Section A

How far could the historian make use of Sources 10 and 11 together to investigate the significance of the *Zollverein* for the German Confederation in 1840?

Explain your answer, using both sources, the information given about them and your own knowledge of the historical context. (20 marks)

Tip

Make sure you use the evidence of the sources to support your points and refer to specific context as you analyse the material. Don't forget to consider the purpose of the author and how this might affect the way that the historian might use the source.

Context is everything

Look at Sources 12-15.

Work in groups.

Take an A3 piece of paper for each source. In the middle of it draw a circle about 18 cm in diameter. Within the circle is the evidence itself, outside the circle is the context.

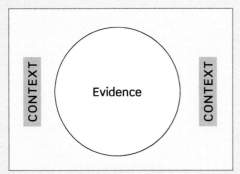

For each source, write a set of statements inside the circle of information that can be gleaned only from the source itself without any contextual knowledge. Outside the circle, write down statements of contextual knowledge that relate to the source. Try to link statements with annotated lines where possible to show how context can change the nature of information that we can take from sources. You may need to compare the sources in this exercise with the sources they were taken from: Sources 8, 11, 17 and 18.

Answer the following question:

Explain why knowledge of context is important when gathering and using historical evidence. Give specific examples to illustrate your point.

The development of the railways

Railway building started in the German Confederation in the 1830s. At first there were small branch lines around major cities and a short line that connected Leipzig with Dresden. The first half of the 1840s saw an explosion of railway building. Driven by speculators, investors and industrialists, the movement of goods was a major factor and by the end of the decade it was possible to move freight from the Ruhr to the ports at Bremen and Hamburg, and freight and passengers from one side of the country to another. By the middle of the 1860s, the intercity network was virtually complete.

Having these rail links helped the German economy tremendously. Agricultural produce could be moved from the south and the east to lucrative markets in western Europe. Similarly, manufactured goods could be quickly taken to ports for export. Railway building also created a demand for engineering skills and steel production. Initially, expertise and material for the new railways had to be imported from Britain, but over time steel from the Ruhr and German engineering took over.

Improved internal communications also had a political impact – quicker communications and easier contact, which then engendered a feeling of common purpose. Individuals could travel between major cities in less than a day. This meant that meetings could be set up quickly and important information

SOURCE 16 Maps showing the growth of the railways in the German Confederation, 1840–80.

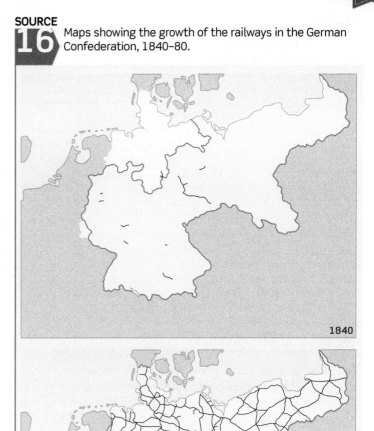

1840

1880

exchanged. For those interested in political change, the ability to communicate quickly with like-minded individuals was a significant improvement. On the other hand, the state would be able to move security forces to sensitive places very quickly. The army high command in Prussia was quick to see the advantages of the railway system. It would use it to gather large numbers of troops quickly in strategically important places. The efficient use of the railway system was one of the significant factors in the Prussian military victories over Austria (1866) and France (1871).

In addition to the development of the railways came the telegraph. This gave people the ability to send information over large distances very quickly. Telegrams between individuals meant that contact could be made in a matter of hours and ideas developed quickly. Also journalists were able to send articles to newspapers and were able to see them in print the next day. The story of great events would thereby travel very quickly and people in places remote from the events would be able to respond within a short time. There were moments when the improvement in communications had a very clear effect on the pace of change.

SOURCE 17

From Freidrich List, *The National System of Political Economy* published in 1841. He is writing about the advantages of the railways.

1 As a means of national defense, it facilitates the concentration, distribution and direction of the army.

2 It is a means to the improvement of the culture of the nation, as it facilitates the distribution and promotes the rapidity of distribution of all literary products, and the results of the arts and sciences. It brings talent, knowledge and skill of every kind readily to market, and increases the means of education and instruction of each individual and of each class and age.

3 It secures the community against dearth and famine, and against excessive fluctuation in the prices of the necessaries of life.

4 It promotes the hygienic condition of the community, as it destroys distances between the sufferer and his means of cure.

5 It promotes social intercourse, and brings friend to friend, and relative to relative.

6 It promotes the spirit of the nation, as it has a tendency to destroy the Philistine spirit arising from isolation and provincial prejudice and vanity. It binds nations by ligaments, and promotes an interchange of food and of commodities, thus making it feel to be a unit. The iron rails become a nerve system, which, on the one hand, strengthens public opinion, and, on the other hand, strengthens the power of the state for police and governmental purposes.

ACTIVITY
KNOWLEDGE CHECK

The economy

1 Study Sources 7 and 8 on page 295. What do they tell us about the changes to the economy within the German Confederation?

2 What was the purpose of the *Zollverein*?

3 List four ancillary consequences (i.e. not to do with its prime purpose) of the *Zollverein*?

4 Find or draw an outline map of the German Confederation. Using the text, the sources and further research, write on the map the important geographical areas and economic activity. Write notes on it that explain the changes to the economy in the first half of the 19th century.

KEY TERM

Industrialisation
The process by which a society changes from production by hand to production by machine. Production by machine is usually concentrated in factories.

Industrialisation and social classes

Industrialisation created the need to bring together large numbers of workers to work in the new factories. This produced a demographic shift, as people left the countryside and moved into the cities where the new factories were being built. This process is known as 'urbanisation'. Within the new cities, the nature of the lower classes was changing. Skilled workers had a new confidence, which was reinforced by their status within factories, the rise in their disposable income and the respect of their peers. As large numbers of workers congregated, they were able to exchange ideas and organise meetings. At the same time there was a rapid growth in the rate of literacy among working people. Although literacy teaching was initially aimed at helping workers to read the Bible, it also led to the popularity of newspapers and journals. As a result, there grew a new awareness of politics among the members of the lower classes.

Industrialisation also led to an increase in people who might regard themselves as 'middle class'. Production on an industrial scale meant high profits for the owners of factories and also those associated with the businesses: merchants, accountants, lawyers, etc. As these middle classes became wealthier and better educated, they began to ask the question as to why they had no say in the running of their country. Not only did the middle classes have the education and the motivation to challenge the existing order, they also had the financial muscle to run political campaigns.

The 1840s also witnessed the birth of a new political movement. Workers' groups were calling for a greater share of wealth and political power. They believed that complete equality was desirable and that stronger members of the group should have a duty to care for weaker members of the group.

This movement became known as 'socialism'. Karl Marx, who was working as a journalist during this period, wrote extensively on political matters and took a keen interest in socialism. In 1847, Marx and his friend Friedrich Engels published a book to define a new and extreme form of socialism called communism. *The Communist Manifesto* would become one of the most influential books in history. One of the earliest 'communist' organisations was the 'League of Outlaws', which wrote a declaration in 1834 that included the line: 'Since all citizens have an equal right to protection, however large the discrepancies in their abilities, equality is the cornerstone of society.'

Urbanisation also contributed to greater social and cultural unity. People in cities began to congregate together to pursue common interests, which they were then able to share with others in different parts of the German Confederation. Athletic clubs, shooting clubs and music and choral societies became popular and festivals were organised where groups could meet and interact. The Lower Rhine Music Festival became a regular feature from 1818 onwards. Moreover, as time went on, German music became a far more significant part of the repertoire and was more 'nationalistic' in nature. *Der Freischutz* by Carl Maria von Weber was particularly popular and the operas of Richard Wagner were based on old German myths and stories.

EXTEND YOUR KNOWLEDGE

Social change and the unification of Germany
Some historians have made a strong case for the unification of Germany having had a significant social and cultural aspect to it. There were Germans who had a strong sense of German similarities that were spread across the Confederation. The German language was a natural unifying factor and a scientific study was undertaken to see the extent to which regional dialects differed. The brothers Grimm, in addition to their famous collection of folk tales, produced a book on German grammar which became a standard work in universities across the Confederation. There was a school of German philosophy that included people like Kant, Hegel and Schopenhauer and German music boasted some of the greatest composers in Europe, such as Beethoven, Brahms and Mendelssohn.

Some historians have also argued that many seemingly innocent activities were, in fact, a front for nationalist groups. They have said that festivals of song or gymnastics were an opportunity for like-minded Germans to meet people from all over the Confederation. It was believed that the authorities could not ban such meetings because they were concerned with sporting or cultural activities rather than political ones.

One cultural area that the authorities did clamp down on was the universities. The Carlsbad Decrees had already singled out students as being potentially dangerous but this was also true of their teachers. At the beginning of the Convention of German Naturalists and Doctors in Berlin in 1828, Alexander von Humboldt told the delegates of the meeting that they represented the unity of Germany.

The economic crisis of 1846-47

Many working people in the German Confederation lived close to the poverty line. This made them vulnerable to changes in the economy. Both agricultural labourers and factory workers could find themselves laid off and facing eviction and starvation. The rapid increase in population (72 per cent in Prussia between 1816 and 1864) only served to exacerbate the situation. That over 400,000 people emigrated to the USA during the 1840s, mostly owing to economic circumstances, illustrates how precarious life could be for many working people.

Life in the countryside was hard. Most of the German agricultural sector was worked by tenant farmers. Often they found that rent was high and low food prices made it hard to earn a living. In East Prussia life was even harder for the landless peasants who worked as casual labourers on the estates owned by the Junkers.

Life in towns was also hard. The availability of factory work was subject to market forces and so workers were often laid off. The rapid expansion of towns meant that they lived in very poor conditions. Houses were badly built and sanitation was often non-existent. Large families might have to live together in one room and ill-health was a constant worry. Epidemics of diseases such as cholera and typhoid were common. Crime was rife.

In 1846, the corn harvest failed. To make matters worse, there was also an outbreak of potato blight which destroyed that year's crop. In 1847, the corn harvest failed again. The consequences of these agricultural problems were far reaching.

Perhaps the most important consequence was that food prices went up. From 1836 to 1844, the price of rye went up by 40 percent but by the middle of 1846, it had gone up by 120 percent since 1836. For most German peasants, potatoes were their staple diet and a failure of the crop meant starvation. Those in the city had to face food shortages and prices that pushed some of them to the edge of starvation. The knock-on effect of this rise in prices was that less was spent on manufactured goods, as families had to prioritise expenditure on food. This in turn lead to a downturn in sales and caused a crisis in manufactured goods. Factories in industrialised areas had to lay off workers, but the hardest hit were the **artisan** class. Already threatened by new production methods and cheap imports, skilled artisans had relied on traditional methods of production, so a downturn in sales hit them very hard.

The reaction to this crisis was desperate. Food riots occurred across the Confederation and workers held demonstrations pressing for better conditions. Ruling elites were nervous that matters might have got out of hand.

KEY TERM

Artisan
A skilled worker who manufactures something by hand: for example, a shoemaker, a weaver or a tailor. Often workers grouped together in guilds in order to keep their profession exclusive and protect their livelihoods.

SOURCE 18 *The Silesian Weavers* by Wilhelm Hübner, 1844. Weavers were particularly badly hit by automated production methods, cheap British imports and the economic crisis of 1846–47.

ACTIVITY
KNOWLEDGE CHECK

Class and the economic crisis

1 Explain how industrialisation changed German society.

2 Why were the consequences of the harvest failures so hard hitting for the lower classes?

3 Study Source 18. What reasons could Wilhelm Hübner have had for painting this picture in 1844?

WHAT WERE THE SHORT-TERM CAUSES OF REVOLUTION, 1846–48?

Middle-class unrest

While the workers and the peasants were faced with a frightening economic situation, there was also dissatisfaction among the middle classes. Their grievances were mostly concerned with power: who held it and how it was applied.

- Reactionary policy almost worked too well. The middle classes, steadily growing in numbers, had been excluded from government in most states within the German Confederation.

- Many autocratic rulers had a very old-fashioned view of things and found it difficult to govern in the light of new changes.

- The economic crisis caused by the harvest failures showed up the inadequacies of the old regimes through their inability to deal effectively with them. For centuries, autocratic regimes had adopted *laissez-faire* attitudes but times had changed and more intervention was perhaps needed in a semi-industrial economy.

- Civil rights were still being abused. Freedom of speech and of the press was still being curtailed by the Carlsbad Decrees and the 1832 recommendations put forward by Metternich.

Part of the difficulty for middle-class liberals and nationalists was that there was no single answer to these problems. Many liberals wanted a more representative form of government. Many nationalists wanted a representative form of government in a unified Germany. It would be unreasonable, however, to believe that a more representative form of government, at least in the eyes of most liberals, would include the lower classes. Universal manhood suffrage was an aim more familiar to socialists and communists than to liberals. In many ways, the middle classes would have been just as alarmed as the ruling elites by the riots and demonstrations of the lower classes. In this respect, the middle classes had to proceed carefully, so that a little change took place in order for them to take a share of power but not so much as to involve workers and peasants in the business of government.

Just before the first harvest failure of 1846, the question of the Danish duchies inflamed nationalist sentiment in the German Confederation. At the end of January 1846, King Christian VIII issued a proclamation, which stated that a new constitution

EXTRACT

The view of the historian David Blackbourn on German liberals of the 1840s, from his book *History of Germany 1780–1918: The Long Nineteenth Century*, 2003.

Liberals were not democrats. True, they criticised the arbitrary state in the name of the 'people', organised petitions, held liberal banquets and other politically based festivities. But liberals were alarmed by the poorest and most ignorant, critical of those they thought of as the 'masses'. They rejected universal manhood suffrage, as they rejected female suffrage, because the poor (like women) were thought to be dependent and suggestible. Independence, based on maturity (of years and judgement), together with a certain level of property and education, was regarded by almost all liberals as a prerequisite of responsible citizenship. The Rhenish liberal Peter Merkens attacked the privileges of the local provincial nobility, but also objected to any broadening of the franchise to the Cologne chamber of commerce that would admit poor fruit peddlers. His colleague David Hansemann denounced popular sovereignty as a 'pernicious theory'. Views like this may have been voiced with unusual firmness by liberal Rhineland merchants, but they were not exceptional. The idea of a pre-1848 liberalism was a society of (male) citizens who were active, industrious, and self-reliant.

would incorporate Schleswig and Holstein into the Kingdom of Denmark. In response, the estates of the two duchies demanded the incorporation of Schleswig-Holstein as a single state into the German Confederation. The leaders of German states were anxious to put pressure on the Danes but not to encourage nationalist feelings within the German Confederation. Fearful of losing a war with the stronger Germans, Christian backed down but not before a nationalist uproar had occurred throughout the Confederation.

The middle classes were able to apply pressure in two ways: first, with large gatherings that produced demands published in documents, and secondly, through the increasing popularity of liberal newspapers such as *Die Deutsche Zeitung* ('The German Newspaper') and *Rheinish Zeitung* ('Rhine Newspaper'). There were two major meetings in 1847. The first of these was held at Offenburg in Baden. Though Baden was already one of the more liberal states in Germany, the delegates at the meeting pushed for further concessions. This partly precipitated the Baden crisis of 1848 (see below). In response to this, moderate liberals called a meeting at Heppenheim in October 1847. The demands of the Heppenheim meeting were:

- an extension of the *Zollverein* customs union to include those German states not currently members in order to bring about unification; this should include Austria

- the participation of the people through elected representatives

- freedom of the press

- reform of the judiciary

- an end to medieval taxes on land and restrictions on its sale

- reduction in the expenses for the standing army and the introduction of a people's army

- a commission of parliamentarians to look into tax reform.

The meetings illustrate the two strands of thinking within the middle classes. The Offenburg meeting was concerned with constitutional issues within Baden and pushed for a liberalisation of government. Although the Heppenheim meeting made some liberal demands, at its heart was the nationalist aim of the unification of Germany.

Liberalism in Prussia

In 1840, the reactionary King Frederick William III died. He was succeeded by his son, Frederick William IV. The new king had a strange mixture of views for a 19th-century monarch. On the one hand, he believed profoundly in the **Divine Right of Kings** and

KEY TERM

Divine Right of Kings
A notion, very popular with monarchists up to the end of the First World War, that monarchs were sent down to earth by God in order to rule countries.

had a vision of a united Germany which would mirror the Holy Roman Empire led by an Austrian emperor. On the other hand, he was willing to adopt measures to appease liberal demands. Upon his accession, Frederick William IV abolished press censorship and restored liberal and nationalist academics to their previous posts. These included Ernst Arndt at Bonn University and the brothers Grimm, who were given posts at Berlin. In 1842, committees were summoned from the provincial estates to meet in Berlin in order to advise the government. Despite these meetings taking place, the advice from these committees was ignored. In 1843, in order to placate the Junkers, press censorship was reinstated, having been abolished in 1840.

It was in 1847 that Frederick William took the biggest step by calling a meeting of a representative body called the Prussian Estates or *Landtag*. Many saw this as the equivalent of a national Prussian parliament. It was not, however, the representative body that many liberals had hoped for. Most of its delegates were aristocrats. The main purpose of the meeting was to vote for a loan to build a railway linking Berlin to East Prussia. While the Prussian Estates agreed to the loan, it also declared that it should meet more regularly. It was at this point that Frederick William dissolved the body.

SOURCE 19

Memorandum to King Frederick William IV from Joseph von Radowitz, minister for foreign affairs, concerning measures to be taken by the Prussian Estates in 1847.

The most powerful force of the present, that of nationality, is the most dangerous weapon in the hands of the enemies of law and order. This fact must be appreciated... if there is to be any insight into present events. Through all hearts flows this desire for a community to develop in Germany, powerful and respected abroad, elevated and in harmony within... This is the only thought that extends beyond parties, to which conflict of different tribes, churches and political doctrines are subordinated. It is therefore the only principle on which a strong state system and society [*Lebensordnung*] can be constructed. It is Prussia's task, with the closest connection with the rest of Germany to pick up the reins lying on the floor and as a true moral authority to create the impetus towards a rebirth of Germany... Measures to be taking were threefold; to strengthen militarily, to extend and develop the protection of law, and to satisfy material needs. To achieve this it was necessary to bind Austria more narrowly to the Confederation, and to overcome the swindle of sovereignty and egoisms of individual governments. The best means to prepare for reform of the Confederation was to call a ministerial conference representing the 17 votes of the inner council of the Confederation. Its task must be to fix the basic principles for national state reform.

The impact of the revolution in France

Since 1789 and the outbreak of the French Revolution, liberals all over Europe had looked to France as the leading liberal state in Europe. The French Revolution itself destroyed the traditional class system in a very violent way and under the motto of 'Liberty, Equality, Fraternity' tried to create a much more equal society. Politically this failed and the French Republic was replaced by the Empire, a virtual dictatorship under Napoleon Bonaparte. The Empire, however, retained some of the vestiges of the liberalism of the French Revolution. Perhaps the most significant of these was the meritocracy.

'Meritocracy' means advancement through ability rather than position. In the ***ancien régime*** of the 18th century, people gained positions of authority because of who they were and what family they belonged to. This meant that the upper classes kept control. As the middle classes became wealthier and better educated, they desired the possibility of gaining positions of power, but they found these opportunities were limited because most of these positions were reserved for members of the aristocracy. As the French Revolution did away with the aristocracy, the way was open for the middle classes to rise on the basis of their ability. During the French Empire, the idea of meritocracy was maintained particularly with regard to the army.

In the German Confederation, the aristocracy still held onto power. The German liberals viewed the French experience with envy. The liberal movement in France had a far greater influence on matters than in Germany. Further French revolutions in 1830 and 1832 sent shockwaves around Europe, causing demonstrations in major European cities. It is no coincidence that when Karl Marx fled from Germany, he went to Paris.

There was some revolutionary activity in the Italian states over the winter of 1847–48, but it was the French Revolution of February 1848 that ignited events all over Europe. On 24 February 1848, the King of France, Louis Philippe, was overthrown and a **republic** was established. Once again, the French had acted on the principle that power resided in the will of the people rather than the will of

KEY TERM

Ancien régime
System of government prevalent in European states during the 18th century where power was concentrated in the hands of the monarch and their advisors.

KEY TERM

Republic
A state governed by an elected parliament and without a monarch.

the monarch. This principle was to be tested in most European countries during the course of the year, as liberals and revolutionaries were inspired by the events of the 'February days'.

The constitutional crisis in Baden

Events in Baden had almost pre-empted the revolution in France. Since 1816, the Baden Assembly had had a second chamber of elected members drawn mostly from the professional classes. The chamber had no powers to pass laws but could lay down motions, some of which were extremely radical in nature. In 1832, it passed a motion criticising the Frankfurt Decrees and their suppression of the press. After much pressure, in 1846, the Grand Duke had agreed to pass a liberal constitution. This meant that Baden had a parliament that was elected on the widest franchise of any German state. This showed other German liberals what gains were possible and gave liberals from Baden a high status. At the Offenburg meeting in September 1847, it was the radical liberals, many from Baden, who took the lead.

SOURCE 20 Demands arising from the Offenburg meeting, September 1847.

1   We demand that our state government disassociates itself from the Carlsbad decrees of 1819, the Frankfurt decrees of 1831 and 1832 and the Vienna decrees of 1834. These decrees are contrary to our inviolable human rights.

2   We demand freedom of the press.

3   We demand freedom of conscience and teaching. The relations of a human being with his God belong to his innermost soul and no external force has the right to intervene... No force should interfere in matters concerning teachers and pupils.

4   We demand that the militarily swear an oath of allegiance to the Constitution.

5   We demand personal freedom. Domination and harassment of citizens by the police should cease. The right of association, the right to enjoy a healthy community life, the right of the people to hold meetings and to speak, in public, the right of the individual to a decent existence, the right to move freely and travel anywhere in the German fatherland should all be henceforth inviolable.

That the Offenburg declaration included references to 'inviolable human rights' was a significant radical step. It would not have been a commonly accepted notion that such a thing as human rights existed. Many states at that time had yet to abolish slavery and the universal declaration of human rights would not be written for another 100 years. Being the most radical German state did not mean that Baden escaped the uprisings of 1848.

Soon after the 'February days', mobs of peasants began to burn the mansions of local aristocrats. On 27 February 1848, an assembly in Mannheim adopted a resolution that called for a **Bill of Rights**. The same demand was soon adopted in Württemberg, Hesse-Darmstadt and Nassau.

KEY TERM

Bill of Rights
A law that establishes the relationship between the people and the monarch. Often this is to establish the rights of the people and their elected body and protect them from arbitrary rule by the monarch.

ACTIVITY
KNOWLEDGE CHECK

Short-term causes of the 1848 revolutions

1   Explain why the middle classes might have desired change but also been nervous of it at the same time.

2   Why would events like the Rhine Crisis of 1840 and the 1846 affair of the Danish duchies help the nationalist cause? Do they underline a weakness with the nationalist movement in Germany?

3   Why were newspapers becoming increasingly influential?

4   Make a list of the ways in which politics in Prussia and Baden were similar and different.

5   Draw a two-circle Venn diagram. Label one of the circles 'Liberals' and the other 'Nationalists'. Within the diagram write down aims and events that relate to one or the other group and those that relate to both.

OUTBREAK OF REVOLUTION IN 1848

The 1848 revolution in Austria

If the political events in Baden were viewed as significant by observers in 1848, what was about to unfold in Austria would have appeared to be seismic.

Once news of events in Paris had reached Vienna, citizens began to compile petitions to deliver to Emperor Ferdinand calling for reform. Early in March, the Viennese took to the streets in their thousands in order to protest against the government and about the economic situation in general. At the same time, the Diet of Lower Austria, which met in Vienna, called for Metternich's resignation owing to the ongoing civil unrest. Metternich sought an assurance of support from the emperor but none was forthcoming. On 13 March, demonstrators clashed with troops on the streets of Vienna and Metternich resigned and fled to London. Emperor Ferdinand appointed a liberal government and made promises about a new constitution. To prevent further clashes, he withdrew the army from Vienna.

EXTEND YOUR KNOWLEDGE

The Austrian Empire
In 1527, the Duke of Austria also became the King of Hungary. The two states then belonged to the same empire until 1918. Unlike the United Kingdom, where having the same monarch led to full political integration, Austria and Hungary always had separate systems of government, except for a brief period between 1848 and 1867. This meant that all laws had to pass through both the Imperial Council in Vienna and the Diet in Budapest. Being politically, linguistically and culturally different sometimes caused friction, as in 1848.

It was events in the rest of the Empire that hampered the government's ability to deal with the revolution in Vienna. In Budapest, the Hungarian Diet saw the opportunity to distance itself from the imperial government in Vienna. It passed laws, which gave control over finance and military affairs in Hungary to the Hungarians and not the emperor's government in Vienna. It also implemented measures designed to limit the activity of Croatian and Romanian nationalists. Czech nationalists in Prague convened a Pan-Slavic congress in June, which called for an end to the oppression of Slavic peoples by German nationalists. In northern Italy, Austrian troops had to withdraw from Milan and take refuge in the fortress area known as the quadrilateral. To make matters worse, Charles Albert, King of Piedmont–Sardinia declared war against Austria on 23 March.

With Austrian troops being tied down in northern Italy, there was little Ferdinand could do against the revolutionaries. In May, he moved his family to Innsbruck and left Vienna virtually to govern itself. Events began to turn in Ferdinand's favour in June when Austrian troops under Prince Windischgratz put down the revolt in Prague. As a reward, Windischgratz was made commander of all the imperial troops outside Italy. He slowly moved his troops back into Vienna and by the end of October had occupied the city and arrested the ringleaders of the revolution. At the same time, the reactionary Prince Schwarzenberg became first minister and moved the Imperial Diet to the Moravian town of Kromeriz. Despite an improvement in the situation, Ferdinand was feeling the strain and was in very poor mental health. He abdicated on 2 December 1848 and was succeeded by his nephew, Franz Josef. In March 1849, the Diet was dismissed and Schwarzenberg issued a new conservative constitution. On 23 March, the Austrians beat the Italians at the Battle of Novara and ended the hopes of Italian nationalists. By the summer of 1849, with the help of a 30,000-strong Russian army, the Hungarian revolt had been put down and the revolutions were over.

The 1848 revolution in the German states

The smaller German states took their lead initially from Baden. In Nassau, a large mob of peasants marched on Wiesbaden and demanded that Duke Adolf abolish serfdom. Similar demonstrations also took place in Württemberg. In Baden itself, the Grand Duke fled and a revolutionary government was appointed. Violence followed a similar pattern as it spread north into Prussian Westphalia, Saxony and Thuringia, as peasants pushed to the brink of starvation attacked the homes of the nobility. There were also demonstrations in the cities, where workers took to the streets to demand better conditions and there was some breaking of factory machinery by skilled workers who felt they had been put out of work by industrialisation.

Serious violence was not necessarily the norm across Germany. Different areas reacted to events in different ways. Violence in the cities was likely to be much more serious than violence in the countryside. An eyewitness in Hardenberg, Bavaria recalled seeing villagers 'streaming out of the forest, pushing wheelbarrows filled with newly chopped wood'. It is perhaps indicative of the parochial nature of German society that locals in Bavaria saw the Europe-wide upsurge in violence and rebellion as an opportunity to steal wood from the local landowner.

THINKING HISTORICALLY   Causation (5b)

Many factors cause historical events. Some are crucial, while some are less important. For some historical questions, it is important to understand exactly what role certain factors played in causing historical change.

Causes of the 1848 revolution in Germany

Bad harvests contributed to a severe economic downturn in 1846 and 1847	Nationalist groups wanted members of the German Confederation to work closer together; some desired a single German state
The structure of government meant that the rising middle classes had no say in the way the country was governed. Therefore liberal groups wanted political reform	The *Zollveriein* had shown that closer economic co-operation could work. There were still, however, some German states that were not members: Austria, for example
The French revolutions had raised questions about the nature of government and showed that violent action could achieve change	Urbanisation had created a situation where workers were more politicised

Work in groups.

1 Rate each of the causes between 1 and 10, where 1 is insignificant and 10 is highly significant. Then compare your ratings with another group. How far did you agree?

2 In your original group, formulate a hypothesis about what would have happened had each of the six causes in turn not been present. Again, compare your hypotheses with another group. How far did you agree this time?

Answer the following questions on your own:

3 Which were the most significant causes of the 1848 revolution in Germany?

4 Think about why it is important for a historian to understand the relative significance of different causal factors.

SOURCE

21 A description of an attack on a customs house in Brunswick in 1848.

The mob began by smashing in the windows and doors; then the tiles were ripped off the roof and the destruction of the building continued, until... it was completely torn down and just the annex was left standing. The records and implements in the building were strewn about and tables and chairs thrown out into the street. The attempt to set the building on fire was thwarted, when the flames which had already encompassed the records and papers were stamped out by the inhabitants of Brunsen who threw a door on the conflagration. At 3 AM, the ruins of the customs building were set on fire, so that it had been completely destroyed.

In Baden, there were still militant elements who were not satisfied with the gains made. A group of armed workers led by Friedrich Hecker and inspired by Gustav von Struve launched an armed uprising in early April 1848. While Struve proclaimed the German state out of a window in Lörrach in West Baden, Hecker started recruiting men for his escapade. Eventually, troops from Baden and Hesse-Darmstadt hunted Hecker down and defeated his small band. Hecker, himself was able to flee. He emigrated to the USA and served in the Union army during the American Civil War.

SOURCE 22
Food riots in Stettin, 1847. A contemporary print from an engraving by G. Nicholls published in the *Illustrated London News*.

Response of the German rulers

The violence soon petered out as governments within the German states made concessions. King Ludwig of Bavaria granted freedom of the press and when this was not enough to appease his subjects, he abdicated in favour of his son, Maximillian. A liberal government was appointed on 20 March. In Saxony, the government resigned on 13 March to be replaced by a more liberal regime, and although violence erupted in May, this was more to do with the perceived failures of the Frankfurt Parliament than lack of progress in Saxony itself. In Württemberg, King William first dismissed his ministers and then replaced them with more liberal figures. Across Germany, concessions granted by the individual regimes caused the initial violence to dissipate. From the end of March, most of Germany had its eyes on the events in the Frankfurt Parliament as it represented the possibility of a new unified German state.

Despite local gains in the individual German states, nationalists and liberals pinned their hopes on the Frankfurt Parliament (see below pages 312–313). It was the speed with which the preliminary meetings were held and the promise that a pre-parliament would prepare the ground for a fully elected parliament that gave the middle class hope that its demands would be met. Without the support of the middle classes, lower-class agitation fizzled out or was brutally put down by government forces.

Reasons for the initial success of the 1848 revolution

The 1848 revolution sent shock waves throughout Europe. It saw the fall of reactionary regimes, most notably that of Metternich in Austria, and showed that liberals and nationalists could make gains against the forces of reaction. There were several reasons for its initial success:

- They had a common purpose, which united the middle and lower classes. Both groups wished to see systems of government change, albeit for different reasons.

- The lower classes were under tremendous economic pressure. Feeling they had nothing to lose, they willingly took part in violent demonstrations.

- Industrial and technological changes had radically altered societies. Reactionary regimes were attempting to govern in the same way that they had before the French Revolution of 1789.

- Radicals in Europe took their lead from the French. The successful February revolution inspired radicals in other parts of Europe and made them confident that they would make progress.

- Increasing cultural unity within the German Confederation convinced nationalists that the time was right for closer political unity.

Summary

The 1840s saw the German Confederation beginning to break free from the reactionary stranglehold. Pan-European liberal ideas had found a receptive audience in the German middle classes and incidents such as the Rhine Crisis and the controversy over the Danish duchies illustrated the strength of German nationalist sensibilities. Economic changes were beginning to transform certain areas into modern industrial conurbations, which meant a burgeoning middle class and a more politicised working class. The economic success of the *Zollverein* had drawn German states closer together and increasing nationalist feeling had found expression in academia and the arts. The same nationalism that had begun to bring Germans closer together, at the same time threatened the Austrians. Their fear of losing their hegemony within the German Confederation was matched by their concern that the nationalist spirit displayed in 1848 in the non-German speaking parts of their empire, would eventually tear the Austrian Empire apart.

ACTIVITY
KNOWLEDGE CHECK

The revolution in Austria and Germany

1 Why would politically aware people throughout the German Confederation be interested in the resignation of Metternich?

2 Explain the two reasons why Austria had to be worried by the rise in nationalist feeling.

3 Study Source 21. How far can you see in this source the reasons for the outbreak of violence during the run up to the 1848 revolutions?

4 How far did nationalism put a break on violence during the early stages of the 1848 revolutions?

ACTIVITY
SUMMARY

1 Write down with full explanations the three most important consequences of industrialisation in Germany.

2 Write a full paragraph explaining why the people in the German Confederation who were liberals might also have been nationalists.

3 Draw three mind maps about the political situation at the end of 1847, one each for Prussia, Austria and Baden.

4 Write a short essay to answer the following question:

How far would a liberal writing in May 1848 have regarded the 1848 revolutions as being successful?

AS Level Exam-Style Question Section A

Why is Source 19 valuable to the historian for an enquiry into the reasons that violence broke out in 1848?

Explain your answer using the source, the information given about it and your own knowledge of the historical context. (8 marks)

Tip
Remember to include material that deals with the author and to show a full appreciation of the context of the question.

WIDER READING

Blackbourn, D. *History of Germany 1780–1918*, Blackwell (2003), chapter 2

Carr, W. *A History of Germany*, Edward Arnold (1989), chapter 1

Clark, C. *Iron Kingdom: The Rise and Downfall of Prussia*, Penguin (2006), chapter 13

Taylor, A.J.P. *The Course of German History*, Hamish Hamilton (1945), chapter 3

Williamson, D.G. *Germany Since 1815*, Palgrave (2005)

2b.2 Failure of revolution, 1848–51

KEY QUESTIONS

- To what extent did the Frankfurt Parliament attain its objectives by 1849?
- What was changed by the Prussian Revolution, 1848–49?
- In what ways can the revolutions of 1848 be seen as a failure?
- How did the revolutions of 1848 change German politics?

INTRODUCTION

The revolutions of 1848 caused a major shift in German politics but for a brief time it then appeared that the status quo had been restored. Major forces of unification and liberal reform convened a parliament that wrote a new constitution for a united Germany and published a declaration of citizens' rights (the Fifty Articles) and yet by the summer of 1849, all that remained of the Frankfurt Parliament and the 1848 revolutions were a few documents and a few memories.

In the longer term, the groundbreaking work done as a result of the revolutions would serve as a background to developments that would bring Germany together and give an example of the kind of state that modern Germany would become.

To a large extent, the events of the revolutionary period were predicated on the relative strengths of the two German powers, Austria and Prussia. Both states experienced serious revolutions in March 1848, where the governments were forced to flee and the monarchs forced to introduce a programme of liberal reform. The situation was, perhaps, worse for the Austrians as Hungary (geographically the largest area in the Habsburg empire) was in open revolt against the Habsburg monarchs until August 1849.

This weakness allowed German liberals to seize the initiative and to call a national parliament at Frankfurt with a view to national unification. There were **counter-revolutions** later in 1848 and the parliament lost influence and the great powers re-asserted their influence. Austria would continue to take the lead in German affairs as it had since 1815 with Prussia playing a secondary role.

KEY TERM

Counter-revolution
Attempts by the authorities to fight back against the forces of revolution and re-establish the situation that had preceded the revolution. This can manifest itself as simply opposition to a revolution as it unfolds or may be the attempt to overthrow a new authority which has been installed by a previous revolution.

EXTRACT

1 The historian A.J.P. Taylor (1906–90, specialist in 19th and 20th century European diplomacy) assesses the impact of the 1848 revolutions across Germany in his book *The Course of German History*, published in 1945.

1848 was the decisive year of German, and so of European, history: it recapitulated Germany's past and inspired Germany's future... Never has there been a revolution so inspired by a limitless faith in the power of ideas: never has a revolution so discredited the power of ideas in its result. The success of the revolution discredited conservative ideas; the failure of the revolution discredited liberal ideas. After it, nothing remained but the idea of Force, and this idea stood at the helm of German history from then on. For the first time since 1521, the German people stepped on to the centre of the German stage only to miss their cue once more. German history reached its turning-point and failed to turn. This was the fateful essence of 1848.

March 1848 – Revolutions in Austria and Prussia

May 1848 – First session of the Frankfurt Parliament

July-August 1848 – Danish War

November 1848 – Prussian Army retakes control of Berlin and ends the revolution

March 1849 – Publication of the German Constitution

May 1849 – Uprisings in Baden and the Palatinate are put down by Prussian troops

1848 Jan	Feb	Mar	Apr	May	June	July	Aug	Sept	Oct	Nov	Dec	1849 Jan	Feb	Mar	Apr	May	June	July

April 1848 – *Vorparlament* makes preparations for the new 'national' assembly

July 1848 – Election of Archduke John of Austria as Imperial Administrator

December 1848 – Fifty Articles published

April 1849 – Offer of the crown of the united Germany is declined by Frederick William of Prussia

October 1848 – Austrian Army retakes control of Vienna

SOURCE 1

The barricades on Kronenstrasse and Friederichstrasse in Berlin on 18 March 1848 from an eyewitness. A coloured lithograph of a painting by F.C. Nordmann (1848).

August 1849 – Hungarian rebels surrender and Habsburg control of all their lands is restored

May 1850 – Revival of the Federal Diet

Aug	Sept	Oct	Nov	Dec	1850 Jan	Feb	Mar	Apr	May	June	July	Aug	Sept	Oct	Nov	Dec	1851 Jan	Feb

March 1850 – The Erfurt Union

November 1850 – The Punctation of Olomouc

EXTRACT

The historian Christopher Clark (1960–, specialist in 19th-century German history) assesses the impact of the 1848 revolutions across Germany in his book, *Iron Kingdom, the Rise and Downfall of Prussia 1600–1947*, published in 2006.

> Yet there was no return to the conditions of the pre-March era. Nor should we think of the revolutions as a failure. The Prussian upheavals of 1848 were not, to borrow A.J.P. Taylor's phrase, 'a turning point' where Prussia 'failed to turn'. They were a watershed between an old world and a new. The decade that began in March 1848 witnessed the profound transformation in political and administrative practices, a 'revolution in government'. The upheaval itself may have ended in failure, marginalisation, exile or imprisonment for some of its protagonists, but its momentum communicated itself like a seismic waves to the fabric of the Prussian (and not only the Prussian) administration, changing structures and ideas, bringing new priorities into government or re-organising old ones, reframing political debates.

TO WHAT EXTENT DID THE FRANKFURT PARLIAMENT ATTAIN ITS OBJECTIVES BY 1849?

The *Vorparlament*

The revolutionary events of February 1848 had caused a shift in power in some German states, notably Baden. In other states where no formal changes in government had taken place, liberals were beginning to have a sense that their influence was about to grow. The Federal Diet also sensed this and in early March began to make concessions to the liberals. Press censorship was abolished across the Confederation and a committee was set up under Dahlmann and given the task of producing a revised constitution. Lacking faith in the unelected Diet's ability to bring about genuine change, leading liberals from south-west Germany held their own meeting at Heidelburg on 5 March 1848.

The most significant conclusion reached by the Heidelberg meeting was the feeling that the Federal Diet would be unable to make the kind of radical changes that the liberals desired. It was decided to call a national parliament in Frankfurt to consist of members from all over the Confederation. A committee of seven was appointed to make the necessary arrangements.

The task of the *Vorparlament*

The committee invited notable liberals and representatives from the state assemblies from all over the Confederation to attend a session that they called a *Vorparlament* or pre-parliament. It was openly acknowledged that the key issue was how to unify Germany, but to become legitimate the body in Frankfurt would have to go through some form of election process in order to call itself a 'parliament'.

The *Vorparlament* first met on 31 March 1848. Between the appointing of the Committee and the first meeting of the *Vorparlament*, events in Vienna and Berlin had changed the situation. What had been political unrest in the south and west of Germany had turned into a full-scale revolution across the Confederation. This had considerably strengthened the hand of those who wished to pursue a policy of radical change.

The task facing the *Vorparlament* was not without difficulty. The terms by which it would be elected, the frequency and conventions of the meetings, the scope of the main body, the organisation of sub-committees and the administration of the whole organisation were all matters that had to be addressed and from a starting point of nothing. Despite the excitement caused by the potential for dramatic change, the *Vorparlament* fulfilled its administrative duties and the first session of the Frankfurt Parliament opened on 18 May 1848.

Many in the *Vorparlament* had hoped for an assembly elected by a broad franchise. All 'Independent' adult males were allowed to vote in the elections. This was interpreted differently in different states. Moreover, many of the elections were indirect, which meant that voters elected a group of people who would then select the delegate to the parliament. As a result of election 'management', the majority of the members could be described as 'middle class'. For example, out of 585, 157 were lawyers, 138 were civil servants and over 100 were teachers. There were only four artisans and one peasant. Another issue in the parliament was that the number of members was not equally balanced across the Confederation. The majority came from the south and west and only two were from Austria (though a few more came later on). Of the 141 Prussian members, over 100 were from the more liberal Rhineland as electoral colleges were given a free choice of whom to nominate and so they favoured delegates with more liberal credentials.

Answer the following:

1 What do you think were the hopes of the members of the *Vorparlament* ?

2 In what ways might the social structure of the Frankfurt Parliament have influenced the extent to which it could pursue radical reform?

The nature and work of the Frankfurt Assembly

The first task facing the new parliament was the establishment of a central **provisional government** for the whole of Germany. Negotiations to this end proved difficult and so it was decided that it would be better for the parliament to elect a leader or 'imperial administrator' to build a government rather than the parliament to seek a consensus between the members. The role was offered by the parliament to the Austrian Archduke John, who was the brother of Emperor Ferdinand and well known for his liberal views. He accepted the role and invited nobles from across the Confederation to serve in the government, including Prince Leiningen, a Bavarian aristocrat and relative of Queen Victoria, as president.

Once a provisional government was in place, they could begin to look at the central task of writing a new constitution for the greater German state. The constitution was a complicated business and committees were appointed to deal with separate parts of it. They began to work from July onwards, looking at how they could incorporate the systems of all the states in the Confederation such that a new constitution would be acceptable to everybody. If they could be successful in this, a major barrier to full unification would have been negotiated.

KEY TERM

Provisional government
A government appointed to run affairs until a more permanent government with greater legitimacy can be set up.

SOURCE

From the *Proclamation of the Imperial Administrator*, Archduke John, on 15 July 1848.

Germans! Your representatives, assembled in Frankfurt, have elected me as the Imperial Administrator. Amidst the declarations of trust, amidst the greetings of goodwill which I have received everywhere and which have moved me, I accepted the leadership of the temporary central administration of our Fatherland.

Germans! After years of pressure total freedom will be granted you. It shall serve you since you have sought it hard and long. It will nevermore be withdrawn since you will know how to preserve it.

Your representatives will complete the German constitution. Await it with trust. The construction will be built seriously, thoughtfully and with the deep love of the Fatherland. Then it will stand as firm and fast as your mountains.

Germans! Your Fatherland will have to withstand severe tests. These will be overcome. Your roads, your rivers will survive, your diligence will find work, your prosperity will increase, if you allow your representatives and me whom you elected to make Germany free and powerful with your help.

However, do not forget that freedom goes hand-in-hand with order and lawfulness. Ensure that these are protected where they are threatened. I shall counteract criminal acts and licentiousness with the full weight of the law. The German citizen must be protected against all punishable acts.

Germans! Let me hope that Germany will live in undisturbed peace. My most sacred duty is to preserve it.

Should, however, German honour or German law be endangered, then the brave German army will be in a position to fight and gain victory for the Fatherland.

AS Level Exam-Style Question Section A

Why is Source 2 valuable to the historian for an enquiry into the hopes of the liberals and nationalists?

Explain your answer using the source, the information given about it and your own knowledge of the historical context. (8 marks)

Tip
Remember to include material that deals with the author and what his overall aims might be for the Frankfurt Parliament and its relations with Austria.

The debate about the shape of the unified Germany

One of the most important questions that the parliament had to face was who should belong to this new Germany. The main problem was that the two major powers, Austria and Prussia, governed areas where the majority of the population were not German. Prussia ruled over Posen, where the majority of people were Polish but this was nothing to the diversity of the Crown lands ruled over by the Habsburg princes. Austria itself was German but this was smaller than Hungary, Bohemia, Moravia, parts of northern Italy, Slovenia, Croatia and Poland. In addition to this, Schleswig had a sizeable Danish minority.

The revolutions of 1848 had worsened relations between the minorities and their German-speaking governments. The Hungarians were in open revolt against the Habsburg emperor and the Czechs formed the Prague National Committee to push for greater autonomy for Bohemia. Czech nationalists also called for a boycott of the elections to the Frankfurt Parliament and when asked to be a delegate, Frantisek Palacky refused on the grounds that he was Czech and not German.

The possible solutions to this issue filtered down into two broad schemes. These became known as the **Grossdeutschland** (*grossdeutsche*, 'great German') and **Kleindeutschland** (*kleindeutsche*, 'little German') solutions. The *Grossdeutschland* solution was to include all of Prussia and all of Austria into a greater Germany regardless of the language of the peoples who lived there. The *Kleindeutschland* solution would exclude non-German speaking areas of Prussia and all of the Austrian Empire.

In the summer of 1848, the Frankfurt Parliament was at its most popular. The assembly had been meeting for several months and appeared to be making progress towards some of its goals. The provisional government had a president and a cabinet and ministries had been set up in order to govern the new German state. Committees were busily working on drafts of new legislation. The appearance, however, of what was happening did not show the serious weaknesses in the new parliament's position.

KEY TERMS

Grossdeutschland solution
This solution to the unification question favoured a Germany consisting of the German-speaking parts of Prussia and Austria, Schleswig-Holstein and Bohemia and Moravia.

Kleindeutschland solution
This solution to the unification question favoured a unified Germany without any lands which belonged to the Austrian Empire.

SOURCE 3

Carl Schurz, a journalist during the revolution and later a politician in America, writing in his memoirs *The Reminiscences of Carl Schurz* (1913).

The political horizon which after the revolution in March looked so glorious soon began to darken. In South Germany, where the opinion had gained ground that the revolution should not have "stood still before the thrones," a republican uprising took place under the leadership of the brilliant and impetuous Hecker, which, however, was speedily suppressed by force of arms. In the country at large such attempts at first found little sympathy. The bulk of the liberal element did not desire anything beyond the establishment of national unity and a constitutional monarchy "on a broad democratic basis." But republican sentiment gradually spread, and was intensified as the "reaction" assumed a more threatening shape.

The National Parliament at Frankfurt elected in the spring, which represented the sovereignty of the German people in the large sense and was to give to the united German nation a national government, counted among its members a great many men illustrious in the fields not so much of politics as of science and literature. It soon showed a dangerous tendency of squandering in brilliant but more or less fruitless debate much of the time which was sorely needed for prompt and decisive action if the legitimate results of the revolution against hostile forces were to be secured.

SOURCE 4

Wilhelm Jordan, Prussian delegate in the Frankfurt Parliament and close ally of Heinrich von Gagern, expressing a view on the Posen issue from the debate in the Frankfurt Parliament, 25 July 1848. Posen was a city in East Prussia which had a majority of Poles living in it.

It is high time that we woke up from that dream like abandonment in which we enthuse for every other nationality under the sun, while we ourselves lie down under humiliating subjugation, with the whole world trampling all over us. It is time we awoke to a healthy national egoism (and I use the expression candidly) which would make the welfare and honour of the fatherland the most important issue in all problems. But this very egoism, without which a people can never become a nation, is described as extremely condemnable by those who sympathise with Poland... Our right is none other than the right of the stronger, the right of conquest. Yes we have done some conquering... In, the West it is only us who have been conquered. In the East we have had the great misfortune of ourselves doing the conquering, and by so doing have provided whole hosts of German poets with the opportunity of writing moving Jeremiads about the various nationalities who have had to succumb to the weight of the German race. If we wanted to be ruthlessly fair, then we must give up not only Poland but also half of Germany... Therefore, I maintain that the German conquest of Poland were a physical necessity. The laws of history are different from the laws of textbooks. History only recognises the laws of nature, and one of these says that a nationality does not possess the right of political autonomy merely because of its existence, but only when it has the strength to affirm itself as a state amongst the others.

A Level Exam-Style Question Section A

How far could the historian make use of Sources 3 and 4 together to investigate the attitudes to nationalism prevalent in the Frankfurt Parliament?

Explain your answer, using both sources, the information given about them and your own knowledge of the historical context. (20 marks)

Tip
Make sure you use the evidence of the sources to support your points and also refer to the context of nationalism and how this may impact on German unification at the time.

Map to show the difference geographically between (from left to right) the *Grossdeutschland*, the *Kleindeutschland* and the Greater Austrian solutions.

Disagreements

The first challenge to the Frankfurt Parliament came during the *Vorparlament* period. Early in March 1848, a group of radicals led by Friedrich Hecker wanted the *Vorparlament* to seize control of Germany and declare itself the rightful government. The majority of the *Vorparlament*, however, were fairly moderate in their views and believed that only through negotiation with the existing princes, would they achieve a united liberal Germany. Increasingly marginalised, Hecker impulsively declared a German Republic with him as its leader. Backed by only a few armed peasants, Hecker was soon chased out of Germany and fled abroad. Also in April 1848, a group of armed German exiles marched from Paris and entered the Rhineland but were quickly dispersed by the local military.

Perhaps a greater challenge facing the parliament came from the major powers within the Confederation: Austria and Prussia. The members attended from both states, and indeed Archduke John accepted the role of imperial administrator, but the attitude of Prussia and Austria towards the Frankfurt Parliament was lukewarm from the start. They both, along with Hanover, refused to allow their soldiers to swear an oath of allegiance to the imperial administrator, safe in the knowledge that there was nothing the parliament could do to enforce this.

EXTEND YOUR KNOWLEDGE

Friedrich Hecker (1811–81)
Friedrich Hecker was a radical politician from Baden, who played a major part in the events of the 1848 revolutions. He was an outspoken critic of the Baden government and, along with Gustav von Struve, wrote the declaration that was passed by the Offenburg Meeting (see above page 307). On becoming a deputy in the Baden Assembly, he attempted to drive forward a more radical programme but was frustrated by the moderates.

Nominated for the *Vorparlament*, Hecker tried to get a motion passed to declare Germany a republic but again was blocked. His last attempt at radical revolution came in April 1848, when he led an armed uprising in Baden but support was limited and it petered out within a couple of days.

Hecker then fled to Switzerland and continued to try to play a role in German politics. He was elected in absentia to the Frankfurt Parliament but was refused permission to take his seat. In September 1848, he emigrated to the United States, where he continued to be politically active and fought for the Union in the American Civil War.

The Danish War

In July 1848, Prussia also indicated that it was set on pursuing its own foreign policy rather than falling into line with policy emitting from the Frankfurt Parliament. In March 1848, a revolution in Copenhagen precipitated the fall of the Danish government and its replacement with a cabinet, which was far more nationalist and far more aggressive. This worried the Germans in Schleswig-Holstein, who took measures to defend themselves against the Danes. The Danes took this as a sign of war and occupied Schleswig. The Federal Diet then asked the Prussians to intervene and Prussian soldiers, fighting on behalf of the Confederation, drove the Danes back into Denmark during April. Once the Frankfurt Parliament had been recognised as having superseded the Federal Diet, they urged the Prussians to pursue the war with greater vigour but the Prussians were sensitive to Austrian opposition to the war and the disapproval of other foreign powers, notably Great Britain. The Prussians concluded their own peace treaty with the Danes in August 1848 at the Swedish city of Malmo. Having been bypassed by the Prussians, the imperial government in Frankfurt resigned in protest.

This illustrates a fundamental weakness of the Frankfurt Parliament. It had a foreign minister with very few ambassadors, a war ministry with no army, the Ministry of Finance with no tax income and a Ministry of the Interior with no right to build, police, or educate. While it was debating great issues such as people's rights or the unification of greater Germany, it was proving to be popular but when it actually came to running the 'country' there were still independent state governments who were not willing to give it power.

The Fifty Articles

Throughout the summer and autumn of 1848, committees of delegates had been working on new legislation. These laws were to enshrine the basic rights of all German people in federal law. The idea that people had rights at all was a revolutionary one. Equality before the law was accepted throughout most of Europe but the Germans at Frankfurt believed that there should be a much wider list of basic rights.

Much of that which found its way into the 'Fifty Articles' or the 'Imperial law regarding the basic rights of the German people' was a reflection of the grievances put forward by liberals and nationalists in the years leading up to 1848. Many of these can be seen in the declarations passed at the meetings of Offenburg and Heppenheim (see above pages 303 and 305). Many of the leading liberals present at those meetings, like Gustav von Struve, were either delegates in the parliament or were actively lobbying.

The publishing of the Fifty Articles in December 1848 was a major achievement by the Frankfurt Parliament and gave many of the members the kind of liberal reform they craved. What it also did was to narrow the focus on those issues which had yet to be resolved. Work on the constitution was progressing steadily but the shape of the new unified Germany had not been decided.

The collapse of the assembly

The attempted exclusion of Austria

Austria had, since the early summer of 1848, played a more active role in the parliament. This was furthered when the Austrian statesman Anton von Schmerling, was appointed minister-president in late September after Leiningen's resignation. One of the first tests of von Schmerling's leadership came in October 1848 when a new uprising of the radical left in Vienna caused the Austrian government to flee the city.

The uprising was soon put down by the Austrian army but an event in the course of this was further to undermine the authority of the Frankfurt Parliament. One of the more radical members from the Frankfurt Parliament, Robert Blum, took part in the Vienna uprising. During it, he was captured by the Austrian army and executed. As a member of the Frankfurt Parliament, he should have had **parliamentary immunity**. The fact that the Austrian government ignored Blum's immunity was indicative that they did not take the Frankfurt Parliament seriously.

The debate was still between the *Grossdeutschen* led by Schmerling the Austrian and the *Kleindeutschen* led by Gagern the Hessian. Initially, the parliament favoured the greater German solution and voted in favour of it at the end of October 1848. The announcement, however, in November 1848, by the new Austrian first minister, Prince Schwarzenberg, that the Austrian Crown lands would not be divided played into the hands of the *Kleindeutschen*. The lukewarm acceptance of Gargern's proposals in Berlin further strengthened the *Kleindeutschen*'s position. The question had been boiled down to the simple issue of whether or not the new Germany should contain Austria.

SOURCE

6 Vote effectively to exclude Austria from the new Germany and thus follow the *Kleindeutschland* solution.

By Region	Yes	No	Abstention	Absent	Total
Prussia	150	30	0	17	197
The rest of north Germany	72	37	0	14	123
South Germany	39	69	0	19	127
Austria	0	88	3	20	111
Total	261	224	3	70	558

By Political Persuasion	Yes	No	Abstention	Absent	Total
Right	24	5	0	9	38
Right centre	163	17	3	22	205
Left centre	23	19	0	7	49
Left	15	117	0	19	151
Independent	36	66	0	13	115
Total	261	224	3	70	558

By Religion	Yes	No	Abstention	Absent	Total
Protestant	167	69	0	25	261
Catholic	42	120	3	36	201
Other	6	7	0	1	14
Not Known	46	28	0	8	82
Total	261	224	3	70	558

Ultimately, it was a mixture of Austrian boldness and Frankfurt's pragmatism that arrived at the resolution. The new Austrian Emperor, Franz Josef, reorganised the Austrian Empire and concentrated more of the power in Vienna. On the back of this, Prince Schwarzenberg suggested to the Frankfurt Parliament that the new Germany be ruled from Vienna and would incorporate all the lands of Austria and Prussia. This was unacceptable to the parliament. When the constitution was finally published in March 1849, the new Germany had the same borders as the old Confederation.

Significance of the weaknesses and political divisions

Radical dissatisfaction with the Frankfurt Parliament

In September 1848, the parliament experienced another challenge to its authority. After the Prussian peace treaty with the Danes was accepted in the parliament by a narrow majority, the left wing organised a mass demonstration in Frankfurt on 18 September. This was attended by thousands of artisans, who demanded that the left-wing members leave the parliament, set up a national convention and continue the war. The left-wing members did not leave the parliament but the crowd set up barricades and had to be dispersed by the military. Two days of violence followed and the authorities declared martial law. During this violence two conservative members were murdered by the mob. On 21 September, radical Gustav Struve led another uprising in Baden and proclaimed a German republic and the nationalisation of all lands belonging to the Church and the State. He and his followers were quickly dispersed and he went into exile. There were also minor disturbances in Württemberg and Cologne.

> **A Level Exam-Style Question Section B**
>
> 'The Frankfurt Parliament had little significance for the working classes.'
>
> How far do you agree with this statement? (20 marks)
>
> **Tip**
> *This question is wider than what the working classes actually did. You need to write about how they affected the actions of other class groups.*

SOURCE 7

Lithograph by Gustav Fischer, published in 1849, criticising the lack of progress made by the parliament at Frankfurt. The caption reads, 'Oh My God! They use everything for nothing. All they do is stay sitting down.'

"O du mein Gott, das nutzt alles nix, deßweg'n bleib'n do alle sitzen."

Divisions within the parliament

Despite the appearance of a unity of purpose, the parliament still divided into different factions. These groups often took their name from the alehouse or café in which they met:

- The 'Steinernes Haus' and the 'Café Milani' were right-wing groups who favoured a strong monarchy and the rule of a narrow elite.
- 'Casino', the 'Augsburger Hof' and the 'Pariser Hof' are examples of liberal groups who wanted a federal state with a strong parliament and the constitutional monarchy.
- The left-wing groups, such as the 'Deustcher Hof 'and the 'Nurnburger Hof' sought a republic based on parliamentary democracy and universal suffrage.

Ultimately, the squabbling between groups within the parliament became more significant than the work of the parliament and the ideas of liberalism and nationalism. As Prussia and Austria began to distance themselves from the parliament, its effectiveness began to decrease.

The last acts of the Frankfurt Parliament

Having a defined state, a constitution and a parliament, all Germany now needed was a monarch. Early in April 1849, a delegation offered the crown of Germany to Frederick William IV of Prussia. Realising that acceptance would cause a war with Austria, he refused. Moreover, as a monarch who believed that he had been given the throne of Prussia by God, he was wary of accepting a throne from an elected body. To have done so would have acknowledged their right to give him the throne and thereby weakened his power.

Austria, following the vote to exclude it, had already withdrawn its members and rejected the constitution; it would not accept a unified Germany without being part of it. Other states, notably Saxony, Hanover and Bavaria soon followed suit. The Prussians ordered their members to leave on 14 May 1849, a move which signalled the end for the Frankfurt Parliament. Elections were called but were never held and a few left-wing radicals that remained attempted to reconvene the parliament in Stuttgart but were dispersed by the Württemberg army.

ACTIVITY
WRITING

Copy out the following paragraph replacing words or phrases with words from the box below. You may need to rewrite some of the sentences. All the words from the box must be used and the meaning should not be changed.

Diet versus parliament

The Federal Diet, sometimes also known as the Federal Convention was an assembly of special selected dignitaries chosen by the governments or monarchs of the member states. It met once a week in the Thurn and Taxis Palace in Frankfurt. It consisted of two parts, a smaller one that decided which laws should be discussed and a larger one that discussed the new laws. It could pass laws but how they were implemented was left to the individual countries that were part of the Confederation. It is seen by historians as an instrument used by statesmen, particularly Metternich, to prevent liberal reform and maintain the status quo. The Frankfurt Parliament was a body which took over from the Federal Diet in July 1848. It was founded as the result of activity against the state governments but its members were elected. It was granted the status as a proper authority due to the participation of the member states, particularly Austria and Prussia. Eventually member states withdrew their members and the parliament collapsed. A few leftover members tried to start it up again in Stuttgart but this failed. The Federal Diet was re-constituted in 1850.

reactionary	rump	executive	Legislature	legitimacy	envoys

ACTIVITY
KNOWLEDGE CHECK

Answer the following questions:

1. Make a list of all the challenges made to the Frankfurt Parliament. Put them in order of significance and write a short explanation of that order.

2. Look at Source 6. What conclusions could be drawn about the nature of the Frankfurt Parliament and Germany itself from these figures?

3. To what extent was the Frankfurt Parliament a success and to what extent was it a failure? Explain your answer and illustrate it with points from the text.

WHAT WAS CHANGED BY THE PRUSSIAN REVOLUTION, 1848–49?

The Prussian Revolution followed close after events in France and south-west Germany. It followed a similar pattern in so far as street violence precipitated concessions and the promise of liberal reform. The government of Frederick William IV, however, though weakened, did not fall. It rode out the troubled times and was able to re-established its authority by 1849.

Events in Berlin and the response of Frederick William IV

What would become the revolutionary mob started out in a rather strange form. There was an area of the Tiergarten (a wooded park in the centre of Berlin) close to the Brandenburg Gate, which was reserved as an area of amusement for the ordinary people. As a result, tents were set up by people offering attractions for the citizens of Berlin. During January and February 1848, this place ceased to be solely a social meeting place and began to be used as a venue for smaller political meetings. These meetings developed into mock assemblies where debates were held and motions were passed.

By 13 March 1848, the crowd gathering around the tents numbered an estimated 20,000. They had begun to petition for political, legal and constitutional reforms. The range of speakers had begun to spread and now included workers and artisans speaking about the state of the economy and the poor standard of living conditions. In the corner of the area, there was even a secession assembly. This smaller assembly, consisting mainly of workers, drew up a petition asking for new laws to protect labour from exploitation.

Alarmed by the size of the group that had assembled by the tents, the Prussian authorities brought soldiers into the capital. What followed were a series of incidents in which both sides tested each other. Men in uniform were attacked in the streets and were told to go out only in large groups. Firearms were discharged accidentally, which gave rise to the rumour that the soldiers were firing on protesters.

SOURCE

8 The report from the Landsrat of the Calau district in Brandenburg to the Oberpresident of the Potsdam Province, March 1848. Calau is about 100 kilometres south of Berlin.

The absence of any post from Berlin on 19th March caused the greatest stress among the people here in Calau and in the vicinity… as there was no doubt that in Berlin the most serious events must have taken place. On the evening of the 19th, more precious information became available from local inhabitants who had left Berlin on the morning of the 19th and there was great consternation as a result of the lamentable bloody clash between the army and the citizens [of Berlin]. The excitement died down, however, when the proclamation of his majesty the king became known and his people trusted him absolutely. On 21st both here and in Vetschau gatherings were organised to express sympathy for the wounded and for the relatives of those killed in Berlin. A large number of the inhabitants of Calau went to Berlin in order to attend the funeral of the fallen. On 22nd memorial services were held in Calau and Lubbenau and on 25th in Senftenburg where citizens and officials in formal address met in front of the Rathaus [town hall] and accompanied by school students, teachers and clergy paraded into the church with a flag with the German colours (black, red and yellow). After the service they moved to the market place where from a platform appropriate speeches were held and a collection made for the widows and orphans of those who fell on 18th and 19th March. Then the meeting broke up peacefully… to be prepared fully for all possible occurrences in Calau for the protection of people and property a home guard has been formed and its leaders elected. At the moment it is not carrying out patrol guard duties as this is at present unnecessary. Only drill is taking place.

The violence came to a head on 18 March. Some decisions had already been taken by the king to introduce liberal reforms but this news had yet to filter through to the crowd, which was gathering in the Palace Square. The king came out onto the balcony and was cheered by the crowd but soon the mood began to change. Soldiers were deployed between the crowd and palace and scuffles broke out. Around 2 p.m., the king lost his nerve. He gave command of the troops to the aggressive General Maximilian von Prittwitz and ordered him to clear the square but that bloodshed should be avoided. The crowd refused to yield and the soldiers resorted to using their sabres and bayonets. Soon barricades were thrown up all over the city and fighting went on between demonstrators and soldiers well into the night.

The removal of the army from Berlin

Taking control of the city was a far more difficult task than the authorities had anticipated. Prittwitz suggested a withdrawal from the city in order that the army could encircle it and bombard it into surrender. The king rejected this and ordered a withdrawal of all the troops from the city to the army camp at Potsdam. He issued a statement calling for calm and guaranteeing the safety of the civilian population. The generals were livid. The king's brother, Prince William, showed his disdain for his brother's actions by flinging his sword at his feet and calling him 'a coward'. William was promptly packed off to London in order to cool down.

The violence was not only limited to Berlin. In Konigsberg, the farthest east of the Prussian cities and thought of as being the most liberal, there were 21 incidents of public unrest. In Silesian Breslau, there were 45 and in Cologne in western Prussia there were 46. There was also rioting and demonstrations throughout the industrialised Ruhr.

The king had had a sense of what was coming and had tried to take measures to avert a revolution. He had announced that the United Estates would be recalled in April and that Prussia would introduce a constitutional system. Censorship of the press was abolished and Frederick William made it clear that he identified with the movement for German unification.

Removing the soldiers from Berlin had put an end to the violence but had left Frederick William terribly exposed. On the afternoon of 19 March, he stood on the balcony of the palace while demonstrators paraded the corpses of those who had died in the fighting. The king took off his hat and bowed his head. This was a terrible humiliation for one of the most powerful monarchs of Europe. Undeterred, he embarked on a daring public relations exercise. He rode his horse out into the city behind a guardsman carrying the red, black and gold flag. He would stop to talk to the local townspeople.

SOURCE 9 Frederick William IV in Berlin in March 1848, as seen by a contemporary observer.

> In the course of the morning of 21st the king appeared in the streets on horseback with the German colours, black, red and gold, round his arm. He was greeted with tumultuous applause... he stooped and said 'I am truly proud that it is my capital, where so powerful an opinion had manifested itself. This day is a great day and ought never to be forgotten. The colours I wear are not my own; I do not mean to usurp anything with them... I want liberty; I will have unity in Germany.' He spoke again of German unity in a proclamation issued on the same day. 'From this day forth the name of Prussia is fused and dissolved in that of Germany.'

If Frederick William was wooing the people of Berlin, the army was still fuming. Traditionally, the army played a very important role in the running of the Prussian state. Ministers were often generals and a career in the army was seen as the highest ambition for sons of the nobility. On 25 March 1848, the king travelled out to Potsdam to speak with his officers. He told them that he was safe in Berlin and that troops would not be returning to the capital. He asked for their renewed loyalty during this difficult time. The officers did not like what they were hearing but were honour bound to obey their commander-in-chief.

The Potsdam speech was a brilliant move by Frederick William. Not only had he pre-empted any attempt by the generals to act unilaterally but he had also made them reaffirm their loyalty to the monarch. More than this, texts of the king's speech were published in the newspapers and reassured Berliners that there would be no return to street fighting. Moreover, the people could see that the king's commitment to the revolution was genuine. Frederick William could now begin the process of assembling a new administration.

The liberal government

Traditionally Prussia had been governed by the nobility, many of whom were generals in the army or landowning Junkers from East Prussia. The government appointed at the end of March 1848, represented a departure from this. Both the prime minister, Gottfried Ludolf Camphausen, and the minister of finance David Hansemann, were liberal businessmen who came from the Rhineland. Other cabinet members may have come from the more traditional areas of society but all had some form of liberal credentials.

KEY TERM

College (political or electoral)
A group which exercises a single vote either to elect a representative or to agree or disagree with an act.

The newly recalled United Estates began to sit during the first week of April. Their first act was to pass a law providing for elections to a Prussian National Assembly. Every adult male was eligible to vote as long as they had lived in the same place for six months and were not in receipt of poor relief. The elections were to be indirect, which meant that the assembly delegates would be selected by electoral **colleges** rather than directly voted for. Though still dominated by the middle and upper classes, the Prussian United Estates had a far greater proportion of artisan and peasant delegates than the counterpart assemblies in Frankfurt and Vienna.

EXTEND YOUR KNOWLEDGE

Ways of voting

There are many different ways that authorities can organise elections:

- The 'first past the post system' is where candidates stand for election in a geographical area. Every voter has a single vote and votes for the candidates of their choice. The candidate with the most votes in that area is elected.

- Proportional representation is where the voter may have two or more choices in ranking order. The votes are counted and then a second round takes places to which the top few candidates go through. The votes for the candidates who did not go through are transferred to one of the candidates who did go through. There may even be a third round. The candidate with the greatest number of votes is elected.

- Indirect elections. Voting elects members of an electoral college in one of the above ways. When elected, the college meets and selects the members of the assembly of their choice.

Prussia favoured the third system, the indirect elections. Often electoral colleges would be dominated by the powerful and the educated, who would seek to elect like-minded deputies. The strong influence of the upper and middle classes in the Prussian National Assembly is partly due to the way in which it was elected.

THINKING HISTORICALLY Interpretations (5c)

Good questions/Bad questions

Below are approaches attributed to three famous historians. They are generalisations for the purpose of this exercise.

Herodotus	Leopold von Ranke	Karl Marx
He looks for the interesting story, the drama and the colourful characters	He is interested in how great men use their influence to bring about change	He is looking underneath the events to see what patterns there are over long periods of time and how ordinary people fit in

Work in groups.

1 Devise three criteria of what makes a good historical question.

2 Consider what you know about the March Revolutions in the German Confederation.

   a) Each write a historical question based on that subject matter.

   b) Put these in rank order, with the best question first based on your criteria.

3 Using a piece of A3 paper, write the names of the three historians so they form a large triangle.

4 Write your questions from 2a) on the piece of paper so that their positions reflect how likely the historians are to be interested by that question. For example, a question about how Frederick William influenced events in Berlin might interest Ranke and possibly Herodotus more than Marx.

5 Add some further questions. Try to think of questions that only one of the three would be interested in.

6 Take it in turns to try to answer the questions you have created in the style of one of the historians. See if the other members of the group can guess which one it was.

Answer the following questions individually using the examples created by the above activity:

7 Does one method of constructing history lead to better reasoning than the others? Explain your answer.

8 Explain why all historians who deploy rigorous methodology are, to an extent, useful sources for the study of the past.

Conservative reaction and counter-revolution

Part of the problem facing the National Assembly from the moment of its inception was the attitude of the king. Although outwardly engaged in the processes of unification and liberal reform, Frederick William was, at heart, deeply conservative. Moreover, he surrounded himself with conservative advisors who were chiefly concerned with protecting the power of the Crown. Faced with the reality of reform, the king proved difficult and recalcitrant in his dealings with the assembly.

By September, the violence of March had long passed and the king felt confident enough to appoint ministers who were more in the mould of the old guard. General Ernst von Pfuel became prime minister and it was hoped that he would appeal to both sides. He was, sure enough, a general in the army but was also an intellectual and a patriot and was popular with the liberals for being tolerant and calm. Even he, however, was unable to bridge the gap between the king and assembly and he resigned on 1 November.

There could have been no clearer sign that the revolution was over than the appointment of Count Friedrich Wilhelm von Brandenburg as prime minister to succeed General Pfuel. The assembly immediately sent a delegation to the king in order to protest about the new appointment. They were summarily dismissed. The next week, Brandenburg presented himself to the assembly and announced that it was adjourned until 27 November and would reconvene in the city of Brandenburg.

SOURCE

10 Leaflet and poster of the Berlin Democratic Club, 3 November 1848. This was a group of influential liberals who sought to lobby the king and parliament.

'It has always been the misfortune of kings that they are deaf to the truth.'

The king received the appointed delegation which delivered the already published message from the National Assembly. After having read it, he folded it up and turned to leave with a curt bow. As President Unruh hesitated about speaking, MP Jacobi intervened and spoke the following words, as the message had expressly ordered the delegation to do:

'Your Majesty! We have not simply been sent here to deliver a message but also, your majesty, to inform you verbally about the true state of the country. With your permission your majesty therefore...'

Here the king interrupted with the word: 'No!'

Jacobi retorted:

'It has always been the misfortune of kings that they are deaf to the truth.'

The king left.

Jacobi in his way portrayed the thoughts of the entire fatherland. May he and his friends not give up their work, at this highly important stage, of representing the threatened interests of the people in Vienna and Berlin and the truth. If this be the case all men will stand firmly with them in order to finally to achieve a basis for freedom and happiness of the people.

Berlin, 3rd November 1848

The Democratic Club

The end of the National Assembly

The assembly saw this adjournment as an infringement of its rights. It called for 'passive resistance' and a tax boycott. Within hours, General Wrangel entered Berlin with 13,000 regular troops and took control of the city. The delegates were dispersed. Two days later, on 11 November, **martial law** was declared, the **militia** was disbanded, political clubs were closed and radical newspapers banned. The king had not only retaken the capital but also had reclaimed the power to run the state as he saw fit.

Some members of the assembly tried to reconvene in Brandenburg on 27 November but were prevented from doing so by the army. The assembly was formally dissolved on 5 December. On the same day the government announced that there would be a new constitution.

AS Level Exam-Style Question Section A

How much weight do you give to the evidence in Source 10 for an enquiry into the strength of the revolutionary movement in November 1848?

Explain your answer using the source, the information given about it and your own knowledge of the historical context. (12 marks)

Tip
Make sure you consider Jacobi's motivation and how that relates to his actions and the overall situation at the time. Then relate it to the question.

KEY TERMS

Martial law
Powers introduced in a state of emergency that give the authorities exceptional powers to arrest, detain and in some cases execute those that it perceives as a threat to law and order.

Militia
Part-time soldiers usually connected to a given area. Often officered by the local gentry and made up of healthy young workers and old veterans who had been stood down from the regular army.

The Prussian constitution

The constitution of 1848

Like the parliament in Frankfurt, the first task facing the Prussian National Assembly was to write a constitution. Unlike the parliament in Frankfurt, a draft document was achieved very quickly. Camphausen had aimed to present the document to the National Assembly on the day of its opening on 22 May 1848. It was, however, delayed and was presented for discussion in June. Frederick William was not happy with the document and insisted that the phrase 'by the grace of God' be inserted to indicate his divine right to rule.

During the next month the Assembly debated the constitution and a second draft was produced. This further reduced the power of the king, provided for a popular national militia and removed the last traces of social and economic privilege enjoyed by the nobility in rural areas. The problem was that for the conservative Right the constitution went too far but for the radical Left it did not go far enough. Fearing that he would be unable to secure a majority in the assembly when it came to a vote on the constitution, Camphausen resigned.

Another pressing issue for the National Assembly was the relationship between the civilian and military authorities. On 31 July in the Silesian town of Schweidnitz, a stand-off between demonstrators and the army turned to violence and 14 civilians were killed. Julius Stein, the deputy for Breslau, presented a motion calling on the army to act in conformity with constitutional values and demonstrate its loyalty to the new political order. This was welcomed by the assembly, which feared that an independent army would be hostile to the cause of liberal reform and still have the wherewithal to reverse the gains of the March revolution. Rudolf von Auerswald, the new prime minister, was reluctant to act on Stein's motion and under pressure from the assembly resigned on 7 September.

Having promised his people a constitution in 1848, it behove Frederick William to make good his promise. However, the Prussian constitution of 1850 was a masterpiece of conservative reaction as it consolidated the power of the monarch and guaranteed the independence of the army.

It provided for an assembly with two chambers: the *Abgeordnetenhaus* or lower chamber and the *Herrenhaus*, or upper chamber. The lower chamber was elected by the system known as three class suffrage. Thus, a third of the deputies were elected by the highest tier of taxpayers, another third by the middle tier of taxpayers and the final third by the lowest tier of taxpayers. This meant that two-thirds of the deputies were elected by the wealthiest strata of society, approximately 25 percent of the population. This gave the lower chamber a majority of conservative deputies. The upper chamber was modelled on the British House of Lords. All its members were nobles and were selected by the king. The lower chamber had very little power and could not vote on matters of legislation or the budget. The upper chamber similarly had no rights on the budget but was allowed to vote on new laws, although it could be overruled by the king.

The constitution itself contained much that was procedural. There were, however, conservative clauses, which could be used against potential opponents. Authorities were once more permitted to censor newspapers and to ban them outright where they saw fit. Freedom of association could also be restricted. The constitution contained detailed plans of how the authorities would react to civil unrest, including plans of how to break the state down into military areas and which troops would be deployed where. It also stated categorically that the army was not bound by the constitution.

ACTIVITY
KNOWLEDGE CHECK

1 How far do you think that Frederick William changed his mind during the course of the revolution? Give examples in your answer.

2 Why were the liberals right to be so nervous about the power of the Prussian army? Explain your answer.

3 How were the conservative right able to re-impose reactionary rule in November 1848?

4 Read Source 10. Why do you think the Democratic Club published that pamphlet in November 1848?

THINKING HISTORICALLY Causation (6b)

Attitudes and actions

Individuals can only make choices based on their context. Prevalent attitudes combine with individual experience and natural temperament to frame the individual's perception of what is going on around them. Nobody can know the future or see into the minds of others.

Context	Action
Frederick William IV had sent the army out of Berlin on 19 March 1848. The National Assembly began to meet in May 1848 and discuss a constitution. Frederick William did not engage proactively with the negotiations regarding the constitution. Different prime ministers (Camphausen, Auerswald, Pfuel) tried to get the king and assembly to work together. They were not very successful. There were signs in the late summer and early autumn of divisions among the revolutionaries. The king appointed Count Frederick William of Brandenburg to be prime minister.	On 9 November 1848, Brandenburg appeared in the National Assembly to tell the deputies that it was dissolved. On the same day, General Wrangel occupied Berlin with 13,000 troops.

Answer the following questions individually and discuss your answers in a group:

1 Why might Frederick William have felt that not co-operating over a new constitution was the right thing to do?

2 To what extent do you think he was monitoring the debates held in the National Assembly?

3 What other information would have been useful to him to help him decide on his course of action?

4 Do you think that the king was surprised when Brandenburg took such a reactionary course of action? Explain your answer.

5 How far should the historian try to understand the context of the beliefs and values of people in the past when explaining why individuals make choices in history?

IN WHAT WAYS CAN THE REVOLUTIONS OF 1848 BE SEEN AS A FAILURE?

As we have seen above, historians have differing opinions as to whether or not the 1848 revolutions were a failure. In terms of attaining their lofty goals of unification and a constitutional liberal state, however, the liberals in 1848 had failed in the short term. The reasons for this lie in the nature of the German Confederation, the dynamic of the revolution and a very narrow strand of genuine support for the Frankfurt Parliament.

The German Confederation was dominated by the forces of conservative reaction. These were principally the army and the Church. It is highly significant that at no point did these institutions throw in their lot with the liberal reforms. The army, most notably in Prussia, was used prudently by the authorities to restore order and protect property but, by and large, was not used as a political weapon. Avoiding an all-out civil war was one of the most important factors that allowed the ruling elites to ride out the revolution and reinstate their authority. The Church also had no wish to see radical change. This was particularly true for the Roman Catholics of the south, who instinctively regarded Catholic Austria as far more benevolent than Protestant Prussia.

Source 11

The Reactionary Victory in Europe, 1849 by the cartoonist F. Schroeder. Originally printed in the periodical *Dusseldorf Monthly* in 1849.

Counter-revolution and the strength of conservative forces across Germany

The revolution of 1848 was largely a middle-class affair. Despite the talk of popular reform and people's rights, the new liberal assemblies in Frankfurt, Berlin and throughout the Confederation were dominated by the middle classes. This 'revolution from the middle' had to walk a fine line. On the one hand, it desired to loosen the grip on power held so tightly by the upper classes but it did not want to liberate the working classes to the extent that the middle classes themselves lost their influence. As the revolution progressed, the radical left became increasingly less satisfied with the reforms being made and demonstrated accordingly. The fear of violence and the overturning of the social order

EXTRACT 3

The modern historian David Blackbourn discusses the survival and resurgence of the conservative elements of Germany in his book *History of Modern Germany 1780–1918*, published in 2003.

The resources of the German regimes went beyond this actual or potential layer of popular support. After a short period when they kept their heads down, court advisors, diplomats, nobles and bureaucrats recovered their confidence and re-emerged. Most important of all, the armed forces of the German princes remained intact. It is striking how rarely troops went over to the revolution in 1848–49 – by contrast with Russia in 1917, say, or Germany in November 1918. Throughout the revolution, Confederation troops drawn from the individual states were garrisoned close to the strategically sensitive areas, in Mainz and Ulm, for example, and were easily able to quell further revolutionary uprising like those of April and September 1848. Every military engagement of 1848–49 showed the superiority of well-equipped conventional troops over the revolutionaries, even when the latter where reinforced by 'volunteer' legions of Hungarians, French and Swiss. That was true of the Austrian and Prussian armies, and of those belonging to Saxony and the smaller states. We should not be surprised by this, given that Habsburg troops eventually defeated even the 170,000 men mobilized by the Hungarian rebels, with little help from the Russian army that Vienna had reluctantly asked for assistance. Generals such as Windischgratz and Wrangel did... much to determine the outcome of the German revolution.

pushed the liberal reformers towards the forces of conservative reaction. The two most powerful groups aiming for change were thus divided.

There were further divisions among the revolutionaries that played into the hands of the conservative right. Artisan **guilds** were still very powerful within urban areas and their members had their own worries about the economic situation. Industrialisation threatened the livelihood of artisans, as the new factories could make goods cheaper and quicker than they could. The artisans saw that the only way to secure their prosperity was a programme of restrictive practices that limited the right of factory owners to make certain goods. Another defence against new cheap goods, particularly from Britain, was the imposition of high import duties to protect the German market and keep it limited to German artisan-made goods. The problem for the revolutionaries was that a cornerstone of liberal ideology was **free trade**. In terms of protecting their businesses, the artisans found a more natural ally in the conservative right.

That the rulers of the German states showed patience was also significant in explaining the lack of short-term progress for the revolution. Frederick William of Prussia recognised how events were unfolding and tried to diffuse the situation. His queen had proved to be incorrect when, during a public appearance, she had told him that 'the guillotine was next'. He had done enough to take the ferocity out of the revolutionary movement. He allowed the assembly to be elected and to meet and though he did not co-operate fully with it, he tolerated it long enough for events to turn in his favour. Ferdinand of Austria also took conciliatory steps towards the revolutionaries as did Maximillian of Bavaria. By appearing to be empathetic, the rulers denied the revolutionaries an object to rail against. True, the revolutionaries still had grievances but the understanding nature of the ruler's reactions had slightly wrong-footed them.

Ultimately the powers of conservative reaction bided their time and struck when the revolution had run out of steam. The Frankfurt Parliament, for all its high ideals, had achieved little in the way of practical progress and in the course of their deliberations the factions had moved further apart. As events moved on it became clear to the various parties that unification at this time was not in their interest but unification and liberal reform by way of a broad consensus sometime in the future was a realisable possibility.

KEY TERMS

Guild
The forerunner to a modern trade union. This was an organisation based on a trade or profession. Membership of the guild was a prerequisite to carry out business in that trade or profession.

Free trade
The policy that all import and export duties be abolished in order that all businesses can compete with each other on an equal basis.

AS Level Exam-Style Question Section B

How accurate is it to say the Frankfurt Parliament was a 'success'? (20 marks)

Tip
Make sure that you write a conclusion where you make a clear judgement and that you support this judgement with a strong substantiated argument.

ACTIVITY
KNOWLEDGE CHECK

1 Lenin said; 'It is only when the "lower classes" do not want to live in the old way and the "upper classes" cannot carry on in the old way that the revolution can triumph.' How far can this explain the failure of the German revolutions of 1848?

2 Look at Source 11, *The Reactionary Victory in Europe*. What statement is this cartoon trying to make about the situation in Europe in 1849?

3 Read Extract 3. What are the main reasons, according to Blackbourn, for the failure of the 1848 revolutions?

4 How far did the vested interests of the different groups prevent any progress in 1848?

The revival of Habsburg power in Austria

The events in Vienna in March 1848 had precipitated alarming events for the Habsburgs all over the empire. It was not just Viennese radicals that were demanding reform but that other minorities were demanding greater powers and, in the case of Hungary, a fully autonomous state.

Much like Prussia, the Austrian authorities went along with the liberal mood of the time. They had little choice. From May 1848, the court 'ruled' from Innsbruck while radical groups and committees shared an uneasy relationship with the Austrian government and, after July, the newly elected Austrian parliament. The army, though still loyal to the emperor, was unable to intercede. The soldiers in Austria were kept in their barracks and the army in Italy under Marshal Radetzky did not dare to venture outside its fortresses.

Military action in Bohemia and Italy

The Austrian authorities made tentative steps to regain their power during the summer. Confident that the regular troops were still loyal to the Crown and more than a match for a revolutionary mob,

General Windischgratz was dispatched to Prague to put down any possibility of a Czech revolt. After Prague had fallen to government troops, the emperor was further buoyed by the news that Radetzky had beaten the Piedmontese at the Battle of Custozza and retaken Milan from Italian nationalists at the end of July. By the end of the summer, the countryside was fully under the control of the monarchy. Only Vienna and the separatist Hungarians remained defiant. Military success was matched by political success in Frankfurt. Archduke John and von Schmerling, it appeared, were leading the Frankfurt Parliament towards a unified Germany in which Austria was still pre-eminent.

Relocating to Innsbruck, though not an ideal situation, served the Habsburg cause well in the long term. It meant that they were not associated directly with the revolution for the three months they were away. Even after the royal family moved back to Vienna towards the end of the summer, they still attempted to keep a fairly low profile. The revolutionaries left much to their own devices began to fall out among themselves. Middle-class liberals had used the city militia to break up workers' protests in August 1848. The workers were protesting about wage cuts for workers on public works. For this they blamed the new Parliament as they realised that the emperor had no authority in this matter.

The retaking of Vienna

In October 1848, another uprising, in protest against the attack on Hungary, once again caused the emperor and his entourage to flee the capital. This time, Windischgratz with 60,000 men moved against Vienna. He was opposed by the radical city militia who numbered 100,000 but these were no match for regular troops. Though the street fighting caused 2,000 casualties, the city was soon back in the hands of the regular army. Many of the citizens welcomed the soldiers as liberators.

The emperor quickly returned to the capital with his advisors. The parliament was dissolved and a new reactionary government was put in place under the leadership of Prince Schwarzenberg. As in Berlin, the discipline and loyalty of the army had triumphed over the disunity of the revolutionaries. As an addendum to the revolution, the feeble-minded emperor Ferdinand, exhausted by the events of the year, was persuaded to abdicate in favour of his nephew, the energetic 18-year-old, Franz Josef.

Defeating the Hungarian rebels

The Hungarian revolution broke out in March 1848 at much the same time as those in Vienna and Berlin. The Hungarians had formed their own government and ruled themselves with impunity for the rest of 1848. Despite opposition from their own national minorities (Croats and Romanians), they had not succumbed to either political pressure or military invasion. It was the defeat of the Austrian-backed Croats at the Battle of Pakozd by the Hungarian revolutionary army which influenced the October uprising in Vienna.

KEY TERM

Campaign
An endeavour carried out by an army or armies. Often this involves an invasion and a series of engagements with the enemy.

General Windischgratz was given the task of putting down the Hungarian rebels and invaded during the spring of 1849. He forced the rebel government to withdraw from Budapest but the **campaign** ran into difficulties and in the end the spring campaign ended with the Austrian army back where it had started on the border.

The campaign was renewed in the summer but with the advantage of the Russians invading from the east. Alarmed by the possibility of revolution spreading to Russian Poland, the tsar had offered troops to help the Austrian cause. Facing a war on two fronts and against armies twice their size, the Hungarian rebels finally surrendered in August 1849.

Weakness of, and divisions among, revolutionaries

Despite the triumph of the conservative right in the Austrian Empire and Prussia and the collapse of the Frankfurt Parliament, there was still revolutionary activity in 1849. It amounted to very little in terms of precipitating political change but the large numbers involved in certain cases are illustrative of the depth of revolutionary feeling that still remained.

The revolutionaries were divided in two ways: geographically and socially. The liberals of Prussia had a different agenda from the liberals of Austria. This is most apparent in the *Grossdeutschland/ Kleindeutschland* question. Moreover, these groups lost influence at slightly different times and their place in the Frankfurt Parliament was taken by more conservative members or a more conservative government at home was instructing them to act differently. Class also played a role as lower-class revolutionaries began to feel that they were not being represented by the liberals of the middle class.

Disturbances, like those in Frankfurt in September 1848 by workers flying the red flag of socialism rather than the red, black and gold of Germany, indicate the rift between the different revolutionary groups.

What undermined the revolutionary cause was that the regular soldiers remained loyal to their rulers. Prussian soldiers in Berlin and Austrian soldiers in Prague and Vienna retained their discipline and were used to restore the power of the conservative regimes. The Frankfurt Parliament used federal troops to disperse rioters and oppose armed uprisings such as the one organised by Hecker (see above page 314). Attempts at violent revolution continued into 1849 but they met with little success.

Disturbances in Saxony and Prussia

There was some rioting in Prussia after the counter-revolution, particularly in Berlin and Breslau but this was put down by the army. In Saxony matters got more serious in May 1849, when the lower house of the Saxon assembly was dissolved. Demonstrators (including the composer Richard Wagner) took to the streets and the king and his government had to leave the capital. A provisional government was declared, but the trouble was confined to Dresden and a force of troops from Saxony and Prussia retook the city within a few days. The revolution was over.

Uprisings in the Palatinate and Baden

The Palatinate saw the most extreme of the violence in 1849. On 18 May, a provisional government was proclaimed at Kaiserslautern. Though this was far from Munich, the capital of Bavaria, it still meant that a major province was in open rebellion. To add to this, in neighbouring Baden, army bases had mutinied at Rastadt and Karlsruhe and Grand Duke Leopold had had to flee the country. Workers and artisans flocked to the revolutionary militia and it is estimated that they numbered almost 30,000.

SOURCE

12 The Battle of Waghausel, 22 June 1849 fought between revolutionary troops and Prussian regulars. Artist unknown. The painting is held by the States Library Picture Archive in Berlin.

Gefecht bei Waghäusel unweit Heidelberg am 22. Juni 1849.

ACTIVITY
KNOWLEDGE CHECK

1 Write down the three most significant events in the return of Habsburg power. Explain your choices.

2 In what ways did the disturbances of spring and summer 1849 increase Prussian influence in Germany?

The ousted authorities called on the Prussians for assistance. In July, two Prussian army corps led by Prince William invaded the Palatinate and put the revolutionaries to flight. On 23 July, Rastadt surrendered and the captured leaders were court martialled and executed.

HOW DID THE REVOLUTIONS OF 1848 CHANGE GERMAN POLITICS?

The ambitions of Prussia and Austria, 1849-51

Joseph von Radowitz

Despite the rejection of the German crown by Frederick William in April 1849, the *Kleindeutschland* solution to the unification question was still appealing to the Prussian elite. A close advisor to the king, Joseph von Radowitz, was given the task of overseeing Prussian foreign policy and sought to revive the plan, initially put forward by von Gagern for a German state led by Prussia but excluding Austria. In May 1849, von Radowitz put the plan to the Austrians who were still militarily engaged in Hungary and northern Italy. Despite offers of military assistance from Prussia to help against the Hungarians, Schwarzenberg, the Austrian prime minister, refused to accept the plan.

For von Radowitz, this was not the end of the matter. He organised the League of Three Kings with Saxony and Hanover. Though grand in title, the league came with conditions. The Saxon king only joined on the condition that the Bavarian king was included. This, of course, made it a League of Four Kings. Hanover, fearful of Prussian domination, would only join if Austria was included in the federal state and 17 other states were persuaded to join. With Prussian troops putting down revolutions in Baden, Württemberg and Saxony, there was some measure of intimidation involved, should the other kings not wish to co-operate.

A new Union

In June 1849, 150 former members of the Frankfurt Parliament agreed that the league would adopt the constitution agreed by the Frankfurt Parliament. Arrangements were put in place for a new assembly consisting of two chambers. In addition, a college of princes would have a veto on any measures that it passed. The election of the assembly would be via the Prussian three-class system, which effectively meant the domination of the wealthier classes.

The Austrian recovery

Austrian military fortunes had recovered by the summer of 1849. The Piedmontese had lost the Battle of Novaro in March and a settlement had finally been signed in August. The Hungarian rebels also surrendered in August. Though the Austrian army was still engaged through the summer, it was clear, particularly when the Russians agreed to invade Hungary, that Austria would have the ability to pursue a far more aggressive policy towards Germany.

An interim agreement was signed between Schwarzenberg and von Radowitz in September 1849 that allowed for joint leadership of Germany by Austria and Prussia until May 1850. For von Radowitz, equality was perhaps the best he could have hoped for but for Schwarzenberg this was hardly the end of the matter. With the empire now firmly under the control of Vienna, he looked towards not only re-establishing Austria's previous controlling position within Germany, but strengthening it.

The Erfurt Parliament

By the time the Union Parliament met in Erfurt in March 1850, there was very little of the union left. The Catholic states of Bavaria and Wurttemberg, nervous of Prussian domination, had decided not to join. Saxony and Hanover, original members of the League of Three Kings, had both seceded for the same reason. Nevertheless, Prussia drove the union forward.

Von Radowitz was not only meeting opposition from outside Prussia. Conservative forces inside Berlin were suspicious of the new assembly and believed that it would revive the liberal agenda of the Frankfurt Parliament. Under pressure from the right, Frederick William announced that he would restrict the union constitution and would not swear an oath of allegiance to it.

ACTIVITY
KNOWLEDGE CHECK

1 Read Source 13. In what ways would this document enhance Prussian power?

2 Why did Prussia pursue the Erfurt Union?

The re-establishment of the German Confederation

The revival of the Federal Diet

To counter the threat of the *Kleindeutschland* solution embodied in the Erfurt Union, Schwarzenberg revived the Federal Diet in Frankfurt in May 1850. Austria naturally assumed the presidency and invited states to send representatives. Ten states, who were not members of the Erfurt Union, sent representatives.

There were now two bodies, each with deputies sent by member states, claiming some rights of governance in Germany. One was led by Prussia and the other by Austria. Civil war within Germany was now a frightening possibility.

SOURCE

13 *Proposal for the League of Three Kings* written by Joseph von Radowitz, a close advisor to King Frederick William, May 1849.

The Government of Prussia, Saxony and Hanover have concluded the following treaty:

1 The Royal Governments of Prussia, Saxony and Hanover conclude in compliance with Article 11 of the German Act of Confederation of 8 June 1815, an alliance with the purpose of safeguarding the internal and external security of Germany and the independence and inviolability of the several German states...

2 All members of the German Confederation may join this alliance...

3 a) The supreme direction of the measures which are to be taken to achieve the aims of the alliance is vested in the crown of Prussia.

   b) An Administrative Council, to which all members shall send one or more representatives, shall be formed to conduct the business of the Alliance.

   c) The Administrative Council may take a final decision on the following matters:

      i The admission of new members to the Alliance.

      ii Steps for the calling of a constituent Reichstag and the direction of its deliberations.

      iii The appointment and direction of civil commissioners to be attached to the military when requests for assistance against internal disturbances are made.

4 Should there be diplomatic negotiations... they shall be conducted by the crown of Prussia and the Administrative Council shall be kept informed of their progress...

Denmark and Hessen-Kassel

There were two potential flashpoints for the war. Fighting had again broken out between Denmark and Prussia over Schleswig-Holstein. Austria, acting on behalf of the Federal Diet, offered to support the Danes against the Prussians. The deployment of Austrian troops fighting for Denmark would certainly have precipitated a war. Under pressure from Russia, however, Prussia signed a peace treaty with the Danes in July 1850.

The accumulating tension finally came to a head in September 1850 in Hessen-Kassel. This was a small electorate, which lay directly in between the eastern and western halves of Prussia. The reactionary elector had tried to force measures through the territorial Diet and had been met by a refusal by the politicians and a mutiny by the army. Unable to rule, he called for assistance from the Federal Diet. The Austrians immediately drew up plans for military intervention by a composite force consisting of troops from Austria, Bavaria and Wurttemberg.

Prussia who already had troops stationed in Hessen-Kassel guarding strategically important roads refused to sanction this. As a kind of compromise, the Diet authorised, on 26 October 1850, troops from Hanover and Bavaria to intervene in Hessen-Kassel and restore the authority of the elector. After skirmishes between Prussian and Federal troops, Schwarzenberg demanded that Prussian troops be withdrawn from Hessen-Kassel.

This proved too much for the Prussians. They **mobilised** their army and events looked as though they would lead to war. On 24 November, backed by Russia, the Austrians demanded a complete withdrawal of Prussian troops in Hessen-Kassel within 48 hours. Prussia agreed to negotiate and a conference was arranged.

KEY TERM

Mobilise
The act of changing the status of the armed forces from peacetime deployment to being on a war footing. Often this involves the rapid movement of troops and the calling up of reserve forces.

The Punctation of Olomouc

The meeting was held in the city of Olomouc (Olmütz in German) in Austrian Moravia at the end of November. The role of the Russians was pivotal, as Prussia knew it could not win a war with Austria if Russia sided with the Austrians. The negotiations did not take long and the Prussians backed down.

The Punctation of Olomouc was signed on 29 November 1850. It was also known, particularly in Prussia, as the 'Humiliation of Olomouc'. With it, the Prussians agreed to demobilise their army and to contribute to joint federal action in Hessen-Kassel. Prussia and Austria agreed to work together to negotiate a reformed German Confederation.

The reformed Confederation never came about. Buoyed by the success at Olomouc, Schwarzenberg pressed for a confederation that included the whole of the Habsburg Empire. He had misread the situation and overplayed his hand. Prussia, quite naturally, opposed the scheme and was supported by foreign powers. Russia particularly, whose influence had limited Prussian power in Germany, were equally keen to see that Austria was not totally dominant either. Britain and France also issued warnings that a German Confederation containing all the Crown lands of Austria would not be conducive to stability in Europe.

SOURCE 14

Otto von Bismarck, Prussian delegate in the Federal Diet, speaking in support of the Punctation of Olomouc in a speech to the Prussian parliament, December 1850.

What kind of war is this? Not an expedition of isolated regiments to Schleswig or Baden, not a military promenade through troubled provinces, but a major war against two of the three great continental powers, whilst the third mobilises on our frontier, eager for conquest and well aware that in Cologne there is treasure to be found which could end the French Revolution and give their rulers the French Imperial Crown. A war, gentlemen, which will begin by forcing us to give up some of the remoter Prussian provinces, in which a large part of Prussia will be inundated by enemy forces, and which will bring to our provinces the full horrors of war. A war, it can be assumed, that the Minister of Public Worship, who has jurisdiction over the servants of religion, peace and love, must loathe to the bottom of his heart [laughter]. A war, which the Minister for Trade and Industry must be convinced will begin by destroying the public welfare entrusted to his care, and which the Finance Minister can only desire when the money can no longer be left in the royal coffers. And yet I would not shrink from such a war, indeed I would advise it, if someone could prove to me that it was necessary, or show me a worthy goal which could only be attained by it and in no other way. Why do large states go to war nowadays? The only sound basis for a large state, and this is what distinguishes it from a small state is state egoism and not romanticism, and it is not worthy of a great state to fight for something that is not in its own interest. Show me, therefore, gentlemen, an objective worthy of war, and I will agree with you.

The only alternative in Germany was the restoration of the Confederation as it had been before March 1848. The only German assembly was the Federal Diet, still dominated by Austria and with the same powers as before the revolution. The Fundamental Rights of the German People (the Fifty Articles) was declared null and void. Constitutions, so readily granted by German princes in 1848 and 1849, were suspended. Reactionary rule was re-imposed.

ACTIVITY
KNOWLEDGE CHECK

1 Why did the Austrians re-call the Federal Diet in 1850?

2 How far was Prussia able to pursue its own policy against Denmark and Hessen-Kassel in 1850?

3 Why do you think that Prussia agreed to sign the Punctation of Olomouc?

4 Read Source 14.

    a) Copy out all the examples of sarcasm in this speech.

    b) Why do you think that Bismarck was in favour of the Punctation of Olomouc?

The significance of revolutionary failure for German nationalism and liberalism

In the three years following March 1848, liberals and nationalists had made significant gains throughout the Confederation and lost them all. Liberal constitutions set out a model for parliamentary government based on a wide franchise and a limited monarchy, were as far away in 1851 as they had been before 1848. Notions of rights and freedoms had come and gone as though blown by the wind.

The liberal and nationalist movements that had been so virulent in the heady days of 1848 were now a shadow of their former selves. Liberals would not find their voice again until the 20th century and nationalists would see their desire for a unified Germany achieved, not by the power of mass popular movements but by the efficiency of the Prussian army and the hard-headed politics of its leaders.

What had changed were ideas. The actuality of a German parliament, governing Germany through a German constitution, had shown that such a possibility existed. What could be achieved once, could be achieved again. Statements of principle could be torn up but, although the statement was gone, the principle would remain. Powerful and popular notions would not be forgotten.

The reactionary rule of the 1850s and the 1860s was, therefore, a different one. It was not the *ancien régime* of the 18th century nor the Restoration Germany dominated by Metternich. It had a character of its own, where conservative ministers, always sensitive to the possibility of popular demonstration, were measured in their approach to government. Social policies, designed to win the support of the masses, were implemented all over Germany. Prussian peasants were freed from their feudal obligations and granted loans from state banks in order to set themselves up as tenant farmers. The abundance of industrial work in the cities kept workers satisfied and the expansion of industry forced economic policy into a more liberal direction.

Perhaps the most significant impact of the German revolutions was the change in the relationship between Austria and Prussia. Before 1848, Prussia had been satisfied to follow the Austrian lead. It recognised that both states had a vested interest in maintaining the status quo and curtailing the possibility of revolution. While Metternich so skilfully managed the continuation of reactionary rule within the Confederation, Prussia was prepared to play second fiddle.

The revolutions, however, had opened up another possibility for Germany. The *Kleindeutschland/Grossdeutschland* argument had shown Prussia that it could be the leading state in a united Germany. That, at a time of Austrian weakness, the Frankfurt Parliament had settled on the *Kleindeutschland* solution demonstrated, at least in the minds of the Prussian leaders that the rest of Germany would be prepared to follow a Prussian lead. The rivalry between Austria and Prussia for **hegemony** in Germany began with the events of 1848 and 1849.

KEY TERM

Hegemony
Unrivalled power in a given area.

Summary

Events of 1848 to 1851 sent seismic waves through the German polity. The major powers of Austria and Prussia were so weakened that an assembly, the Frankfurt Parliament, could lay claim through popular support to be the rightful government of the United Germany. The fact that Austria and Prussia had to deal with the Frankfurt Parliament and, indeed, had to introduce liberal reform in their own states is testimony to their weakness and the strength of feeling of the liberals and the nationalists. Ultimately, the ruling elites regained their strength and the liberal gains were reversed. It is perhaps a reasonable argument to state that the 1848 revolutions changed much in the short term and much in the long term but very little in the medium term.

ACTIVITY
SUMMARY

1 Make a list of all the gains made in 1848 by liberals and nationalists.

2 Why did the great powers (Britain, France and Russia) go along with events in the summer of 1848?

3 Why were the forces of reaction able to mount a counter-revolution in the autumn of 1848?

4 How far had conservative rule re-established itself by the end of 1850?

WIDER READING

Blackbourn, D. *History of Germany 1780-1918*, Blackwell (2003), chapter 3

Carr, W. *A History of Germany 1815-1985*, Edward Arnold (1987), chapter 2

Clark, C. *Iron Kingdom*, Allen Lane (2006), chapter 14

Taylor, A.J.P. *The Course of German History*, Hamish Hamilton (1945), chapter 4

2b.3 Austro-Prussian rivalry, 1852–66

KEY QUESTIONS

- How far did economic and political setbacks weaken Austria's position by 1862?
- To what extent did Prussia take the lead in the industrialisation of the German Confederation?
- How effective were reforms in Prussia in enabling it to rival Austria?
- Why was Prussia able to achieve pre-eminence in Germany by 1866?

INTRODUCTION

It seemed as though the events of 1848 and 1849 had exhausted the people's belief in Germany's ability to take part in politics. That so much effort had gone into the actions undertaken during the revolution to no avail was soul-destroying for the liberals and nationalists. If their enthusiasm was on the wane it was matched by the complete lack of opportunity to push forward the liberal and nationalist agenda. The forces of conservative reaction dominated the German Confederation, just as they had in the time of Metternich.

It was, perhaps, fortunate that other matters came to the fore during the 1850s. Industrialisation, which had touched certain areas of Germany before 1850, now became its chief concern. This process brought about massive social and economic change not only in the cities but in the countryside as well. These changes not only affected day-to-day life but also the political climate of the Confederation. When people began to be more aware of issues on a national and, indeed on a **supranational** level, rather than just a local level, governments had to be accommodating to popular opinion.

By the end of the 1850s, the old *Kleindeutschland/Grossdeutschland* question had once again resurfaced. In terms of the two powers, Austria and Prussia, it was very much the same Austria who had reinstated the Federal Diet that was moving into the 1860s but it was in no way the same Prussia. Austria had the same monarch, the same empire, the same aspirations and the same problems. The Prussians, on the other hand, had a new king, new industry, new railways, a reformed army with new weapons and an ambitious new first minister, Otto von Bismarck. In the summer of 1866, Austria and Prussia would fight a war that would radically alter the course of European history.

1852 – Death of Prince von Schwarzenberg and the beginning of autocratic rule in Austria

1854 – Crimean War

1859 – War between Austria and France/Piedmont

1859 – Establishment of the *Nationalverein*

1851	1852	1853	1854	1855	1856	1857	1858	1859	1860

1853 – Treaty between Austria and the *Zollverein*

1860 – Reform of the Prussian Army proposed

HOW FAR DID ECONOMIC AND POLITICAL SETBACKS WEAKEN AUSTRIA'S POSITION BY 1862?

Ostensibly, in the 1850s, it appeared that Austrian dominance of the German Confederation was as strong as it had ever been. The Punctation of Olomouc had been a Prussian climbdown that left Austria unchallenged. The Federal Diet had been reinstated at the behest of the Austrians and their influence, particularly in the Catholic states of southern Germany, was as strong as ever. There were, however, problems in their multinational empire and signs that their hegemony in Germany would not be maintained.

Absolutism

In 1852, the first minister of Austria, Prince von Schwarzenberg, died. He was not replaced but Emperor Franz Josef, the self-proclaimed 'first servant of the state', took over his duties. Working from five in the morning till midnight, the emperor ruled the empire. Ministers from the Schwarzenberg era remained and Alexander Bach, minister of the interior, was a particularly close advisor and, in the eyes of many, Schwarzenberg's successor.

Aspects of liberal government had been introduced but were short lived. The interior minister Franz Stadion's liberal constitution, which had been passed in March 1849, had never been enacted and had been totally discarded following the Punctation of Olomouc in 1851. The Reichsrat, an imperial assembly, met but had little power. The army was loyal to the emperor. Thus with an emperor who was also the first minister, Austria had become an **absolutist** state.

Political influence in Germany

The Punctation of Olomouc and the recall of the Federal Diet had reduced Prussian influence. Austria was clearly the dominant power in the Confederation. Aside from maintaining this supremacy, Austria could openly improve its situation by moving towards a *Grossdeutschland* unification. This would only be achieved by moving the lesser German states closer diplomatically to Austria and at the same time weakening the Prussian position.

The *Grossdeutschland* plan was revived by the minister of commerce, Karl Ludwig von Bruck. Von Bruck was a merchant who had made a fortune trading out of Trieste. He had a grandiose vision of a super state which he called *Mittel-Europa*. At a time when the maritime powers, particularly Britain and France, were building vast overseas empires, he believed that the German destiny lay in the east and the Balkans. A vast German Empire incorporating all the Habsburg Crown lands and ruled by Germans was the aim. Steps were taken towards this with the abolition of the Erfurt Union but that was the extent of Austrian progress.

> **KEY TERM**
>
> **Absolutist**
> An absolutist system of government is where the monarch has the right to rule the state as they see fit. Often the monarch is above the rule of the law.

1861 – William I becomes King of Prussia

1863 – William of Prussia snubs Franz Josef of Austria and refuses to attend a meeting at Frankfurt

1863 – Revolt in Russian-controlled Poland

| 1861 | 1862 | 1863 | 1864 | 1865 | 1866 | 1867 | 1868 | 1869 | 1870 |

1862 – Otto von Bismarck appointed first minister of Prussia

1864 – War with Denmark

1866 – Seven Weeks' War between Austria and Prussia

AS Level Exam-Style Question Section B

How far was there Austrian domination of the German Confederation during the 1850s? (20 marks)

Tip

Make it very clear what you regard as 'secure' in this context and use this to drive the judgements throughout the answer.

The Austrians were keen to use the Federal Diet to undermine the Prussian position. They worked with lesser states to vote against the Prussians. The lesser states enjoyed this as it gave them, at least from their own perspective, a raised status. It also reinforced notions of the Austrian ascendency within Germany. The Diet, however, had no real power to affect matters and the issues that they voted on were often trivial and of little concern to state governments.

The Crimean War

The war, which took place on the Crimean peninsula and parts of modern day Bulgaria, altered the system of European security set up in 1815. It did not directly involve Prussia and Austria but had an effect on relations between the two and their place within the Confederation. The war had been caused by Russian ambitions to gain territory from the ailing Ottoman Empire. Alarmed by the prospect of Russia making strategic gains in the Balkans and perhaps even in the Eastern Mediterranean, Britain and France declared war. The war lasted from 1854 to 1856.

While not actually declaring war, Austria was alarmed enough at events to **mobilise** its army to guard against a Russian invasion. It seemed natural to go to the Federal Diet and make a firm request for assistance from the German states in the form of troops. Prussia refused point blank. Other states were similarly reluctant to provide troops for a potential Austrian war in the Balkans. It was the first time that Austria had been defeated in the Federal Diet since it had been reconvened.

Prussia was quick to make political capital out of this. It painted the Austrians as expansionist warmongers who were only interested in using German resources to expand their own empire in the east. If the notion of *Mittel-Europa* was remote in 1853, it was completely dead by 1854. Prussia, on the other hand, had made progress in its pursuit of the *Kleindeutschland* solution.

Economic and financial problems

Austria was faced with the same issues facing other central European states but was slower in dealing with them. It did not abolish feudal ties in the countryside as quickly as the Prussians had and were also slower to exploit natural resources.

Part of the initial problem was that the revolution had taken much longer to resolve than in the German states. Moreover, the resolving of it in the German states had meant deploying the regular army, usually Prussians with a few detachments of supporting troops, on a couple of occasions. There were some small demonstrations that took place but these were contained fairly easily. The Austrians, on the other hand, had been forced to mount major campaigns. The re-taking of Prague and Vienna had taken tens of thousands of troops and a major war against Piedmont-Sardinia had been fought to preserve Austrian power. The subjugation of the Hungarian insurrection had taken over a year and had consisted of two major invasions. Politically, this was damaging for Austria but this was overcome at Olomouc. Financially, the effect was far longer lasting.

The cost of the military actions of 1848 and 1849 left the Austrian government significantly short of money. At a time when Prussia had tax surpluses which it used to fund economic growth, the Austrians were scratching around for tax income simply to balance the books. This gave the Austrian government far less scope to encourage investment.

Also Austria had a political system that did not encourage innovation. While the Prussians were able to walk the fine line between political conservatism and economic liberalism, the Austrians found this more difficult. An absolutist state with power held in the hands of the emperor looks to the emperor. He was not inclined to concern himself much with economic policy. While ministers like Bruck saw the advantages of industrialisation and economic development, conditions were not as conducive as elsewhere in the Confederation. Railway building was also given over wholly to private enterprise. This meant that coverage was not as substantial as it was in northern Germany. Unlike their Prussian counterparts, the Austrian general staff actively discouraged railway building, deeming it a waste of resources.

This is not to say that the Austrians did not pursue economic growth. Seeing the rapid advances made in Germany, there was certainly a policy to stimulate investment, particularly towards the end of the decade. There was some liberalisation of the manorial system, particularly in the German-speaking lands, and tenant farmers were encouraged to purchase their farms and set up on their own. Where the Austrians lagged behind the Prussians was in having the financial resources to lend money on quite the same scale.

ACTIVITY
KNOWLEDGE CHECK

1 Describe the style of government adopted by Austria in the years following the Punctation of Olomouc.

2 What were the main problems facing Austria between 1852 and 1862?

3 To what extent would supporters of the Austrian government have regarded the 1850s as a successful decade for Austria?

Rejection from the *Zollverein*

Austria had made overtures to get into the *Zollverein* since the 1830s but to little avail. Following the revolutions, Schwarzenberg came up with a scheme to absorb the *Zollverein* into the Austrian Customs Union thus creating one massive central European free trade area.

The problem was that the Austrian Customs Union amounted to Austria alone whereas the *Zollverein* contained virtually every other state in the Confederation. Prussia had been proactive in the early 1850s and had persuaded both Hanover and Oldenburg to join. This gave them coverage of virtually the whole of Germany with the exception of Austria.

As the 1850s progressed, Prussian industrial development pushed them ahead of the Austrians. Though the Austrians had a political pre-eminence within the Confederation, they were unable to use this influence in the industrial sphere. Prussia was able to use its economic might in order to prevent smaller states from entering into any agreement with the Austrians.

In 1853, Bruck was able to negotiate a treaty with the *Zollverein*. This slightly lowered duties between the two areas but did little else. The fact that Austria was negotiating with the *Zollverein* as a separate entity only reinforced the perception that the *Zollverein* was a Prussian organisation and that Austria was a foreign body.

SOURCE

1 Letter from Karl Ludwig von Bruck to Prince von Schwarzenberg in 1850, outlining his ideas for a Central European Customs Union.

Austria has, above all, one thing to prevent, namely that, the Zollverein, due to expire at the end of 1852, should be renewed before the Austro-German Customs Union is irrevocably settled on a sure foundation. Such a renewal would bind all the German states for twelve years longer to Prussia's will in all national economic affairs. If Prussia were to see her supremacy assured for so long a time, she would scarcely be persuaded to enter the Customs Union with Austria – even though it offered the most convincing economic advantages – and to share, to that degree, her supremacy with her. The matter would, however, stand quite differently, if the renewal of the Zollverein were put in question by several of its members, or if it were made dependent upon the previous achievement of a Customs Union with Austria; for rather than endanger the intellectual and economic supremacy that she gained through the Zollverein, Prussia would prefer an attempt to share it with Austria…

Perhaps one might also mention that Austria herself, notwithstanding the political differences still outstanding unreservedly offers her hand to help forward this unity, because she does not wish to withhold these advantages from the nation any longer and because she hopes to succeed through this unity in settling agitation on other matters…

The Prussians made a miscalculation in 1862 which might have changed the situation. Prussia negotiated a bi-lateral trade agreement with France, the chief purpose of which was to block any further attempts by Austria to join the *Zollverein*. This backfired when Austria accused Prussia of arrogantly regarding the *Zollverein* as a Prussian institution. Other *Zollverein* members backed the Austrian position, notably Bavaria and Württemberg, who refused to sanction the treaty. This added to a tension that was already building (see below).

ACTIVITY
KNOWLEDGE CHECK

1 Why was it so important for Prussia to keep Austria out of the *Zollverein*?

2 To what extent do you think Prussian economic development was dependent on the *Zollverein*?

3 Would it be fair to describe Austria as economically backward compared with Prussia in the 1850s? Give examples to illustrate your answer.

4 Read Source 1. What arguments does Bruck put forward for a Central European Customs Union to include Austria?

International setbacks

In 1815 at the Congress of Vienna, a system was set up to keep the peace in Europe. It was known as the '**Concert of Europe**'. This system assumed that the five great powers (Britain, France, Prussia, Austria and Russia) would not fight each other. Together, or individually with the others' consent, they would 'police' the rest of Europe to prevent unrest. Each of the powers was allocated spheres of influence. The Italian peninsula was to be overseen by Austria.

KEY TERM

Concert of Europe
Devised in 1814–15 largely by Metternich of Austria and Castlereagh of Britain, it was a system by which the larger powers in Europe would police the smaller ones and resolve issues through diplomacy rather than warfare.

Italy, like Germany, was a collection of independent states. Within Italy there was also a movement that wished to unify into a single Italian nation state. Austria sought to prevent this and used its military might to this end. Piedmont-Sardinia, the most powerful of the Italian states, had already fought the Austrians in 1848 to try to break the Austrian hold on Italy. In 1859, it would try again.

The difference was that in 1859, Piedmont had the help of France. Napoleon III, the nephew of Napoleon I, had become the French emperor following the revolution of 1848 and sought to aggrandise France much in the same way that his uncle had. A combined Piedmontese-French army defeated the Austrians at the battles of Magenta and Solferino and over 40 years of Austrian hegemony in Italy was broken.

The effect of the war of 1859

The loss of the war of 1859 sent shockwaves through Austria. It lost physical territory as Lombardy was annexed by Piedmont as part of the peace treaty but also it lost its position of influence over the rest of the Italian peninsula. In Germany, Austria's standing with the other states was reduced considerably as it considered losing to France as a German humiliation. Financially, the war further stretched Austrian resources and precipitated a wave of political reform to try to put government finances back on an even keel.

Lombardy had been part of the Habsburg Crown lands since the early 16th century. Not only did Austria feel its loss as a blow to its prestige but also its industry and commerce had economic effect. Strategically it retained the quadrilateral, an area of fortifications vital to Austrian security in the area, but had, of course, lost the major population centre of Milan. At a point when the assumption in Austria was that the empire was going to get bigger, losing a prosperous area like Lombardy was a massive psychological blow.

In the Confederation, the perception of Austrian power was radically altered. The military successes of 1848 and 1849 were in the distant past. Now, the Austrian army had lost a major war with another European power in a matter of weeks. Economically, Austria was being outpaced by other German states, notably Prussia, and the Federal Diet was no longer the Austrian puppet that it had been in the early 1850s. Franz Joseph believed that he could make good the losses in Italy by making gains in Germany, a policy that was, perhaps, ill-advised. In many ways, the war of 1859 created a situation that would eventually lead to a *Kleindeutschland* unification under Prussian leadership.

Government finances were in a fairly precarious state even before 1859. Before the war, Franz Joseph had refused to expand the army, even though his advisors thought that a reaction to Prussian army reform would be prudent. The fact was, as the emperor saw it, they could not afford to pay for army reform. The declaration of war in April 1859 caused a run on the banks even before any fighting had actually taken place, making it even more difficult for the government to find credit. After the fighting had taken place, the government needed to pay all the bills for the summer campaign, a hefty sum that it had problems finding. Franz Josef and his advisors believed that the only solution was a reformed tax system based on a popular mandate. As a result, they initiated a programme of political reform in order to create a constitutional system based on a monarch and a parliament.

EXTEND YOUR KNOWLEDGE

Austria and tactical doctrine in the early 19th century
The 18th century had been dominated by armies who fought in long lines and used musket fire to try and break the enemy. The instances of close-quarter fighting were few. During the French Revolutionary Wars and the Napoleonic Wars, the French conquered Europe by switching to 'shock' tactics by which their soldiers would charge the enemy at the earliest opportunity and use the momentum of their rapid movement to break the enemy's spirit and thereby win the engagement. The British used terrain to prevent the rapid charge and thereby fire tactics were seen as dominant doctrine by 1815.

The Austrians retrained along French lines after their disastrous defeats against Napoleon in 1805 and 1809 but following the Congress of Vienna reverted to 'fire' tactics after the British model. In 1859, the French won the battles of Magenta and Solferino by using 'shock' tactics which overcame Austrian 'fire' tactics. The Austrian armies again retrained, adopting the French 'shock' doctrine. This played into the hands of the Prussians in 1866, whose 'fire' tactics with their new breech-loading needle gun proved highly effective against the masses of Austrian infantry as they sought to charge the Prussian lines.

Austria did pursue a programme of military reform as a result of its defeat in 1859. Most significantly, it switched **military doctrine**. Since, the Napoleonic Wars, the Austrian army had favoured 'fire' tactics, by which it would keep its distance from the enemy and fire at them. The French army had, since the French Revolutionary Wars, favoured 'shock' tactics, by which it would advance at great speed and seek to close with the enemy as quickly as possible. In 1859, the impetus gained by French 'shock' tactics caused panic in the Austrian army and thereby won the battles (and the war) for the French and Piedmontese. Learning its lesson from this, the Austrian army switched its training and adopted 'shock' tactics. This move would have grave consequences during the Seven Weeks' War in 1866.

KEY TERM

Military doctrine
The way in which armed forces fight wars.

ACTIVITY
KNOWLEDGE CHECK

1 Why, do you think that France and Italy declared war on Austria in 1859?

2 How did the loss of the war affect Austria?

TO WHAT EXTENT DID PRUSSIA TAKE THE LEAD IN THE INDUSTRIALISATION OF THE GERMAN CONFEDERATION?

Development of the *Zollverein*

There were two significant developments of the *Zollverein* during the 1850s. These were the addition of Hannover and Oldenburg, two of the larger north German states, which had hitherto refused to join, and the granting of the right for *Zollverein* officials to negotiate international tariffs (see Chapter 1, pages 297–9).

Having Offenburg and Hannover as members from 1854 gave the *Zollverein* coverage of all the states of the Confederation, apart from Austria, Mecklenburg-Schwerin and Schleswig-Holstein. This represented the *Kleindeutschland* solution to the unification problem. For the Prussians, having an almost *Kleindeutschland* economic union was seen as a useful forerunner to a potential political union. Excluding the Austrians, therefore, became the main aim of Prussian policy towards the *Zollverein*. For the Austrians, gaining entry or making alternative arrangements became very important (see below). Giving the *Zollverein* and its assembly greater power only served to further isolate the Austrians.

SOURCE

Map of the *Zollverein* in 1854.

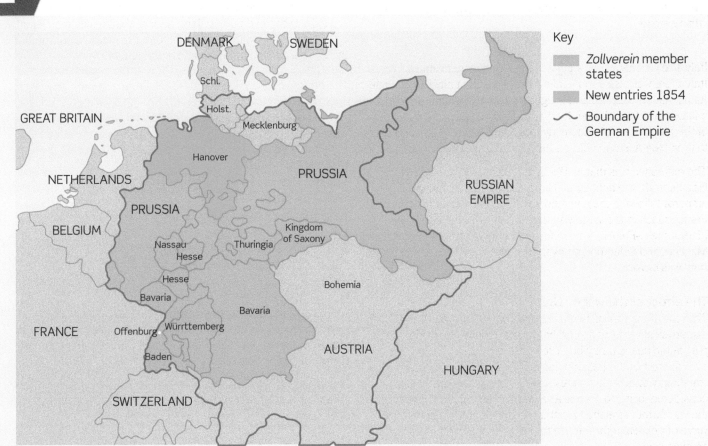

The existence of the *Zollverein* was very helpful to the expanding German economy. As businesses expanded, they had a large internal free market, already set up, at their disposal. That this free market had the ability to negotiate with foreign governments on behalf of its members gave it a lot of influence and enabled it, in many cases, to negotiate favourable terms.

Financial strength

Having already seen the effects of industrialisation in Britain, the Prussians were acutely aware of its potential advantages. This included private investors and state governments alike. While industrialisation in Britain came about as a result of individuals who were innovative and entrepreneurial, in Prussia the state governments played a far greater role in encouraging development. This was not necessarily through direct investment aside perhaps from railways and canals, but more through the creation of conditions conducive to industrialisation. This included a tax system which fell more heavily on land owners and consumers rather than industrial enterprises, liberal company and banking law and the encouragement of chambers of commerce.

Smaller banks saw the opportunity to make money and combined forces to create larger **investment banks**. The Darmstadter und Nationalbank (1853), the Handelgesellschaft (1856) and the Disconto-Gesellschaft (1851) were all **joint stock banks** which were founded in order to provide venture capital for industry. The Disconto-Gesellschaft was founded in Berlin by David Hanseman, who had been minister of finance under Camphausen and Auerswald in 1848. One of the bank's chief functions was to underwrite state loans for the Prussian government.

Increased industrial production

Economic growth and industrial development comes in waves. At times, it is slow and languid and other times dynamic and quick. The 1850s and 1860s represent, perhaps, the most dynamic change in the process of German industrialisation. Statistics indicate that levels of production increased rapidly. For example, in 1846 the German Confederation mined 3.2 million tonnes of coal a year. By 1860 that figure had risen to 12.3 million tonnes a year and by 1870 to 29.4 million tonnes. By 1865, 3 million tonnes a year was being mined. It is estimated that production in all sectors rose an average of 4.8 percent in the 20 years following 1850 but in more dynamic sectors like the railways, the figure was more like 14 percent.

Increased production was driven by new and expanding companies. These firms needed more workers and attracted people to move from the countryside into the cities (urbanisation). They were also able to draw from the growing population. For example, Alfred Krupp, initially a steel producer and later an armaments manufacturer, employed 60 men in 1836. By 1865, this had reached 8,000 and doubled to 16,000 less than ten years later. The Phoenix iron foundry, which was founded in 1851, had a workforce of 4,500 by 1870. In the Saarland, the number of miners quadrupled from under 5,000 in 1850 to around 20,000 in 1870.

Advantages of the Prussian industrial revolution

Industrialising later than some other countries, such as Britain, gave Prussia something of an advantage. It was not simply a case of copying the machinery and factories from Britain but developing them in a different way. The Prussians could utilise the latest technology in the building process rather than having to upgrade existing machinery. A comparative study between the Ruhr coalfield and the South Wales coalfield has shown that the Prussian mines were larger and more efficient because they were able to take advantage of new and more efficient machinery. The Prussians began to use **coke** to smelt iron to make steel, as the British were doing, but Prussian steel plants were on average much bigger than their British counterparts. New efficiency meant that Prussia could not only compete effectively in the market within the German Confederation but also begin to challenge Britain's domination of the export markets.

New and old industries

A boom in traditional industries also gave rise to new ones. An example of this is the chemical industry. Chemical companies were originally founded to produce dyes for the textile industry; companies like Bayer and BASF diverged into areas such as fertilisers, explosives and

SOURCE
3

The Krupp works at Essen in 1865. An example of German industrial might.

pharmaceuticals. Engine manufacturers provided machinery for the new factories and for the railways. In Rhineland-Westphalia, the number of steam engines grew from 650 in 1849 to around 10,000 in the 1860s. Not only were there more of them, but they were far more powerful.

The construction sector also enjoyed a boom during these years. Entrepreneurs wanted factories building, often utilising new techniques and materials such as steel and needing to be designed so as to be able to incorporate steam engines and machinery. The expanding population needed housing and so **brownfield sites** within cities were utilised, as were new sites on their outskirts (greenfield sites). Towns felt an increasing level of civic pride and so grander public buildings were constructed. In Prussia alone, over a million new buildings were built in the two decades following 1850 and the investment in non-agricultural buildings increased four-fold. In addition to employing vast numbers of builders and labourers, the construction sector also stimulated other areas such as brick manufacturing, wood production, steel production and furniture manufacturing.

Another area stimulated by the new industry was **consumer goods**. Larger urban populations with higher levels of disposable income needed items to buy. Previously, these would have been handmade by Prussian artisans or cheap imports, most probably from Britain. By the 1850s, Prussia was in a position to produce goods that could compete in these markets. An illustration of this is that almost a quarter of all people employed in manufacturing in Prussia were engaged in the production of apparel – shoes, hosiery, clothes, and hats.

Food processing also became a growth area as demand in urban areas grew. The beet sugar industry in Prussia became the world leader, with export revenue from sugar exceeding that from coal or machinery. The worldwide renown of items such as the frankfurter and the hamburger are further testimony to the success of the German processed food industry.

KEY TERMS

Brownfield site
An area of undeveloped land which had previously been built on. A 'greenfield' site is an area of undeveloped land which has not been built on.

Consumer goods
Everyday items used by ordinary people in their everyday lives.

ACTIVITY
KNOWLEDGE CHECK

1 Do some research on the Ruhr and Silesia. Why were these obvious areas for industrialisation?

2 How did heavy industry stimulate growth in other sectors?

3 Why was it an advantage for Prussia to be able to examine the industrialisation process in Britain?

Agricultural reform

Though industry was becoming more and more important, agriculture was still by far the largest economic sector. In 1852, 55 percent of all workers worked in the agricultural sector, which provided the largest part of the German Confederation's GDP.

The end of the feudal arrangements was a great stimulus for change. Freed from the medieval arrangements of dues and service, farmers could now look at farming as purely a commercial operation. This meant that there were incentives to improve efficiency. It paid off for tenant farmers to take out loans in order to improve their land and state banks were more than willing to lend money. Special low interest loans were also made available by the state for peasants to buy their farms outright: 600,000 of them took advantage of this. Large landowners looked upon agriculture as a business and began to introduce efficiency measures on their estates. Some landowners took back their tenanted farms and consolidated them into bigger units, the former tenants becoming salaried workers. **Marginal land** was also brought under cultivation, so that a greater percentage of the land was being utilised for food production.

New methods also brought improvements. The uses of new fertilisers caused yields to rise. Guano was imported from Central and South America to make fertilisers but it was **potash** mining that gave the Prussians an advantage. Traditionally, potash had been manufactured by burning wood in large quantities but in the 1850s it was discovered that there was, in Prussia, a large amount of natural potash that could be mined. Having a worldwide monopoly in natural potash not only benefited Prussian farmers but it was also a high export product in its own right.

New crops also opened up new possibilities for Prussian agriculture. Wheat was still the staple crop, particularly in East Prussia, and there was a very strong export demand for Prussian grain until the Americans flooded the market towards the end of the 19th century. The coming of the railways meant that farmers could reach more distant markets within Europe and so it benefited them to diversify. One of the most successful crops was sugar beet. Not only was it well suited to the European climate but its expansion coincided with sugar's transformation from being seen as a luxury to being regarded as a staple. Moreover, the new sugar beet industry led the way with many of the innovations that helped efficiency in growing other crops. Rapeseed oil cake, used mostly in animal feed, also became popular which meant that farmers could grow oil-seed rape as a reliable cash crop.

The expansion of the railways and state investment

Industrialisation gave a boost to the railway industry but also the railway industry gave a boost to industrialisation. At no other time in Prussia's history would this symbiotic relationship be so dynamic.

Railways were being built by a mixture of private enterprise and state funded infrastructure projects. Individual entrepreneurs built railways with a view to making a profit and so they were built piecemeal. State governments had a different view, as they saw the overall economic and strategic benefit of a comprehensive railway network. Thus, where lines were not being built by private enterprise, state governments would step in to ensure that there was a reasonable coverage of the country. Both Bavaria and Baden had state-funded railways, but it was really in Prussia where the state set out to control the rail network. Funded by the new income tax of 1851, Prussian state spending on railways increased dramatically either in building new lines or nationalising existing ones.

This expansion of the railway sector created a demand for heavy industry. There was a continual demand for more steel for new lines, locomotives and wagons, creating an expansion of the steel industry. Once in place, the new railways transported other German steel products to new markets quickly and cheaply. Coal was also needed to power the locomotives and so much of the increased coal output was used by the new railways. The new trains transported coal that was being increasingly needed to power engines in the new factories and to heat homes.

SOURCE 4 Railway building in the German Confederation, 1841–70.

	Austria (1)	Prussia	Germany (2)
1841	351	375	681
1847	1,048	2,325	4,306
1850	1,357	2,967	5,856
1860	2,927	5,762	11,089
1865	3,698	6,895	13,900

(1) Only the part in the German Confederation

(2) States in the Confederation excluding Prussia and Austria

The railways brought a reduction in transport costs which affected manufacturing across the board. Consumer goods now had access to many more markets and well-made and cheap items could generate large profits for the company manufacturing them. It also caused the agricultural sector to diversify. Farmers were no longer restricted to growing crops or raising animals which would sell on the local market or were for a standard export market, such as wheat. The ability to deliver fresh food over long distances meant that **niche markets** for items such as soft fruit, for example, could be exploited. This in turn widened the diet of German people who had access to a far larger variety of foodstuffs.

> **KEY TERM**
>
> Niche market
> A market where demand is not widespread but the desire for the product is high. This means that consumers are willing to pay a higher price for it.

ACTIVITY
KNOWLEDGE CHECK

1 Why did food production change so dramatically in the 1850s?

2 To what extent would you describe the railways as the single most important factor driving economic change in Prussia in the 1850s?

3 To what extent had Prussia become the dominant economic force in the German Confederation by 1860?

HOW EFFECTIVE WERE REFORMS IN PRUSSIA IN ENABLING HER TO RIVAL AUSTRIA?

The pre-eminence of von Radowitz as Frederick William's chief advisor did not even last until the conference at Olomouc in 1850 where it was agreed to reinstate the German Confederation. He was replaced by Otto von Manteuffel, initially as foreign minister, though later von Manteuffel became the first minister. Von Manteuffel would remain in post throughout most of the 1850s. Though conservative by inclination, he saw that the days of the *ancien régime* were over and believed that the traditional ruling gentry needed to exercise power through a constitutional framework.

Von Manteuffel believed that it was the role of government to mediate between different interests in society. The ultra-conservatives, thinking they had totally defeated the revolution, expected to return to the situation that had existed before 1848. Despite the reverses of the counter-revolution, liberals and nationalists were still there and were waiting for a new opportunity to press forward their claims. The working classes had yet to find an organised voice though there were signs of an embryonic **socialist** movement.

> **KEY TERM**
>
> Socialist and socialism
> Socialism is a way of organising a society in which major industries are owned and controlled by the government rather than by individual people. Often socialist movements are organised by middle-class intellectuals but appeal in the main to working people.

The pressure on von Manteuffel was to manage a state that, at the same time, desired to be politically conservative but economically liberal. This brought the first minister into conflict with the ultra-conservatives and the monarch but also gave him support from the more moderate conservatives. These moderates saw that Prussia needed a more liberal approach to economic matters in order to stimulate economic growth, industrialisation and better agricultural efficiency. By the 1860s, this new liberalism had made its presence felt with a liberal majority in parliament.

Otto von Manteuffel's reforms

Political reforms

Von Manteuffel oversaw a transformation of the state bureaucracy from a small amateurish collection of state ministries to a civil service, which would have been recognisable by modern observers. Under the old system, officials had largely done as they were asked by the powerful elites on an ad hoc basis. There were some systems in place but these would have been easily overridden by individual instruction. The new bureaucracy was based on processes and layers of management. Systems take the strain when a modern state becomes too complex for individuals to manage. This reduces the possibility for individuals to act on their own initiative, unless, of course, they are in charge.

Von Manteuffel's new bureaucracy was an important tool for political control. The expansion of the police force, particularly the **secret police**, gave the government far more information about possible dissent. Von Manteuffel employed spies to watch his political opponents and procure for him important documents. It was even rumoured that Crown Prince William was under surveillance.

> **KEY TERM**
>
> Secret police
> Organisation within the police whose task it is to keep people who the state regards as politically dangerous under surveillance. Famous secret police services include the Gestapo, the KGB and the Stasi.

Another area that the bureaucracy improved was tax collection. The new income tax of 1851 and a greater efficiency of collecting other taxes meant that the Prussian government had a very healthy income throughout the 1850s and the 1860s. This allowed it to further improve the civil service, increase spending on the military and invest in economic projects such as railway building.

Economic reforms

The loosening of state controls gave a major boost to economic development. The government's reluctance to charter joint stock banks, on the basis of not wishing to risk public funds, had given rise to a number of banks run by private partnerships with limited liabilities. The conservatives believed that these banks would encourage high-risk speculation. In 1856, the cabinet drew up new legislation to restrict joint stock banks but von Manteuffel, under pressure from leading businessmen, was able to block this initiative. Following this, government restrictions on the activities of joint stock banks were eased and more capital was made available.

In the coal and iron industries, government supervision was also slackened. Entrepreneurs were freer to develop sites that they saw as having potential without the red tape of the previous era. The greater availability of capital turned this potential into reality.

Von Manteuffel and the press

Von Manteuffel put an end to press censorship but this was not for liberal reasons. He understood that retributive action was often too late and that the 'harm' had already been done. Closing down radical newspapers, for example, would prevent them from printing more but would do nothing to get rid of those copies which had already been printed and circulated. Moreover, asking publications to submit material for approval by the censor was cumbersome and ineffective in a sector with so many newspapers and journals.

Manteuffel's idea was to work with the press in order to shape its output. He created an office in the civil service, the press agency, whose task was to provide the press with government-friendly stories. Part of this process, unavoidably, was that officials had a far more personal relationship with editors. Through these relationships, co-operative editors were given far greater access to government information than less co-operative editors. The government would not enter into political debate with the newspapers directly but would do so through their press agency. These relationships were also extended to the foreign press.

The government also bought a newspaper. *The Deutsche Reform* would serve as the government mouthpiece and support its policies. Other newspapers, which were sympathetic to the government, would be given subsidies and special access privileges.

Liberalism and nationalism and the *Nationalverein*

Continuation of reactionary governments

By the end of 1850, it was clear that the liberal and nationalist movements had failed to achieve their aims from the revolutions in 1848. Germany was still ruled by individual state governments and not by a single German parliament. The Federal Diet, dominated as it was by reactionary Austria, was a wholly inadequate instrument of federal governance. In Austria, the constitution had been abolished and rule returned to the autocracy of the emperor. In Prussia, the constitution of 1850 had been so conservative as to make it clear that liberal reform would not be possible.

Liberals and nationalists had much cause to reflect on the failures of 1848. In many ways it had been the split in their own ranks that had done so much to undermine their efforts. They knew that, as long as German rulers could rely on the loyalty of the armed forces, they could not hope for success. Only a mass uprising could deliver the kind of liberal national Germany that was hoped for but when faced with mass action, the middle-class liberals had balked and had allied themselves with the forces of conservative reaction.

The potential for liberal gains

And yet there were some signs for optimism. The main factor that had kept Germany separate before 1848 was the co-operation between Austria and Prussia. Both powers saw that it was in their best interest to work together. After 1848, it was the rivalry between Austria and Prussia that prevented

German unification. In one sense, both powers wanted a more federal state but only with their domination. The result of this rivalry was the preservation of the status quo in Germany. Liberals had hoped that this rivalry would become unequal and create conditions conducive to liberal reform.

SOURCE 5

A memorandum to Frederick William on the need for social welfare, written in 1850 by Leopold von Ranke, Professor of History at the University of Berlin.

For he who serves the state with his life has also a claim on it for support. The soundest policy would be to satisfy this claim, since as a matter of fact it is dangerous to train year after year the entire youthful population in the use of arms, and then alienate a large and physically perhaps the most vigorous part, leaving it exposed to the agitation of the enemies of all order. Either we must exempt the propertyless from duty to serve in the army, or we must place them under an obligation to the state even after their period of service by the prospect of gainful employment.

Changes to the economy were also a potential gain for the liberals. Despite suspicions about liberalism in general, some conservative leaders were quick to see the advantages of a more liberal economic policy. Free trade and free movement of labour were very much on the same lines as freedom of association and freedom of the press.

The growth of the socialist movement among the urban working classes was also a sign of change. Some liberals hoped that the conservative elite would form a natural alliance with the middle-class liberals in order to negate the threat posed by the socialists. Liberals desired change, some wanting radical change but there were few who were willing to undergo a proletariat uprising in order to achieve this.

The *Nationalverein*

The victory of France over Austria in the war of 1859 (see below) caused a stir throughout the Confederation. In September 1859, the *Nationalverein* (National Union) was founded by a group of influential liberals. It was a pressure group with the sole aim of promoting German unification. It was the first popular movement that covered the whole Confederation. The members of the *Nationalverein* believed in the *Kleindeutschland* solution though the government in Prussia was suspicious of it.

The *Nationalverein* was in no way a mass movement. Membership was limited to the professional classes in the north German states. A request from the workers in Leipzig that membership be opened in 1863 was rejected. At its height, the association numbered 25,000 members and was able to send speakers to many public gatherings and to have a great effect on popular opinion.

The *Nationalverein* needed to be careful in the way that it managed Austria and the southern German states. In 1860, it declared that both Austria and Bohemia were part of the German Fatherland. In 1862, south German radicals formed their own *Deutscher Reformverein* in direct opposition to the *Nationalverein*. The new organisation, however, which only had 1,500 members at the height of its popularity did not have the same influence as its older counterpart.

SOURCE 6

The Founding declaration of the *Nationalverein*, 14 August 1859 at Eisenach, in the Grand Duchy of Saxe-Weimar.

The current dangerous state of affairs in Europe and Germany and the need to subordinate politically partisan demands to the great common cause of German unification have brought together a number of men from different German lands – some belonging to the democratic, some to the constitutional party – to reach an agreement on bringing about a uniform German constitution and on what needs to be done to achieve such a goal.

The same have – following up on the Eisenach Declaration of the 17th and the Hanover Declaration of the 19th of July 1859 – come to an agreement on the following points:

1. In the current international political situation we perceive great perils for the independence of our German fatherland, which tend to be increased rather than decreased by the peace concluded between Austria and France.
2. These perils are ultimately caused by Germany's flawed overall constitution, and they can only be eliminated by a prompt alteration in this constitution.
3. To this end it is necessary for the German Federal Diet to be replaced by a solid, strong, and lasting central government for Germany, and for a German national assembly to be convened.
4. Under the current circumstances, the most effective steps toward achieving this end can only emanate from Prussia; it is essential, therefore, to work toward getting Prussia to assume the initiative.
5. Should Germany be directly threatened from abroad in the near future, the leadership of German military forces and the diplomatic representation of Germany abroad are to be transferred to Prussia until such time as a German central government is definitively constituted.
6. It is the duty of every German man to support the Prussian government to the best of his ability, insofar as its efforts proceed from the assumption that the mission of the Prussian state essentially coincides with Germany's needs and mission, and insofar as its activity is directed toward the introduction of a strong and free overall constitution for Germany.
7. From all German patriots,* whether they belong to the democratic or the constitutional party, we expect that they will place national independence and unity above the demands of their party, and that they will work together harmoniously and tenaciously to attain a powerful constitution for Germany.

ACTIVITY
KNOWLEDGE CHECK

1 Explain how von Manteuffel's reforms benefited Prussia.

2 How fair would it be to describe the Prussian government as reactionary?

3 Read Source 5. Leopold von Ranke was a Prussian aristocrat. Are you surprised by what he wrote to the king?

4 Make a list of similarities and differences between the *Nationalverein* and the liberal-nationalists of 1848.

KEY TERM

Regent
A nominated person (usually a prince or princess) who takes the place of a monarch who is no longer capable of ruling or is too young to rule.

A Level Exam-Style Question Section B

'Prussia had become the most modern state in the German Confederation by 1866.'

How far do you agree with this statement? (20 marks)

Tip
Make sure that you make it very clear what you mean by 'modern' before you apply it to Prussia and other states in the German Confederation. Try to make it a broad definition.

KEY TERMS

Autocracy
A government where supreme power is concentrated in the hands of one person.

Landwehr
The Landwehr was the Prussian militia. It consisted of two groups: the first line Landwehr, which might be called upon to serve with the regular army during wartime and the second line which might be called up but would be allocated non-fighting tasks.

The regency and accession of William I

By 1858, Frederick William had suffered a series of strokes and was not capable of ruling Prussia. This meant that his brother William had to step in and rule as **regent** in his place. The regency lasted until 1861 when Frederick William died and William was crowned king.

William was already 60 years of age when he became regent and so had a fair amount of experience of public life. He was different from his brother in that he was closely associated with the army. He had been a soldier all his life and preferred the company of soldiers. The generals were pleased that the ruler of Prussia was now 'one of their own'.

Throughout the 1850s, however, William had modified his political views somewhat. By the time he became regent, he was no longer the hothead who had been bundled out of the country to cool down while the events of March 1848 unfolded. Realising that the situation had changed, William had kept contact with liberals in Prussia, convinced that one day they would be helpful if Prussia were to push for a *Kleindeutschland* unification. He still had a traditional approach to politics, believing that as an anointed monarch he was answerable only to God. He walked a fine line between pragmatic politics and **autocracy**.

William's first act as regent was to sack von Manteuffel and his cabinet. His first government consisted of a mixture of liberals and conservatives. Temperamentally, William might have preferred a cabinet of conservatives but the moderate liberals had just won a small majority in parliament in the elections of 1858 and so he could not ignore them. Given that the constitution of 1850 limited the power of parliament, however, he was in no way going to allow them to govern Germany. That was the role of the king.

Reform of the army

Upon becoming regent William was very enthusiastic about strengthening the army. The military tradition in Prussia was long and distinguished and William saw himself very much as the heir of Frederick the Great, the military genius who ruled Prussia in the 18th century.

The Prussian army had changed little since the end of the Napoleonic Wars in 1815. It had only fought in anger against the small Danish army over Schleswig and Holstein and bands of revolutionaries since then. The mobilisation of 1859 in response to the events in Italy (see below) drew into sharp focus its deficiencies. This gave William and the generals the opportunity to push for reform.

In 1860, William appointed General Albrecht von Roon as minister for war. He quickly introduced a bill to reform the army. This aimed to double the size of a re-equipped army and reduce the role of the **Landwehr**. Military service in the regular army was to be increased from a minimum of two years to three years and service in the regular army reserve from two to five years. These reforms were consistent with the kinds of reform programmes carried out in all the major European powers.

There was, however, a major political fall-out from these proposals. Liberals feared that the army was an instrument of the king and the ultra-conservatives. They remembered how, in 1848, Wrangel had used the army to re-occupy Berlin after the break-up of the National Assembly. They feared that a 'royal' army could be used this way again. The reduction in importance of the Landwehr, the 'people's army', also roused their suspicions. Many believed that the Landwehr could potentially be used to check the power of the regular army during a revolutionary situation, should one occur and by reducing the Landwehr, the government was increasing the power of the army and thereby the conservatives.

The constitutional crisis, 1860–62

Early in 1860, the government presented two bills to parliament. One was concerning the proposed reforms of the army and the other for the military budget. William saw these matters as separate. The constitution gave him authority over the army and so the reform bill should be rubber-stamped. The parliament may debate the budget since finance was part of their remit and may also request some amendments. The problem was that parliament saw the two bills as intrinsically linked.

Parliament made the reform bill dependent on the budget bill. Thus it passed the budget bill but only provisionally and there was much dissent about the army reform. Nevertheless, William pushed on with army reform regardless of the protests in parliament. Partly as a result of this, 17 members from the liberal faction broke away and formed the Progressive Party in January 1861.

Alarmed by the shift to the left, William dissolved parliament and called fresh elections. The new chamber that assembled at the end of 1861 contained over 100 Progressive Party members and only 15 ultra-conservatives. William's plan had backfired badly. The new parliament was just as unwilling to approve the army reforms as its predecessor. Undeterred, he repeated the process in the spring of 1862 but with the same result.

William was left with a stark choice – defer to parliament or abandon the constitutional system and return to a system of absolutism. Some advisors like Edwin von Manteuffel (Otto's cousin) took a hard line, advising William to dispense with parliament and rule on his own. Others, like General Roon, advised a more conciliatory course of action. William offered to abdicate in favour of his son in order to resolve the situation but was persuaded against this. Roon advised a different solution and so, on 22 September 1862, William appointed a new first minister, Otto von Bismarck.

EXTEND YOUR KNOWLEDGE

Otto von Bismarck (1815–98)

Otto von Bismarck was born in Schonhausen, the son of a Prussian Junker. Well educated and multilingual, he embarked upon a career in the law and then the civil service before returning home to manage the family estates upon the death of his mother in 1839. In 1847, he became a deputy in the short-lived United Estates and went on to represent Prussia in the Federal Diet during the 1850s.

Bismarck was pious and cynical in equal measure but had an immense self-confidence. He saw himself as a man of destiny who history had placed at the centre of events at a time of great change. He was fiercely loyal to the Prussian king, William I, though their relationship was tempestuous – often their meetings would descend into slanging matches. He habitually smoked cigars, drank heavily and ate enormous meals and in 1883, his weight had reached 114 kg. Personally he was ruthless and vindictive but could also be charming and witty. He invariably got his own way.

He served as the first minister of Prussia from 1862 to 1871 and chancellor of Germany from 1871 to 1890. He led Prussia through three victorious war: against Denmark in 1864, against Austria in 1866 and against France in 1870. Although a Prussian patriot rather than a German nationalist, he is seen by historians as the main protagonist in the process of German unification.

The impact of Bismarck's appointment

Otto von Bismarck was from a Junker family, who had studied law and pursued a career as a civil servant. In 1847, he entered politics and was elected as a member of the short-lived Prussian National Diet. He then served as Prussian delegate in the Federal Diet in Frankfurt from 1851 to 1859 and as ambassador to Russia from 1859 to 1862. Bismarck was seen as an ultra-conservative but was, perhaps, more accurately a loyal supporter of the monarchy. He was also a pragmatist and became well known for his '**realpolitik**' approach.

Initially, Bismarck sought to come to a compromise with the liberal parliament. His initial proposals for negotiations revolved around a larger army but one in which compulsory minimum service remained at two years. On advice from Edwin von Manteuffel, the king refused to support these negotiations and Bismarck was forced to withdraw. This led to Bismarck reappraising his own situation and a radical shift in his approach.

KEY TERM

Realpolitik
Realpolitik is politics based on power and practical considerations rather than ideologies or principles.

SOURCE

From Otto von Bismarck's 'Iron and blood' speech to the Budget Committee of the Prussian Parliament, 30 September 1862.

There are members of the National Association... who have stated that all standing armies are superfluous. Well, what if a public assembly had this view! Would not a government have to reject this? – There was talk about the "sobriety" of the Prussian people. Yes, the great independence of the individual makes it difficult in Prussia to govern with the constitution (or to consolidate the constitution?); in France things are different, there this individual independence is lacking. A constitutional crisis would not be disgraceful, but honourable instead. – Furthermore, we are perhaps too "well-educated" to support a constitution; we are too critical; the ability to assess government measures and records of the public assembly is too common... This may sound paradoxical, but everything proves how hard constitutional life is in Prussia. – Furthermore, one is too sensitive about the government's mistakes; as if it were enough to say "this and that [cabinet] minister made mistakes,['] as if one wasn't adversely affected oneself. Public opinion changes, the press is not [the same as] public opinion; one knows how the press is written; members of parliament have a higher duty, to lead opinion, to stand above it. We are too hot-blooded, we have a preference for putting on armour that is too big for our small body; and now we're actually supposed to utilize it. Germany is not looking to Prussia's liberalism, but to its power; Bavaria, Württemberg, Baden may indulge liberalism, and yet no one will assign them Prussia's role; Prussia has to coalesce and concentrate its power for the opportune moment, which has already been missed several times; Prussia's borders according to the Vienna Treaties [of 1814–15] are not favourable for a healthy, vital state; it is not by speeches and majority resolutions that the great questions of the time are decided – that was the big mistake of 1848 and 1849 – but by iron and blood.

Realising that his own position was entirely dependent on the king, Bismarck abandoned the attempt to compromise and switched to a policy of open confrontation. The military reforms were put fully into operation and the government levied fresh taxes to pay for them. Civil servants were warned that any disobedience of the government or involvement with the opposition would lead to immediate dismissal. This naturally brought declarations of outrage from the parliament but in reality they were powerless to do anything. The king was now fully assured of Bismarck's loyalty and Edwin von Manteuffel began to lose influence at court.

Bismarck's position was now improved with the king but he was extremely unpopular in the country. Election results in 1863 returned an even more hostile parliament with only 38 pro-government deputies. The king expressed real fears about a revolution and the possibility of being guillotined. It was only perhaps, Bismarck's success with foreign powers that kept him in post. He successfully blocked Austrian attempts to reform the Confederation and join the *Zollverein* in 1863 and engineered ***rapprochement*** with Russia, formalised in the Convention of Alvensleben in February 1863 (see page 352). In the end, it was success in war that secured Bismarck's position, beginning in 1864 with the war against Denmark.

> **KEY TERM**
>
> *Rapprochement*
> The establishing of, or having, friendly relations. Usually applied to nation states.

ACTIVITY
KNOWLEDGE CHECK

1 Why do you think that William dismissed von Manteuffel as first minister?

2 Make a list of things that William and Bismarck had in common.

3 Why was Bismarck's position so precarious, with regard to Edwin von Manteuffel on the one hand and parliament on the other, in 1862 and 1863?

4 Read Source 7. What is Bismarck saying about the issues facing Prussia?

WHY WAS PRUSSIA ABLE TO ACHIEVE PRE-EMINENCE IN GERMANY BY 1866?

Bismarck's aims

There were two main issues facing Bismarck's government in the early 1860s: how to increase Prussian influence within the German Confederation at the expense of Austria and how to negate the possibility of liberal reform within Prussia. Both these issues exercised Bismarck's mind but in the end positive outcomes were achieved in both areas via a single strand of policy.

Bismarck felt that it was better to take on a foreign enemy than to fight off an internal revolution. He also thought that Prussia and Austria were on a collision course over Germany. There is a debate among historians about whether or not he had a detailed grand scheme but the two notions suggested that a foreign war was a distinct possibility in the mind of Bismarck in the years at the beginning of the 1860s. He is alleged to have told Benjamin Disraeli in 1861 that he would declare war on Austria at the first opportunity, tear up the Confederation and unite the German states under Prussian leadership. A war with Austria would not only quieten dissent at home but also serve to change the situation within the Confederation. The only question was whether or not a reformed Prussian army could match the defeated but retrained Austrians.

Historians have identified the process of German unification from 1859 to 1871 as a revolution from above. It was not the groundswell of popular opinion that found voice in the liberal nationalists of 1848, nor the middle-class members of the *Nationalverein* but the realpolitik of Bismarck, his cynical opportunistic diplomacy and the effectiveness of the modernised Prussian army.

Austria attempts to reform the Confederation

The events of 1859 caused a major shift in Austrian policy. Financially limited and economically losing ground to Prussia and unable to rely on the subtle threat of military power, Franz Josef had to find a different means to pursue Austrian aims within the Confederation. Absolutism was replaced with liberal reform.

This popularist policy proved effective in moving some of the states towards supporting Austria, particularly in the Diet. The southern Catholic states, Baden, Bavaria and Württemberg, had always been geographically and religiously closer to Austria than to Prussia but Austria, with its liberal reforms, was now more comforting to their strong liberal movements. As Bismarck began to flex his diplomatic muscles, they were pushed even further into the Austrian camp. Bismarck had served as Prussian delegate in the Diet and so he was well known to the statesmen of the Confederation.

One scheme that Austria proposed was for joint military action. The plan was that a 'German' army led by Austria would retake Lombardy and restore German pride. The Prussians were lukewarm to the idea of Prussian troops in far-off Italy but saw the opportunity to stake their claim for parity. They would only accede if the leadership of the Confederation force was shared equally between Austria and Prussia. The Austrians declined and the plan was forgotten.

One notion at the heart of Bismarck's early policy was that Prussia should be seen as an equal partner with Austria. This was an idea that the Austrians would not tolerate. In 1861, the state of Saxony, which was neither in the Austrian or Prussian camp, proposed a scheme for a tripartite organisation of three equal partners within the Confederation: Austria, Prussia and the smaller states. Austria, not willing to acknowledge Prussian equality, countered with a modified proposal. Prussia rejected both the Saxon scheme and the Austrian modification outright. It countered with a proposal for a united Germany led by Prussia.

SOURCE 8

From letters from the Austrian foreign minister, Johann Bernhard von Rechberg, to Otto von Bismarck in September 1865.

Permit me, honoured friend, to express my opinion openly.

You know that I give myself with the whole of my soul to the task of maintaining in the future the harmony that has once more been brought about between Austria and Prussia... You will grant to me, most honoured friend, that a sincere and loyal recognition of Austria's oneness with Germany is one of those essential conditions without which Austria cannot feel at home in the Prussian Alliance. The fact gives the answer to the question, what inexplicable magic is contained for us in the simple word 'Tariff-Union' [Zollverein]. The value of this word is, I admit, one of those things that are imponderable, but the value of our position as a German Power is also imponderable...

The present question, whether Austria shall withdraw from her right to be included in a tariff-union, and thus acknowledge that in a politico-commercial connection she does not belong to Germany, I must, as an Austrian minister, answer in the negative... If we persist in our claim to a tariff-union, it is... because Austria is a German power, and cannot allow a common German institution to be closed to her on principle, nor permit herself to be treated as a foreign nation by her own associates in the Confederation. 17 September 1865

To make matters worse, the commercial treaty that Prussia signed with France in 1862 made the other *Zollverein* members nervous. Unilateral action on the part of a pan-German organisation sent a clear message. Bavaria and Württemberg looked to Austria for support but Austria was not a member of the *Zollverein* and short of military action could do little to intervene directly. What Austria did instead was to further propose a reform of the Confederation.

A Level Exam-Style Question Section A

How far could the historian make use of Sources 1 and 8 together to investigate the attitudes to the *Zollverein* prevalent in the Austrian government during the 1850s and 1860s?

Explain your answer, using both sources, the information given about them and your own knowledge of the historical context. (20 marks)

Tip

Make sure you use the evidence of the sources to support your points and also refer to the struggle between Prussia and Austria and how economic matters relate to this.

A meeting was called by Schmerling, the Austrian first minister, for August 1863. All the German princes were to attend and the agenda was to be the reform of the Confederation in order to move towards a position of greater unity. The main proposals were:

- periodic congresses of the German princes
- the establishment of a directory of five ministers
- the creation of a national assembly of 300 deputies drawn from the deputies of state parliaments.

The meeting was chaired by Franz Josef and was convened at Frankfurt. All the important princes of Germany attended along with their ministers, except one – the King of Prussia.

On Bismarck's advice, William had refused the first summons to attend the meeting. When the second summons arrived, his nerve weakened and he agreed to go. On hearing this, Bismarck met the king. He argued vehemently against attendance on the grounds that Prussia would be outvoted and thereby be committed to a scheme which would only secure Austria domination within the Confederation. Bismarck's threat of resignation was enough and after a long and heated discussion, William agreed not to attend.

Even without Prussia, the meeting carried on. Franz Josef chaired the discussions and the Austrian proposals were carried, with some minor modifications. The victory such as it was, was a hollow one. Without Prussian agreement nothing could be done. The princes returned home and things went on as before. The beneficiaries, if there were any, were the smaller states. Prussian isolation and Austrian impotence meant that neither was in a position to dominate the Confederation. The '**Third Germany**', as it had become known, was, perhaps, more independent in 1863 than it had been for generations.

KEY TERM

Third Germany
All the German states other than Prussia and Austria.

SOURCE

9 A meeting of German princes organised by Franz Josef of Austria in 1863 in order to reform the German Confederation. On advice from Bismarck, William I of Prussia did not attend this meeting thus preventing reform from taking place.

THINKING HISTORICALLY Change (6a)

Below are some different types of history that historians may identify. Sometimes historians will concentrate on one area and produce 'thematic' histories.

Political History   Economic History   Social History

Religious History   Military History   International History

These are thematic histories, where a historian will focus on a particular area with a particular focus. For example, an economic history of the kingdom of Prussia in the 1800s would focus on industrialisation and the agrarian reforms of the middle of the century, whereas a political history of the empire would focus on von Manteuffel and Bismarck and their domestic policy. An international historian would be more concerned with the interaction of Prussia with other powers, particularly the wars of 1864, 1866 and 1871.

Work in groups.

Write a definition for each type of history.

These are events of the strand of change (the process by which Prussia became dominant in Germany) that goes through the period 1852 to 1866.

1850	1851	1854	1859	1862	1864
The Punctation of Olomouc	The founding of the Phoenix iron works in Prussia	The expansion of the *Zollverein* but not including Austria	The founding of the *Nationalverein*	The appointment of Otto von Bismarck as first minister	The Dreyse needle gun makes its debut in a major war

Answer the following questions:

1 What kind of history is represented by each of these events?

Look at events from 1850 and 1854.

2 Are these the same area of history?

3 How important were these events to Austrian domination of the German Confederation?

4 How did Austrian influence differ from the political sphere to the economic sphere?

5 How did these events affect each other?

6 What other two events had an impact on the significance of the Dreyse needle gun?

7 What was the religious aspect of the *Nationalverein*?

8 What types of history are not represented by these events? Is this a reasonable omission?

Work in pairs.

Write a statement attacking 'thematic history'.

Write three statements defending 'thematic history'.

Explain why 'thematic history' occurs.

ACTIVITY
KNOWLEDGE CHECK

1 How far does the idea that Bismarck 'had a plan' fit in with his adherence to the principles of realpolitik?

2 What effect did the war of 1859 have on Austria's political position within the German Confederation?

3 Read Source 8. What do you imagine Bismarck would have thought while he was reading this letter?

4 Look at Source 9. Why do you think that Franz Josef arranged to have this photograph taken despite the absence of William I of Prussia?

The significance of the Polish revolt

In January 1863, there was a revolt in Russian-controlled Poland. It did not directly involve Prussia but it allowed Bismarck to influence the international situation in such a way that subsequent events would play into Prussian hands.

As soon as the news came through about the Polish insurrection against the Russians, the Prussians acted. Troops were dispatched into all those areas of Eastern Prussia with a sizeable Polish community. Bismarck was keen that Poles within Prussia would not be tempted to join their compatriots in Russian Poland and revolt against Prussian rule.

At the same time, Bismarck sent General Alvensleben to St Petersburg, ostensibly to offer support but really to drive a wedge diplomatically between Russia and France. Both parties tacitly understood that neither had a desire to see Prussian troops in Russian Poland but there was much in the gesture. Russian relations with Austria had soured since the Crimean War and Bismarck needed to count on Russian neutrality if he was to move against Austria. Franco-Russian relations did cool later in the year but not as a direct result of Prussian moves. The Alvensleben Convention did, however, prepare the way for the war with Austria in 1866.

Austrio-Prussian intervention in Denmark

In 1863, King Frederick VII of Denmark died without leaving a direct male heir. The next in line was Christian of Glucksburg. Christian expected that this succession also included the dukedom of Schleswig-Holstein. The succession to Schleswig-Holstein was disputed by Prince Frederick of Augustenburg, who felt that he had a better claim to the dukedom. Danish nationalists saw their opportunity to incorporate Schleswig-Holstein into Denmark and demonstrated in Copenhagen to force the young king's hand. Meanwhile, delegates at the Federal Diet, outraged at the prospect, voted to support Prince Frederick.

Austria and Prussia were alarmed by both sides of the affair. Clearly they would oppose the Danish move but did not wish to be seen to be encouraging German nationalism, partly because they wished to drive unification for themselves, but also because they were nervous of how France might react. Seeing that they had a mutual interest, the Austrians and the Prussians insisted that matters be dealt with in line with the 1852 Treaty of London, which had resolved the previous conflict over Schleswig-Holstein.

Acting in unison, as no one could have envisaged a few months earlier, a joint ultimatum was presented to the Danes. They refused to comply and Schleswig was invaded by a mixed force of Prussians and Austrians. The fighting was not without difficulty for the German forces but by the summer, Schleswig had been taken and the Danes forced to sue for peace.

Both Austria and Prussia had achieved their aims. Neither wanted to make the Danish subservient to nationalist aims or provide an opportunity for the Federal Diet to behave like a national parliament. Austria, rightfully fearing that Bismarck aimed to annexe the duchies for Prussia, had prevented this and recovered

some creditability for its armed forces into the bargain. Bismarck had removed the Danes from German politics and though Prussia had to share the duchies with Austria, he knew that once the hegemony question in Germany was resolved in Prussia's favour, the duchies would pass to Prussia and become part of his united Germany.

Another important aspect of the Danish War was the performance of the armies. Shaken by the defeat in 1859, the Austrian army had retrained itself along French lines. The new tactics worked well and Austrian formations performed credibly and with a good deal of confidence. General Wrangel, the Prussian commander, was so impressed with one Austrian attack that he rushed over to the Austrian brigade commander and kissed him on the cheeks. If the Prussians had been dismissive of Austria's military prowess, the Danish War gave them cause to think again.

What did divide the two armies, for those who chose to look closely enough, was the equipment. The powerful rifled field guns made by Prussian engineering companies like Krupp made short work of Danish defences. In one attack in April, the Prussians stormed entrenched positions on a hilltop and managed to inflict more casualties than they took – normally an attacking army would expect to lose more men then a defending one. The Danish War also saw the debut of a new Prussian infantry weapon. The **Dreyse needle gun** would revolutionise warfare in the 19th century.

KEY TERM

Dreyse needle gun
Traditionally infantry firearms had been loaded by dropping the bullet down the barrel and then ramming it down with a small rod. It was held there with cartridge paper and the gunpowder was loose. The needle gun had bullets that came ready made with their brass cartridges which contained the required amount of gunpowder. On pulling the trigger, a small needle was released which struck the base of the cartridge, which set off the gunpowder and fired the bullet. The gun was loaded through the breech. This meant that the needle gun had a far higher rate of fire and could be loaded from a prone or kneeling position. Standing soldiers still using muzzle loading guns were a far better target than the Prussians who were able to lie down.

Bismarck's preparation for war

The victory over the Danes had given Bismarck a level of popularity in Prussia. He had used the kudos of the war to win over the working classes. He sought an alliance between them and the conservative right based on patriotic nationalism. In this way, he hoped to isolate the liberal middle classes.

If he needed an excuse to go to war with Austria, he hoped that the resolution of the Danish problem might give him one. The war had ended with Denmark ceding both duchies jointly to Austria and Prussia. It was left to them to work out the practical arrangements. Of course, the problem for Austria was that the duchies were very remote from the other Habsburg Crown lands and quite close to Prussian territory in the west. Austria proposed that it cede both duchies to Prussia in return for land in Prussian Silesia. Bismarck refused. Another Austrian proposal was to make both duchies an independent state under Prince Frederick. Bismarck refused this as well. In the end, it was Bismarck's solution that was agreed.

The Convention of Gastein, signed in August 1865, gave Schleswig to Prussia and Holstein to Austria. For Prussia, this was a far preferable outcome. It could claim to have acted reasonably and split the spoils. In reality, in the event of a war between Austria and Prussia, any troops in Holstein would be cut off from Austria and so the duchy was virtually indefensible. Moreover, Bismarck could use any activity by the pro-Augustenburg as evidence that Austria was trying to undermine the Convention. The resolution was no guarantee of peace.

Bismarck also used diplomacy to improve the Prussian position. To put further pressure on Austria, Bismarck negotiated a treaty with the newly formed kingdom of Italy. It provided for mutual support should either state find itself at war with Austria. The Italians had unified most of the peninsula but Venice was still under Austrian control. Tentative negotiations were also undertaken with France in an attempt to buy its neutrality. Bismarck offered the French territorial compensation for their neutrality in the event of a Prussian victory. It turned out that Napoleon III, the French emperor, had acquired similar concessions from the Austrians.

ACTIVITY
KNOWLEDGE CHECK

1 Why was the situation in Russia with regard to the Poles such a problem for Prussia?

2 What did the Danish War teach the Prussian and Austrian armies about each other's strengths and weaknesses?

3 How far was the Convention of Gastein a sustainable solution to the problem of the duchies?

Prussian Initiatives in the Federal Diet

On 9 April 1866, Bismarck surprised the Federal Diet by calling for a national German Parliament based on universal male suffrage. The reaction to the arch-conservative proposing the most liberal of reforms was naturally cynical. While debating this, troop movements in Italy caused alarm in Vienna and Austria responded by mobilising its forces. The Prussians then fully mobilised their armed forces. A motion in the Diet on 9 May asked the Prussians to explain their mobilisation.

The Austrians were anxious to move the weight of the Confederation against the Prussians. At the end of May, they passed the responsibility for the Danish duchies onto the Federal Diet. Claiming that this broke the Gastein Convention, Prussia occupied Holstein. Austria countered by proposing a resolution calling for the mobilisation of Confederation forces against Prussia. When the Diet approved this, the Prussian delegate walked out, declaring that Prussia considered the Diet dissolved. Five days later, Italy declared war on Austria and Prussia followed suit.

SOURCE

10 A memorandum from Field Marshal Helmuth von Moltke to William I in 1861 discussing new weapons and tactics.

It is generally acknowledged that the great improvement in firearms will entail a substantial change in fighting methods in future wars.

There are no experiences to draw on yet, because the [new] weapons had not achieved their current perfection during the last campaigns, and they were employed on terrain that reduced the impact of firepower from a distance.

Therefore, the influence of the new firearm on tactics can only be derived in theory from its nature and characteristics. The firearm requires: visibility of the target, knowledge of its distance, and calm delivery of fire.

If these conditions are met, then the Prussians' rifled guns will hit any target within a range of 2500 paces [2000 metres] with approximately equal accuracy, to the extent that the human eye is still capable of clearly recognizing an object. A troop of people or horses, [or] a [piece of] artillery constitute target objects that can be hit at least once with two shots. With this heightened accuracy, the artillery achieves an enhanced effectiveness for its shells from percussion and explosion, so that it will be impossible for troops drawn up in close formation to stay put under fire from a rifled battery at a distance of a quarter mile.

On an open plain the enemy can only find protection by movement and scattered formations.

The Prussian infantry rifle is still capable of combining its great accuracy at up to 600 paces [480 metres] with the possibility of extraordinarily rapid fire, an indisputable advantage if its application is saved for the really decisive moments of battle. Within this extended sphere of activity for infantry, even enemy swarms in loose formation are incapable of holding out when unprotected and at a standstill.

AS Level Exam-Style Question Section A

Why is Source 10 valuable to the historian for an enquiry into the reasons why Prussia won the Seven Weeks' War in 1866?

Explain your answer using the source, the information given about it and your own knowledge of the historical context. (8 marks)

Tip
Remember to include material that deals with the author and his perspective but also to include material relating to the context of the Prussian army in the early 1860s.

The summer campaign

The war consisted of a short summer campaign and two major battles, Sadowa (or Koniggratz) and Custozza. The Battle of Sadowa was fought between the Prussians and the Austrians and was an overwhelming victory for the Prussians. Custozza was fought in northern Italy and was an overwhelming victory for the Austrians. Success in Italy counted for little, however, as the Prussian army pushed towards Vienna and the Austrian government realised the situation was hopeless and sued for peace. The Confederation had also suffered reverses against the Prussians and followed suit.

The reasons for the speed of the Prussian victory are contentious among historians. Some cite the quality of the general staff on the Prussian side against the weaknesses of Austrian leadership but both sides had mobilised efficiently and both armies were well supplied. There seemed to be little difference in the quality of the troops, as the Austrian performance in Denmark and Italy would indicate. The more advanced economy of the Prussians did not have time to exert its influence in such a short campaign and though the Krupp cannons were effective, the Austrians also possessed modern artillery. The one aspect where there was a significant difference was in the infantry weapon, the Dreyse needle gun.

**SOURCE
11**

A contemporary illustration of Prussian troops cheering their generals at the Battle of Sadowa, 1866.

The Dreyse needle gun was standard issue to the Prussian army. It had bullets in brass cartridges and was loaded through the breech (the end near the firer). The Austrians were armed with the Minie rifle, which had bullets in paper cartridges and was loaded through the muzzle (the hole at the end of the gun furthest away from the firer). This had two major effects on the fighting. The first was that the rate of fire by the Prussians could be up to five times as fast as the Austrians. The second was the needle gun could be loaded lying down or kneeling. Men had to stand to load a Minie rifle. The discrepancy between weapons was only exacerbated by the Austrians retraining. That the Austrians were attempting to fight at close quarters with bayonets gave the Prussians the opportunity to adopt defensive positions and fire at the enemy. The results at the Battle of Sadowa were over 44,000 Austrian casualties, over five times the Prussian number.

The significance of the Seven Weeks' War

In under two months, total Prussian hegemony had been established in Germany. Events following the war would progress in the direction that Bismarck wanted. The Austrians had been totally defeated and the Federal Diet would continue only if Prussia willed it. What Bismarck did not have, however, was a free hand.

With two Prussian armies bearing down on Vienna, Bismarck was acutely aware of the changes to the European balance of power. The prospect of a united Germany under Prussian leadership was not simply a German matter. Alarm bells were ringing in London, Paris and St Petersburg at the possibility of a new central European power, probably the most powerful on the continent. Thus, Bismarck stopped short and reassured the British, French and the Russians that a negotiated peace was all that he desired. Assuaging the fears of the foreign powers negated the possibility of them intervening and Bismarck was freer to negotiate the shape of the new Germany.

SOURCE

12 The Nikolsburg memorandum from Otto von Bismarck to William I, urging peace with Austria, 24 July 1866.

Regarding the negotiations with Austria to find a basis for peace, I respectfully beg your majesty to allow me to lay before you the following considerations:

It seems to me of the greatest importance that the present favourable moment should not be missed.

By your majesty's declared acceptance en bloc of the proposals of his Majesty the Emperor of the French, the danger of France's taking sides against Prussia, which by diplomatic pressure could easily turn into active participation, has been eliminated.

As a result of the instructions given to Count Goltz [the Prussian ambassador in Paris] on Your Majesty's orders, it has been possible to secure in addition from the Emperor Napoleon the definite assurance... that he will not only allow the direct annexation of four million in North Germany, but will himself recommend it, without any mention of compensation for France.

But the wavering of the Emperor in the last few weeks, and the pressure of public opinion in France, raise definite fears that, if the present concessions were not quickly converted into fact, then there could be a new about-face. We cannot count on support from the other great powers for further, or even these, Prussian demands. Your Majesty has observed in the letters of HM the Emperor of Russia with what alarm he views the Prussian conditions. His minister, Prince Gortschakov, has also expressed the wish to know these conditions, both through Your Majesty's ambassador in St. Petersburg and Baron Oubril in Berlin.

The family connexions of the Russian Imperial house with German dynasties give rise to the fear that in further negotiations sympathy with them will carry great weight. In England, public opinion begins to veer towards Your Majesty's military victories but the same cannot be said of the government, and it can only be assumed that it will recognise the *faits accomplis*. The double declaration of Austria that it will withdraw from the German Confederation and agree to a reconstruction of it under Prussian leadership without Austria's participation, and that it will recognise everything that Your Majesty thinks fit to do in North Germany, provides all the essentials that Prussia demands of her.

What was clear was that Austria's hopes of a major role in the new Germany were finished. Without the threat of her military power, Prussia could not be coerced. She would have to accept whatever solution Bismarck proposed and hope that support from France and Russia would mollify the terms. Moreover, Austria would lose Venice in the peace treaty and only retain a small part of the Tyrol of her Italian possessions. Within months the Hungarians would have revolted and demanded a new arrangement for the empire that would become the Dual Monarchy in 1867.

ACTIVITY
KNOWLEDGE CHECK

1 Was it inevitable that Prussia would have to fight the Confederation as well as Austria in 1866? Explain your answer.

2 Read Source 10. What is it about the new weapons that gave von Moltke such confidence?

3 Why did Prussia win the Seven Weeks' War so quickly?

4 Read Source 12. Why was Bismarck so keen to make peace with Austria when Vienna was at the mercy of the Prussian army?

EXTRACT
1 From William Carr, *Germany 1815 to 1985*, published in 1987.

Contemporaries expected a long war ending in an Austrian victory. In Paris the betting odds were four to one in her favour. Austria had the active military support of the larger German states, whilst Prussia had only one ally of consequence, Italy, and she was heavily defeated on land at the battle of Custozza and at sea in the battle of Lissa. Moltke thought a hard fight certain and Bismarck talked of falling in battle... Contemporaries were wrong about the war... The Prussian victory was due not to great numerical superiority – in Bohemia 221,000 Prussians faced a combined Austrian and Saxon army of 215,000 – but to the meticulous planning of Moltke and the superior fire power of the new needle gun.

THINKING HISTORICALLY Evidence (5b)

Arguments and opinions
Look at Sources 10–12 and Extract 1.

Work in groups.

1 Why is evidence important in history?

2 Study Sources 10 and 11. How does the information in Source 10 help to explain the action in Source 11?

3 Study Sources 10 and 12.

   a) How do these sources disagree about the prospects for further success against Austria?

   b) Does the evidence in Source 12 mean that Bismarck is ignoring von Moltke's point of view? Fully explain your answer.

4 Read the extract from William Carr's book in Extract 1. Does the information in Source 10 make Carr wrong about Moltke's attitude? Fully explain your answer.

5 Do Bismarck and Carr agree about Austrian military prowess?

6 What other evidence would Carr have used to put together the text in Extract 1?

7 Carr writes about how people believed that an Austrian victory was a possibility in 1866. Should we discount Carr's history because Sources 10 and 11 show aspects of a Prussian victory? Fully explain your answer.

Summary

The period from 1852 to 1866 saw a shift of power within Germany. In 1852, the primacy of Austria was unchallenged. By 1866, Prussia was so dominant a force that she was in a position to unify Germany under her leadership.

Austria lost ground throughout the period. The difficulty of managing her vast empire with so many different minorities drew attention away from the German question. Her government also found it difficult to collect the amount of tax needed to maintain a large army and invest in industrialisation and economic development. In 1849, it had relied on the army to bring Hungary and Italy back under control and it was the threat of military action that kept it as the major power within the Confederation. Defeats by France in 1859 and Prussia in 1866 so undermined Austria as a military force it was unable to negotiate with other countries from a strong position. The struggle for supremacy in Germany between Austria and Prussia ended in 1866 on the battlefield at Sadowa.

The lowest point for Prussia was, perhaps, the Punctation of Olomouc, or as many Prussians referred to it, the 'humiliation'. Throughout the 1850s, Prussian industrialisation and then army reform transformed the state and gave it the potential to challenge Austria. Events also played themselves out in Prussia's favour. The War of 1859 broke the myth of Austrian invincibility and came at a time when Prussia was reforming its own armed forces. A key factor in the Prussian government's ability to influence events was the tax surplus, which gave them the power to spend where it felt it was necessary. The contrast with the Austrian fiscal position could not be starker. It was Bismarck's skilful manipulation of both national and international politics and the effectiveness of the Dreyse needle gun that put Prussia on the verge of unifying Germany under their leadership.

ACTIVITY
SUMMARY

1 What changes took place in the German Confederation between 1852 and 1866?

2 How important were economic factors in overturning Austrian domination of Germany, 1852–66?

3 For each of the following give them a rating of their importance in the unification process up to and including 1866 (10 being very important, 1 being not important). Explain why you have given them this rating: Otto Von Bismarck, William I, Franz Josef, Otto von Manteuffel, Field Marshal Von Moltke, Louis Napoleon III, King Christian of Denmark.

WIDER READING

Blackbourn, D. *History of Germany 1780-1918*, Blackwell (2003), chapters 5 and 6

Carr, W. *A History of Germany*, Edward Arnold, (1989), chapter 3

Green, A. *Fatherlands State building and Nationalism in Nineteenth Century Germany*, Cambridge University Press (2001)

Taylor, A. J. P. *The Course of German History*, Hamish Hamilton (1945), chapter 5

Williamson, D.G. *Germany Since 1815*, Palgrave (2005)

2b.4 Prussia and the *Kleindeutschland* solution, 1866–71

KEY QUESTIONS

- What was the significance of Prussia's role in Germany, 1866-67?
- Why were Prussia's relations with France so important?
- Why did Prussia need to win the Franco-Prussian War?
- Why was Prussia so successful in unifying Germany?

INTRODUCTION

The geographical spread of the states within the German Confederation meant that events within the Confederation would always be of interest to the powers that surrounded it. In the east, Prussia and Austria both shared borders with Russia, and Austria also shared a border with the Ottoman Empire. In the west, France, Belgium and Holland bordered Prussia, Bavaria, Oldenburg and Baden and in the south, Austria shared borders with Italy. In addition, the possibility of a shift in the European **balance of power** was of interest to Britain who regarded stability in Europe as central to her trade interests.

Up to 1866, the European powers had only exerted a mild influence on the German Confederation. Often Austria and Prussia had worked together to maintain the status quo and when opposed to one another, in matters such as the *Zollverein*, there had always been an element of balance in that one would not go so far as to provoke the other into war. The Seven Weeks' War had destroyed all that (see pages 356–357).

The situation at the end of the summer of 1866 was very different. The question of German unification had been answered by the *Kleindeutschland* solution by virtue of Prussia's victorious armies. The details were yet to be thrashed out but it was clear that any ambitions that Austria had to lead the Confederation were now over. Bismarck, however, was not able to proceed without caution.

The Seven Weeks' War had gone far better than Bismarck could have hoped. Even the most confident of the Prussian generals could not have hoped for such a decisive victory as Sadowa. Nor could they have hoped that the forces of the other states of the Confederation would have proved to be so ineffective. And yet, Bismarck realised, a punitive peace with Austria would just create instability. The Austrians, looking for revenge, could decide to combine with France against Prussia. This could also suit the French as it would keep the German Confederation divided and weak. He realised that, as in Italy, unification would be by increments not in a single sweep.

August 1866 – Peace of Prague and founding of the North German Confederation

April 1867 – First sitting of German Reichstag Ratification of the North German Confederation with William of Prussia as its king and Bismarck as chancellor

| 1866 | 1867 | 1868 | 1869 |

May 1867 – Establishment of the Dual Monarchy in Austria

April 1867 – Luxembourg Crisis

May 1867 – Treaty of London

Louis Napoleon Bonaparte was the nephew of Napoleon I, French Emperor from 1804 to 1815. He had lived in exile before the revolution of 1848 but had returned and been elected president. In 1852, he had made himself emperor. Like his famous uncle, Louis Napoleon was interested in French **aggrandisement**. Therefore, he took a keen interest in European diplomacy and was quick to act when he felt that France had something to gain, as in 1859 in Italy.

The potential unification of Germany caused alarm in Paris. Germany had the possibility of growing more powerful than France, with a larger population and a far greater land area, giving the Germans access to greater resources. Having weakened the Austrians in 1859, it was in France's interest to make sure that power was checked as early as possible.

KEY TERM

Aggrandisement
To enhance power, wealth, position or reputation of an individual, group or nation state.

WHAT WAS THE SIGNIFICANCE OF PRUSSIA'S ROLE IN GERMANY, 1866–67?

The chief concern for Bismarck and the Prussian leadership was a resolution to the Seven Weeks' War that would be sustained in Prussia's favour. The fighting was finished very quickly but all sides had to agree a treaty by which a lasting peace could be engineered. Having won the war, Prussia held a powerful position but did not want to force too harsh a peace treaty on the Austrians, as this would invariably cause a renewal of the fighting at a later date. On this basis, the Prussian delegation, led by Bismarck, met their Austrian and Italian counterparts in Prague in August 1866.

The Treaty of Prague

William I of Prussia had wished to press home his advantage both on the battlefield and during negotiations. With the Austrian army broken, he had wanted to occupy Vienna and humiliate Franz Josef. There was even excited talk of annexing Austria altogether. Only by threat of resignation did Bismarck get his way and William backed down.

Above all else, Bismarck was anxious for a peace that was lenient to Austria. His demands only related to the Confederation and its organisation. It was accepted by both sides that Prussia was now the leading state within the Confederation and that it was Prussia's will that would prevail. The Austrians, so long kept outside the *Zollverein,* were now excluded from German affairs as the Confederation was abolished by the treaty.

Five days before the treaty was signed, Bismarck engineered a new military alliance which was to pave the way for further developments that would lead to the creation of a new state. The North German Confederation was an agreement between the states of northern Germany to co-operate on military matters but the underlying understanding was that it was a precursor to a federal state. Bismarck got the states to agree to the alliance on the basis that those who had fought against Prussia

January 1870 – Spanish Candidacy

July 1870 – Ems Telegram

14 January 1871 – German Empire proclaimed at Versailles

| 1870 | 1871 | 1872 | 1873 |

August 1870 – Start of the Franco-Prussian War

September 1870 – Battle of Sedan

28 January 1871 – French surrender

would not have to pay war indemnities and those who had been neutral or fought with Prussia were given guarantees that local rights would not be infringed.

War indemnities aside, the treaty was lenient on the other combatants. Bavaria, Württemberg, Baden and the Grand Duchy of Hesse were to continue independently of the North German Confederation, though they were still members of the *Zollverein*. Austria was expected to pay indemnities to Prussia but would lose no territory to her northern neighbour. Where Austria would lose out was in the south.

Italy had entered the war, indeed started it, with the aim of wrestling control of Venetia from the Austrians. Although defeated decisively on the battlefield, Italy came to the peace conference as the victor by virtue of its alliance with Prussia and demanded its spoils accordingly. At first the Austrians refused to concede to Italian demands. It was difficult for them to see the Italians as being part of the winning side when they had lost on the battlefield. In the end, Austria agreed to give Venice to France. The French in turn gave it to their Italian allies. Austria had not wished to cede the territory directly to Italy and the French proved convenient go-betweens.

The annexation of the north German states

Though Bismarck was anxious to tread carefully, he was keen to stamp out anti-Prussian sentiment in northern Germany. The king and the generals wanted far more decisive action by Bismarck to expand Prussian power but he was keen to restrain them as he wanted the dust to settle in order to consolidate Prussian gains within the new North German Confederation. The major states of the north, who had fought against Prussia and lost, were annexed and became part of Prussia. This included Hanover, Hessen-Kassel, Nassau and Frankfurt. The long-running Schleswig-Holstein question was answered when the already occupied duchies became part of Prussia.

The one exception to this was Saxony. Potentially the most powerful of Prussia's German enemies, Saxony had deployed a corps of 32,000 to aid the Austrians, which had fought at the Battle of Sadowa. Bismarck could have deposed the King of Saxony and annexed his lands as he did to the King of Hanover but Bismarck was reluctant to have too many dispossessed monarchs loose in Europe. Moreover, as Saxony bordered Bohemia, it was strategically important. The Prussians therefore invited Saxony to join the North German Confederation, which meant that the King of Saxony would retain his throne and Saxony itself would have some notion of equality with the Prussians. The Saxons accepted.

SOURCE 1

Taken from a letter from Sir Henry F. Howard, British envoy to Bavaria to the British foreign secretary Lord Stanley, 3 December 1866.

My Lord,

The Prussian annexations have no doubt considerably advanced the unification of Germany, but the process of consolidation will be a slow one, because they were effected by conquest and contrary to the will of the population of the annexed countries, and the general state of Germany after the war is anything but settled or satisfactory.

In Hanover, the people… are unable to reconcile themselves to the expulsion of their dynasty, to the total extinction of their separate existence and independence, and to the loss of their own institutions, more liberal than the Prussian and in many respects superior to the latter. The Prussians, as I am credibly informed, meet with ill will and opposition from all classes of the population, with the exception of a portion of that in the towns and in the provinces annexed to Hanover in 1815.

As regards the Duchy of Holstein, it appears to me that, once separated by Treaty from Denmark, under whose rule, notwithstanding certain drawbacks, it enjoyed a prosperity which it has not since known, its lot, as annexed to Prussia, will be a happier one than were it to be erected, as was in contemplation, into a mere Vassal State.

In Bavaria, the Austrian Alliance is entirely abandoned, and public opinion points to the necessity of an alliance with Prussia, more particularly against French aggression, but at the same time the predominant, feeling of the country seems at present opposed to such a sacrifice of its independence as would be entailed by an accession to the Northern Confederation as contemplated by Prussia. Had Prussia really intended the formation of a Federal State on an equitable basis, Bavaria and the remaining independent States would, there is every probability, have been ready to join it.

The North German Confederation

The treaty that established the North German Confederation as a military alliance stipulated that if no agreement had been reached to establish a German federal state by August 1867, then the treaty would expire. As the states which might have seen an advantage in slowing down the process had already been annexed by Prussia, Bismarck was able to proceed with optimism.

Bismarck began drafting the new constitution in late 1866 and presented it to the first sitting of the new Reichstag (Imperial Parliament) in February 1867. After negotiations, it was accepted in April 1867 and came into force in July. The North German Confederation had become a federal nation with Bismarck as its chancellor and William as its head of state.

SOURCE

2 A contemporary German journalist, Julius von Eckardt, writing in his memoirs about life in the North German Confederation.

I never breathed in my life a more invigorating air than the one which blew in the autumn of 1866 through North Germany. It cast an incomparable spell over us. One felt as if one were standing at the threshold of a new period, a period which promised miracles. One lived under the impression of a surprise which had come so suddenly and with such overwhelming fullness that the patriots who a short while before had been full of fears and sombre premonitions suddenly felt like dreamers.

ACTIVITY
KNOWLEDGE CHECK

1 Why do you think that Bismarck was so intent on a lenient peace with Austria?

2 Why was Bismarck reluctant to annex all the north German states after the Seven Weeks' War?

3 Study Source 1. According to Howard, how do the Germans feel about the events of 1866?

4 Study Source 2. How far does the journalist agree with Howard? Why might this be?

The north German Reichstag

The Reichstag itself is an indication of Bismarck's flexible approach to politics. He feared the liberal middle classes and saw that there was the possibility of an alliance between the conservative upper classes and the patriotic working class. The victories over Denmark and Austria had changed Bismarck's popularity. The pariah of 1863 had become the national hero in 1866. Seeing an opportunity, Bismarck called elections for the Prussian parliament at the height of the war with Austria (on the same day as the Battle of Sadowa, 3 July 1866). The results saw the liberal majority in the Prussian parliament reduced from over 100 to a mere six. Bismarck believed that patriotism would be even firmer among the workers across the North German Confederation; the Reichstag of the new North German Confederation was elected by universal manhood **suffrage,** which meant that every man over 25 had the vote.

The make-up of the new Reichstag was not quite what Bismarck had wanted. A hung lower house consisted of roughly one-third conservatives, one-third liberals and one-third anti-Bismarck delegates. The National Liberals were the biggest individual party and Bismarck had to court their support in order to get any laws passed. As they saw Bismarck as the unifier of Germany, they were willing to co-operate with him to that end. They agreed rules over the military budget and a number of unifying reforms that consolidated the new state.

The practicalities of unification caused Bismarck to shift his position. In granting universal manhood suffrage, he alienated the ultra-conservatives who proceeded to vote against him. The more moderate conservatives formed their own party, the Free Conservatives, and formed a coalition with the National Liberals that backed the government (see page 364).

see page 364

AS Level Exam-Style Question Section A

Why is Source 1 valuable to the historian for an enquiry into the reasons why Prussia won the Seven Weeks' War in 1866?

Explain your answer using the source, the information given about it and your own knowledge of the historical context. (8 marks)

Tip
Remember to include material that deals with the author and his perspective but also to include material relating to the context of the Prussian army in the early 1860s.

KEY TERM

Suffrage
The right to vote in electing public officials and adopting or rejecting proposed legislation. Universal suffrage means all adults having the vote, although at certain points in history and in certain places, universal suffrage means universal manhood suffrage.

The Bundesrat

The Reichstag was, however, only the lower chamber of the Confederation's parliament. The Upper House was the Bundesrat, or Federal Council. This was made up of delegates sent by the individual states. These were representative of the governments who acted in the interests of their respective states. The structure of the council had been decided by Bismarck. Of the 43 members of the Bundesrat, 17 were from Prussia. Saxony had four but most states had only one.

Sessions of the Bundesrat were chaired by the chancellor. Decisions were taken by a simple majority vote. With a guaranteed bank of 17, Bismarck only needed to persuade another five in order to gain a majority. All laws needed the agreement of the Reichstag, the Bundesrat and the monarch. Having control of the Bundesrat and the monarch gave Bismarck an automatic veto on new legislation.

Was the new Germany a parliamentary democracy?

On the face of it, the North German Confederation was the most liberal constitutional monarchy in Europe. Even in Great Britain, where parliament ruled with very little consultation with Queen Victoria, there was no universal manhood suffrage. With a **bicameral parliament**, featuring a lower chamber elected by universal manhood suffrage, Bismarck could justifiably claim to be moving liberalism forward. There was, however, more of a veneer of liberalism within Germany than anything very substantial.

The Reichstag, in reality, had very little power. The military budget, which amounted to 90 percent of the federal expenditure, was in the hands of the chancellor not the Reichstag. The remaining budget could only be debated and passed every three years. During negotiations for the constitution, Bismarck conceded the right to debate the budget every year and agreed to revisit the question of the military budget in 1872. It may have been that Bismarck had adopted an extreme position with regard to the rights of the Reichstag in order to be seen to grant concessions that would result in a compromise position that he had secretly aimed for all along. In any case, when the constitution was finally approved, the Reichstag was still severely limited in its ability to stand in Bismarck's way.

> **KEY TERM**
>
> **Bicameral parliament**
> A legislative assembly consisting of two separate chambers.

Prussia's relationship with south German states

Ideally, Bismarck would have wished to incorporate the south German states in the new Germany. He was, however, aware of France's increasing alarm at the possibility of a new super-power in central Europe and also that Austria regarded the Catholic states as part of its sphere of influence. He thought that the status of the south German states was not yet settled but did not think that the time was right, in 1866 and 1867, to go to war with France and he was mindful of the need for *rapprochement* with Austria, which he considered a necessary ally to maintain stability in central Europe.

There were some talks concerning a South German Confederation, which came to nothing. Bismarck was opposed to anything rivalling the North German Confederation and felt that at some later date, the south Germans would become part of a united Germany. Having the south German states independent also suited the French for strategic reasons – having a more powerful block on its eastern border would raise concerns about security. Of the south German states, the leaders of Baden expressed the view that they would rather be in a German state led by the Prussians.

The condition of Austria

Though Bismarck had taken great pains to keep Austria intact, the internal situation was anything but stable. Aware of its weakened international status, the Austrian government began to address the Hungarian problem. Hungarian nationalists had not forgotten the war of 1849 and still resented the imposition of rule from Vienna. The Austrian chancellor Friedrich Ferdinand von Beust, began negotiations with Hungarian nobles led by Ferenc Deak at the beginning of 1867 and reached an agreement by the spring. The Austro-Hungarian Compromise, as it became known, was ratified by the Hungarian parliament in May 1867.

What the compromise laid out was internal independence for Hungary. It would have its own parliament and its own budget. Franz Josef would be crowned King of Hungary to make it clear that the king of Hungary and the emperor of Austria were two separate positions. Military matters and foreign affairs were still to be run centrally but for the most part Hungary was free to run its affairs as it saw fit. This arrangement became known as the Dual Monarchy, which was to last for a further 50 years.

This arrangement was advantageous to everybody involved. For Franz Josef it was a way of shoring up his empire and reducing the risk of internal dissension. The Hungarians got virtual autonomy but still retained the advantages of belonging to a large modernising state with what was still a powerful army. For Bismarck it diverted Austrian attention away from what was going on in Germany. He would have been delighted when, in 1870, the Hungarian parliament voted against aiding the French in the Franco-Prussian War, despite Chancellor Buest's desperate desire for revenge for 1866.

Creation of the *Zollparlament*

Though political unification between the North German Confederation and the southern states had not been achieved in 1866/67, there was, at least, still the *Zollverein*. As the economic ties which bound the southern states to the *Zollverein* became stronger with increased industrialisation, it became more difficult to break.

To bring the southern states closer to the north, a new initiative was launched in 1867. Delegates from the southern states were invited to attend the Reichstag when matters pertaining to the *Zollverein* were being debated. Similarly, delegates were also sent to the Bundesrat on the same terms. These bodies were seen as separate from the usual organs of the North German Confederation and were given the titles *Zollparlament* and *Zollbundesrat*.

EXTRACT 1

From A.J.P. Taylor, *The Course of German History*, published in 1961.

In 1866, German national feeling so far as it existed, was almost united against Prussia; in 1870 nationalist professors killed Frenchmen from their university chairs, but the real war was fought by a Prussian officer class to whom national enthusiasm was altogether repugnant.

EXTRACT 2

From W. Carr, *A History of Germany 1815–1985*, published in 1987.

Most liberals had no such reservations [about unification]. For them the War of 1870 was the culmination of the national revolution begun in 1866. The onward march of events since 1866 had been little short of miraculous in their eyes, and led easily to the growth of an exaggerated national pride.

EXTRACT 3

From E.J. Passant, *A Short History of Germany 1816–1945*, published in 1969.

The preamble to the Constitution makes clear the conservative nature of the new Prusso-German Empire. It does not emanate from the German people. It is a grant from the rulers of the several states. Bismarck had arranged that Prussia should not merge into Germany, particularly into democratic Germany.

EXTRACT 4

From D. Blackbourn, *History of Germany 1780–1918*, published in 2003.

Bismarck breached monarchical solidarity in the war with Austria, to nationalist applause, and followed this by introducing universal manhood suffrage over the heads of the liberal opposition. Like Napoleon III, he believed that enfranchising the lower classes would swamp liberalism.

THINKING HISTORICALLY | Evidence (6a)

Arguments and facts

Most of the fighting in 1866 and 1870 was done by Prussian soldiers.

1 Read Extracts 1 and 2. Does this fact make Extract 1 more valid than Extract 2? Explain your answer.

2 Read Extracts 2 and 3. Extract 2 talks about a liberal national revolution, Extract 3 about Bismarck making 'arrangements'. Which source is better supported by the facts as you understand them? Explain your answer.

3 How do Extracts 3 and 4 disagree about the level of support that Bismarck had from ordinary people. Does this make one of them wrong? Explain your answer.

4 If we accept that the sources are all factually correct, how do we explain the differences in them?

If this was a move by Bismarck to promote further unity, it slightly backfired. The *Zollparlament* members from the North German Confederation were the normally elected members of the Reichstag. The delegates from the southern states had to be specially elected. The National Liberals in the south had hoped that these elections would serve as a **referendum** on unification and show that the feeling in the southern states was to join with the north. This was not to be the case. Local issues and parochialism proved stronger. Many Roman Catholics in the south were distrustful of Protestant Prussia. In the end, the elections returned 49 delegates against union to 35 delegates for union.

KEY TERM

Referendum
A vote on a single issue.

Bismarck was not unduly concerned by this. He had seen that the unification of the north had been achieved not by popular politics or economic union but by war. He knew that France would never agree to the southern states becoming part of Germany because they would not want a direct border with a large power. Therefore the southern states would only become part of Germany after a victorious war with France.

SOURCE 3

Bismarck in conversation with a member of the Prussian parliament, March 1867.

Unhappily I believe in a war with France before long – her vanity, hurt by our victories, will drive her in that direction. Yet, since, I do not know of any French or German interest requiring a resort to arms, I do not see it as certain. Only a country's most vital interests justify embarking on war – only its honour, which is not to be confused with so-called prestige. No statesman has a right to begin a war simply because, in his opinion, it is inevitable in a given period of time. If foreign ministers had followed their rulers and military commanders into the field, History would record fewer wars. On the battlefield – and, what is far worse, in the hospitals – I have seen the flower of our youth struck down by wounds and disease... You may rest assured that I shall never advise His Majesty to wage war unless the most vital interests of the Fatherland require it.

Bismarck and the National Liberals

In the first five years of his ministry, Bismarck had consolidated the conservative regime in Prussia. He had led Prussia in two wars, both of which extended Prussian territory and eradicated the power of two other states in Germany (Denmark and Austria). Practical success masked the shifts in the ideological position that he had had to make in order to achieve this success.

During the first years of his ministry, Bismarck had relied on support from the conservatives. As the Prussian parliament was dominated by the liberals, he found it difficult to rule with parliament and so he ruled without it. Both the wars were a welcome distraction from the troubles of internal Prussian politics. In 1866, during the war with Austria, elections returned a Prussian parliament with a far greater balance between conservatives and liberals.

In the wake of the victory over Austria, Bismarck decided that it was time to heal the schism between government and parliament. He granted parliament an indemnity bill, which was in effect an open acknowledgement that the government had acted 'unconstitutionally'. This split both the factions. The ultra-conservatives were appalled that the government should be so conciliatory towards liberalism but moderate conservatives continued to support Bismarck. The Progressive Party, still holding out against Bismarck, began to break up and from it came a small group of radical liberals and a newly formed National Liberals. Bismarck now had a solid core of supportive centre ground delegates.

William had initially appointed Bismarck as a bulwark of the ultra-conservatives against the forces of progression and reform. Putting practicalities above ideology, Bismarck saw that maintaining an ultra-conservative regime would not be possible. As unification became more of a possibility, he positioned himself with that aim in mind and made concessions to the National Liberals that gave him an advantage rather than sticking with a position that was driven by ideology.

As the National Liberals dominated the Reichstag, an alliance with them was to Bismarck's advantage. He gave way on certain issues such as election by secret ballot or the right to an annual debate on the budget but held firm on key issues of ministerial privilege or the right to control the military budget and decide foreign policy.

ACTIVITY
CONSOLIDATION

1 Why is it surprising that Bismarck decided to elect the Reichstag by universal manhood suffrage?

2 Describe the balance of power between the Bundesrat and the Reichstag.

3 Why was Austria unable to make a new challenge to Prussia after 1866?

4 Why was the *Zollparlament* so significant?

5 Study Source 3. Why would Bismarck express these sentiments to a member of the Prussian parliament?

WHY WERE PRUSSIAN RELATIONS WITH FRANCE SO IMPORTANT?

Napoleon III and Bismarck

Louis Napoleon Bonaparte was elected the president of the Second French Republic in 1848. After a coup d'etat in 1851, he became the emperor of the Second Empire (Napoleon III). In an attempt to make clear the link to his uncle, Napoleon I, Louis Napoleon reformed French institutions, rebuilt Paris and enlarged the French Empire. In Europe, his foreign policy was proactive and at times, aggressive.

Seeking to increase French influence in Europe made France a natural ally for Prussia in the years before 1866. As France sought to challenge Russia during the Crimean War (1854–56) and then Austria (1859), Prussian neutrality was very important. When Bismarck became the first minister of Prussia in 1862, he understood that reducing Austrian power was a common goal for both France and Prussia. He also understood that unifying Germany would pose a strategic threat to France and that it would be unlikely to stand by while Bismarck brought the whole of Germany together under Prussian leadership.

Louis Napoleon was not ideologically against the notion of German unification. Indeed, his sense of nationalism was strong. He did, however, recognise that a united Germany would shift the balance of power and would not be to France's advantage. When Italy had unified, France was given territory in Savoy as compensation. It was rumoured that he had been given vague promises by Prussian representatives that the same might happen should Germany unify. Louis Napoleon voiced his concerns but allowed the events of 1866 to unfold as they did.

Deutschlands Zukunft ('Germany's Future'). A cartoon published in 1870 in the Austrian satirical magazine *Kikeriki*. The caption reads 'Germany's future, will it fit under one hat? I believe it is more likely to come under a Pickelhaube!' The pickelhaube helmet was standard issue of the Prussian army.

Louis Napoleon saw foreign policy as his own personal area and, perhaps, was more inclined to be led by his heart than his head. Bismarck also took the lead in foreign policy but conducted himself with opportunistic cynicism. After 1867, Louis Napoleon became ill and had to rely on his advisors more and more. Bismarck was at the height of his powers.

The significance of the Luxembourg Crisis

As a small duchy between the new North German Confederation, Luxembourg was a possible area for French compensation for the unification of Germany. Moreover, the Concert of Europe had assumed a French interest in Luxembourg. An initial solution, put forward by the French ambassador in Berlin for France to gain part of the Rhineland, was rejected by Bismarck. As the land in question was Bavarian, this rejection served a double purpose; it slightly provoked the French and served to help convince the Bavarians that they would be better off with Prussia. Following this, French attention moved to Luxembourg. There was, however, a very practical stumbling block as, since the Congress of Vienna in 1815, the fortress city of Luxembourg had contained a Prussian garrison.

Evidence would suggest that Bismarck offered mild encouragement to the French. Indeed, he also mentioned the French-speaking areas of Belgium in addition to the largely French-speaking Luxembourg. By involving Belgium, Bismarck was demonstrating his flair for foreign policy. Belgium was guaranteed by Britain by the Treaty of London of 1839. Any French proposals would inevitably meet with British opposition. Louis Napoleon saw that Luxembourg was a more likely avenue of success.

EXTEND YOUR KNOWLEDGE

The breakdown of the Concert of Europe

The unification of Germany and its international consequences were part of a larger change in relations between countries in Europe. Following the Congress of Vienna in 1815, a system of congresses was set up to resolve the international disputes in Europe. This became known as the Concert of Europe. Though the congress system fell out of favour in the early 1820s, the idea that the major powers would work together in order to prevent war carried on long after. It only broke down with the Crimean War when Russia was opposed by Britain and France.

The idea that the major powers had spheres of influence remained even after the Crimean War. This idea was used skilfully by Bismarck to give Prussia an advantage. For example, the Austrian focus on Italy led it into the War of 1859 and also caused it to fight a war on two fronts in 1866. Similarly, the French focus on the Low Countries (Luxembourg, Holland and Belgium) meant that it was an obvious assumption to think that territorial compensation for France should come in that area. When Prussia annexed territory in north Germany, there was no outcry, partly because north Germany had long been recognised as Prussia's sphere of influence.

The Duke of Luxembourg was also the King of Holland. Louis Napoleon opened negotiations with the offer of compensation should Luxembourg become part of France. Bismarck gave the impression to the Dutch that Prussia would not be against such an arrangement. The king, who had little interest in Luxembourg and needed the money, was ready to agree to the scheme. Then, in the early spring of 1867, Bismarck began to play politics.

The escalation of the Crisis

Leaking the news of French designs to the German press was the first move in Bismarck's posturing. He began to make speeches referring to Luxembourg as 'German' and declaring that its surrender to France would be an affront to German nationalism. He also cited the right of Prussia to maintain a garrison, which was granted by international treaty and that any move by France to acquire Luxembourg would break that treaty.

Louis Napoleon, despite being unwell, did not take this matter lying down. French propaganda tried to stir up the locals in Luxembourg against the Prussians and anti-German demonstrations took place across the duchy. He also tried to convince the King of Holland that Prussia had designs on Dutch territory and offered French military intervention should the North German Confederation move against Holland.

SOURCE

Louis Napoleon III in conversation with Lord Augustus Loftus, British ambassador to Berlin in 1868, published in *The Diplomatic Reminiscences of Lord Augustus Loftus 1862–79* (1894).

I [Lord Augustus Loftus] had a long conversation with His Imperial Highness on the day after his arrival. It then appeared to me that his attention was mostly, if not entirely, occupied with the present and future of Germany. He disclaimed any identification with the present ministry or policy of France, and frankly said that he was in opposition to the government, and that, consequently, his opinions were purely private and personal. He spoke of the reconstruction of Germany saying that what had been done was not a fait accompli, and recognised by France. He did not seem to entertain any hopes, or even a wish, that what had been so far affected could be altered. He even said that the absorption of the smaller northern states was of no importance to France. 'But', observed His Imperial Highness, 'the unification of Germany under Prussia is still in progress. The Zollverein parliament is a step further to the absorption of southern Germany. Where is this to end? What limit is to be placed to the Germany of the future – or, rather, to Prussia.

'Then again,' said His Imperial Highness, 'if the principle of nationality is carried out – the legitimate grounds for such a policy – what will become of the 8 millions of Austro-Germans? Will their turn come next? And how will it be possible for them to avoid being drawn into the same vortex?

'It may be very well to say that Germany is not an aggressive power, but who can say when she may not become so? And that she may not someday reclaim Alsace and Lorraine, or seek to unite within her boundaries the Russo-German provinces of the Baltic?

'You English have chosen to withdraw yourselves from the political arena of Europe, and this abstention of England from active participation in European politics is a great misfortune for Europe, and will later prove to be a great misfortune for herself.

'There are two points on which England keeps a watchful and jealous eye – namely, Belgium and Constantinople. If any idea is ever mooted which could menace the independence of Belgium, England will immediately raise her voice. If Russia discloses any secret design on Constantinople, there again you raise a cry of alarm. But as regards the change brought about and in operation in Germany you are apparently apathetic, and foresee no danger likely to affect your interests.

'Let a Germany be constituted, but let its limits be fixed and final, so that it may not be led to aspire to future aggrandisement; and let the arrangement concluded be placed under European guarantee.

Bismarck sought to maintain the momentum against France when he 'leaked' information about secret military alliances that he had made with the south German states. This showed the French that the buffer zone that they thought they had in the neutral and independent south German states was non-existent.

The resolution of the crisis

In the end, the king of Holland proposed to sell Luxembourg to the French for 5 million guilders but only if the king of Prussia agreed. The king of Prussia did not agree and, moreover, Bismarck hinted strongly that any concessions to France would be viewed in Germany as a **_casus belli_**. Bismarck then appealed to the European powers to help find a solution.

> **KEY TERM**
>
> *Casus belli*
> A reason to start a war.

A Conference was held in London and was attended by representatives of the countries involved and all the other European powers. The compromise that was agreed was that the Prussian garrison should be withdrawn and that Luxembourg's independence and neutrality would be guaranteed by the great powers.

The crisis had opened further the rift between the North German Confederation and France. Louis Napoleon felt that he had reason to be particularly aggrieved. Promises to compensate France for the unification of north Germany had not been kept and he had to face the French people having been humiliated by Bismarck. The withdrawal of the Prussian garrison from Luxembourg was of little consequence to the French who had expected at one point to gain territory.

For Bismarck, the 1867 Treaty of London was a triumph. For the small price of moving the Prussian garrison out of Luxembourg, he had completely checked the possibility of French expansion along the whole of its northern and eastern border. The integrity of both Belgium and Luxembourg was now guaranteed by the great European powers. Moreover, he had made appeals to 'German', not 'Prussian' patriotism. His ability to stir up German national sentiment was an indication that his machinations to build a German nation were working.

1 Why did Bismarck secretly hint that France would be compensated after the Seven Weeks' War?

2 How far would a French annexation of Luxembourg have suited all the parties involved?

3 Why did Bismarck create outrage at the Luxembourg plan?

4 How far could the resolution of the Luxembourg Crisis be seen as a victory for Bismarck?

The Hohenzollern candidature and the Ems telegram

A year after the resolution of the Luxembourg Crisis, another issue arose which came between France and the North German Confederation. A revolution in Spain had forced Queen Isabella to flee. The interim Spanish government tried to replace her with a member of a royal European house. In February 1870, an offer was made to Prince Leopold **Hohenzollern**-Sigmaringen, a member of the Catholic branch of the Prussian royal family.

KEY TERM

Hohenzollern
The surname of the royal family of Prussia, Swabia and latterly, Romania.

Leopold's father, Prince Karl Anton, accepted provisionally on Leopold's behalf but could not commit to the scheme without first consulting William I of Prussia, as head of the Hohenzollern family. Understanding the reaction that it would cause in France, William was reluctant to sanction the candidacy. He knew that the French reaction would be extremely hostile. They would see it as a German attempt to encircle France. Bismarck, however, saw things differently. He persuaded William that widening the power base of the Hohenzollern dynasty would be good for Germany. William agreed on the proviso that Leopold himself wished to proceed. Leopold had thought better of it and refused.

With Leopold's refusal, the matter could have ended but Bismarck thought otherwise. He sent Prussian agents to Madrid with large bribes so that influential Spaniards would keep up the pressure for Leopold's candidacy. He also put pressure on the Hohenzollern family, arguing that the candidacy would do much for German power within Europe. Leopold changed his mind and William gave his consent.

The news of the candidacy

The plan to announce the candidacy was put in place in June 1870. Bismarck was to send a document to Madrid accepting the throne on Leopold's behalf. The document would be taken immediately to a session of the Spanish parliament where a vote would be taken to ratify the document and proclaim Leopold king. Unfortunately, due to a mix-up at the Prussian embassy, the document arrived in Madrid at a time when the Spanish parliament was not sitting. It became inevitable that news of the document would leak out before it had been **ratified** by the Spanish parliament. The news reached Paris on 3 July 1870.

KEY TERM

Ratify/ratification
The approval and formal sanctioning of a proposal usually by a body. By ratification the action gains a legal status.

SOURCE

The Hohenzollern princes discuss ascension to the Spanish throne. From the diary of Major Max von Versen, Bismarck's agent in Madrid, 19 June 1870.

The Hereditary Prince [Leopold] said that with a heavy heart but with the consciousness of acting in the interest of the state he asked the King's permission to accept. The letter was worded in such a way that the Hereditary Prince intimated that he was making a sacrifice for the renown of the family and the wealth of the Fatherland; but it was at the same time phrased so that the king only needed to reply: 'no objection.' The Hereditary Prince repeated what he had said to me already several times, namely, that he had to say this because he was not acting either from self-interest or on any special impulse, and did not want to appear as a 'climber'. Bucher induced the younger brother of King Frederick William IV of Prussia, Prince Karl Anton, to accompany this letter of the Hereditary Prince's with one of his own to the King in which he said: 'only on grounds of family law did his son thus apply for permission and he trusted the king would have no injections to make.' The question now arose as to who was to go to the King. Bucher looked at me as if I should be the one. I said the best thing would be for Herr Bucher to go, for the King is furious that I am not at Posen. Then there came various scruples on Prince Karl Anton's part. What would France say about it? Would it not give rise to complications? I said: 'Bismarck says that is just what he is looking for.'

The reaction of the French was heated. Louis Napoleon who had believed the matter of the candidacy to be at an end was apoplectic, encouraged in his anger by Empress Eugenie, who was a Spanish royal and related to the deposed Queen Isabella. Moreover, Louis Napoleon had a new foreign minister, Antoine Gramont, who had an aggressive disposition and was fiercely anti-German. A telegram was sent to Berlin asking the Prussian government to withdraw the candidacy and making it clear that the French would not accept such a state of affairs. Gramont sent the French ambassador, Count Benedetti, to seek an audience with William to discuss the candidacy as a matter of urgency.

The Ems telegram

William was not in Berlin at the time and Benedetti had to follow him to the spa town of Ems, where he was taking the waters. Benedetti advised William that proceeding with the candidacy would upset the European balance of power and that Leopold's acceptance of the Spanish crown would lead to war.

William was conciliatory with the French ambassador. He assured him of Prussia's friendship for France and that he would seek to resolve the situation. On 12 July 1870, Karl Anton withdrew the candidacy on his son's behalf. William now regarded the matter as settled.

William's view was not shared by Bismarck. The affair now appeared to be a French diplomatic victory as William had backed down in the face of French pressure. Bismarck felt humiliated and threatened to resign. The continuation of the affair by the French saved him having to consider it.

Gramont, the French foreign minister, was not satisfied with William's assurance. He instructed Benedetti to seek a further meeting with William and push for further concessions, namely William's personal assurance that the candidacy would not ever be renewed. William, feeling that his previous assurances and the telegram that Karl Anton had sent to the Spanish government were enough, refused to see Benedetti. This snub was felt keenly in Paris.

SOURCE

7 The Ems telegrams, 13 July 1870, showing the original conversation between the French ambassador, Count Benedetti, and Kaiser Wilhelm I. Below is the version as edited and released by Bismarck. The French requested that the Prussians would not back any candidate from the Hohenzollern family for the Spanish throne.

The original:

M. Benedetti intercepted me on the Promenade in order to demand of me most insistently that I should authorize him to telegraph immediately to Paris that I shall obligate myself for all future time never again to give my approval to the candidacy of the Hohenzollerns should it be renewed. I refused to agree to this, the last time somewhat severely, informing him that one dare not and cannot assume such obligations *à tout jamais*. Naturally, I informed him that I had received no news as yet, and since he had been informed earlier than I by way of Paris and Madrid, he could easily understand why my government was once again out of the matter.

Since then His Majesty has received a dispatch from the Prince[*] [Charles Anthony]. As His Majesty has informed Count Benedetti that he was expecting news from the Prince, His Majesty himself, in view of the above-mentioned demand and in consonance with the advice of Count Eulenburg[**] and myself, decided not to receive the French envoy again but to inform him through an adjutant that His Majesty had now received from the Prince confirmation of the news which Benedetti had already received from Paris, and that he had nothing further to say to the Ambassador. His Majesty leaves it to the judgment of Your Excellency whether or not to communicate at once the new demand by Benedetti and its rejection to our ambassadors and to the press.

The version edited by Bismarck:

After the reports of the renunciation by the hereditary Prince of Hohenzollern had been officially transmitted by the Royal Government of Spain to the Imperial Government of France, the French Ambassador presented to His Majesty the King at Ems the demand to authorize him to telegraph to Paris that His Majesty the King would obligate himself for all future time never again to give his approval to the candidacy of the Hohenzollerns should it be renewed. His Majesty the King thereupon refused to receive the French envoy again and informed him through an adjutant that His Majesty had nothing further to say to the Ambassador.

Gramont and his supporters were now pushing Louis Napoleon towards war. The French papers were full of the diplomatic affront caused to France by William's refusal to see the French ambassador. Some even went so far as to doubt his promise over the withdrawal of the candidacy. Parisians took to the streets to demonstrate against the Prussians.

In the meantime, William had sent a telegram to Bismarck outlining the nature of his discussion with Benedetti. The telegram itself was a straightforward document which told of the encounter between the two and what passed between them. Bismarck received the telegram while having dinner with generals Von Moltke and Roon. Taking a pen, he then removed certain parts of the message without adding or amending anything. The edited telegram was then released to the German press.

A Level Exam-Style Question Section B

'Prussia achieved her aims in both the Luxembourg Crisis and the Hohenzollern candidacy.'

How far do you agree with this statement? (20 marks)

Tip
You will need to clearly define what you understand were Prussia's aims so that you can measure the extent to which they were achieved.

What had been sent as a mere description of events now read as the preamble to a confrontation. It seemed that William having given way over the candidacy was now refusing to compromise. The day after appearing in the German newspapers, the edited telegram appeared in the French press and added to the outrage of the snub to their ambassador.

Bismarck knew that the disclosure of the telegram in Paris would cause uproar. Public opinion, backed by the empress, the government and the army, demanded war. Sure enough, on 19 July 1870, Louis Napoleon declared that the French Empire was at war with Prussia.

EXTEND YOUR KNOWLEDGE

The power of public opinion
Before the 19th century, public opinion could only be expressed in demonstrations by the mob. We see this in the Peasant's Revolt in England in 1381 or during the French Revolution of the 1790s. Manipulating public opinion was simply a case of rabble-rousing to get the crowd onto your side.

During the first half of the 19th century, there was an explosion in literacy among working people making newspapers more powerful because they were more widely read. This was recognised by the leaders of the German states when they passed the Carlsbad Decrees that allowed governments to censor the press. The nature of the 1848 revolutions shows how this change in literacy and the press had affected society. Before 1848, most popular action had been focused on local, usually economic matters. The revolutions of 1848, particularly in the German states, had a strong element of ideology and were about issues on a national and sometimes international level.

Both Bismarck and Louis Napoleon understood the need to consider public opinion, even though both governed in a fairly autocratic way. That they both played the injured party very publicly moved the press to support them and gave rise to a great outpouring of nationalistic sentiment. They were both able to use this to their advantage in the run-up to the war and during the fighting itself.

1 Why do you think the Spanish wanted a monarch that was a close relation of the King of Prussia?

2 Why did Bismarck want to continue to push the candidacy even when the Hohenzollern's had lost interest?

3 What does the editing of the Ems telegram tell us about Bismarck and his methods?

4 Why was it so important for Bismarck that it was France who declared war on Prussia?

The outbreak of war

The fact that it was the French who had declared war on the Prussians was not lost on Bismarck. Diplomatically, he could play the injured party in all the royal courts of Europe. Moreover, the French had only declared war on Prussia itself but given the nature of the North German Confederation, it included the other parts as well. Geographically and politically the southern German states were drawn in. They had alliance agreements with the north Germans and if the French were to attack Prussia, they would need to march their armies through the south German states. It has gone down in history as the Franco-Prussian War but in many ways it was a Franco-German war.

The German army – though dominated by Prussians – was quick to mobilise. By the beginning of August, 500,000 men had been deployed on the French border. The strategically designed railways, which consisted of six separate lines running into the border area, were utilised to the full. The French were slower to organise their army but could muster 180,000 around the fortress town of Metz. The Germans were commanded by General von Moltke, the French by Emperor Louis Napoleon, though Marshals Bazaine and MacMahon commanded the field armies.

Unlike the Seven Weeks' War, the Germans did not enjoy such a marked advantage in their infantry weapons. The needle gun was still the standard rifle for the German infantry but the French were equipped with chassepot rifles, which outranged the needle gun. They also had the millaitreuse, which was a very early form of machine gun. Where the Germans did have a significant advantage was in their heavy weapons. Their breech-loading rifled cannons, produced in the main by the Krupp company, had a higher rate of fire and were more accurate than the French **muzzle**-loading guns.

KEY TERMS

Muzzle
The muzzle is the end of the gun barrel where the bullet exits the gun.

Siege
A military operation where one side is surrounded by the other side and contained within a fortress or a city. The aim of the army carrying out the siege is to force the besieged army to surrender owing to lack of supplies, which would save having to fight them.

The Siege of Metz

Due to the speed of their mobilisation, the Germans crossed the French frontier during the first days of August. In response, the French sent two corps to occupy the town of Saarbrucken on the German side of the border. German progress meant that the French were in danger of being cut off and so they had to withdraw. Three German victories in three days during the first week of August pushed the French army away from the border. Wissembourg (4 August), Spicheren (5 August) and Worth (6 August) were small-scale engagements but all gave the clear message that the Germans were better organised than the French.

The French retreated back into the fortress at Metz, where they were soon surrounded by the Germans. Two attempts to break out from the fortress, at Mars-le-Tour (15 August) and Gravelotte (18 August) were defeated and the **siege** maintained. Louis Napoleon had escaped but had left over 150,000 of his best troops holed up in the fortress to play no further part in the war. They would surrender at the end of October.

The Battle of Sedan

In an attempt to relieve the forces at Metz, Louis Napoleon and MacMahon formed the Army of Chalons and began to approach Metz from the north west. Moltke took three corps from the force besieging Metz and formed the Army of the Meuse and ordered it to link up with the Prussian Third Army to block the approaching French. The two sides met at Sedan on 1 September 1870.

The strategic necessities of the battle played into the German hands. The French had to break out from Sedan towards Metz in order to relieve Bazaine. This meant that they had to attack German positions. Again the needle gun proved its worth along with the 600 breech-loading cannons. When the French attacks faltered, the Germans were able to surround large pockets of French troops and force them to surrender. By midday the battle was over and the French had lost 17,000 casualties.

By the end of the day over 100,000 French soldiers were prisoners of the Germans, including the emperor.

In real terms, this should have brought the war to an end. Indeed, MacMahon was negotiating peace with Moltke and Bismarck on behalf of the emperor. After all, the only professional French soldiers left that were not German prisoners were holed up in the fortress at Metz. Then news came through of events in Paris. Louis Napoleon had been deposed, the Second Empire abolished and the Third Republic declared. The war would continue.

The second phase of the war

The new French government raised a citizen's army, which gathered in the south. It even invited Garibaldi, the Italian revolutionary, to command the Army of the Vosges. Enthusiasm carried the French a long way and, while they made it difficult for the Germans, they were no match for professional troops. There was also the call for a guerrilla war against the invaders but that came to little.

SOURCE
8
Letter from Otto von Bismarck to William regarding the tension between civilian and military leadership of the war and potential negotiations with the French government, December 1870.

Your Majesty has deigned to grant permission to my most humble request that no initiatives for negotiations with the enemy would be undertaken on our part, so as to avoid the impression that we were in need of a quick peace and to give no rise to attitudes that deceit and gullibility might associate with it. Along these lines, I implied to Lieutenant Colonel von Bronsart [Prussian staff officer] this morning that the proposed step did not seem unproblematic to me. I believed, however, that lacking any more detailed knowledge of the situation, I ought not to raise my objections against the proposed step. In all of this, I assumed that before the supreme order was given, I would have ample opportunity to report to Your Majesty myself on a matter that touches upon my own area of responsibility. I deemed such an order all the less imminent as the dispatch of the letter was supposed to be delayed until information about the capture of Orleans came in, news of which I still have not received by this afternoon. I had no doubt that I would be permitted beforehand to report to Your Majesty in person on the subject of negotiations with the French government, and for that reason had not put crucial weight on my discussions with Lieutenant Colonel Bronsart. Instead, I had reserved the right to raise my fundamental and formal reservations not with the General Staff but with Your Majesty. On principle, I did not agree with this step at all, because any German initiative for negotiations is misunderstood and abused in Paris; and because I believe that there should be no communication on the part of the *military* that would accommodate the current French government. . . Formally, I had wished to propose to Your Majesty a different version of the letter, namely the use of German. On another occasion, I will take the liberty of humbly suggesting this for general practice, because German officers and civil servants are always at a disadvantage if they are officially required to use French in correspondence with the enemies, who necessarily have better command of their mother tongue.

May Your Royal Majesty graciously allow me, in light of this incident, to make the respectful general request: that Your Majesty may graciously order that I be consulted in all military talks that touch upon political issues, and that I be authorized to direct to the General Staff any questions concerning the military situation, about which I, as Foreign Minister and Prime Minister, believe information is required.

ACTIVITY
WRITING

Source analysis
Study Source 8.

1 Identify any words or phrases that need extra information in order to be understood.

2 Rewrite those phrases including the extra information to make the meaning clear. Try to make them as concise as possible.

3 Rewrite the whole letter in under 80 words.

Moltke believed that the quickest way to end the war was to take Paris. He knew that the Germans did not have enough troops to occupy the whole of France. The siege of Paris began in late September and was to last almost six months. The provisional republican government in Paris was cut off from the rest of the country but still tried to co-ordinate resistance but with very few professional soldiers left there was little it could do. Eventually, Paris surrendered on 28 January 1871 and the war was finally over.

Louis Napoleon (left) and Bismarck (right) in conversation following Louis Napoleon's capture at the Battle of Sedan, September 1870. Painted in 1878 by Wilhelm Camphausen, official artist of the Prussian army during the Franco-Prussian War.

The significance of the international situation 1870

The Franco-Prussian War had come at an ideal time for the Germans. The international situation could scarcely have been more favourable. France had hoped to rally the support of the other powers but a mixture of good fortune and Bismarck's planning had prevented this.

Louis Napoleon viewed Austria as a natural ally against Prussian expansion. Certainly there were those in Austria for whom revenge for 1866 was very important. The leading figure among these was von Beust, the chancellor. The problem for him was that the re-organisation of the empire had weakened the power of the cabinet in Vienna. The Hungarian parliament feared that another war against Prussia, particularly a victorious one, would strengthen the German Austrians and might have led to a reduction in Hungarian autonomy. They would naturally vote against it. There were also those Austrians who remembered the humiliation of 1859 and were unwilling to commit the Austrian army to support the French.

The Russians were equally not inclined to aid the French cause. Russia's prime concern was to gain territory at the expense of

Turkey and also to strengthen her naval situation in the Eastern Mediterranean. France had always been a strong supporter of Turkey and had, of course, fought alongside it against Russia during the Crimean War. As former ambassador to Russia, Bismarck had good contacts and Russia had valued Prussia's support over the Polish revolt.

The last of the five great powers in Europe were the British. Traditionally, France was Britain's greatest rival and so Britain was inclined to work against the French wherever possible. Britain was pursuing a policy of 'glorious isolation' from Europe and concentrating on her overseas possessions. Germany had no overseas colonies and so did not much concern British foreign policy, whereas the French had the second biggest overseas empire and had, during the 1860s, begun to colonise Indo-China (modern day Vietnam, Laos and Cambodia). To raise even further British suspicions of France, the Luxembourg affair had raised the spectre of the one cause that Britain would get involved in on the continent, namely the sanctity of Belgium. Even by entertaining the thought of annexing Belgian territory to France, Louis Napoleon had set alarm bells ringing in London. French discomfort was by no means unwelcome to the British.

France's diplomatic isolation played into Bismarck's hands. Not only could the North German Confederation conduct a war with France without foreign intervention, he also had the south German states, who felt they were far better with Prussia rather than rely on France against Prussia. The Germans had more men under arms than the French and superiority in artillery and organisation. In little over a month, the French professional army had been destroyed. The war carried on for a further five months to reach its inevitable conclusion. It was then that Bismarck faced a new challenge, to unify Germany without provoking foreign intervention.

ACTIVITY
KNOWLEDGE CHECK

1 Why did the Germans win the Franco-Prussian War?

2 Study Source 8. Why was it so important for Bismarck that the army high command should not enter into negotiations with the French?

3 In what ways did the international situation in 1870 favour Bismarck's position?

WHY DID PRUSSIA NEED TO WIN THE FRANCO-PRUSSIAN WAR?

The Franco-Prussian War was the last stage in the process, the culmination of Bismarck's dream of a *Kleindeutschland* solution. Clever diplomacy by Bismarck had isolated the French and German military superiority had defeated them. At stake during the peace negotiations was more than simply the end of the war, it was the future of the German nation.

Increased support for German nationalism

For decades, German nationalism had been a force that largely belonged to the middle class. Pan-German sentiment had been the preserve of the educated and the politically active. The working classes were often too busy struggling to survive to take part in abstract debates about the shape of nation states. Socialism as a political force was in its infancy. The ruling elites had too much of a vested interest in maintaining their power and saw nationalism as a dangerous concept. They took practical steps to stamp it out. In 1848, the nationalist liberals made their play and were brutally put down.

Nationalism, however, was not simply a statement of political will. It was played out on a much more subtle level between ordinary people through very straightforward interaction. Every point of contact between people from different states, where they touch upon a common idea or activity was feeding into the cause of nationalism. Every tacit acknowledgement of commonality was building a German idea. It could be the product of a single great man with a single great idea or the sum of countless ideas in the heads of countless people.

Movements of popular culture drew in the masses better than liberal rhetoric ever could. The German Gymnastic Association

was banned by the Carlsbad Decrees in 1819 in many states, as politicians saw it as being politically dangerous. Many of the associations were revived in the 1840s. They provided contacts between people from all over Germany during the three decades in the run up to unification. Choral societies performed a similar role as choirs toured around different parts of Germany singing 'German' music.

How the wars affected nationalism

The Seven Weeks' War of 1866 caused some ambivalence among the nationalists from an ideological and emotive perspective but was encouraging from a practical one. Among Prussian patriots the war was a Prussian triumph and a desire to unify Germany as a result of the war could be interpreted as German nationalism but also as Prussian supremacy and domination. To residents of the states who would form the North German Confederation, there was a fine line between seeing the process as the unification of Germany or the annexation of independent states by Prussia. In southern Germany, people were suspicious of Prussian motives and mindful of their local independence, but the lure of German unification was there.

In some ways, the French war galvanised the nationalist feeling within Germany. There seemed to be an obvious choice between the supremacy of a Prussian-led Germany or France. Politically and culturally, the sympathy of the majority of Germans was with Berlin, however Bavarian or Hanoverian they might have felt. On a more practical level, it served the purpose of the Prussian Germans that the threat from France was closest to those areas of Germany which were most remote from Prussia. Therefore, the south German states had to ally with the north Germans to counter the threat of a French invasion. If anything, the French occupation of Saarbrucken reinforced this point to the south German states.

There is, of course, nothing like a successful cause for attracting people. The lightning victory of 1866 was an indication of Prussian superiority over Austria. Nationalists saw that the Prussian military could be the force to make a unified Germany. Prussia had a strong economy and a strong first minister. Austria, however, was in disarray. The dual monarchy compromise did little to contradict the idea that Austria's influence in Germany was finished. The Franco-Prussian War was clearly a German endeavour and a German victory. Even before Germany actually existed, it was clear that it was a German force that had defeated the French, not just a Prussian one. The pride in the victory spread across the whole of Germany.

Strengthening of Bismarck's position

Bismarck's power had never been greater and would never be as great again. He had the European powers in such positions that, should he proceed carefully, there would be no interference. In the east, Russia adopted a policy of neutrality as long as Austria did the same. Thus, the one checked the action of the other. Of course, Austria objected to Bismarck's moves to incorporate the south German states but could do little without alerting the Russians. Britain had little interest in continental Europe and if France's attention were drawn away from their overseas colonies so much the better.

As the defeated power, France did not have much choice but to agree to the peace conditions. In addition to paying indemnities for the cost of the war, the territories of Alsace and Lorraine were given up by France and incorporated into the new German Empire.

The most difficult negotiations that Bismarck would have to face would be those with the south German states, particularly Bavaria. No one was in much doubt that the *Kleindeutschland* solution would finally be reached when the four states were absorbed into the North German Confederation. The issue was how this would be achieved and what freedoms would be lost by the governments of these states and what privileges would remain. Bismarck was aware that this was his moment but was also aware that different groups needed to be placated to maintain a lasting arrangement.

The creation of a German Empire

As soon as the French Army surrendered at Sedan, Bismarck was able to begin negotiations with the south German states. Baden and Hesse both declared their desire to join the North German Confederation, while Württemberg was more circumspect. The real problem was Bavaria.

Second in size to Prussia, Bavaria demanded an equal voice to Prussia in the new Germany. Bismarck could not be seen to be giving in to these demands and by a mixture of pressure and conciliation tried to modify Bavaria's position. He used the upsurge in nationalist feelings to put pressure on those who were resisting unification by planting stories in the newspapers. Once Baden and Hesse had declared for unification, all he needed to do was to split Württemberg from Bavaria to leave them isolated. By allowing Württemberg to keep its postal service and armed forces, Bismarck had done enough to win over opinion in Württemberg and it agreed to join Germany. Bismarck had successfully divided Württemberg and Bavaria. Allowing Bavaria to keep its postal service and armed forces also, Bismarck conceded for them a permanent seat on the military committee of the Bundesrat. Seeing that they were swimming against the tide, the Bavarians accepted unification.

The issue of head of state was potentially a difficult one. As a federal state, the new Germany retained local rulers and local governments. King Ludwig II of Bavaria would thereby remain king of Bavaria just as the Duke of Baden would remain the duke of Baden. The natural position of one who rules over kings is an emperor. The obvious candidate was William, King of Prussia. King Ludwig opposed this suggestion on the basis that as kings, William and he were of the same rank. In the end he was bought off by Bismarck with a massive bribe, and even sent the letter (drafted on his behalf by Bismarck) inviting William to take the imperial crown.

The exact title of the new head of state was to prove controversial. William wanted to be the 'Emperor of Germany' while Bismarck

SOURCE 10   A letter from Otto von Bismarck to King Ludwig II of Bavaria, taken from M. Gorman, *The Unification of Germany* (1989).

It is not my commission, however, but that of the German people and their history to thank the Most Serene Bavarian dynasty for Your Majesty's German politics and the heroism of Your army. I can only assure that, as long as I live, I will be devoted and obedient to Your Majesty in reverent gratitude, and I will always consider myself lucky if ever I get a chance to be at Your Majesty's service.

With respect to the question of German Kaiserdom, it is in my respectful estimation important above all that its proposal [should] first originate with none other than Your Majesty and certainly not with the representative body of the people. The title would be compromised if its origin were not in the well-considered initiative of the most powerful among the princes joining the confederation. I have taken the liberty of handing over to Count Holnstein, upon his request, a draft statement to be directed to my most gracious King [Wilhelm of Prussia] and, with some necessary revisions to that version, to the other allies. This statement is based on the idea that indeed fills the hearts of the German tribes: The German Kaiser is their countryman, the King of Prussia their neighbour; only the German title shows that the privileges connected with it derive from the voluntary transfer by the German princes and tribes. History teaches us that the great dynasties of Germany, including the Prussian one, would not be diminished in their prominent European position through the existence of a German emperor elected by them.

suggested 'German Emperor'. Though subtle, the difference was enough to rouse passions. The 'Emperor of Germany' is an indication that the incumbent is clearly the ruler of Germany. 'German Emperor' simply means that the title holder is an emperor and a German. Bismarck was sensitive to the political implications of this. He knew it would be far more acceptable for the other German princes to have a 'German Emperor'. As ever, Bismarck won the argument and William took the title; 'by the grace of God German emperor and king of Prussia'. In order to cement this, the Grand Duke of Baden shouted out during the coronation, 'long live his imperial and royal majesty Emperor William!' William knew that Bismarck had put him up to it and refused to speak to Bismarck for a number of days after it.

The coronation took place, not in Berlin but in Paris. This again shows Bismarck's sensibilities towards the non-Prussian German elites. He chose to stage the coronation in the Hall of Mirrors at the Palace of Versailles, which had been built to show the power of Louis XIV of France. Not only did it provide the most sumptuous of neutral venues (being outside Germany it did not favour one German venue over another) but was also a reminder of the German victory over the French, a unifying cause for a moment of unification. The coronation also took place on 18 January 1870, a full ten days before the war officially ended, when nationalist sentiments were at their most enflamed.

SOURCE 11

Letter from King Ludwig II of Bavaria to William I of Prussia, 7 December 1870.

After the adhesion of Southern Germany to the German Constitutional Alliance the Presidential rights vested in your Majesty will extend over all German States. In consenting to those rights being vested in a single hand I have been influenced by the conviction that the interests of the whole German Fatherland and its allied Sovereigns will be effectually promoted by this arrangement. I trust that the rights constitutionally possessed by the President of the Confederation will, by the restoration of the German Empire and the German Imperial dignity, be recognised as rights exercised by your majesty in the name of the entire Fatherland, and by virtue of the agreement affected between its Princes. I have therefore proposed to the German Sovereigns, conjointly with myself, to suggest to your Majesty that the possession of the Presidential Rights of the Confederation be coupled with the Imperial Title.

> **A Level Exam-Style Question Section A**
>
> How far could the historian make use of Sources 10 and 11 together to investigate the issues regarding the creation of the German Empire in 1871?
>
> Explain your answer, using both sources, the information given about them and your own knowledge of the historical context. (20 marks)
>
> **Tip**
> *Make sure you use the evidence of the sources to support your points and also consider the information that the sources are not telling you.*

SOURCE 12

William proclaimed emperor in the Hall of Mirrors, Palace of Versailles, on 18 January 1871. *The Proclamation of the Germany Empire* by Anton von Werner, painted in 1885. It was commissioned by the Prussian royal family to commemorate the 70th birthday of Otto von Bismarck.

KEY TERM

Reich
German for 'empire'. The 'First Reich' was the Holy Roman Empire and the 'Third Reich' was the Nazi state.

Positive reactions to unification

Liberals within Germany were quick to proclaim the new Empire or **Reich**. Many saw it as the culmination of a long process by which the nation, which had always existed, was made one by its inherent superiority. It was simply the material domination of Prussian-led Germany over Austria and France but a moral one also. Bismarck had gone from being the arch conservative to the darling of the nationalist liberals. His ability to outfox the diplomatic brains of Europe and navigate the affairs of state so skilfully was admired not just in Germany but throughout the world.

It was not only in Germany that the new state was proclaimed. Writers in other countries praised German efficiency. In Britain reforms to education and the armed forces were a direct result of the success of Prussia and the Germans. Queen Victoria wrote at the time about the German triumph 'of civilisation, of liberty, of order and of unity… over despotism, corruption, immorality and aggression'. There was still something of an adherence to the old belief that victory in war is an indication of the will of God.

THINKING HISTORICALLY | Cause and Consequence (6a)

Seeing things differently

Different times and different places have a different set of ideas. Beliefs about how the world works, how human societies should be governed or the best way to achieve economic prosperity, can all be radically different from our own. It is important for the historian to take into account these different attitudes and be aware of the dangers of judging them against modern ideas.

Ruling elites and the conduct of war

Up to the 20th century, ordinary people may have expected to have played little or no part in politics. Nations were led by great men but nationalism was an idea that had yet to be fully defined, particularly in a German context. Bismarck used popular opinion where it suited him to gain an advantage, particularly when he could whip up nationalist sentiment. He felt that the popular classes were easily manipulated into reacting to events in a certain way, particularly when it was a matter of patriotism. He introduced universal manhood suffrage at a time when he felt that the ordinary man was not capable of following the liberal argument and would simply vote for his betters or for his heroes.

Answer the following questions:

1 Look at Source 9. Why do you think Louis Napoleon is pictured talking calmly to Bismarck after he was captured? How might you have expected him to react?

2 Explain the difference between the nationalism that arose in 1848, the nationalism in reaction to the military victories of 1866 and 1870 and the support a modern person might give to their nation's football team.

3 How far do you think it mattered to Bismarck whether or not the people of Luxembourg felt truly 'German' or not?

4 Do you think that Bismarck regarded democracy as the ultimate aim for a modern state? So why did he introduce universal manhood suffrage?

5 How important is it for historians to deal with events in the context of the beliefs and values of people in the past as well as seeing them as part of a greater pattern?

Dissenting voices

Not every German was delighted at the way that events had unfolded. Some liberals regarded the new Germany as simply a Greater Prussia. They were fearful of Bismarck's cynicism and the power of the Prussian army. Gervinus, a liberal historian and one of the Göttingen Seven, warned that Germany would become a militaristic and aggressive state while Georg Herwegh, a poet and liberal activist, said that unity without freedom was worthless. There were those who had, in 1848, dreamed of a unified state brought together through a mass social and cultural movement and had instead witnessed unification brought about by the power of the Prussian military. Though in the minority, some people felt that the end did not justify the means.

The significance of the Treaty of Frankfurt, 1871

Signed on 10 May 1871, the treaty brought the Franco-Prussian War to an end. There were three main significant decisions contained in it:

- The French would pay a war indemnity of five billion francs, payable over five years.

- The territories of Alsace and Lorraine would be annexed to the new German Reich.

- The French would recognise the new German Reich under the leadership of Emperor William.

The indemnity was a standard clause for a defeated power. As France had declared war on Prussia, it could be cast as the aggressor and therefore it was reasonable for it to pay the cost of the war. An occupation force of German troops would remain in the eastern part of France until the money was paid.

France had no choice but to recognise the new Germany, as did the other European powers. Any meaningful objection would have meant joining the war – a war that France had already lost. In recognising the new Germany and coming to arrangements over trade that formed some of the clauses of the treaty, France did not lose anything. Losing Alsace and Lorraine, on the other hand, struck deep into the French psyche. It formed the basis for a whole political movement of the late 19th century: 'the **Revanchment**' and was a major contributing factor to the start of the First World War in 1914.

Bismarck was aware that taking Alsace-Lorraine would infuriate the French. He thought that the humiliation of defeat would have been enough to make France an implacable enemy of Germany. He was interested in making sure that France was too weak to attack Germany and that along the common border, German security was as good as it could be.

Moreover, in annexing Alsace and the northern part of Lorraine, the Germans were working along nationalist lines. Most of the inhabitants spoke German dialects and thought of themselves as culturally and racially German. Strasbourg had been a major German city since the ninth century. Not many people in the territories themselves raised much of an objection. The uproar in Paris at this slight against the French nation was massive.

Another of Bismarck's concerns was strategic. In absorbing Alsace-Lorraine, he placed a buffer zone including the Vosges Mountains between France and Baden and Bavaria. Not being the first line of defence was reassuring for the newly unified south German states. That the fortress town of Metz was also part of Alsace-Lorraine gave the German army the use of those fortifications against the French.

> **KEY TERM**
>
> Revanchment
> French for 'revenge'. The Revanchment was a political movement in France in the late 19th century, the sole purpose of which was to reverse the territorial settlement of the Treaty of Frankfurt.

SOURCE

13 Preliminary peace treaty between Germany and France, 26 February 1871. This later formed the basis of the Treaty of Frankfurt.

1. France renounces in favour of the German Empire all her rights and titles over the territories situated on the east of the frontier hereafter described... The German Empire shall possess these territories in perpetuity in all sovereignty and property... The frontier, such as it has been described, is marked in green on two identical copies of the map of the territory forming the government of Alsace.

2. France shall pay His Majesty the Emperor of Germany the sum of 5 milliards [billion] francs. The payment of at least 1,000,000,000 francs shall be effected within the year 1871, and the whole of the remainder of the debt in the space of three years, dating from the ratification of the present treaty.

3. The evacuation of the French territory occupied by German troops shall begin the ratification of the present treaty by the National Assembly sitting at Bordeaux. Immediately after that ratification, the German troops shall quit the interior of Paris, as well as the forts on the left bank of the Seine and within the shortest possible delay... they shall entirely evacuate the *departments* as far as the left bank of the Seine... The garrison of Paris is excepted from this disposition, the number of which shall not exceed 40,000 men, and the garrisons indispensably necessary for the safety of the strongholds.

The evacuation of the departments between the right bank of the Seine and the eastern frontier by German troops shall take place gradually after the ratification of the Definitive Treaty of Peace and the payment of the first 500,000,000 of the contribution stipulated by Article 2...

> **AS Level Exam-Style Question Section A**
>
> How much weight do you give to the evidence in Source 13 for an enquiry into the peace settlement following the Franco-Prussian War?
>
> Explain your answer using the source, the information given about it and your own knowledge of the historical context. (12 marks)
>
> **Tip**
> *Make sure you consider the reasons why the Germans demanded each clause and therefore what motivated them.*

1 What effect did the Franco-Prussian War have on German nationalism?

2 Why do you think the distinction between 'German Emperor' and 'Emperor of the Germans' was so important to those involved?

3 Study Source 10. How does Bismarck refer back into history to persuade Ludwig to accept William as emperor?

4 Why do you think certain Germans were unhappy about the unification?

5 Why did Bismarck annex Alsace-Lorraine even though he knew that it would infuriate the French?

WHY WAS PRUSSIA SO SUCCESSFUL IN UNIFYING GERMANY?

The role of Bismarck

In the 1840s, the Scottish philosopher Thomas Carlyle wrote; 'the history of the world is but the biography of great men.' This was countered by an argument put forward by the philosopher Herbert Spencer who wrote; 'You must admit that the genesis of a great man depends on the long series of complex influences which has produced the race in which he appears and the social state into which that race has slowly grown… Before he can remake his society, his society must make him.' This argument between the notion that great men make things happen through their own will and that much larger movements allow things to happen is very pertinent to Bismarck. He was definitely a great man but did not operate in isolation.

There is certainly no doubt that Bismarck played a significant role in the unification of Germany. He changed the politics in Prussia and later within the North German Confederation. He freed himself from ideology and was able to pursue policies that would make practical gains. His management of European diplomacy through the 1860s created the ideal conditions for Prussia to capitalise on its military victories. Without Bismarck, events would have taken a different course.

Initially, Bismarck was appointed as first minister in order to safeguard the ultra-conservative Prussian government. Faced with a liberal majority in the Prussian parliament, William felt that he needed a hardline conservative to protect his rights as king. By identifying himself with unification and leading Prussia through successful wars, Bismarck safeguarded his own position and William's privileges. He realised, however, that he could not swim against the tide of liberalism. He made some concessions to the liberals, such as universal manhood suffrage, to win them over to his side but was able to find the most common ground in the unification process. By 1871, Bismarck was supported by a broad coalition between moderate conservatives and nationalist liberals, who had been swept along on a tide of patriotism. The instruments of state, however, in both Prussia and Germany allowed the government and the monarch to keep hold of the reins of power.

It was Bismarck's belief in the idea of realpolitik that allowed him the flexibility to respond to events. He could be ruthless in pursuit of his goals, such as with the annexation of Hanover in 1866 or the bombardment of Paris in 1870 and then conciliatory, as with Austria after the Seven Weeks' War or with Bavaria in 1870. Dogmatic leaders driven by ideology cannot be opportunistic in this way. Some have argued that realpolitik is cynical and Bismarck was certainly not above the use of bribes and secret deals to get what he wanted. His subterfuge during the Hohenzollern candidacy involved deceiving those on his own side and the bribe that he gave Ludwig II in 1870 remained secret for many years. One thing we can say is that without Bismarck's willingness to bend, Prussia would not have been able to take advantage of opportunities in the same way.

Nation states, at any given time, have issues that they regard as important and other issues they regard as unimportant. If Bismarck is to be praised for his diplomacy during the 1860s, it is that he understood exactly what those issues were for each state. His use of Italy as an ally during the Seven Weeks' War meant that Austria had to dispatch half its fighting force to northern Italy rather than using the whole of Austria's might to oppose Prussia. Similarly, his manipulation of the Luxembourg Crisis pushed Britain further away from France.

Perhaps Bismarck's contribution was to manage events as they arose in a way that led to his ultimate goal of uniting Germany. There were other factors, of course, over which he had no control.

Military strength

Prussia had long been a militaristic state. Since the beginning of the 18th century, the army was the monarch's most prized possession. Frederick William I searched all over Europe for tall men to be in his guards regiments and Frederick the Great (Frederick II) fought many military battles between 1740 and 1786. The Napoleonic wars had been a setback for the Prussian army but it reformed during the 19th century and by the1860s was well organised, well equipped and morale was high.

The Prussians took a scientific view of warfare and their staff college was probably the most advanced in Europe. Carl von Clausewitz's book, *On War*, became a standard for military leaders throughout the world and illustrates the general approach that the Prussians had towards warfare. It was through this approach that the Prussians were able to utilise the railways to make sure that armies were mobilised quickly and were kept well supplied. Officers had good maps and the chain of command was clear.

Technology played a very important part in the victories of the Prussian army. The needle gun outclassed the Austrians in 1866 and breech-loading artillery outclassed the French in 1870. The railways kept the soldiers supplied with ammunition, so that they could keep firing and food so they could keep going.

The Prussians also benefited from the tactical and **strategic** errors of the opposition. The Austrian conversion to 'shock' tactics after 1859 played into the hands of the rapid firing Prussians and was a significant factor in the Austrian defeat at Sadowa. In 1870, the French allowed half their forces to be manoeuvred into the fortress at Metz, where they sat out the rest of the war. Had the French still had two mobile field armies, the campaign might have played out differently.

Economic factors

The strength of the Prussian economy was important in allowing Prussia to take the lead in Germany. Prussia became the leading industrial state within the Confederation during the 1850s. This allowed it to dominate the *Zollverein* and control investment in capital projects.

Prussia's control of the *Zollverein* was a precursor to a unified Germany. By the late 1860s, it contained virtually all the territory that would form the new Germany and had bodies that resembled those of a nation state such as the *Zollparlament*. The exclusion of Austria from economic matters within the Confederation was highly significant as it was happening long before the political exclusion following the Seven Weeks' War. The *Zollverein* was like an embryonic *Kleindeutschland* solution.

The discrepancy in tax income between Prussia and Austria should not be underestimated. The Prussians were able to make money available for capital projects such as railway building and the founding of heavy industrial plants. They were also able to make loans for tenant farmers to buy their farms and invest in modern agricultural equipment. The Austrians, drained by wars in Italy and Hungary, were struggling to balance the books and thereby did not enjoy the freedom that the Prussian government had. When the moment came for army reform at the end of the 1850s, the Prussian government had the money to re-equip the army with modern weapons. The Austrian government listened to the **tactical** arguments against breech-loading rifles but decided against them because this saved it from the problem of finding the money to pay for them. Consequently, the outcome of the Seven Weeks' War is partially rooted in economic matters.

KEY TERMS

Strategic
Identifies the way in which nation states conduct wars.

Tactical
Describes the way that soldiers operate on a battlefield.

AS Level Exam-Style Question Section B

How accurate would it be to state that the reaching of the *Kleindeutschland* solution in 1871 was entirely the result of Bismarck's policy of realpolitik? (20 marks)

Tip
Make sure you consider both sides of the question and come to a balanced conclusion.

German nationalism

Tension existed between the idea of German nationalism and Prussian nationalism. How far did people perceive the *Kleindeutschland* solution as a unified Germany excluding Austria, which was led by Prussia or dominated by Prussia? Was the new Germany in 1871 really Germany or just Greater Prussia? Perhaps in a federal state, there are always these tensions between individual states and the nation.

The nationalists of 1848 certainly believed that nationalism was a movement consisting of a broad consensus. They thought that German unity was going to be the obvious result of historical development. Many of them hoped that it would be linked into some kind of liberal political reform. The events of 1848 and 1849 showed that this would not be the case, at least in the short term. During the 1850s nationalism lost ground as the old system prevailed.

The wars of the 1860s gave the nationalists a second chance if they were willing to reframe their thinking. Like Bismarck, they would have to adapt if their sole aim was a unified Germany. Some, like Gervinus or von Gagern were unable to do this and disappeared into obscurity. Most others forged an intellectual and emotional alliance with Bismarck and were willing to be led as long as they were moving towards their shared goal. Though unthinkable in 1862, an alliance between Bismarck and the National Liberals was not so surprising in 1870.

Victory in war also helped to raise nationalist sentiment. In 1866, this was not so clear but in 1870, it was clearly portrayed as Germans winning a German war. Bismarck was quick to use nationalism for his own ends, particularly during the Luxembourg Crisis. This wave of popular sentiment, exemplified by victorious troops and marching bands, was utilised by Bismarck as he sought to win over more reluctant factions to the idea of German unification.

The international situation

Napoleon I had, perhaps flippantly, rejected talent among his generals and said that he preferred 'lucky' ones. Luck played some part in the unification of Germany, perhaps not more so than in the field of international diplomacy.

Ostensibly, the whole of Europe was against German unification. Why would they not be? Who would not have been proportionately weakened by a German super state? And yet the European powers allowed the process to run its course.

The breakdown of the Concert of Europe was massively important. Had the system been sustained, Prussia would have been coerced by the other four powers to maintain the status quo. It was the weakness of Turkey that proved to be the decisive factor, as Russia was looking (and would look, up to the end of the First World War) to exploit Turkish weakness to increase its own power. This set the Russians on a path against Britain and France, who saw a strong Turkey as vital to their own strategic interest in the Eastern Mediterranean. This distracted attention away from the German question.

The ambition of France to revive its glorious Napoleonic Empire also played into Prussian hands. The War of 1859 wounded Austria and created a unified Italy that posed more of a threat than the splintered states created at the Congress of Vienna. The re-establishment of Austrian hegemony in Italy and revenge against the French isolated Austria from the western powers and she was left without major allies when war with Prussia broke out in 1866.

Bismarck very cleverly isolated the countries with whom the Prussians were about to have a war. The one possible ally of Austria that would have made the difference was Russia. Bismarck had, however, co-operated with Russia over the Polish insurrection while at the same time he knew that Austria and Russia were drifting apart over issues in the Balkans. Knowing that Italy was afraid of Austria, negotiating a military pact with the new kingdom was fairly straightforward. He was able to keep the French out of affairs in 1866 with vague promises of territorial compensation for France, though when France pressed its claim, he made it look like the aggressor and used the issue of Belgium to isolate France from Britain. Using the Ems telegram to provoke the French into declaring war played into Bismarck's hands; as the injured party, the Germans were only sorting out the mess created by French aggression.

ACTIVITY
KNOWLEDGE CHECK

1 Explain why Bismarck was so crucial to the unification of Germany.

2 How significant was the *Zollverein* in the events following the Seven Weeks' War and the Franco-Prussian War?

3 How far was it luck that created a favourable international situation in the late 1860s and how far was it Bismarck's clever diplomacy?

Revolution from above or revolution from below?

The question that has been asked by historians is whether the unification of Germany was a revolution from above or below? In essence was the change brought about because of the will of the ruling elite or because there was a mass movement which desired it and brought about the conditions by which it could happen? The answer, as is so often the case, lies somewhere in the middle.

The case for the revolution from below lies in the causes and the events of 1848 along with the broader social and cultural movements that were prevalent in Germany at this time. The vision of the men of 1848 was, at different times and different places, supported by large numbers. Demonstrations such as at the Heppenheim Festival indicate this. The relative power of the Frankfurt Parliament in the summer of 1848 indicated how far the consensus stretched and the inability of either Austria or Prussia to challenge this underpins the argument of its popularity. The failure of 1848 to deliver a tangible outcome was a blow to the nationalist liberal cause but ideas once sown cannot be easily reclaimed. Being genuinely close to the possibility of a unified Germany made the idea a reality for countless thousands of Germans.

That movements of social and cultural unification were going along underneath the great events should not be underestimated. The contact between peoples of different states but with the same language and culture was unification in very subtle ways. The inter-relations between institutes of higher education also played an unseen role. To illustrate this point it is worth citing academics such as Friedrich Dahlmann, one of the Gottingen Seven, who, during his lifetime held posts in Schleswig-Holstein, Hanover, Saxony and Prussia (East and West). He was not a parochial Mecklenburger but a German who saw little difference in the places he worked. The perception of German culture: literature, music, art and history which transcended state boundaries played a role in setting conditions that minimised the opposition to the unification when it came.

The case for revolution from above is clear. The scheming of Bismarck, the weakness of Austria, Prussian manipulation of the *Zollverein* and the Prussian victories in the wars against Austria and France are all causes of the unification of Germany. The change itself was so significant in the way that it altered the balance of power in Europe, that the only way to push through change was at the point of a bayonet (or the muzzle of a needle gun). Understanding this, Bismarck manipulated situations that allowed him to exploit Prussian military success to the end of unifying Germany under Prussian rule.

Of course, the two extremes of revolution from above and revolution from below have a very strong relationship. The political outcomes of the wars should always be considered with the progress made in cultural unity. The impact of the meeting of exercise clubs or the singing of Bach cantatas is unmeasurable and yet without them, how would the German psyche have developed? How far could the armies of Prussia have swept all before them? Political change can be forced in the short term through the power of weapons but it can only be sustained when the masses of the people are prepared for it. Cultural unity, along with the debates in the Frankfurt Parliament concerning the nature of Germany, had prepared the ground for Bismarck and Von Moltke. Great men, as with great events can, perhaps, only be born of their time.

ACTIVITY
SUMMARY

1 What was the most significant factor in the reaching of the *Kleindeutschland* solution in 1871?

2 Make a list of the five most significant successes that Bismarck achieved in the years up to 1871. For each of these explain your choice.

3 To what extent was the unification of Germany a revolution from above?

WIDER READING

Carr, W. *A History of Germany*, Edward Arnold (1989), chapter 4

Farmer, A. and Stiles, A. *The Unification of Germany, 1815–1919*, Hodder Education (2007), chapter 4

Gorman, M. *The Unification of Germany*, Cambridge University Press (1989), chapter 5

Whitfield, B. *Germany 1848–1914*, Heinemann (2000), chapter 4

Preparing for your AS Level Paper 2 exam

Advance planning

1. Draw up a timetable for your revision and try to keep to it. Spread your timetable over a number of weeks, and aim to cover four or five topics each week.
2. Spend longer on topics which you have found difficult, and revise them several times.
3. Above all, do not try to limit your revision by attempting to 'question spot'. Try to be confident about all aspects of your Paper 2 work, because this will ensure that you have a choice of questions in Section B.

Paper 2 overview:

AS Paper 2	Time: 1 hour 30 minutes	
Section A	Answer 1 compulsory two-part sources question	8+12 marks = 20 marks
Section B	Answer 1 question from a choice of 3	20 marks
	Total marks =	40 marks

You should familiarise yourself with the layout of the paper by looking at the examples published by Edexcel. The questions for each section are followed by eight pages of lined paper where you should write your answer.

Section A question

Each of the two parts of the question will focus on one of the two contemporary sources provided. The sources together will total around 300 words. The (a) question, worth 8 marks, will be in the form of 'Why is Source 1 useful for an enquiry into…?' The (b) question, worth 12 marks, will be in the form of 'How much weight do you give the evidence of Source 2 for an enquiry into…?' In both your answers you should address the value of the content of the source, and then its nature, origin and purpose. Finally, you should use your own knowledge of the context of the source to assess its value.

Section B questions

These questions ask you to reach a judgement on an aspect of the topic studied. The questions will have the form, for example, of 'How far…', 'To what extent…' or 'How accurate is it to say…'. The questions can deal with historical concepts such as cause, consequence, change, continuity, similarity, difference and significance. You should consider the issue raised in the question, consider other relevant issues, and then conclude with an overall judgement.

The timescale of the questions could be as short as a single year or even a single event (an example from Option 2C.2 could be, 'To what extent was Russia's involvement in the First World War responsible for the fall of the Provisional Government in 1917?'). The timescale could be longer depending on the historical event or process being examined, but questions are likely to be shorter than those set for Sections A and B in Paper 1.

Use of time

This is an issue which you should discuss with your teachers and fellow students, but here are some suggestions for you.

1. Do not write solidly for 45 minutes on each question. For Section A it is essential that you have a clear understanding of the content of each source, the points being made, and the nature, origin and purpose of each source. You might decide to spend up to ten minutes reading the sources and drawing up your plan, and 35 minutes writing your answer.
2. For Section B answers you should spend a few minutes working out what the question is asking you to do, and drawing up a plan of your answer before you begin to write your response.

Preparing for your AS Level exams

Paper 2: AS Level sample answer with comments

Section A

Part A requires you to:

- identify key points in the source and explain them
- deploy your own knowledge of the context in which events took place
- make appropriate comments about the author/origins/purpose of the source.

Study Source 20 (page 305) before you answer this question.

Why is Source 20 valuable to the historian for an enquiry into the reasons for the outbreak of the revolutions of 1848?

Explain your answer using the source, the information given about it and your own knowledge of the historical context. (8 marks)

Average student answer

This source shows that people thought that their lives were being restricted. The fact that the 'the Carlsbad decrees of 1819, the Frankfurt decrees of 1831 and 1832 and the Vienna decrees of 1834… decrees are contrary to our inviolable human rights' shows a resentment against the powers of the Confederation. By demanding 'freedom of the press' they show that the press was not free and the people at Offenburg wanted this to change. The Offenburg meeting demanded that these restrictions should be lifted.

This is a weak opening paragraph because it does not explain how these things relate to the question. The quotes are used to illustrate the inferences made without being subjected to any kind of evaluation.
It could be improved by explaining what these ideas show us about the mood in 1847.

The source shows some people in certain parts of the Confederation were resentful of the influence of the larger powers. The 'Carlsbad Decrees' and the 'Vienna Decrees' were signed and imposed by Austria. People in Baden would not like to be dominated by the Austrians and wanted greater freedom from their domination. Baden is in the west of Germany, which is a long way from Austria which is in the east. They would not be happy that decisions taken by the Austrian government would have such a serious effect on their lives.

There is a clear dislike here for the powers of governments. When the people express the desire for 'personal freedom' without the 'domination and harassment of citizens by the police' they are expressing dissatisfaction with the government in Baden. There was bound to be a revolution because the people wanted to force the authorities to respect these rights.

This paragraph focuses on the geographical positioning of Baden and Austria but also the relative influence of the Austrian court on the Confederation. It does address fully the reasons why people in Baden might not be happy with Austrian domination.

It could be better if there was a little more depth to the argument about Austrian domination and reference to the Metternich system. Some of the source could be quoted as an example of how Austrian influence was affecting the lives of the people of Baden.

This paragraph deals partly with the feelings of the people who attended the Offenburg meeting and their grievances and has used quotes from the source to support this. There is some attempt to link this to the question.

What the question demands is an understanding of the value of the source for this specific enquiry. It should explain why the delegates from the meeting thought that such a list of demands was advisable and what this shows us about their ideas about the situation.

Verdict

This is an average answer because:

- it does not make clear connections between the source and the question
- it does not use the context of the source to explain its value

- it does not explain the significance of the issues raised in the answer, particularly where quotes are used.

Use the feedback on this answer to rewrite it, making as many improvements as you can.

Paper 2: AS Level sample answer with comments

Section A

Part B requires you to:

- interrogate the source
- draw reasoned inferences
- deploy your own knowledge to interpret the material in its context
- make judgement about the value (weight) of the source in terms of making judgements.

Study Source 14 (page 331) before you answer this question.

How much weight do you give the evidence of Source 14 for an enquiry into the reasons why Prussia complied with the Punctation of Olomouc?

Explain your answer using the source, the information given about it and your own knowledge of the historical context. (12 marks)

Average student answer

The speech by Bismarck is valuable because it shows Prussia's attitude towards the Punctation of Olomouc. He shows the possible consequences of a war between Prussia and the three other continental powers (Russia, Austria and France): 'A war, gentlemen, which will bring to our provinces the full horrors of war.' He also says that war is only worth fighting when there is something to be gained, though he does not say what that gain might be. There is an early indication of Bismarck's realpolitik approach when he says that 'and it is not worthy of a great state to fight for something that is not in its own interest'.

In some ways the source is not valuable for a historian. Bismarck is only one man expressing an opinion. Just because he was from an influential Junker family and was speaking to the Parliament does not mean that he is stating the ideas that are held by the Prussian government or ordinary Prussians. As an arch conservative, he will say things that show the monarchy in a good light and so it is when he says, 'large parts of Prussia will be inundated by enemy forces' he implies that the king was saving Prussia from a horrific fate by signing the Punctation.

Prussia had no choice but to sign the Punctation. The Austrian army was larger than Prussia's and had been aided by the Russian army in defeating the Hungarians in 1849. The Austrian Army was therefore battled hardened and ready to mobilise for another war which the Prussian army was not. The lukewarm attitude of some to the Erfurt Union, not just the Roman Catholic states of the south, meant that the Prussians were unwilling to stand on their own against Austria to challenge their dominance within the Confederation. Also, there were those in Prussia, including conservatives like Bismarck, who felt that the German Confederation dominated by the forces of reaction led by Austria was far more in Prussia's interest than the force of national-liberalism.

This paragraph deals partly with the reasons why Prussia felt that they had no choice but to sign the Punctation. It does include some contextual information relevant to this.

What the question demands is that the reasons why the Punctation was signed are compared and contrasted with the information contained in the source. The source needed to be used in relation to these issues in order to deal with the demands of the question.

This is a weak opening paragraph because it does not address the significance of what the source contains. It makes a point and illustrates it with a quote but the point amounts to little more than a paraphrase of the quote.

It could be improved by explaining how the context of the recent events impacts on the opinions being expressed and the weight that would be given to the source.

In this paragraph there is an attempt to look beyond the source and deal with Bismarck and the context. It does make some attempt to address the issue of why the Punctation was signed.

It could be better, if the material more fully explored the reasons why Prussia felt compelled to sign the agreement and how far these reasons were and were not reflected in Bismarck's speech.

Verdict

This is an average answer because:

- it does not make clear connections between the source and the question or use the context of the source to explain its limitations

- it does not explain the significance of the issues raised in the answer, particularly where quotes are used.

Use the feedback on this answer to rewrite it, making as many improvements as you can.

Paper 2: AS Level sample answer with comments

Section A

Part A requires you to:

- identify key points in the source and explain them
- deploy your own knowledge of the context in which events took place
- make appropriate comments about the author/origins/purpose of the source.

Study Source 20 (page 305) before you answer this question.

Why is Source 20 valuable to the historian for an enquiry into the reasons for the outbreak of the revolutions of 1848?

Explain your answer using the source, the information given about it and your own knowledge of the historical context. (8 marks)

Strong student answer

The demands of the Offenburg meeting show that people were unhappy with restrictions upon their personal freedom but were more concerned with the impact of this on how they could act politically. Acts like the 'Carlsbad Decrees of 1819' were created to restrict political movements rather than simply being an attack on personal liberty. Point 5 addresses the issues of 'freedom of association' and the 'right to hold meetings and to speak'. The main impact of these was felt by the middle-class liberals, the group who will be the driving force behind the revolutions of 1848. The Offenburg Meeting itself broke the law but it is very much the opinion of those present that it was the law that was wrong not the holding of the meeting.

> By recognising that the Offenburg Meeting was part of a political struggle, the answer sees the context of the source. It uses well selected details from the source to back this up. It acknowledges the authors of the source and their role in the revolutions.

The source hints slightly at a unification agenda. In point 5 it mentions 'the right to move freely and travel anywhere in the German fatherland'. This takes the scope of the meeting slightly beyond the borders of Baden. Moreover, in point 3, the demands state that 'No force should interfere in matters concerning teachers and pupils' which also could be seen as a matter directly affecting unification. The Gottingen Seven were sacked by the government of Hanover but the fallout was felt throughout the Confederation. The creation of the Frankfurt Parliament shows how far the issue of unification was at the centre of the revolutions of 1848. The authors of this source were therefore not only liberals but nationalists, although the local nature of the meeting (in Baden) meant that they might not have been so confident in pushing forward a wholly nationalist agenda.

> In this paragraph there is an attempt to look beyond the source and deal with the broader issue of unification. This shows that the candidate is aware that it is a major factor of the revolutions and is able to relate this to the source in question.

The fact that the revolutions dealt with the issues raised by then Offenburg Meeting is an invaluable indication of its value for the historian. The Frankfurt Parliament passed 'The Imperial Act concerning the Basic Rights of the German People' in December 1848 which is almost a direct mirror of the demands of the Offenburg Meeting. If the Frankfurt Parliament, saw its business as removing certain boundaries to liberty and if those boundaries correspond to the demands of the Offenburg Meeting, then the demands of the Offenburg Meeting are indeed a valuable resource for any historian studying the causes of the 1848 revolutions.

> This paragraph identifies the most important point as to why the source will be a valid one for a historian studying the reasons for the outbreak of revolution in 1848.

Verdict

This is a strong answer because:

- it makes clear connections between the source and the question and it uses the context of the source to show how it relates to the question

- it selects relevant parts of the sources and explains why they are important in relation to the question.

Paper 2: AS Level sample answer with comments

Section A

Part B requires you to:

- interrogate the source
- draw reasoned inferences
- deploy your own knowledge to interpret the material in its context
- make judgement about the value (weight) of the source in terms of making judgements.

Study Source 14 (page 331) before you answer this question.

How much weight do you give the evidence of Source 14 for an enquiry into the reasons why Prussia complied with the Punctation of Olomouc?

Explain your answer using the source, the information given about it and your own knowledge of the historical context. (12 marks)

Strong student answer

The speech by Bismarck shows that he is making the best of a bad situation. The Prussians, in avoiding a war that they could not win, have gained something. Bismarck reinforces the point that avoiding 'the full horrors of war' is a kind of victory. It is entirely understandable that the Prussian establishment would wish to put this spin on these events. Bismarck, as a conservative supporter of the monarchy, a fairly reasonable indicator of how the monarchy may have viewed the events. The source indicates prevalent attitudes of those in power and has some weight in arriving at an overall judgement.

> This paragraph explains why the source portrays the signing of the Punctation as it does. An inference is made about the Prussians gaining something and this is explained by examining Bismarck's motivation for speaking in this way. It then makes a direct statement regarding the weight of this.

In 1850 Bismarck was of minor importance and the speech has only been preserved because of his actions from 1862 onwards. It should be judged in this light and given weight accordingly. While we can make assumptions about what the Prussian government would wish the interpretation to be, we cannot take it for granted that Bismarck spoke for them. Moreover, we cannot take his word that a war with Austria would be a disaster for Prussia as no evidence of the relative strengths of the armies is available. Also, the fact that the Frankfurt Parliament offered the German throne to Frederick William IV would indicate that there was some genuine support for a *Kleindeutsch* solution within the Confederation. Not addressing these issues keeps the reasons why the Punctation was signed unclear and therefore the source bears less much weight.

> This paragraph shows that the source material has been evaluated against the demands of the question and a judgement regarding its weight has been made. It also offers justification of the argument by citing contextual information and arrives at a conclusion which draws the argument to a close.

Although the source reveals something about Bismarck's and Prussia's view of the relationship with Austria, it implies a different possibility in the future. Bismarck states: 'The only sound basis for a large state, and this is what distinguishes it from a small state is state egoism and not romanticism, and it is not worthy of a great state to fight for something that is not in its own interest.' This implies that opposing Austria was not in Prussia's interest but also it could be inferred that Bismarck would support Prussian opposition to Austria if it were in its interest. The source contains some reasonable deductions about what may have occurred in the days leading up to the signing, particularly from the point of view of a conservative Prussian monarchist. For this reason, it would be given some weight by a historian making an inquiry into why the Prussians signed the Punctation but would need corroborating by other sources.

> This paragraph attempts to come to an overall judgement about the weight of the source.

Verdict

This is a strong answer because:

- it makes inferences from the source and deploys material from the source to support them
- it shows a deep awareness of context and brings it into the answer when appropriate to the question
- it sticks to the question to arrive at a clear judgement.

Paper 2: AS Level sample answer with comments

Section B

These questions assess your understanding of the period in depth. They will ask you about the content you learned about in the four key themes, and may ask about more than one theme. For these questions remember to:

- give an analytical, not a descriptive, response
- support your points with evidence
- cover the whole time period specified in the question
- come to a substantiated judgement.

How accurate is it to say that the role of Bismarck was the most important factor in the unification of Germany? (20 marks)

Average student answer

Bismarck was a Prussian Junker from a wealthy background. He entered politics in the 1850s, serving in the Federal Diet as a delegate from Prussia. In 1862, he was appointed First Minister by William I because he was a conservative and the king thought that Bismarck would help protect the power of the monarchy from the liberals. Bismarck led Prussia into key wars with Denmark in 1864, Austria in 1866 and France in 1870. The war of 1864 was won with the help of Austria and Prussia gained influence in Schleswig-Holstein. In the war of 1866, Prussia beat Austria with the help of Italy. After the Prussian victory at Koniggratz, the Austrians surrendered and Bismarck was able to form the North German Confederation. From here, Prussia took on the French in 1870 and beat the French Army very quickly but then was held up by the siege of Paris. It was largely because of these wars that he was able to unify Germany in 1871. To answer the question, it is necessary to look at other factors in the unification of Germany in order to fully assess whether Bismarck was the most important factor.

Bismarck did a lot of things that caused the unification of Germany. He helped to stabilise the government in Prussia. When he first became the First Minister the king was very unpopular in Parliament and the liberals there refused to work with the government. Bismarck turned this around by winning wars against the Danes and the Austrians. This made Bismarck and the king more popular. He also pushed through army reforms in Prussia even though the National Assembly were against them. After the victory in the War of 1866, he allowed an indemnity act which meant that he admitted that the government had been collecting illegal taxes since 1862. Eventually, he organised a coalition between the national liberals and the moderate conservatives, which helped him to rule the new North German Confederation after 1866. This made things much more stable by 1870.

This paragraph gives information about the subject matter of the essay but does not address the issues raised by the question. It needs to deal with the issue of what it means to be the 'most important factor' by explaining exactly what would constitute 'important'. There is also, perhaps, too much descriptive writing.

In this paragraph the material covers some of the important things that Bismarck did in the process of German unification. These points are relevant to the question but reasons for their importance to the process of unification remain implicit.

To make this better, the reasons why these things are important need to be fully explained with a close regard to the words of the question.

Bismarck was also good at dealing with other countries. When Denmark was threatening, he arranged for the Austrians and the Prussians to fight side by side. Two years later, he was very careful to make sure that Russia did not want to interfere in the dispute between Austria and Prussia – Bismarck had made it clear how important was Prussia's help with the Polish Revolt for the Russians. Similarly, he made a lenient peace with the Austrians to make sure that they did not want revenge. When the French declared war on Prussia in 1870, the Austrians did not wish to join in. This meant that Prussia was free to win the victories at Gravelot St Privat and Sedan. From there the Prussian armies were able to march on Paris and put it under siege in September 1870. There were many in the Prussia leadership who wanted to punish Austria severely but it was Bismarck who argued against this. Bismarck's skill at diplomacy made the right conditions for the Prussian victories in the wars against Austria and France.

Without Bismarck, Prussia would not have been so strong and would not have been able to win the wars that they won so easily. This would have meant that Germany would not have been unified so quickly. On the other hand, other things were also important. The skill of the army and their technological advantage, particularly over the Austrians, was also important because without them, Bismarck could not have won the wars on his own and therefore could not have unified Germany. It was through these wars that the Peace of Prague in 1866 and the Treaty of Frankfurt in 1871 were signed and the unification of Germany was made possible.

There is an explanation here of how Bismarck was important to diplomacy and how this helped Prussia in their wars with Austria and France. It does not explain why these wars were important in the process by which Germany was unified.

To make this paragraph better, it needs to take these points further and explain how these impacted on the process, led by Prussia and Bismarck, that culminated in the unification of Germany.

This concluding paragraph is too short. It makes the link between success in the wars and the unification of Germany but does not go into depth about how these things were inter-related. Also it does not explain the relative importance of the role of Bismarck and does not arrive at a judgement about whether or not he was the most important factor.

This conclusion needs to directly address the question about Bismarck being the 'most important factor' and come to a judgement. It then needs to fully explain why this judgement is reached and what evidence has been cited to support it.

Verdict

This is an average answer because:

- it does not give a direct and supported answer to the question
- it does not fully explain the significance of the issues raised in the answer
- although there is an attempt to answer the question based on the criteria the argument is not always substantiated with evidence.

Use the feedback on this answer to rewrite it, making as many improvements as you can.

Paper 2: AS Level sample answer with comments

Section B

These questions assess your understanding of the period in depth. They will ask you about the content you learned about in the four key themes, and may ask about more than one theme. For these questions remember to:

- give an analytical, not a descriptive, response
- support your points with evidence
- cover the whole time period specified in the question
- come to a substantiated judgement.

How accurate is it to say that the role of Bismarck was the most important factor in the unification of Germany? (20 marks)

Strong student answer

In order to assess the significance of Bismarck's role in the unification of Germany, those events which arose from his direct intervention, need to be identified. They should be measured against those events over which Bismarck had no control and the two compared and contrasted. By doing this the events should also be judged as to how far they rank as important with the process of unification and not simply as important in themselves. As the first minister of the Prussian state from 1862 onwards, Bismarck naturally played a pivotal role in the unification process. It was his management of foreign affairs, politics within the Confederation and affairs within Prussia that created the right conditions for unification to take place. On the other hand, factors like the quality of the Prussian Army and the willingness of other Germans to support unification, cannot solely be attributed to Bismarck's intervention.

> This paragraph sets out the criterion against which the question is going to be judged and suggests an overall shape that the argument will take.

Bismarck played a massive role in the diplomacy of the 1860s, which made the conditions favourable for German unification. This placed Prussia in an advantageous position with regard to the other European powers. For example, in the run up to the Seven Weeks' War, Bismarck pursued a pro-Russian policy over the Polish Insurrection (1863–65). It was this, and Bismarck's close personal contacts in St Petersburg that kept Russia out of the events in Germany in 1866. He was also clever in his manipulation of the French claim for compensation following the Peace of Prague in August 1866. By suggesting that Luxemburg was a possibility, he was then able to stir up nationalist feeling against the French and by suggesting that France might take Belgian territory as compensation, Britain was brought into the matter against the French. Moreover, he cleverly provoked the French into making the first step in the Franco-Prussian War of 1870. It was Bismarck's manipulation of the issue of the Spanish candidacy and his editing of the Ems telegram which provoked France into declaring war. This made it much harder for other powers to join in against the Prussians, as the French were clearly the aggressors. These events were very much centred on Bismarck personally and might have taken a different turn with a different Prussian minister.

> In this paragraph the events are explained with regard to the role of Bismarck.

Bismarck was skilled at managing the other states within the German Confederation. He saw that Prussia could unify Germany from above but also that popularity was needed. His alliance with the National Liberals was a very important part of this. He appealed to German sentiment in Schleswig-Holstein and drew support for the Danish War from across the whole Confederation. It was Bismarck who isolated Austria and, facing a choice of France or the North German Confederation, manoeuvred the southern German states into signing military treaties with the Germans. This then meant that south German troops fought alongside Prussian ones in 1870. Bribing the King of Bavaria to propose William of Prussia as Emperor is another example of

> This paragraph makes a judgement about the way that he managed the German Confederation. It explains why his role was particularly important but also cites other factors that were also influential.

how Bismarck managed events within the Confederation to Prussia's advantage. On the other hand, there were factors within the Confederation that preceded the influence of Bismarck. The legacy of the 1848 revolutions was that liberals throughout the Confederation had already known a period where German unification looked possible and so they were prepared for it when it started to happen throughout the 1860s. Moreover, the social movements that created a sense of cultural unity, such as gymnastic societies or choral groups, were factors that were beyond Bismarck's power. It could be argued that politically, creating the right conditions within Germany for unification was an important part of Bismarck's contribution.

Bismarck had little to do with the success of the Prussian Army. The Army reforms were brought in before Bismarck was made First Minister although he did have some influence over their implementation after 1862. The technological superiority of the Prussian Army was a mixture of industrial advancement and German innovation. This led to the development of the Dreyse Needle Gun and the Krupp breech-loading cannon which proved to be decisive in the fighting. These developments were down to Prussian innovation and industrial power rather than being due to personal intervention by Bismarck. Industrialisation was underway before Bismarck's premiership and the decision to use the needle gun and breech-loading artillery was not his. On the other hand, the tax income needed to finance the production of the weapons in order for the army to be equipped with them was down to Bismarck's government. The campaign plans and the speed of mobilisation were matters for the General Staff under Von Moltke and Bismarck would have little influence in these things. Where perhaps Bismarck was important was the speed with which he exploited the victories. The Peace Treaty after the Seven Weeks' War was negotiated in under a month and the German Empire was proclaimed at Versailles while the French War was officially still going on. Though the victories were not down to Bismarck, he played a very important role in their exploitation.

> This paragraph explains the other side of the argument by examining the things that Bismarck did not play a significant personal role in, though it does explain how Bismarck was able to exploit these successes.

As the leader of the victorious power Bismarck's role was pivotal in the events that led to the unification. Armies can only win battles and no matter how complete the victories, it is the politicians that use them to an advantage. The context of the armies' success and the fact that the success in 1870 was a 'German' success rather than simply a Prussian one owes much to Bismarck's management. It was Bismarck who exploited nationalist feelings, Bismarck who separated Austria from Germany while maintaining reasonably friendly relations with Austria and Bismarck who manoeuvred the Bavarian king to propose William as Emperor of the new German Empire in 1871. On the balance, therefore, Bismarck was the most important factor.

> The conclusion answers the question directly. It goes through the main reasons why Bismarck was important and arrives at a judgement that has been substantiated by the evidence and the explanation throughout the essay.

Verdict

This is a strong answer because:

- it answers the question throughout
- it uses the issue of the question to set criteria so that a judgement is made against something tangible

- it selects relevant evidence and deploys to support the arguments being made.

Preparing for your A Level Paper 2 exam

Advance planning

1. Draw up a timetable for your revision and try to keep to it. Spread your timetable over a number of weeks, and aim to cover four or five topics each week.
2. Spend longer on topics which you have found difficult, and revise them several times.
3. Above all, do not try to limit your revision by attempting to 'question spot'. Try to be confident about all aspects of your Paper 2 work, because this will ensure that you have a choice of questions in Section B.

Paper 2 overview

AL Paper 2	Time: 1 hour 30 minutes	
Section A	Answer 1 compulsory source question	20 marks
Section B	Answer 1 question from a choice of 2	20 marks
	Total marks =	40 marks

You should familiarise yourself with the layout of the paper by looking at the examples published by Edexcel. The questions for each section are followed by eight pages of lined paper where you should write your answer.

Section A question

This question asks you to assess two contemporary sources totalling around 400 words, and will be in the form of 'How far could the historian make use of Sources 1 and 2 together to investigate…?' Your answer should examine each source separately, and you should make three points on each source: the value of its content: its nature, origin and purpose; and then you should use your own knowledge of the context of the source to assess its accuracy and value. Finally, you should make a few concluding points on the two sources taken together as a set.

Section B questions

These questions ask you to reach a judgement on an aspect of the topic studied. The questions will have the form, for example, of 'How far…', 'To what extent…' or 'How accurate is it to say…'. The questions can deal with historical concepts such as cause, consequence, change, continuity, similarity, difference and significance. You should consider the issue raised in the question, then other relevant issues, and conclude with an overall judgement.

The timescale of the questions could be as short as a single year or even a single event (an example from Option 2C.2 could be, 'To what extent was Russia's involvement in the First World War responsible for the fall of the Romanovs in 1917?'). The timescale could be longer depending on the historical event or process being examined, but questions are likely to be shorter than the those set for Sections A and B in Paper 1.

Use of time

This is an issue which you should discuss with your teachers and fellow students, but here are some suggestions for you.

1. Do not write solidly for 45 minutes on each question. For Section A it is essential that you have a clear understanding of the content of each source, the points being made, and the nature, origin and purpose of each source. You might decide to spend up to ten minutes reading the sources and drawing up your plan, and 35 minutes writing your answer.
2. For Section B answers you should spend a few minutes working out what the question is asking you to do, and drawing up a plan of your answer before you begin to write your response.

Preparing for your A Level exams

Paper 2: A Level sample answer with comments

Section A

You will need to read and analyse two sources and use them in tandem to assess how useful they are in investigating an issue. For these questions remember to:

- spend time, up to ten minutes, reading and identifying the arguments and evidence present in the sources; then make a plan to ensure that your response will be rooted in these sources
- use specific references from the sources
- deploy your own knowledge to develop points made in the sources and establish appropriate context
- come to a substantiated judgement.

Study Source 1 (page 337) and Source 6 (page 345) before you answer this question.

How far could the historian make use of Sources 1 and 6 to investigate the tension between Prussia and Austria between 1850 and 1864?

Explain your answer, using both sources, the information given about them and your own knowledge of the historical context. (20 marks)

Average student answer

There was a great deal of tension between Prussia and Austria between 1850 and 1864. They were rivals for supremacy in Germany and each sought to weaken the other. The Punctation of Olomouc in 1850 gave Austria power over her rival but control of the Zollverein meant that Prussia could keep Austria weak.

Source 1 is a letter from Bruck to Schwarzenberg. In it he talks about his ideas for a Central European Customs Union which he hopes will replace the Prussian-led Zollverein after 1852. He writes about this because he was the minister responsible for finance and he wants to get Schwarzenberg on his side. He does this by showing Schwarzenberg how the customs union would benefit Austria and Germany because he talks about 'greater power' and better 'shipping routes' and more 'overseas trade'. Despite this, he is not convinced that Prussia would agree to it. He writes that 'If Prussia were to see her supremacy assured for so long a time, she would scarcely be persuaded to enter the Customs Union with Austria' but if some of the other German states would be closer supporters of Austria then the Prussians 'would prefer an attempt to share it with Austria'. Bruck is trying to improve his power with Schwarzenberg. In the 1850s Austria was an autocracy which meant that all the power was held in the hands of the Emperor. If Bruck could have created a Customs Union led by Austria, he would have been able to enhance his power within the Austrian government.

Source 6 is a declaration by the Nationalverein from 1859. It shows how they would like to unify Germany under Prussian leadership. It shows the need for a German constitution and a body that

> This is a weak opening paragraph because it simply gives an overview of some of the contextual content. It does not address the central issue of the question, which is how useful these sources are for a particular enquiry.
>
> To make it better, it needs to address the question and clearly state what the issues are both with the nature of the enquiry and an overview of the strengths and weaknesses of the sources.

> This paragraph is an overview of one source. Much of it is simple description, where the quotes either form part of that description or are paraphrased and used as supporting material for that paraphrasing. It describes what Bruck was trying to do or what he was thinking rather than how his background and position might affect the things that he would be likely to say.
>
> To make this paragraph better, it needs to be more analytical about why Bruck is presenting his case in this way and to bring in far more contextual information to place the source within the history being studied. Far more focus needs to be on the issue of tension between the two states. Also some information from Source 36 would be helpful for a direct contrast.

was 'solid, strong, and lasting' to replace the Federal Diet. The Nationalverein were very clear that 'under the current circumstances, the most effective steps toward achieving this end can only emanate from Prussia' but then most of the members of the Nationalverein were Prussian so they would have been biased in this. The source also mentions the 'dangerous state of affairs in Europe' and that German unification is the answer to that. In Point 1 it talks about the 'peace concluded between Austria and France' which refers to the War of 1859 that they fought over Italy. Perhaps the Germans feel that a weaker Austria would turn to Germany to look to strengthen itself and that a victorious France posed more of a threat. This meant that Germany had to unify and to give the power to Prussia. This was the kleindeutsch solution proposed by the Frankfurt Parliament. This is very similar to the Erfurt Union when Prussia tried to make a new Germany without Austria. This shows that the tension between Austria and Prussia was a main cause of the unification of Germany.

Both sources are written because the people want something. Source 1 is a letter from a minister who wants Austria to be in a German Customs Union. He will want the first minister to do the things he wants and he is trying to persuade him. Source 6 is a statement by an organisation that wants to unify Germany under Prussian leadership (the Kleindeutsch) solution. They want to show Prussia as powerful and Austria as a threat. The historian has to think about these things when he is using them to write his history.

Both sources are useful because they give the historian a view of the tension between Austria and Prussia with a view from both sides. Bruck is a member of the Austrian government and the Nationalverein are Prussian nationalists. In this way, both sources cannot be trusted fully. Bruck as a minister, is trying to improve his position, so it would help him to be as accurate as possible in his judgement about the situation – he would look bad if things turned out differently to how he had seen it. On the other hand, he would also want to proceed in a way that gives him more power. The Nationalverein, similarly, have a singular purpose and it is worth bearing in mind how many people actually contributed to the drawing up and publishing of the document. It is in the interest of the Nationalverein to push forward Prussia and provoke Austria. The historian should be careful not to assume just because an organisation, made up mainly of middle-class liberals, came into existence that it represented the feelings of the majority of Prussians and/or Germans. The historian needs to be careful of how they would use both documents for these reasons.

This paragraph is an overview of the second source. It describes much of the content and deploys quotes in the paragraph to illustrate or form an integral part of the description. There is some contextual knowledge but this is not related to the source in terms of its usefulness for the enquiry.

To improve this paragraph, the contextual information needs to be linked with the source throughout and an explanation added showing how this relates to the issue of tension between the two states. Some explanation of what the Nationalverein was and how it came into being would also be helpful. Some material from Source 1 which could be used to provide a comparison with Source 6 and how they jointly relate to the question would also improve this paragraph.

This paragraph deals with the motivation of the authors of the sources and thereby their purpose. It makes brief statements about what the purpose might be without explanation as to why this is the case. There is no direct comparison made between the sources.

To improve this paragraph, the purpose should be compared between the two sources with a direct comparison and some contextual knowledge used to show how these sources came into being. The significance of these sources for the historian studying this enquiry should also be addressed with regard to their provenance and purpose. This material does not necessarily need a paragraph of its own but could be integrated into other paragraphs.

This paragraph is an attempt to provide the essay with a conclusion. It does provide a direct answer but lacks any substantiation.

To improve this, a full explanation of why these sources are useful is needed. The more solid arguments should be emphasised as they will clinch the view that the writer is attempting to put forward. The claims put forward by the writer should be supported where appropriate, with quotations from the sources.

Verdict

This is an average answer because:

- it does not make clear connections between the sources and the question
- it does not use the context of the sources to explain its value
- it does not explain the significance of the issues raised in the answer, particularly where quotes are used
- it does explain why the provenance and purpose of the sources impact on judgements about their utility.

Use the feedback on this answer to rewrite it, making as many improvements as you can.

Paper 2: A Level sample answer with comments

Section A

You will need to read and analyse two sources and use them in tandem to assess how useful they are in investigating an issue. For these questions remember to:

- spend time, up to ten minutes, reading and identifying the arguments and evidence present in the sources; then make a plan to ensure that your response will be rooted in these sources
- use specific references from the sources
- deploy your own knowledge to develop points made in the sources and establish appropriate context
- come to a substantiated judgement.

Study Source 1 (page 337) and Source 6 (page 345) before you answer this question.

How far could the historian make use of Sources 1 and 6 to investigate the tension between Prussia and Austria between 1850 and 1864?

Explain your answer, using both sources, the information given about them and your own knowledge of the historical context. (20 marks)

Strong student answer

The relationship between Prussia and Austria had been changed by the events of 1848–50. Prior to 1848, Germany had been dominated by Austria under Metternich aided by the Prussians, though the Zollverein, as Bruck states, had partially excluded Austria from economic affairs. As the political situation changed, so the economic arrangements became more important and the aims of the Nationalverein mirrored the structure of the Zollverein. The debates in the Frankfurt parliament about the nature of a unified Germany had led to the polarisation of ideas into the kleindeutsche and grossdeutsche solutions. What both the sources indicate is how far the Zollverein and the Nationalverein aimed towards a kleindeutsche solution and sought to exclude Austria from the future German nation. A historian would look to these documents to help to shed some light on the reasons for this development.

One of the most significant bodies within the German Confederation was the Zollverein. Established by Prussia in 1818, it had grown by the early 1850s to include virtually every other German state, with the notable exception of Austria. It is in this context that Bruck, the Minister of Commerce, wrote to Schwarzenburg, the First Minister in 1850. As the Zollverein was 'due to expire' in 1852, it was very important that Austria gain admittance or put forward an alternative scheme before Prussia might 'see her supremacy assured for so long a time'. As this is an internal document, Bruck is able to be candid and offers reasons for making the Zollverein an important part of Austrian policy but also how it might be of benefit to Germany as a whole. It would be of interest to the historian that Bruck sees the significance of the Zollverein at a time when Austria was about to re-assert its political dominance of the Confederation through the Punctation of Olomouc. The Nationalverein was certainly sensitive to Austrian domination of the Confederation when it declared that 'it is essential, therefore, to work toward getting Prussia to assume the initiative [in the struggle for German unification]'. Though it is not surprising that Bruck should take a very proactive view of getting Austria into the Zollverein, a historian would perhaps note that Prussia was successful in keeping the Austrians out and therefore this would increasing be a source of tension throughout the 1850s and early 1860s. This tension may well have been exacerbated by Prussian industrial growth and the healthy tax returns compared with a much more stagnant Austrian economy and much lower tax returns.

> This paragraph successfully sets out the context of the tension between Prussia and Austria with reference to the sources. It places it in the context of post-revolution Germany with reference to the key ideas about unification, the *grossdeutsche* and *kleindeutsche* solutions.

> This paragraph relates tension to the Zollverein. It explains the reasons behind Source 6 and places it in the context of the 1850s. It also introduces Source 1 for a brief comparison and finishes with an appraisal that deals with the issue of a historian using the sources for a specific purpose.

Although economic matters were important, the primary causes of tension between Austria and Prussia were political. The Erfurt Union had been an attempt by Prussia to force through a kleindeutsche solution and this is very much reflected in the Nationalverein declaration when it refers to 'the assumption that the mission of the Prussian state essentially coincides with Germany's needs and mission, and insofar as its activity is directed toward the introduction of a strong and free overall constitution for Germany'. This had alarmed Austria and had led to the negotiations at Olomouc in November 1850. The Punctation, or humiliation as many Prussians saw it, may have asserted Austrian domination in the short term but in the long term it was a point to be redressed. It is this alluded to by the declaration in clause 1 when it states that the 'peace concluded between Austria and France' presents 'great perils for the independence of our German fatherland'. Bruck's letter may have been written before the Punctation (only the year is given) and therefore was written in a political context that was much less certain. By ignoring economic matters, the Nationalverein declaration implies that this area is secure and that it is on the political front that matters need to be challenged. As an individual, and Minister of Commerce, Bruck has a far less global view than the group of activists who wrote the declaration. This would make the individual opinions stated by Bruck far more specific than the overall aims of a new political organisation. Moreover, the fact that the declaration was written for a wide public audience will make it slightly different in tone to Bruck's personal letter. In this sense, the historian must be careful when using them together to make claims about the history he is investigating.

There are some issues for the historian to be aware of while trying to use these documents in conjunction. Although both are documents which suggest future action, one is by an individual minister in private correspondence and the other is a manifesto by a large political organisation. Moreover, they are not necessarily thinking about exactly the same thing. Bruck is thinking about Austria's standing within the Confederation. He wrote about 'closer political links' being a result of Austrian participation in a Custom Union but does not go on to state the aim of unification. On the other hand, The Nationalverein declaration makes unification its clear aim when it says, 'the German Federal Diet to be replaced by a solid, strong, and lasting central government for Germany' and that 'the most effective steps toward achieving this end can only emanate from Prussia'. Moreover, we do not have a Prussian government position, although we know that Bismarck would, in the course of time, invoke the nationalist sentiments expressed in the declaration, particularly following the Danish War in 1864 but this is not evidence provided in the source. These documents do, however, provide some evidence of both sides and their attitudes towards each other during the period stated and therefore they would be useful for the historian investigating the tension between Austria and Prussia during the period stated and could be used as supporting material for claims that they might make.

This paragraph relates the context of the 1850s to the declaration of the Nationalverein in 1859. It deals with the information given when speculating about the exact date of Bruck's letter and explains why this may be important. At the end the difference between the authors and the intended audience is explained and related to the demands of the question.

This highlights the difference in intent between the documents and warns of the potential problems of not comparing like with like. It addresses the question directly and alludes to material already covered in the answer in order to support the stated judgement.

Verdict

This is a strong answer because:

- it makes clear connections between the sources and the question
- it uses the context of the sources to show how they relate to the question
- it sustains focus and develops a clear and balanced argument
- there is a clear judgement which follows on from the arguments put forward.

Paper 2: A Level sample answer with comments

Section B

These questions assess your understanding of the period in depth. They will ask you about the content you learned about in the four key themes, and may ask about more than one theme. For these questions remember to:

- give an analytical, not a descriptive, response
- support your points with evidence
- cover the whole time period specified in the question
- come to a substantiated judgement.

To what extent had Austria lost its position as the leading state in the Confederation by 1864? (20 marks)

Average student answer

Austria was the leading state in Germany because of the Metternich system. Then the revolutions of 1848 forced Metternich to leave and Austria lost its place as the leading state in Germany and was replaced for a time by the Frankfurt Parliament. This Parliament debated the solution to the problem of German unification and had to decide between the grossdeutsche solution and the kleindeutsche solution. The grossdeutsche solution was to unify Germany and include the German-speaking lands of Austria and the kleindeutsche solution was the unification of Germany excluding Austria and dominated by Prussia. In the end, they chose the kleindeutsche solution and offered the German crown to the King of Prussia. He did not accept this because he was afraid of Austria. They re-asserted their dominance of Germany when they forced the Prussians to sign the Punctation of Olomouc in 1850.

The War of 1859 was lost by Austria. They fought the French over Italy and lost because the French were allied to the Piedmontese. The Austrians lost two battles at Solferino and Magenta and then surrendered. This meant that the Austrians lost land in northern Italy but also they were no longer able to tell the Italian states what to do. In Germany, the other German states saw that Austria was vulnerable to military action and it made them more confident in challenging Austria. The Prussians were able to defy the Austrians in 1863, when King William did not attend a meeting called by Franz Josef, the Austrian Emperor. This shows how much more confident the Prussians were because the Austrian Army was not so powerful. This means that the Austrians had lost their leading position by 1864.

This paragraph describes some of the relevant background information. It is the start of the process and thereby the start of the story. It fails to address the demands of the question.

To make this paragraph better, it needs to deal directly with the demands of the question. This means that it needs to closely examine what it means to be the leading state in a loose Confederation and what power and influence a leading state might have. It then needs to briefly assess how far this situation changed up to 1864.

This paragraph describes what happened in the War of 1859. It does state a result of this that is implicitly linked to the question and then it draws a conclusion based on this.

To improve this paragraph, the writing needs to immediately address the question and examine how far this war influenced the decline of Austrian power within Germany. It needs to take a deeper analytical look at the impact of the war and explain more fully the importance that it has in reducing Austria's role as a leading state. It could also introduce a counter argument as a balance to the argument being made.

In the Danish War of 1864, Austria and Prussia fought side by side. The war was fought over control of the duchies of Schleswig and Holstein. The Austrian Army fought just as well as the Prussians and showed them how good they were. After the war, the Austrian Army occupied Schleswig which shows that the Austrians were still powerful because the duchies were a long way from Austria but next to Prussia, so the Prussians had to allow an Austrian Army to be next to Prussia. During the war of 1866 (The Seven Weeks' War), the Austrian Army was badly beaten by the Prussians and this proved how bad the Austrians were. This was when Prussia became the leading state of Germany and took over from Austria. This meant that the kleindeutsche solution was the final outcome of the struggle between Prussia and Austria.

Austria was not allowed to join the Zollverein. This meant that they were losing their economic position. Prussia's economic power was growing, particularly during the 1850s when they were rapidly industrialising. Government tax income helped the Prussians to invest in things like railways. The Austrians could not invest so much in these things because they did not have the same income as the Prussians. This economic power meant that Prussia was able to dominate the Zollverein and keep Austria out. Other states, like Bavaria who might have wanted Austria to take part, were unable to get their way because Prussia was so powerful.

Austria went from being the leading state through the Metternich system to losing wars which meant that they lost their position. If they had been better at wars, they would have kept their leading position within Germany and would not have been overtaken by Prussia in 1866.

This paragraph deals with the Austrian role in the War of 1864. It draws a limited conclusion about what this means for the role of Austria as the leading state in the Confederation. It relates this to the larger context in a limited way. It also includes material which is outside the timeframe and would be ignored by the examiner.

To make this a better paragraph it should focus on the War of 1864 and look at how the relationship between Prussia and Austria had changed since the Punctation of Olomouc. From this a substantiated judgement could be offered.

This paragraph describes briefly the differences in economic development between Austria and Prussia. It fails to provide any kind of explanation which would help to address this material to the question.

To make this paragraph better, the Zollverein needs to be used as an example of how Austria might not have been the leading state in all areas. Also the connection between economic matters and political ones needs to be fully explained and how it relates to the question of Austria being the leading state within the Confederation or not.

This concluding paragraph is too short. It describes the overall process and makes a counter-factual statement about their proficiency at fighting wars.

To improve this paragraph it needs to directly answer the question. It then needs to compare and contrast the most significant points raised in the essay and use them to formulate a judgement about the extent to which Austria had lost its position by 1864.

Verdict

This is an average answer because:

- it does not give a direct and supported answer to the question
- it does not explain the significance of the issues raised in the answer.

Use the feedback on this answer to rewrite it, making as many improvements as you can.

Paper 2: A Level sample answer with comments

Section B

These questions assess your understanding of the period in depth. They will ask you about the content you learned about in the four key themes, and may ask about more than one theme. For these questions remember to:

- give an analytical, not a descriptive, response
- support your points with evidence
- cover the whole time period specified in the question
- come to a substantiated judgement.

To what extent had Austria lost its position as the leading state in the Confederation by 1864? (20 marks)

Strong student answer

The political supremacy of Austria within the Confederation had been re-affirmed by the Punctation of Olomouc in 1850 and the break-up of the Erfurt Union. A major cause of the Prussian climb-down had been the success of the Austrian Army with victories over the Piedmontese and the Hungarians in 1849 and the feeling that Prussia was militarily much weaker than Austria and, due to its long borders and divided territories, strategically vulnerable. It could be argued that economically, Austria was never the leading state in the Confederation as they were never members of the Zollverein. This was amplified in the 1850s by the difference in the relative tax income between the Austrian and Prussian governments. There were events and trends up to 1864 which damaged Austria's standing but it would be debatable to say that it had 'lost its position'.

> This paragraph sets out an overview of the issues. It partly states the case for seeing Austria as the leading state but also challenges the assumption of the question. The last sentence indicates a recognition that this is a 'debate'.

Loss of military reputation affected Austria's position. The War of 1859 dented the reputation of the Austrian Army which hitherto had been unbeaten since the Napoleonic Wars. By losing the war to France, Austria's status as a great European power was dented and this caused Prussia to re-assess the idea that Austria could not be challenged militarily. Moreover, the prestige was further affected by their loss of hegemony in the Italian peninsula and the loss of industrial and commercial assets in Lombardy. The Prussian Army reforms of 1860, however, would imply that Prussia did not believe itself to be capable of a military challenge to Austrian supremacy even after these losses and therefore, while unwelcome, the loss of the war with France did not do much to lessen Austrian power within the Confederation. On a purely military basis, the fact that the Austrians held their own during war with Denmark in 1864 would suggest that the War of 1859 did not have a major impact on their place as the leading state within the Confederation.

> In this paragraph the answer deals with the military situation. It explains the consequences of the War of 1859 but frames its impact by citing the War of 1864 as evidence as to the extent of the effect of the defeat to France.

In a political sense, the Punctation of Olomouc continued to symbolise Austria's leading role until after 1864. Though lacking the perceived influence of the Frankfurt Parliament, the Federal Diet was still dominated by Austria and the external difficulties with the French and Italians did little to undermine this and neither did the internal difficulties caused by the adoption of autocracy or the change to constitutional monarchy. It is true that the loss in 1859 made the Prussians a little more confident but this would not be fully the case until 1863 when Bismarck vetoed Austrian plans to reform the Federal Diet, by advising William I not to attend the meeting called by Franz Josef. In 1864, the Austrians got their way over the Danish War and played the part that they wanted to play, eventually occupying Schleswig. The Federal Diet followed the Austrians lead in this. It could be said that without the Seven Weeks' War of 1866, 1863 would just be a blip in the continuation of Austrian dominance. In the context of what was to follow, however, the veto of 1863 was a clear indication that Prussia regarded itself as having parity with Austria and therefore Austria had partly lost its leading position by 1864.

> This paragraph makes a judgement about the political domination of Austria. It argues that the non-attendance of William I of Prussia at the meeting is evidence that Prussia felt that it had political parity with Austria. A conclusion is then drawn from this.

Economically, Austria was not the leading power in the Confederation. Being kept out of the Zollverein would have been a slight were it not for the shift in economic strength that took place during the 1850s. That cash-rich Prussia had been able to manage investment to a far greater extent than the Austrians, who were having difficulty in paying for their wars and therefore balancing the books, gave the Prussians even greater influence within the Zollverein and meant that the Austrians were unlikely to be admitted. Even during the crisis of 1862, when the Prussians overplayed their hand by negotiating with France on their own, the Austrians were unable to improve their position. As time went on, matters got worse for the Austrians and better for the Prussians. A key example of this is the building of railways. By 1864, the Prussians had linked virtually every major city to the rail network while the Austrians were still some years from achieving this. They did not, therefore, lose their leading position economically because they never had that position to lose.

It is reasonable to argue that Austria had lost its position as leading state in the Confederation by 1864. The loss of the War of 1859 had reduced their military reputation and Prussia had seen the opportunity to be regarded at least as equal. The conduct of the War of 1864 indicates that Austria and Prussia were operating as equal partners which would imply that Austria had lost its leading position. The fact that the Prussians ignored the meeting of 1863 and thereby prevented the Austrians from leading a reform of the Confederation also shows that the Austrians had lost some ground politically, though the fact that the meeting was called by them in the first place, indicates that they regarded themselves as having some form of leading role, as did the other princes who attended the meeting. The ongoing exclusion of Austria from the Zollverein indicated Austria's economic weakness compared to Prussia and so there was no leading state status to lose economically. Of course, in 1864, no one could have anticipated the results of the war in 1866, but even that Prussia would have been in a position to contemplate a war with Austria, suggests that there had certainly been some shift in the balance of power within the Confederation in the years leading up to it.

> This paragraph challenges the assumption of the question by arguing that economically Austria was not the leading state. It gives evidence of the discrepancy in tax income and Prussian management of the Zollverein and ends with a judgement which directly answers the question.

> The conclusion answers the question directly. It uses the most compelling evidence from the body of the essay and uses it to support the direct answer.

Verdict

This is a strong answer because:

- it answers the question throughout and analyses the key relationship between Austria and Prussia
- it uses the issue of the question to set criteria so that a concluding judgement is made against something tangible
- it has a wide range of evidence which is used to support the points made
- it is well organised and communication of material is clear and precise.

Index

Acknowledgements

The authors and publisher would like to thank the following individuals and organisations for permission to reproduce photographs and text in this book.

Photographs

(Key: b-bottom; c-centre; l-left; r-right; t-top)

akg-images Ltd: 183, 311, 326, 341, De Agostini Picture Lib./A. Dagli Orti 230, Deutsches Historisches Museum, Berlin 298, 302, Imagno 318; **Alamy Images:** Classic Image 40, Mary Evans Picture Library 26, 58, 79, National Geographic Image Collection 6, North Wind Picture Archives 37, 45, The Art Archive 126, World History Archive 93; **Bridgeman Art Library Ltd:** Germanisches Nationalmuseum, Nuremberg (Nuernberg), Germany 292, Private Collection/Ken Welsh 372; **Corbis:** 308, Bettmann 354, Hulton-Deutsch Collection 350; **Getty Images:** De Agostini/N. Marullo 206, DeAgostini 178, Hulton Archive 63, 82, Illustrated London News/Hulton Archive 187; **Irvin Department of Rare Books and Special Collections, University of South Carolina Libraries:** 190; **Bildarchiv Preussischer Kulturbesitz:** 329, 365; **Library of Congress:** 15, 115, 133; **Mary Evans Picture Library:** 33, 51, 65, 69, 88, 105, 111, 197, 224, 234, 241, 255, 375, Douglas McCarthy 217, Epic/Tallandier 335, Everett Collection 120, INTERFOTO/History 167, INTERFOTO/Sammlung Rauch 194, 290, Peter Higginbotham Collection 100, The National Archive, London 10, 17; **TopFoto:** HIP 245, 260

Cover images: *Front:* **Getty Images:** Universal History Archive/UIG

All other images © Pearson Education

Figures
Figure 1.1, p.169 adapted from 'Italy in 1815' by Professor George Rhyne, http://users.dickinson.edu/~rhyne/232/Three/Italy_1815.htm, copyright © Professor George Rhyne; Figure p.287 from *Access to History: The Unification of Germany 1815–1919*, 3/e, by Farmer, A. & Stiles, A., Hodder Education, 2007, p.4, map 1.1. Reproduced by permission of Hodder Education; Figure p.297 adapted from 'The German Zollverein 1834–1919' by Amine Raihani, http://italiangermanuni.wikispaces.com/Zollverein, licensed under a Creative Commons Attribution Share-Alike 3.0 License; and Figure p.299 from 'Eisenbahnen in Deutschland 1835–1885' compiled by Andreas Kunz, and Figure p.339 adapted from 'States within the Northern German Confederation, 1867' from IEG Maps (Staaten im Deutschen Bund, 1848) compiled by Michael Hundt, Cartography Joachim Robert Moeschl, Editor Andreas Kunz, copyright © IEG/A. Kunz 2000, http://www.ieg-maps.uni-mainz.de.

Tables
Table p.295 from *Handbuch der deutschen Wirtschafts- und Sozialgeschichte*. Hrsg. v. Hermann Aubin / Wolfgang Zorn, Band 2: Das 19 und 20 Jahrhundert, Klett-Cotta, Stuttgart, 1976, p.313. Reproduced with permission; Tables pp.295, 298 from *The Unification of Germany* by Michael Gorman, Cambridge University Press, 1989, pp.34–35, based on statistics from C.M. Cipolla, *The Emergence of Industrial Societies*, The Fontana Economic History of Europe, Vol. 4, 1973. Reproduced with permission from Cambridge University Press; Table p.317 from *The Frankfurt Parliament 1848–49* by Frank Eyck, Macmillan, 1963, pp.358–361. Reproduced by kind permission of the Estate of Frank Eyck; and Table p.342 from *Austria, Prussia and the Making of Germany 1806–1871* by John Breuilly, Pearson Education, 2011, p.106, Table 8.5, copyright © 2011. Reproduced by permission of Taylor & Francis Books UK.

Text
Extract p.28 from *Labour and Reform: Working Class Movements, 1815–1914* by Clive Behagg, Hodder Education, 1991, p.66. Reproduced by permission of Hodder Education; Extracts pp.71, 74 from *The History of Trade Unionism 1666–1920* by Sydney and Beatrice Webb, 1920. Reproduced with permission from the Webb Memorial Trust; Extract p.75 from *The Congress of 1868* by A. E. Musson, 1968, p.32. Reproduced by permission of Trades Union Congress, London; Extract p.91 adapted from 'Subsidies paid in Loaves of Bread in England in 1700s' by Luiza Chwialkowska, *National Post (Canada)*, 12/12/2000, A6, National Post, a division of Postmedia Network Inc. Reproduced with permission; Extract p.92 from 'The 1832 Royal Commission of Inquiry into the operation of the Poor Laws', http://www.victorianweb.org/history/poorlaw/royalcom.html, Source: The Victorian Web; Extract p.99 from *The Workhouse* by Jennie Walters, www.jenniewalters.com. Reproduced by kind permission of Jennie Walters, author of the Swallowcliffe Hall series; Extract p.119 from 'Capitalism and Slavery: a Critique' by Roger Anstey, *Economic History Review*, Vol. 21, (2), pp.307–320, August 1968, copyright © 2008, John Wiley and Sons; Extracts pp.119, 135 from *Bury the Chains: The British Struggle to Abolish Slavery* by Adam Hochschild, Macmillan, 2005, pp.5, 236, 366, copyright © Adam Hochschild, 1998, 2005. Reproduced by permission of Macmillan and Houghton Mifflin Harcourt Publishing Company. All rights reserved; Extract p.121 from *Capitalism and Slavery* by Eric Williams, University of North Carolina Press, 1944, p.211, copyright © 1944 by the University of North Carolina Press, renewed 1972 by Eric Williams. New introduction by Colin A. Palmer © 1994; and Extracts pp.121, 128 from *Econocide: British*

Slavery in the Era of Abolition, 2/e by Seymour Drescher, The University of North Carolina Press, 2010, pp.114, 170–171, copyright © 2010 by the University of North Carolina Press. Used by permission of the publisher, www.uncpress.unc.edu; Extracts pp.122, 125, 129, 134 from *A Short History of Slavery* by James Walvin, Penguin Books, 2007, pp.157, 163, 187, copyright © James Walvin, 2007. Reproduced by permission of Penguin Books Ltd; Extract p.128 from *A Mad, Bad and Dangerous People? England 1783–1846* by Boyd Hilton, Oxford University Press, 2006, p.185. Reproduced by permission of Oxford University Press, www.oup.com; Extract p.136 from *Empire & Slavery* by Patrick Richardson, Longman, 1968. Reproduced by permission of Pearson Education Ltd; Extracts pp.170, 172, 174, 244 from *Italy in the Age of the Risorgimento, 1790–1870* by Harry Hearder, Longman, 1983, pp.108, 125, 178. Reproduced by permission of Taylor & Francis Books UK; Extracts pp, 177, 180, 205, 209, 220, 229, 237, 257 from *The Italian Risorgimento*, 2nd edn by Martin Clark, Routledge, 2009, pp.30, 45, 79, 97, 111–113, 119. Reproduced by permission of Taylor & Francis Books UK; Extracts pp.174, 177, 201, 237 from *Italy: A Modern History* by Denis Mack Smith, University of Michigan Press, 1959, pp.20, 21, 37; Extracts pp.183, 189, 222, 229 from *The Risorgimento* by Agatha Ramm, The Historical Association, 1962, pp.12, 14. Reproduced by permission; Extracts pp.195, 244 from *Modern Italy* by Denis Mack Smith, Yale University Press, 1997, p.29. Reproduced by permission of Yale University Press and University of Michigan Press; Extracts pp.199, 277, 278 from 'The Situation of Italy', *The Spectator*, 21/05/1853, p.13 http://archive.spectator.co.uk. Reproduced by permission; Extracts pp.200, 218, from *Risorgimento* by Lucy Riall, Palgrave Macmillan, 2009. Reproduced by permission; Extract p.201 from *The Sterner Plan* by Raymond Grew, Princeton University Press, 1963, copyright © Princeton University, 1963. Reproduced by permission; Extracts pp.204, 245 from *Cavour* by Denis Mack Smith, Routledge, 1985, p.xi, and Extracts pp.234, 235 from *Garibaldi: A Portrait in Documents* by Denis Mack Smith, Passigli Editori, 1982, pp.30–1. Reproduced by kind permission of the author; Extracts pp.205, 219, 232, 235, 247, 249, 253, 254, 267, 269 from *The Making of Italy 1796–1866* by Denis Mack Smith, Palgrave Macmillan, 1988, pp.106, 215, 222, 318–319, 333, 367, 368, 384–385, 392, 405, copyright © Denis Mack Smith 1968, 1988. Reproduced by permission of Palgrave Macmillan; Extract p.211 from *Cavour* by Harry Hearder, Routledge, 1994, pp.89–91. Reproduced by permission of Taylor & Francis Books UK; Extracts pp.213, 225 from *The Struggle for Mastery in Europe 1848–1918* by A.J.P. Taylor , Oxford University Press, 1971, pp.103, 124. Reproduced by permission of Oxford University Press, USA; Extract p.218 from *Garibaldi* by Lucy Riall, Yale University Press, 2008. Reproduced by permission; Extract p.222 from *The Political Life and letters of Cavour* by Arthur James Beresford Whyte, Oxford University Press, 1930, pp.271–272. Reproduced by permission of Oxford University Press; Extract p.227 from *Mazzini* by Denis Mack Smith, Yale University Press, 1996, p.112. Reproduced by permission; Extract p.235 from *Garibaldi and the Making of Italy* by George Macaulay Trevelyan, Phoenix, 1911, pp.124–125. Reproduced by kind permission of the Estate of George Macaulay Trevelyan; Extract p.243, 282 from *Modern Italy 1871–1995*, 2nd edn by Martin Clark, Longman, 1996. Reproduced by permission of Taylor & Francis Books UK; Extract p.261 from

Access to History: The Unification of Italy, 3rd edn by Andrina Stiles and Robert Pearce, Hodder Education, 2006, pp.138–139. Reproduced by permission of Hodder Education; Extracts pp.288, 301, 303, 305, 313, 323, 384, 386 from *Fragen an die Deustche Geschichte English Edition*, German Bundestag Publications Section, 1993, pp.63, 74, 99, 101, 144. Reproduced with permission from German Bundestag; Extracts pp.290, 298 from *The Unification of Germany* by Michael Gorman, Cambridge University Press, 1989, pp.28, 38. Reproduced with permission from Cambridge University Press; Excerpts p.297 from 'Hostility to Trade', by John Prince-Smith, 1843, pp.345, 394–397 from The Founding Declaration of the Nationalverein, 14/08/1859, p.348 from Bismarck's 'Blood and iron' speech, 30/09/1862, p.353 from A Memorandum from Field Marshal Von Moltke, 1861, translated by Jeremiah Riemer for the German History in Documents and Images website, http://germanhistorydocs.ghi-dc.org/. Reproduced by permission of The Friends of the German Historical Institute and the translator; Extracts pp.303, 326, 363 from *The History of Germany 1780–1918 The Long Nineteenth Century* by David Blackbourn, Blackwell Publishing, 2003, p.116, 193. Reproduced via Copyright Clearance Center; Extracts pp.304, 314 from *Open University Course A321: The Revelations of 1848, Unit 3, Document collection*, translated by E. Huber, Open University Press, 1976, pp.60, 77–78, copyright © The Open University Press; Extracts pp.306, 307 from *The European Revolutions 1848–51* by Jonathan Sperber, Cambridge University Press, 2005, p.130. Original source: Andreas Duwel, Sozialrevolutionarer Protest und konservative Gesinnung. Die Landbevolkerungdes KonigreichsHanover und des hersogtums Braunschweigin der Revolution von 1848–1849. Frankfurt 1996, p.83. Translation reproduced by permission of Cambridge University Press; Extracts pp.310, 363 from *The Course of German History: A Survey of the Development of German History since 1815* by A.J.P. Taylor, Routledge, 2001, pp.69, 126. Reproduced by permission of David Higham Associates; Extracts pp.312, 327 from *Iron Kingdom, the Rise and Downfall of Prussia 1600–1947* by Christopher Clarke, Allen Lane 2006, Penguin Books 2007, pp.476, 501, copyright © Christopher Clarke, 2006. Reproduced by permission of Penguin Books Ltd; Extract p.320 from *Germany Since 1815: A Nation Forged and Renewed* by Dr David G. Williamson, Palgrave Macmillan, 2005, p.393, and Extract p.321 from *Nineteenth Century Europe*, reprint edition by Stephen Brooks, Palgrave Macmillan, 1983. Reproduced with permission of Palgrave Macmillan; Extracts pp.330, 369 from *Documents of German History* ed. Louis L. Synder, Rutgers University Press, 1958, copyright © 1958 by Rutgers, the State University. Used by permission of Rutgers University Press; Extracts pp.331, 355, 385, 387 from *Bismarck and Europe* ed. by William Norton Medlicott and Dorothy K. Coveney, Hodder & Stoughton, 1997; Extracts pp.337, 394, 396, 397 from *The Foundation of the German Empire* ed. Helmut Bohme, translated by Agatha Ramm, Oxford University Press, 1971, p.78. Reproduced by permission of Oxford University Press, www.oup.com; Extract p.345 from *Restoration, Revolution, Reaction* by Theodore S. Hamerow, Princeton University Press, 1966, p.211, copyright © 1958 Princeton University Press. Reproduced via Copyright Clearance Center; Extracts pp.356, 363 from *A History of Germany 1815–1985* by William Carr, Hodder Arnold, 1987, pp.100, 104. Reproduced by permission of Hodder Education; Extract p.361 from *The Mind of*

Germany The Education of A Nation, by Julius von Eckardt, translated by Hans Kohn, Charles Scribner's Sons, 1961. Reproduced by kind permission of the Estate of Immanuel Kohn; Extract p.363 from *A Short History of Germany 1815–1945* by E.J. Passant, copyright © Cambridge University Press, 1959. Reproduced with permission; Extract p.364 from *Bismark* by Alan Warwick Palmer, Scribner, 1976, p.133. Reproduced by permission of The Marsh Agency Ltd on behalf of the author; Extract p.368 from *Bismarck and the Hohenzollern Candidate for the Spanish Throne* by Georges Bonnin, Chatto & Windus, 1957, pp.277–278. Reproduced with kind permission from Jean Bonnin and Lynn (Morfydd) Bonnin. Look out for Georges Bonnin's autobiographical publication, about his experiences and observations at the Nuremberg Trials, due in 2016. See www. jeanbonnin.com; and Extracts pp.371, 374 from Otto von Bismarck, Die gesammelten Werke [*The Collected Works*], ed. Gerhard Ritter and Rudolf Stadelmann, Friedrichsruh ed, 15 vols, Vol. 6b, nos.1932, 1950, Berlin, 1924–1932, translated by Dr Erwin Fink for the German History in Documents and Images website, http://germanhistorydocs.ghi-dc.org/. Reproduced by permission of The Friends of the German Historical Institute and the translator.

Every effort has been made to contact copyright holders of material reproduced in this book. Any omissions will be rectified in subsequent printings if notice is given to the publishers.